Th Standard Lesson Commentary 1995-96

International Sunday School Lessons

published by

Standard Publishing

Eugene H. Wigginton, *Publisher*

Richard C. McKinley, *Director of Curriculum Development*

James I. Fehl, *Senior Editor*   Hela M. Campbell, *Office Editor*

Jonathan Underwood, *NIV Editor*

Second Annual Volume

STANDARD PUBLISHING
Cincinnati, Ohio

Cover design by Listenberger Design Associates, Indianapolis.

© 1995
The STANDARD PUBLISHING Company
division of STANDEX INTERNATIONAL Corporation
8121 Hamilton Avenue, Cincinnati, Ohio 45231
Printed in U.S.A.

In This Volume

Special Features

Autumn Quarter, 1995

Theme: *The Story of Christian Beginnings (Acts)*

Writers

Lesson Development ....*Orrin Root*
Verbal Illustrations ....*Charles R. Boatman*
Discovery Learning ....*Mark A. Taylor*

What Do You Think? ....*Kenton K. Smith*
Reproducible Activities......................*Beth Muskopf*

Winter Quarter, 1995-96

Theme: *God's Promise of Deliverance (Isaiah)*
God's Love for All People (Jonah, Ruth)

Writers

Lesson Development ....*Roger W. Thomas* (1, 2)
Doug Redford (3-5)
Steve Hooks (6-9)
Ralph Sims (10, 11)
William Gwaltney (12, 13)

Verbal Illustrations.....................*Richard W. Baynes*
Discovery Learning ....*Ron Davis*
What Do You Think? ....*Charles E. Cook* (1-9)
Jonathon Stedman (10-13)
Reproducible Activities ....*Jonathan Underwood*

Spring Quarter, 1996

Theme: *Teachings of Jesus*

Writers

Lesson Development ....*Edwin V. Hayden*
Verbal Illustrations ....*C. Barry McCarty*
Discovery Learning.........................*Dennis E. Glenn*

What Do You Think? ....*Kenton K. Smith*
Reproducible Activities ....*Jonathan Underwood*

Summer Quarter, 1996

Theme: *A Practical Religion (James)*
God Is With Us (Psalms)

Writers

Lesson Development.......................*John W. Wade*
Verbal Illustrations...................*James G. VanBuren*
What Do You Think? ....*David Baynes*
Reproducible Pages.....*Mike McCann* (1, 2, 5, 8, 9)
Phil Haas (3, 4, 6, 7)
Mark Plunkett (10-13)

Discovery Learning ....*Mike McCann* (1, 2, 5)
David H. Ray (3, 4)
Phil Haas (6, 7)
Alan Weber (8, 9)
Mark Plunkett (10-13)

A Wonderful Thought

Surely one of the most wonderful thoughts we can entertain is that God, the Creator of all things, loves us. Not just some of us, but all of us. The Bible tells us so. And then it shows what He has done to prove His love for us.

The studies in the 1995-96 Sunday school year (which are highlighted by the color panel in the chart below) speak eloquently of God's love. Some of our studies look back to when God was preparing Israel to be the people through whom He would eventually bless the whole world. His love for Israel and for all peoples, and His desire for fellowship with us, are seen in the Winter and Summer Quarters.

The incarnation and death of God's Son, by which atonement was made for the sins of mankind, were the crowning demonstration of divine love. While He was among us, Jesus taught. His teachings and the noble life they inspire also reveal the Father's love. We'll see this in the Spring and Summer Quarters.

When Jesus' redemptive work was completed, it was time to announce the gospel of God's love. The exciting story of the proclamation of the gospel on Pentecost, and the resulting birth and rapid growth of the church, will be the focus of the lessons in the Autumn Quarter.

International Sunday School Lesson Cycle
September, 1992—August, 1998

YEAR	AUTUMN QUARTER (Sept., Oct., Nov.)	WINTER QUARTER (Dec., Jan., Feb.)	SPRING QUARTER (Mar., Apr., May)	SUMMER QUARTER (June, July, Aug.)
1992-1993	Old Testament Personalities (Old Testament Survey)	Good News for All (Old Testament Survey)	Believing in Christ (John)	Following God's Purpose (Ephesians, Philippians, Colossians, Philemon)
1993-1994	The Story of Beginnings (Genesis)	The Story of Jesus (Luke)	Good News for God's People (Romans) Set Free by God's Grace (Galatians)	God Redeems a People (Exodus, Leviticus, Numbers, Deuteronomy)
1994-1995	From the Conquest to the Kingdom (Joshua, Judges, 1 and 2 Samuel, 1 Kings)	Jesus the Fulfillment (Matthew)	Christians Living in Community (1 and 2 Corinthians)	A Nation Turns From God (1 and 2 Kings, Amos, Hosea, Micah, Isaiah)
1995-1996	The Story of Christian Beginnings (Acts)	God's Promise of Deliverance (Isaiah) God's Love for All People (Jonah, Ruth)	Teachings of Jesus (Matthew, Mark, Luke)	A Practical Religion (James) God Is With Us (Psalms)
1996-1997	God's People Face Judgment (2 Kings, Jeremiah, Lamentations, Ezekiel, Habakkuk)	New Testament Personalities	Hope for the Future (1 and 2 Thessalonians, Revelation)	Guidance for Ministry (1 and 2 Timothy, Titus) A Call to Faithfulness (Hebrews)
1997-1998	God Leads a People Home (Major Prophets, Minor Prophets, Nehemiah)	God's People in a Troubled World (1 and 2 Peter, 1, 2, 3 John, Jude)	The Gospel of Action (Mark)	Wisdom for Living (Job, Proverbs, Ecclesiastes)

Introducing *The NIV Standard Lesson Commentary*

At last! Here is a user-friendly Uniform Lesson commentary based on the *New International Version* Scripture text. Teachers familiar with the *Standard Lesson Commentary* will immediately feel at home with this volume. Many features here are the same as in that popular resource (based on the King James Version). Whether or not you have used the *Standard Lesson Commentary* before, however, you will quickly find *The NIV Standard Lesson Commentary* a helpful companion in preparing your Sunday school lessons.

LESSON DEVELOPMENT

The first page of each lesson clearly identifies the title, Scripture, current unit, and lesson aims for the session. A thumb tab identifies the date the lesson will be taught so that it can be found quickly. The date is repeated on each page at the top outside corner.

The first item in the lesson development is a brief rationale for the lesson: "**Why Teach This Lesson?**" Tying the lesson theme to contemporary life, this section puts application at the forefront of your preparation. Then comes the lesson treatment itself, following a three-point structure: introduction, exposition, and conclusion. The **introduction** provides background and other useful information to set the stage, tie the current lessons with earlier ones, and generally give you a handle on the context for the current lesson.

What follows is a **verse-by-verse Scripture exposition.** The text is printed in the *New International Version,* usually one verse at a time. Bold type sets the text off from commentary so you can read it easily, even if you just want to read through the passage without comment at first. The commentary is interspersed so you can relate the comments to the specific Scripture passage it illuminates.

The **conclusion** leans heavily toward **application,** giving specific examples of how the principles of the lesson Scripture can be put to practice in real life.

Verbal illustrations, usually two in each lesson, help to illuminate the concepts of the lesson. These are usually found in the exposition section, providing yet another tool for you to illustrate the point of the Scripture. These are set off in block quotes so they can be easily found or easily jumped over if you choose not to use them.

MARGINAL NOTES

Many of the most helpful features of this lesson commentary are found in the margins. Occasionally the text suggests some interesting point for discussion. These issues are raised under the heading of "**What Do You Think?**" The question is raised, sometimes from more than one perspective. The Scripture in the main section is relevant, and other Scriptures may also be suggested. No answers are given, however, because these are questions without pat answers. These will encourage your students to wrestle with the big issues without being trite.

"**Visuals**" are pictured in the margins, also. These are reproductions of the classroom visuals available from Standard Publishing each quarter to help your students visualize the points being made. Again, these appear in the margin alongside the Scripture or other part of the lesson where they are most appropriate.

Daily Bible readings, points to remember, and even prayer ideas are included in the margin near the end of each lesson.

DISCOVERY LEARNING

For teachers who like to involve their students in the learning process, a page of **Discovery Learning** is included in each lesson. These alternate lesson plans are designed to get the students busy in Bible study and application to discover for themselves the timeless truths of the Scriptures. Each discovery learning plan includes an activity to begin the lesson, a Bible study activity, and an application activity.

The last page of each lesson is a **reproducible page**. These, too, are designed to involve the students in discovery learning. Sometimes they are an integral part of the discovery learning plan. At other times, they provide optional activities that may be introduced at various points in the lesson. Marginal "Option" notes frequently call your attention to an activity on this page. Or you can start with the whole page and build your lesson plan around it, using the other resources in this book.

OPTIONS

This is a lesson planner with lots of options! No matter what style you prefer—lecture, discussion, activities—you'll find resources to plan a great lesson. If you like variety, this will help you design an easy-to-teach lesson unique to your personality and that of your class. Or, if you like a ready-made plan you can teach with minimal preparation time, you'll find that, too. It's all here.

PLANNING SHEET

Use the lesson planning sheet on page 10 to plan each of your lessons. The page is reproducible, so you can use it to fill in the blanks and plan out your complete lesson each week. List the options and features you have chosen for each lesson, and use it to guide you quickly and easily from one activity to the next.

Index of Printed Texts, 1995-96

The printed texts for 1995-96 are arranged here in the order in which they appear in the Bible. Opposite each reference is the page number on which the passage begins in this volume.

Cumulative Index

A cumulative index for the Scripture passages used in *The NIV Standard Lesson Commentary* for September 1994—August 1996 is presented here for your convenience.

Lesson Planning Page

List the aims here, either directly from the lesson or revised to suit your individual needs.

LESSON AIMS

Begin with an opening activity like the illustration from the beginning of the lesson, "Into the Lesson" from the Discovery Learning page, a discussion question, or some other appropriate opener.

GETTING STARTED

List in order the activities you will use. These include discussion questions, activities from the discovery learning page and the reproducible page—as well as key points from the commentary section.

LESSON DEVELOPMENT

I.

II.

III.

How will you bring the lesson to a climax, stressing the key point and desired action steps?

CONCLUSION & APPLICATION

Dismiss the class with an activity that reinforces the Bible lesson.

CLOSING ACTIVITY

Autumn Quarter, 1995

Theme: *The Story of Christian Beginnings (The Book of Acts)*

Special Features

Lessons

Unit 1. Beginnings in Jerusalem

Unit 2. Witnessing in Judea and Samaria

Unit 3. Spreading the Gospel Into All the World

About these lessons

This study reviews the exciting story of the birth of the church on Pentecost and its rapid growth in the months and years following. Lessons focus on key events and persons in the life of the early church and in the spread of the gospel to lands beyond Palestine.

Sep 3
Sep 10
Sep 17
Sep 24
Oct 1
Oct 8
Oct 15
Oct 22
Oct 29
Nov 5
Nov 12
Nov 19
Nov 26

Thinking of Beginnings

by Orrin Root

Mommy, where did I come from?" Mommy finds it hard to answer the childish question, and so does Daddy. Consequently the silly story of the stork is handed down from generation to generation, even in places where never a stork is seen.

Though hard for parents to answer, the question is important. The child comes from Daddy and Mommy. To a large extent, what they are determines what the child is. Soon people begin to notice that he or she has Daddy's eyes or Mommy's nose. More important things are inherited too, like intelligence and musical talent.

Of course, care and training also have a part in shaping the child. Scholars debate endlessly the relative importance of heredity and environment. But in normal circumstances parents provide the environment as well as the heredity, so their influence is doubled.

BEGINNING OF THE CHURCH

Where did the church come from? It came from God. It is composed of people born of God (John 1:12, 13). Such people are only human, of course. They have human faults and follies and failures, and these are reflected in the church. But people born of God show also a likeness to the Father. They show something of His strength and truth and justice, coupled with something of His mercy and compassion and love. These too are reflected in the church.

How can we know what the church ought to be and do? One way is to consider its beginning and early growth, while the apostles were with it. Jesus had given them three years of intensive training when He was with them on earth. For their postgraduate training He had given them the Holy Spirit in an extraordinary way. They were baptized, submerged, overwhelmed in the Spirit (Acts 1:5). They were under His influence so completely that they could not make a mistake in their teaching. The Spirit guided them into all truth (John 16:13).

How could anyone know the apostles were guided by the Holy Spirit and were not just promoting their own ideas? How can we know it now? The Spirit made His presence known by doing things no man can do.

By the gate of the temple lay a beggar, a middle-aged man, a cripple who had never walked. To him Peter said, "In the name of Jesus Christ of Nazareth rise up and walk." The man rose to his feet and went into the temple, "walking, and leaping, and praising God" (Acts 3:1-10). Most of the miracles are not described so fully, but there must have been hundreds of them. Who could deny that God was with those apostles?

Guided by the Holy Spirit, Luke recorded how the church began and grew. From his record we take our Sunday school lessons this quarter. It will not be hard to find suggestions for Christian living and church growth today.

The thirteen lessons are divided into three units. Here is a preview.

SEPTEMBER

UNIT 1. BEGINNINGS IN JERUSALEM

Lesson 1. About forty days after Jesus rose from the dead, He instructed His apostles to wait for the Holy Spirit to bring them power from on high. Then they were to testify for Jesus in widening circles till they reached the uttermost part of the earth. Having said this, Jesus rose from the earth and vanished in a cloud.

Lesson 2. On the Day of Pentecost the Holy Spirit came. Upheld by His power, the apostles faced a huge crowd and declared, "God hath made that same Jesus, whom ye have crucified, both Lord and Christ." The message carried conviction, and about three thousand persons were baptized in the name of Jesus Christ for the remission of sins.

Lesson 3. The church gained more attention when Peter and John brought healing to a lame man, but this brought no joy to the rulers who had managed the death of Jesus. They arrested Peter and John, but to the ruling council the apostles declared that Jesus is the only Savior.

Lesson 4. The apostles' teaching and miracles of healing continued till the whole group of apostles were arrested and ordered not to teach about Jesus. But the apostles answered, "We ought to obey God rather than men."

UNIT 2. WITNESSING IN JUDEA AND SAMARIA

Lesson 5. The Christians spent all their time listening to the apostles' teaching. Some soon ran out of money, but the others took care of them. Seven good men were chosen to manage the care of the poor.

Lesson 6. A young Pharisee by the name of Saul took the lead in opposing the church. He searched Jerusalem for Christians and put them in jail, but many escaped by fleeing to other towns of Judea and Samaria. They took the gospel wherever they went. The apostle Philip converted many Samaritans, and then won a traveler from Ethiopia.

Lesson 7. Saul was vigorously extending his persecution of Christians, but Jesus stopped him on the road to Damascus. The leading persecutor became a leading evangelist.

Lesson 8. For some time the gospel was preached only to Jews, but God's plan was wider. The gospel was meant for all nations, and God used some unusual methods to help the Jewish Christians learn that.

Lesson 9. Christians fleeing from persecution took the gospel to Gentiles as well as Jews in Antioch. A great church grew up in that Gentile city. Grateful for the gospel, it sent financial aid to the Christians in Judea.

OCTOBER

UNIT 3. SPREADING THE GOSPEL INTO ALL THE WORLD

Lesson 10. The church at Antioch had many prophets and teachers. The Holy Spirit called two of them to work elsewhere. Saul and Barnabas carried the gospel through Cyprus and Asia Minor. Saul now was called Paul, and this trip is known as Paul's first missionary journey.

Lesson 11. Lesson 8 told how God convinced Jewish Christians that Gentiles could be Christians too. That was not questioned again, but at Antioch some Jewish Christians taught that Gentiles who become Christians must become Jews also. After some earnest discussion, that error was repudiated.

Lesson 12. Paul set out on his second missionary journey, taking Silas with him. A vision from God led the evangelists to take the gospel into Macedonia. The lesson centers on their work in Philippi, where they were beaten and jailed. However, an earthquake opened the jail, the jailer became a Christian, and Paul and Silas were released with apologies.

Lesson 13. An event from Paul's third missionary journey completes our series. Fakers failed to match God's miracles, and former fakers used their books of magic for a public bonfire. A simple statement of Scripture summarizes our series: "So mightily grew the word of God and prevailed."

These lessons bring us thirteen highlights from a magnificent book. Still the thirteen printed texts total only 198 verses of Scripture. This is less than one-fifth of the 1007 verses in the book of Acts. We trust the highlights will be so exciting that every student will eagerly read the other four-fifths of Acts as the studies proceed.

NOVEMBER

A Gospel for All Time

by Alan G. Ahlgrim

Jesus was never boring. What He said and did jolted people to attention. The same was true of the apostles, who led in establishing the church in the first century. Whenever the gospel was shared and put into practice as Christ intended, the impact was great. The same can and should be true today; unfortunately, in the experience of too many people the church is dull, not dynamic.

A letter from a "Dear Abby" column illustrates the point. The letter was written in response to another article involving a churchgoing woman whose minister asked her (loudly) every Sunday morning, "Where is your husband today?"

The letter writer related that her mother-in-law was also a churchgoing woman, but that her father-in-law seldom accompanied her. One day the minister visited their home, and her father-in-law couldn't hide fast enough. Sure enough, the minister cornered him and asked him why he never came to church.

Her father-in-law replied, "Because the seats are too hard and you talk too long!" The minister never mentioned her father-in-law's absence after that!

For many people these days the thought of being involved in the church is just about as exciting as watching paint dry. In their thinking, the words *church* and *boring* are synonymous. And, tragically, they may also feel that the church has always been as they perceive it to be today. Nothing could be farther from the truth.

THAT'S EXCITING!

Recently I was impressed once again by the excitement created by the gospel in the early days of the church. Not long after Jesus had been raised from the dead, the apostles began to preach boldly that Jesus was the long-awaited Messiah. Thousands in Jerusalem believed and were baptized. From that beginning on Pentecost, the church continued to enjoy phenomenal numerical growth. Because the apostles had been specially empowered by the Holy Spirit, people in and around Jerusalem brought their sick to them for healing. Teaching was intense. Christ was magnified. Growth was constant. Opposition was unrelenting. Great faith was evident. It was exciting to be a part of the First Church of Jerusalem!

I wonder, could the church stir up so much excitement, support, and opposition in our time?

POWER IN EXPECTATIONS!

On one occasion, the famous nineteenth-century preacher Charles Spurgeon was talking to a young preacher, "feeling him out." Spurgeon said to the young man, "You really don't expect much to happen in your pastorate, do you?"

The man replied, "Well, no. . ."

Spurgeon almost exploded, "Then you won't see much happen, either!"

Spurgeon was right on target. It is said that life is often a self-fulfilling prophecy. The meaning is that while we don't always get what we want in life, in the long run we do get just about what we expect.

Many in the church today consider the gospel to be merely an historic record rather than a personal resource. They read the Bible for information rather than inspiration. They attend classes or services as a routine—expecting simply to hear about God rather than to encounter God.

What the church needs is a revival of expectation. We are serving almighty God, who dramatically interrupted the routines of the citizens of Jerusalem on the Day of

Pentecost two thousand years ago. He is perfectly capable of interrupting our routines as well. Whenever people come together with that sort of expectancy, worship and fellowship become electric.

What sort of expectations do you have of the gospel? The present time is replete with extraordinary opportunities for the gospel. Spiritual darkness abounds, and the challenge for the Christian messenger is great. But the power of the gospel dispels that darkness, and the gospel's Author promises to be with His servants to meet the challenges involved in confronting the spiritual darkness of this world.

The early church enjoyed great growth, not despite the difficulty and hostility of their culture, but because of it.

Could the same happen today? If the church vigorously undertook the mission given it by the Master, could we not expect Him to bless our efforts to save the lost and thus bring glory and honor to His name?

THE CHALLENGE TO CHANGE

Clinton T. Duffy was for many years the warden of San Quentin prison and an outspoken advocate of convicts. He was a tough man, but a fair man. He was a man who believed in others.

Someone once challenged Warden Duffy, questioning his attitude toward criminals. His critic said, "Warden, you should know that leopards don't change their spots!"

Duffy snapped back, "You should know that I don't work with leopards. I work with men, and men change every day!"

The gospel is all about change. That is the meaning of repentance. It is a change of heart, of mind, of the direction of one's life. That was the theme of the apostles and evangelists in the early church, as the message of forgiveness and redemption through Jesus Christ was first heralded to a sin-burdened society.

One observer of contemporary church life suggests that the appeal of modern evangelism is not so much for repentance, a true change of heart, as it is for enlistment. The task of the church, however, has not changed. We are to extend to lost sinners the challenge of the high calling and standard of Christ. We are to do so with the certain knowledge that sinners can change, and that when they do they will find a warm welcome with the Lord.

The challenge to change is not reserved only for those who are outside of Christ. The Lord's people must always be willing and ready to accept change, and to change, in order to advance the cause of Christ.

A few years ago a woman asked how the old, urban church she attended, which was dying, could be enlivened. She said, "Everybody in the congregation is old, and the community is young. The church members are from well-to-do families, and the surrounding community is poor." The preceding summer approximately sixty children from the community attended VBS, but she lamented that on the Sunday after VBS the church offered no programming for the children. In fact, she said that when some of them returned to the churchyard and asked if they could come in, the chairman of the board went out and locked the gate!

If the church of the twenty-first century is to be Christ's church, if it is to grow as the church of the first century grew, there must be openness and acceptance among the church's leaders and members alike. The people in the book of Acts were challenged to set aside their prejudices and self-interests. They were called to stretch their faith and to grow in love regardless of the changes that were involved.

No wonder the number of Christians grew, nay, multiplied in the church's early days! The gospel was changing lives. People were living in a different and dynamic way because of the message of God's love and grace in Jesus Christ.

PERSONAL COMMITMENT

The gospel made its impact on the world of the first century because of persons such as Peter and Stephen and Paul and Silas. Men on a mission. Men totally committed to Jesus Christ.

The world watched with wonder at the sacrifice these and many others made for Christ and for others. It still does. That is why a tiny Albanian woman known as "Mother Theresa" has had such an impact in our time. She is admired by peasants and honored by presidents. Everyone is impressed with her humble spirit, exemplified by her expression, "I'm just a pencil in the hand of God."

The success of the gospel in any age depends on such commitment by the followers of Christ. Are there others today who are serving Him quietly and faithfully, sharing the blessings of the gospel with the downtrodden and despairing? Surely. And just as most faithful servants of the past were never mentioned in the Bible, most today will never win the acclaim of men. That doesn't mean, however, that they are not witnessing boldly and effectively for Christ. By the fruits of their labors, namely the souls who have been rescued from the stranglehold of sin by the grace of God through Christ Jesus, these servants are proving that the gospel of Christ is God's power unto salvation in our time.

THE PROMISE OF THE SPIRIT'S POWER

LESSON 1

WHY TEACH THIS LESSON?

Waiting. It's one of the hardest tasks we can be assigned. We don't like to wait. We want to act. "Lead, follow, or get out of the way!" "Don't just stand there—do something." "Just do it."

But sometimes, we have to wait. And the disciples show us how. As they awaited the gift promised by the Father, they spent time together, they praised God, they restored the number of apostles to twelve. And they prayed—"continually."

We all wait for the return of Jesus. We also wait for other things—answers to prayer, results of tests, the return of a loved one. What do we do while we wait? This lesson challenges us to use our waiting time wisely: praising God, sharing with other believers, and praying—continually!

INTRODUCTION

Dawn crept over the rippling waters of Galilee and pushed the darkness from the streets of Bethsaida. People came early to Simon Peter's house, asking for Jesus. But Jesus was not there. He had risen "very early in the morning, while it was still dark," and gone out to find a solitary place for prayer (Mark 1:35).

A. PAUSE FOR PRAYER

Crowds of people pressed upon Jesus so urgently that he could scarcely find time to eat (Mark 6:31). Yet Jesus knew the value of a pause for prayer. Thronging multitudes were eager to hear and to be healed, but still he managed to slip away and pray alone (Luke 5:15, 16). One time he spent the whole night in prayer (Luke 6:12). And Jesus taught that his disciples "should always pray" (Luke 18:1).

B. LESSON BACKGROUND

This week we begin a series of studies from the book of Acts. That book finds its background in the book of Luke, an earlier work of the same author. That background is enhanced by similar records written by Matthew, Mark, and John.

After more than three years of teaching, Jesus gave his life at Calvary to redeem lost sinners. On the third day he rose triumphant over death. For a while he taught again, and sent his disciples to take his message of salvation to all the world. Then he rose to Heaven and took his place at God's right hand.

The book of Acts begins where the book of Luke ends, adding some details of the last minutes before Jesus rose visibly to the sky; and there we begin our study.

I. TIME OF WAITING (ACTS 1:1-5)

The disciples of Jesus were to testify for him "in Jerusalem, and in all Judea and Samaria, and to the ends of the earth" (Acts 1:8). What a tremendous task! But

DEVOTIONAL READING
ACTS 1:21-26

LESSON SCRIPTURE
ACTS 1

PRINTED TEXT
ACTS 1:1-14

LESSON AIMS

After this lesson a student should be able to:

1. List what is said in the passage about the Holy Spirit.

2. Compare the disciples' wait for the promise from God with modern Christians' waiting for God's promises.

3. Support fellow believers with their presence and prayers.

KEY VERSE

But you will receive power when the Holy Spirit comes on you; and you will be my witnesses in Jerusalem, and in all Judea and Samaria, and to the ends of the earth. —Acts 1:8

What Do You Think?

The excuse, "I'm too busy," is possibly the most common reason people give for refusing to accept some task in the church or for failing to perform some spiritual duty—including prayer. Jesus was an extremely busy person, but he made time for what was most important. (See p. 17, "Pause for Prayer.") When we are too busy for prayer, we need to ask ourselves, "Busy with what?" Any worthwhile activity that commands our time could be done better if we lifted it in prayer to our heavenly Father and sought the strength and guidance he willingly offers.

What do you think? What are some specific, practical ways "busy people" can be sure to make time for prayer?

Visuals for These Lessons

The Adult Visuals/Learning Resources packet contains classroom-size visuals for use with the lessons in the Autumn Quarter. The packet is available from your supplier. Order No. 192.

Visual 1 of the visuals packet (below) is a chart of the resurrection appearances of Christ. Visual 14 (not shown) illustrates the theme for the quarter.

they were not to plunge into preaching instantly when the Master said good-bye. They were to wait for "power from on high" (Luke 24:49).

A. The Former Book (vv. 1, 2)

1. In my former book, Theophilus, I wrote about all that Jesus began to do and to teach.

The *former book* is the book of Luke, which records much of what Jesus did and taught. It too is addressed to *Theophilus,* of whom we really know nothing more.

2. ...until the day he was taken up to heaven, after giving instructions through the Holy Spirit to the apostles he had chosen.

The former book ends with *the day* in which Jesus *was taken up to Heaven,* adding merely that the apostles afterward "stayed continually at the temple, praising God" (Luke 24:50-53). Verse 8 of our text records the outstanding commandment that he had given not long before he rose to Heaven. *Through the Holy Spirit* seems to mean that Jesus gave this commandment with the guidance of the Holy Spirit, who had given him power and guidance all through the years of his ministry. The commandment in verse 8 was given several times in different words (e.g., Matthew 28:18-20; Mark 16:15, 16). Jesus did give other commands before he ascended. We see one in verse 4 of our text. But over them all towers the great command to carry the gospel to the whole world.

B. Proof of Resurrection (v. 3)

3. After his suffering, he showed himself to these men and gave many convincing proofs that he was alive. He appeared to them over a period of forty days and spoke about the kingdom of God.

Jesus' *suffering* means the suffering he endured leading up to, and including, his death. He died and was buried, but afterward *he showed himself . . . and gave many convincing proofs that he was alive.* Read about some of them in Luke 24:36-43 and John 20:19-29. Notice the list of witnesses in 1 Corinthians 15:3-8. There can be no doubt that Jesus actually died and returned to life. The apostles saw him at various times during *forty days* after his resurrection—perhaps many more times than are recorded. He taught them about *the kingdom of God,* saying much that is not included in the record.

C. Command to Wait (v. 4)

4. On one occasion, while he was eating with them, he gave them this command: "Do not leave Jerusalem, but wait for the gift my Father promised, which you have heard me speak about.

Jesus met his disciples in Jerusalem in the evening following his resurrection (John 20:19). During the following forty days he was with them sometimes in Galilee (John 21; Matthew 28:16-20). But near the time of his ascension he was with them in Jerusalem again, and he told them to stay there. That did not contradict the order to go to all the world; it merely postponed their going. They were to wait for a specific thing before starting out: a *gift.* It was a gift that had been promised by *the Father,* but the disciples had heard the promise from Jesus. The next verse tells about this promised gift.

D. Promise of Power (v. 5)

5. "For John baptized with water, but in a few days you will be baptized with the Holy Spirit."

More than three years earlier, John the Baptist had startled Israel with his fervent call to repent and be baptized. Many people were wondering whether John was the long-expected Christ, but John said the Christ would be far greater than he. He added, "He will baptize you with the Holy Spirit and with fire." (Luke 3:15, 16). John went on to explain the baptism in fire. The Christ will judge the people of earth, separating wheat from chaff, and "he will burn up the chaff with unquenchable fire" (Luke 3:17). John gave no explanation of the baptism with the Holy Spirit, but now Jesus mentioned it as the thing promised by the Father to the apostles. In a few days they would be baptized with the Holy Spirit. Acts 2:1-4 describes that baptism. The apostles were submerged, overwhelmed, by the Holy Spirit. They were under his influence so completely that he used their voices to speak in languages unknown to them, but known to some of the hearers (Acts 2:5-11).

Verse 8 of our text adds that the apostles would receive power along with their baptism with the Spirit. In the second chapter of Acts it is apparent that they received power to speak in unknown languages. They also received power to do miracles of healing (Acts 3:1-8). They received power to endure persecution and resist the orders of ungodly rulers (Acts 4:18-20). Furthermore, the Holy Spirit guided them into all truth (John 16:12, 13). He gave them power to understand the kingdom of Christ, a kingdom not of this world (John 18:36). He gave them power to teach God's word without any error, and that is our assurance that we can trust the Bible that was written by them and other men likewise guided by the Holy Spirit.

II. TIME OF PARTING (ACTS 1:6-11)
A. THE FATHER'S SECRET (vv. 6, 7)
6. So when they met together, they asked him, "Lord, are you at this time going to restore the kingdom to Israel?"

It seems quite evident that the apostles did not yet understand the nature of God's kingdom, a kingdom not of this world, a kingdom of love instead of force, a kingdom ruling only those who choose to be ruled by it. They were thinking of Israel triumphant, supreme among the nations of the world, as it had been in the time of Solomon. They were asking if the time had come to restore Israel to that ancient glory.

7. He said to them: "It is not for you to know the times or dates the Father has set by his own authority.

Jesus did not give a lecture on the true nature of the kingdom. In time the Holy Spirit would guide the apostles to that truth, and they would come to understand that the kingdom would win, not by killing people, but by making friends out of enemies. They would come to understand that the kingdom is vastly larger than Israel, drawing its citizens from all the nations of the world. For the time being, Jesus was content to deal with the question that was asked: was it then time for the kingdom to take charge and be triumphant? That was not for the apostles to know. The time of triumph was God's secret, and it still is (Matthew 24:36).

B. THE APOSTLES' TASK (v. 8)
8. "But you will receive power when the Holy Spirit comes on you; and you will be my witnesses in Jerusalem, and in all Judea and Samaria, and to the ends of the earth."

The *power* that would come with the Holy Spirit has been discussed briefly in the comments on verse 5. With that power the apostles had a job to do. Jesus spoke these words in or near *Jerusalem. Judea* was the area around that city; *Samaria* was just north of Judea. But these places were only a tiny beginning. The testimony about Jesus was to explode into all the world. In the lifetime of those apostles it spread rapidly on the east and north sides of the Mediterranean Sea, as we shall see as we continue our studies in Acts. We have no similar book to tell us how swiftly

WHAT DO YOU THINK?
Acts 1:8 records Jesus' plan for the spread of the gospel, and the plan was carried out as he designed it. The gospel was first proclaimed in a city, the city of Jerusalem, and from there it spread into the surrounding regions. Later, Paul followed this same plan, centering his evangelistic efforts in major cities, such as Corinth, Philippi, and Ephesus, and then witnessing the spread of the gospel into surrounding areas. (See Acts 19:8-10.) It is obvious that in our own time major cities must still be prominent centers of evangelistic activity.

(USE THIS QUESTION IF YOU ARE IN AN URBAN OR SUBURBAN CHURCH)
What is your church doing to reach the city? What more can it do? How can individual Christians be a part of this evangelistic effort?

(USE THIS QUESTION IF YOU ARE IN A RURAL CHURCH)
But what of us who are not located in a city? How can we be involved—individually and as a church—to spread the gospel?

HOW TO SAY IT

Alphaeus. Al-FEE-us.
Bartholomew. Bar-THOL-o-mew.
Bethsaida. Beth-SAY-uh-duh.
Iscariot. Iss-CARE-e-ut.
Matthias. Muh-THIGH-us.
Theophilus. Thee-AHF-ih-luss
   (th as in thin).
Zealot. ZEL-ut.

WHAT DO YOU THINK?

Another aspect of Jesus' plan was its worldwide vision, its ultimate focus on "the ends of the earth." We today must not become nearsighted, focusing all our prayer and energies into our own church and community; we must embrace that same worldwide vision.

How can our church be sure we are focusing on the worldwide vision for Christ's church? How can we as individuals help in this effort?

WHAT DO YOU THINK?

The promise of the two angels standing by at Jesus' ascension is but one of many promises of Jesus' return. Their gentle rebuke suggests that we need to be active while we await that event.

How does one who anticipates the imminent return of the Lord differ from one who does not? What is different about that person's work, attitudes, and service for the Lord?

Is it obvious from your own behavior that you are anticipating his return? Why or why not? What one change can you make that will reflect that expectation? (See also Matthew 24:45-51.)

and far the gospel went in Egypt and Mesopotamia and India in those early years. Today there is urgent need for followers of Jesus to take the gospel back to the land of its beginning, and to the wide areas where Communism has suppressed it for decades, and to the teeming millions of India and China and the isles of the sea— *to the ends of the earth.*

THE KUDZU EFFECT

"Kudzu." It's almost like saying, "the plague." Kudzu is a fast-growing vine—up to a foot a day!—with bright green leaves and grape-scented purple blossoms. In the 1930s it was widely planted in the southern part of the United States. Its deep network of thick roots tenaciously holds the soil, so it seemed a perfect means of stopping soil erosion. But the plant became a relentless monster, covering millions of acres across the South and killing all other vegetation in its path.

Belatedly, beneficial uses for this once-maligned plant are being found. Its roots are rich in starch and B vitamins, and its leaves and vines are a potential source of ethanol for fuel.

Christianity must have seemed like kudzu to the people in the first century. Its Founder had commissioned his followers to start where they were (Jerusalem) and to cover the world with the Christian message. To its enemies, Christianity must have seemed like a force that would destroy everything the Jewish world stood for and also consume the whole pagan world in the process. Try as they might, they could not stamp it out.

Christ's Great Commission is still in effect. If we will enthusiastically heed his charge to us to cover the world with the gospel, the world may finally come to appreciate its marvelous benefits!

          —C. R. B.

C. THE PARTING (v. 9)

9. After he said this, he was taken up before their very eyes, and a cloud hid him from their sight.

Luke's earlier book records that Jesus had led the apostles out to the Mount of Olives east of Jerusalem. From that spot the visible body of Jesus *was taken up* into thin air till it vanished in *a cloud.* Luke 24:50, 51 records that Jesus was blessing the apostles as he left them; Mark 16:19 adds that "he was taken up into heaven and he sat at the right hand of God."

D. THE PROMISE OF RETURN (vv. 10, 11)

10. They were looking intently up into the sky as he was going, when suddenly two men dressed in white stood beside them.

No doubt these were angels, who took the form of *men* to communicate with the apostles. Their *white* apparel symbolized their perfect holiness.

11. "Men of Galilee," they said, "why do you stand here looking into the sky? This same Jesus, who has been taken from you into heaven, will come back in the same way you have seen him go into heaven."

Jesus will come back as he went, in a visible body. "Every eye will see him" (Revelation 1:7). He vanished in a cloud; he will come back in clouds, but "with power and great glory" (Matthew 24:30, 31). It was useless for the apostles to stand gazing at *the sky.* Jesus was not coming back that day. They had a job to do before his return.

HOPE-PRODUCING PROMISE

World War II began for the United States on December 7, 1941, when the Imperial Japanese armed forces bombed Pearl Harbor. Within hours of that bombing, the Japanese attacked Hong Kong, Malay, and the Philippines. Many feared that the flag of the rising sun would soon fly over every nation on the western side of what we now call the Pacific Rim.

The Philippine islands quickly fell prey to the Japanese onslaught. General Douglas MacArthur, commander of United States Armed Forces in the Far East, was forced to retreat with his overpowered troops. When he was ordered to withdraw from Philippine soil, General MacArthur made a promise that was to become famous. He vowed, "I shall return." And so he did. As the Japanese were later driven out of the Philippines, General MacArthur returned as conquering hero.

During the week before his crucifixion, Jesus spoke of his triumphant return to earth (Matthew 24). When he stepped off the soil of the Judean hillside and ascended into Heaven, this hope-producing promise was given again, this time by two angels standing by. The enemy, Satan, was strong and controlled the hearts of many in the land. But the apostles took courage in Jesus' promise and, against all odds, began a resistance movement against the forces of evil that continues to this day. The hopeful heart of every Christian is still empowered by Jesus' words: "I shall return!"
—C. R. B.

III. TIME OF PRAYING (ACTS 1:12-14)

Prompted by angels, the apostles stopped gazing at that cloud into which their Master had soared. They had a big job to do, but they were not to plunge into it that day or the next. First they must wait for "power from on high" (Luke 24:49).

A. THE PLACE (v. 12)
12. Then they returned to Jerusalem from the hill called the Mount of Olives, a Sabbath day's walk from the city.

The apostles must have been filled with awe as they walked down the western slope of *the Mount of Olives*, across the bridge over the Kidron Valley, and into the gate of *Jerusalem*. That was where Jesus had told them to wait (Luke 24:49), and probably not one of them set a foot outside the city wall before the Spirit came with the promised power.

B. THE PEOPLE (v. 13)
13. When they arrived, they went upstairs to the room where they were staying. Those present were Peter, John, James and Andrew; Philip and Thomas, Bartholomew and Matthew; James son of Alphaeus and Simon the Zealot, and Judas son of James.

Here Luke lists the eleven apostles who remained. Judas Iscariot had committed suicide after betraying Jesus (Matthew 27:3-5). Apparently the eleven were all lodging together *upstairs* in a *room* in Jerusalem. It seems, however, that this room was only for sleeping and perhaps for eating. Luke ends his earlier book with the statement that the apostles "stayed continually at the temple, praising God." That seems to indicate that most of their waking hours were spent there. Other followers of Jesus could gather with them in the spacious court of the temple (Acts 1:15).

C. THE PRAYING (v. 14)
14. They all joined together constantly in prayer, along with the women and Mary the mother of Jesus, and with his brothers.

In his earlier book Luke records that Jesus was followed in Galilee by many women whom he had rescued from demons and diseases. They showed their gratitude by helping to support him (Luke 8:1-3). Some of them followed him to Jerusalem, where they saw him die on the cross and watched as his body was laid in the tomb. They were the first of Jesus' followers to find his tomb empty on the

PRAYER

You have created us, O God, and we are sure you know our needs better than we do. Thank you for setting before us what we need of work and rest and worship. May we use all of these well and wisely to extend your kingdom and glorify your name. In Jesus' name. Amen.

THOUGHT TO REMEMBER

Our time off is to prepare us for our time on.

DAILY BIBLE READINGS

Monday, Aug. 28—The Spirit's Prediction (Acts 1:15-20)

Tuesday, Aug. 29—God Works Through the Spirit (Zechariah 4:1-6)

Wednesday, Aug. 30—Empowered by the Spirit (Matthew 12:22-28)

Thursday, Aug. 31—The Holy Spirit's Work (John 16:1-15)

Friday, Sept. 1—Life in the Spirit (Romans 8:11-17, 26, 27)

Saturday, Sept. 2—The Spirit Gives Life (2 Corinthians 3:1-6)

Sunday, Sept. 3—God's Affirmation (1 John 4:13-18)

WHAT DO YOU THINK?

Many churches place in their bulletins the slogan, "Enter to worship; depart to serve." How can the church's gatherings on the Lord's Day better prepare believers for service?

What can be done to encourage specific acts of service in the following areas?

- *Evangelism*
- *Assisting a needy family*
- *Encouraging a missionary*
- *Other needed activities*

---

first day of the week, and to hear angels say he had risen from the dead (Luke 23:49, 55; 24:1-10). No doubt some of them were *the women* who gathered with the apostles after Jesus returned to Heaven. Jesus' *mother* was there too. Jesus had committed her to the care of his beloved disciple John (John 19:25-27). *His brothers* also were with the group. About six months before he died, they still did not believe in him (John 7:5). Apparently his resurrection had convinced them.

Probably all these men and women met with the apostles in the temple (Luke 24:53) rather than in the upper room. The big outer court of the temple had room for all of them, plus any other believers who wanted to be with them (Acts 1:15).

Prayer was not the only activity of the group in the days of waiting. One item of business was the choice of Matthias to take the place of Judas Iscariot, so the number of apostles again was twelve (Acts 1:15-26). Still Luke writes, *They all joined together constantly in prayer.* Thanksgiving must have had a large place in their praying. After the terrible tragedy of Jesus' death, their hearts were overflowing with gratitude because he was alive, because he had all power (Matthew 28:18), because the movement to which they had given their lives would go on and grow. Still there was reason for concern. The rulers who had contrived the death of Jesus were still ruling, and they would be no less hostile to Jesus' followers. There must have been earnest prayer for courage, for determination, for wisdom, and for the promised guidance and power of the Holy Spirit.

CONCLUSION

How busy we are! We have to work forty hours a week. The round of home duties is endless; the tasks are not done till it is time to begin them again. Children have duties too, and parents have to take them to music lessons and sports events, to school and to parties. We can hardly stop for a deep breath. But our work does not fill all our needs.

We need to eat, and we find time to do it. Is spiritual nourishment less necessary than physical? We take time off to have a tooth pulled or an appendix removed. Is the health of our spirits less important than the health of our bodies?

We need vacations. When God was making laws for a nation, he established three vacations every year; and he decreed how they should be spent. All Israel must go to an appointed place for fun and fellowship and worship: the Passover feast in spring, the Day of Pentecost in summer, the feast of Tabernacles in autumn. Do you choose a vacation time in which you can attend a Christian convention, conference, or camp?

When God was making laws for a nation, he required a weekly day of rest (Exodus 20:8-11). Part of it was used for worshiping together. Now most of us work five days a week and have two days off. But do we rest? And how many of us worship? Are we neglecting some of our most urgent needs?

Jesus' people had endured the terrible grief of his death and the tremendous joy of his resurrection. They had lived through forty days of excitement in which they met with Jesus again and again in places widely separated. So Jesus told them to take some days off before plunging into the work that would keep them busy for the rest of their lives. Wisely through those days they "all joined together constantly in prayer."

Prayer, worship, Scripture study, communion with God—certainly these are some of our most urgent needs. Then let us take time for these—but let us never imagine that they take the place of work, either the work by which we earn a living or the Christian work by which we build God's kingdom. Our time off is to prepare us for our time on.

Discovery Learning

This page contains an alternate lesson plan emphasizing learning activities. Classes desiring such student involvement will find these suggestions helpful. The next page is a reproducible activity page to further enhance discovery learning.

LEARNING GOALS

As students participate in today's class session, they should:

1. List what is said in the passage about the Holy Spirit.

2. Compare the disciples' wait for the promise from God with modern Christians' waiting for God's promises.

3. Support fellow believers with their presence and prayers.

INTO THE LESSON

Divide the class into groups of three to five members each. In each group ask each member to tell about an occasion when they have prayed for something but had to wait for a long time for the answer. Allow about two minutes per person. (Announce to the class every two minutes that it is time to hear from another person in the group. This way everyone should get a chance to contribute.)

After everyone has shared in the groups, take about five minutes to discuss some or all of the following questions with the whole class:

• What did you think as you waited for your prayer to be answered?

• How did you feel when the answer was delayed so long?

• Was there anything you could do to hasten the answer?

Make the transition to the Bible study by announcing that today's lesson involves waiting, as the disciples waited for the coming of the Holy Spirit.

OPTION

Before class write each of the letters of the word *wait* on a different sheet of construction paper. Begin today's session by giving the four sheets to four class members, one sheet each. Ask the four members to stand before the class and to display the letters. Then ask them to arrange themselves so that they spell a word. When they have formed the word *wait*, thank them and mount the letters on a bulletin board or the wall.

Ask the class members to turn to a partner and discuss, "The most difficult wait I ever endured." After three minutes, ask volunteers to share with the whole class.

Ask, "What makes waiting difficult? Has waiting become easier or more difficult for you as you have become older?"

Tell the class that this week's study focuses on the apostles in the weeks after Christ's resurrection and on his order for them to wait.

INTO THE WORD

Ask the students what they already know about the background of the book of Acts. List major points on the chalkboard or newsprint. Explain that the current quarter comprises a study of the story of Christian beginnings. Fill in with additional information given in the "Lesson Background" (page 17).

Read the Scripture, Acts 1:1-14. Have the students work in small groups to find information about what the Holy Spirit is and does. They should be able to find the following:

The Holy Spirit gives instruction (v. 2).

The Holy Spirit is a gift (v. 4).

There is a "baptism" of the Holy Spirit (v. 5).

The Holy Spirit gives power (v. 8).

The Holy Spirit speaks through the mouths of men (v. 8).

After reports of information about the Holy Spirit, ask students to read through the rest of Acts 1. They should be looking for the ways the disciples spent their time as they waited for the promise of the Holy Spirit to come to them. Give them about ten minutes to do this search. Then as a whole group discuss these activities of the disciples. Did they use their time wisely? What else could they have done?

INTO LIFE

Ask students, "What are some of God's promises to us today for which we must wait?"

"How should we spend our waiting time?"

"How can we help one another in the waiting?"

Try to get class members to be specific in answering.

OPTION

Use the second activity, "Watch and Pray," on page 24.

Close the class by praying for people you know who face difficult days because of illness, family problems, loss of jobs, or because they are seeking God's will for new direction, etc. Pray that God will help you know the best way to be supportive of those people to make their wait more bearable.

Old Testament Holy Spirit

The Spirit of God is evident throughout the Old Testament, but it was not given to all believers as promised in the New Testament. Examine following Scriptures to compare the different roles of the Holy Spirit.

SCRIPTURE	OCCASION	RESULT
Exodus 31:1-11		
Numbers 11:24, 25		
Judges 6:33-35		
1 Samuel 10:10		
1 Samuel 16:13, 14		
2 Samuel 23:2		
1 Chronicles 12:18		
2 Chronicles 24:20		
Job 33:4		

Watch and Pray

As the apostles waited for the promised Holy Spirit, they joined with the other believers in prayer. Listed below are some items that may well have been included in their prayers. Next to each item, write one or two similar reasons for prayer that you find in your life and in the life of your church.

Thanksgiving (for the promises being fulfilled in their lives) _____

Courage (to face the opposition of the rulers) _____

Wisdom (to bear witness of Christ effectively) _____

The Holy Spirit (for the promised gift to come) _____

THE HOLY SPIRIT COMES IN POWER

LESSON 2

WHY TEACH THIS LESSON?

The amazing events of Pentecost were nothing short of dramatic. With a great audio-visual display, God called attention to his Spirit-inspired messengers so they could proclaim the gospel message.

The events that followed, while often less noticed, were equally dramatic. People shared freely and generously with virtual strangers. They worked and worshiped together for the glory of Christ. They knew and expressed the joy of forgiveness.

It is this second set of events you will want to duplicate among your own class members. The coming of the Spirit is significant, in that it validates the message, the truth of the gospel. But it is the steadfastness, the generosity, and the joy of the early church you want to see become the norm for your class today.

INTRODUCTION

Who has seen the wind?
        Neither you nor I:
But when the trees bow down their heads,
        The wind is passing by.
                —Christina Georgina Rossetti

The wind is invisible, but that does not mean it is not real and powerful. We see results of it. We also hear the sound of it and feel its breath on our faces. If the wind is strong, its force is felt on the whole body.

The Greek language uses the same word to mean either wind or spirit. This reminds us that a spirit is somewhat like a wind. We do not see him, but sometimes we plainly see the results of what he does.

A. ABOUT SPIRITS

We know very little about spirits. Being neither visible nor tangible, they elude scientific investigation. But we can learn a little about them from the Bible.

Angels are spirits (Hebrews 1:14). Usually unseen, they take visible forms when it suits God's purpose for them. In the lesson text for last week we read of two of them who appeared as men (Acts 1:10, 11). The New Testament does not tell us that bad spirits take visible forms, but sometimes they take possession of living human beings. For example, a demon robbed one man of sight and speech (Matthew 12:22). Of course, the Holy Spirit, the Spirit of God, does nothing but good. He is the Spirit who has a major part in this lesson study.

B. LESSON BACKGROUND

Last week we read that Jesus rose from the dead, taught his disciples at different times and places during forty days, and then rose from the Mount of Olives to

---

DEVOTIONAL READING
Acts 2:16-24
LESSON SCRIPTURE
Acts 2
PRINTED TEXT
Acts 2:1-4, 14a, 29-33, 37-39, 44, 45

LESSON AIMS

After this lesson students should be able to:

1. Describe the events, message, and resulting fellowship of the believers of Pentecost.

2. Express confidence of salvation in Christ.

3. Participate in the body life of the church, as described in Acts 2:42-47.

KEY VERSE

Peter replied, "Repent and be baptized, every one of you, in the name of Jesus Christ for the forgiveness of your sins. And you will receive the gift of the Holy Spirit."
                —ACTS 2:38

LESSON 2 NOTES

OPTION

The reproducible on page 32 includes an activity to help the students explore what the text reveals about the Holy Spirit. Use it to begin your study of the lesson text.

HOW TO SAY IT

Ananias. An-uh-NYE-us.
Sapphira. Suh-FYE-ruh.
Sheol. SHE-ol.

Heaven. He told his disciples to go into all the world and preach the gospel to everyone. But he told them to wait in Jerusalem till the Holy Spirit would come to them with power. Today we'll read of the fulfillment of that promise.

I. COMING OF THE SPIRIT (ACTS 2:1-4)

Waiting and praying, the apostles must have thought often of Jesus' promises concerning the Holy Spirit. The Spirit would be their comforter, their encourager. He would teach them all things; he would remind them of what Jesus had said (John 14:26). He would guide them into all truth; he would glorify Jesus (John 16:13, 14). So for ten days they waited.

A. THE SOUND OF HIS COMING (vv. 1, 2)

1. When the day of Pentecost came, they were all together in one place.

The word *Pentecost* means fiftieth. That was the Greek name given to the Jewish festival that came on the fiftieth day after the Sabbath of the Passover celebration (Leviticus 23:15, 16). The Old Testament calls it the Feast of Weeks (Exodus 34:22) because it came seven weeks after the Passover.

They seems to mean the apostles, for they are mentioned at the end of chapter 1. The *place* where they were is not named. The apostles were staying in an upper room in Jerusalem (Acts 1:13), so that may be the *place*. At the same time, they were "continually at the temple" (Luke 24:53). Apparently they slept in the upper room, but spent much of their waking time in the temple, where the big courtyard provided room for other believers to gather with the apostles and join in their prayers (Acts 1:14, 15). Thus, the *place* mentioned in our text was probably in the temple. A big crowd promptly gathered there (v. 6).

2. Suddenly a sound like the blowing of a violent wind came from heaven and filled the whole house where they were sitting.

This does not indicate that any wind was felt or that anything was blown away; there was only *a sound* like that of a swift and powerful *wind*. It came from the sky above, and it *filled the whole house where they were sitting*. This *house* may have been one of the porches of the temple, open on the side toward the wide court of the temple where a crowd could gather.

B. THE SIGN OF HIS COMING (v. 3)

3. They saw what seemed to be tongues of fire that separated and came to rest on each of them.

As there was a sound of wind without any wind (v. 2), so also there was the appearance of *fire* without any fire. No fuel was being burned; the apostles were not scorched when something that looked like fire *came to rest on each of them*. Apparently there was something that looked like a big flame dividing into twelve flames that rested on the apostles. How big were those flame-like *tongues*? We are not told; but surely they were big enough to be seen by everyone in the crowd that gathered, and big enough to point out the apostles as the center of this amazing event.

C. THE RESULT OF HIS COMING (v. 4)

4. All of them were filled with the Holy Spirit and began to speak in other tongues as the Spirit enabled them.

When the sound like wind was heard and the tongues like fire were seen, the unseen Holy Spirit filled the apostles. As Jesus had put it in his promise (Acts 1:5), they were baptized with the Holy Spirit. They were submerged, covered. So completely were they under the Spirit's influence that he *enabled them* to *speak in other tongues,* in different languages that were unknown to them.

Verses 5-13 tell more about this phenomenon. Though these languages were unknown to the speakers, each language was known to some of the hearers. Hearing the wind-like sound that filled the house where the apostles were, people came quickly to see what was going on. These people included Jews from many nations. They had come to Jerusalem for the feast of Pentecost. Now men of many nations were hearing the languages of their homelands, and they were amazed. They recognized the speakers as men of Galilee, a province not noted for breadth of culture. But here some Galileans were speaking the languages of Parthia and Media and Elam, of Egypt and Crete and Arabia. That was astounding. True, some jokers scoffed that the speakers must be drunk. But those who understood knew they were hearing about "the wonders of God." We are not told what wonders were described; but it is easy to suppose the apostles were reporting some of the marvelous miracles of Jesus, some of his matchless teaching, the facts of his wonderful resurrection.

II. MESSAGE OF THE SPIRIT (ACTS 2:14a, 29-33)

Whatever the apostles were saying in different languages, it was part of the Spirit's message. It served to get the attention of the people, and to turn their thoughts to God. Now came the time for the heart of the message; and it glorified Jesus, as Jesus had said the Holy Spirit would do (John 16:14).

A. PROPHECY OF DAVID (vv. 14a, 29-31)

14a. Then Peter stood up with the Eleven, raised his voice and addressed the crowd.

Had the twelve apostles scattered among the people, speaking to different national groups? We are not told; but if they had been scattered they now came together. Eleven of them stopped talking, and Peter spoke as the Spirit guided him.

Peter stated that the apostles were not drunk, but that God was fulfilling the prophecy of Joel 2:28, 29, which promised that he would pour out his Spirit on his servants, causing them to prophesy (Acts 2:14-21). Then Peter announced that God had raised Jesus from the dead (Acts 2:22-24). He quoted David's words from Psalm 16:10: "You will not abandon me to the grave, nor will you let your Holy One see decay" (see Acts 2:25-27). The *King James Version* has "hell" instead of "the grave," but the Greek has *hades* and the Hebrew of the psalm has *sheol.* Both these terms mean the place of the dead, and sometimes mean the grave, not Hell. The quotation from the psalm provides the basis for Peter's words in verse 29.

29. "Brothers, I can tell you confidently that the patriarch David died and was buried, and his tomb is here to this day.

It is plain that the words quoted from the psalm do not refer to David himself. God did leave *David* in the grave, and his body did decay. His *tomb* was still there for all to see. What David wrote in the psalm referred to someone else, not to David.

30. "But he was a prophet and knew that God had promised him on oath that he would place one of his descendants on his throne.

David *was a prophet,* inspired to speak God's message, not his own. He knew *God had promised* that one of David's *descendants* would be the Christ, the Messiah, the Redeemer and King of God's people.

31. "Seeing what was ahead, he spoke of the resurrection of the Christ, that he was not abandoned to the grave, nor did his body see decay.

As a prophet, David wrote of *the Christ,* who was to come centuries later. He wrote that God would not leave the Christ in *the grave,* and that the Christ's body would not *decay.*

WHAT DO YOU THINK?

Scoffers were present on the Day of Pentecost. Today also there are those who scoff at the Christian faith. It is noteworthy that Peter calmly and briefly dismissed the scoffers' suggestion that he and the other apostles were drunk (see Acts 2:14, 15). Obviously he was not intimidated or distracted by the scoffers. Likewise, a Christian today should not allow scoffers to distract him or her from fulfilling the important task of proclaiming the gospel to those who hunger for it.

How can we do this? What traits and behaviors are characteristic of a Christian who is unintimidated by the scoffers of the world?

Peter threw down a challenge when he declared the apostles "witnesses of the fact" of the resurrection. He put the burden of proof on the unbelievers to prove, if possible, that the apostles were mistaken in saying that Jesus had been raised from the dead.

There was much that verified his claim: the empty tomb, the many eyewitness reports, the transformation of the apostles, and the miraculous display of the Holy Spirit's power on Pentecost.

Unbelievers, now as then, offer naturalistic explanations for these facts. How can Christians today challenge unbelievers to consider the facts and respond to the truth?

Confronted with their sin of having killed the Messiah, the convicted hearers on Pentecost cried out, "What shall we do?" Our aim, too, is to lead people to see that Jesus is the Christ and the one whom God sent to save us from our sins. To great numbers of people Jesus is nothing more than a notable teacher. We must demonstrate that Jesus is the unique Son of God, that he suffered and died on the cross to atone for the sins of mankind, and that his resurrection from the dead is a historical reality. Every human being must either accept the atonement for sin that he provided on the cross or reject it and face the terrible consequences.

What are some specific ways we can challenge the people of the world to come to this position? What was it that influenced you to believe in Christ?

B. Prophecy Fulfilled (vv. 32, 33)

32. "God has raised this Jesus to life, and we are all witnesses of the fact.

Now Peter turned from the prophecy to its fulfillment. As a matter of fact, God did raise Jesus from the dead. He was not left in the grave; his body did not decay. The twelve apostles could testify positively that Jesus was alive after his death—and who would call them liars as they stood there with those spectacular flames upon them?

33. "Exalted to the right hand of God, he has received from the Father the promised Holy Spirit and has poured out what you now see and hear."

Besides being raised from the dead, Jesus had been received into Heaven and given a place at God's *right hand*. Furthermore, Jesus had *received from the Father the promised Holy Spirit,* and had passed that promise on to his disciples (Acts 1:4, 5). To fulfill that promise, Jesus had sent the Holy Spirit with a sound like that of wind and with flames that looked like fire. Verses 34 and 35 add David's prophecy that the Christ would be thus exalted: "The Lord said to my Lord: 'Sit at my right hand until I make your enemies a footstool for your feet'" (See also Psalm 110:1). David's prophecies of the Christ were fulfilled in Jesus. This makes it plain that Jesus is the Christ. So Peter's sermon soared to its climax: "Let all Israel be assured of this: God has made this Jesus, whom you crucified, both Lord and Christ" (v. 36).

III. RESULT OF THE MESSAGE (ACTS 2:37-39, 44, 45)

It was clear that something supernatural was happening. The sound like wind, the tongues like fire, the many languages—none of these could be explained in ordinary ways. Then with clear reasoning Peter showed that Jesus was the Christ foretold by David. The people were convinced.

A. Question and Answer (vv. 37-39)

37. When the people heard this, they were cut to the heart and said to Peter and the other apostles, "Brothers, what shall we do?"

Has your heart ever felt the pang of realizing that you have done a monstrous wrong? If so, you know something of how the people felt on that Day of Pentecost. All their lives they had been hoping and praying for the Messiah to come. Now he had come, and they had killed him (v. 36). God had raised him from the dead. He was living and ruling from Heaven. His kingdom would go on; but what would become of his killers? Was there any possible way to escape the destruction they deserved? In desperation they cried, *What shall we do?*

38. Peter replied, "Repent and be baptized, every one of you, in the name of Jesus Christ for the forgiveness of your sins. And you will receive the gift of the Holy Spirit.

Peter answered with two commands and a promise. The first command was to *Repent.* Renounce your rejection of the Christ, grieve over his murder, vow to follow him faithfully for the rest of your lives. The second command was *be baptized.* Wash away your sin (Acts 22:16). Separate yourself from sin: die to it. Be buried in baptism and rise to a new life (Romans 6:1-4). Do this *in the name of Jesus Christ* to secure *the forgiveness of your sins.* Then came the promise: *You will receive the gift of the Holy Spirit.* The Spirit of God, who has produced all the wonders of Pentecost—he will be given to you; he will live in you; he will give you power for what you have to do as followers of the Messiah. Some students take a different view of this promise. They think the promised gift is not the Spirit himself, but the forgiveness and salvation the Spirit gives. We need not debate the exact meaning of the promise, for as a matter of fact the Spirit does live in every faithful follower of Christ (1 Corinthians 6:19, 20). He does give power for Christian service. This does not mean he gives all Christians the same power he gave to the apostles. Not all speak in other tongues. Not all do miracles of healing. Not all are inspired to speak God's truth without error. The Spirit gives different abilities to different people (1 Corinthians 12). Each Christian should recognize his or her ability, and use it well (Romans 12:6-8).

39. "The promise is for you and your children and for all who are far off—for all whom the Lord our God will call."

Sinners are not all beyond redemption. Even murderers of the Christ can be saved in the way just outlined. Such a promise is extended to sinners everywhere: those in Jerusalem at Pentecost, their *children* of all generations to come, and *all who are far off*. The promise is for all who will accept it. At that time, Peter may have thought that last phrase meant all the faraway Jews; but the Spirit who inspired Peter knew it meant people of all nations, even such depraved heathen as are described in Romans 1:28-32. Acts 10 records how Peter afterward learned to understand as the Spirit did.

What we have been reading is only a summary of Peter's sermon at Pentecost. He had much more to say (v. 40). Many hearers were persuaded. On that day three thousand of them accepted his message and were baptized (v. 41).

ACTING ON THE EVIDENCE

A real-estate partnership in which Allen Fehr was involved was audited by the Internal Revenue Service in 1985. The IRS ruled that Mr. Fehr owed $17,632 in taxes for four years, so he sent in a check for that amount. His canceled check came back with his next bank statement. But in the next six months, Fehr received four increasingly threatening, computer-generated letters demanding that he pay his taxes and adding penalties to the bill. Each time he phoned the IRS and explained the facts.

Over a period of two years' time, more than twenty-five letters and phone calls were exchanged between Fehr and the IRS. Even copies of the canceled check did not change the IRS's position! Finally, when the IRS threatened to seize all of his property, Fehr decided to tell a newspaper columnist who printed his sad story of governmental intransigence. Soon a human being at the IRS sent an apology and a refund check! It seems that Fehr had overpaid his taxes by nearly one thousand dollars!

Not everyone is as immune to the reasonable presentation of facts as some government agencies and their computers. When the first gospel sermon was preached, at least three thousand persons believed the evidence of Jesus' death and resurrection and acknowledged the implication of those facts for their personal salvation. The facts are still the same for us, as well. The sensible person will respond to them in the same way as those first Christians did.

—C. R. B.

B. NEW WAY OF LIFE (vv. 44, 45)

44. All the believers were together and had everything in common.

Visitors in Jerusalem for the feast of Pentecost included people from all over Palestine and from many foreign countries as well. As we noted, three thousand of them accepted Jesus and were baptized (v. 41). Most of these did not go back to their faraway homes, but stayed in Jerusalem to be taught by the apostles (v. 42). Naturally some of them were soon out of money, but others were willing to share. No one thought that what he had was his own; it was the common property of the group (Acts 4:32).

45. Selling their possessions and goods, they gave to anyone as he had need.

With unlimited generosity, people even sold their property and shared the proceeds. They turned the money over to the apostles to be distributed to the needy (Acts 4:34, 35). No one had to go out and get a job instead of "staying in school,"

PRAYER

How gracious you are, our heavenly Father! For all of us sinners you have provided a way of salvation, and you have given us the Holy Spirit and the power to walk in that way. Continue to give us strength and courage that we may be faithful forever. In Jesus' name we pray. Amen.

DAILY BIBLE READINGS

Monday, Sept. 4—Baptized With the Spirit (Matthew 3:7-12)

Tuesday, Sept. 5—Empowered by the Spirit (Luke 1:8-17)

Wednesday, Sept. 6—Speaking With Boldness (Acts 4:27-31)

Thursday, Sept. 7—Direct Communication (Acts 13:6-12)

Friday, Sept. 8—Holy Spirit and Joy (Acts 13:47-52)

Saturday, Sept. 9—Insight From the Spirit (Luke 2:22-32)

Sunday, Sept. 10—The Spirit as Teacher (1 Corinthians 2:10-16)

WHAT DO YOU THINK?

Not all of the practices of the church in Jerusalem were adopted by congregations elsewhere. Changes were made to suit particular times and needs. Obviously we are not free to change the doctrines or practices that the New Testament clearly sets forth for the church to follow, but changes may well be needed in man-made customs and methods. If a church perceives that a certain tradition or method has passed beyond usefulness, or if felt needs are not being met, that church would do well to make some changes.

Suggest some principles that may guide a congregation in establishing new practices or discontinuing old ones.

as it were, and being taught by the inspired apostles. The wisdom of this intensive schooling became apparent when persecution drove the disciples out of Jerusalem. Then they were so well trained that they could be preachers of the gospel wherever they went (Acts 8:1, 4).

The believers had all things common (v. 44), but this was not *communism* in the modern sense of the term. The funds were given voluntarily: no one was required to give (Acts 5:4). Ananias and Sapphira were punished, not for keeping part of their money, but for lying about it (Acts 5:1-11). Not all of the property owners sold their property. A woman named Mary kept her house in Jerusalem and shared the house instead of the money (Acts 12:12). With this happy sharing and intensive teaching, the church continued to grow day by day (Acts 2:47).

CONCLUSION

What a tremendous lesson this is! How many conclusions might be drawn from it! Let's think a little about the Holy Spirit's coming in power.

A. THE SPIRIT AND POWER

Himself unseen, the Spirit came with a roaring sound and a spectacular sight. To the apostles he gave amazing powers: power to talk in languages that they had not learned, power to heal the sick by miracles, power to teach God's word with never an error.

However, the Spirit did not give them power to get rich and live in luxury. Nor did he give them power to escape suffering and persecution. Soon the apostles were imprisoned and beaten (Acts 5:17-42). Soon James was killed (Acts 12:1, 2). Old tradition says all the apostles except John died for their faith.

A few disciples besides the apostles received miraculous powers (Acts 8:5-8), but more did not. And while we today identify with that greater number, nearly all of us have power to learn. Are we studying God's Word enough to make use of that power? Some of us have power to teach. Are we teaching, or are we turning away because it is too much work? Some of us have executive ability. Are we leading or loafing in the church? Some of us have a fine ability to be helpful to others. Are we using or wasting it? Most of us have power to give of our means. Are we giving liberally? (See Romans 12:6-8.) And if our faithful service brings persecution, do not all of us share the apostles' power to endure it?

B. THE CHANGING, CHANGELESS CHURCH

Pentecost is often called the birthday of the church. The newborn church was a robust infant, but an infant does not live like a ten-year-old, and a ten-year-old does not live like an adult. Some features of the young church soon changed, but some things never change.

Members of the first church abandoned jobs and businesses to listen daily to the apostles' teaching. That practice was not continued in other congregations, but no church will prosper and grow unless it gives attention to teaching.

Members of the first church "were together, and had everything in common" (Acts 2:44). That was not a general practice among other churches at that time; but in all times and everywhere, Christians share with brothers and sisters in need.

People came into the fellowship of the first church by being convinced that Jesus is the Christ, by turning away from their sins to obey him, by being baptized in his name for the forgiveness of sins. In the fellowship of the church they continued steadfastly in Christian worship and life (Acts 2:42). These are some of the things that never change.

Discovery Learning

This page contains an alternate lesson plan emphasizing learning activities. Classes desiring such student involvement will find these suggestions helpful. The next page is a reproducible activity page to further enhance discovery learning.

LEARNING GOALS

As students participate in today's class session, they should:

1. Describe the events, message, and resulting fellowship of the believers of Pentecost.

2. Express confidence of salvation in Christ.

3. Participate in the body life of the church, as described in Acts 2:42-47.

INTO THE LESSON

Before class prepare enough slips of paper to provide one slip for everyone who will attend your class. On one-third of the slips write, "A sermon that pointed me in a new direction." On another third of the slips write, "The day I became a Christian." On the final third write, "A time when I shared the gospel."

Give a slip to each member as he or she enters the classroom. To begin the session, instruct the members to stand and either (a) find another person whose slip has the same phrases as his own or (b) trade slips with another class member and then find someone whose slip matches his new one.

Once everyone has a partner, the couples should spend three minutes talking with each other about the topic on their slips. Then ask volunteers to share briefly their responses with the whole class.

Tell the class that the necessity of preaching and conversion are two of the major topics dealt with in our lesson text.

INTO THE WORD

Allow class members to examine the entire second chapter of Acts in this session. Accomplish this by dividing the chapter into four sections:

1. What the Holy Spirit did (vv. 1-13)
2. What Peter claimed (vv. 14-36)
3. How the people responded (vv. 37-41)
4. What the first church was like (vv. 42-47)

Write these four headings on the chalkboard before class. Have the verses that correspond to each heading read aloud to the class by four class members. Then tell your students that they may choose a learning activity to help them explore one of the paragraphs further. Describe each of these options to your class:

1. Write a newspaper account describing the events recorded in verses 1-13.

2. Make a simple outline of Peter's sermon recorded in verses 14-36.

3. Imagine that you were in the audience when Peter preached his sermon. Then write a diary entry in which you explain your response to his message. Especially consider verses 37-41 as you write.

4. Make a comparison chart. For each of the first church's activities described in verses 42-47, list a comparable activity that you see happening in the church today.

If you have at least twelve class members, have them divide into four groups so that each of the four activities is undertaken. Allot about ten minutes for these activities. Then let each group share with the whole class so all will have an overview of Acts 2.

INTO LIFE

Suggest to the class that three categories of people can be identified in this chapter:

• Messengers with a mission.
• Hearers who needed to repent.
• Believers who were helped by their fellowship with one another.

Ask, "Who from Acts 2 falls into each category?"

Then have your students return to the same groups in which they did their Bible study. Suggest to them that in their groups they tell each other in which category they believe they belong, and why.

Read the following three questions aloud as your students listen with their eyes closed and heads bowed:

1. Does any obstacle stand in the way of your salvation? Do you need to take any of the steps Peter commanded in Acts 2?

2. Do you have a mission to share the gospel with someone? Whom could you tell this week?

3. What place have you taken in the local fellowship of believers? Are you doing your part to make your congregation effective in the service of Christ?

On this third point, you might want to suggest the topics under "The Believers in Action," on page 32. Have each student do some self evaluation on each point. (Or photocopy the page and distribute it.)

Close your time together with a discussion of how your class can work together to reproduce the spirit and activity of the early church as described in the text. End with a prayer circle, praying for God's Spirit to use each member of the class in service for God.

Topic: Holy Spirit

Using ideas from today's Scripture texts, write a word that begins with each of the following letters that relates to the Holy Spirit.

A_____   M_____

B_____   N_____

C_____   O_____

D_____   P_____

E_____   R_____

F_____   S_____

G_____   T_____

H_____   U_____

I_____   V_____

J_____   W_____

K_____   Y_____

L_____   Z_____

The Believers in Action

Listed below are some of the activities of the first believers in Jerusalem. (See Acts 2:42-47.) Next to each one, describe how you can be involved in similar activities today.

The apostles' teaching _____

Fellowship _____

The breaking of bread _____

Prayer_____

Being together _____

Sharing their possessions _____

Praising God _____

The Story of Christian Beginnings
Unit 1. The Promise of the Spirit's Power
(Lessons 1-4)

HEALING AND PREACHING

LESSON 3

WHY TEACH THIS LESSON?

There was a time when being a Christian was considered a virtue. In fact, almost everyone wanted to be *thought* a Christian, even if the person made no attempt to conform to the standards of the Scriptures.

That time is all but gone today. Christians are portrayed in the media as narrow-minded, hypocritical, and ignorant. Any good the church has done is largely ignored, while the bad is grossly exaggerated. Mobs have invaded and disrupted worship services, professing Christians have been fired from their positions, and occasionally physical violence has even been used against Christians. More and more, your students will find themselves facing opposition. The example of Peter and John in today's lesson will help them to take their stand.

INTRODUCTION

It's pleasant to be popular—but it's dangerous. Jesus said, "Woe to you when all men speak well of you, for that is how their fathers treated the false prophets" (Luke 6:26).

False prophets in ancient times abandoned the truth to say what people liked to hear, and disaster came to prophets and people together. In our time, a popular entertainer may value applause more than decency. A popular preacher may put the offering ahead of the truth. But William Cullen Bryant put it well:

Truth, crushed to earth, shall rise again;
The eternal years of God are hers;
But Error, wounded, writhes in pain,
And dies among his worshippers.

A. THE POPULAR JESUS

Surely Jesus was the most popular teacher in Israel. People flocked to him from all over the country (Matthew 4:25). His teaching and his miraculous healing were a magnet that drew them (Luke 5:15).

But Jesus was not popular with "all men." The elite of Israel opposed him strongly—the highly educated men, the priests, the ruling class, the accredited teachers. Finding no other way to counter Jesus' popularity, the rulers killed him.

B. LESSON BACKGROUND

Jesus warned his disciples, "'No servant is greater than his master.' If they persecuted me, they will persecute you also" (John 15:20). After Jesus went back to Heaven, his followers found that they had inherited both his popularity and his opposition. Their miracles, their good way of life, and their teaching won the favor of the people in Jerusalem, and the young church grew rapidly (Acts 2:43-47). But Jesus' followers gained no favor with the rulers, as we see in our text.

I. MIRACLE (ACTS 3:1-8)

"Many wonders and miraculous signs were done by the apostles" (Acts 2:43).

Sep
17

DEVOTIONAL READING
ACTS 3:18-26

LESSON SCRIPTURE
ACTS 3:1—4:31

PRINTED TEXT
ACTS 3:1-8; 4:5-12

LESSON AIMS

After participating in this lesson one should be able to:

1. Tell why and how Peter and John faced opposition from the religious rulers, and how they responded.

2. Compare the hostility of the council toward the apostles with the hostility modern Christians sometimes face.

3. Describe how a Christian may boldly yet courteously share the gospel in the face of antagonism.

KEY VERSE

Peter said, "Silver or gold I do not have, but what I have I give you. In the name of Jesus Christ of Nazareth, walk." —Acts 3:6

The relative importance of material wealth and the power of Jesus is illustrated by visual 3 of the visuals packet.

WHAT DO YOU THINK?

Our society clings to the idea that any problem can be solved if enough money is spent on it. However, crime, illicit drug usage, teenage pregnancy, and homelessness are among our society's problems that seem unaffected by great sums of money poured into programs to combat them.

When Peter and John met the lame man, they offered a solution that silver and gold could not provide. The church still holds the key to such change. It is found in the gospel with its promise of "a new creation" (2 Corinthians 5:17).

What then should be the church's response to the social problems of our day? What guidelines would you suggest for a proper balance between spending money to address social ills and spending for evangelism? Suggest Scriptures to support your conclusions.

This is repeated with emphasis in Acts 5:12-16. Luke does not pause to discuss many of these miracles, but a sample is recorded in our text.

A. MAN IN NEED (vv. 1-3)
1. One day Peter and John were going up to the temple at the time of prayer—at three in the afternoon.

Three o'clock was one of the daily times of public prayer in Jerusalem. Apparently *Peter and John* were going to attend the prayer meeting. It seems that they and other disciples spent much of their time in Solomon's Porch (Acts 3:11; Acts 5:12). This was a roofed colonnade at the east side of the big outer court, the temple court that was open to all the people, Jews and Gentiles alike. The prayer meeting was held in a smaller court inside the big one. This inner court was on a higher level and surrounded by a wall with signs warning Gentiles that they would be killed if they entered.

2. Now a man crippled from birth was being carried to the temple gate called Beautiful, where he was put every day to beg from those going into the temple courts.

This unfortunate man had been *crippled from birth*. He was now more than forty years old (Acts 4:22). He was so crippled that he could not work for a living. He could not even walk, but family members or friends *carried* him each day and *put* him at the *gate called Beautiful*. It was a good place for a beggar, for many worshiping people are generous people. The gate was a huge one. Its doors, made of brass and richly decorated, towered seventy-five feet above the crippled man. If Peter and John were coming from Solomon's porch, they came naturally to this gate, for it was on the east side of the inner court.

3. When he saw Peter and John about to enter, he asked them for money.

There is nothing here to indicate that the beggar knew *Peter and John*. He asked them for a donation just as he asked anyone else who passed him to *enter* the temple.

B. MEETING A NEED (vv. 4-7)
4. Peter looked straight at him, as did John. Then Peter said, "Look at us!"

Probably most persons who responded to the beggar's plea just dropped small coins without stopping. But this pair stopped, not only looking at the man, but also asking him to look at them.

5. So the man gave them his attention, expecting to get something from them.

We can imagine that the man looked up very eagerly. If these two wanted to call special attention to their giving, probably the gift would be a big one. And indeed it was, though the man as yet had no inkling of the nature of it.

6. Then Peter said, "Silver or gold I do not have, but what I have I give you. In the name of Jesus Christ of Nazareth, walk."

Perhaps the beggar's heart sank at Peter's first words. He could expect no more than a copper coin if the giver had no *silver or gold*. But how his heart must have leaped as Peter finished! We can only guess how much this man knew about Jesus, but surely he had heard much. Only months earlier, Jesus had received a tumultuous welcome in Jerusalem (Luke 19:35-40). He had come into the temple and had "looked around at everything" (Mark 11:11). The next day he had driven the crooked merchants from the temple court (Mark 11:15-17). The crippled man at the Beautiful gate must have seen some of the excitement. He must have heard more from passers-by at the gate and from those who carried him to and from his begging place. Among other things, he must have heard of marvelous miracles. Now *in the name of Jesus Christ of Nazareth* he was called to *walk*. Hope must have surged within him at the words.

7. Taking him by the right hand, he helped him up, and instantly the man's feet and ankles became strong.

Peter helped with his hand as well as his voice. The lame man made an effort, and suddenly his useless feet were as useful as anyone's.

MORE THAN EXPECTED

Insurance fraud hurts us all. Some people have taken to staging traffic collisions and then filing claim for imaginary—although very expensive—injuries. But it doesn't always work as planned.

Recently, the driver of a car on the freeway swerved in front of a semitrailer truck. Since trucking companies insure their vehicles and because large trucks cannot stop quickly, it seemed like a perfect insurance fraud setup. But it backfired. Instead of merely bumping the car from behind, the truck jackknifed and overturned on top of the car, crushing it. One of the car's occupants was killed. The driver of the car and the two surviving passengers were arrested on suspicion of insurance fraud and faced the prospect of being charged with murder as well. All three got more—and worse!—than they expected.

The lame man at the temple gate wished only for a gift of a few coins, perhaps enough to help his family pay for his care. But because those whom he asked for help were God's servants, he received far more—and far better!—than what he had been looking for!

When with pure hearts we seek blessing from God, we will not be disappointed. Perhaps what we receive will be different from what we expected. It may be far better!

—C. R. B.

C. JOY AND PRAISE (v. 8)

8. He jumped to his feet and began to walk. Then he went with them into the temple courts, walking and jumping, and praising God.

The man did not need time to learn to walk. He was perfectly capable of *walking, and jumping* as well. He had to go up a flight of stairs to the inner court of the temple, but stairs were no obstacle to his nimble feet. He was also *praising God,* and certainly not in whispers. Imagine the amazement of people gathering for the prayer meeting. Day by day they had seen this man at the gate, helpless and hopeless—but look at him now! (Acts 3:9, 10).

This man had been laid at the temple gate daily (v. 2). Peter and John and other apostles must have passed him again and again. He may have been there when Jesus had come into the temple and looked around (Mark 11:11). After that, Jesus had taught daily in the temple (Luke 19:47). Naturally we wonder why this lame man had not been healed before.

We can only answer that Peter and John were directed by the Holy Spirit. It was the Spirit, not the apostles, who chose the time for the miracle. No doubt he chose a time when the miracle would most accomplish its purpose.

This reminds us again of the purpose of miracles. They did help needy people, but they were not done for that purpose alone. If they had been, God could have healed from Heaven without any help from Peter and John.

The miracle had two other purposes. First, it caught the attention of many people. Second, it showed that God's power was with the apostles. This encouraged people to believe that the apostles spoke God's truth.

Don't we still need to attract attention to the gospel of Christ? Don't we still need to convince people that the gospel is really God's message? Of course we do. Then why aren't miracles as common now as they were in the days when the church was just beginning? Perhaps for the same reason that teenagers and adults

OPTION

An activity on the reproducible page, "Unbounded Joy," will help your students explore further the subject of receiving more than expected. See page 40.

HOW TO SAY IT
Annas. AN-nus.
Caiaphas. KAY-uh-fus or
    KYE-uh-fus.
Pharisees. FAIR-ih-seez.
Sadducees. SAD-you-seez.
Sanhedrin. SAN-huh-drun or
    San-HEED-run.

don't receive the same care that little babies do. The miracles were a special help for a newborn church while it was just getting started.

II. TROUBLE (ACTS 4:5-7)

Prayer meeting in the inner court must have been a bit unsettled that day. When it ended, the healed man clung to Peter and John as they went back to Solomon's Porch. People from the prayer meeting went along. Others saw the excitement and came to see what was happening. To the gathering crowd Peter explained that he and John had not done this miracle. It was the work of God, who did it to glorify Jesus, his Son whom men had crucified but God had raised from the dead. Peter declared that Jesus is the Christ foretold by the prophets. He urged the people to repent, to have their sins blotted out, to become followers of the crucified and risen Messiah (Acts 3:11-26). But before the sermon was finished, there was trouble.

The priests in charge of the temple were angry and grieved because Peter was lauding Jesus. They were doubly grieved because he was proclaiming the resurrection of the dead. The priests were Sadducees (Acts 5:17), and Sadducees did not believe in any resurrection (Acts 23:8). So they came and brought with them the chief of the temple police and put the apostles in jail (Acts 4:1-3).

A. HOSTILE RULERS (vv. 5, 6)

5, 6. The next day the rulers, elders and teachers of the law met in Jerusalem. Annas the high priest was there, and so were Caiaphas, John, Alexander and the other men of the high priest's family.

The day was near its end when Peter and John were arrested, so the two were jailed for the night (Acts 4:3). The next day the men in authority were assembled to deal with the prisoners. These verses seem to describe the Sanhedrin, sometimes called the Council, which was both legislature and supreme court. It included not only the chief priests, but also *elders* and *teachers of the law*. Probably some of these were Pharisees instead of Sadducees (Acts 23:6). Pharisees believed in resurrection, but not the resurrection of Jesus. They had opposed Jesus throughout his ministry. They envied his popularity; they were angry because he did not respect all their traditions; they were annoyed because he exposed their hypocrisy. The priests (Sadducees) had also opposed Jesus during his ministry. They too envied his popularity, but they also differed with him theologically (cf. Matthew 22:23-32). Pharisees and Sadducees had their differences and disputes, but they had cooperated to condemn Jesus and persuade the Roman governor to have him crucified. Now they would cooperate in an effort to compel Jesus' followers to stop talking about him.

B. HOSTILE QUESTION (v. 7)

7. They had Peter and John brought before them and began to question them: "By what power or what name did you do this?"

The Sanhedrin had about seventy members. They were seated in a semicircle, and probably dressed in elaborate robes. It was an assembly well designed to intimidate a pair of fishermen from Galilee, who now were *brought before them*, with hostile eyes on three sides of them. These seventy men were the rulers. Power among the Jews belonged to them, and they certainly had not authorized these Galilean visitors to lecture in the temple. Then *by what power or what name* had these impudent fishermen done what they had done?

III. INSPIRED ANSWER (ACTS 4:8-12)

The assembly of rulers was impressive, but Peter and John were not intimidated. Their power came from a higher authority, and they knew it.

WHAT DO YOU THINK?

The first question directed to Peter and John by the members of the council—"By what power or what name did you do this?"—exhibits their extreme prejudice. Among themselves they admitted that these apostles had performed a great miracle (Acts 4:16), but there is no record of their crediting Peter and John with being God's instruments of healing. So today the church's critics frequently seem inclined to regard Christians as meddlers and troublemakers, while virtually ignoring the vast amount of good that is done by believers who feed the hungry, minister to the sick, teach the illiterate, and comfort the brokenhearted.

Why do you suppose this is so? What action, if any, should Christians take to balance the scales?

A. Inspired Preacher (v. 8)

8. Then Peter, filled with the Holy Spirit, said to them: "Rulers and elders of the people!

Jesus had given his apostles instructions and a promise for times like this. When they were called into court for obeying him, they were not to sit up all night to plan their defense. The words would be given to them. Jesus said, "It will not be you speaking, but the Spirit of your Father speaking through you" (Matthew 10:17-20). Now Peter was *filled with the Holy Spirit,* and he spoke the words that the Spirit gave him. Courteously he acknowledged that the hostile men before him were in fact *rulers and elders* of his *people,* the Jews.

B. Good Deed (v. 9)

9. "If we are being called to account today for an act of kindness shown to a cripple and are asked how he was healed. . . .

These words exposed the awkward position of the rulers. They had arrested two men, kept them in jail overnight, and brought them into court to be questioned, not for some crime done or alleged, but for a deed that was unquestionably good, the healing of a helpless man. The seventy must have been squirming uncomfortably as Peter continued.

C. Good Doer (vv. 10-12)

10. "Then know this, you and all the people of Israel: It is by the name of Jesus Christ of Nazareth, whom you crucified but whom God raised from the dead, that this man stands before you healed.

Peter was very glad to answer the question of verse 7. He wanted not only those judges, but also *all the people of Israel,* to know that *Jesus Christ of Nazareth* had supplied the power for the healing done in his name. Peter added a reminder that those very judges had condemned Jesus to death and had persuaded the Roman governor to order him crucified. God had reversed their decision and had brought Jesus back from the dead. If the rulers were squirming before, this certainly did not make them any more comfortable.

11. "He is 'the stone you builders rejected, which has become the capstone.'

Psalm 118 sings praises to God for his gracious help. Among other things, it sings of a stone that was rejected by builders, but nevertheless became the chief cornerstone of a structure. The psalm adds, "The Lord has done this, and it is marvelous in our eyes" (vv. 22, 23). Directed by the Holy Spirit, Peter said that stone is Jesus. The judges in the council were the builders that rejected Jesus. Nevertheless, Jesus is the chief cornerstone of a magnificent structure, his church (Ephesians 2:19-22). "The Lord has done this, and it is marvelous in our eyes."

12. "Salvation is found in no one else, for there is no other name under heaven given to men by which we must be saved."

So the Holy Spirit and Peter brought the speech to its end. Jesus not only is the power that gave healing to this helpless man; he is also the only hope of *salvation* for all mankind, including the judges who condemned him.

The rulers must have known from the beginning that they had no case against Peter and John. They hoped to frighten those Galilean fishermen into silence. But their effort had backfired. The fishermen were unabashed; the rulers were frustrated and probably furious. But what could they do? To add to their discomfort, the healed man also had been brought into court. There he stood, a living refutation of anything that might be said against Jesus (Acts 4:14). Those judges themselves knew the man well. Often they had seen him lying helpless in his begging place. There was no way to deny that a notable miracle had been done (v. 16). The rulers

What Do You Think?

In today's atmosphere of tolerance for religious diversity, it may seem unbecoming of Christians to insist that Jesus Christ is the exclusive way to salvation and eternal life. Nevertheless, it is the only way we can be true to the New Testament. (See John 14:6; Acts 4:12.)

What are some ways Christians can insist that "salvation is found in no one else" and still be attractive witnesses to our pluralistic society?

WHAT DO YOU THINK?

The lesson writer observes, "It is helpful to be as critical of our own opinions as we are of an opponent's opinions." Do you agree or disagree? Why?

PRAYER

Heavenly Father, how good it is to have in our hands the Holy Bible, your inspired Word! How good it is to see the noble example of our Savior and his saints of ancient times! By your grace may we find the truth you want us to know. Then may we hold it firmly and proclaim it boldly, for Jesus' sake. In his name. Amen.

THOUGHT TO REMEMBER

Be sure you're right; then go ahead.

WHAT DO YOU THINK?

Unfortunately, courtesy and respect seem to be rare today—even among Christians. Yet rudeness and ridicule, while sometimes effective in winning an argument with another individual, only serve to drive the other person farther away from the truth and from us. It is a hollow victory to "win the battle, but lose the war."

Christians more than any other people should be able to contend for the truth in a courteous manner. Suggest some guidelines for doing this.

could only go on with their effort to scare the apostles. With threats they "commanded them not to speak or teach at all in the name of Jesus" (vv. 15-18). Peter and John may have been scared, but they were not silenced. Firmly they replied, "Judge for yourselves whether it is right in God's sight to obey you rather than God. For we cannot help speaking about what we have seen and heard" (vv. 19, 20).

When Peter and John were released from custody, they and other disciples joined in prayer—not for freedom from trouble, but for courage to go on with their work and for continuing miracles to show that God was with them (Acts 4:21-31). Their prayer was answered: they did go on with their work, the miracles did continue—and more trouble came, as we shall see next week.

CONCLUSION

Two messages for us leap from the pages of this lesson: one on the negative side, and one on the positive.

A. NEGATIVE

On the negative side, we must not fall into the sin of the rulers. They clung tenaciously to their mistaken opinion even when it drove them to murder. Jesus was not one of them; he did not respect all their traditions. Therefore they reasoned that he could not be the Christ, the Son of God. This seemed so obvious that they shut their eyes to the evidence and plunged into battle against him. Unable to win with reason or argument, they used their political power to kill him. Then they tried to stop his followers from speaking about him.

Of course you and I are not in a position to commit legal murder if someone disagrees with us, and of course we are not so unreasonably set in our opinions anyway. But don't you know someone who is? A man stoutly declares that the kind of car he drives is the best kind there is, and he is not even listening when you extol the virtues of your car. A lady is likewise devoted to one brand of tea, or detergent, or computer. She will not even consider any other brand. A teacher presents his theory of evolution as if it were a compilation of well-known facts. If you raise a question, he brands you as ignorant. A preacher says his understanding of the millennium is the one and only correct one. Your opinion is silly, he says. A campaign orator tells outrageous lies about his opponent. If you raise an objection, he shouts you down.

Even with the Holy Spirit in our hearts and the Holy Bible in our hands, most of us Christians know we are not so fully inspired as Peter was. We can be wrong, but we can learn. It is helpful to be as critical of our own opinions as we are of an opponent's opinions. It helps if we keep our minds open and try to understand the positions of those who disagree with us. It helps if we look for points of agreement as well as points of disagreement. We can learn, if we are willing to learn.

B. POSITIVE

On the positive side, when our position is clearly the one taught by God's Word, we need to hold it as firmly as Peter and John held theirs. We must cling to truth and right regardless of the consequences. We must speak out for the Lord, though it brings upon us the scorn of scholars, the threats of foes, and the pity of friends. So let us join the apostles in prayer for courage rather than comfort.

At the same time, let us note that the apostles spoke courteously, even to those who were not courteous. Likewise Jesus spoke with courtesy to Pilate, the governor who pronounced him innocent and ordered him to be crucified. Let us follow in the footsteps of our Lord so that, "speaking the truth in love, we will in all things grow up into him who is the Head, that is, Christ" (Ephesians 4:15).

Discovery Learning

This page contains an alternate lesson plan emphasizing learning activities. Classes desiring such student involvement will find these suggestions helpful. The next page is a reproducible activity page to further enhance discovery learning.

LEARNING GOALS

As students participate in today's class session, they should:

1. Tell why and how Peter and John faced opposition from the religious rulers, and how they responded.

2. Compare the hostility of the council toward the apostles with the hostility modern Christians sometimes face.

3. Describe how a Christian may boldly yet courteously share the gospel in the face of antagonism.

INTO THE LESSON

Before the class session begins, write each of the following phrases on half sheets of paper, one phrase on each:

1. Places in the *world* that are *hostile* to the gospel of Christ.
2. Places in our *country* that are *hostile* to the gospel of Christ.
3. Places in our *community* that are *hostile* to the gospel of Christ.

A. Places in the *world* that are *friendly* to the gospel of Christ.
B. Places in our *country* that are *friendly* to the gospel of Christ.
C. Places in our *community* that are *friendly* to the gospel of Christ.

Begin today's session by dividing your class into groups of between five and seven students each. Give each of the groups a different piece of paper, using the phrases from numbers 1-3 above. If possible, provide each group with a large sheet of paper and a felt-tip marker. Each group is to jot down ideas in response to its assigned phrase. The "places" need not necessarily be specific geographical names; they could be labels for situations, such as "any class taught by my English professor at the university."

After allotting five minutes to complete the assignment, ask the groups to display their lists. Read a few items from each one.

Then repeat the process, this time assigning the groups the phrases lettered A-C. After five more minutes, read a few of the items from each group's list.

Tell the class that from the church's earliest days there were those who were hostile to the gospel. Nevertheless, amid that hostility, the gospel flourished. Today's study can provide some clues as to how we can spread the gospel today, even in the face of those who are antagonistic toward the claims of Christ.

INTO THE WORD

Use the same groups for Bible study that were formed for the introductory activity. Each of the groups should assume the identity of one of the main characters in the biblical event we are studying today: Peter, John, the lame man, the Jewish authorities, and the citizens of Jerusalem. Each group is to try to determine the thoughts and feelings of its assigned character when the events in today's Scripture text occurred.

Tell your class members to listen carefully as volunteers read aloud the following five paragraphs of Scripture: Acts 3:1-10, 11-16; 4:1-7, 8-12, 13-22. Then ask each group to answer this question: "What did our character think and feel when the events recorded in these paragraphs occurred?"

You may want to make a chart on your chalkboard. Down the left side of the board, list all the characters or groups named above. Across the top write each of the Scripture references. Allot six or eight minutes for the groups to discuss the question. Then complete your chart as someone from each group reports the group's findings to the whole class.

INTO LIFE

Discuss the following questions:
1. What can we do that will draw attention to the message of Jesus?
2. What can we learn from Peter and John regarding—
   a. the content of our message to a lost world?
   b. the best way to present the message?
   c. how to react when the message is resisted?

Challenge class members to think of the situation in their lives when sharing the gospel is most difficult. Can they find any clues in the example of Peter and John to help them to know how they should respond?

If you have time, allow class members to share their personal strategy with others in their small groups. Then they can pray for each other in their groups before the class is dismissed.

Spreading the Gospel

From the healing of one crippled beggar, many lives were changed by the power of the Holy Spirit. Fill in the boxes to trace this chain reaction as one person rejoiced in what the Lord had done for him. (The first box has been filled in for you.)

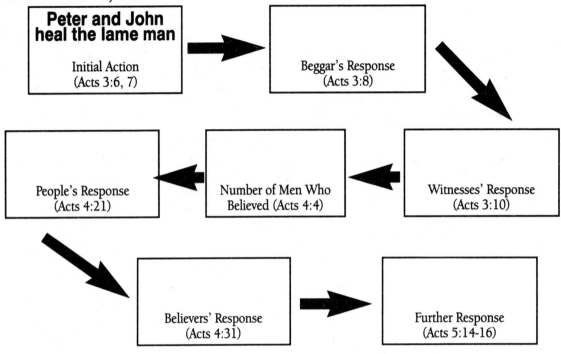

Peter and John heal the lame man

Initial Action
(Acts 3:6, 7)

Beggar's Response
(Acts 3:8)

People's Response
(Acts 4:21)

Number of Men Who
Believed (Acts 4:4)

Witnesses' Response
(Acts 3:10)

Believers' Response
(Acts 4:31)

Further Response
(Acts 5:14-16)

Unbounded Joy

In our lives we pray for God's blessings, we pray for God's intervention. The crippled beggar was expectant. He anticipated gold or silver. His healing gave him overwhelming joy. Recall a time when your prayer was answered beyond all expectation.

What was your situation? _____

What did you expect? _____

What did you receive? _____

How did you express your joy? _____

How has your life been different as a result? _____

The Story of Christian Beginnings

Unit 1. The Promise of the Spirit's Power
(Lessons 1-4)

OBEDIENT TO THE SPIRIT

LESSON 4

WHY TEACH THIS LESSON?

"Choose for yourselves this day whom you will serve," challenged Joshua long ago (Joshua 24:15). There was nothing unusual about *that* day. The same choice is set before us *every* day. In the security of the Sunday school classroom, the right answer is easy, "We must obey God rather than men." In the not-so-secure world of the office or plant or classroom, however, the choice is more difficult.

In today's lesson, we will see how that choice was made in the face of a serious threat to the lives of the apostles. We will also see an occasion of God's providence. Together, these events can give your students a view that God will reward and protect those who take their stand for him. That assurance should make the right choice not so difficult even when students have left the security of the classroom.

INTRODUCTION

Sometimes the Christian way is perplexing. For example, when John the Baptist was explaining the meaning of repentance, he said, "The man with two tunics should share with him who has none" (Luke 3:10, 11). So I am a bit disturbed when I look in my closet and see two coats. Does that mean my repentance is not real?

My bank account is disturbing too. Jesus said, "Do not store up for yourselves treasures on earth" (Matthew 6:19). Should I close that bank account and give the money to the poor? But on the other hand, Paul recognized the principle that "children should not have to save up for their parents, but parents for their children" (2 Corinthians 12:14). Isn't it reasonable and right to put aside a part of my earnings so my children will not have to pay my rent when I have to live in a nursing home?

A. EASY DECISIONS

On the other hand, some decisions are easy even if they are costly. If the neighbors have to flee their burning home in a snowstorm, we take them in even if our house is full already. If we have a chance to make a million by defrauding our friends, or even by defrauding our enemies, we turn it down. Fraud has no place in the Christian life.

Likewise easy was the apostles' decision. Jesus told them to tell his gospel to the world; the rulers of Jerusalem told them to shut up. The apostles said, "We must obey God rather than men" (Acts 5:29). It was the only choice possible for Christians, even if they were flogged for it (Acts 5:40).

B. LESSON BACKGROUND

Last week we read that Peter and John were arrested and ordered not to talk about Jesus anymore. When they were released, other disciples joined them in prayer. They did not pray that none of them would be arrested. They prayed for boldness to keep on spreading Jesus' message, and they prayed for continuing miracles to show God's presence and power (Acts 4:29, 30). Both prayers were answered. They "spoke the word of God boldly" (Acts 4:31), and miracles were

DEVOTIONAL READING
ACTS 4:32-37
LESSON SCRIPTURE
ACTS 4:32—5:42
PRINTED TEXT
ACTS 5:17-32

Sep
24

LESSON AIMS

After this lesson a student should be able to:

1. Describe the continuing opposition faced by the apostles and how they dealt with it.

2. Suggest some modern situation in which Christians are forced to choose "to obey God rather than men."

3. Identify at least one way the individual, the class, or the church together can take a stand "to obey God rather than men."

KEY VERSE

Peter and the other apostles replied: "We must obey God rather than men!" —Acts 5:29

LESSON 4 NOTES

multiplied (Acts 5:12-16). "More and more men and women believed in the Lord and were added to their number" (Acts 5:14). This did not please the rulers who had ordered the apostles to stop their preaching.

I. IN AND OUT OF JAIL (ACTS 5:17-21a)

The apostles made no secret of their disobedience to the rulers. Their meeting place was Solomon's porch, a huge roofed colonnade in the big outer court of the temple. They also took their ministry of healing out into the streets of Jerusalem, and people from other cities came flocking to be healed. No one, ruler or commoner, could fail to see what was going on (Acts 5:12-16).

A. IN JAIL (vv. 17, 18)

17. Then the high priest and all his associates, who were members of the party of the Sadducees, were filled with jealousy.

The high priest was the highest official among the Jews. *All his associates* were other leaders among the priests. These belonged to *the party of the Sadducees.* Though they conducted the ceremonies of worship, they were more political and less religious than the Pharisees, who were proud of their devotion to the Scriptures and to their traditions.

These leaders were not used to having their orders ignored. The apostles were ignoring their order very obviously, and were becoming very popular with the people at the same time. As a result, the priests *were filled with jealousy.*

18. They arrested the apostles and put them in the public jail.

Peter and John had been arrested before, but now it seems that all twelve of *the apostles* were seized. They were put *in the public jail* like common criminals, to be held till the ruling council, the Sanhedrin, could deal with them.

A JEALOUS HEART

Few sins are more common than jealousy, and Christians must constantly guard against it. One may be jealous of another's singing voice, exceptional teaching or speaking ability, or simply the winsomeness of a godly personality. We all know that jealousy is not an attitude of a godly heart.

The Sadducees were among the spiritual leaders of Israel, but they were jealous of the apostles. The apostles were honest and sincere men doing God's will by bringing people to Christ.

Jealousy should have no place in those who are committed to the service of God. It only disrupts the work. May our concern be that God alone will receive glory and praise for the talents he has given to each of us.

—C. R. B.

B. OUT OF JAIL (vv. 19-21a)

19, 20. But during the night an angel of the Lord opened the doors of the jail and brought them out. "Go, stand in the temple courts," he said, "and tell the people the full message of this new life."

The supreme rulers of the Jews put these men in prison, but the supreme Ruler of Heaven and earth sent his messenger to release them. Obviously the guards were helpless; possibly they were blinded so they could see nothing, or possibly they were sleeping on duty. It seems that they did not even know the prisoners were gone. Had they known, surely they would have reported it. It seems that the guards were totally ignored as the angel led a dozen men out of the prison and sent them to go on with their work of preaching the gospel *in the temple courts,* under the very noses of the hostile authorities.

Sidebar (left column)

OPTION

Use the reproducible activity, "Nobody Said It Was Easy," on page 48 to explore the concept of facing opposition.

HOW TO SAY IT

Ago (Greek). AH-go.
Archegos (Greek). are-kay-GOSS.
Arche (Greek). are-KAY.
Gamaliel. Guh-MAY-lih-ul.
Pharisees. FAIR-ih-seez.
Sadducees. SAD-you-seez.
Sanhedrin. SAN-huh-drun
　　or San HEED-drun.

21a. At daybreak they entered the temple courts, as they had been told, and began to teach the people.

Again the record does not pause to deal with details. What time of night was it when the apostles were released? Did they have time to eat and sleep before they went back to their teaching? We can only wonder about such questions. But early in the morning, as soon as anyone would be there to hear, the apostles went back into the temple and kept on teaching God's message to all who would listen.

II. IN CUSTODY AGAIN (ACTS 5:21b-26)

Of course the amazing escape could not long be hidden, and of course the apostles could not hope to teach very long without another interruption. Perhaps that was the reason they started early in the morning. In the meantime, the high priest and his associates were going about their business, never suspecting that their prisoners were no longer in jail.

A. COURT IN SESSION (v. 21b)

21b. When the high priest and his associates arrived, they called together the Sanhedrin—the full assembly of the elders of Israel—and sent to the jail for the apostles.

The high priest and his associates lost no time in pressing their case. Messengers were sent to summon the members of the Sanhedrin, the ruling council of Israel. Probably the call went out on the day the apostles were arrested, but it was not until the following day that the council was assembled. This was a full meeting. The high priest thought the apostles were a serious threat, and he meant to deal with them with all the power of his government. So the whole council assembled, and probably the high priest explained the reason for the meeting. Then the bailiffs were sent to bring the prisoners before the court.

B. PRISONERS MISSING (vv. 22-24)

22, 23. But on arriving at the jail, the officers did not find them there. So they went back and reported, "We found the jail securely locked, with the guards standing at the doors; but when we opened them, we found no one inside."

What a shock! A bit of routine duty turned into an amazing puzzle. At the prison everything seemed to be in perfect order. The doors were properly shut and *locked.* The *guards* on duty were alert. But the jail was empty!

24. On hearing this report, the captain of the temple guard and the chief priests were puzzled, wondering what would come of this.

There must have been a lot of sound and fury: questioning of the bailiffs who had found the jail empty, questioning of the guards who had been on duty at the prison, shouted charges and fearful denials. The priests must have been furious; the guards must have been frightened. But no one could explain what had happened. There had been an impossible escape, and priests and police were afraid that was only a beginning. What would this affair grow into? They could only guess.

C. PRISONERS RECAPTURED (vv. 25, 26)

25. Then someone came and said, "Look! The men you put in jail are standing in the temple courts teaching the people."

Someone brought news to the agitated gathering. Was it good news or bad? The prisoners had not gone beyond reach of the police—but possibly the priests would have been happier if the escapees had gone to Egypt or Rome. They were right there *in the temple courts,* and right back at the work of telling about Jesus. As the priests saw it, that was bad news!

Visual 4 of the visuals packet highlights a principle Christians must follow when facing moral or ethical choices.

WHAT DO YOU THINK?

What a tremendous surge in the growth of the kingdom of God would result if Christians everywhere were to imitate the apostles and say, "I am going to tell other people about Jesus Christ, and I am not going to let anyone or anything intimidate me." We are all capable of persistence, and many demonstrate that capability in various ways. One may say, "I am determined that I'm going to own a better car," or, "I will learn to use a computer or know the reason why." If we can persist in such mundane matters, surely we can focus this capacity for persistence in winning others to Jesus Christ.

Why, then, does such persistence for the sake of the gospel seem so rare today? What does it take to motivate someone to imitate the apostles' persistence? How can Christians support one another in this persistence?

26. At that, the captain went with his officers and brought the apostles. They did not use force, because they feared that the people would stone them.

The captain probably was chief of the temple police. He took a group of *officers* and went to arrest the *apostles* again. Those prisoners had caused so much trouble that the police might have been inclined to treat them roughly, but *they feared that the people would stone them.* The apostles were teaching a crowd of people, and the many helpful miracles made the speakers popular with the people (Acts 5:13). The crowd might get rough with the police if the police got rough with the apostles. So the police approached with respect, and the apostles let themselves be arrested.

III. COURT IN ACTION (ACTS 5:27-32)

At last the seventy assembled judges had the prisoners before them. Nothing was said about the mysterious escape from jail the previous night—or if something was said, it is not recorded. Perhaps the judges preferred not to say or hear anything about it. They proceeded promptly with the case at hand.

A. ACCUSATION (vv. 27, 28)

27. Having brought the apostles, they made them appear before the Sanhedrin to be questioned by the high priest.

This court did not proceed as a modern one does, with an unbiased presiding judge who listens while two lawyers develop the case, one for the prosecution and one for the defense. The duty of all the seventy judges was to examine witnesses and develop the case both against and for the defendants. But in this case, the judges themselves were accusers and prosecutors. The high priest made their accusation.

28. "We gave you strict orders not to teach in this name," he said. "Yet you have filled Jerusalem with your teaching and are determined to make us guilty of this man's blood."

The high priest really brought two accusations against the apostles. The two were related, but not the same.

First, the high priest said the apostles had disobeyed the plain command of the council. Two leaders among them, Peter and John, had been given *strict orders* "not to speak or teach at all in the name of Jesus" (Acts 4:18). In fact, the command had been accompanied by threats, though the threats were not mentioned here (Acts 4:17, 21). In spite of a plain order and forceful warning, the apostles had *filled Jerusalem* with their forbidden *teaching.* They had openly defied the command of the ruling council, right in the court of the temple, and all Jerusalem knew about it.

Second, the high priest said that the apostles intended to make the members of that council *guilty* of Jesus' blood: that is, they meant to show that those judges were guilty of killing Jesus. The high priest ignored the fact that he and his helpers had cried, "Let his blood be on us and on our children!" (Matthew 27:25). But now, with the apostles on trial before them, the high priest and all the council wanted to deny that they were responsible for Jesus' death.

B. DEFENSE (v. 29)

29. Peter and the other apostles replied: "We must obey God rather than men!

The apostles did not deny that the charges were true. They had indeed disobeyed the command of the ruling council, and they had indeed shown that the members of that council were guilty in the death of Jesus. Their defense was simple. They were obeying the order of a higher authority. The Lord God Almighty had told them what to say, and no court on earth had a right to countermand his order.

A HIGHER POWER

The Twelve-Step program of Alcoholics Anonymous has helped a multitude of people overcome their addiction to alcohol. In one of these "steps," the recovering addict acknowledges that only "a Power greater than ourselves" is sufficient to help him.

An illegitimate power—alcohol or any other drug, undisciplined carnal desire, or another person—can cause us untold suffering. In fact, anything or anyone who comes between us and God will lead us into disaster.

In the early days of the church the apostles had to choose whether or not they would submit to the religious authorities, whose demands conflicted with what God commanded of them. Yielding to the power of the authorities could have guaranteed the apostles' physical safety, but it would have jeopardized their spiritual well-being, since it would have caused them to violate God's will.

Their decision to obey God reflected their obedience to a higher power. It also attested to their personal integrity, for God's command coincided with their own experience in seeing the risen Christ.

—C. R. B.

C. EXPLANATION (vv. 30-32)

30. "The God of our fathers raised Jesus from the dead—whom you had killed by hanging him on a tree.

These were plain facts that the apostles had been declaring, and now they declared them again. *The God of our fathers,* Jehovah, the one real and living God, the Almighty—he had raised Jesus from the dead. The apostles knew this beyond the shadow of a doubt, and they announced it at every opportunity. And before God raised up Jesus, these members of the council killed him. True, Roman soldiers drove the nails and raised the cross, and they did it at the order of the Roman governor, Pilate. But Pilate gave the order because these rulers insisted.

31. "God exalted him to his own right hand as Prince and Savior that he might give repentance and forgiveness of sins to Israel.

God not only raised Jesus from the dead, but also *exalted* him. *To his own right hand* means God seated Jesus at a place of honor at his right hand (cf. Mark 16:19). The *King James Version* reads "with his right hand," meaning that by his own authority and power God exalted Jesus. Either of these translations expresses a truth, and the Greek text can have either meaning.

The English word *prince* comes from Latin and originally meant one who takes the first part. The Greek word is *archegos,* which originally meant a first leader or chief leader (from *arche,* first, and *ago,* to lead). Such is the place God has given to Jesus, though men crucified him. As Paul puts it, "Therefore God exalted him to the highest place and gave him the name that is above every name, that at the name of Jesus every knee should bow, in heaven and on earth and under the earth, and every tongue confess that Jesus Christ is Lord, to the glory of God the Father" (Philippians 2:9-11). See also Ephesians 1:20-22.

God exalted Jesus not only to be a chief leader, but also to be a *Savior.* Part of what that means is seen in the phrases that follow. To *give repentance . . . to Israel* means to give Israel an opportunity and a reason to repent, to give an urging to turn away from wrongdoing and become obedient to the chief leader, Jesus. To those who grasp that opportunity, those who do repent and obey Jesus, he gives *forgiveness of sins.* Compare Peter's inspired call in Acts 2:38. Thus sinners are saved from sin and death; thus they become children of God.

32. "We are witnesses of these things, and so is the Holy Spirit, whom God has given to those who obey him."

WHAT DO YOU THINK?

Some political candidates speak out for "law and order" as though that were the most pressing issue of our time. Of course, "law and order" is a Christian concern. First Timothy 2:1-4 urges us to pray for governmental authorities and suggests that the general peace and quietness these rulers can promote will provide an atmosphere conducive to effective evangelism. At the same time we recognize that tougher laws and penalties, better equipped police forces, and larger prisons are inadequate solutions to the problem of lawlessness. People need to be changed, radically changed, and "grace and discipleship" are best suited to do that.

What can we do to increase our efforts to bring God's grace to our society?

THOUGHT TO REMEMBER

"We must obey God rather than men!"

PRAYER

Heavenly Father, how good it is that you have provided a plain way of repentance and forgiveness! May we not only enjoy these ourselves, but also bring many others to enjoy them with us. In Jesus' name, amen.

DAILY BIBLE READINGS

Monday, Sept. 18—Noah's Obedience (Genesis 6:13-22)

Tuesday, Sept. 19—Obedience Better Than Sacrifice (1 Samuel 15:19-26)

Wednesday, Sept. 20—Pious Talk Not Enough (Matthew 7: 15-23)

Thursday, Sept. 21—Wise Builders (Matthew 7:24-29)

Friday, Sept. 22—To Love Is to Obey (John 14:15-23)

Saturday, Sept. 23—Lying to the Spirit (Acts 5:1-11)

Sunday, Sept. 24—Faithful and Counted Worthy (Acts 5: 33-42)

WHAT DO YOU THINK?

Paul tells Christians to rejoice in all situations (Philippians 4:4). James agrees, calling on Christians to rejoice even in trials (James 1:2). The apostles demonstrated such faith when they rejoiced at being counted worthy to suffer shame for Christ (Acts 5:41).

How different such an attitude is from that of our culture! The world continually tells us we deserve happiness—carefree pleasure. What are some important factors in developing such a counter-culture attitude as the apostles displayed?

How can doomed sinners know that Jesus is ready to give them repentance and forgiveness? He has sent his *witnesses* to tell them; he has sent the very apostles that the angry rulers were trying to silence. Another witness is *the Holy Spirit.* Not only was he guiding the apostles in all they said; he was also showing his presence by giving the power to work countless miracles (Acts 5:12-16).

Thus the prisoners not only confessed their disobedience to the supreme court, but also repeated it. Again they spoke of Jesus; again they accused those rulers of killing him. Now in addition they accused them of trying to silence Jesus' witnesses, and in so doing to silence the Holy Spirit himself.

We can imagine the fury of the rulers. The next verse says, "They were furious and wanted to put them to death." The killers of Jesus proposed to kill his witnesses. That would silence them!

In that heated moment, one cooler head prevailed. Wise old Gamaliel had the prisoners removed while he reasoned with his colleagues. There had been other troublesome movements, he said. He mentioned two of them specifically. In each case the leader had died, and the movement had faded away. So Jesus' movement would fade, said Gamaliel, if it was not of God. If it was of God, he warned, these judges would find themselves fighting against God, and they could not win (vv. 33-39).

This calm reasoning prevailed—to a degree. The rulers gave up their plan to kill the apostles, but they gave them a beating and repeated the command "not to speak in the name of Jesus." So the prisoners were released, and "day after day, in the temple courts and from house to house, they never stopped teaching and proclaiming the good news that Jesus is the Christ" (vv. 40-42).

CONCLUSION

"We must obey God rather than men." Hardly anyone will dispute that, except one foolish enough to say in his heart, "There is no God" (Psalm 14:1). Still, this general agreement gives rise to a number of questions:

1. If men order us to disobey God, of course we obey God as the apostles did. But in most circumstances, God tells us to obey the laws of men (1 Peter 2:13-15). Then why are our jails filled to overflowing?

2. God says we ought to renounce stealing and work to earn a living and to share with the needy (Ephesians 4:28). Then why do we have shoplifters in stores, bankers defrauding depositors, and graft in government?

3. God says one should earn his own living (2 Thessalonians 3:10-12). Then why is there a growing craze for something for nothing? Why is gambling legalized in more and more places? Why do states themselves have lotteries? Why do even churches conduct gambling games?

4. God says fathers should bring up children in the training and instruction of the Lord, but without exasperating them (Ephesians 6:4). Then why do we need officers and courts to deal with parents who abuse their children?

5. God says husband and wife are one flesh (Genesis 2:24). He says he hates divorce (Malachi 2:16). Then why are the divorce courts so busy?

Wise men can multiply answers to any of these questions, but there is one answer that fits them all: Many people are not obeying God.

What can be done about it? Stricter laws? Stiffer penalties? More police? These may be needed; but with or without them, it is very hard to get unbelievers to act like Christians. For more obedience to God, his people today can do nothing better than what the apostles did long ago: "They never stopped teaching and proclaiming the good news" (Acts 5:42). As a result, their number continued to increase as more and more people turned to the Lord.

Discovery Learning

This page contains an alternate lesson plan emphasizing learning activities. Classes desiring such student involvement will find these suggestions helpful. The next page is a reproducible activity page to further enhance discovery learning.

LEARNING GOALS

Students in today's class session should:

1. Describe the continuing opposition faced by the apostles and how they dealt with it.

2. Suggest some modern situation in which Christians are forced to choose "to obey God rather than men."

3. Identify at least one way the individual, the class, or the church together can take a stand "to obey God rather than men."

INTO THE LESSON

Ask the class members to turn to the people seated near them and dream aloud what a world of true believers would be like. How would people treat one another? What would the class structure be like? Where would the money be? Then ask what could break the cycle of peace generated by a community of Christians?

State to the class that this harmonious relationship is the situation that was present in the early church at the time reported in the text for today's lesson. Believers were living one in heart and mind and they were sharing everything with those who had need.

INTO THE WORD

Summarize the events recorded in Acts 4:32-36 and 5:1-11. Then have a volunteer read Acts 5:12-16 aloud to the class. Afterwards, lead one of the following Bible-study activities:

FINISH THE STORY

Tell your students that you will continue reading from Acts 5, stopping at key points in the story. After each stop, your students should discuss how the story could continue from there, based on the happenings to that point.

Divide the class into groups of five to seven students each. After each stop, let the students discuss in their groups for three or four minutes. Then lead the whole class in discussion. As you do so, focus on the motivations of the main characters in the story.

Stop after these verses: 18, 20, 21, 23, 25, 28, and 32.

CORRECT THE ORDER

Give each student a copy of the following list of statements and quotations. Working individually, the students are to arrange the items in chronological order. Have each

student compare his or her list with another student's before you announce the correct order. (The numbers are included here for your reference.)

(4) "Go to the temple and preach the gospel."

(7) "The jail was locked, but no one was inside!"

(5) The apostles preached the gospel in the temple early in the morning.

(3) During the night an angel opened the doors of the jail and freed the apostles.

(11) "God raised Jesus from the dead, and wants to give forgiveness to Israel."

(2) The council put the apostles in jail.

(10) "We must obey God, not men."

(6) The officers went to the jail, but the apostles were not there.

(1) The high priest and his associates were extremely angry with the apostles.

(9) "We told you not to teach about Jesus."

(8) "The men you put in jail are teaching the people in the temple!"

After either activity, have a student read aloud the following verses: Acts 4:1-3, 7, 10, 13, 18-21; 5:12, 17-20, 27-29. Lead the class in discussing these questions: Why did the apostles behave as they did? What word would you choose to describe the apostles' behavior?

INTO LIFE

In recent years, Christians in the western world have had a more difficult time witnessing and living the life they believe God has called them to. Even wearing religious symbols to the work place or talking about exciting answers to prayer have brought punitive responses from secular policy makers in some businesses, and the U.S. Congress considered making a legal ban on such activities. With that in mind, discuss the following questions.

In the growing hostility against Christians, how does a public school teacher speak out in favor of Christianity? How much can be said without putting that teacher's job at risk?

What should be the Christian's stand toward the display of a Nativity scene on public land?

Should Christians pay taxes on their church property? Why or why not?

What are other areas where Christians face opposition? What are our responsibilities in obeying God and not man in these situations?

Nobody Said It Was Easy!

God never promised us that as Christians we would live without turmoil and opposition. Instead he promised us that he would be with us and strengthen us so that he might be glorified. Study the following Scriptures and learn what God's Word tells us about persecution and opposition.

SCRIPTURE	LESSON TO BE LEARNED
Psalm 11:2	
Psalm 37:32	
Matthew 5:10	
Matthew 10: 16-28	
Mark 8:35	
Mark 13:9-13	
Luke 6: 6:22, 23	
John 17:14-19	
Romans 8:17; 35-37	
2 Corinthians 12:10	

What conclusions can be reached after examining these Scriptures?

Therefore, I must live my life . . .

CHOSEN TO SERVE
LESSON 5

WHY TEACH THIS LESSON?

Anyone who is looking for a church that never has a problem will likely be searching for a lifetime. Even the first church, in Jerusalem, did not last long before a problem arose.

What we find in this lesson, then, is not a plan for avoiding problems. Instead, we find a plan for dealing with problems.

Key to the solution of any problem is spiritual leadership. Stephen, one of the seven, illustrates this principle beautifully. As you use this lesson to present the plan of dealing with a troublesome situation, hold up the model of Stephen. Challenge your students to be problem solvers in the spirit of Stephen.

INTRODUCTION

Susanne had a little pain in her side. It hampered her golf swing, and her drive fell short. A friend joked that she was getting old, and Susanne joked right back.

The pain grew worse. At the ninth hole Susanne apologized and dropped out. A friend advised her to see a doctor, but she only laughed. "Nah. It'll go away."

The pain did go away, but it came back now and then. It never bothered Susanne at work, and not often at home. She gave up golf.

Susanne never liked housework. When the pain interfered with that, she got a girl to do it for her. But the little pain grew bigger and came more frequently.

At last Susanne did go to her doctor. She had to take time off for a series of tests. The doctor looked grim as he gave his report: "You have a tumor—a big one. I wish you had come to us a year ago."

A. LITTLE PAINS AND BIG PAINS

Almost any church has a little pain now and then. It's a trivial thing—a complaint from one crank, grumbling in one Sunday school class, one teacher with some shady notions. We like to ignore it, hoping it will go away. Sometimes it does, but sometimes it comes back bigger than it was before. Sometimes we ignore a little pain till it becomes a big pain, and big trouble.

B. LESSON BACKGROUND

The background of this lesson is seen in the lessons before it.

Lesson 1. Alive from the dead, Jesus told his disciples to take his message of salvation to the whole world—but first to wait for the Holy Spirit to come with power from on high. Then the Lord ascended to Heaven.

Lesson 2. Empowered by the Holy Spirit, the apostles in Jerusalem began to sound Jesus' call to repentance and salvation. Three thousand people responded in a day, and others responded in the days that followed. Sharing their funds so all could live, the new disciples met daily to be taught by the apostles.

Lesson 3. Drawn by miracles, throngs of people listened as the apostles proclaimed Jesus' message of salvation. Angry priests had Peter and John arrested. The ruling council ordered them not to teach about Jesus—but the two and the other apostles kept on teaching.

DEVOTIONAL READING
ACTS 7:54—8:3
LESSON SCRIPTURE
ACTS 6:1—8:3
PRINTED TEXT
ACTS 6:1-14

Oct
1

LESSON AIMS

After this lesson students should be able to:

1. Tell how the church responded to problems that arose from within and from outside the church.

2. List some principles for dealing with both big and little problems in the church.

3. Commit themselves to being part of a solution whenever a problem develops in the church.

KEY VERSE

They presented these men to the apostles, who prayed and laid their hands on them.

—Acts 6:6

LESSON 5 NOTES

WHAT DO YOU THINK?

When problems arise, the human response is either to ignore them or to fret over them. If we view them instead as opportunities, we will more likely deal with them promptly and relish the challenges they pose rather than dread the damage they may do. Church leaders should train themselves to face a problem with the question, "How can we handle this to make the church stronger and to build a firmer faith in the people involved?" Acts 6:1-7 shows how a potentially divisive problem in the church at Jerusalem was turned into an occasion for developing new leadership and initiating a fresh advance in evangelistic success.

That can also happen in our church, if…. If what? What do you think?

OPTION

Use the activity on page 56, "Prayer and the Ministry of the Word," to explore ways of following the same pattern the apostles followed to free spiritual leaders to do their ministry.

Lesson 4. All the apostles were arrested, whipped, and commanded to stop teaching about Jesus. But the apostles had orders from a higher authority. So the church continued to grow, not by twos and threes, but "more and more" (Acts 5:14). Rapid growth brought a problem within as well as opposition from without.

I. A PROBLEM SOLVED (ACTS 6:1-7)

Problems arise in any new enterprise and in any church that is growing rapidly. Blessed is the church that does not ignore them till they grow big, but deals with them promptly and wisely, with goodwill and good sense.

A. PROBLEM (v. 1)

1. In those days when the number of disciples was increasing, the Grecian Jews among them complained against the Hebraic Jews because their widows were being overlooked in the daily distribution of food.

Those days is a general term meaning the time of the events recorded in the previous chapters of Acts. In that time the apostles were vigorously telling about Jesus, and the rulers of Jerusalem were vigorously objecting. In spite of the opposition, *the number of the disciples was increasing.* About a hundred and twenty disciples gathered before the Day of Pentecost (Acts 1:15). On that great day three thousand more were added (2:41). Thereafter there were daily additions (2:47) until the number of men became about five thousand (4:4). We can only guess at the number of women, but Acts 5:14 adds that "more and more men and women" came into the fellowship. This rapid growth not only disturbed the opponents, but also brought difficulties in the church itself.

The Hebraic Jews were natives of Palestine, the Jewish homeland. *The Grecian Jews* were Jews who had been born in other lands or had lived away from Palestine a long time. Many of these Grecian Jews had come to Jerusalem for the feast of Pentecost and were among the three thousand who accepted Christ that day. Instead of returning to their homes abroad, they stayed in Jerusalem to learn more about the Christian way. New disciples who lived in Palestine also left their jobs to listen to the apostles' teaching daily (Acts 2:46, 47). Grecians and Hebrews alike pooled their resources so all could eat (Acts 2:44, 45). The apostles received contributions and provided for the needs of all (Acts 4:34, 35), including a *daily distribution of food.* This task became more difficult as the number of disciples increased by thousands. In time, the Jews from abroad began to complain that *widows* among them were not getting their fair share. Widows were especially likely to be overlooked because they had no husbands to look out for them, and opportunities to look out for themselves were extremely limited in that culture. Women were very dependent on the men in their lives, and here it was men who noticed and remedied their plight.

B. SOLUTION (vv. 2-4)

2. So the Twelve gathered all the disciples together and said, "It would not be right for us to neglect the ministry of the word of God in order to wait on tables.

The apostles were the ones making the daily distribution, so they were the ones being criticized. Instead of reacting with anger, the apostles moved to solve the problem. Instead of imposing a solution by their own authority, they involved *all the disciples,* including the complainers, in the process.

The twelve apostles were specially chosen and taught by Jesus, and specially empowered by the Holy Spirit, for the purpose of teaching *the word of God.* It was not reasonable or *right* for them to get so tied up in the distribution of food or funds that they could not give most of their time to the work for which they had been called and prepared.

3. "Brothers, choose seven men from among you who are known to be full of the Spirit and wisdom. We will turn this responsibility over to them.

The apostles proposed to have *seven men* take over the *responsibility* of distributing funds or food. Why did they choose seven? Probably because the apostles, guided by the Holy Spirit, judged that seven were needed to do the job well. The seven were to be chosen by the entire congregation rather than by the apostles, but the apostles described the kind of men who should be chosen. They should be *full of the Spirit*. All Christians receive the gift of the Holy Spirit (Acts 2:38). Those who are full of him are those who give themselves completely to his leading. They needed to be *full of…wisdom*, wise enough to recognize the Spirit's leading, wise enough to resist selfish people who wanted more than their share, wise enough to find and help the modest needy who made no demands. They should be men whose character was not doubted—*known* to be full of the Spirit and wisdom. The word for *known* here comes from the word generally translated "witness." These were men whose lives bore witness to their Spirit-filled wisdom.

4. "… and will give our attention to prayer and the ministry of the word."

With seven other good men to see that everyone was properly fed, clothed, and sheltered, the apostles could give their full time to preaching and praying.

FOOD FIGHTS

An unusual type of "food fight" was reported in the *Journal of the American Medical Association* a while back. Two brothers engaged in a contest—with chili peppers as their weapons! The winner ate twenty-five of them in twelve minutes. In truth, however, he was the loser, because the capsaicin—the "hot" ingredient in the peppers—burned through the wall of his intestine! Surgery was required to repair the damage.

Different still was the food fight that occurred between the Grecian and Palestinian Jews in the early church. The Grecians complained that their widows were not being treated as well as the widows of the Hebrews in the daily distribution of food. The apostles realized that the church would only lose in this situation, so they immediately proceeded to rectify it.

In the church, we should have no concern for winning some battle over anything that would set one Christian above another. We are children in the same "family," and our Father wants no fights among us.   —C. R. B.

C. THE CHOSEN MEN (vv. 5, 6)

5. This proposal pleased the whole group. They chose Stephen, a man full of faith and of the Holy Spirit; also Philip, Procorus, Nicanor, Timon, Parmenas, and Nicolas from Antioch, a convert to Judaism.

The proposal was so obviously sensible that it *pleased the whole group*. It was no small task to choose seven men in a congregation numbering thousands. We are not told how the choice was made; but with the guidance of the Holy Spirit and the goodwill of the people, it was made.

6. They presented these men to the apostles, who prayed and laid their hands on them.

The ordination ceremony was simple. The apostles *prayed*, doubtless asking God's blessing and help for the seven in the huge task they were undertaking. Then the apostles *laid their hands on them*. It seems probable that this gave the seven something of the divine inspiration and miraculous power that the apostles had. It is recorded that Stephen soon afterward did miracles (v. 8), and so did Philip (Acts 8:6). Those two quickly became notable preachers. We have no record of what the other five did.

Visual 5 of the visuals packet lists qualities needed by any who would hold a position of responsibility in the church.

WHAT DO YOU THINK?

Acts 6:3 gives the qualifications for the seven men who would direct the distribution of food. Qualifications for elders or deacons are spelled out in 1 Timothy 3:1-13 and Titus 1:6-9. Certainly anyone who helps plan worship services, develops evangelistic or educational programs, or contacts people in need of benevolent assistance should be a Christian who will represent Christ and the church well. The qualifications of "full of the Spirit and wisdom" are no doubt appropriate. But what about custodial duties, or cutting the grass? Are there ministries for which no qualifications are necessary? If so, what? If not, why not?

WHAT DO YOU THINK?

Acts 6:6 mentions prayer as an important feature in setting people aside for service in the church. It seems reasonable to suppose that prayers ought to be offered that each person entering some ministry would receive strength and guidance through the

Holy Spirit and that each would grow in spiritual wisdom. Specific requests should be made for such matters as the discipline to do the job well, the patience to work with people who are slow to cooperate, and the graciousness to handle criticism well. It would be appropriate also to pray that our fellow Christians will resist the temptation to misuse their authority (See 3 John 9, 10.)

What do you think about having an "ordination" service for new workers in various ministries of the church, to offer such prayers as these? The apostles publicly prayed for the seven men selected in Acts 6; is that the pattern for all ministries in the church? For some? When is an "ordination" in order?

WHAT DO YOU THINK?

Acts 6:7 records that a great number of the priests became obedient to the faith. Like Saul of Tarsus, some of these priests had once thought that they "ought to do all that was possible to oppose the name of Jesus" (Acts 26:9). Now they embraced the faith they once tried to destroy. These priests surely were in a position to know the falseness of the rumor circulated from within their ranks that Jesus' body had been stolen from the tomb (See Matthew 28:11-15.) They now recognized as well that the miracles the apostles were performing testified to the divine authority of the apostles' message concerning Jesus Christ.

How does the conversion of former enemies of the gospel affirm your own faith? What kind of motivation does it provide for your own obedience?

D. CONTINUING PROGRESS (v. 7)

7. So the word of God spread. The number of disciples in Jerusalem increased rapidly, and a large number of priests became obedient to the faith.

The complaint of the Grecians was answered quickly and in a satisfactory way. Thus dissension in the church was nipped in the bud, and progress continued as before. *The word of God spread:* the gospel was preached to more and more people, and more and more of them responded to it. *The number of disciples ... increased rapidly.*

Amazingly, even *a large number of priests became obedient to the faith.* The priests had been leaders of the opposition (see Acts 4:1-3; 5:17, 18). Now a large number of them became believers. The priests were in a position to know how unfounded the opposition was. The time came when many of them could no longer go along with the savage effort to silence the truth, and so they took their place with the persecuted ones who told the truth.

II. ANOTHER CONFLICT (ACTS 6:8-10)

As the church in Jerusalem grew, members of the church were growing in usefulness and service, as every Christian ought to do. Seven men were chosen for a special kind of service, and apparently they did it well. Soon some of them were serving in another way. The last part of our text tells about Stephen.

A. NEW MIRACLE WORKER (v. 8)

8. Now Stephen, a man full of God's grace and power, did great wonders and miraculous signs among the people.

In verse 5 Stephen is described as "full of faith and of the Holy Spirit"; now he is described as *full of God's grace and power.* It seems that the Holy Spirit had given him power to do *great wonders and miraculous signs.* We suppose these were miracles of healing such as the apostles had been doing (Acts 3:1-8; 5:12-16).

B. NEW OPPONENTS (v. 9)

9. Opposition arose, however, from members of the Synagogue of the Freedmen (as it was called)—Jews of Cyrene and Alexandria as well as the provinces of Cilicia and Asia. These men began to argue with Stephen.

In the first century B.C. the Roman general Pompey took some Jewish prisoners and deported them to Rome where they were sold into slavery. Subsequently they were freed, and some of them returned to Palestine. The *Freedmen* are thought to have been chiefly descendants of these people. Some think this verse describes just one synagogue, which also included *Jews of Cyrene and Alexandria,* and people of *Cilicia and Asia.* Other students think each of these national groups may have had a separate synagogue. Be that as it may, some of these people began *to argue with Stephen.* Apparently Stephen was spreading the message of Jesus. Apparently, too, the opponents accepted the official position of the priests and Pharisees—they thought Jesus was a dead rebel. So they arose to argue with Stephen. We are not told where the disputing occurred.

C. DEFEATED OPPONENTS (v. 10)

10. But they could not stand up against his wisdom or the Spirit by whom he spoke.

Stephen had been well taught by the apostles. He knew the facts of Jesus' life and death and resurrection. He knew the Old Testament prophecies the Lord fulfilled. He knew the miracles that showed the presence and power of God. *The Spirit by whom he spoke* was the Holy Spirit, who guided his use of facts and arguments. Those who tried to debate with him were defeated at every point.

III. UNFAIR OPPOSITION (ACTS 6:11-14)

Unable to stand against the truth, Stephen's opponents launched a campaign against the man who told the truth. It was a campaign of falsehood after falsehood, but with enough semblance of truth to make it more dangerous than outright lying.

A. FALSE ACCUSATION (v. 11)

11. Then they secretly persuaded some men to say, "We have heard Stephen speak words of blasphemy against Moses and against God."

Somehow, perhaps with bribes, the defeated debaters persuaded some men to bring this false accusation. *Words of blasphemy* are slanderous words, insulting words. No examples are given in the text, but we recall that Jesus had quoted Moses' law and then had added something different: "You have heard that it was said to the people long ago, 'Do not murder, and anyone who murders will be subject to judgment.' But I tell you that anyone who is angry with his brother will be subject to judgment" (Matthew 5:21, 22). See other examples in the verses that follow in that chapter of Matthew. Stephen may have quoted such sayings, and the accusers may have said they were an insulting denial of Moses' law. Of course, Moses' law was God's law, so the same words could be twisted to appear as an insult to God.

B. FALSE ARREST (v. 12)

12. So they stirred up the people and the elders and the teachers of the law. They seized Stephen and brought him before the Sanhedrin.

Before this time, action against the apostles had been started by priests and other Sadducees. The action against Stephen was more like a grassroots movement started by common people and their teachers. But Stephen was taken to the same *Sanhedrin* that had tried to silence the apostles, a council composed of both Sadducees and Pharisees.

C. FALSE TESTIMONY (vv. 13, 14)

13. They produced false witnesses, who testified, "This fellow never stops speaking against this holy place and against the law.

The earlier accusation was that Stephen had spoken against Moses and God. Now in the courtroom the witnesses added that he had spoken against *this holy place,* that is, the temple, or perhaps the city of Jerusalem. This charge is made more specific in the next verse.

14. For we have heard him say that this Jesus of Nazareth will destroy this place and change the customs Moses handed down to us."

Jesus once had said, "Destroy this temple, and I will raise it again in three days." He said that of his body, not the stone temple (John 2:19-21). But the saying was twisted and used against him at his trial (Matthew 26:60, 61). At another time Jesus had plainly predicted the destruction of the whole temple (Matthew 24:1, 2). At yet another time he had mourned over the coming fall of Jerusalem (Luke 19:41-44). Stephen may have mentioned some of these things, and the witnesses at his trial could have twisted them into a declaration that Jesus would destroy the holy place. Their purpose was to make it appear that Stephen was intent on destroying the whole Jewish system, temple and customs and all.

Chapter 7 of Acts records the outcome. When Stephen had a chance to speak for himself, he briefly surveyed the long history of Israel. He reminded the rulers that their forefathers had resisted the will of God again and again through all that long history. Then he declared that the present rulers also were resisting God's will, for they had killed the Christ.

HOW TO SAY IT

Cilicia. Sih-LISH-i-uh.
Cyrenians. Sye-REE-ni-unz.
Nicanor. Ny-CAY-nor.
Nicolas. NICK-o-lus.
Parmenas. PAR-me-nus.
Prochorus. PROCK-o-rus.
Timon. TY-mon.

WHAT DO YOU THINK?

False witnesses accused Jesus; more false witnesses accused Stephen. False witnesses continue to accuse Christian people today. Christians are misrepresented in the media and ridiculed on college campuses.

What is the proper response to such abuse? In the cases of Jesus and Stephen, such charges resulted in death! Is that what modern Christians have to look forward to? What, if any, resistance should Christians offer today?

PRAYER

Father, we confess that we have not matched the earnestness of the first Christians. We pray that you will so guide our choices and our actions that we shall be better teachers of truth and winners of souls. In Jesus' name. Amen.

THOUGHT TO REMEMBER

You can do better.

DAILY BIBLE READINGS

Monday, Sept. 25—Willing to Serve (Psalm 40:4-10)

Tuesday, Sept. 26—Ready to Serve (Isaiah 6:1-8)

Wednesday, Sept. 27—Joy in Service (Psalm 126)

Thursday, Sept. 28—Shared Benefits (John 4:31-38)

Friday, Sept. 29—Christ's Example (Matthew 20:20-28)

Saturday, Sept. 30—Serving Through Hardships (1 Thessalonians 2:1-9)

Sunday, Oct. 1—God's Reward (Ephesians 6:1-8)

The rulers reacted with fury, but Stephen looked up to the supreme Ruler. Raising his eyes, he called out, "Look … I see heaven open and the Son of Man standing at the right hand of God."

That was the last straw. The persecutors dragged Stephen out of town and stoned him to death. So Stephen became the first Christian martyr—but the church went on and on.

SO MANY WAYS TO LIE

Identical twin brothers played on a high school basketball team. Before one game the coach mistakenly listed only one of them in the official scorebook. He was injured in the first half. At halftime, the coach told his brother to put on the injured player's jersey and not check in with the officials. This made him a false witness, since telling the truth about the coach's oversight would have drawn a technical foul.

The ruse worked. After the game, however, the coach's conscience bothered him. He turned himself in to the officials, and he and one of the twins were given a one-game suspension.

The difference between this coach and those who opposed Stephen and the gospel is that the latter seem to have had no conscience. They knowingly brought false witnesses to the council to testify against Stephen. But this wasn't just a game with a technical foul or even a suspension at stake; it was to become a matter of life and death for Stephen.

Lying seems so prevalent in modern society that many are inclined to take it for granted. Misleading advertising, insurance fraud, and cutting corners on quality are just a few examples of lying that have gained tacit acceptance in our society. Christians are called to live by a higher standard of truth.

—C. R. B.

CONCLUSION

Jesus said, "I will build my church and the gates of Hades will not overcome it" (Matthew 16:18). We can depend on that. The Sadducees and the Pharisees could not kill it when it was small; Satan and all his hosts cannot kill it now that it is big.

But while the church cannot be killed, it can be hurt. We want to be among those who heal, not those who hurt. Again we have a lesson with two messages for us. Let's call them A and B.

A. HURTS LITTLE AND BIG

A little wound can be cleansed with peroxide and protected by a bandage till it heals, but a little wound untreated can develop gangrene and require an amputation.

Shall not every little hurt in the church be treated and healed with tender loving care? If it is not, before long there will be some big hurts to deal with.

B. ARE YOU READY?

If ardent personal evangelists like Stephen were being stoned today, how many of us would be ardent enough to earn that fate?

It is easy to see that popular media, popular entertainment, and popular tastes are becoming more un-Christian and more obscene. Protests, petitions, and boycotts have some effect, but not enough. It is hard to get non-Christians to act like Christians. The original Christians devoted themselves to making more Christians. Three thousand grew swiftly to five thousand, and then multitudes were added (Acts 2:41; 4:4; 5:14). Can we duplicate that effort and that result? Are you ready to do your part?

Discovery Learning

This page contains an alternate lesson plan emphasizing learning activities. Classes desiring such student involvement will find these suggestions helpful. The next page is a reproducible activity page to further enhance discovery learning.

LEARNING GOALS

As students participate in today's class session, they should:

1. Tell how the church responded to problems that arose from within and from outside the church.

2. List some principles for dealing with both big and little problems in the church.

3. Commit themselves to being part of the solution whenever a problem develops in the church.

INTO THE LESSON

Write the heading "Church Problems" on your chalkboard. Begin today's session by asking the class to brainstorm a list of problems a congregation could face. List their suggestions under the heading on the chalkboard.

As you read the list, have the class help you to decide whether each problem is a "little" problem or a "big" one. Label the "little" problems "L" and the "big" ones "B."

Tell the class that the lesson text reveals how the church in its early days dealt with a "little" problem and then a "big" one. The class will discover principles for dealing with each kind in this week's discussion.

INTO THE WORD

Give a brief review of the first four lessons of this quarter. Use the thoughts presented in the "Lesson Background" section, which is included in the "Introduction."

Using the following questions, lead class members to explore the lesson text. You may find it helpful to write on the chalkboard the italicized words from each question as you ask it.

1. Who were the *Grecian Jews?* How were they different from the *Hebraic Jews?*

2. Who were the *twelve?*

3. Why didn't the twelve take care of the *daily distribution* themselves?

4. What were the *qualifications* for the seven men who would perform the daily distribution? What principle may be seen in this regarding the selection of persons for responsible positions of service in the church?

5. It has been noted that the *seven men* who were chosen, had Greek names. If the seven were Grecian Jews, what principle for problem-solving does this suggest?

6. How do we know that the problem concerning the daily distribution was resolved? What was the *result* for the church?

7. Why was *Stephen* opposed? Who opposed him?

8. What *methods* did Stephen's opponents use to undermine him?

9. *What happened* to Stephen?

If class members do not remember what happened to Stephen, share the comments under verse 14.

INTO LIFE

We have seen that early on in its existence the church faced two problems: a "little" problem and a "big" problem. Ask someone to identify each. Then divide the class in half. Ask one half to write a brief list of principles for solving "little" church problems. The other half should make a list of principles for solving "big" church problems. If your class numbers more than sixteen, divide each half into smaller groups.

The "little" problem group may suggest principles such as the following:

1. Deal with the problem promptly.

2. Leaders should not try to do every task in the church, but should enlist the help of responsible persons and delegate authority to them.

3. Even leaders who minister to "physical" needs of people should be spiritual people.

4. No job is unimportant. We should ask God to bless and guide every ministry.

The "big" problem group may suggest principles such as the following:

1. The gospel is often a threat to those who won't accept it.

2. Don't expect integrity from the gospel's opponents.

3. Don't compromise God's message or your principles in the face of opposition.

4. God can use even hardship or persecution to accomplish his purposes.

Discuss these questions with your class:

• Which does a congregation typically experience more, "little" problems or "big" problems"?

• Which are a bigger threat to the life and health of the church? Why?

Ask, "How can Christians prepare themselves to be a part of the solution to either kind of problem?" As students give suggestions, list them on your chalkboard. After a few minutes, challenge class members to choose one of the ideas and decide how he or she can act on it during this week.

Prayer and the Ministry of the Word

The apostles needed to concentrate on their ministry in the word, so seven men were chosen to relieve them of the duty of "waiting tables." Spiritual leaders of the church today also need to do give their attention to "prayer and the ministry of the word." How can this be arranged?

List below a number of activities that should take priority for spiritual leaders. Some categories are suggested; list specific activities under each one. (For example, "study" is an activity that prepares for teaching.) Feel free to add other categories also.

Evangelism

Teaching

Shepherding of members

Other

Now list some activities that often consume a leader's time but are not priority ministries for such leaders. Again, some categories are suggested.

Office work

Building maintenance

Financial concerns

Next to each activity in the second group, write an estimate of how much time per week you think it would take to get these tasks done.

Now, can you think of some people who would be willing to work at these tasks to free your leaders for their ministry? What qualifications are necessary to be used in these positions?

If other members can be enlisted to contribute an hour or two per week to deal with these kinds of church business, the work will get done, and those involved in service are likely to become more enthusiastic about the church and its ministries. In time, they may even develop an interest in becoming leaders themselves!

PHILIP:
WITNESS TO OUTCASTS

LESSON 6

WHY TEACH THIS LESSON?

The Lord's Great Commission is to make disciples. Sometimes that involves addressing large crowds. At other times it means talking to one person in a lonely place. On occasion it is the role of a noted "evangelist," while on others it is simply the role of believers who tell of Jesus wherever they go.

Both models are seen in today's lesson. Philip, who came to be known as "the evangelist," proclaimed the gospel to many in the city and to a single individual on a desert road. Always he told of Jesus. His example is a worthy challenge to us today.

INTRODUCTION

About the year 1890, my grandfather bought a farm from a western homesteader. The house was a rickety frame structure that threatened to fall apart from its own weight; but it sheltered Grandpa for the rest of his life, and later became my birthplace.

The old house didn't last long after that. The cellar caved in, the building tilted at a terrifying angle, and some joints pulled apart.

My parents were devastated. They were a young couple with two babies, barely making a living on a small farm—and now they had no place to live.

But God was gracious, a moneylender was reckless, and my parents were no strangers to hard work. The house they built was bigger and far better than the old one had ever been.

A. BENEFITS OF DISASTER

How many times disaster has proved to be beneficial! The empire trembled when much of Rome was destroyed by fire in A.D. 64. But the new Rome that rose from the ruins was a much finer city. Likewise the new Chicago that followed the famous fire of 1871 was bigger and better—and more fireproof. So was the new San Francisco that rose after the terrible earthquake in 1906.

In Jerusalem, persecution shattered the new church soon after it began. But fragments of the shattered church landed in other towns of Judea and Samaria, and soon there were many churches. The gospel of Christ was starting its journey "to the ends of the earth."

B. LESSON BACKGROUND

In earlier lessons we have seen that priests had the apostles of Jesus arrested and taken to the ruling council, where they were whipped and ordered not to talk about Jesus anymore. Then some of the common people dragged Stephen to the same council, and he was stoned to death.

At that point an ardent young Pharisee named Saul took the lead in persecuting the followers of Jesus. He had watched and approved as Stephen was stoned.

DEVOTIONAL READING
ACTS 8:9-24

LESSON SCRIPTURE
ACTS 8:4-40

PRINTED TEXT
ACTS 8:5, 6, 26-38

Oct
8

LESSON AIMS

After this lesson a student should be able to:

1. Describe how Philip shared the gospel publicly and one-to-one.

2. Name some principles for effective evangelism based on Philip's experience.

3. Choose someone with whom to share the gospel, using one or more of the principles identified in the lesson.

KEY VERSE

Then Philip began with that very passage of Scripture and told him the good news about Jesus.
—Acts 8:35

Angrily he arrested the Christians and put them in jail (Acts 7:57—8:3). Probably the ruling priests assigned a squad of police to help him as he invaded every house where disciples were thought to be.

It was no small task that Saul undertook. There were thousands of Christians. Most of them left Jerusalem before he could catch them. They went to other towns of Judea and Samaria (Acts 8:1). Some of them went to more distant places as we shall see in later lessons. Wherever they went, they took the good news of salvation with them (Acts 8:4). So churches sprang up in many towns of Judea and Samaria.

I. THE GOSPEL IN SAMARIA (ACTS 8:5, 6)

It is surprising to see that the scattered Christians went to Samaria as well as Judea. For centuries there had been more hard feeling than friendship between Jews and Samaritans. Jews regarded Samaritans as half-breed Jews, and Samaritans responded with indignation. But probably the fugitives were safer in Samaria than in Judea, which was closer to the vengeful enemies in Jerusalem.

Of course, Samaritans were not all alike. Jesus found a cordial welcome in one town (John 4:1-43). Another town refused to let him stay overnight (Luke 9:51-53). Probably the scattered disciples likewise were more welcome in some towns than in others, but they "preached the word wherever they went" (Acts 8:4).

A. THE PREACHING (v. 5)

5. Philip went down to a city in Samaria and proclaimed the Christ there.

Last week the central figure in our lesson was Stephen; this week it is Philip. Like Stephen, Philip was one of the seven men chosen to manage the distribution of funds or food to the needy in the church (Acts 6:1-6). Like Stephen, Philip became a good preacher of the gospel. But Philip was one of those who escaped from Jerusalem and took the message elsewhere.

The Greek word here for *proclaimed* means to announce. It is the word used of a royal herald who proclaims the message of a king. In the New Testament, it is the word used of a preacher who proclaims the gospel, the message of the King of kings. As Peter had done on Pentecost, Philip announced that Jesus is the Christ promised by ancient Scriptures, and that people should believe in him, repent of their sins, and be baptized in Jesus' name.

B. THE RESULT (v. 6)

6. When the crowds heard Philip and saw the miraculous signs he did, they all paid close attention to what he said.

Like Stephen, Philip had been given power to do miracles. Verse 7 describes some of them. These miracles quickly convinced the Samaritans that Philip was a true herald of Heaven, proclaiming God's own message. Consequently many of them believed Philip and were baptized (v. 12). "There was great joy in that city" (v. 8), both because of the healings and because of the promise of salvation.

The twelve apostles had stayed in Jerusalem when the other disciples of Jesus had fled (Acts 8:1). Now two of them came to help in Samaria. With prayer they laid their hands on some of the new converts (vv. 14-17). It seems that this imparted to those converts the same inspiration and miraculous power that Philip had received. These, then, could take the place of Philip. Philip was free to move on to another field.

GOOD NEWS FOR EVERYONE

There are probably more "Good Samaritan" hospitals in the world today than there are Samaritans. Only about five hundred Samaritans are known to exist. From

HOW TO SAY IT

Candace. CAN-duh-see.
Theophilus. Thee-AHF-ih-lus
*   (Th as in thin).*

WHAT DO YOU THINK?

The lesson writer points out that the Greek word for pro-claimed in Acts 8:5 is "used of a royal herald who proclaims the message of a king." It is not likely that any herald of ancient times would have announced his king's message in a timid and hesitant manner. Instead, he would have spoken clearly and confidently. Why, then, are so many Christians timid about proclaiming Jesus? How can we display more of the confidence and power of the royal herald?

Also, since he represented the king, the herald would have been careful to present only the king's message. He surely would not have mixed his opinions with the king's proclamation. What, then, is the place for our opinions about spiritual matters? When is it right and when is it wrong for us to ex-press these to other people? What can we do to be clear in distin-guishing God's truths from our speculations?

biblical times to the present, these people have been considered outcasts. Their low social ranking is seen in the fact that Jesus' story about one "good Samaritan" put him in a role contradictory to what people normally thought of Samaritans.

In Jesus' day, Samaritans were so despised that many Jews would not walk through Samaria on the way from Judea to Galilee and vice versa.

It is remarkable, therefore, that Philip took the initiative to preach Christ to the Samaritans. The reason he did so is found in the description of this godly man (Acts 6:3-6). He was a man filled with the Spirit of God.

Christians who allow themselves to be led by God's Spirit will look down on no one, but will see all persons as worthy of receiving the gospel of God's love.

—C. R. B.

II. THE GOSPEL ON THE HIGHWAY (ACTS 8:26-35)

You or I, or even Philip, might think it was unwise for an able evangelist to leave a field where people were responding to the gospel. But Philip had his orders from One wiser than any of us. It was time for him to move on.

A. NEW FIELD (v. 26)

26. Now an angel of the Lord said to Philip, "Go south to the road—the desert road—that goes down from Jerusalem to Gaza."

Desert does not mean sandy waste like the Sahara; it means deserted, uninhabited. The road to Gaza led through range land, the kind of country where Abraham and Isaac pastured their flocks. But what can an evangelist do in empty country like that?

B. NEW PROSPECT (vv. 27, 28)

27. So he started out, and on his way he met an Ethiopian eunuch, an important official in charge of all the treasury of Candace, queen of the Ethiopians. This man had gone to Jerusalem to worship.

Knowing where the order came from, Philip obeyed. *On his way, he met* the man whom the Lord was sending him to meet: a man of Ethiopia.

This Ethiopia was not the same as the country we now call by that name. Its boundaries are not described exactly, but it included the upper Nile Valley south of Egypt. Some students conclude that its population included Africans from the south, Egyptians from the north, and Arabians from the east. We have no description of *Candace,* the *queen.* We learn here several things, however, about the man Philip was to meet:

1. He was a *eunuch,* as were many attendants in royal courts. They were thought to be more docile, more loyal, more dependable than normal men; and they were not likely to become involved in scandalous behavior with ladies of the court.

2. The man held a position of trust and great authority: he was the queen's treasurer.

3. He *had gone to Jerusalem to worship.* This indicates that he was Jewish, for Jerusalem was the Jews' central place of worship. Was he a native Ethiopian of African, Egyptian, or Arabian descent, who had been converted to the Jewish religion? Was he a native of Ethiopia born of Jewish ancestors who had moved to Ethiopia generations earlier? Was he a slave, a descendant of Jews who had been captured and enslaved long before? Was he a native of Palestine who had gone to Ethiopia and risen to a high position as Joseph had done in Egypt and Daniel had done in Babylon? For these questions we have no answers.

28. And on his way home was sitting in his chariot reading the book of Isaiah the prophet.

A Christian's duty to tell others of Jesus is the theme of visual 6 of the visuals packet.

WHAT DO YOU THINK?

The Ethiopian was reading the Scriptures. Naturally, there is great potential for a spiritual breakthrough when a person is willing to read the Bible. Paul told the Thessalonians, "When you received the word of God, which you heard from us, you accepted it not as the word of men, but as it actually is, the word of God, which is at work in you who believe" (1 Thessalonians 2:13). The Scriptures can bring conviction of sin and faith in the saving Christ to the unsaved person who gives attention to these inspired writings. The Christian who needs wisdom to resolve a problem or strength to resist a temptation will find in the Scriptures the help needed to achieve a mighty victory to the glory of God.

What about one who is unconvinced about the Word of God? What can a Christian do to present the gospel to such a one as that?

WHAT DO YOU THINK?

The Bible is a book the average human being can understand. That does not mean a person cannot profit from guidance supplied by mature and experienced students of God's Word, however. Some beginning students may not understand the difference between the Old and New Testaments, and so they require instruction regarding the purpose of each. Others may have difficulty comprehending the divine character and mission of Jesus Christ, but with assistance they can be led to the key passages that spell that out. Philip's question to the Ethiopian, "Do you understand what you are reading?" (Acts 8:30), is still an appropriate one to ask a Bible reader. Such guidance, offered in a spirit of loving concern, may evoke from a modern-day Bible student the same openness as was displayed by the Ethiopian.

Of course, that question can also be asked with an air of superiority, which will be offensive to the reader. What are some guidelines to be sure one offers such help in a loving and helpful way and does not—even inadvertently—convey a disparaging attitude?

It is clear that the man was starting to go back home to Ethiopia, but questions arise instantly. Was he traveling alone? Wouldn't a high official of Ethiopia have at least a servant to drive the chariot and take care of the horses when they stopped for the night? It seems quite probable that such an official would travel with armed and mounted guards. But if the man had any companions, they are not mentioned in the record. Possibly the official thought it was safer to travel alone and incognito.

People who remember the horse-and-buggy days know it is possible to read while driving a slow-moving horse, and horses do not move very rapidly when they have to keep going all day. But wouldn't it be helpful to have someone else do the driving? For our study, the important thing is what the man was doing as he traveled. He was *reading the book of Isaiah the prophet.*

C. NEW OPPORTUNITY (vv. 29-31)

29. The Spirit told Philip, "Go to that chariot and stay near it."

Now we know why Philip was sent to this desert place. This chariot carried the man whom God was sending his preacher to meet.

30. Then Philip ran up to the chariot and heard the man reading Isaiah the prophet. "Do you understand what you are reading?" Philip asked.

The Ethiopian was reading aloud, and Philip recognized the words of Isaiah. His question was well designed to open the way for his preaching. No one in Israel—no one in the world—understood those words of Isaiah till he saw how they were fulfilled in Jesus.

31. "How can I," he said, "unless someone explains it to me?" So he invited Philip to come up and sit with him.

The man was wise enough to realize that he did not understand the prophecy, and wise enough to rejoice in the prospect of finding some help with it. He invited Philip to join him in the chariot.

D. SCRIPTURE READING (vv. 32, 33)

32, 33. The eunuch was reading this passage of Scripture: "He was led like a sheep to the slaughter, and as a lamb before the shearer is silent, so he did not open his mouth. In his humiliation he was deprived of justice. Who can speak of his descendants? For his life was taken from the earth."

This is a part of what we call Isaiah 53:7, 8. That chapter sings tenderly of God's servant persecuted and killed, though innocent, yet destined to share with the great. What we see in Acts is a free quotation from the Greek version of Isaiah that was commonly used in New Testament times. It is not exactly like the passage as we see it in our version of Isaiah, but any version of the prophecy is fulfilled in Jesus.

E. EXPLANATION (vv. 34, 35)

34. The eunuch asked Philip, "Tell me, please, who is the prophet talking about, himself or someone else?"

The man of Ethiopia asked a question that puzzled all the scholars of Israel. Obviously the prophet was singing of someone—but whom? Was the song about Isaiah *himself*? He was despised and rejected and persecuted, perhaps killed; but how could it be said that we are healed by Isaiah's wounds? (Isaiah 53:5). How could it be said that Isaiah would justify many (Isaiah 53:11)? If Isaiah was singing of *someone else,* the same questions remain unanswered. Some students suggested that Isaiah might be singing about the nation of Israel. That nation would indeed suffer much, but what Israelite would believe that his nation might ever die? (Isaiah 53:8).

35. Then Philip began with that very passage of Scripture and told him the good news about Jesus.

Jesus! In all history, no one else fits the description written by Isaiah. Innocent as any sheep, Jesus was led to the slaughter, never opening his mouth to scream a protest. He was humiliated in every possible way, and just judgment was taken away from him. Who can say anything about Jesus' descendants (v. 33), since he died without any children? Yet there are millions of his spiritual descendants, people who have been born again through him, and have become God's children. In them "he will see his offspring" (Isaiah 53:10).

Philip may have led his hearer through that fifty-third chapter of Isaiah step by step. He may have emphasized especially "by his wounds we are healed" (v. 5) and other statements of redemption. He may have cited other prophecies too, such as those of David that Peter had used on Pentecost (Acts 2:25-36). As Peter had done, Philip made a convincing case: Jesus is the Christ foretold by the prophets of God.

III. EAGER CONVERT (ACTS 8:36-38)

We have no way of knowing how long Philip continued to preach Jesus. He may have gone on for hours. Certainly many hours could be used in discussing Old Testament prophecies and the wonderful way Jesus has fulfilled them. No doubt the Ethiopian felt his conviction growing stronger with every passing mile.

A. INQUIRY (v. 36)

36. As they traveled along the road, they came to some water and the eunuch said, "Look, here is water. Why shouldn't I be baptized?"

Obviously Philip's preaching of Jesus had included information about baptism. We are not told what Philip had said about it; but we are sure it did not contradict what Peter had said as recorded in Acts 2:38. He may have said much more than is written there. Luke was writing this record thirty years after the church began. He addressed it to Theophilus, who already had been instructed in the Christian way (Acts 1:1; Luke 1:3, 4). Christian teaching about baptism was well known to Theophilus and others like him. There was no need for Luke to repeat it.

B. CONFESSION (v. 37)

37 (footnote). Philip said, "If you believe with all your heart, you may." The eunuch answered, "I believe that Jesus Christ is the Son of God."

This verse is not found in the oldest known manuscripts of Acts, and so it is left out of many English versions, or rendered as a footnote as in our text. It seems probable that Luke did not write it; but of course Philip did not baptize this man without being assured that he believed in Jesus Christ. Whoever wrote the verse, undoubtedly it shows one form of confession that was used among early Christians. Perhaps it originated as a footnote to inform readers and later someone who was copying the book wrote it into the text.

C. BAPTISM (v. 38)

38. And he gave orders to stop the chariot. Then both Philip and the eunuch went down into the water and Philip baptized him.

Here we see an indication that the Ethiopian traveler had someone else driving the horses. One does not give a command to a chariot itself. It seems probable that the driver held the horses while Philip and the Ethiopian left the chariot. No doubt the two took off their outer robes, at least. Luke does not include details, but gives the essential facts. The two men waded into the water, and Philip baptized the man of Ethiopia.

WHAT DO YOU THINK?

Philip "began at the same Scripture, and preached unto him Jesus." The person and work of Jesus Christ are so much the focus of the Bible that one could easily make a transition from countless Scripture passages to a gospel presentation. Suggest some Scriptures that would easily and naturally open the door to a gospel presentation.

NOTE

Your students may offer many such passages. If discussion lags, suggest Psalm 23, with its description of the Lord as shepherd, one could lead into a consideration of Jesus as the Good Shepherd who has given his life for the sheep (John 10:11). Any passage that speaks of sin provides an occasion for one to describe the Savior from sin. Any that refer to God's love and mercy provide an obvious opportunity. Any that make mention of death open the door to a discussion of Jesus as the victor over death and the grave.

OPTION

Use the reproducible activity page (64) to help your students discover applicable principles of evangelism from this lesson text.

THOUGHT TO REMEMBER

Not enjoyment, and not sorrow,
Is our destined end or way;
But to act that each tomorrow
Finds us farther than today.

WHAT DO YOU THINK?

It is vital for Christians who have received the gospel to find ways of passing that message on to others. If we who have received the good news of salvation in Jesus Christ do not share it with those who are still bound by sin, they will never know the redemption he offers. Additionally, we maintain our own spiritual vitality by sharing the teaching we have received.

With that in mind, how would you answer a Christian who said he wants to wait until he grows more in his faith before he attempts to share the gospel with anyone? Could you share a personal testimony of the benefits of sharing your faith?

PRAYER

Truly, our Father, you have set before us the standard of excellence: "the whole measure of the fullness of Christ" (Ephesians 4:13). Strengthen us and help us as we push on toward that standard. In Jesus' name, amen.

DAILY BIBLE READINGS

Monday, Oct. 2—A Leper Cleansed (Matthew 8:1-4)

Tuesday, Oct. 3—Harlots Accepted (Matthew 21:28-32)

Wednesday, Oct. 4—Tax Collectors Justified (Luke 7:24-30)

Thursday, Oct. 5—A Sinner Forgiven (Luke 7:36-50)

Friday, Oct. 6—Paradise Promised (Luke 23:32-43)

Saturday, Oct. 7—Outcasts Brought In (Isaiah 6:1-3, 10-12)

Sunday, Oct. 8—Faith Generated in One Cast Out (John 9: 24-38)

"When they came up out of the water, the Spirit of the Lord suddenly took Philip away" (v. 39). Apparently the preacher simply vanished. "The eunuch did not see him again." The traveler must have been greatly puzzled, but "he went on his way rejoicing." He had good reasons for joy. He now understood that puzzling prophecy. Much more than that, he was forgiven, cleansed, redeemed. He was a new man, born again as a child of God.

A NATURAL RESPONSE

During the Gulf War of 1991, many American soldiers found that being in the desert so far from home stimulated them to do some serious thinking. One GI said, "[When I get home] every day when I walk in the door, I'm going to kiss my wife and tell her I love her." He also said that when his daughter asked to go with him on an errand, he would no longer refuse her.

As the troops waited for the war to begin, chaplains reported that soldiers were reading their Bibles more and going to church services more often. Of course, skeptics say this is just the natural response to the threat of imminent battle. The old saying is that "there are no atheists in foxholes," but after the loneliness and danger of the battle are past, most people go back to their old ways.

The Ethiopian treasurer, traveling on the deserted road to Gaza, also turned to the Scriptures, and in his case it made a lasting difference. Exhibiting sincere interest in the Word of God, he accepted the help of Philip, whom God had sent to him. Philip's preaching led the Ethiopian to faith in Christ. The man's response was the natural one for an honest seeker: he heard the gospel message, understood what God had commanded him to do, and then eagerly obeyed. We do well to follow the Ethiopian's example whenever we come to a new understanding of what God expects of us.   —C. R. B.

CONCLUSION

The church is not designed to stand still. Every Christian can be a growing Christian. "Jesus Christ is the same yesterday and today and forever" (Hebrews 13:8). But God's people on earth are on the move—or ought to be.

A. A GROWING CHRISTIAN

Philip was chosen for a specific job, the care of the poor (Acts 6:1-6). But now we see him as a great preacher of the gospel, successful with many in the city, successful with one in the desert. After that he preached his way up the coast "until he reached Caesarea" (Acts 8:40). Thirty years later he must have been aging; but still he was known as "the evangelist," the teller of good news (Acts 21:8).

B. A PROGRESSING CHURCH

Did Philip abandon the job he was chosen and ordained to do? No, that specific job ceased to exist. The church passed into a new phase, and the work the seven had done was no longer possible. They did their job well when the multiplying thousands of Christians were in Jerusalem. When those thousands scattered, no seven men could care for all the poor. If only a dozen Christians were in a village, all of them knew one another's needs. If three hundred settled in a town, perhaps they had their own committee. Quickly the church adapted to the new situation.

C. PUPILS BECOME TEACHERS

In Jerusalem the church members had listened to the apostles' teaching. When they scattered, all of them became teachers (Acts 8:4). Hebrews 5:12 criticizes Christians who ought to be teachers, but still need to be taught the basics. Are we too easily content to keep receiving teaching without ever giving it to others?

Discovery Learning

This page contains an alternate lesson plan emphasizing learning activities. Classes desiring such student involvement will find these suggestions helpful. The next page is a reproducible activity page to further enhance discovery learning.

LEARNING GOALS

As students participate in today's class session, they should:

1. Describe how Philip shared the gospel publicly and one-on-one.

2. Name some principles for effective evangelism based on Philip's experience.

3. Choose someone with whom to share the gospel, using one or more of the principles identified in the lesson.

INTO THE LESSON

Before class write the following open-ended sentences on poster boards, one sentence per board. Display the posters in your classroom before your students arrive. (Or simply write one or two of the statements on your chalkboard.)

"The biggest barrier to spreading the gospel today is…"

"The last time I tried to share the gospel with a non-Christian…"

"My first thought when I hear a sermon about evangelism is usually…"

"The first time someone tried to talk with me about becoming a Christian…"

Use these sentences in one of the following two ways:

Option 1. Give each student a piece of paper. Have each choose one of the incomplete sentences and write the statement and a completion for it on his or her paper. Students are not to sign their names. Collect the papers and read them to the class.

Option 2. Have each student find a partner. Then each is to complete one of the statements and share it with his or her partner. After ninety seconds, ask volunteers to share their answers with the whole class.

If any of your students have had positive experiences sharing the gospel with a non-Christian, ask them to relate those experiences now. Then ask, "What makes us hesitant sometimes to share the message of Christ with a friend?"

Tell the class that today's Bible study will examine the experience of a successful evangelist. Perhaps this study will help us in our sharing of the gospel.

INTO THE WORD

Distribute a handout on which you have written the following sentences. (Use the reproducible page, 64, for this activity.)

He was open to God's leading.

He obeyed when he understood what God required.

He was eager to share the gospel.

He searched the Scriptures diligently.

He relied on God's Word, not his own experiences, to lead the seeker to Christ.

He hungered to know the truth.

He understood the place of Christ in prophecy.

He combined faith with action.

He permitted no social barriers to hinder his preaching to the lost.

His faith in Christ caused him to rejoice.

Arrange your class members in groups of about five. Tell them to examine this list of statements and decide whether each sentence describes the apostle Philip or the Ethiopian official in this week's text. Give them about five minutes, and then ask for their answers. (The first sentence describes Philip. Then the sentences alternate describing the Ethiopian and Philip. Members may feel that some of the sentences describe both of the men.) As you read each sentence aloud, come to agreement on each. Students should then mark "P" or "E" beside each sentence on their handouts.

Next have your class members look at the "P" sentences and in their groups discuss these questions regarding the sentences: "How did Philip demonstrate this principle? Why is this an important principle for serving as a successful evangelist?"

The students may discuss any or all of the sentences in their groups. After another five minutes, consider each principle and discuss it with the whole class.

INTO LIFE

Ask class members to decide which of the principles for evangelists seems most important to them. If you have time, members may discuss this in their groups before volunteers share with the whole group.

Ask them whether they know anyone who might be receptive to the gospel. We are to share the gospel with the whole world, but some in our world would be more easily won than others. It is wise to focus particularly on those who seem receptive.

Have the students remain in their groups and close this session by praying that they will seize their opportunities to be evangelists during the coming week.

Which One?

Read Acts 8:4-40. Then examine this list of statements and decide whether each sentence describes the apostle Philip or the Ethiopian official. Mark a **P** in the blank before each statement that refers to Philip and an **E** in each one that refers to the Ethiopian.

_____ He was open to God's leading.

_____ He obeyed when he understood what God required.

_____ He was eager to share the gospel.

_____ He searched the Scriptures diligently.

_____ He relied on God's Word, not his own experiences, to lead the seeker to Christ.

_____ He hungered to know the truth.

_____ He understood the place of Christ in prophecy.

_____ He combined faith with action.

_____ He permitted no social barriers to hinder his preaching to the lost.

_____ His faith in Christ caused him to rejoice.

Look again at each statement you marked with a **P.** Use them to compile a list of principles for effective evangelism. Write them below.

Look at the statements marked **E.** What can you learn from them to help you determine when someone may be receptive to the gospel?

Personal Path to Evangelism

Philip took advantage of the opportunity in front of of him to lead the Ethiopian to Christ. Philip was obedient and his obedience allowed another to accept the Good News and salvation. Our own lives put us in very different circumstances but nevertheless opportunities exist for us to be evangelists. Examine the following Scriptures to find principles necessary for us to be evangelists.

Luke 24:49	Ephesians 6:19-20	Mark 5:19	1 John 1:1-3
Acts 1:8	John 14:13-14	Mark 7:31f	1 Corinthians 16:9

Principles:

SAUL BECOMES A DISCIPLE

LESSON 7

WHY TEACH THIS LESSON?

Acts is a book of evangelism. Throughout this quarter we have seen, and will see many more times, how early Christians shared their faith and won new disciples. The obvious application is that we ought to be sharing our faith as well.

But many of us are hesitant. Will people think we are strange—or part of a cult—if we are bold with our witness? Might we actually drive away some who would otherwise have become Christians if we had not "messed things up"? Is there any use sharing Christ with the thoroughly secular and immoral neighbor?

Today's lesson will reassure your students that sharing the gospel is worth every effort. If as unlikely a prospect as Saul of Tarsus could be converted and then become the apostle Paul, then the power of the gospel is effective even to change the immoral and secular neighbors in our own town.

INTRODUCTION

Most of us have heard of John Newton. Early in life he was engaged in the slave trade, transporting people to lives of bondage. Somehow the gospel of Jesus reached him. Touched and transformed, John Newton became a Christian minister, calling slaves of sin to be transported to lives of freedom in Christ. He was the man who gave us the words to our beloved hymn "Amazing Grace."

A. TRANSFORMING POWER

The power of Almighty God is no less amazing than his grace. He transforms sinners into saints, millions of them. Besides, he sometimes transforms those who already are devoted to him. Moses was a shepherd for forty years, but God made him the leader of a nation. David was a shepherd, too, but God made him king. Amos was a southern farmer, but God sent him north to prophesy to the people of Israel. And then there was Saul of Tarsus.

B. LESSON BACKGROUND

Saul was born in Tarsus of Cilicia, but we meet him first in Jerusalem. There he was a student under Gamaliel, a famous teacher of the Jews (Acts 22:3).

Gamaliel advised restraint in dealing with the Christians who filled Jerusalem with their teaching (Acts 5:33-39), but Saul would have none of that. It seemed to him that these Christians were bent on destroying the ancient religion of Israel, and he could see nothing to do about it but to destroy the Christians. He stood by with approval when Stephen was stoned to death, and then he took the lead in hunting down other Christians and jailing them (Acts 8:1-3). But God Almighty had other plans for Saul.

I. HALT! (ACTS 9:1-6)

Saul's campaign failed to accomplish its purpose. Instead of giving up their faith, the Christians gave up their homes. They scattered into the many towns and villages of Judea and Samaria. They took their faith with them, and they told about it wherever they went (Acts 8:1-4). Churches sprang up all over those

DEVOTIONAL READING
MATTHEW 4:17-22
LESSON SCRIPTURE
ACTS 9:1-31
PRINTED TEXT
ACTS 9:1-6, 10-20

Oct
15

LESSON AIMS

After completing this lesson a student should be able to:

1. Tell how Saul of Tarsus changed from a persecutor to a Christian, including the role of Ananias.

2. Describe some situations in which Christians today might hesitate to share the gospel.

3. Plan a way to share the gospel in a difficult situation.

KEY VERSE

This man [Saul] is my chosen instrument to carry my name before the Gentiles and their kings and before the people of Israel.
—Acts 9:15

WHAT DO YOU THINK?

Jesus told Saul, "It is hard for you to kick against the goads" (Acts 26:14; see note below). Some students believe the Lord was referring to a struggle within Saul—pangs of conscience, memories of mournful women and children. Others believe God had been using external forces—e.g., the preaching of Stephen.

What do you think? What kind of goads do you believe the Lord was using to urge Saul to repent of his murderous ways? What kinds of goads is he using to call the people of this country to repentance? The people of our community? The people of our church?

NOTE

The King James Version includes the words, "It is hard for thee to kick against the pricks" (i.e., "goads") in verse 5. Verse 6 begins, "And he trembling and astonished said, Lord, what wilt thou have me to do? And the Lord said…." Most modern versions do not include these readings, as they are not in most of the manuscripts we have of Acts. The material in verse 5 is found in Acts 26:14 (where Paul tells of the event to King Agrippa). The question in verse 6 is included in Paul's account of his conversion in Acts 22:10. Apparently, some scribe copying the text attempted to harmonize this account with Paul's later reports and added the words here. They are doubtless actual parts of what happened but were probably not included in Luke's account of the event here.

areas, and soon in regions far beyond them. Now Saul could see nothing to do but to follow the Christians wherever they went, to hunt them down and lock them up.

A. FURIOUS PERSECUTION (vv. 1, 2)

1, 2. Meanwhile, Saul was still breathing out murderous threats against the Lord's disciples. He went to the high priest and asked him for letters to the synagogues in Damascus, so that if he found any there who belonged to the Way, whether men or women, he might take them as prisoners to Jerusalem.

Damascus was about a hundred forty miles from Jerusalem, far outside the area ruled by the Jews. At this time it was subject to Aretas, king of Arabia (2 Corinthians 11:32). Apparently the Jewish rulers in Jerusalem had a treaty allowing them to discipline Jews in Damascus. No doubt Saul learned that a strong church was growing stronger there. Still furiously continuing his persecution, he asked the high priest for papers authorizing him to arrest any Christians found in Damascus and take them to Jerusalem. He must have taken along a squad of police as he set out for that foreign city.

B. SUDDEN STOP (vv. 3-6)

3. As he neared Damascus on his journey, suddenly a light from heaven flashed around him.

The journey was near its end when it was interrupted suddenly. It was about noon, but the light from heaven was brighter than the sunlight (Acts 22:6; 26:13). **4. He fell to the ground and heard a voice say to him, "Saul, Saul, why do you persecute me?"**

In fear and reverence, Saul fell to the ground, and so did those who were traveling with him (Acts 26:14). Then a voice called Saul by name. That must have been as terrifying as the light, especially when the voice accused, Why do you persecute me? The men traveling with Saul heard the voice (v. 7), but saw no one and did not understand the words that were spoken (Acts 22:9). **5. "Who are you, Lord?" Saul asked. "I am Jesus, whom you are persecuting," he replied.**

Whoever was speaking in that unearthly light was entitled to be called Lord. Saul was sure of that, but he did not know who it was. Fearfully he asked, Who are you?

I am Jesus! What a shock! Till that moment Saul had felt sure Jesus was a dead impostor. He had thought he was persecuting disciples of that dead man, liars who were also traitors to country and faith and God. Suddenly Saul's whole frame of mind collapsed. Those disciples were not liars and traitors after all. They were right! Jesus was alive just as they said—alive and ruling in Heaven! Saul himself was the liar, the traitor to country and faith and God! What shame, what grief, what terror must have crushed the man as he cringed on the ground under that blinding light! **6. "Now get up and go into the city, and you will be told what you must do."**

From Paul's own account we learn this message came in response to his question, "What shall I do, Lord?" (Acts 22:10). No longer resisting the Lord, Saul was broken, shamed, terrified. He was ready to do whatever Jesus said. It is notable that Jesus did not tell him what to do to be forgiven and saved from his sin. Last week we read that an angel sent Philip to the Gaza road, and the Holy Spirit told him to join a passing chariot. Now we read that Jesus himself stopped Saul's persecution. But neither angel nor Spirit nor Jesus explained the way of salvation. That work has been given to Christians, and no one is going to do it for us. So now Jesus sent Saul on to Damascus. There a human messenger would tell him what to do.

LIGHT FROM HEAVEN

"Shooting stars" are small particles of matter in the solar system that streak into earth's atmosphere and, in a brief burst of light, are vaporized. Sometimes, however, a much larger mass of matter bursts into our thin envelope of air. On these occasions, the meteorite burns with a brilliant light and strikes the ground with tremendous force.

Several thousand years ago a meteorite traveling at forty-three thousand miles per hour hit the earth near what is now Flagstaff, Arizona. We can still see the result: a crater nearly six hundred feet deep and more than three-fourths of a mile across—an amazing effect for such a brief, bright event!

Saul of Tarsus was bent on destroying the church. He was a zealous defender of the law and saw the church as a threat to Judaism. The light from heaven and the accompanying message that came to Saul comprised only one brief event in human history. But the enormous change that took place in Saul's life as a result was a force to be recognized. Saul's zeal for the law was changed into zeal for Christ, and the world bears the marks of that change.

Will what we do for Christ give evidence that we have seen that "light from heaven"?
—C. R. B.

II. THE LORD'S MESSENGER (ACTS 9:10-16)

Saul was blinded by that terrific light, but his companions could see, so they led him on to Damascus. For three days Saul remained in utter darkness, eating nothing, drinking nothing, waiting to be told what to do (vv. 8, 9). And he was praying (v. 11).

A. ORDER (vv. 10-12)

10. In Damascus there was a disciple named Ananias. The Lord called to him in a vision, "Ananias!" "Yes, Lord," he answered.

It seems that *Ananias* was a Jew of Damascus who had been won to Christ. He had heard of Saul's persecution in Jerusalem (v. 13). Now *in a vision* he heard the Lord speak to him. He may have been surprised and startled, but apparently he was not so frightened as Saul had been. He responded promptly and waited to hear more.

11. The Lord told him, "Go to the house of Judas on Straight Street and ask for a man from Tarsus named Saul, for he is praying.

Saul was *praying*. No doubt he was praying, among other things, for someone to come and tell him what to do, as Jesus had promised (v. 6). Ananias was to be God's answer to that prayer.

12. "In a vision he has seen a man named Ananias come and place his hands on him to restore his sight."

Blind Saul was being prepared to receive God's messenger. Already he had seen *a vision of a man named Ananias* coming to restore his sight with a touch. When the vision would become reality, Saul would have no doubt that Ananias was really God's messenger.

B. PROTEST (vv. 13, 14)

13. "Lord," Ananias answered, "I have heard many reports about this man and all the harm he has done to your saints in Jerusalem.

Christians coming from Jerusalem naturally had told why they came, and Ananias had *heard many reports* of Saul's furious campaign.

14. "And he has come here with authority from the chief priests to arrest all who call on your name."

A "street called Straight" in Damascus is the subject of a photo, which is Visual 7 of the visuals packet.

HOW TO SAY IT
Ananias. An-uh-NYE-us.
Aretas. AIR-ih-tas.
Cilicia. Sih-LISH-i-uh.
Gamaliel. Guh-MAY-lih-ul.

OPTION

"Three Disciples," on page 72, is a reproducible Bible study activity that will help your students explore this text by noting the actions of three of the main characters involved—Saul, Ananias, and Barnabas.

WHAT DO YOU THINK?

In Damascus, the blinded Saul spent much time praying, no doubt asking for someone to come with that word of instruction that Jesus had promised him. Ananias was the answer to that prayer.

We may have neighbors, fellow workers, or other acquaintances who are hurting enough that they are crying out to God for help. They may need to hear God's message of salvation, or they may be Christians who are desperate for a listening ear or a word of counsel. It is an exciting thought for us to realize that we can be answers to such people's prayers.

How can one develop the sensitivity to recognize when he or she can be an answer to someone's prayer? What qualities mark the person who is quick to recognize the needs of others and who is just as quick to respond to such needs?

Apparently Christians were still coming from Jerusalem to Damascus. News of Saul's coming and his purpose had arrived ahead of him. Should Ananias go looking for the man who was looking for him with the intention of taking him to Jerusalem to be punished?

C. ORDER REPEATED (vv. 15, 16)

15. But the Lord said to Ananias, "Go! This man is my chosen instrument to carry my name before the Gentiles and their kings and before the people of Israel.

Incredible as it seemed, Jesus' worst persecutor was to become his best preacher. Fervent Jew though he was, Saul was to be a special messenger to *the Gentiles.* He was to stand before *kings.* He was to speak also to his own people, *the people of Israel.* Everywhere he was to take Jesus' *name.* He was to proclaim Jesus, the Christ, the Son of God. He was to sound Jesus' call and his promise of salvation. This assurance must have quieted Ananias's fear, but still we wonder if his voice trembled a little as he walked up to Judas's house and asked for Saul.

16. "I will show him how much he must suffer for my name."

The persecutor would become the persecuted. Saul had caused suffering to the Christians; he would be a Christian, and would himself *suffer.*

NOT SUCH A MONSTER, AFTER ALL

Boris Karloff portrayed "Frankenstein" as a horrific monster in the famous 1931 film. Through the years since then, a whole series of Frankenstein movies have followed, using the same monstrous motif for the title character.

In 1993, however, a made-for-television movie portrayed Frankenstein as a far more human being—a person with normal human longings for acceptance and companionship. Ironically, this more accurately depicts the character as Mary Shelley, his creator, portrayed him in her 1818 novel. It turns out that Frankenstein is not such a monster, after all.

Saul of Tarsus was "breathing out murderous threats" against the church (Acts 9:1). When Ananias first heard that Saul was coming to Damascus, he must have trembled to think of the pain and suffering the church might soon endure at the hands of this monster. So it must have been an incredible surprise when the Lord revealed that the world would soon see a different, converted Saul. When the sin was washed from Saul's heart, he would be seen as not such a monster, after all!

As difficult as it may be to believe that some hardened sinners can change, we should never doubt the life-changing power of God.   —C. R. B.

III. SAUL TRANSFORMED (ACTS 9:17-20)

Can you imagine how Saul felt? For three long days he could not tell day from night. He was blind. For three long days he had nothing to eat—not even a drink of water. For three long days he prayed. We know of only one communication he received in those days: a vision of "a man named Ananias." But the three days ended.

A. THE LORD'S MESSAGE (vv. 17, 18a)

17. Then Ananias went to the house and entered it. Placing his hands on Saul, he said, "Brother Saul, the Lord—Jesus, who appeared to you on the road as you were coming here—has sent me so that you may see again and be filled with the Holy Spirit."

Besides what is recorded here in the verse before us, the Lord's message to Saul included the plain command, "Receive your sight" (Acts 22:13). It also included this: "And now what are you waiting for? Get up, be baptized and wash your sins away, calling on his name" (22:16). But the main purpose of verse 17 in our text is to show that Ananias came exactly as Saul in the vision had seen him coming (v. 12). By that Saul was sure that Ananias was really the Lord's messenger.

18a. Immediately, something like scales fell from Saul's eyes, and he could see again.

Ananias's word and touch were effective: instantly Saul could see. It was as if *scales* had been covering his eyes, and now were gone.

B. THE LORD'S NEW MAN (vv. 18b-20)

18b. He got up and was baptized.

Saul did this in response to Ananias's plain urging (Acts 22:16). It was not necessary for Ananias to explain the meaning of baptism. Saul must have known what the apostles had been teaching in Jerusalem. But Ananias did mention the feature most reassuring to Saul at the moment: this was the way to get rid of his sins. His sins must have been a heavy burden on his mind and soul through all those days since Jesus had appeared to him on the way.

19. And after taking some food, he regained his strength. Saul spent several days with the disciples in Damascus.

Instead of going back to Jerusalem or going home to Tarsus, Saul stayed for a time with *the disciples in Damascus.*

20. At once he began to preach in the synagogues that Jesus is the Son of God.

Saul was not one to be quiet about his new conviction. Promptly he began to reason with the Jews *in the synagogues,* teaching the same doctrine that had brought death to Stephen in Jerusalem, the same truth for which the disciples had been driven from Jerusalem and had scattered at least as far as Damascus, the same teaching that Saul had been trying to stop.

It may have been soon after this that Saul went away to Arabia for a time (Galatians 1:15-17). We do not know how long he stayed in Arabia or what he did there; but we can imagine that he spent long days restudying the Scriptures of the Old Testament and seeing how perfectly Jesus fulfilled the prophecies of the Christ. Jesus had called Saul to be a minister and a witness; Jesus would send him to testify far and near (Acts 26:16-18). He was Christ's apostle, for the word *apostle* means "one who is sent." Saul was an apostle as surely and as fully as were the other twelve apostles (2 Corinthians 11:5). He was filled with the Holy Spirit (Acts 9:17), guided and inspired as the other apostles were.

From Arabia Saul returned to Damascus and resumed his teaching in the synagogues. Unbelieving Jews tried to argue with him, but they were defeated (Acts 9:22) just as those in Jerusalem had lost their debates with Stephen (Acts 6:9, 10). Soon Saul began to learn how he must suffer for the Lord's name (Acts 9:16). Unbelievers plotted to kill him—apparently involving the civil authorities in the attempt—but disciples helped him to escape (Acts 9:23-25; 2 Corinthians 11:32, 33).

CONCLUSION

You Don't Have to Stay the Way You Are. That is the intriguing title of a book that appeared some years ago. If you are not what you would like to be, or if you are not what you ought to be, you can change. It's true. People are changing all the time.

A. FROM SINNERS TO SAINTS

One of the most momentous changes in the world transforms a sinner to a saint. In the language of the New Testament, every Christian is a saint. The name means a person is set apart, dedicated. Even when one fails to live up to one's dedication, he or she is still dedicated, still a saint.

WHAT DO YOU THINK?

Saul certainly had no lack for zeal—either as persecutor or later as preacher. Yet many Christians and whole churches seem to have no zeal. They may blame this on the preacher for the quality of his sermons or the church's leaders for their inability to develop appealing programs. But these cannot be used as excuses for lack of zeal, which each Christian is personally responsible for maintaining (Romans 12:11). How can a Christian or a church rekindle zeal for serving Christ?

WHAT DO YOU THINK?

In the New Testament, all believers are referred to as "saints" (see Romans 1:7; Philippians 1:1). That term does not mean that Christians have achieved absolute holiness or perfect piety. It signifies that God has called us and set us apart to lives of holiness. If we regularly think of ourselves and our fellow Christians as saints, we may be reminded of our obligation to cultivate holiness in every thought, word, and deed.

What would be different in our church if everyone began thinking this way? What victories would be won for the Lord? What old wounds would be healed?

What would it take for some of us to begin thinking this way and to spread that attitude around?

PRAYER

How unfailing is your love, our Father! For us you gave your only Son. Stir our hearts anew, we pray, awaken our love, arouse our energy until we do your work as well as it was done by your saints of old. In Jesus' name. Amen.

THOUGHT TO REMEMBER

"Never be lacking in zeal, but keep your spiritual fervor, serving the Lord" (Romans 12:11).

DAILY BIBLE READINGS

Monday, Oct. 9—How Paul Became a Disciple (Galatians 1:11-19)

Tuesday, Oct. 10—Called to Preach to Gentiles (Acts 22: 12-21)

Wednesday, Oct. 11—Benefited From Roman Citizenship (Acts 22:22-29)

Thursday, Oct. 12—Plot Against Paul's Life (Acts 23:6-15)

Friday, Oct. 13—Paul Preaching in Rome (Acts 28: 23-31)

Saturday, Oct. 14—Paul's Care for the Church (1 Thessalonians 3)

Sunday, Oct. 15—Saul on the Damascus Road (Acts 9:1-9)

In a former lesson we read that three thousand persons became saints in a single day, the Day of Pentecost. That is unusual, but the same kind of change is going on day by day.

Most of us who read this book have made the change from sinner to saint. Now we are the people who help others make it. Are you doing that? You don't know how? Read the second chapter of Acts to see how Peter appealed to people who believed the Bible. Read Acts 17:16-31 to see how Paul appealed to people who did not believe the Bible. Put their messages in your own words and adapt them to the sinners you know. If you're not very good at that, you can increase your offerings for the support of people who are.

B. FROM IGNORANT TO INFORMED

Some people sin without knowing it. Saul is a prime example. After he learned the truth, he said he had been "a blasphemer and a persecutor and a violent man," but he had done it "in ignorance" (1 Timothy 1:13). When he tried to stop the preaching of the gospel, he thought he was defending God's truth against a lie. When he learned the truth, he found that he had been defending a lie against God's truth. Then he called himself the worst of sinners (1 Timothy 1:15).

The Lord took an unusual way to inform Saul of the facts. He came in a blinding light to prove that he had risen from the dead. Most people learn the facts in other ways, or not at all. Now the facts of Jesus' life and death and resurrection, verified by competent witnesses, are set down in black and white for all to read. Those who do not read the record need someone like you or me to tell them—and your duty and mine is to meet their need. Whom have you told in the past week, or the past year?

Sometimes a careless unbeliever says, "When Jesus comes to me as he came to Saul, then I'll believe." Thoughtless, thoughtless! Do you really want Jesus to call you as he called Saul? Do you want to spend the rest of your life in earnest, ardent preaching of the gospel to nations and kings and the children of Israel? Do you want to endure prison and beating, cold and hunger, shipwreck and peril? (2 Corinthians 11:24-28). Jesus came to call Saul to all that—to make him a minister and a witness, an apostle to the world in spite of terrible persecution (Acts 26:16-18).

That meeting with Jesus on the road to Damascus did not take away Saul's sin and make him a saint. It made him a convicted sinner, a remorseful, penitent sinner, a frightened, blinded, grieving sinner, fasting and praying—but still a sinner. It remained for him to wash away his sin in baptism, even as you and I have done, or can do (Acts 22:16).

C. FROM INDOLENT TO ENERGETIC

The Lord rebuked the church at Ephesus because it had left its first love. Once it had labored earnestly for the Lord, labored vigorously and long, and had loved it. Now it was content to drift, content with its accomplishments, content with its reputation, content with its past. To that church Jesus called, "Remember the height from which you have fallen! Repent and do the things you did at first" (Revelation 2:1-7).

Seldom has any church matched the zeal and fervor of the first church in Jerusalem. Despite the frowns of religious leaders, it became a shining light that beckoned sinners to repent and live. Despite the fury of the government, it became a training school that made its members preachers of the gospel. When persecution drove those members from Jerusalem, they "preached the word wherever they went."

Is that first love still alive in your congregation? Is it still alive in your heart? If not, hear the call of the Master: "Repent and do the things you did at first"!

Discovery Learning

This page contains an alternate lesson plan emphasizing learning activities. Classes desiring such student involvement will find these suggestions helpful. The next page is a reproducible activity page to further enhance discovery learning.

LEARNING GOALS

As students participate in today's class session, they should:

1. Tell how Saul of Tarsus changed from a persecutor to a Christian, including the role of Ananias.

2. Describe some situations in which Christians today might hesitate to share the gospel.

3. Plan a way to share the gospel in a difficult situation.

INTO THE LESSON

Make copies of the next page for your students. Or write the words *HATE* and *LOVE* on the chalkboard with enough space to add three more words, one word per line, between them.

Divide the class into groups of three to five members each. Ask each group to attempt to change the word *hate* into *love* by changing just one letter at a time to form not more than three words between them.

Allow just five or six minutes for this activity. If none of the groups has done it in that time, call time and reveal the answer. If one has, celebrate the victory and ask that group to reveal the answer. (A possible solution is HATE, DATE, DOTE, DOVE, LOVE.)

Observe that changing "hate" to "love" is a drastic change. Today's lesson text reveals how the gospel can make just as dramatic a change in one's life. For most of us, that change is gradual, like changing one letter at a time in our opening activity. For others, it may come suddenly. For Saul of Tarsus, the change was quick and extreme. He, indeed, went from hate to love!

INTO THE WORD

Before class mark four copies of Acts 9:1-31 to highlight the speeches of God, Saul, and Ananias and the non-dialog parts (for a narrator). Pick four people who will read those parts in class.

Then assign each group (same groups as before) one of the personalities who played an important role in this Scripture: Saul, Ananias, and Barnabas.

The group (or groups) that takes Saul should answer these questions, using Acts 9:1-25 as a guide:

What was he doing? (Going to Damascus with orders from the high priest in Jerusalem to arrest Christians.)

What happened? (He was struck down by a great light; Jesus appeared to him; he was blinded; he was led into Damascus; he spent three days praying and fasting; a disciple named Ananias came and healed his blindness, shared the gospel with him, and baptized him.)

What was the outcome? (He became a disciple and a preacher. He himself was persecuted.)

What can we learn from Saul's experience? (Several answers may emerge here. Certainly we can learn that even the most unlikely prospect can be changed by the power of the gospel.)

The group that takes Ananias should answer these questions (from Acts 9:10-25):

What was his role? (He healed Saul, shared the gospel with him, and baptized him.)

What was his attitude? (Fear, at first; then love. Obedience in spite of fear.)

What was the outcome? (He was able to minister to Saul's need; a great victory was won for the church.)

Is there anything we can learn from Ananias's experience? (Again, this may vary. One lesson is that obedience is required even when the situation is frightening.)

The group that takes Barnabas should answer these questions (from Acts 9:23-31):

What was his role? (He helped Saul gain acceptance in Jerusalem.)

What was his attitude? (Acceptance.)

What was the outcome? (Saul was able to fellowship with the Christians in Jerusalem.)

Is there anything we can learn from Barnabas's experience? (The main lesson is acceptance, encouragement.)

Give the groups ten minutes for discussion. Then bring the whole group together and have a spokesperson from each group report on the group's observations.

INTO LIFE

Ask, "With which person do you best identify—Saul, Ananias, or Barnabas? Why?" After some have shared, ask for some ideas on how Christians might share the gospel in some difficult situations. For example, a friend's mate has been diagnosed with a serious, even terminal, illness; a co-worker is struggling with relationships at work; a close neighbor confides in you that the in-laws have treated him/her badly. What would an "Ananias" or a "Barnabas" do in each situation?

Dramatic Change

The following words are very different—exact opposites! Yet you can change hate into love in just four steps, changing one letter at a time. Try it. There's just one thing: each change you make must result in an actual word, correctly spelled!

HATE

___ ___ ___ ___

___ ___ ___ ___

___ ___ ___ ___

LOVE

Three Disciples

SAUL

Read Acts 9:1-25 and answer the following questions.
What was he doing?
What happened?
What was the outcome?
What can we learn from Saul's experience?

ANANIAS

Read Acts 9:10-25 and answer the following questions.
What was his role?
What was his attitude?
What was the outcome?
Is there anything we can learn from Ananias's experience?

BARNABAS

Read Acts 9:23-31 and answer the following questions.
What was his role? (He helped Saul gain acceptance in Jerusalem.)
What was his attitude? (Acceptance.)
What was the outcome? (Saul was able to fellowship with the Christians in Jerusalem.)
Is there anything we can learn from Barnabas's experience?

The Story of Christian Beginnings

Unit 2. Witnessing in Judea and Samaria
(Lessons 5-9)

GENTILES RECEIVE THE SPIRIT

LESSON 8

WHY TEACH THIS LESSON?

Racial tension is a chronic problem in our society. Government has tried to ease it, education has tried to ease it, even the church has tried to ease it, but yet it continues. In fact, many of the so-called solutions have only made the problem worse!

But this is not a hopeless situation. What is required is treating the problem and not just the symptoms. What is needed is the gospel of Jesus Christ!

The conversion of Cornelius, the first Gentile Christian, is proof that previously warring races can be reconciled. This lesson may be the catalyst to solving racial problems in our churches and communities today. That is our prayer!

INTRODUCTION

No one of another race is to go inside the barrier around the temple and enclosure. Anyone who is caught will be responsible for his own death, which will follow.

Those words were carved in stone, and stones inscribed with them were built into the wall that separated the sacred inner court of the temple in Jerusalem from the big outer court that anyone might enter. That wall and that warning were fitting symbols of the agelong separation of the Jews from all the other people of the world. From the time of Abraham, he and his descendants knew they were a people set apart, a people God had chosen for his own.

A. THE JEWISH CHURCH

When the church of Jesus began in Jerusalem, all its members were Jews. It seems that none of them even dreamed that Gentiles ever would be included. Jesus was Israel's Messiah; his blessings were for Israel. So they thought.

Jesus had told his apostles to go to all the world and preach to every creature (Mark 16:15). Apparently they thought that meant every Jewish creature, for Jews then were scattered through all the known world. Saul was specifically sent to Gentiles (Acts 26:16-18), but the brethren in Jerusalem did not know that yet.

The Holy Spirit had come to guide the apostles into all truth (John 16:13). He inspired their preaching, and it was wonderfully effective. But Jesus wanted people of all nations in his church. That was truth, too, but it seems that Jewish minds were so firmly closed to it that the Spirit had to use extraordinary methods to teach it to them. In unusual ways two messages came, one to a Gentile and one to a Jew.

B. LESSON BACKGROUND

Cornelius was not a Jew, but neither was he a pagan. He was a Roman, an officer in the foreign army that occupied the Jews' country. But Cornelius believed in the real God, as the Jews did; and he lived in godly ways. He prayed much, and he was generous in sharing his wealth (Acts 10:1, 2). This officer was stationed in

DEVOTIONAL READING
ACTS 10:9-23

LESSON SCRIPTURE
ACTS 10:1—11:18

PRINTED TEXT
ACTS 10:30-39, 44-48

Oct
22

LESSON AIMS

After the completion of this lesson students should be able to:

1. Explain how God removed obstacles that had prevented the spread of the gospel to Gentiles.

2. List some barriers that hinder the spread of the gospel today.

3. Suggest a way to remove at least one barrier to personal evangelism.

KEY VERSE

Then Peter began to speak: "I now realize how true it is that God does not show favoritism but accepts men from every nation who fear him and do what is right."   —Acts 10:34, 35

LESSON 8 NOTES

HOW TO SAY IT

Caesarea. Sess-uh-REE-uh.
Cornelius. Kor-NEE-lih-us or
   Kor-NEEL-yus.

OPTION

  Use the reproducible activity,
"Breaking Down the Barriers," on
page 80 to explore this text.

NOTE

  Some manuscripts of Acts also
mention fasting here, so it is in-
cluded in the King James Version.
Cornelius may have been fasting,
but we cannot be sure.

the seacoast city of Caesarea, the headquarters of the Roman governor of Judea and Samaria.

A heavenly angel appeared to Cornelius, but he did not explain the way of salva-tion. The angel told Cornelius to send for Simon Peter, who then was staying at Joppa, more than thirty miles down the coast. Peter would tell Cornelius what he ought to do. Cornelius promptly sent three men to ask Peter to come (vv. 3-8).

About noon the next day, a vision came to Peter in Joppa. He was praying alone when he saw a big sheet let down from Heaven with all kinds of animals in it. A voice invited hungry Peter to kill an animal and eat.

Peter objected. Such meat would not be kosher. It would be impure; it would be "unclean."

The voice spoke again: "Do not call anything impure that God has made clean" (vv. 9-16).

While Peter was wondering what the vision meant, the messengers arrived from Cornelius. Plainly the Holy Spirit told Peter to go with them. Then Peter began to see what the vision meant. He should not call those messengers unclean, Gentiles though they were. He invited the men to stay for the night, and the next day he started to Caesarea with them. Knowing full well that strict Jews at Jerusalem would criticize him for that, Peter asked some Jewish Christians to go along and be wit-nesses of what was going to happen (vv. 17-23).

In Caesarea, Cornelius was ready for them. He had called together his relatives and friends to hear whatever message Peter would bring. Violating the traditional law of the rabbis, Peter went into that Gentile house and asked why Cornelius had sent for him (vv. 24-29).

I. A READY AUDIENCE (ACTS 10:30-33)

What excited expectancy must have filled that house! A Jew was coming to tell the Roman what he ought to do. Such a visit was extraordinary and cause for the belief that the message was one of divine import. But that was not all: a shining angel had told the Roman to send for that Jew. Surely, then, there would be a mes-sage from God! So there must have been a breathless hush while Cornelius ex-plained why he had sent for Peter.

A. ANGEL'S MESSAGE (vv. 30-32)

30. Cornelius answered: "Four days ago I was in my house praying at this hour, at three in the afternoon. Suddenly a man in shining clothes stood before me.

Cornelius explained exactly why he had sent for Peter. Counting days in the way then customary, he told what had happened *four days ago*. On the first two of those days his messengers had traveled to Joppa; on the third and fourth days they had returned with Peter and other Jewish Christians. On the first of those four days Cornelius had prayed at the customary Jewish hour of prayer, about *three in the afternoon*. As he was praying an angel appeared (Acts 10:3), whom Cornelius described as *a man in shining clothes*.

31. "… and said, 'Cornelius, God has heard your prayer and remembered your gifts to the poor.

First, the angel assured Cornelius that God had both heard his prayer and taken note of his generous giving. Prayers are more likely to be answered when the one who prays is a sincere worshiper and an unselfish giver.

32. "'Send to Joppa for Simon who is called Peter. He is a guest in the home of Simon the tanner, who lives by the sea.'

The angel was specific. Simon Peter would have a message for Cornelius, and the angel told exactly where Simon Peter was to be found. Why didn't the angel tell

Cornelius to go to Peter instead of inviting Peter to come to him? For one thing, God surely knew Cornelius would bring a houseful of relatives and friends to hear the gospel with him. For another thing, God was bringing about a change in Peter as well as a change in Cornelius. He was breaking down Peter's lifelong aversion to people who were not Jews, and bringing Peter into a Gentile's house was a part of the process.

B. MESSAGE OBEYED (v. 33)

33. "So I sent for you immediately, and it was good of you to come. Now we are all here in the presence of God to listen to everything the Lord has commanded you to tell us."

Cornelius obeyed the angel *immediately*. Though it was midafternoon when the angel came, Cornelius called his men and started them on their way that very day. That shows how eager he was to get whatever message Peter would bring. Since a heavenly angel ordered the invitation, Cornelius was sure Peter had done right in coming, even though it was contrary to the traditional rules of his people (Acts 10:28).

Now Peter was there, and many Gentiles were there to hear him. They realized that they were *in the presence of God;* before them was the man whom God's angel had told them to call; they were sure they would hear from him what God had commanded him to say. Was ever an audience more ready for a sermon?

IMPORTANT INFORMATION

The "information superhighway" is the latest place one may go to find information. With a computer, a modem, and the appropriate software, one can gain access to many sources that provide an amazing variety of information.

Cornelius was a devout, God-fearing, generous man. God had important information for Cornelius—the saving gospel of Christ—so he commanded Cornelius to send for Simon Peter, who would deliver the message to him.

Peter was an eyewitness of the ministry, death, and resurrection of Christ. He would give Cornelius all the information necessary to establish faith in Christ and lead to salvation.

God saw fit to have the testimony of Peter and other eyewitnesses recorded for us in his Word, so that we too may learn of salvation and how we may share in it. That's better than even the *latest* in modern technology can do!

—C. R. B.

II. A PLAIN MESSAGE (ACTS 10:34-39)

Peter, too, could see that God had arranged this meeting. God's angel had told Cornelius to send for him; God's Spirit had told Peter to come (Acts 10:19, 20). Now he had come, and he had no message except the gospel of Jesus. It was plain that God wanted him to give that message to these Gentiles.

A. IMPARTIAL GOD (vv. 34, 35)

34. Then Peter began to speak: "I now realize how true it is that God does not show favoritism.

God not show favoritism; that is, God does not favor any person because that person is a member of a particular group, or holds a high position, or is rich, or is powerful. From the Old Testament Peter knew that God does not favor any person for such reasons, and people should not (Deuteronomy 1:17; 16:19; 2 Chronicles 19:7). Now he realized, perhaps for the first time, that it applied to everyone. God does not give special favor to anyone just because one is a Jew.

WHAT DO YOU THINK?

Cornelius's statement in Acts 10:33b expresses an appropriate sentiment for us as we congregate for worship on the Lord's Day. It reminds us that when we assemble for worship we are coming as a body into the very presence of God. All mental distractions and all unkind or judgmental thoughts toward other persons should be set aside and replaced by humility and reverence before God. It reminds us that one of the reasons for our assembling is to receive instruction from God's Word. We ought not to judge the elements of the worship service on the basis of their entertainment value. God may want us to hear a call to repentance or an exhortation to share our faith with others—messages that may not be entertaining.

How can a congregation encourage such an attitude in its members? Suggest some specific ideas.

Visual 8 illustrates verse 34. It is pictured on page 76

WHAT DO YOU THINK?

Obviously, if our Heavenly Father does not favor anyone because of outward circumstances, neither should any human being. Like Peter, a person may accept this concept easily in principle, but have difficulty applying it to specific circumstances. Perhaps one has grown up with a negative stereotype regarding persons of different races, or nationalities, or economic classes. Or perhaps one had an unpleasant experience involving a person of one of these groups and transferred his or her feelings for that person to the whole group.

How can a Christian set aside such feelings and practice the love and acceptance of God? What may result if we fail to do this? What kind of victories result when we succeed?

Visual 8.

WHAT DO YOU THINK?

Peter noted, almost in passing, that Cornelius and other Roman army officers knew of Jesus' career (Acts 10:37-42.). If the claims that Peter and the apostles made about Jesus were fictional, people who knew the facts of Jesus' life would have challenged and discredited them. Peter's assumption that Cornelius knew enough of Jesus to know that the message Peter brought was true verifies that it was.

How does this consistency affirm your faith in Christ? Do you think sharing this information would be helpful to one who was still coming to faith in Christ? Why or why not?

35. ". . . but accepts men from every nation who fear him and do what is right.

God does not show favoritism; but he does favor faith and righteousness. Cornelius was a Roman, outside the chosen nation; but he won God's attention by sincere worship and goodness.

B. JESUS THE SAVIOR (vv. 36-38)

36. "You know the message God sent to the people of Israel, telling the good news of peace through Jesus Christ, who is Lord of all.

God now was using Peter to send a message to Cornelius and other Romans, and it was the same message that *God sent to the people of Israel* by Peter and others. It was a message of *peace through Jesus Christ.* Jesus is the Christ, the Messiah, the one whom God has chosen to be prophet and priest and king. Those who believe in him and obey him are forgiven, cleansed, purified. Therefore they are at peace with God. They are God's children, and brothers and sisters of one another. Therefore they are at peace among themselves. Jesus the Savior is also the Lord—the commander, the ruler, the owner—and he *is Lord of all.* Now Peter was learning that *all* means Gentiles as well as Jews.

THE GOD WHO CARES FOR ALL

"Flu" and the common cold do not show favoritism. We all come down with these afflictions in spite of our best efforts to avoid them.

In the days before antibiotics, every family, it seems, had a favorite remedy for these ailments. For example, some treated sore throats by blowing sulfur through a straw against the back of the throat or by rubbing kerosene on the neck. It was thought you could keep germs away by hanging around your neck a bag containing fried onions or asafetida—a foul-smelling gum resin from Oriental plants.

Sin is the common ailment of the human spirit, but fortunately for us all, God loves the people of all races and nationalities alike. His remedy for the disease that destroys our souls is the same for all: fear God, do what is right, and trust in Christ and obey him.

—C. R. B.

37. "You know what has happened throughout Judea, beginning in Galilee after the baptism that John preached.

Cornelius was an officer in the Roman army. He and others like him were in Palestine to keep the peace, to prevent any rebellion against Rome. They were alert to every movement among the Jews. They knew that the crowds had flocked to John the Baptist. Some of them had been in those crowds, listening to see whether John was stirring up insurrection. After John was put in prison, Jesus came to Galilee with his teaching. Crowds then flocked to him. Again the Romans listened but heard no call to rebellion. The Romans knew that Jesus had been crucified; and they knew the teaching of his resurrection had filled Jerusalem and had spread *throughout Judea.* Because they were watching for any sign of rebellious uprising, the Romans were aware of the facts and the teachings of this religious movement; but until this time, both Romans and Jews had thought that movement was strictly a Jewish matter. Now both were beginning to see that it included Romans as well.

38. ". . . how God anointed Jesus of Nazareth with the Holy Spirit and power, and how he went around doing good and healing all who were under the power of the devil, because God was with him.

Cornelius and his friends knew the basic facts of Jesus' ministry; but Peter now gave a brief summary of them, emphasizing God's part in what was done. *God anointed Jesus of Nazareth with the Holy Spirit.* Luke 4:18 records Jesus' own statement of the same fact, as he declared the prophecy of Isaiah fulfilled in himself. In the *power* of the Holy Spirit, Jesus *went around doing good.* Jesus encountered many who were *under the power of the devil.* Whether the oppression was in the form of demons or sickness or crippling deformity, Jesus released those who were oppressed. Why was he able to do such marvelous miracles? *God was with him.*

C. RELIABLE WITNESSES (v. 39)

39. "We are witnesses of everything he did in the country of the Jews and in Jerusalem. They killed him by hanging him on a tree."

Peter and the other apostles were with Jesus during his three-year ministry. They could testify about what he had done all over the Jewish country and in Jerusalem.

Verses 39-43 record that Peter went on to mention other important facts:

1. Jews and Romans crucified Jesus.

2. God raised Jesus from the dead and showed him to the apostles so they could testify positively that he was alive after he died.

3. Jesus told the apostles to testify that God had named Jesus to be the judge of the living and the dead.

4. All the prophets also testify of Jesus, that all who believe in him will have their sins forgiven.

III. A HAPPY ENDING (ACTS 10:44-48)

Peter had been speaking of the work of God. Now God acted again, acted in a way that surprised both Romans and Jews.

A. SURPRISE! (vv. 44-46a)

44. While Peter was still speaking, the Holy Spirit came on all who heard the message.

Peter might have said much more if he had not been interrupted; but he was interrupted, and the interruption certainly was from God.

45. The circumcised believers who had come with Peter were astonished that the gift of the Holy Spirit had been poured out even on the Gentiles.

The circumcised believers were the six Jewish Christians who had come from Joppa with Peter (Acts 10:23; 11:12). The six must have found themselves in a turmoil as Peter's speech went on. No doubt Peter had told them of his vision in Joppa. No doubt he had said the Holy Spirit told him to go with Cornelius's messengers. So they had come along, and they had gone with Peter into a Gentile home, but they may have wondered whether that was the right thing to do. They must have wondered even more as Peter was speaking. Peter said whoever believed in Jesus would be forgiven (Acts 10:43). Was it possible that he was going to tell them to repent and be baptized—those foreigners, even those in the army of the enemy? Then came the Holy Spirit.

46a. For they heard them speaking in tongues and praising God.

This was how the Jewish Christians knew the Holy Spirit had come to the Gentiles. *They heard them speaking in tongues,* as the apostles had done when the Holy Spirit had come to them on the Day of Pentecost (Acts 2:4). Nothing is said here of a sound like wind or a sight like fire such as appeared on Pentecost. Whether these were present or not, the tongues were clear evidence of the Spirit's presence.

B. QUESTION (vv. 46b, 47)

46b, 47. Then Peter said, "Can anyone keep these people from being baptized with water? They have received the Holy Spirit just as we have."

Peter's vision had taught him not to call anything unclean when God had cleansed it (Acts 10:15). The Holy Spirit had told Peter to go with Cornelius's men (Acts 10:19, 20). He had learned that a shining angel had told Cornelius to send

WHAT DO YOU THINK?

A person who attempts in a naive and impractical way to improve the conditions under which other people live is derisively called a "do-gooder." Such an individual is regarded as meddling in other people's business and trying to impose his or her life-style or values on them. How is this different from the example of Jesus, who "went around doing good" (Acts 10:38)? How can we imitate our Savior as we go about our daily activities—being sure we are "doing good," not being a "do-gooder"?

PRAYER

How grateful we are that salvation is not offered to one nation only! What a blessing it is to be included among the saved! We ask for wisdom and strength both to live as saved people ought to live and to share the good news of salvation with others. In Jesus' name. Amen.

OPTION

The reproducible activity, "Personal Evangelism," on page 80 will help your class members from a plan to obey the Great Commission.

THOUGHT TO REMEMBER

"Whoever wishes, let him take the free gift of the water of life" (Revelation 22:17).

DAILY BIBLE READINGS

Monday, Oct. 16—Nations Blessed Through Abraham (Genesis 22:15-19)

Tuesday, Oct. 17—All Families to Worship God (Psalm 22:27-31)

Wednesday, Oct. 18—Israel a Light to the Nations (Isaiah 49:1-7)

Thursday, Oct. 19—All Peoples to Serve God (Daniel 7:13-18)

Friday, Oct. 20—Gentiles, Fellow Heirs (Ephesians 3:1-6)

Saturday, Oct. 21—Gentiles Welcomed (Romans 15:7-21)

Sunday, Oct. 22—All Are Invited (Revelation 22:12-21)

for him. Now the Holy Spirit had come to a group of Gentiles. At last Peter was fully convinced. The Lord wanted those Gentiles to be saved and accepted in his church. Peter saw no way to escape that conclusion, so he put the question to the Jewish Christians who had come from Joppa with him. Could any of them see a reason why these Romans should not be baptized? No objection was made. All of the Christians were convinced along with Peter.

C. BAPTISM (v. 48)

48. So he ordered that they be baptized in the name of Jesus Christ. Then they asked Peter to stay with them for a few days.

So the first Gentiles accepted the Savior and came into the fellowship of the church. *They asked Peter to stay with them* for some days, and no doubt he did stay to teach them more about the way of the Lord.

CONCLUSION

The obvious conclusion is the one Peter reached. God wants both Jews and Gentiles in his church. Jesus meant what he said when he told his disciples to make disciples of *all nations* (Matthew 28:19, 20).

This now is so well known that we can hardly realize what a difficult conclusion it was for the Jews. It was hard for Peter, and he had some explaining to do when he went back to Jerusalem. When he explained, however, all the Jewish Christians came to the same conclusion, and they were gracious enough to praise God because Gentiles also could be saved (Acts 11:1-18).

Some other conclusions have been drawn from this text, and not all of them are as plain and inescapable as that one.

A. PURPOSE OF THE TONGUES

Since Cornelius and his friends were the first Gentiles to become Christians, some students have concluded that Jews and Gentiles become Christians in different ways. Jews are called to repent and be baptized, they say (Acts 2:38), but Gentiles must wait for the gift of tongues or some other startling experience to show that the Holy Spirit has come to call them.

We do not find that conclusion verified as we read on through the book of Acts. We read that people became Christians in many places, but we do not read that Jews and Gentiles did it in different ways. All of them believed in Jesus; all of them turned away from wrongdoing to follow him; all of them were baptized.

Why was the gift of tongues given to Cornelius and his friends? It was not to convince them that Jesus is the Christ, the Savior, the Lord. That was done by the message Peter brought. The gift of tongues was given to do what it did do: it convinced Peter and the other Jews that God wanted to save Gentiles and accept them in his church.

B. PURPOSE OF THE RECORD

Some students are puzzled because Peter did not tell the Gentiles to repent and they did not say they believed in Christ. This reminds us again that Luke wrote this story briefly, not taking time to record all the details of each event. Surely Peter did not have these people baptized without some assurance that they believed in Jesus and wanted to follow him. We do not need to know exactly how that assurance was given.

The tenth chapter of Acts was not written to teach us how one becomes a Christian. It was written to record how the Jews learned that God wants Gentiles in his church—and it does that very well.

Discovery Learning

This page contains an alternate lesson plan emphasizing learning activities. Classes desiring such student involvement will find these suggestions helpful. The next page is a reproducible activity page to further enhance discovery learning.

LEARNING GOALS

As a result of participating in today's class session, the students should:

1. Explain how God removed the obstacles that had prevented the spread of the gospel to Gentiles.

2. List some barriers that hinder the spread of the gospel today.

3. Suggest a way to remove at least one barrier to personal evangelism.

INTO THE LESSON

Send one person out of the room. Tell the person privately that he or she will attempt to unite a divided class.

Have the men go to one side of the room; women to the other. Further separate the groups by having men 5'10" tall and under go to one corner and taller men go to the other corner. Similarly. women of 5'4" tall and under go to one corner and those over 5'4" to the other corner.

Ask the class to imagine they are part of a society that believes these groups should never mingle, let alone worship with one another. No mere human can promote interaction among them.

Now ask the person who left earlier to enter and try to get the groups united. Allow this to go one for just a few minutes. Then call time and ask the groups what it would take for them to be convinced that God wanted them to worship and praise him as a united people. Would a dream and a messenger convince them? Tell them that in today's lesson Peter is convinced that God wants Gentiles and Jews alike to worship and praise him.

INTO THE WORD

Read the inscription that is carved in stone in the wall separating the sacred inner court of the temple from the outer court. (See page 73.) Discuss how this would affect the relationship between Gentiles and Jews. Continue by giving other background from the "Introduction."

After this discussion, have a volunteer read the lesson Scripture, Acts 10:30-48. Then form groups of four to six members. Give each group one of the following sets of instructions. (You may photocopy page 80 to assist in this.)

ODD-NUMBERED GROUPS:

Use Acts 10:1-48 to answer the following questions:

1. Where was Peter when he had the vision? (On the roof at the home of Simon the Tanner, in Joppa.)

2. What was his first reaction to the message in the vision? (Horror. He refused to eat on religious grounds.)

3. What convinced him the message was legitimate? (The Holy Spirit's message that he should go with the messengers, Cornelius's account of his own vision.)

4. How might he have reacted? (He could have hardened himself to the message and refused it.)

5. What barriers did Peter break down? (By inviting the messengers into the house and by going to the home of Cornelius, Peter violated traditions that had separated Jews and Gentiles for centuries. The racial barrier was collapsing. By taking six others with him, he was breaking down the barrier of peer pressure. [These would support his story when his actions were challenged by Jewish Christians in Jerusalem, Acts 11:1-18.])

EVEN-NUMBERED GROUPS:

Use Acts 10:1-48 to answer the following questions:

1. Where was Cornelius when the angel appeared? (In his house in Caesarea.)

2. What was his first reaction to the angel? (Fear.)

3. Why was Cornelius singled out? (God was responding to Cornelius's prayers and generosity.)

4. What was his reaction to the order? (Immediate obedience.)

5. What barriers did Cornelius break down? (Cornelius ignored the racial barrier that normally separated Jews and Gentiles. He also did not let his position and status keep him from seeking guidance from a Galilean fisherman. Barriers of wealth and status were no obstacle for him.)

After about fifteen minutes, select various people to share answers from their groups.

INTO LIFE

In this century we have erected different kinds of barriers from the ones experienced by the Gentiles and Jews. In the same groups that answered the questions, have members list five barriers that prevent, or at least hinder, the spread of the gospel today. Then have them brainstorm ways to break down those barriers. Encourage them to consider situations within their own community and how they might personally make a difference. Share ideas with the whole class. End with prayer that each one might remove a personal barrier to communicate with one other person to bring that person to salvation.

Breaking Down the Barriers

Read Acts 10:1-48. Then answer one or both sets of questions below.

PETER:

1. Where was Peter when he had the vision?

2. What was his first reaction to the message in the vision?

3. What convinced him the message was legitimate?

4. How might he have reacted?

5. What barriers did Peter break down?

CORNELIUS

1. Where was Cornelius when the angel appeared?

2. What was his first reaction to the angel?

3. Why was Cornelius singled out?

4. What was his reaction to the order?

5. What barriers did Cornelius break down?

Personal Evangelism

Many books have been written to instruct Christians how to share their faith. Most of them suggest that making friends and deepening those relationships is the most effective method for bringing others to Christ. Think about a friendship you have that might lead to that person's salvation. God may not come to you in a vision, but he has paved the way for you to share your faith.

Write the name of one person you know who is not a Christian. _____

What could you do to encourage a deeper friendship with that person? _____

What kinds of activities do both of you enjoy? _____

Is that person experiencing any difficulty in his or her life right now? _____

How soon can you make contact with that person? _____

What will you say or do to deepen the relationship? _____

THE CHURCH AT ANTIOCH

LESSON 9

WHY TEACH THIS LESSON?

In an earlier lesson we met Barnabas, the "Son of Encouragement" (Acts 4:36) of the early church. Later we saw his encouraging spirit in action, as he convinced the believers in Jerusalem that Saul's conversion was genuine (Acts 9:26, 27). Today we see him in action again, encouraging the church at Antioch and enlisting Saul in service—service that would eventually eclipse his own ministry.

This lesson provides an excellent model for Christians in your class and everywhere to follow. Hold up the example of Barnabas as a challenge to put service ahead of recognition, and the needs of the church ahead of personal needs.

INTRODUCTION

Problems come with growth. A baby soon outgrows the rattle and other toys of infancy, and has to have more costly things. A boy outgrows his jeans at an alarming rate, and needs new ones. Parents have to make sure he does not outgrow his habit of willing obedience along with his jeans.

Parents must also make sure the child grows into new things as well as out of old ones: new tasks, new responsibilities, new strength of character. A growing child learns to pick up his clothes and keep his room neat, to wash dishes or rake leaves, to be kind to little sister, and to put homework before television.

A. PROBLEMS OF A GROWING CHURCH

The church in Jerusalem was growing, not by ones and twos, but by thousands (Acts 2:41, 47; 4:4; 6:7). Problems came with growth. Some members were penniless; but the others took care of them, even selling houses and lands for that purpose (Acts 4:32-37). Persecution soon arose; but the disciples clung nobly to their faith, even when they were jailed and beaten (Acts 5:17-42). They were driven from their homes, but they took the gospel with them and started churches all over Judea and Samaria (Acts 8:1, 4). Two weeks ago we saw that they went beyond these areas to Damascus (Acts 9:1, 2), and probably the Ethiopian of lesson 6 carried the good news beyond Egypt to the upper valley of the Nile.

All these actions seem to have come as naturally as a child's growth in stature, but the Father in Heaven had to use some extraordinary methods to persuade the growing church to accept the responsibility of taking the gospel to the Gentiles as well as to the Jews (Acts 10). That, too, was done, and the way was opened for bearers of the good news to go to the ends of the earth.

B. LESSON BACKGROUND

In previous lessons we have seen three great forward movements for the strength of the church and the glory of God:

1. The church in Jerusalem grew in spite of persecution, and spread swiftly to places farther and farther away.

2. One of the church's most furious persecutors became one of its most fervent preachers. Then Saul was persecuted! Fleeing Damascus to save his life, he went to Jerusalem; fleeing from there, he went to his native land, to Tarsus (Acts 9:1-30).

DEVOTIONAL READING
ACTS 12:1-11

LESSON SCRIPTURE
ACTS 11:19-30; 12:24, 25

PRINTED TEXT
ACTS 11:19-30; 12:24, 25

LESSON AIMS

After this lesson students should be able to:

1. Explain how the churches in Jerusalem and Antioch helped and supported one another.

2. Suggest some ways in which Christians and churches sometimes need support today.

3. Develop a plan to increase personal help and support to a church or missionary.

Oct
29

NOTE

Discuss the "Problems of a Growing Church" with a "What Do You Think?" discussion starter on the next page.

KEY VERSE

He was glad and encouraged them all to remain true to the Lord with all their hearts.
—Acts 11:23

LESSON 9 NOTES

WHAT DO YOU THINK?

As in first-century Jerusalem, today's growing churches encounter a variety of problems. Consider some of the problems of growing churches and suggest some solutions:

- *The need for physical facilities*
- *Integrating new members into the fellowship and service of the church*
- *Overtaxing the church's leaders*
- *What are some other problems? Suggest some solutions.*

WHAT DO YOU THINK?

The experience of the early church demonstrates that persecution can actually contribute to the growth of the church. Persecution puts Christians face to face with the elements of risk and sacrifice, and brings into sharp focus the difference between the things that are temporal and what is eternal. Although we often shrink from difficult challenges, we may actually be drawn to them. To face the risk of being persecuted because of our faith can strengthen our determination to be faithful disciples and stir up our zeal to witness and win others to Christ. Also, it can heighten our awareness of our fellowship with Christ and the reality of our hope of eternal life in him (Philippians 3:10).

Do you think your church would grow or diminish in the face of persecution like that under Saul before his conversion? Why? What could you do to be sure you could endure?

3. By special revelations from God, Peter was convinced that the Lord wanted his gospel taken to Gentiles as well as Jews (Acts 10). The church accepted that conviction and assumed the new responsibility (Acts 11:1-18).

During the study of this week's lesson we see these three movements coming together. The church continued to spread farther and farther from Jerusalem. More and more Gentiles accepted the gospel and came into the fellowship of the church. Saul left Tarsus and came into the mainstream of the story.

I. THE GOSPEL IN ANTIOCH (ACTS 11:19-21)

Luke's record moves swiftly over great events, seldom pausing to note the passing of time. Uncertainly we estimate that this lesson begins about eight years after that great Day of Pentecost when three thousand people accepted the call of Christ (Acts 2:41). Events recorded in the few verses of our text then took perhaps about six more years.

A. PREACHING TO JEWS (v. 19)

19. Now those who had been scattered by the persecution in connection with Stephen traveled as far as Phoenicia, Cyprus and Antioch, telling the message only to Jews.

Stephen was the first of Jesus' disciples to be killed for his faith (Acts 6:8—7:60). His death was followed by the furious persecution that drove most of the Christians out of Jerusalem (Acts 8:1). Now we see them moving northward. *Phoenicia* was an area on the east coast of the Mediterranean and north of the Jews' country. *Cyprus* was the big island that still wears that name. *Antioch* was an important city near the coast and farther north than Phoenicia. It was about three hundred miles from Jerusalem. Disciples of Jesus did not reach all of these places at the same time, of course. Probably the progress recorded in this verse took several years, and during those years Peter took the gospel to Cornelius and other Gentiles in Caesarea, as we saw in last week's lesson. Following the custom established when they were first driven from Jerusalem, these scattered disciples "preached the word wherever they went" (Acts 8:4). But they preached it only to Jews.

B. PREACHING TO GENTILES (v. 20)

20. Some of them, however, men from Cyprus and Cyrene, went to Antioch and began to speak to Greeks also, telling them the good news about the Lord Jesus.

Cyrene was located on the south side of the Mediterranean, west of the land of Egypt. Jews from there had been among the many thousands in Jerusalem on the Day of Pentecost. After becoming followers of Jesus, they had stayed in Jerusalem to be taught by the apostles. Now they, along with fellow believers who hailed from Cyprus, were fleeing from the terrible persecution in Jerusalem.

These Jews *from Cyprus and Cyrene* had lived among Gentiles, perhaps all their lives. They had done business with Gentiles, been friends with Gentiles. They were not so keenly aware of Jewish separation as the Jews of Palestine were. In *Antioch* some of them came in contact with Gentiles and gave the message of Christ to them as they did to Jews. Probably Peter already had preached to the Gentiles in Caesarea, but we do not know whether the preachers in Antioch knew that or not.

C. SUCCESS (v. 21)

21. The Lord's hand was with them, and a great number of people believed and turned to the Lord.

We are not told just how *the Lord's hand* worked to help these preachers. Perhaps the Lord guided their speech by the Holy Spirit. Perhaps he gave them good weather for outdoor preaching. Perhaps he worked in ways unknown to us to prevent interruptions and heckling. These men were doing what the Lord wanted them to do. He helped them in ways not described, *and a great number of people believed and turned to the Lord.*

BREAKING THE BONDS OF CULTURE

When Irving Berlin died in 1989 at the age of 101, he had long been recognized as one of the great American songwriters. His songs have been sung by generations of Americans.

One of his most popular songs was written simply as a tune for the 1942 movie, *Holiday Inn.* The song was "White Christmas," and it has become an all-time favorite. And who can forget "God Bless America," as sung by Kate Smith in the dark days of World War II?

Berlin was a Russian Jewish immigrant. His music, however, was American in essence, reflecting as it did the way Americans felt. He broke the bonds of culture to become an artist whose craft has blessed Americans of many and varied backgrounds.

When the gospel first spread out into the Mediterranean world, it was a message preached by Jews to other Jews. But some of those who carried the message realized it could—and should—bless everyone, not just Jews but Gentiles as well. Thus, Jewish Christians from Cypress and Cyrene came to Antioch proclaiming salvation to anyone who would listen. The blessing of God on their work is a reminder to the church in every age that the gospel must never be bound by any human limitation.

—C. R. B.

II. HELP FROM JERUSALEM (ACTS 11:22-26)

If there were some strict Jews from Jerusalem among the disciples in Antioch, they may have been disturbed when they saw many Gentiles becoming disciples. They may have hurried a messenger to Jerusalem to see what the mother church would say about this development. Whether in this way or some other, news of the church in Antioch soon reached Jerusalem.

A. BARNABAS (vv. 22-24)

22. News of this reached the ears of the church at Jerusalem, and they sent Barnabas to Antioch.

By this time the followers of Jesus in *Jerusalem* knew about Peter's preaching to the Gentiles, and they were convinced that evangelizing the Gentiles was right (Acts 11:1-18). They sent one of their members to *Antioch*, not to criticize, but to help. *Barnabas* was a man who could do that. He himself was from Cyprus (Acts 4:36), so he was probably accustomed to living among Gentiles and dealing with them. He would find joy in the salvation of Gentiles, and rejoice in the building of a great church in Antioch. On the other hand, he was thoroughly trained in the Way of the Lord. If anything was out of order in the church at Antioch, he would see it. He would move to correct it, but he would move gently and with reason, not with angry accusation.

23. When he arrived and saw the evidence of the grace of God, he was glad and encouraged them all to remain true to the Lord with all their hearts.

Large numbers of people, many of them Gentiles, were turning to the Lord, taking their place among the saints. Very plainly Barnabas could see that *the grace of God* was working in Antioch, and *he was glad.* Happily he *encouraged them all.* Most of Antioch was pagan, and there were many temptations to worldly wickedness. Barnabas urged the new disciples to give wholehearted loyalty to their new Master, Jesus.

HOW TO SAY IT

Agabus. AG-uh-bus.
Antioch. AN-tee-ock.
Barnabas. BAR-nuh-bus.
Caesarea. Sess-uh-REE-uh.
Cyprus. SYE-prus.
Cyrene. Sye-REE-nee.
Phoenicia. Fi-NISH-uh.

24. He was a good man, full of the Holy Spirit and faith, and a great number of people were brought to the Lord.

The record shows that Barnabas was notably unselfish and *good* at helping and encouraging others. He sold his property to provide for the poor (Acts 4:36, 37). He stood by Saul when the other disciples were afraid of him (Acts 9:26-28). He insisted on giving John Mark a second chance (Acts 15:36-40). With good reason the apostles named him Barnabas (his real name was Joseph). The nickname means encourager (Acts 4:36). In our text we see him encouraging brethren to be faithful to Christ. Apparently he also encouraged others to come to Christ, *a great number of people were brought to the Lord*. Barnabas was *full of the Holy Spirit;* he put his selfish wishes aside and followed the leading of the Spirit. He was full of *faith:* he believed in Christ, trusted him, and was faithful to him.

B. SAUL (vv. 25, 26a)

25. Then Barnabas went to Tarsus to look for Saul.

Here is one more example of help and encouragement given by Barnabas. The growing church at Antioch needed workers as capable and vigorous as Saul, and Saul needed just such a place to work. Barnabas planned to help both the church and Saul by bringing them together.

26a. And when he found him, he brought him to Antioch.

It seems that Saul was easily persuaded to go with Barnabas to Antioch. Perhaps he felt indebted to Barnabas because Barnabas had helped him in Jerusalem (Acts 9:26-28); probably he was eager to share his faith in Jesus, and Antioch was a fine place to do so.

C. PROGRESS (v. 26b)

26b. So for a whole year Barnabas and Saul met with the church and taught great numbers of people. The disciples were called Christians first at Antioch.

For a whole year these two worked together in Antioch, *and taught great numbers of people.* Antioch was a big city and many people needed to hear of Jesus. And all who became followers of the Master needed to be taught how to follow him better. It was a busy year.

The disciples were called Christians first at Antioch. There is nothing in our English text to tell who first gave the disciples their new name, and scholars have various ideas. Some think the followers of Jesus gave themselves that name, as followers of Luther call themselves Lutherans. Some think the pagan people of Antioch first used the name, perhaps in derision. Some think the Lord himself first gave the name *Christians.* These note that the Greek word used here for *called* is used often in the New Testament to speak of calls or revelations or warnings from God (Matthew 2:12, 22; Luke 2:26; Acts 10:22; Hebrews 8:5; 11:7; 12:25). Whoever used the name first, the Christians themselves accepted it as an honorable name (1 Peter 4:16).

WHAT'S IN A NAME?

Pulitzer Prize winner Jack Smith, who was a daily columnist for the *Los Angeles Times* for years, was fascinated by unusual names. One column in 1989 told of an obituary in a New Orleans newspaper that noted the passing of Zenda Gloyce Smith, who left sisters Brenda Loyce, Glenda Joyce, Lenda Royce, Renda Floyce, Flenda Boyce, Quanda Doyce, and Benda Noyce.

Some people have names given by parents in a fit of misguided creativity. Others choose an unusual name for themselves to attract attention. The name given to those who accepted Jesus as Savior was certain to attract attention. *Christian*—one who belongs to Christ—says that one has identified oneself with him who fulfilled God's

WHAT DO YOU THINK?

Of the several suggestions for the origin of the name Christian, *which do you think is most likely? Why?*

Whatever the origin of the name Christian, *it is an appropriate name for the followers of Christ to wear. The name identifies us with Jesus Christ and reminds us that we belong to him (Galatians 3:29; 5:24). It serves as a worthy focus for our witness to others. As Christians we represent Jesus Christ, and we are concerned about leading other people to believe in him and to follow him.*

What are some of the privileges of being called a "Christian"? What responsibilities come with wearing that name?

messianic promise to the Jews. All who follow Christ should be proud to wear that name—and that name alone—as an indication of where their spiritual allegiance lies.

—C. R. B.

III. HELP TO JERUSALEM (ACTS 11:27-30; 12:24, 25)

Men of Cyprus and Cyrene brought to Antioch the good news of salvation (Acts 11:20), but those men had learned the good news in Jerusalem and carried it from there to Antioch. So the Christians in Antioch were deeply indebted to those in Jerusalem, and the time came for them to make a payment on their debt.

A. FORECAST AND FAMINE (vv. 27, 28)

27. During this time some prophets came down from Jerusalem to Antioch.

Prophets are people whom the Lord chooses to receive messages directly from him and deliver them to people on earth. Perhaps these men came *from Jerusalem to Antioch* to add to the help that Barnabas and Saul were giving. In the days before the New Testament was written, Christians needed such inspired prophets to teach them the proper way for Christians to live. The church in Antioch was growing so rapidly that it needed more teachers to give God's word to the new members. So the prophets brought help from Jerusalem, but another result of their coming was that help would be sent back to Jerusalem.

28. One of them, named Agabus, stood up and through the Spirit predicted that a severe famine would spread over the entire Roman world. (This happened during the reign of Claudius.)

Agabus spoke *through the Spirit;* that is, he said what the Holy Spirit told him to say. Human beings often guess about the future, but the Spirit knows. The prediction was from Heaven, not from Agabus; and it soon proved to be true. Luke, writing some years after this prediction, was able to inform the reader when the prophesied *famine* had occurred. Since it affected *the entire Roman world,* it was fitting to date it by the Roman emperor who was in power at the time. *Claudius* Caesar was emperor from A.D. 41 to A.D. 54.

B. HELP SENT (vv. 29, 30)

29. The disciples, each according to his ability, decided to provide help for the brothers living in Judea.

The famine was everywhere (v. 28). Food was scarce and expensive. However, the Christians *in Judea* suffered more than others because they had used their savings, and even sold their real estate, to provide a living for all of them while they were listening daily to the apostles' teaching (Acts 2:43-47). The rich among them had been reduced to poverty by caring for the poor. Now they were all poor, and the brethren in Antioch wanted to care for them. Those in Antioch had profited spiritually by receiving the gospel from Judea and being saved from sin and death; now those in Judea would profit materially by receiving funds from Antioch and being saved from starvation. Later Paul would write that such repayment was both a debt and a pleasure (Romans 15:26, 27).

The church did not require a certain amount from each member, but each gave *according to his ability;* each one gave as much as he thought he could afford.

30. This they did, sending their gift to the elders by Barnabas and Saul.

These chosen messengers had lived in Jerusalem and had worked with the Christians there. They were trusted both by the givers in Antioch and by the receivers in Jerusalem. Still these two did not attempt to distribute the offering among the Christians in Judea. They took the money *to the elders.* There were congregations in many towns of Judea, and probably by this time each congregation had a

---

OPTION

The reproducible page (88) contains a word-search puzzle that may provide an enjoyable way to review today's lesson.

WHAT DO YOU THINK?

Among the disciples at Antioch each person gave "according to his ability" for the purpose of aiding the Judean Christians. (See also 1 Corinthians 16:1, 2.) How can one honestly determine what is his or her "ability" to give? Why is it that some Christians with lesser incomes actually give more (often in actual amount, not just in percentage) than some wealthier members?

How many Christians today do you suppose actually give according to their "ability" and not according to their "convenience"? How can Christians be encouraged to practice better stewardship?

DAILY BIBLE READINGS

Monday, Oct. 23—Christian Living (Romans 12:1-13)

Tuesday, Oct. 24—One Body With Many Gifts (1 Corinthians 12:12-20, 27-31)

Wednesday, Oct. 25—Prayer for a Church (Ephesians 1:15-23)

Thursday, Oct. 26—The Church as a Unit (Ephesians 4: 1-16)

Friday, Oct. 27—Paul's Care of the Churches (2 Corinthians 12:14-21)

Saturday, Oct. 28—Guidelines for Christian Conduct (Titus 3:1-11)

Sunday, Oct. 29—Guidelines for Church Leaders (1 Timothy 3:1-7)

little group of wise and godly elders to oversee its work. In the earlier days of the church, the apostles had distributed food or money among the needy. Then a committee had been chosen for that important work (Acts 4:34, 35; 6:1-6). Now that the disciples were scattered to many towns in Judea, the elders took up the work of distribution. No doubt they already were distributing such funds as were available in Judea; now the increase in funds would be a blessing to many brethren.

C. BACK TO ANTIOCH (12:24, 25)

24. But the word of God continued to increase and spread.

The first part of chapter 12 tells how Herod began to persecute the Christians in Palestine. This was Herod Agrippa I, grandson of the Herod who was ruling when Jesus was born. He killed the apostle James, and put Peter in prison. But an angel set Peter free, and not long after, Herod died a miserable death. The disciples of Jesus were still preaching the word of God, and that word kept on growing in power and influence. More and more people became Christians.

25. When Barnabas and Saul had finished their mission, they returned from Jerusalem, taking with them John, also called Mark.

Barnabas and Saul, having delivered the funds from Antioch to the elders in Judea, went back to Antioch to continue their work there. *John, also called Mark,* went with them. This young man was a relative of Barnabas (Colossians 4:10), though Barnabas came from Cyprus (Acts 4:36, 37) and John Mark probably lived in Jerusalem with his mother (Acts 12:12). So three good Christian workers went to Antioch, the Christian frontier. This set the stage for our next lesson.

CONCLUSION

We have been considering the progress of the early church. It was then directed by apostles of Jesus, and it was tremendously successful. For both these reasons, its activities may well be a pattern for those of the church today. Let's look briefly at three kinds of activity.

A. GROWING

Swiftly the church grew till it numbered many thousands in Jerusalem. When those thousands were driven out of town, they took the gospel with them, and growth was increased rather than stopped.

How did they do it? They "preached the word wherever they went" (Acts 8:4). If the church is not growing so rapidly today, is it because we are not so vigorous and enthusiastic in spreading the message?

B. TEACHING

The first Christians continued in the apostles' teaching, among other things (Acts 2:42). New Christians in Caesarea asked Peter to stay awhile, and no doubt he stayed and taught them (Acts 10:48). Barnabas and Saul spent a year in Antioch, and "taught great numbers of people" (Acts 11:26). Teaching is vital in any growing church. Members must learn how to serve Jesus, and how to take his invitation to others.

C. CARING

The Christians in Jerusalem took care of one another, so none among them were without food and clothing and shelter (Acts 4:34, 35). Sharing "everything they had" (v. 32) was not continued in all churches, but generous giving was and is. Christians in Antioch shared with those in Judea, and Christians today share with needy brethren near and far.

Discovery Learning

This page contains an alternate lesson plan emphasizing learning activities. Classes desiring such student involvement will find these suggestions helpful. The next page is a reproducible activity page to further enhance discovery learning.

LEARNING GOALS

As a result of participating in today's class session, a student should:

1. Explain how the churches in Jerusalem and Antioch helped and supported one another.

2. Suggest some ways in which Christians and churches sometimes need support today.

3. Develop a plan to increase personal help and support to a church or missionary.

INTO THE LESSON

On a chalkboard or a poster at the front of the classroom, write the following statement:

"The only duty of missionaries is to preach the good news of salvation through Jesus Christ."

Post a plus sign (+) on the wall to the students' right and a minus sign (-) on the wall to the left. When everyone arrives, tell the class that the plus sign symbolizes strong agreement with the statement and the minus sign strong disagreement. Ask the class members to consider where their opinions fall between strong agreement and strong disagreement, and then to line up at the appropriate spot.

Ask someone on the extreme end of the plus side to explain why he or she believes that way. Do the same for the minus side. Take another three to five minutes for a general discussion of the issue. The class should come to a consensus that preaching the gospel is the *main* duty of missionaries, but not the *only* duty. Teaching, medical help, and famine relief are just a few of the additional activities that might be mentioned.

Note that today's lesson will reveal how the early church balanced preaching the gospel with ministering to physical needs.

INTO THE WORD

Have a good reader read aloud the Scripture for the day, Acts 11:19-30; 12:24, 25.

Explain that this seems to have been a time of relative quiet for the church. No unsettling problems are observed in these verses. The size of the church increased and spread.

In small groups, have class members discuss the following questions:

• Who were the prominent leaders of the church at this time? (The apostles, Barnabas, elders [see 11:30]; Saul was becoming a prominent leader.)

[James the brother of Jesus was also prominent, or was becoming prominent; see his role in the Jerusalem Conference of Acts 15.]

• What are some major events that took place in this time frame? (The church at Antioch was founded. The name *Christian* began to be used. A famine was predicted. James the brother of John was martyred. Peter was imprisoned and miraculously released. Herod died.)

• Why might the disciples have been given the name Christian at this time and in this place? (See comments on verse 26 in the commentary section.)

Next, have each group use the text to formulate a question they might have about the people or the events recorded, or about some principle gleaned from this passage. Each group then chooses a messenger to take their question along with answers to the other questions to another group. That person will share his/her group's answers with the next group and ask the new question. If there is time or if the class is large enough, the messengers could continue to several more groups, taking the questions and answers. If every group doesn't have a chance to hear all of the additional questions, discuss them with the whole class for a few minutes.

INTO LIFE

Summarize the ideas under the "Conclusion" section, page 86 (growing, teaching, sharing). Ask the class how Christians today send support to other Christians and churches. List ways that support may be given.

If your class already gives significant support to another church or missionary, discuss how your commitment might be strengthened as a class and as individuals. If you do not have an outside commitment, discuss what you might do to fulfill the phrase "They will know we are Christians by our love."

OPTION

Provide a list of the missions currently supported by your church. Discuss ways your class can encourage the people or organizations your church supports. You might begin writing letters, or send special packages for birthdays, Christmas, and anniversaries. You might increase your financial support. You can certainly pray.

Find the Word

Twenty-five words from Acts 11:19-30 are hidden in the puzzle below. Read the text; then see how many of the words you can find. (The words are listed at the bottom of the page in case you need a little help.)

```
W B S F G I P J T C M G R X R D Z B S G S S
C J U A P R O P H E T S N J K X S T V C U Q
K E R T U G L B C X T T U I E F E X A B K J
G U P U Z L F L G B T D I D Z P V T A F N Y
R T Y V X E A M C Q E E Y O H A T G K G P T
S I C R U B C G A L E V E F E A G M O Z G
W E G C D I E Y F T X C N C R U K K T O R O
Z I L I U Q C R X I H A S E T E C J V D V Z
H P U P K M M E B C L R D C N U F M E N S Y
H S Q F I C P N V P Q G J C W U F M E E S Y
L Q I S Z C Z E O R E L O V Q V D E N W A B
P I K T P X S K Z L J U R D T K T S U S B E
K K S E Z T Y I D X R A J C R C E S Q I A L
F S W E J U C E D A H C O I T N A A G A N I
A W U V N E R V G W C W V Z N F Y G H U R E
M G U S R S F E A I C I N E O H P E R P A V
I S Z S R G D Z P N O I T U C E S R E P B E
N V O G U A M Z E P C H R I S T I A N S P D
E M H N G V T A I C M E L A S U R E J M E T
```

Choose any five of the words you have found and write a brief description or identification of each.

1.

2.

3.

4.

5.

The Story of Christian Beginnings

Unit 3. Spreading the Gospel Into All the World

(Lessons 10-13)

MISSION TO GENTILES

LESSON 10

WHY TEACH THIS LESSON?

Missions is a much talked about but little acted on subject in many churches. It seems most everyone believes in the importance of missions, but few want to participate, either in the going or in the supporting.

Today's lesson reports what might be called the birth of missionary work, as Barnabas and Saul launch their first missionary journey. We read of a church that committed the missionaries to the grace of God. We read of both hardships and victories on the field. And we read of a church eager to hear the results of the trip. If we continued reading, we would soon be reading of another missionary journey.

Who draws the bigger crowd at your church, the gospel singer/entertainer or the visiting missionary? To what field are more young people challenged to enter, business or missions? When all is said and done on the topic of missions, has there been too much said and too little done?

Use this lesson to challenge the priorities of your students so that missions is seen as the exciting participation in the grace of God that it is!

INTRODUCTION

Missionary work has long been recognized as an important part of our Christian service. Many of us feel guilty because the money spent in spreading the gospel abroad is only a small fraction of the budget of the local congregation. On the other hand, some Christians would stop missionary work altogether. "All the money we can raise is needed right here at home," they say.

The New Testament does not record that objection by early Christians. Still, something extraordinary was needed to propel them to take the gospel of Jesus Christ into new fields.

A. RELUCTANT OUTREACH

In Jerusalem the first Christians were on fire with the gospel, and the church grew amazingly (Acts 2:41; 4:4; 5:14; 6:1). Yet we do not read that they carried the gospel beyond Jerusalem till persecution came. That misfortune did not lessen their enthusiasm. They took the gospel with them and formed churches all over Judea and Samaria. Philip's great work in Samaria is an example (8:1, 4-8).

Enthusiastic as they were, the scattered disciples offered the gospel only to Jews. It took special acts of God to convince the apostle Peter that salvation was for Gentiles too. With the help of those acts of God Peter then convinced the other Christians, and they rejoiced to know that God wanted to save all of mankind (Acts 10:1—11:18).

B. LESSON BACKGROUND

It seems that the church at Antioch was the first big congregation among the Gentiles. It was started by Christians scattered from Jerusalem, and helped greatly by others sent from that city. Grateful for such help, the Christians in Antioch were generous in sending help of another kind to their brethren in Judea (Acts 11:19-30). But still a special order from the Holy Spirit was needed to involve the

DEVOTIONAL READING

Acts 13:13-26

LESSON SCRIPTURE

Acts 13, 14

PRINTED TEXT

Acts 13:1-5; 14:1-7, 24-27

LESSON AIMS

After this lesson students should be able to:

1. Summarize the events, obstacles, and results of Paul and Barnabas's first missionary journey.

2. Compare the challenges faced by modern missionaries to those faced by Paul and Barnabas.

3. Support missionaries with prayers, money and visits.

Nov
5

KEY VERSE

They gathered the church together and reported all that God had done through them and how he had opened the door of faith to the Gentiles.

—Acts 14:27

LESSON 10 NOTES

church at Antioch in a great missionary work. That is what we shall see in this week's lesson.

I. SENDING MISSIONARIES (ACTS 13:1-5)

Barnabas and Saul were the men sent by the Antioch church to carry its offering to the famine-stricken Christians in Judea. When that service was completed they went back to Antioch, taking with them John Mark, a young kinsman of Barnabas (Acts 12:25; Colossians 4:10).

A. ABUNDANCE IN ANTIOCH (v. 1)

1. In the church at Antioch there were prophets and teachers: Barnabas, Simeon called Niger, Lucius of Cyrene, Manaen (who had been brought up with Herod the tetrarch) and Saul.

Prophets were people to whom God revealed special messages to be delivered to others. They were teachers, of course; but there were other *teachers* who had no special revelations, but taught what they had learned from prophets and from Scripture.

Antioch had capable teachers in abundance. Five of them are named in this verse. *Saul* is named last in this distinguished list, but soon we shall see him becoming the leading character of the remainder of the book of Acts.

B. CALL TO SHARE (v. 2)

2. While they were worshiping the Lord and fasting, the Holy Spirit said, "Set apart for me Barnabas and Saul for the work to which I have called them."

It is not clear whether *they* means the five prophets and teachers named in verse 1 or the whole church in Antioch, which also is mentioned in verse 1. We should probably picture a group, either five prophets and teachers or the whole congregation, engaged in worship. *The Holy Spirit said, Set apart for me Barnabas and Saul for the work to which I have called them.* Perhaps the Spirit also told what that work was. Luke does not record that here, but leaves us to discover it as we read on in the record. The Spirit was calling on the church to give up two of its five fine teachers so they could work in fields where now there were no Christian teachers at all.

C. RESPONSE (v. 3)

3. So after they had fasted and prayed, they placed their hands on them and sent them off.

With fasting and earnest prayer, the two men were set apart, dedicated to the work the Spirit had called them to do. Probably the hands laid on them indicated the approval and blessing of the church. *Sent them off* is more accurately translated "let them go." The Holy Spirit was sending these men (v. 4), but the church was releasing them with its blessing.

SET APART AND SENT OUT

"Greetings!" the letter began. Many citizens received from the draft board a letter with that ominous salutation. The recipient of the letter was being drafted into military service.

Imagine the surprise of Nathan Matt several years ago when he received a letter from Uncle Sam saying, "Greetings! A match of computer files has indicated that you may be required to register with the Selective Service." Mr. Matt was not unwilling to serve his country, but he was seventy-eight years old! The "invitation" to register was later rescinded with the explanation that there had been a computer error.

HOW TO SAY IT

Antipas. AN-tuh-pas.
Attalia. At-uh-LYE-uh.
Cyrene. Cy-REE-ne.
Derbe. DER-be.
Iconium. Eye-KO-nee-um.
Lucius. LEW-shus.
Lycaonia. LIK-uh-O-ni-uh.
Lystra. LISS-truh.
Manaen. MAN-uh-un.
Niger. NYE-jer.
Pamphylia. Pam-FILL-e-uh.
Perga. PER-guh.
Pisidia. Pih-SIS-ee-uh.
Salamis. SAL-uh-miss.
Seleucia. See-LEW-shuh.
Sergius Paulus. SIR-ji-us PAHL-us.

WHAT DO YOU THINK?

The church at Antioch gave up two of its finest teachers to send them into the mission field. Today, churches are often almost jealous to keep their best teachers. They prefer to send good "prospective" teachers and leaders to help start a new congregation in the area, or to be trained for specialized Christian work, or to serve on a mission field.

How can a church develop a greater eagerness to send its best into new fields? Do you think such a practice would be harmful or helpful to the sending church? Why?

In response to the guidance of the Holy Spirit, the church at Antioch "drafted" Barnabas and Saul from their midst for special service for Christ. The church set them apart and sent them out as evangelists to distant places.

When mobilizing for a great campaign—whether military or evangelistic—the leaders must recognize and evaluate the need, find the personnel to meet the need, and then give them complete support. The world still needs the gospel. Is the church still willing to make the commitment of personnel and resources?   —C. R. B.

D. *Starting the Journey (vv. 4, 5)*

4. The two of them, sent on their way by the Holy Spirit, went down to Seleucia and sailed from there to Cyprus.

Antioch was about fifteen miles from the Mediterranean coast. *Seleucia* was its seaport. From there, Barnabas and Saul went by ship to the island of *Cyprus,* nearly a hundred miles away. Since the Holy Spirit was sending them, it may be supposed that he told them where to go; but we can hardly think he put money in their pockets for the fare on the ship. Since nothing is said about finances, many students suppose the church at Antioch provided funds for the trip.

Cyprus was the former home of Barnabas (Acts 4:36, 37); but if he now met any relatives or old friends, there is no record of it.

5. When they arrived at Salamis, they proclaimed the word of God in the Jewish synagogues. John was with them as their helper.

Salamis was the port city on the east side of Cyprus. There the missionaries left the ship and began their work, and now we see what work the Holy Spirit had called them to do. *The word of God* they announced was of course the news of Jesus, the Christ and the Savior. They spoke *in the Jewish synagogues,* but here in Gentile country probably many in the audiences were not Jews. There were people who were forsaking the old pagan religions in those days, and some of them were learning from the Jews about the real God. In Jewish synagogues the missionaries often found Gentiles who believed in God and worshiped with the Jews.

In writing Acts, Luke did not often tell just what the preachers said. However, he did record three sermons so we can see not only the substance of the Christian message, but also the different ways of presenting it. Acts 2:14-40 records a sermon to Jews in Palestine. Acts 13:16-41 tells how the gospel was presented to an audience of Jews and Gentiles in a synagogue. Acts 17:22-31 shows how Paul preached to intelligent Gentiles who did not believe in the one true God.

Last week we read that John Mark went from Jerusalem to Antioch with Barnabas and Saul (Acts 12:25). This young relative of Barnabas set out with them on their missionary journey to assist them in their work.

II. MISSIONARIES AT WORK (ACTS 14:1-7)

Barnabas, Saul, and John Mark went through the island of Cyprus from east to west. Luke tells us that in part of one sentence, but pauses longer to tell of their encounter with an evil sorcerer (Acts 13:6-12). At this point we see a change that is not fully explained. Barnabas and Saul were teaching a government official called Sergius Paulus. Luke comments that Saul "was also called Paul" (Greek, *Paulus*). Through the rest of Acts, the man who has been called Saul is called Paul instead. It seems, too, that Paul now moved into the leadership of the team. We have been reading of "Barnabas and Saul" (13:2, 7); now we shall be reading of "Paul and his companions" (13:13) and "Paul and Barnabas" (13:43, 46, 50).

From the west end of the island, the missionaries sailed north to the mainland. At that point John Mark left the party and went back to Jerusalem (Acts 13:13). Paul and Barnabas pushed inland to Antioch, not the Antioch from which they had

Option

Use the reproducible map activity on page 96 to have your students trace the route of Paul and Barnabas's journey.

What Do You Think?

We are not told why John Mark returned to Jerusalem. Perhaps the missionaries changed their plan, and John was not prepared for a longer than anticipated journey. Perhaps he became fearful of the hazards of travel, or grew homesick. Some have suggested he resented what appears to have been a change in leadership, from his relative Barnabas to Paul. Or maybe there was some other reason.

What do you think? What was the likely reason for his return? What, if anything, can we learn from the experience?

started, in Syria, but another city of the same name, this one in Pisidia. In Acts 13:14-52 we have a more complete record of their success there, and the opposition that was aroused. This thrilling story is too long to be included in a single Sunday-school lesson, so we bypass it and go to chapter 14. There a short passage gives a fine example of the kind of work the missionaries were doing and the kind of opposition they faced.

A. SUCCESSFUL PREACHING (v. 1)

1. At Iconium Paul and Barnabas went as usual into the Jewish synagogue. There they spoke so effectively that a great number of Jews and Gentiles believed.

Iconium was about eighty miles southeast of Antioch. It may have taken three or four days to make the trip on foot.

The missionaries found both *Jews and Gentiles* in the *synagogue* in Iconium. The preaching probably was very much like that in Pisidian Antioch (Acts 13:16-41). It was convincing to *a great number* of those who heard. They *believed* the message, believed that Jesus is the Christ, the Savior, the Son of God; so of course they were baptized and became Christians.

B. SUBTLE OPPOSITION (v. 2)

2. But the Jews who refused to believe stirred up the Gentiles and poisoned their minds against the brothers.

As usual when the gospel was preached, some of the hearers *refused to believe.* If those unbelievers tried to argue with the preachers, they found themselves defeated by Scripture and reasoning, as unbelieving Jews in Jerusalem had been (Acts 6:9, 10). So the unbelieving Jews began a campaign of slander among *the Gentiles,* not only the Gentiles in the synagogue meetings, but Gentiles of influence throughout the city. They were able to convince some that all the excitement produced by these visitors would have bad results.

C. PREACHING AND POWER (v. 3)

3. So Paul and Barnabas spent considerable time there, speaking boldly for the Lord, who confirmed the message of his grace by enabling them to do miraculous signs and wonders.

We can only guess how long Paul and Barnabas stayed in Iconium. Possibly it was several months. They kept on *speaking boldly* in spite of frowns and perhaps threats from leading Jews and influential Gentiles. The missionaries could be bold because they were speaking *for the Lord.* The *King James Version* has speaking "in the Lord" here, possibly indicating that God gave them wisdom and courage. They were speaking *the message of his grace,* that grace by which sinners are redeemed. The Lord *confirmed the message* they preached by *enabling them to do miraculous signs and wonders.* The *signs and wonders* are not described; probably they were miracles of healing such as the apostles had done in Jerusalem (Acts 5:12-16). These helpful miracles made it more and more difficult for the opponents to discredit the preachers.

D. DIVIDED CITY (v. 4)

4. The people of the city were divided; some sided with the Jews, others with the apostles.

No doubt Paul and Barnabas taught people all through the week as well as in the synagogue on the Sabbath. Their miracles attracted attention. Everyone in Iconium knew these preachers had powerful opposition. Naturally many people were loyal to their local leaders, who said these strangers were fakes. But more and more people were being convinced that Paul and Barnabas were God's messengers. The opponents saw themselves losing, and they became desperate.

E. VIOLENT OPPOSITION (v. 5)

5. There was a plot afoot among the Gentiles and Jews, together with their leaders, to mistreat them and stone them.

Unchecked, this desperation would soon erupt in physical violence. We are not told what kind of *plot* was being developed. Perhaps it involved trumped up charges in a court of law. More likely, it was to be some kind of ambush. The desired end was to have Paul and Barnabas stoned to death.

F. MOVING ON (vv. 6, 7)

6. But they found out about it and fled to the Lycaonian cities of Lystra and Derbe and to the surrounding country.

Probably Paul and Barnabas heard from several sources that a plot was being made against them. Probably many new Christians were ready, willing, and able to protect them, meeting violence with violence. But war in the streets has no place in the Christian way of spreading the gospel. Jesus once told his messengers to be "shrewd as snakes and as innocent as doves." He said, "When you are persecuted in one place, flee to another" (Matthew 10:16, 23). Wisely, then, Paul and Barnabas flitted away like harmless doves before anyone was injured physically.

Lycaonia was a region southeast of Iconium. At this time it was included in the Roman province of Galatia. *Lystra* was only a day's walk from Iconium, and Derbe only a day's walk farther on. The messengers went to both of these cities, and our text seems to suggest that they also spent some time in the villages of *the surrounding country*.

7. . . . where they continued to preach the good news.

The work of the missionaries was not stopped; it was only moved to other fields. But the opponents followed to Lystra, and this time the preachers did not move on soon enough to escape physical injury (Acts 14:19, 20). Still they continued their work in nearby Derbe (Acts 14:20, 21). From Derbe they turned back to revisit and strengthen the Christians in Lystra, Iconium, and Pisidian Antioch (Acts 14:21-23).

III. MISSIONARIES BACK HOME (ACTS 14:24-27)

The last part of our text takes up the story as Paul and Barnabas moved southward from Antioch toward the Mediterranean Sea.

A. PREACHING ON THE WAY (vv. 24, 25)

24. After going through Pisidia, they came into Pamphylia.

Antioch was in the extreme north of the region called Pisidia. To reach the sea, the missionaries had to travel south, *through Pisidia*, and *into Pamphylia*, which lay between Pisidia and the sea.

25. And when they had preached the word in Perga, they went down to Attalia.

Perga was a town in Pamphylia. It seems that Paul and Barnabas had passed through the town on the outward journey without stopping to preach (Acts 13:13, 14). Now they did stop to preach the gospel there, but we are not told how long they stayed. Soon they went on to *Attalia* on the coast.

B. REPORTING TO THE HOME CHURCH (vv. 26, 27)

26. From Attalia they sailed back to Antioch, where they had been committed to the grace of God for the work they had now completed.

WHAT DO YOU THINK?

In Antioch Paul and Barnabas "had been committed to the grace of God" before they set forth on their missionary travels (Acts 14:26). In Acts 13:3 we read that prayer was a prominent feature of the act of sending out Paul and Barnabas. We should give some thought to our prayers for missionaries. It is inadequate merely to append to our prayers the request, "Lord, bless all the missionaries." If we are to commit them to the grace of God, we must pray that their faith will remain strong in the face of disappointment and adversity; we must request that he will keep in mind their dependence on his wisdom and guidance. What are some other practical ways we can commit our missionaries to the grace of God?

WHAT DO YOU THINK?

Upon their return to Antioch, Paul and Barnabas described "all that God had done through them." When missionaries visit our church, it is natural for us to want to know something of the land in which they labor or the unusual characteristics of the people among whom they minister. Our main interest, however, should center around their efforts at sowing the gospel seed and the harvest that has resulted from such sowing. Their reports should lead us to rejoice anew in the power of the gospel and to praise God.

With this in mind, suggest some items or topics that would be most appropriate for a mission report. Do you think it would be appropriate to send such a list to a missionary and request that kind of report? Why or why not?

Visual 10 of the visuals packet shows that there are to be no limits to the preaching of the gospel.

PRAYER

Father in Heaven, we are your children because your people through centuries passed the gospel on and on till it came to us. We do want to do our part in passing on that same gospel. Help us, then, to see our part more clearly and do it better. Through Christ we ask it. Amen.

THOUGHT TO REMEMBER

"Go into all the world and preach the good news to all creation" (Mark 16:15).

DAILY BIBLE READINGS

Monday, Oct. 30—*Witnessing in Cyprus (Acts 13:6-12)*

Tuesday, Oct. 31—*Witnessing in Antioch in Pisidia (Acts 13: 13-25)*

Wednesday, Nov. 1—*Paul's Sermon Continues (Acts 13: 26-39)*

Thursday, Nov. 2—*Gentiles Happy (Acts 13:40-52)*

Friday, Nov. 3—*Mistaken Identity (Acts 14:8-18)*

Saturday, Nov. 4—*Churches Revisited and Strengthened (Acts 14:19-23)*

Sunday, Nov. 5—*The Christian's Loyalty (Matthew 10:34-39)*

It seems that the missionaries did not revisit the Christians on Cyprus on the way back home. At Attalia they took a ship and sailed directly to *Antioch*, the city in Syria from which they had started their trip, where their fellow Christians had committed them to God's grace as they set out on the work to which the Spirit had called them (Acts 13:1-3). Now they had *completed* the task to which they had been sent, and they were going back home.

27. On arriving there, they gathered the church together and reported all that God had done through them and how he had opened the door of faith to the Gentiles.

We can imagine how joyfully the Christians in Antioch met to hear the report of their missionaries. Modestly and factually, Paul and Barnabas did not tell what they had done; they told what *God had done through them.* It may have taken hours to tell about all their adventures, but Luke summarizes it in a sentence: God *had opened the door of faith to the Gentiles.* He had opened it earlier in Caesarea (Acts 10:1—11:18). He had opened it wide in Antioch (Acts 11:19-24). Now he had opened that same door of faith to Gentiles in a string of towns in Asia Minor—and there was more to come, as we will see in later lessons.

A REPORT ON A GREAT ADVENTURE

The Lewis and Clark Expedition blazed a trail westward across an uncharted wilderness. In 1803, U.S. President Thomas Jefferson proposed such a venture as a means of exploring the vast region west of the Mississippi River. Much of this area was part of the Louisiana Territory, which had been purchased that year from France.

Meriwether Lewis and William Clark and their company left Saint Louis in May, 1804, and headed up the Missouri River. Late in 1805 they reached the Pacific Ocean. In May, 1806, they began their homeward journey, reaching Saint Louis four months later. The expedition's report contributed enormously to America's knowledge of its new territory.

Whenever a venture into uncharted regions is made, it is fitting that a detailed report of the expedition's findings be given to those who commissioned the venture. So it was with the church's first major missionary effort—Paul and Barnabas's evangelistic tour of Cyprus and Asia Minor. The report of this pioneer mission spoke of momentous accomplishments, as the men described how God had opened the door of faith to the Gentiles.

—C. R. B.

CONCLUSION

As we consider the church described in the New Testament, we are struck by its rapid growth: both the growth of the local congregation and the beginning of new congregations. If we take that church as a model for the church of today, we need to be concerned about both of these kinds of growth.

A. PERSONAL EVANGELISM

In former lessons we have seen that Christians from Jerusalem "preached the word wherever they went" (Acts 8:4). They were well prepared because they had left their jobs for intensive training by the apostles. Such intensive training was not a model for all the churches: it was not copied in the churches of Judea and Damascus and Antioch. But couldn't your church benefit from a course in personal evangelism taught by someone skilled in that work?

B. UNITED EFFORT

In our lesson for today we have seen that the church in Antioch had five fine teachers, and ordained two of them to teach where there were no Christian teachers at all. How does the missionary effort of your congregation compare with that?

Discovery Learning

This page contains an alternate lesson plan emphasizing learning activities. Classes desiring such student involvement will find these suggestions helpful. The next page is a reproducible activity page to further enhance discovery learning.

LEARNING GOALS

This session will help students to:

1. Summarize the events, obstacles, and results of Paul and Barnabas's first missionary journey.

2. Compare the challenges faced by modern missionaries to those faced by Paul and Barnabas.

3. Support missionaries with prayers, money, and visits.

INTO THE LESSON

Give each student a blank sheet of paper. Then read the following sentences and ask the students to write a completion to each one.

1. When I hear the word *missionary,* my first thought is…

2. One way to describe the missionary work of our congregation is…

3. I feel most like a missionary when…

After class members have completed the sentences on paper, allow several to share them with the class.

Tell the class that today we will consider the missionary activity of the church in its early years to see what lessons there are for the church's missionary efforts today.

INTO THE WORD

Before class prepare nine pieces of paper on which you have written the following information, one place or person on each.

Antioch—Apparently the first large church that included Gentiles in its membership.

Barnabas—A faithful Christian who, along with Saul, was sent by the church in Antioch to take its offering to the famine-stricken Christians in Judea.

Simeon Niger—A teacher in the Antioch church. *Niger* means "black"; he probably had black hair and a dark complexion.

Lucius of Cyrene—A teacher in the Antioch church whose hometown was a city in north Africa.

Manaen—A teacher in the Antioch church who was brought up as the companion of Herod the tetrarch or who was his foster brother. This Herod, also known as Herod Antipas, was the ruler of Galilee and Perea during the earthly ministry of Jesus.

Seleucia—The seaport for Antioch. Antioch lay about fifteen miles inland.

Cyprus—An island in the eastern part of the Mediterranean off the coast of Syria.

Salamis—The port city on the east side of Cyprus.

John—Also known as John Mark, he was a young relative of Barnabas. John had accompanied Barnabas and Saul when they returned to Antioch from Jerusalem after delivering the Antioch church's gift to the needy saints in Judea.

Distribute the papers to class members; then read Acts 13:1-5 aloud. Next, have the class members with the papers read the information on them to the class. (Have the papers read in the order shown above.)

Review the lesson text with the following questions:

• How many teachers were in the church at Antioch? (Five.)

• How did the church know to send Barnabas and Saul on this missionary journey? (By the Holy Spirit.)

• How did the church set them apart? (With fasting, prayer, and the laying on of hands.)

Connect this passage with Acts 14 by presenting thoughts given in the two paragraphs immediately under the heading "Missionaries at Work," pages 91, 92. Then read 14:1-7, 24-27 aloud. (If you have time, read all of chapter 14.) Read verse 27 a second time.

Have class members work in groups to list the events of Paul and Barnabas's missionary journey that the two would have been sure to share with their friends in Antioch. As groups report, list their suggestions on the chalkboard.

OPTION

Use the map on the next page to review Paul and Barnabas's journey. Make a copy for each student.

INTO LIFE

Discuss these questions with the class:

1. How do the obstacles faced by Paul and Barnabas compare with obstacles we face today when we try to spread the gospel?

2. How do you suppose Paul and Barnabas felt about their missionary experience? What aspects of it would make them want to do further missionary work?

3. How do the experiences of Paul and Barnabas affect your feelings about spreading the gospel?

Distribute a list of missionary efforts your congregation sponsors and have the students examine the list. Then close with prayer, asking God to help each person see how he or she can become more involved in these efforts.

Map of Paul's First Missionary Journey

Using a Bible atlas, locate the cities listed below on the map. Then use a pen to trace Paul and Barnabas's first missionary journey (Acts 13, 14).

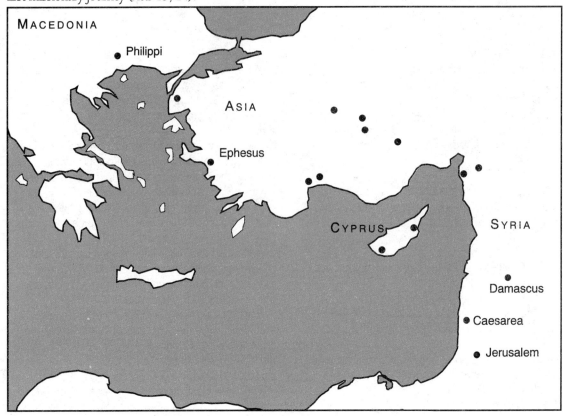

Next to the name of each city below write one thing that happened to Paul and Barnabas in that city.

1. Antioch (in Syria) _____

2. Seleucia _____

3. Salamis _____

4. Paphos _____

5. Perga _____

6. Antioch (in Pisidia) _____

7. Iconium _____

8. Lystra _____

9. Derbe _____

10. Lystra _____

11. Iconium _____

12. Antioch (in Pisidia) _____

13. Perga _____

14. Attalia _____

15. Antioch (in Syria) _____

THE JERUSALEM CONFERENCE

LESSON 11

WHY TEACH THIS LESSON?

"I have a right to my opinion." That usually settles the matter. It seems we all want to hold on to the right to form our own opinions, so no one will challenge such a statement.

Unfortunately, it's just not so. Where matters of truth and reality are concerned, we do not have a right to our own opinions. Who would stand by and allow a mother to serve her child spoiled milk because it was her opinion that such milk was healthful?

In the church, there are matters of opinion in which we must grant one another the freedom to hold what opinion he will. But we never have the right to hold an opinion that contradicts God's revealed truth. The spoiled milk of our opinions must never be allowed to substitute for the "pure spiritual milk" of God's word (1 Peter 2:2). Use today's lesson as a reminder of that fact.

INTRODUCTION

A man convinced against his will
Is of the same opinion still

Thus a poet notes what most of us have noted, too. People are inclined to cling to their opinions. Sometimes we cling to an opinion because we like it. Why else does anyone ignore the piled-up evidence and say cigarette smoke is not really harmful? Then sometimes we cling to an opinion just because it is ours. We have stated it strongly, and we don't want to admit that we have been wrong. Years ago Grandpa declared that peanuts will produce more if they are planted in the dark of the moon. He declares it still, even though a neighbor plants when the moon is full and has a better crop.

A. A TREASURED OPINION

God chose the Jewish people to be his own. That is a fact, not an opinion. However, many of the Jews took that to mean they were above the rest of the world and must be strictly separate forever. That was their opinion, and they liked it. Not many of them recalled that God chose them for the purpose of bringing a blessing to all the world (Genesis 12:3).

B. LESSON BACKGROUND

The first Christians were Jews, and for a while they supposed that no one but Jews would ever be Christians. Lesson 8 reviewed how God convinced Peter that Gentiles also would be redeemed. Peter convinced the other Jewish Christians, and they praised God (Acts 11:18). They were convinced, but some of them were convinced against their will.

DEVOTIONAL READING
ROMANS 3:21-31
LESSON SCRIPTURE
ACTS 15:1-35
PRINTED TEXT
ACTS 15:1, 2, 6-18

LESSON AIMS

After this lesson a student should be able to:

1. Tell what doctrinal problem developed in the early church and how the problem was resolved.

2. List some principles for resolving conflict as demonstrated by the participants in the Jerusalem conference.

3. Discuss how these principles can help to resolve a specific modern conflict.

Nov
12

KEY VERSE

We believe it is through the grace of our Lord Jesus that we are saved. —Acts 15:11

WHAT DO YOU THINK?

The apostles were divinely inspired to impart truth to the church, and the church was "devoted … to the apostles' teaching" (Acts 2:42). It seems strange, then, that there was any debate on a doctrinal issue.

Why do you think Paul did not just declare God's truth and end the matter in Antioch? Or why didn't Peter and the other apostles in Jerusalem simply announce God's will in the matter? What was the reason for the conference and discussion? What benefits do you think may have been gained over simply declaring the truth and expecting that to end the matter?

WHAT DO YOU THINK?

Paul and Barnabas determined that Christians not be bound by Jewish law. Christ died to set us free from the law. For one to return to it, therefore, would signify that that person had no part in the grace of God (Galatians 5:1-4).

Paul surely knew the apostles in Jerusalem would confirm his teaching. The Spirit would not give contradictory messages! So the Conference in Jerusalem did not establish the truth of Paul's message but confirmed it.

What do you think they would have done if going up to Jerusalem had not been an option? How would the conflict have been resolved without potentially yielding to those who were wrong? How can disputes today be determined according to the truth of God's will and not by human consensus?

I. PROBLEM (ACTS 15:1, 2, 6)

After the events recorded in chapters 10 and 11 of Acts, no one could deny that God wanted Gentiles to become Christians. Then the exclusive Jews took a different turn in their thinking. "Certainly Gentiles can become Christians," they said. "That's great. But they must become Jews, too."

A. DISPUTE (vv. 1, 2a)

1. Some men came down from Judea to Antioch and were teaching the brothers: "Unless you are circumcised, according to the custom taught by Moses, you cannot be saved."

These men brought a teaching not heard in Antioch before. They said being Christian is not enough, and that Gentile Christians could not be saved unless they would also become Jews—*circumcised according to the custom taught by Moses.*

2a. This brought Paul and Barnabas into sharp dispute and debate with them.

The new teachers were mistaken. *Paul and Barnabas* knew it, and they said so. The new teachers did not back down. The debate grew long, and perhaps heated.

B. SEARCH FOR SETTLEMENT (v. 2b)

2b. So Paul and Barnabas were appointed, along with some other believers, to go up to Jerusalem to see the apostles and elders about this question.

Probably the new teachers claimed to be giving the true teaching of the original church in Jerusalem. Paul and Barnabas made the same claim, but their teaching was contradictory. The Christians in Antioch thought this question was important enough to deserve a reliable answer. Therefore, they sent a delegation to Jerusalem to find out what the original church was teaching. Paul and Barnabas were included. Probably some of their opponents were in the group, too, plus some of the Antioch Christians who had taken no part in the debate. *The apostles and elders* could answer the question.

C. WISE LEADERS (v. 6)

6. The apostles and elders met to consider this question.

In verses 4 and 5 we read that the Christians in Jerusalem met with the apostles and elders to greet their brethren from Antioch. Paul and Barnabas told about their missionary journey. They had brought many Gentiles to Christ, but had not told them to become Jews. Then some Christian Pharisees stood up to agree with the new teachers who had lately gone to Antioch. They said all those Gentile Christians must become Jews and keep the Old Testament laws.

This was the question now to be considered by *the apostles and elders.* Apparently the whole congregation still was present (v. 12), but the leaders *met* in a little group to talk about *this question* before the congregation.

NOTHING NEW ALLOWED

In mid-eighteenth-century England, English wool was made into English woolens, and it was done by hand. England's craftsmen took pride in their work. Then came the Industrial Revolution, and with it came social turmoil. Machines were costing people their jobs.

One night in 1811, in England's Spen Valley, two hundred armed men in masks (or otherwise disguised), began what led to a wave of guerrilla warfare. They smashed the new textile-making machines that were threatening their way of life. They came to be known as Luddites, after Ned Ludd, who years earlier in a fit of anger had destroyed his father's knitting frame. Their rebellion lasted only five or six years, but the name *Luddite* has been applied to any opponent of new ways of doing things, especially when new technology is involved.

In its early years the church was troubled by spiritual Luddites. They were more concerned with keeping their traditions than they were with what God so obviously was doing in the world. Through his appointed messengers God was leading Gentiles to Christ, but these Jewish Christian "Luddites" could only say, "Everyone has to come to God *our* way."

God clearly has revealed that he seeks the salvation of every person, and he has provided the way. Let us not cling to any tradition that would impede his will.

—C. R. B.

II. TESTIMONY (ACTS 15:7-12)

A. SIMON PETER (vv. 7-11)

7. After much discussion, Peter got up and addressed them: "Brothers, you know that some time ago God made a choice among you that the Gentiles might hear from my lips the message of the gospel and believe.

It is not likely that there was much dispute among apostles and elders; but others were allowed to join in the *discussion,* and there were those who disagreed with the Christian Pharisees. All of those who wished to speak had their opportunities, and then *Peter got up* to give his testimony. He reminded the gathering that he had been the first to take the gospel to the Gentiles, not by his choice, but by God's.

8. "God, who knows the heart, showed that he accepted them by giving the Holy Spirit to them, just as he did to us.

Peter continued to emphasize the decisive part *God* had played in the matter—God *who knows the heart* and cannot be deceived by outward appearance or pretense. He had given those Gentiles *the Holy Spirit,* just as he had given to the apostles on the Day of Pentecost (Acts 2:1-4; 10:44-46). This was God's own testimony in favor of the Gentiles of Cornelius's household.

9. "He made no distinction between us and them, for he purified their hearts by faith.

In the matter of being saved and becoming children of God, there is *no distinction* between Jews and Gentiles. This is indicated by God's own testimony. What makes a difference is *faith.*

10. "Now then, why do you try to test God by putting on the necks of the disciples a yoke that neither we nor our fathers have been able to bear?

The Pharisees in the church were putting God on trial. They were contesting his decision, not Peter's or Paul's. God had shown himself ready to accept the Gentiles who came by faith; the Pharisees wanted to require more than God did. The law was *a yoke,* a burden that had proved to be too much for the Jews then present and for all of their ancestors. The Jews who came to Christ came admitting their failure. They were not righteous according to the law. They looked to Jesus to forgive them, to take away their sins, to make them righteous because of their faith. Now Gentiles were coming to Christ in the same way, and the Pharisees wanted to put on them the law that already had proved to be inadequate. That was absurd.

11. "No! We believe it is through the grace of our Lord Jesus that we are saved, just as they are."

The grace of our Lord Jesus Christ is, of course, his undeserved favor. That was the only hope of the Jewish Christians (*we*), even the Pharisees who had been most zealous for the law. The law could not save them. The Lord's grace could, and it could save the Gentiles (*they*) as well.

BY LAW OR BY GRACE?

We all admit that we need laws. But the average layman is sometimes puzzled by the workings of the legal mind.

NOTE

In the previous lesson we noted how Luke had changed the order of mentioning these two missionaries. "Barnabas and Saul" had become "Paul and Barnabas," indicating that Paul had become the leader of the team instead of Barnabas. Here, in Jerusalem, where Barnabas had a high reputation among the leaders of the church, Barnabas is listed first again. Perhaps Barnabas, in his usual encouraging manner, took the lead to encourage the church to accept the Gentiles without reservation.

Visual 11 of the visuals packet shows that no one has the right to require more than God requires for a person to be saved.

A while back the *New Jersey Law Journal* explained in profound "legalese" why an insurance company was legally able to rescind a life insurance policy after the death of the insured. The man's survivors received no benefits from the policy because it was discovered that, in applying for coverage, he had knowingly withheld the information that he had diabetes.

Most of us would say, "Fair enough," if his death had been caused by an undisclosed health problem. But in this case, the man was found in the trunk of his car, *shot to death!* A legal technicality seems—to the layman, at least—to have voided the facts in the case. But then the law seems not to have any room for grace.

The exclusive Jewish Christians were more concerned with points of the law than they were with the grace of God. Apparently they preferred to see Gentile God-seekers crushed by the weight of God's law than to see them enjoy the liberating grace of God in Christ, by which Jews and Gentiles alike are to be saved.

Not even the noblest person can bear the weight of God's law. The fact of our sin mocks our demands that God save us because we have obeyed him. We simply can't be that good! Only his grace can save us.   —C. R. B.

B. PAUL AND BARNABAS (v. 12)

12. The whole assembly became silent as they listened to Barnabas and Paul telling about the miraculous signs and wonders God had done among the Gentiles through them.

When Peter had finished his testimony, *Barnabas and Paul* spoke again. They had told about their mission before (v. 4), but now they emphasized the *miraculous signs and wonders* that *God had done among the Gentiles through them.* Barnabas and Paul had not done those miracles; God had done them. That was clear evidence that God had been with the missionaries and had given his approval to their work. In that God-approved work they had led Gentiles to become Christians without becoming Jews.

III. SCRIPTURE (ACTS 15:13-18)

The testimony of Peter was plain and powerful. It had convinced the Christians in Jerusalem before (Acts 11:1-18), and now it convinced them again. The testimony of Barnabas and Paul added strength to the conviction. Now another speaker added the testimony of the Holy Scriptures. Who could argue with that?

A. PROPHECY OF AMOS (vv. 13-17)

13. When they finished, James spoke up: "Brothers, listen to me.

When Barnabas and Paul had finished what they wanted to say, the next speaker was *James*. James the brother of John was no longer living on earth (Acts 12:1, 2), so we conclude that this James was "the Lord's brother" (Galatians 1:19); that is, a half brother of Jesus, a son of Joseph and Mary (Mark 6:3). James became a leader in the Jerusalem church, and author of the book of James. In the meeting we are considering, he rose to bring the discussion to its conclusion.

14. "Simon has described to us how God at first showed his concern by taking from the Gentiles a people for himself.

Simon was the original name of the disciple we usually call Peter. James began his speech by recalling what Simon Peter had said in the meeting only a short while before. Peter had recalled *how God at first showed his concern* for the Gentiles. Before any of the Jewish Christians were ready to welcome Gentiles into the church, God himself had gone to them, *taking from the Gentiles a people for himself;* that is, bringing some of them to become Christians. How God did that is recorded in Acts 10. It had been thoroughly discussed in the church at Jerusalem, and the Jewish Christians had agreed that God wanted Gentiles to be saved along with Jews (Acts

WHAT DO YOU THINK?

Still today some believers wish to impose "yokes" of personal opinion on others. It may concern forms of recreation—attending movies in theaters, watching television, and many other such matters. Or it may concern the observance of certain holidays that the person believes should not be observed by Christians. On and on the list may go.

What is the difference between holding an opinion and using an opinion as a "yoke"? How can Christians be sure to hold their opinions in a fair and reasonable way and not as a yoke on other believers?

And doesn't the Bible give some restrictions that ought to be imposed on believers? How can we be sure to impose only legitimate scriptural restrictions and not yokes of our own opinions or understanding? (See Romans 15:1, 2; 1 Corinthians 10:31; 16:14.)

11:1-18). In the meeting we are now reading about, Peter needed only a few words to remind the brethren of that earlier decision.

15. "The words of the prophets are in agreement with this, as it is written:

James first recalled that God himself had acted to have Gentiles received among his people (v. 14). Then James stated that the same thing was shown in *the words of the prophets* and *written* in the Old Testament that was revered by all Jews, Christian and non-Christian.

16. "'After this I will return and rebuild David's fallen tent. Its ruins I will rebuild, and I will restore it.

James chose Amos 9:11, 12 as an example of the prophecies that foretold God's acceptance of Gentiles. The first part of that chapter foretells the destruction of Israel, but not total destruction (Amos 9:8-10). In our text we are reading God's promise to rebuild it.

Probably Amos gave his prophecy between 760 and 750 B.C. In 722 or 721 B.C. the Assyrians overcame northern Israel and scattered its people in foreign lands. The southern tribe of Judah survived then, but in 586 B.C. the Babylonians destroyed Jerusalem and took the people of Judah to Babylon as captives. Thus the nation was destroyed, but not utterly. This fulfilled the prophecy of Amos 9:8-10. God preserved a remnant of the nation in Babylon, and about 536 B.C. He brought it back to Jerusalem and rebuilt the nation according to Amos's prophecy quoted in our text. The next verse explains why God rebuilt the ruined nation of Israel.

17. "'That the remnant of men may seek the Lord, and all the Gentiles who bear my name, says the Lord, who does these things.'

God did not restore the nation of Israel for its own sake only. He had designed that nation to bring into the world the Savior, Jesus, a man of David's line, who would lead not only Jews, but all the rest of mankind, to seek after the Lord. The non-Jewish people are described as *all the Gentiles*. God intended the good news of salvation for everyone. Of course, the offer of salvation does not rob people of their freedom to choose. Salvation is offered to all, and God wants all to be saved (2 Peter 3:9). Those actually saved are those who accept the Savior, Jesus—those who make him their Lord and obey him. Then they *bear* his *name*; that is, they are known as God's people.

Like many prophecies of Scripture, this one from Amos has more than one fulfillment. First, God did rebuild David's tent—his kingdom, his nation—after it had fallen into captivity. He used that nation to bring the Savior into the world and lead all kinds of people to seek God. But in a second and greater fulfillment, God is even now building up the tent of David, the church that is ruled by Jesus Christ. On the human side, Jesus is David's descendant and heir to his throne. Therefore, the kingdom of Christ is fittingly called the tent of David. But now people from all the nations of the world are brought into it.

Verse 17 ends with a reminder that this prophecy is not from Amos, but from *the Lord*, Jehovah, the Creator of Heaven and earth. He is the one *who does these things*. Through Amos he told what he would do; he did it and is doing it still.

B. COMMENT OF JAMES (v. 18)

18. "... that have been known for ages."

The quotation from Amos ends with verse 17, and now James adds his comment. From the beginning of the world God has known what he was going to do. He foretold much of it through the prophets. People understood the prophecies so poorly that they killed the Son of God, the Savior of the world. God raised him to life and glory. After that, even the people who knew Christ best and followed him most eagerly were only gradually coming to understand what God had known all

WHAT DO YOU THINK?

Some longtime Christians may say, "I have held my opinions for many years, and I am not likely to change them now." Certainly the longer we have held a view—or the louder we have proclaimed it—the harder it is to change. How can we be open to changing our opinions when they have been with us for a long time or have been especially cherished? How can we be supportive of opinionated believers without condoning false opinions, lovingly urging a change without condemning the individuals? Suggest some examples.

OPTION

Use the reproducible activity on page 104 to review the text and to apply its conflict-resolving principles to problems of today.

PRAYER

Our Father in Heaven, your love for us is so plain that we can never doubt it. We know every plan of yours is for our good as well as for your glory. Help us then to subdue our stubborn wills and bring every thought and word and act in line with the teaching of your holy Word. In Jesus' name. Amen

THOUGHT TO REMEMBER

God's way is best.

DAILY BIBLE READINGS

Monday, Nov. 6—Difficulty of Keeping the Law (John 7:14-24)

Tuesday, Nov. 7—Justification by Faith (Galatians 2:11-21)

Wednesday, Nov. 8—Forgiveness of Sins (Acts 10:39-43)

Thursday, Nov. 9—Righteousness Bestowed by Christ (Isaiah 53:7-12)

Friday, Nov. 10—Approval From the Council at Jerusalem (Acts 15:19-29)

Saturday, Nov. 11—Letter Received With Rejoicing (Acts 15:30-35)

Sunday, Nov. 12—Grace for All (Romans 3:21-31)

along and had revealed through the prophets. Slowly, and with special urging by the Holy Spirit, Jewish Christians were learning that the offer of salvation is for all people, that the duty of Christians is to take it to all people, and that all people who earnestly follow Jesus are equally acceptable to God. Though that was learned with difficulty, it was learned thoroughly. All around the world today, God is building up "the tent of David," the church of Jesus Christ.

CONCLUSION

Christians of today are much like those early Christians. We, too, like our own opinions, and we cling to them vigorously. We had better examine our thinking and be sure we do not cling to any opinion that opposes the will of God.

A. DON'T BE AFRAID TO CHANGE

The first Christians thought only Jews would ever be Christians, but they changed their thinking when God made his will known. Then some of them tried to keep their mistaken opinion in another form, insisting that Gentiles become Jews in order to be Christians. That opinion also was abandoned after the discussion we have seen in our lesson text. It was not in accord with God's will.

In our day, not many Christians doubt that God wants all kinds of people to be saved. But do you know of a Christian who has some reservations in his own mind? "Sure," he says, "I'm delighted to have all kinds of people come to Christ, people rich and poor, people educated and illiterate, people of all races and nations—but please, not in our congregation. Let's keep our church like it is." And if we will not do that, some members will move to a congregation that will.

Let's search the Scriptures. Can we find any indication that God does not want every person in our community to be in our church? If any opinion or wish of ours is not in line with God's will, let's change it.

On the other hand, enthusiastic Christians can go too far in demanding that every congregation include all kinds of people in its membership. Some years ago a Christian writer described a church in New Mexico that included Mexican Americans, Chinese Americans, Japanese Americans, Hindu Americans, and some assorted aliens. The description closed with the ringing declaration, "God wants every congregation to be just like that!"

In a rural church in Ohio, an elder chuckled. "Where shall we get all those kinds of people?" he asked. "Shall we hire a bus and bring them fifty miles from Columbus? It just happens that all the people we know have European ancestors —Italian or French or Russian or Norwegian or English."

In our search of the Scriptures, we do not find that God wants our congregation to include any more kinds of people than live in our community; but we do not find that he wants it to exclude any of the kinds of people who do live there.

B. LET GOD DECIDE

The Jewish Christians at Jerusalem gave up their treasured opinion because it was not in line with God's will. That is a noble example for us to follow.

Not all of those early Christians so nobly gave up their old opinion, however. There were some who kept on teaching that Christ is not enough, that Gentiles who become Christians must also become Jews and keep the Jewish law in order to be saved.

Paul had a forceful answer for that. If you think Christ is not enough, he said, if you look to the law for salvation, then "Christ will be of no value to you at all . . . you have fallen away from grace" (Galatians 5:2-4). That is a bad example—one for us to avoid. Let God decide. Accept his will. He is always right.

Discovery Learning

This page contains an alternate lesson plan emphasizing learning activities. Classes desiring such student involvement will find these suggestions helpful. The next page is a reproducible activity page to further enhance discovery learning.

LEARNING GOALS

Students in today's class should:

1. Tell what doctrinal problem developed in the early church and how the problem was resolved.

2. List some principles for resolving conflict as demonstrated by the participants in the Jerusalem conference.

3. Discuss how these principles can help to resolve a specific modern conflict.

INTO THE LESSON

Use one of the two following activities to introduce the theme of this study:

• Display a poster on which you have written the following statements:

Conflict Is a Sin and Must Always Be Avoided.   **Conflict Is Inevitable and Always Shows Progress.**

Ask students to decide which statement best describes their opinion about conflict in the church. If they feel uncomfortable with either extreme, ask them what they *do* believe about conflict between Christians. Divide the students into groups of three and ask each group to write one sentence that describes their thinking about conflict.

• Have someone read aloud the "Introduction" to this lesson. Then ask, "What are some subjects concerning which there are conflicting opinions among Christians today?" List as many as students identify in ninety seconds. Write their suggestions on sheets of paper, one suggestion per sheet. Tape the sheets to the wall.

Tell the class that in this session we will look at how the church in New Testament times handled conflict, and we will look for principles to help Christians deal with conflict in our time.

INTO THE WORD

Set the stage for Bible study by reviewing last week's lesson. Then divide the class into four groups and assign to each of the groups one of the four persons listed below. As you read today's lesson text aloud, each group is to listen to discover the perspective of its character:

1. A Christian Pharisee
2. A Gentile Christian
3. Paul
4. Peter

After the Scripture is read, have class members divide into groups of three or four. Each group is to write a brief paragraph retelling the story from the point of view of its assigned character. Allow seven or eight minutes for the groups to write; then ask to hear some of the paragraphs.

If time is short, the groups may simply list the thoughts and emotions they think their characters might have had. As the paragraphs or lists are shared, answer questions or fill in gaps with information from the lesson comments.

Next have members work in pairs or in groups of three to prepare a list of principles for solving church conflicts. They should base their lists on the model set by the apostles and elders as recorded in Acts 15.

Give class members at least ten minutes to make their lists; then, as volunteers share items from their lists, write them on your chalkboard. As each item is shared, ask other groups or students if they had written down the same or a similar thought.

If time is short, you may want to suggest some principles to your class members and ask them to find how they are demonstrated in this text. Some possible principles from Acts 15 for resolving church conflicts are,

1. Consult church leaders.

2. Confer with leaders from another congregation.

3. Keep discussing until consensus is reached; don't take sides or leave a meeting angrily.

4. Analyze what God says about the issue. Keep studying till you can see how all his pronouncements and actions related to an issue agree with each other.

5. Be open to God's will, not committed to your own opinions.

(This list may also be helpful if you use the activity on page 104. See "General Principles," the middle section.)

INTO LIFE

• Refer to the sheets you taped to the wall earlier (if you chose the second "Into the Lesson" activity). Select some of the subjects listed on the sheets and discuss how principles from Acts 15 can help resolve conflicts concerning them. Close the class session with prayer.

• If you chose the first "Into the Lesson" activity, or if you have time to do both "Into Life" activities, distribute copies of the reproducible page (page 104), and allow time for the students to complete them. Then discuss the "Current Conflict" section, making plans to address some current issue dividing your class or your church.

The Jerusalem Conference

Read Acts 15:1-21. Under the heading labeled **Original Information** identify the issue that caused conflict in the text and then list the steps that were taken to resolve that issue. From that, write some **General Principles** for conflict resolution. Finally, in the space at the bottom, identify a **Current Conflict** in your own class or church and apply the general pattern to solving your own problem.

ORIGINAL INFORMATION
  The Issue (vv. 1, 5) _____

  Steps taken to resolve the conflict:

  (v. 2) _____

  (v. 6) _____

  (vv. 7-11) _____

  (v. 12) _____

  (vv. 13-18) _____

  (v. 19) _____

GENERAL PRINCIPLES
   (If help is needed here, the teacher has some suggested principles on page 103 of the *Commentary.*)

CURRENT CONFLICT
  The Issue_____

  Steps you might take to resolve the conflict:

A GOSPEL FOR THE WHOLE WORLD

LESSON 12

WHY TEACH THIS LESSON?

We have been watching the spread of the gospel. From Jerusalem it went first to Jews in Judea and Samaria. Then it reached to Gentiles—especially in Antioch. From there a great missionary work was launched, reaching to Cyprus and Asia Minor. Today, we see it reach into Europe. From a wealthy businesswoman to a Roman jailer, we see acceptance of the gospel coming from a variety of people.

It is easy to see only our own church or churches like ours. The record in Acts shows us the gospel is for every people group, people like us and people very different from us. Challenge your class to look beyond themselves to explore how they may share in reaching more peoples with the power of the gospel.

INTRODUCTION

Since the collapse of the Soviet Union, countless missionaries have flooded into the countries where Communist governments had promoted atheism for many years. Churches are growing even in China, where a Communist government still rules, and encouraging news comes from countless other fields around the world.

Yet, after two thousand years, how far we are from fulfilling the magnificent vision of the Master! He said, "Go into all the world and preach the good news to all creation" (Mark 16:15).

A. GOD'S GREAT VISION

Since the very beginning of the church, how constantly God has been pushing his people to go farther and do more!

The first Christians in Jerusalem won multiplied thousands of people to the Lord, but they seemed quite content to stay in that city till persecution drove them out. We wonder if God permitted the persecution for that purpose.

Those who were scattered "preached the word wherever they went" (Acts 8:4), but they preached it "only to Jews" (11:19). Lesson 8 reviewed the extraordinary methods God used to persuade them that the good news was for Gentiles, too.

Apparently Antioch was the scene of the first great church among the Gentiles. The Christians there were devoted and enthusiastic, but it took a special word from the Holy Spirit to send two of their best workers out through the island of Cyprus and into Asia Minor. Lesson 10 reviewed their trip for us.

B. LESSON BACKGROUND

Last week's lesson pictured a human effort to restrict church growth by compelling all Christians to become Jews. With the leading of the Holy Spirit, the church repudiated that effort.

Paul and Barnabas then planned a second trip, intending to revisit the churches they had started before. After a sharp difference of opinion, they

DEVOTIONAL READING
Acts 15:36—16:5
LESSON SCRIPTURE
Acts 15:36—16:40
PRINTED TEXT
Acts 16:9, 10, 13-15, 25-34

LESSON AIMS

After this lesson a student should be able to:

1. Describe how the gospel first spread to Europe and some of the immediate results.

2. Tell how different individuals have responded to gospel teaching.

3. Identify individuals or groups they or their church are uniquely positioned to reach with the gospel.

KEY VERSE

NOV 19

After Paul had seen the vision, we got ready at once to leave for Macedonia, concluding that God had called us to preach the gospel to them.

—*Acts 16:10*

Lesson 12 Notes

separated and formed two missionary teams instead of one. Barnabas and John Mark went to Cyprus; Paul and Silas went to the churches on the mainland (Acts 15:36-41).

At Lystra, young Timothy joined Paul and Silas (Acts 16:1-5). After visiting the churches that were started earlier, the three went on to the west, apparently expecting to preach in cities of Asia. This was not the great continent we now call Asia; it was the Roman province at the west end of that continent.

The missionaries must have been surprised when the Holy Spirit told them not to preach in Asia. They thought then of going north to Bithynia, but the Spirit vetoed that idea, too. So the trio pressed on to the west till they were stopped by the sea at Troas (Acts 16:6-8). We can imagine that they were greatly puzzled. The gospel was for everyone. Why should they not preach it in Asia or Bithynia? What did the Spirit want them to do?

How To Say It

Aegean. A-JEE-un.
Antioch. AN-tee-ock.
Bithynia. Bih-THIN-ee-uh.
Cilicia. Sih-LISH-i-uh.
Cyprus. SYE-prus.
Derbe. DER-be.
Galatia. Guh-LAY-shuh.
Lydia. LID-i-uh.
Lystra. LISS-truh.
Macedonia. Mass-eh-DOE-nee-uh.
Neapolis. Nee-AP-o-lis.
Phrygia. FRIJ-ee-uh.
Philippi. Fih-LIP-pie or FIL-ih-pie.
Syria. SEAR-ee-uh.
Troas. TRO-az.

I. ANSWERING A CALL (ACTS 16:9, 10)

Soon the missionaries learned what the Spirit had in mind. As at other times, God's vision was wider than man's. These preachers of the gospel were not only to leave the little province then called Asia; they were to leave the huge continent that now has that name. They were going to Europe!

Some Bible students make much of that, calling it the first coming of the gospel to a new continent. Of that we cannot be sure, but it is the first *recorded* evangelism in Europe.

In any case, the coming of the gospel to Europe proved to be vastly important. From Europe the faith spread to America; from Europe and America came most of the men and money for the great worldwide missionary movement of the nineteenth and twentieth centuries. Thus Europe became an important station on the gospel's journey to "the ends of the earth."

A. VISION (v. 9)

9. During the night Paul had a vision of a man of Macedonia standing and begging him, "Come over to Macedonia and help us."

Macedonia was not far away, though it was on another continent. It was the country just north of Greece.

Option

Use the reproducible map activity on page 112 to trace the apostles' movements through the events of today's lesson.

B. RESPONSE (v. 10)

10. After Paul had seen the vision, we got ready at once to leave for Macedonia, concluding that God had called us to preach the gospel to them.

Paul and his companions had no doubt about the meaning of the vision. It was God's call. He wanted these missionaries to preach the gospel in Macedonia. *At once* they began looking for a ship that would take them to the place where God wanted them.

Notice the change in the pronouns. *They*—Paul, Silas, and Timothy—came to Troas (v. 8). But *we* prepared to go to Macedonia, sure that the Lord had called *us*—Paul, Silas, Timothy, *and Luke,* the writer of this record. Where did Luke come from? Why did he join the party at this point? Was he already known to any of the missionaries? Obviously Luke was a modest historian. He told us nothing about himself.

II. CONVERTING A LADY (ACTS 16:13-15)

The missionaries boarded a boat that carried them more than a hundred miles northwest across the Aegean Sea to the coast of Macedonia. Landing at Neapolis, they went inland to Philippi (Acts 16:11, 12).

A. PRAYER MEETING (v. 13)

13. On the Sabbath we went outside the city gate to the river, where we expected to find a place of prayer. We sat down and began to speak to the women who had gathered there.

Chief city though it was, Philippi probably did not have enough Jews to maintain a synagogue. But there was a prayer meeting by a river outside the city. The missionaries learned about that and took their message to it. Apparently only women attended, but the visiting teachers were welcomed and given a chance to speak.

B. ATTENTIVE LISTENER (v. 14)

14. One of those listening was a woman named Lydia, a dealer in purple cloth from the city of Thyatira, who was a worshiper of God. The Lord opened her heart to respond to Paul's message.

Lydia was a businesswoman. Probably she was a prosperous one, for *purple* dye is rare and costly, obtained from shellfish. The word *cloth* in our text is supplied by the translators; the Greek word involved literally means "dealer in purple." Lydia may have sold the cloth, or the dye, or finished garments of purple, or all three.

This lady had come from *the city of Thyatira* in the province of Asia, which the missionaries had just left behind. Luke says Lydia *was a worshiper of God*. Probably that means she was not Jewish, but had forsaken the mythical religions of the pagans to worship the real God whom the Jews worshiped. Such Gentiles were described as devout (Acts 10:7) or as God-fearing (Acts 10:2; 13:26; 17:4, 17). Often they were found meeting with Jews in the synagogues.

Lydia's conversion was not accomplished by Paul's personality or Paul's eloquence alone; *the Lord opened her heart*. Some may debate about how God opens a human heart, but in this case one way is obvious. The Lord opened Lydia's heart by means of the message she heard from Paul. It was the Lord's message, and it accomplished his purpose. That message, the gospel, is "the power of God for the salvation of everyone who believes" (Romans 1:16). By means of that message God opened Lydia's heart *to respond to* (she accepted) the message.

C. CHRISTIAN HOSPITALITY (v. 15)

15. When she and the members of her household were baptized, she invited us to her home. "If you consider me a believer in the Lord," she said, "come and stay at my house." And she persuaded us.

In obedience to the message she heard and accepted, Lydia was *baptized*. So was *her household*. This included members of her family, if she had a family living with her. Whether she had a family or not, her household probably included household servants. It may also have included employees who helped with her business. How many there may have been we have no way of knowing. Whoever they were, they, too, listened to the gospel, and the Lord opened their hearts to receive it. So the mistress of the house and her household became Christians together.

Then Lydia *invited* Paul, Silas, Timothy, and Luke to *stay at* her *house*. Here is another indication that the lady was prosperous. She had room for four house guests. The four may have been reluctant to accept her generous hospitality. As a rule, Paul liked to share the gospel without cost to those who heard it (1 Corinthians 9:18). But Lydia wouldn't take no for an answer. She *persuaded* them to accept her offer.

III. CONVERTING A JAILER (ACTS 16:25-34)

A slave girl in Philippi was possessed by a demon. Evil though he was, the spirit knew many things unknown to humans. Using the girl's voice, he made her an excellent fortune-teller, and she earned a lot of money for her owners.

WHAT DO YOU THINK?

Paul found people receptive to the gospel at a place of prayer. Today we often hear non-Christian people mention that they pray to God. Do you think that suggests an opening for the gospel, or is it just idle talk designed to keep us from suggesting they need to be more spiritual? Explain. If you think it may provide and open door for the gospel, explain how one might take advantage of that opening.

If such people's prayers are mere "bargaining" sessions, or if they address God as if he were a glorified "genie," how might we focus the person's attention on the real God who answers real prayers?

WHAT DO YOU THINK?

Lydia's eagerness to provide lodging for Paul and his companions reminds us of the zeal for service that new converts often have. The church's leadership needs to be aware of the new convert's enthusiasm and should challenge that person to serve Christ and the church in ways that are appropriate to his capability. Within the new convert's family and circle of friends there may be several unsaved individuals with whom he can share his newfound faith. But he may need help in this.

A new convert can be given responsibilities in the church that will help her become better acquainted with her new brothers and sisters in Christ.

What are some specific tasks a new convert can do without being asked to do too much too soon, or being overwhelmed with ministry tasks that require more maturity than a new convert has?

Visual 12 is a photo of the ruins of the Agora (AG-uh-ruh) in Philippi, where Paul and Silas were haled before the city magistrates.

WHAT DO YOU THINK?

In the midst of cruel and unjust treatment Paul and Silas prayed and praised God. We who are Christians also face adversity at times. Do we differ from our non-Christian neighbors in the way we handle unpleasant experiences? Or do we complain just as bitterly as they and strike back just as viciously at those who have wronged us? Our testimony for Christ demands that we respond to adversity with patience, steadfastness, and even praise. Hebrews 13:15 urges us to "continually offer to God a sacrifice of praise." Praise and thanksgiving represent worthy sacrifices to God when they are offered on occasions in which we are tempted instead to complain.

How can we develop a faith that can praise God even in the tough times? How can we encourage one another in this regard?

Impelled by the demon, the girl followed the missionaries day by day shouting, "These men are servants of the Most High God, who are telling you the way to be saved" (v. 17).

Paul was grieved, probably both because the girl was mistreated and because God's servants do not want the support of demons. In the name of Jesus, Paul ordered the demon to go away and leave the girl alone.

Owners of the girl were furious. Now they had an ordinary slave instead of a high-priced fortune-teller. They dragged Paul and Silas to the marketplace, where judges were sitting to decide whatever cases were brought to them.

Instead of voicing their real complaint, the accusers appealed to racial prejudice. They said these Jews were teaching customs that were not legal for Romans. Without waiting for evidence, the crowd raised a great cry against Paul and Silas.

Roman authorities liked to prevent rioting at all costs. These judges appeased the crowd by having Paul and Silas stripped, beaten, and put in jail. So these innocent men were sitting in the maximum security cell with their feet locked in the stocks. All this is told in verses 16-24, which are not included in our text.

A. BIG EARTHQUAKE (vv. 25, 26)

25. About midnight Paul and Silas were praying and singing hymns to God, and the other prisoners were listening to them.

At *midnight* there must have been utter darkness in the inner prison, but Paul and Silas were not sleeping. They could not lie down comfortably because their backs were bruised and bloody from their beating. They could not sit comfortably because their feet were locked in the stocks. So they *were praying and singing hymns to God.* Other *prisoners* were awake, too, and probably they were surprised to hear prayers and praises instead of curses.

PRAISING GOD IN STRANGE PLACES

Most people would not expect to find a church in the trailer of an eighteen-wheel "big rig," but Ken Taylor operates a permanent chapel at a truck stop in Southern California. He drove the open road for thirty years and knows how to speak to the spiritual needs of truckers.

Several ministries to professional drivers have "truck-stop churches" located across the United States and Canada. Drivers who have tired of the irreverent chatter coming over their CB radios, or who are looking for strength to resist the temptations that loneliness brings, find in such chapels a haven where they can praise God and seek his guidance.

Praising God can bring positive change to even the worst of situations. It was so in the prison in Philippi. Jail would seem to be a strange place to praise God, but that is where Paul and Silas were doing it! Even though they were unfairly imprisoned, they gave glory to God. Their praise not only raised their own spirits, but it also had a profound impact on at least one other man and his entire household. Praising God can change lives—our own and others'.   —C. R. B.

26. Suddenly there was such a violent earthquake that the foundations of the prison were shaken. At once all the prison doors flew open, and everybody's chains came loose.

This was no tiny tremor; it was *a violent earthquake.* It was strong enough to shake *the foundations of the prison,* but it was a divinely directed quake. Instead of shaking down stone walls, it opened locked *doors.* It unlocked the stocks from the feet of Paul and Silas and unfastened whatever *chains* and fetters were restraining other prisoners.

B. NARROW ESCAPE (vv. 27, 28)

27. The jailer woke up, and when he saw the prison doors open, he drew his sword and was about to kill himself because he thought the prisoners had escaped.

Apparently the *jailer* had an office in the prison and was sleeping there. Awakened by an earthquake, he collected his senses and looked around. It must have been shocking to see the open doors. Death was the routine punishment for a guard who let prisoners escape, and this guard preferred suicide to execution. Without waiting to be sure the prisoners were gone, he drew his sword to *kill himself.*

28. But Paul shouted, "Don't harm yourself! We are all here!"

How did Paul know what the jailer was doing? Perhaps the Holy Spirit revealed it to him; or perhaps there was a lamp in the office, and Paul could see through the open doors. In either case, his shout brought a narrow escape to a jailer on the verge of death.

C. IMPORTANT QUESTION (vv. 29, 30)

29. The jailer called for lights, rushed in and fell trembling before Paul and Silas.

If there was a lamp in the office, apparently it was not suitable for carrying. But the jailer had helpers nearby. At his call they quickly brought a torch or lantern. He *rushed* into the dungeon. Why did he go to Paul and Silas rather than the other prisoners? It seems plain that he knew enough about these two to convince him that they were somehow allied with the power that sent the earthquake. In reverent awe he *fell* down before them. He was *trembling* with fear of the supernatural, and perhaps also because he was unnerved by his narrow escape from death.

30. He then brought them out and asked, "Sirs, what must I do to be saved?"

The jailer did not remain prostrate for long. Probably Paul and Silas told him they were only men and were not to be worshiped. So he rose and *brought them out* of the dungeon. Where did he take them then? We are not told; but as soon as he brought them to a suitable place he asked the question that was on his mind.

What must I do to be saved? What did this pagan mean by that? He was already saved from the earthquake and from suicide, so he was not asking about those. He must have been thinking of the kind of salvation Paul and Silas preached about. This indicates that he already knew something about these men. Perhaps he knew a fortune-teller had said they taught the way of salvation (vv. 16, 17). Maybe he had been told about their preaching, or even had heard them preach. Surely he was not yet fully informed about salvation, but he wanted to know how to get it.

D. IMPORTANT ANSWER (vv. 31, 32)

31. They replied, "Believe in the Lord Jesus, and you will be saved—you and your household."

The preachers gave a short answer that needed a long explanation. See verse 32.

32. Then they spoke the word of the Lord to him and to all the others in his house.

The earthquake came at midnight (vv. 25, 26). Most of the remaining hours of the night may have been used in presenting *the word of the Lord* to the jailer and his family and servants.

E. PROMPT OBEDIENCE (vv. 33, 34)

33. At that hour of the night the jailer took them and washed their wounds; then immediately he and all his family were baptized.

Ashamed of his part in mistreating these men, the jailer did what he could to make amends. He gave a simple treatment to the backs that had been injured by a brutal beating (vv. 22, 23). Now that he and his *family* had heard the gospel and believed it, they were *immediately . . . baptized.*

WHAT DO YOU THINK?

If an unbeliever were to ask us, "What must I do to be saved?" would we be able to provide the necessary information? Or would we say, "Why don't you talk to my preacher or to one of the elders in my church?" What if the preacher and the elders are not available at the particular moment when one who is seeking this information is in the best frame of mind to receive an answer to the question. Or what if the individual is not comfortable discussing his or her spiritual needs with someone other than us? How can each Christian be always ready to give an answer (1 Peter 3:15)?

PRAYER

Our Father, all around us we see people who need Jesus. Help us to get their attention, convince them with the message of salvation, baptize them in the name of Jesus, and teach them to do all he has commanded. In Jesus' name. Amen.

THOUGHT TO REMEMBER

People need Jesus.

DAILY BIBLE READINGS

Monday, Nov. 13—Solving a Mother's Need (Exodus 2:1-10).

Tuesday, Nov. 14—God's Response to His People's Cry (Exodus 3:1-8)

Wednesday, Nov. 15—Caring for a Fellow Traveler (Luke 10:25-37)

Thursday, Nov. 16—The Spirit's Response to Our Cry (Romans 8:12-17)

Friday, Nov. 17—Timothy Enlisted as a Helper (Acts 16:1-8)

Saturday, Nov. 18—Arrested for Helping a Slave Girl (Acts 16:16-24)

Sunday, Nov. 19—Released for Continued Ministry (Acts 16:35-40)

34. The jailer brought them into his house and set a meal before them; he was filled with joy because he had come to believe in God—he and his whole family.

When the baptisms were completed, it was time for a happy breakfast together. Preachers and converts rejoiced because the *jailer* and his *family* had been turned "from darkness to light, and from the power of Satan unto God" (Acts 26:18)—and there was joy in Heaven, too (Luke 15:7).

MEETING CHRIST IN PRISON

On June 17, 1972, five men were arrested for breaking into the headquarters of the Democratic National Committee in a Washington, D.C., office building. By mid-summer of 1973, what had appeared at first to be a simple burglary had become the Watergate scandal.

Charles Colson was one of the presidential aides who went to prison for his complicity in the Watergate affair. In prison he met Jesus Christ, and Colson's life was turned around. He has since become a highly respected Christian spokesman. He has written several Christian books, is a regular columnist in a major Christian magazine, and is the founder of a Christian ministry to people in prison.

Centuries earlier in Philippi, another prison ministry was conducted. Two innocent men had been imprisoned, but their demeanor in the prison that night was so unusual, so amazing in light of the circumstances, that the jailer was moved to inquire about his own salvation. That very night, through the assistance of Paul and Silas, the jailer met Jesus. Since we never know what circumstances may incline a person's heart to the gospel of Christ, we should always be ready to share the message whenever the opportunity presents itself.   —C. R. B.

CONCLUSION

In two sections of our text we see two very different people who became Christians. One was a wealthy and cultured lady who believed in God. The other was a jailer who seemed heartless and unfeeling. There is no indication that he believed either in God or in the mythical deities of the pagan.

Our world likewise has different kinds of people, but they all need Jesus. Our task is to bring all of them to him. Let's note how that was done in Philippi.

A. GETTING ATTENTION

It was easy to get Lydia's attention. She was glad to hear the gospel. There are many like her in the world about us, but they do not come looking for us. We have to go to them.

It was harder, from a human perspective, to get the jailer's attention, but not for the Lord. After the earthquake the jailer was very attentive. With no earthquake to help us, we need to think about how to get the attention of uncaring unbelievers.

B. GIVING THE MESSAGE

When people are listening, the same message applies to each of them. All have sinned, and salvation is offered to all. There is no salvation except through Jesus.

C. OBEDIENCE

Lydia and the jailer heard the same message, and both responded with prompt obedience. First they were baptized. Then they showed their allegiance to their new Master by ministering to the needs of his servants.

D. JOY

In any time and place, there is joy in turning "from darkness to light, and from the power of Satan to God" (Acts 26:18).

Discovery Learning

This page contains an alternate lesson plan emphasizing learning activities. Classes desiring such student involvement will find these suggestions helpful. The next page is a reproducible activity page to further enhance discovery learning.

LEARNING GOALS

As students participate in today's session, they should:

1. Describe how the gospel first spread to Europe and some of the immediate results.

2. Tell how different individuals have responded to gospel teaching.

3. Identify individuals or groups they or their church are uniquely positioned to reach with the gospel.

INTO THE LESSON

Ask your class members to pair off, and have each pair complete one of the following incomplete sentences:

1. "The person who first told me about Christ was…."

2. "The last time I talked with someone else about the gospel was…."

3. "I became a Christian because…."

4. "The main reason people become Christians is…."

Allow a few class members to share their sentences with the whole class; then tell your group that today we will study some dramatic conversions to Christ that occurred on one of Paul's missionary trips.

INTO THE WORD

Write the three major headings of the lesson outline on your chalkboard:

    I. Answering a Call

    II. Converting a Lady

    III. Converting a Jailer

To consider the first point, ask a volunteer to read Acts 16:6-10 aloud while the class listens to hear what the Spirit *wanted* Paul to do, and what the Spirit *did not want* Paul to do. Then discuss. Refer to maps in your classroom or reproduce the map on page 112 to locate the places mentioned in this text. Do the same as you read verses 11 and 12 aloud. Observe that this is the first record of the gospel's being preached in Europe. Apparently God wanted the gospel taken into Europe at this particular time even though there were still many in Asia who had not yet heard the word. Discuss why this might have been. Possible ideas include people (i.e. Lydia and the jailer) who were receptive; available messengers were still in Asia, but Paul and his company were uniquely positioned to take the gospel into Europe.

Now consider points II and III together. Have one class member read verses 13-15 aloud followed by another class member's reading verses 25-34 aloud. As the two

read, the rest of the class should listen for *similarities* and *differences* in these two conversion accounts. (Summarize verses 16-24 so class members will understand why Paul and Silas were in prison.)

Divide the class into groups of from three to seven. Each group should list the similarities and differences in the accounts. If you wish you may give these study groups the following questions to get them started.

1. How many heard the message?

2. How many responded?

3. What prompted them to respond?

4. How did they respond?

After six minutes, ask the groups to share their findings. As they do, list the similarities and differences.

Discuss this with your class: "If Acts 16:13-34 were the only passage in the Bible available for your study, what could you learn about…

(a) … how to share the gospel message?"

(b) … how to become a Christian?"

(c) … what it means to a person to become a Christian?"

INTO LIFE

Before class, type the following two quotes on cards, one quote per card.

Give the cards to two different class members. Ask each card holder to read his or her quote aloud. After each is read, let the class members comment, basing their comments on today's Bible text. (Appropriate references are provided after each quote for the teacher's convenience.)

• "I don't understand why things are going so badly for me. I was certain that I was doing God's will, but in the last month, all I've had is trouble. I'm tempted to give up on Christ and the church." (vv. 19-25)

• The church people I know are sour, sullen, and out-of-touch. Why would anyone want to become a Christian anyway? Aren't a good salary, a decent home, and healthy family enough to bring anyone happiness?" (v. 34).

Have the students reassemble in the groups in which they did their Bible study earlier. Give each group a copy of one of the quotes and ask them to discuss it. Observe that each of us individually, and our church as a whole, are uniquely positioned to take the gospel to some particular person or group.

Conclude your class with guided prayer on the theme, "God, help me to understand where and with whom you want *me* to share the gospel message."

A Gospel for the Whole World

Trace the journey of Paul and Silas on the map below. Locate each of the cities or regions below, and note at least one significant event that happened in each.

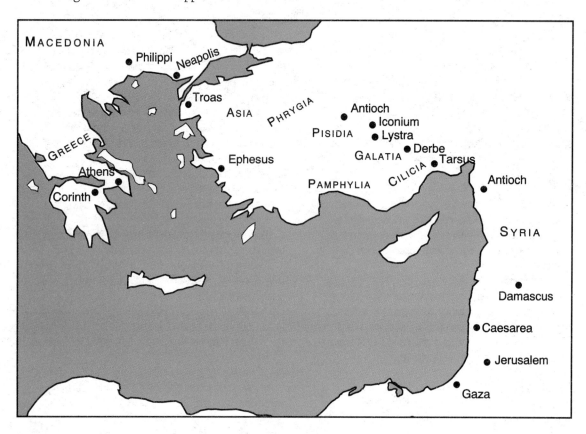

Antioch _____

Syria _____

Cilicia _____

Derbe _____

Lystra _____

Phrygia _____

Galatia _____

Troas _____

Neapolis _____

Philippi _____

The Story of Christian Beginnings

Unit 3. Spreading the Gospel Into All the World
(Lessons 10-13)

THE POWER
OF THE GOSPEL

LESSON 13

WHY TEACH THIS LESSON?

This lesson is the conclusion to our study of Acts. Here we note the conclusion of Paul's second missionary journey and his launching the third. In all of it, we see the power of God at work—the power of the gospel.

This lesson, like the ones before it, are intended to display God's power. Different human beings are highlighted as they carry that powerful gospel, but it is the same God.

Remind your students of that fact. Remind them, too, that the same God continues to be at work in that same gospel. Challenge them to be ones whom God uses today in this life-giving work.

INTRODUCTION

Last week in our lesson we read that Paul and Silas were midnight prisoners in Philippi; but before morning an earthquake opened the prison, and the jailer became a Christian. City officials then were eager to get those preachers out of their jail and out of their town. After their release Paul and Silas and Timothy moved on; but Luke stayed, probably to continue teaching the new Christians.

A. PAUL'S SECOND MISSIONARY JOURNEY

That was early in Paul's second missionary journey. Philippi was his first stop on the European continent. From there he went on to other cities of Macedonia. Souls were won in each place, but unbelieving Jews became so hostile that Paul soon moved on.

From Macedonia he went south to Greece. He taught in Athens for a while, and then spent about two years in Corinth. After that he was ready to bring his second journey to its close.

Paul's friends Aquila and Priscilla went with him from Corinth to Ephesus. They were tentmakers with whom Paul had worked in Corinth. The two of them stayed in Ephesus while Paul went on to attend a Jewish feast in Jerusalem and to visit Antioch before starting his third journey. All this is told in Acts 16:35—18:23.

B. LESSON BACKGROUND

Before Paul came again to Ephesus, another traveling Jewish teacher arrived. He was Apollos, from Alexandria in Egypt. He was well versed in the Scriptures, enthusiastic, and eloquent. Like Paul, he taught about Jesus; but unlike Paul, he did not understand Christian baptism. He taught baptism as it was taught by Jesus' forerunner, John the Baptist.

Priscilla and Aquila quickly saw the defect in his teaching. They did not oppose him in the synagogue, but took him home with them and "explained to him the way of God more adequately." When he went on to Corinth, he was a better preacher than he had been before (Acts 18:24-28).

DEVOTIONAL READING
ACTS 18:18-28

LESSON SCRIPTURE
ACTS 18:18—19:41

PRINTED TEXT
ACTS 19:1-6, 11-20

LESSON AIMS

After the study of this lesson a student should be able to :

1. Tell how the power of the gospel was demonstrated during Paul's ministry in Ephesus.

2. Compare changes made in Ephesus with changes that have been observed in modern experience—and with changes that need yet to be made.

3. Commit themselves to sharing the gospel with the lost so those persons may experience its life-changing power.

KEY VERSE

The word of the Lord spread widely and grew in power.   —Acts 19:20

Nov
26

LESSON 13 NOTES

Visual 13 is a map that you will find useful for tracing Paul's movements through this lesson.

OPTION

There is a reproducible map on page 112. (Perhaps you used it in lesson 12.) Make copies for your students to follow the events of this lesson.

HOW TO SAY IT

Alexandria. Al-ex-AN-dree-uh.
Apollos. Uh-POL-us.
Aquila. ACK-wih-luh.
Artemis. AR-teh-miss
Denarius. dih-NAIR-ee-us.
Drachma. DRAK-ma.
Ephesus. EF-eh-sus.
Macedonia. Mass-eh-DOE-nee-uh.
Philippi. Fih-LIP-pie or FIL-ih-pie.
Priscilla. Prih-SIL-uh.
Sceva. SEE-vuh.

I. TEACHING NEW DISCIPLES (ACTS 19:1-6)

Meanwhile, Paul was starting his third missionary journey. First the apostle went again to visit the churches he had started on his first journey (Acts 18:23). Then he continued on westward into the province of Asia. On the second journey the Holy Spirit had told him not to preach there (Acts 16:6), but now the time had come.

A. REVEALING QUESTION (vv. 1, 2)

1a. While Apollos was at Corinth, Paul took the road through the interior and arrived at Ephesus.

Paul traveled westward through the high country in the province of Asia and came to the seacoast at *Ephesus,* the principal city of Asia. *Apollos* by then had left Ephesus and was at *Corinth.*

1b, 2. There he found some disciples and asked them, "Did you receive the Holy Spirit when you believed?" They answered, "No, we have not even heard that there is a Holy Spirit."

Disciples here means Christians, disciples of Jesus. In Ephesus Paul found some of them who were strangers to him. He asked a question that would help him know how much they had been taught. Had they received the Holy Spirit? No, these disciples had not even heard that there was a Holy Spirit.

B. TWO BAPTISMS (vv. 3-5)

3. So Paul asked, "Then what baptism did you receive?" "John's baptism," they replied.

Again Paul asked a question that would help him understand what these disciples had been taught. Most disciples of Jesus were baptized "in the name of the Father and of the Son and of the Holy Spirit" (Matthew 28:19). If these disciples had never heard of the Holy Spirit, what kind of baptism was theirs?

The disciples answered easily. They had been baptized with the kind of baptism John the Baptist taught. That was the only baptism Apollos knew when he came to Ephesus (Acts 18:25). Therefore we suppose these disciples were some that Apollos led to Christ before Priscilla and Aquila taught him more about baptism. After learning from Priscilla and Aquila, Apollos went on to Corinth without giving the added knowledge to all those whom he had converted.

4. Paul said, "John's baptism was a baptism of repentance. He told the people to believe in the one coming after him, that is, in Jesus."

Now Paul had the opportunity to explain to these disciples what was lacking in their teaching. John baptized people who repented of their sins. So do Christian teachers now. John told them to believe in a Redeemer who was yet to come. Christian teachers tell people to believe in a Redeemer who has already come and has given his life to redeem them. Repentant believers now are baptized into Christ (Galatians 3:27) and into his death (Romans 6:3). In him they are members of his body (1 Corinthians 12:27). This involves much more than John's baptism did.

5. On hearing this, they were baptized into the name of the Lord Jesus.

We need not suppose all this was done in a few minutes. Perhaps Paul talked with these disciples several times, explaining how Christian baptism is different from the baptism John taught. Perhaps they saw some of his miracles (vv. 11, 12), and were convinced that he was truly God's messenger. The outcome was that *they were baptized* again, this time *into the name of the Lord Jesus.*

C. POWER OF THE HOLY SPIRIT (v. 6)

6. When Paul placed his hands on them, the Holy Spirit came on them, and they spoke in tongues and prophesied.

About twelve men were in this group of disciples (v. 7). Some or all of them were given certain miraculous powers, not when they were baptized, but *when Paul placed his hands on them*. It seems that the apostles imparted such powers to selected Christians in this way.

To prophesy is to receive messages directly from God and to pass them on to people on earth. In the early days of the church, it was very helpful to have some prophets in a congregation. They brought divine guidance when as yet there was no New Testament for a guide.

Speaking in tongues is described in Acts 2:1-11. The apostles spoke in languages that they themselves did not know, but people in the audience did. This served two purposes. First, it enabled people to hear the message in their native languages. Second, it was a sign that the speakers were inspired by the Holy Spirit. We do not know whether the disciples in Ephesus were from different countries or not. If not, speaking in tongues still served to show the inspiration of the Holy Spirit.

II. MIRACLES DONE AND ATTEMPTED (ACTS 19:11-14)

Paul taught in the synagogue in Ephesus till the opposition of unbelievers became vigorous. Then he found a schoolroom or "lecture hall," where he kept on teaching for two years. Many people of the province of Asia came to Ephesus on business or on vacations. It seems that some of them listened to Paul and carried his message back home, "so that all the Jews and Greeks who lived in the province of Asia heard the word of the Lord" (vv. 8-10). Our text goes on with what happened in Ephesus.

A. MIRACLES DONE (vv. 11, 12)
11. God did extraordinary miracles through Paul.

God did the miracles, but he did them *through Paul* so people could know Paul was God's man. Then they would believe that the message Paul brought was God's message.

12. So that even handkerchiefs and aprons that had touched him were taken to the sick, and their illnesses were cured and the evil spirits left them.

It was not necessary for Paul to touch or even see the sick and demon-possessed. Bits of cloth that Paul had touched were all that was needed to heal the sick and drive out demons.

B. MIRACLES ATTEMPTED (vv. 13, 14)
13. Some Jews who went around driving out evil spirits tried to invoke the name of the Lord Jesus over those who were demon-possessed. They would say, "In the name of Jesus, whom Paul preaches, I command you to come out."

The Jewish historian Josephus tells of an exorcist named Eleazar. By means of a certain kind of root said to be prescribed by Solomon, along with incantations said to be composed by Solomon, this man claimed to draw a demon out through the nose of an afflicted man. Similar methods may have been used by other Jewish exorcists.

Not all of Paul's miracles were done through handkerchiefs and aprons, as told in verse 12. Sometimes Paul was with someone possessed with a demon. By the authority of Jesus, he ordered the demon to leave. Seeing how effective this was, the exorcists thought Paul had a better incantation than they had. So they tried to use that better incantation.

Luke tells us of these exorcists without commenting on the source or validity of their skill. It says they were *driving out evil spirits,* so they must have been successful

OPTION

The imaginative activity on the reproducible page 120 will provide an interesting review and visual demonstration of how the power of the gospel spread from person to person and place to place in the early days of the church.

WHAT DO YOU THINK?

The Jewish exorcists attempted to counterfeit the power of the gospel. In what ways do people today offer a counterfeit gospel, a gospel that is attractive but which lacks any true power? How can the church guard against such a counterfeit gospel?

What Do You Think?

As a result of the preaching of the gospel and the miracles attendant to it, "the name of the Lord Jesus was held in high honor" in Ephesus (Acts 19:17). Do you think his name is held in high honor in your community? Why or why not? What would happen to your worship services if the issue of holding the name of Jesus in "high honor" were kept primary? What changes, if any, do you think would be made? What changes would be made in the lives of individual Christians if this were their primary aim in life? What can you do this week to give "high honor" to the name of Jesus?

Note (v. 16)

The word translated all is usually rendered both, so that reading is seen in some English versions. Some students therefore conclude that only two of Sceva's seven sons were involved in this incident. However, the Greek word is undoubtedly used for more than two in some contexts. In Acts 23:8, for example, the word is clearly used of three.

at least part of the time. If they were successful all or even most of the time, it would be surprising indeed that they would change their practice to imitate Paul. That they *went around* plying their trade makes us wonder if they didn't stay in an area only long enough to be exposed as mostly fraudulent; then they had to hurry on to the next town.

14. Seven sons of Sceva, a Jewish chief priest, were doing this.

We are not told whether these seven were or were not the only ones who tried to use Paul's incantation, but these have special mention because of the startling result of their effort.

III. TRIUMPH OF TRUTH (ACTS 19:15-20)

These vagabond exorcists were not apostles of Christ. They were not even Christians. If they could do the same miracles Paul did, then Paul's miracles would not show that he was God's spokesman. But Sceva's sons soon learned that they could not do what Paul was doing.

A. Disaster to Fakers (vv. 15, 16)

15. [One day] the evil spirit answered them, "Jesus I know, and I know about Paul, but who are you?"

The demon knew he had to obey Jesus, and he knew Paul was Jesus' authorized apostle. But the words Paul spoke had no power when they were spoken by an unauthorized person. Power over demons was not in the words, but in Jesus.

16. Then the man who had the evil spirit jumped on them and overpowered them all. He gave them such a beating that they ran out of the house naked and bleeding.

In last week's lesson we read of a demon who gave a girl such superhuman knowledge that she became a fortune-teller (Acts 16:16). Now we are reading of a demon who gave a man such superhuman strength that he was able to attack all seven of the would-be exorcists at once. In the melee that followed, he tore off their clothes and beat them so badly *that they ran out of the house naked and bleeding.*

B. Honor to Jesus (vv. 17, 18)

17. When this became known to the Jews and Greeks living in Ephesus, they were all seized with fear, and the name of the Lord Jesus was held in high honor.

News spread swiftly from person to person, especially the spectacular story of seven naked exorcists streaking through the streets. Already the city was buzzing with news of the miracles God did through Paul. Now the buzzing was doubled by added information. Spoken by Paul, the name of Jesus brought healing to the sick and put demons to flight. Spoken by traveling exorcists, the same name brought a beating to the speakers. That was awesome. Reverent fear fell on those who heard about it. One who wanted to speak against Jesus would hardly dare do it, and most were eager to speak in favor of him. So his name *was held in high honor.*

18. Many of those who believed now came and openly confessed their evil deeds.

God's miraculous power working through Paul, coupled with the disaster to Sceva's sons, convinced many people that Paul was telling the truth: that Jesus is indeed the Son of God and the Savior of people on earth. Day after day believers were coming to Paul and other Christians to tell of their faith and to tell also of the wrongs they had done but now intended to do no more.

C. From Darkness to Light (vv. 19, 20)

19. A number who had practiced sorcery brought their scrolls together and burned them publicly. When they calculated the value of the scrolls, the total came to fifty thousand drachmas.

Sorcery seems to be a general term for various kinds of occult divination and magic. Perhaps it includes the exorcisms practiced by the likes of the sons of Sceva. Christians turned away from these superstitious and deceitful practices. *Their scrolls* were scrolls of papyrus or parchment with instructions about those practices. Instead of selling the costly scrolls to get their money back, the Christians made a public bonfire of them. Thus they testified that they were renouncing all forms of pagan magic as they embraced the Christian faith. Someone interested in statistics added up the cost of the books that were burned: *fifty thousand drachmas.* The value of a Greek drachma was about the same as that of a Roman denarius. In Jesus' parable in Matthew 20:1-16, a denarius appears as a day's pay for a working man. We see that a man would have to work seven days a week for nearly 137 years to earn the price of all those books!

WHAT SHALL WE DO WITH THE PAST?

Some people idealize the past, trying to live in it. An unusual form of this regard for a past era came to light a couple of years ago. At the time a French "performance artist" named Orlan had undergone the fifth of seven cosmetic surgeries scheduled over a four-year period. She called it "art by personal body transformation." Orlan's goal was to change her face and body so that she would be a reincarnation of Renaissance ideals of feminine beauty.

There are other ways to live in the past. Most of us know of people who continue to live in their own past, burdened with guilt for a sin they committed (or some good deed they left undone). We may know others who refuse to change attitudes or actions that have caused trouble for them and their families for years.

The sorcerers and magicians in Ephesus who became Christians set a good example for us all. In public they destroyed the instruction manuals for the occult practices by which they had made their living. It was a forceful demonstration that they had turned from the past, and were committing themselves to a new way of life in Christ.

In coming to Christ, one should turn from all that was evil or destructive in his or her past. And by making a public commitment to Christ, one places positive moral pressure on oneself to follow through with his or her commitment to Christ.

—C. R. B.

20. In this way the word of the Lord spread widely and grew in power.

The books of magic were worthless, but *the word of the Lord* is of eternal worth. The gospel Paul preached was and is "the power of God for … salvation" (Romans 1:16). In Ephesus that word was growing more influential and effective as it was turning souls from darkness to light and from the power of Satan to God (Acts 26:18). The defeat of Sceva's sons helped it grow, and so did the public bonfire of books. Christians sacrificed fifty thousand drachma, but they gained "an inheritance that can never perish, spoil or fade" (1 Peter 1:4).

The rest of chapter 19 in Acts brings further evidence of the growth of the word of God in Ephesus. That word turned many of the Ephesians to the real God, and those who made money from false religions were alarmed. They aroused a mob to chant the praises of Artemis, favorite goddess of the pagan city. But their demonstration proved to be as powerless as their goddess. When they had yelled themselves hoarse, the town clerk dismissed the assembly—and the word of God kept on growing.

CONCLUSION

"The Power of the Gospel"! That is our lesson title, and it is a good one. The gospel, the good news of salvation in Jesus Christ, was at work in Ephesus. It was

---

WHAT DO YOU THINK?

The believers' destruction of occult literature in Ephesus raises the question of what we should do with spiritually or morally damaging literature that has come into our possession. Many Christians are wary of the idea of book-burning. Nevertheless, the example of the believers in Ephesus reminds us that immoral, anti-Christian books or magazines have no place in our homes. What would be a Christ-honoring way of purging such material from our homes and lives?

WHAT DO YOU THINK?

By burning their books of sorcery, the Ephesian converts openly declared that the way of Jesus was far superior to their former lifestyle. What are some practical ways we can declare that the life Jesus offers is a better, happier life than that offered by the world?

PRAYER

How good it is to know that boundless power belongs to you, our Father! Considering the various abilities that you have given to us, we give you our heartfelt thanks. As we try to use your gifts for your glory, we look to you for guidance as well as for power. In Jesus' name. Amen.

THOUGHT TO REMEMBER

*To the work! To the work! We
are servants of God,*

*Let us follow the path that our
Master has trod;*

*With the balm of his counsel
our strength to renew,*

*Let us do with our might what
our hands find to do.*

—*Fanny J. Crosby*

WHAT DO YOU THINK?

*The lesson writer uses the
building of a house to illustrate
what is involved in building the
church of the Lord Jesus. How
might each of the following facts
about building a house be compared to building the church?*

*• A house must rest on a foun-
dation.*

*• A house is constructed ac-
cording to a plan.*

• Building a house is expensive.

*• The construction of a house
brings together the skills of many
workers with differing skills.*

DAILY BIBLE READINGS

*Monday, Nov. 20—Leader of
Synagogue Converted (Acts 18:
1-11)*

*Tuesday, Nov. 21—Apollos
Strengthens Believers (Acts 18:
24-28)*

*Wednesday, Nov. 22—Idolatry
Threatened by the Gospel (Acts
19:21-34)*

*Thursday, Nov. 23—Order
Restored by Clerk's Logic (Acts
19:35-41)*

*Friday, Nov. 24—Paul's
Thanksgiving and Confidence
(Romans 1:8-17)*

*Saturday, Nov. 25—The
Spirit's Power in Christ (Luke
4:14-21)*

*Sunday, Nov. 26—Power to
Give Eternal Life (John 17:1-5)*

working powerfully, turning people from darkness to light, and from the power of
Satan to God.

Yet we must remember that the gospel is God's power (Romans 1:16). God was
at work in the gospel, transforming lives, saving souls, building the church. We can
give the gospel all the credit it deserves without taking any credit away from God.

In the first part of our text, we read that the Holy Spirit gave to some Christians
the miraculous power to speak with tongues and to prophesy—and the Holy Spirit
is God. In the middle of our text we read that the name of Jesus defeated diseases
and demons—and Jesus is God. In the end of our text we read that the word was
growing and prevailing—and it was God's word.

A. GOD AND HIS SON AND HIS SPIRIT

There is only one God. There are three divine beings, the Father, Son, and Holy
Spirit; but in some way the three are one. This may be too much for us to understand, but it is not too much for us to believe.

The Son is the one who became man and gave his life for us. That seems plain
enough. The Spirit is the one who lives in us if we are Christians. That seems plain
enough too—or is it? When the Spirit comes to live with us, the Father and Son
come too (John 14:23).

Perhaps we can never explain exactly how the three are one even while they are
three, nor do we need an explanation. We can be sure they are one in will and purpose. We cannot please one of them without pleasing all of them; we cannot grieve
one of them without grieving all of them; we cannot serve one of them without
serving all of them. Let us take care to serve and please them, and never to grieve
them.

B. GOD'S POWER AND OUR TASK

Trying to give God's gospel to a dying world, we find many people who are un-
interested and some who are hostile. If only we could heal the sick as Paul did!
Then people would listen. God is no respecter of persons. Perhaps a simple illustration will help us understand.

When we plan to build a house, we take our plans to the proper authorities and
get a building permit. That authorizes us to build the whole house. When the
foundation is laid, we do not need another permit for the walls; when the walls are
erected, we do not need another permit for the roof.

"I will build my church," said Jesus (Matthew 16:18); but he is building it
through the efforts of his people on earth. As the building began, he gave some of
those people his own miraculous power. Like a permit displayed at a building site,
that power told everyone that the builders were authorized. As we continue to
build according to the original plan, it is not necessary for every worker to display
the same evidence of authority. Our task is to be sure we build according to the
plan.

If we fail to follow the plan, if we put a wall where there is no foundation, if we
substitute wood or straw where stone is called for, we can be sure the building in-
spector will know (1 Corinthians 3:11-15).

The divine plan is in the New Testament. Let us follow it. Instead of pleading for
power God has not given us, let us use the abilities he has given, and use them
with the same earnestness and tireless persistence that Paul displayed.

God's power is winning souls and building the church. But in that task God's
power is powerless unless we use it. We depend on him for power; he depends on
us to make it effective. If we fail in our task, he must look for other workers—but
remember what happens to salt that loses its flavor (Matthew 5:13).

Discovery Learning

This page contains an alternate lesson plan emphasizing learning activities. Classes desiring such student involvement will find these suggestions helpful. The next page is a reproducible activity page to further enhance discovery learning.

LEARNING GOALS

After this session, students should:

1. Tell how the power of the gospel was demonstrated during Paul's ministry in Ephesus.

2. Compare changes made in Ephesus with changes that have been observed in modern experience—and with changes that need yet to be made.

3. Commit to sharing the gospel with the lost so those persons may experience its life-changing power.

INTO THE LESSON

Write this question on your chalkboard before pupils arrive: "How do we feel about *power?*" Distribute newspapers and magazines, and ask your students to find advertisements or articles that suggest answers to the question. After several minutes let volunteers show what they have chosen and tell how their examples answer the question.

Option. Instead of this activity, or after it, conduct two sixty-second brainstorming sessions. First, have class members mention everything they can think of that is *good* about power. Second, have them mention everything they can think of that is *bad* about power. Then ask, "Well, which is it? Is power good or bad?" Discuss.

Observe that today's lesson looks at good power, the power of God manifested in connection with the preaching of the gospel in the days of the church's infancy.

INTO THE WORD

To connect this lesson's text with that of last week's lesson, deliver a brief lecture based on the information given in the "Introduction" section. After that, your students will be prepared to examine today's Scripture text. Tell them that in this session we will consider Acts 19:1-20 to discover how the power of the gospel was demonstrated in the ancient city of Ephesus.

Divide your class into groups of from three to seven students each. In their groups they are to divide the text into four sections and consider each section separately. The four sections are as follows: verses 1-7; 8-10; 11, 12; and 13-20. For each of these sections, group members should answer these questions:

1. How was the power of the gospel demonstrated?

2. Why was the power needed?

3. What did the power accomplish?

Allot ten to fifteen minutes for group study. Then let the groups share their conclusions and discuss as a class.

OPTION

Give each student a sheet of paper on which you have written the three questions above (leave plenty of blank space after each question for answers). Or write the questions on the chalkboard and give each student a sheet of blank paper. Read the whole text three times, pausing after each of the incidents recorded (after verses 7, 10, 12, and 20). For each section of the text, class members should write down answers to the first question after the first reading, to the second question after the second reading, and to the third question after the third reading.

Then discuss the following questions:

1. How are John's baptism and Christian baptism the same? How are they different?

2. Why did the seven sons of Sceva want to drive out demons? Why were they unable to do so in the incident recorded in our text?

3. How did the failure of the sons of Sceva affect the community? The church?

INTO LIFE

Divide the class into groups of two or three, and ask them to answer these questions:

1. Which example of the power of the gospel in this text strikes you as most remarkable? Why?

2. Why were the Jews and Greeks in Ephesus afraid after the incident with the evil spirit (vv. 15-17)? Why might some people today fear the gospel?

3. Which of the following quotes comes closest to representing how this passage makes you feel?

- "When I see how God's power was manifested in New Testament times, I feel dissatisfied. I wish I could see his power unleashed in the same way today."
- "This lesson reminds me that the gospel is the only power that can truly change lives today. I'm thankful for the changes the gospel is making in our world."
- "I'm reminded of my own need for the gospel's power to rid my life of sin and set me on a productive course."

In the discussion, be sure it is noted that the power of God through the gospel is still "the power of God for the salvation of everyone who believes" (Romans 1:16). While God's power may be expressed in different ways today, it still changes lives and provides eternal salvation. Discuss how your class can work together to share the gospel with someone, or a group of people, who need the power of the gospel to be brought into their lives.

The Power of the Gospel

Look up each Scripture reference and fill in the blanks, usually with a place name to show how the power of the gospel reaches out to change lives and make a difference. (Not every city on Paul's journeys is mentioned.)

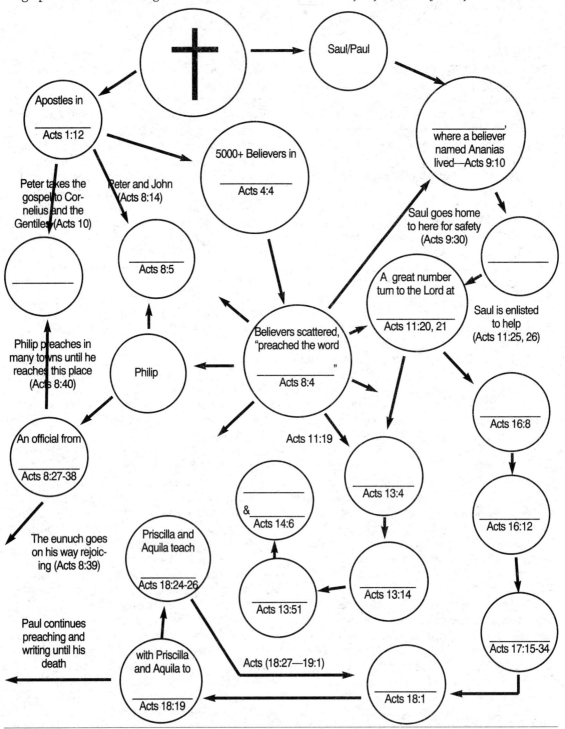

Saul/Paul

Apostles in
_____
Acts 1:12

_____,
where a believer named Ananias lived—Acts 9:10

5000+ Believers in
_____
Acts 4:4

Peter takes the gospel to Cornelius and the Gentiles (Acts 10)

Peter and John (Acts 8:14)

Saul goes home to here for safety (Acts 9:30)

_____
Acts 8:5

_____

A great number turn to the Lord at
_____
Acts 11:20, 21

Saul is enlisted to help (Acts 11:25, 26)

_____

Philip preaches in many towns until he reaches this place (Acts 8:40)

Philip

Believers scattered, "preached the word
_____"
Acts 8:4

_____
Acts 16:8

An official from
_____
Acts 8:27-38

Acts 11:19

_____
Acts 13:4

_____ &
_____
Acts 14:6

_____
Acts 16:12

The eunuch goes on his way rejoicing (Acts 8:39)

Priscilla and Aquila teach
_____
Acts 18:24-26

_____
Acts 13:51

_____
Acts 13:14

_____
Acts 17:15-34

Paul continues preaching and writing until his death

with Priscilla and Aquila to
_____
Acts 18:19

Acts (18:27—19:1)

_____
Acts 18:1

Winter Quarter, 1995-96

Theme: God's Promise of Deliverance (Isaiah)

Special Features

Lessons

Unit 1. The Coming of a New Day

Unit 2. The Ministry of the Suffering Servant

Theme: God's Love for All People (Jonah, Ruth)

About these lessons

Israel's deliverance, the Messiah's kingdom and rule, and the ministry of the Suffering Servant are the focus of the lessons based on the book of Isaiah. The studies in Jonah and Ruth explore God's love for all people.

Dec 3
Dec 10
Dec 17
Dec 24
Dec 31
Jan 7
Jan 14
Jan 21
Jan 28
Feb 4
Feb 11
Feb 18
Feb 25

The Coming of a New Day

by Roger W. Thomas

Anticipation! If there is one word that describes the Christmas season, it is this one. Children grow more and more excited each day. Parents hustle from store to store trying to finish the last-minute shopping. Grandparents look forward to the family gatherings and the renewal that comes from seeing the joy and laughter in the faces of the little ones. Unfortunately, much of the anticipation is focused on matters of secondary importance.

In part to help correct some of this imbalance, many churches observe Advent, a period of special spiritual emphasis at this time of the year. Advent prepares the soul for Christmas. Lasting for nearly a month, Advent provides an opportunity to look toward the coming of the annual celebration of Christ's birth while also drawing attention to the additional promises of Christ's second coming.

Based on the Old Testament prophecies of Isaiah, the lessons of Unit 1 of this quarter's study are all about anticipation. Living seven centuries before Christ, the prophet and his people faced difficult times. Political tensions and warring neighbors threatened to engulf tiny Judah. On the home front, religious indifference and even apostasy were destroying the once great faith of Israel.

Into this cauldron the Lord sent Isaiah to deliver a message of impending judgment and future deliverance. Unit 1 concentrates on the promises of deliverance that would come eventually to the faithful of God. Some of the promises were short-term, but most were to be fulfilled in the distant future. All, however, would be fulfilled—that was the important thing!

Lesson 1 examines the words of comfort extended to a people in distress. Times were tough and they were going to become tougher. The prophet already had announced God's judgment. Now a time had come for a word of consolation. The promises of this lesson, as with many in Isaiah, look forward to the day when the Messiah would come. This "anointed one" would be the great fulfillment of all of God's promises. In this lesson, the one who would prepare the way for the Messiah is introduced. The New Testament identifies this forerunner as John the Baptist.

Lesson 2 speaks of God's everlasting salvation promised to his people. Isaiah reminded the people that past blessings came because the Lord was faithful in fulfilling his promises to Abraham and Sarah. Just as certain was the fulfillment of his promise of everlasting salvation in the future. Despite the darkness of the moment, the people were told to look forward to a coming day of justice and righteousness.

Lesson 3 sounds a note of joy and celebration. In this lesson, the promise of the coming Messiah becomes more personal and specific. He is described as a child yet to be born who would usher in a great day of peace, justice, and righteousness. The text will be recognized as one that is frequently read during the Christmas season. We can only imagine the amazement and mystery that surrounded these words when first heard by the people of Isaiah's day.

Lesson 4, the Christmas lesson, starts with Isaiah's promise of a Deliverer coming from the line of David and moves to a review of the events surrounding the birth of Jesus. Consideration will be given to the qualities possessed by the Messiah as a result of the special endowment of the Holy Spirit, qualities that would enable him to rule well and to deal fairly with both the wicked and the righteous. The Messiah's righteous dealings with all, and the era of peace he will usher in, are presented in strikingly dramatic terms.

Lesson 5 will move from the promises of Christ's coming to the continuing fulfillment of those promises through the preaching and teaching of the gospel. The study will examine further ways in which Jesus fulfilled the purpose of the Messiah's coming.

These lessons can provide an important part of our preparation for this season, in which Christ's coming is celebrated. In addition, learning the lasting lessons of Isaiah can help prepare us for the great and coming day of Christ's glorious return.

Singing at Midnight

by Stephen M. Hooks

When Paul and Silas came to Philippi, they soon were confronted by a hostile mob. "Jews," the rioters called them, "advocating customs unlawful for us Romans to accept or practice" (Acts 16:21). Without semblance of a trial, the magistrates ordered them stripped and beaten, and then threw the two into jail (vv. 22-24).

The prisons in those days must have been dismal, miserable places, designed to enslave the spirit as well as the body. Men had been known to cry and to curse in such jails; and some, in the midst of bleak despair, had even taken their own lives. We venture to say that never in all the dark days of that gloomy old dungeon in Philippi had a prisoner ever been known to sing. And yet, at midnight, in the darkest hour of their darkest night, Paul and Silas sang. Confident that if God was for them no one could stand against them, they gave voice to their faith and filled the prison with the strains of sacred song.

I do not know what song they chose, what lyric or melody they felt best suited the occasion. Perhaps it was one of the psalms that proclaim the Lord "a very present help in trouble"; or maybe it was one of the Servant Songs of Isaiah. These compelling songs (42:1-4; 49:1-6; 50:4-9; 52:13—53:12) were written to be sung in "jail." Anticipating the Babylonian exile of the Jewish nation (586-539 B.C.), the Servant Songs were composed by the prophet to reassure the exiles that through obedient submission to the divine will, their suffering would serve a purpose that would reach far beyond their own race and their own generation.

The central figure in the songs is the "Servant of the Lord." According to the book of Isaiah, this servant is collectively the Israelite nation or, more particularly, the "remnant" of the penitent exiles, whose faithful endurance of their bondage would become the means by which God would redeem his people from their captivity and restore them to the promised land. Yet, at the same time, these prophecies anticipate some special individual in the future who would arise to suffer for the sins of all humanity. This "Servant," the New Testament tells us, is Jesus the Messiah (Acts 8:34, 35).

Each lesson in this unit is devoted to one of the songs and explores some aspect of the Servant's ministry.

Lesson 6 considers the dynamics of the servant's call—how Israel was chosen by God and empowered by him to proclaim his truth to all the nations. This servant would not act coercively but gently; through spiritual influences of sacrifice and grace the servant (Israel) would bring his world to God. Even so, the Servant (Christ) would later say, "But I, when I am lifted up from the earth [crucified], will draw all men to myself" (John 12:32). God's Servant would compel people to righteousness, not by driving them, but by drawing them with the irresistible power of his sacrificial love.

Lesson 7 explains what God was going to accomplish through his servant. According to the prophet, the captivity of Judah would not just punish them for their apostasy; it would also serve a redemptive purpose. Through their suffering, the repentant exiles would "restore" Israel by paying the penalty of the nation's apostasy and thereby pave the way for their reconciliation with God. It would also "save" the nations by illustrating the truth that those who submit to the true and living God will, in due time, be rewarded.

Lesson 8 begins to explore the price the servant must pay to do the Lord's will. In spite of rejection and persecution, the servant was determined to see his task through to the end. We'll see that the servant was instructed by suffering—taught that those who wait upon the Lord will eventually find the strength to persevere.

Lesson 9 gives the student nothing less than a prophetic glimpse of Calvary. In the final and most compelling of the Servant Songs (52:13—53:12), the prophet predicts the Servant's victory and what it would accomplish. In a paradox only God could construct, suffering and death—the very symbols of defeat—are made the means to victory for the Servant and his people. Rather than overpowering the enemy, the Servant submits to him. Instead of smiting his foes, he is smitten. Instead of taking lives, he gives his own. And the God who "works in mysterious ways" turns that which appears to be a humiliating defeat into glorious victory.

God's Love for All People

by Ralph E. Sims

"Valentine Love" is found in the Bible, but not as a description of the attitude of God toward his created beings. God's love is deeper and more encompassing than this kind of affection, and his is a perfect love.

Lessons 10-13 of this quarter form a unit entitled, "God's Love for All People." Based on the Old Testament books of Jonah and Ruth, the lessons illustrate dramatically that God's love causes him to work for our good at all times. We see the hand of God at work, even though the persons in these biblical accounts were not aware of it at the time. If we do not see God's hand as obviously in events of today, we may be sure that it is there. His attitudes toward people are the same as in Bible times, as is his concern for the ways in which his people are to fulfill his will.

FEBRUARY

Lesson 10 opens with a simple enough picture. We see that Jonah, a prophet of God, was told by God to go to Nineveh and deliver a message of warning against the people's wickedness. Instead of doing as he was directed, Jonah attempted to run away, hoping to escape from God's presence.

Jonah's disobedience seems to have been prompted by more than an unwillingness to do a particular job. Jonah had a genuine aversion to going to Nineveh. He may have been afraid of "foreigners." He may have feared a language barrier. He may have been racially prejudiced. He simply may have wanted to stay in a comfortable ministry. Perhaps, like many today, he just wanted to keep the *status quo*.

Jonah seems to have had the attitude that God would be able to find him if he stayed home in Israel, but that he would be free from the all-seeing eye of God if he fled to the other end of the Mediterranean Sea.

Jonah's reaction to his opportunity revealed much about him, and we will find it instructive to reflect on his reaction. We can learn much about ourselves if we reflect on our responses to the routine things of life, particularly when those events are not of our choosing.

Lesson 11 shows that when the word of God is proclaimed clearly and forth-rightly it is effective in bringing the results that God desires. God's will is going to be done. The people of Nineveh listened to God's message when Jonah finally delivered it to them. They repented in sackcloth and ashes, and God was true to himself in forgiving them.

Although he was physically where God wanted him to be, Jonah was still running from God. For some reason Jonah was displeased because the wicked Ninevites repented of their sins and by so doing escaped the destruction he had warned them of. He could not understand why God would "go easy" on these people. God's mercy baffled the prophet. Every Christian would benefit by giving serious attention to the effective power of the Word of God. Some today, like Jonah, have a preconceived notion of what God will do, expect God to do it, and are upset when that expectation is not carried out.

Part of what makes God's grace amazing is that he still loved Jonah, and he loves others like him in spite of themselves.

Lesson 12 presents a picture of the working of God's love in the lives of Naomi and Ruth—two ordinary women of different ethnic backgrounds. This mother and her daughter-in-law became the principals in a story of God's love that involved no miracle, such as in the account of Jonah. Naomi was an Israelite whose love for God and his law was reflected in her everyday life. Ruth was a Moabite woman who was drawn into the circle of that love.

Because of famine, Naomi's family left their native land and settled in Moab. In that foreign land Naomi's husband died, and her two sons married daughters of the people of Moab. After some time Naomi's sons died also. From the human standpoint, the young widows would have been wise to return to their own homes. One of them did. Ruth, however, had responded to the love of her mother-in-law, and a great bond based on God's love grew between them. So when Naomi left Moab to return to her homeland, Ruth accompanied her, became part of Naomi's people, and accepted Naomi's God.

Lesson 13 depicts a part of the culture of early Israel that is foreign to us. It was the custom for a brother or the nearest kinsman of a deceased Israelite to care for his widow and to father children in behalf of the deceased member of the family. Although Boaz was not the closest relative of the deceased in this case, he was willing to fulfill that responsibility and provide for Ruth. So through Boaz this woman who was not of Israel was again the recipient of God's love. Through Jesus Christ, the great descendant of Boaz and Ruth, the love of God was shed upon all nations of the world.

A Love Like God's

by Paul S. Williams

I don't ever want to return to that place!" That is not an uncommon response from people heading home after a visit to New York City. While some are energized by its pace and vibrancy, others see only the crime-riddled streets and graffiti-stained concrete canyons. They can't wait to get away from New York and its dizzying collection of 178 ethnic groups and 116 languages.

After my first visit to New York City, I was one of those who vowed never to return. And now I live and work in the New York City metropolitan area! I never intended to work in or near a city, or to be involved in cross-cultural ministry. I always thought I would stay in the Midwest, remaining comfortably in the culture in which I was reared. God seemed to have other plans for me. In that I am not alone.

COMFORTING THE AFFLICTED; AFFLICTING THE COMFORTABLE

"Comfort, comfort my people," the Lord told Isaiah (Isaiah 40:1). And that is often the role of one who answers the call of God. On the other hand, as Jonah discovered, the call of God is not always what one might expect or desire. While God comforts the afflicted, on occasion he may find it necessary to afflict the comfortable! Jonah didn't want to go to Nineveh. God had other plans for him.

It is difficult to see beyond our own fences to the fields that lie in the distance, rich and ready for cultivation. It is difficult to leave the comfort and familiarity of home to move to a new land or a foreign culture. It is difficult to do the work necessary to see others as God sees them. But it is only when we attempt that task that we begin to understand and reflect the true character of Christ.

The churches of the New York City metropolitan area meet annually for several gatherings. It is always a rich experience to hear five or six languages spoken and music presented in seven or eight distinctly different cultural styles. Participating in such a gathering becomes a reminder that we can never understand the fullness of Christ until we see it reflected in cultures other than our own. Coming together, we appreciate the richness of the unity we have in the midst of such cultural diversity.

It is a fact, however, that resistance to change and hesitancy to embrace people and things that are strange and unfamiliar, run deep. I understand Jonah's reluctance to go to Nineveh. I also understand God's purpose for sending him. God was concerned about the hundreds of thousands of people who lived in that city, and Jonah was God's man to meet that need. Today God is concerned about the more than nineteen million people of metropolitan New York City—and six billion people in the world!

To show concern for those of another culture does not always require a public presence in their midst, such as Jonah's. God is concerned not only for the millions and the billions, but for the individuals. Perhaps we can answer God's call by touching just one life at a time.

Reaching out to those of another culture may mean giving oneself in service to others, such as feeding the hungry in the teeming city of a developing nation. It may mean using vacation time to build a mission hospital abroad. It may mean a public and visible proclamation of the Word of God after the manner of Jonah. Or, like Ruth, it may mean finding the courage to care for that person whom God has already placed in your path whose cultural background differs from yours.

CALLED TO BE FAITHFUL

Whether in the public arena or in the quiet events of everyday life, God wants us to make the effort to "cross over" to others. He has chosen only one method to bring the good news to those who need to hear. God's word must come through us—culturally bound and woefully inadequate vessels that we are.

Yet he has chosen us to take the good news to the cities and villages of the world—in Asia, in Europe, in America, in Africa, in Australia. He has chosen us to announce the good news that Jesus came to make crooked ways straight. He has given us the ministry of reconciliation: to tell everyone that God was reconciling the world to himself in Christ. May we have the courage to move beyond our cultural limitations and zones of comfort to respond to his awesome and mighty call.

At times I still am uncomfortable in New York City. In those times I am reminded that God did not issue the call to an easy life. He did not call us to be successful. He called us to be faithful. May we be faithful indeed.

God's Promise of Deliverance
Unit 1. *The Coming of a New Day*
(Lessons 1-5)

A TIME
OF COMFORT

LESSON 1

WHY TEACH THIS LESSON?

"If only for this life we have hope in Christ, we are to be pitied more than all men" (1 Corinthians 15:19). "Brothers, we do not want you to be ignorant about those who fall asleep, or to grieve like the rest of men, who have no hope" (1 Thessalonians 4:13). "Praise be to the God and Father of our Lord Jesus Christ! In his great mercy he has given us new birth into a living hope…" (1 Peter 1:3).

Hope. It is central to the Christian message. It is a source of strength. It is what sets us apart from the world. And it is the underlying theme of today's lesson. If the exiles in Babylon could find comfort in the promise of a return to Zion, how much more will we be comforted with a reminder that the ultimate fulfillment of Isaiah's prophecy is for us. Exiled in a world of sin, we soon will be restored to fellowship with the Father!

Whatever struggles your students face, offer them hope through today's lesson.

INTRODUCTION

A. THE POWER OF HOPE

People come in two basic models. The big difference in people is not that some are rich and others are poor, or that some are learned and others less so. It is that some have hope and others do not. This is the difference that makes all the difference in the world.

One who has hope knows that the world is not an accident governed by chance or luck, but is the careful product of a wise and caring Creator. One who has hope is convinced that every person has a purpose and a place in the scheme of things.

Without hope, there are no better tomorrows. Hope means believing that "what is" need not determine "what will be."

Hope is the conviction that as long as God is here, even darkness can be turned into light. Hope is the secret that keeps some people going when others have long since quit.

Some interesting information has been discovered by scientists who research human nature and the keys to survival under difficult circumstances. One research project, for example, investigated coal mine disasters in an effort to discover why some men survived and others did not. One common thread seemed to stand out among survivors. Generally, those who survived were those who expected to escape. Those who believed they were doomed seldom lived. Interestingly, even with miners in the same cave-in under the same circumstances, those who gave up often died first. Those who kept trying to dig their way out because they thought it possible often lasted longer, even though they used more precious oxygen and energy in the effort.

Survival was not determined solely by the circumstances or the miners' physical condition, but by attitude. Some had hope, a reason to hang on. Others did not!

DEVOTIONAL READING
2 CORINTHIANS 7:2-7
LESSON SCRIPTURE
ISAIAH 40:1-11
PRINTED TEXT
ISAIAH 40:1-11

LESSON AIMS

This lesson is designed to help the student:

1. Recall or paraphrase expressions from Isaiah 40:1-11 that indicate comfort.

2. Explain how Isaiah's prophecy can comfort us today.

3. Plan to share the comforting truths in personal ministry to those who need comfort.

KEY VERSE

Comfort, comfort my people, says your God. Speak tenderly to Jerusalem. —Isaiah 40:1, 2

VISUALS FOR THESE LESSONS

The Adult Visuals/Learning Resources packet contains classroom-size visuals designed for use with the lessons in the Winter Quarter. The packet is available from your supplier. Order No. 292.

Visual 1 of the winter visuals packet calls to mind the teaching of Isaiah 40:8. Visual 14 (not shown) is a time line for use throughout this quarter.

HOW TO SAY IT

Ahaz. AY-haz.
Asaph. AY-saf.
Hezekiah. Hez-eh-KYE-uh.
Jotham. JO-tham.
Uzziah. Uh-ZYE-uh.

When we are faced with difficulties or hardships, the key to overcoming is often not so much the depth of the problems but the degree of our hope. People of faith who believe that God will deliver them often can endure far more than those who believe that they are left to their own devices.

The message of this season of anticipation of Christmas is hope. These weeks are a time to look forward and know that something is going to happen, that God is going to act. It remind us that God's promises are worth waiting for.

B. LESSON BACKGROUND

Isaiah the prophet lived in Jerusalem in the eighth century B.C. He prophesied in the days of four kings of Judah: Uzziah, Jotham, Ahaz, and Hezekiah. These were difficult times for Judah. Relations were not good with her sister nation, Israel, to the north. Assyria to the east and Egypt to the south were casting threatening shadows across the entire Middle East. During Isaiah's lifetime, Israel would fall to Assyria, and her people would be carried away into captivity.

The politicians in Judah thought that their nation would survive only if they made peace with their more powerful neighbors. Isaiah, on the other hand, insisted that survival depended on the nation's making peace with God. Treaties and alliances with the military powers of the day would prove futile, he preached. If Judah refused to return to God, she would surely follow the way of Israel. In fact, Isaiah prophesied that Judah would indeed be carried away into captivity—not by Assyria, however, nor by Egypt, but by Babylon (Isaiah 39:5-7), a nation yet to rise as a dominant world power. Isaiah also prophesied that Judah's punishment in captivity would be followed by their return to their own land (1:25-27).

The captivity that Isaiah prophesied concerning Judah would not begin until more than one hundred years had passed, and the return would occur seventy years after that. It is little wonder that his countrymen scoffed at his prediction of defeat and captivity. Likewise, his assurance of a return from captivity had no meaning for them. However, a hundred and fifty years later the Jews were actually captives in Babylon. There that prediction from an ancient book came to them as a word of comfort, providing hope in a time of despair.

Isaiah's prophecy was partly fulfilled when the Jews returned to Jerusalem. It was partly fulfilled when Jesus came to redeem mankind from sin's bondage. It will be completely fulfilled when Jesus returns and God's new order is fully manifested.

Rightly has Isaiah been called the great "gospel" prophet of the Old Testament. He more than any other Old Testament prophet points to the coming Messiah. Filled with tantalizing hints and bold predictions that would someday be fulfilled in and through Jesus, Isaiah's book is a preview of Matthew, Mark, Luke, and John.

The book of Isaiah divides into two basic sections: chapters 1-39 and chapters 40-66. The messages of the two sections are vastly different. The first section deals largely with the themes of judgment and doom. The latter section, which opens with our lesson text, promises blessings that will eventually follow the years of captivity and that will extend not only to the Jewish people, but to all the nations of the earth.

Chapter 40 begins the latter section of Isaiah with a promise of comfort and deliverance. Our text serves as an introduction to the entire second half of Isaiah. The text divides into four parts, representing four voices, or messages, about the future of God's people.

I. THE VOICE OF PARDON (ISAIAH 40:1, 2)

A. THE SOURCE OF COMFORT (v. 1)

1. Comfort, comfort my people, says your God.

The previous chapter, which concluded the first section of Isaiah, ended with the prediction that at some point in the future Judah would suffer captivity in Babylon. This chapter jumps ahead to the promise of release and restoration that would eventually follow.

The Hebrew word rendered here as *comfort* literally means "to breathe again." It perfectly describes the sensation of relaxing and taking a deep breath after a period of peril and difficulty. It is repeated twice for emphasis. The prophet, writing many years earlier, exhorted the people in captivity to be comforted. God, however, was the real Comforter of his people (Isaiah 12:1; 49:13; 51:3, 12).

My people and *your God* are reminders of the Lord's faithfulness to his people, even though Judah had been judged by him and sent into exile. He was "their" God, not a stranger. Judah had not ceased to be his people.

B. THE MEANS OF COMFORT (v. 2)

2. Speak tenderly to Jerusalem, and proclaim to her that her hard service has been completed, that her sin has been paid for, that she has received from the LORD's hand double for all her sins.

Speak tenderly is literally "speak to the heart." This was a message for the soul, for the innermost needs and desires of the people. The expression was meant to quiet the people's fears and anxieties as they languished in captivity. There was nothing superficial about it. *Jerusalem* personified to represent the people of God.

The term *hard service* stands for the long period of hardship that Judah experienced in her captivity. Remember, Isaiah was speaking of a time more than a century into the future. Because of the certainty of God's faithfulness, he spoke as if the events had already occurred.

Judah's greatest comfort would come from pardon. The God of grace and mercy would forgive the sins of the past. *She has received from the LORD's hand double* is not intended to suggest that Judah was punished with twice the severity that she deserved. It means, instead, that she had received her full measure of suffering and that she need not fear further vengeance. (Compare Isaiah 61:7.)

This promise of God was the basis for the people's hope. Knowing that his punishment for their sins was complete, they could live in hope that better times would be coming.

Likewise, the gospel of Christ is a message of hope to a lost world. It gives assurance that God offers forgiveness and grace for a person's sin. Only those who refuse to avail themselves of the offer of the Savior are doomed. "Whosoever will" can know the comfort and reassurance of God's pardon.

II. THE VOICE OF PREPARATION (ISAIAH 40:3-5)

A. THE KING ANNOUNCED (v. 3)

3. A voice of one calling: "In the desert prepare the way for the LORD; make straight in the wilderness a highway for our God.

In ancient times, a visit by a king would be preceded by his messenger announcing the event. Preparations were to be made for his coming. The way was to be cleared, and the people properly attired.

Using this image, the prophet indicated that God's people in captivity must ready themselves for his coming to them to restore them to the homeland. The prophet spoke figuratively. The preparation they needed to make was spiritual. Whatever hindrances—political, spiritual, or others—that stood in the way of the return were to be removed.

Students of the New Testament know that there was a deeper meaning in this prophecy of Isaiah. His words were also prophetic of John the Baptist, the herald

WHAT DO YOU THINK?

In the midst of difficult and painful experiences, one may lose perspective. When suffering is intense over time, it tends to distort reality. One's view of God gets smaller and smaller; thus the problems grow larger and larger. It then becomes easy to confuse the temporary with the eternal—the suffering seems as if it will never end.

The promises of comfort and hope in Isaiah 40 are addressed to just such a situation. They must have seemed incredible to Judah in captivity, and they may well seem incredible to suffering people today.

Suggest some situations in which Isaiah's message of hope is needed today. Who needs this comfort? (Suggest some specific individuals.) Why do they need it? How can this message be communicated to them?

WHAT DO YOU THINK?

Since we have read the New Testament, we recognize verse 3 in the text as a prediction of John the Baptist and his ministry of preparing the people of Israel for Jesus and his ministry. With that aspect of the prophecy fulfilled, what is left for us? Is there still a need for a voice calling in the desert? If so, what? How can we be involved in preparing the way of the Lord?

(Be sure to note verse 5.)

who prepared a people to receive the Messiah (Matthew 3:1-17). John came in a literal wilderness to announce the coming of the King and to call the nation to prepare for his coming. John made it clear that only repentance properly prepares one for a visit from the King. According to John, sins must be abandoned, wrongs righted, and commitments made to follow the way of the master.

B. THE KING ANTICIPATED (v. 4)

4. "Every valley shall be raised up, every mountain and hill made low; the rough ground shall become level, the rugged places a plain.

The prophet continues the figure regarding the preparations that were to be made for the visit of royalty. The *rough* and uneven places were to be smoothed out and leveled to facilitate the monarch's coming. So captive Judah was to prepare herself to receive the Lord and the redemption he was bringing. The proud and the self-righteous must be humbled. The poor and weak, the downcast and oppressed, must be *raised up* and encouraged. The crooked and wicked must be called to change their ways. They must "straighten up."

Likewise, Christ Jesus is ready and waiting to come into any life that is prepared for his coming. However, into the life that does not desire him, he will not come.

C. THE KING REVEALED (v. 5)

5. "And the glory of the LORD will be revealed, and all mankind together will see it. For the mouth of the LORD has spoken."

When all of the preparation was completed, God's glory would be revealed. Judah would be delivered from Babylon by the power of God, and by this act God's glory and majesty would be shown to the nations.

All mankind together will see it clearly suggests a work of God that would go far beyond the return of the Jews to Jerusalem. When Christ came to earth, he revealed the glory of God (John 1:14; 2:11; 2 Corinthians 4:6; 2 Peter 1:16). This "revealing" will be completed when he comes again (Matthew 16:27; Revelation 1:7).

III. THE VOICE OF PROTECTION (ISAIAH 40:6-8)

A. THINGS TEMPORARY (vv. 6, 7)

6. A voice says, "Cry out." And I said, "What shall I cry?" "All men are like grass, and all their glory is like the flowers of the field.

The voices falling on the prophet's ear are not identified. Perhaps they were angels. The first point of their discourse was that all human conditions are only temporary. *All men* are finite. There are no exceptions.

On the surface this might seem to be anything but a word of comfort and encouragement (v. 1). Quite the contrary! In the context it is good news, because even the power of the Babylonians and the captivity in which Israel would be held would pass away.

God's glory is radiant and overwhelming. It is eternal. Human *glory*, on the other hand, is weak and temporary. The term here refers to the outward beauty and attractiveness of human life. Physical strength diminishes with time. Eventually frailty rules where power once reigned.

7. "The grass withers and the flowers fall, because the breath of the LORD blows on them. Surely the people are grass.

The illustration of grass and flower is repeated for emphasis. The expression *breath of the Lord* brings to mind the force of the hot east wind that can blow out of the desert and quickly wither the heartiest of crops. When the Spirit of the Lord (the same Hebrew word is translated "spirit," "breath," or "wind") blows in judgment upon men, they perish.

WHAT DO YOU THINK?

It is difficult for us to see any value in pain or suffering, but the Bible affirms that there is. One of the most obvious benefits is that we may grow in the virtue of patience (1 Peter 2:20). In addition, hardship and difficulty can produce a strength and firm resolve in our character, qualities essential for growth and maturity (1 Peter 5:10).

How have you matured through hardship? What lessons has suffering taught you?

How can this reassurance be communicated to one who is suffering? How would you express it so that the message does not sound trite or "Pollyanna"?

WHAT DO YOU THINK?

That all men—and women— are grass and destined to fade and wither and die does not at first glance appear to be a message of hope! What is hopeful about this situation? How does the contrasting message—"the word of our God stands forever"—change that gloomy sounding statement into one of hope?

(Note the lesson writer's comments on verses 6-8.)

B. THINGS PERMANENT (v. 8)

8. "The grass withers and the flowers fall, but the word of our God stands forever."

The second and most important element in the discourse of the voices (see comment under verse 6) is seen here. Whereas everything in the world is finite, God is infinite. Nations, rulers, and governments come and go, but what God says stands forever. He is completely dependable.

The word of our God refers to the promises of the Lord. Here is the great comfort for a people facing adversity. The powers that create the troubles will fade, but the God who delivers will remain.

Peter quotes this passage and applies it to the gospel (1 Peter 1:23-25). Jesus used a similar image to call his disciples to greater dependence on the everlasting Lord (Matthew 6:30; also see 1 John 2:17).

SUSTAINING LIFE

Where I live, lawn mowing is normally a once-a-week job. One recent summer, however, it was different. The weather was so dry in July and August, I didn't mow my lawn for six weeks! Without water, grass withers quickly and flowers fade fast.

Even with adequate moisture, plant life grows through a predictable and comparatively short cycle of "bud, blossom, fruit"—and then dies. In cold climates, the whole process, from green to brown, lasts only a few weeks.

With this analogy, the prophet makes a point about mortality: "All men are like grass." Human life is short—here today, gone tomorrow. And all the good we do is soon forgotten, like a fading corsage taped to a dresser mirror. As wise King Solomon wrote, "That which now is in the days to come shall all be forgotten" (Ecclesiastes 2:16, *King James Version*).

Christians, however, can survive the "Solomon syndrome." Flesh is mortal, but God's Spirit in us is eternal. And "the word of our God stands forever." Even Solomon admitted, "I know that everything God does will endure forever" (Ecclesiastes 3:14). Let us live our brief span keeping eternity's values in view.   —R. W. B.

IV. THE VOICE OF POWER (ISAIAH 40:9-11)

A. GOOD NEWS: GOD IS HERE (v. 9)

9. You who bring good tidings to Zion, go up on a high mountain. You who bring good tidings to Jerusalem, lift up your voice with a shout, lift it up, do not be afraid; say to the towns of Judah, "Here is your God!"

Here begins the great news of comfort to which the previous verses of this text have been leading. The preparation spoken of in them is complete. God was returning to reign in Jerusalem. The fallen city and nation would be restored.

The message was to be heralded from the highest mountains. It was to be proclaimed with the strongest possible voice and without fear. The Lord was with his people once again, and this good news was for all of Judah.

The message sounds strikingly like that of John the Baptist, who, when identifying the Messiah, declared to those from Jerusalem and the villages of Judah, "Look, the Lamb of God!" (John 1:29). At the heart of John's preaching was the good news, "The kingdom of heaven is near" (Matthew 3:2).

B. GOOD NEWS: GOD IS GREAT (v. 10)

10. See, the Sovereign LORD comes with power, and his arm rules for him. See, his reward is with him, and his recompense accompanies him.

God would come in power to his people, assembling his flock and taking it back to Jerusalem. *His reward is with him.* This may be a reference to the salvation bestowed upon the people, or it may refer to the fact that the accomplishment of his purposes is God's own reward.

WHAT DO YOU THINK?

It is not uncommon for mature Christians to experience pain and suffering. Jesus said we would (John 15:18-21). In suffering, we share many of Jesus' experiences. He faced hostility. Our world is still hostile to Christianity. He did not receive justice. Injustice is still widespread. He was misunderstood, rejected, and persecuted; so are Christians today. Sometimes when Christians experience such suffering, they wonder why. Paul suggests the answer: "So that we can comfort those in any trouble with the comfort we ourselves have received from God" (2 Corinthians 1:4, New International Version).

Recall some of the hard times and suffering you have experienced. How have these experiences equipped you to comfort others? How are you using your opportunities to pass on God's comfort?

OPTION

The reproducible activity, "Paralyzed or Energized?" on page 134 will help you lead a discussion on dealing with discouragement. You can lead a good discussion with or without distributing copies of that page.

LET US PRAY

Lord, there is much about life and the troubles of this world that we don't understand. Sometimes the problems seem just too big to handle. But we know that you are concerned about your people, and that if we trust you, all will be well one day. Help us to be faithful through good days and bad. In Jesus' name we pray. Amen.

THOUGHT TO REMEMBER

The difference between defeat and victory is often perseverance. The key to perseverance is hope!

HOME DAILY BIBLE READINGS

Monday, Nov. 27—Short-sighted Behavior (Isaiah 39:1-8)

Tuesday, Nov. 28—Declaration of Sin (Micah 3:1-8)

Wednesday, Nov. 29—Prayer for Blessing on the King (Psalm 72:1-14)

Thursday, Nov. 30—The Appeal of Good Tidings (Isaiah 52: 1-10)

Friday, Dec. 1—The Lord Will Restore (Isaiah 49:1-10)

Saturday, Dec. 2—Gift of Abundant Life (John 10:1-11)

Sunday, Dec. 3—Prayer for Deliverance (Psalm 86:8-17)

The great consolation for God's people is that at the time God deems it appropriate, he will act and make all things right and just. He is worth waiting for, even during times of difficulty and hardship.

C. GOOD NEWS: GOD IS GOOD (v. 11)

11. He tends his flock like a shepherd: He gathers the lambs in his arms and carries them close to his heart; he gently leads those that have young.

Many in our time may be unfamiliar with a gentle, caring shepherd, but it was not unfamiliar to the ancients. Even for those who know little of shepherds and sheep, the message of a gentle, compassionate guardian comes through loud and strong. The Lord has special concern for the young, the weak, and the vulnerable, who are unable to care for themselves.

In these closing verses of our text we see two aspects of the Lord's coming to rescue his people from their captivity in Babylon and to lead them back to their homeland—namely, his strength and his gentleness. In a larger way this prophecy speaks of the coming of the Lord in the person of Christ—in his first and in his second coming.

His first coming revealed his meekness and humility, for he came as "the Lamb of God, who takes away the sin of the world" (John 1:29). Jesus referred to himself as the Good Shepherd, who was concerned for his sheep.

Christ's second coming will reveal his "strong hand." Then he will "reign for ever and ever" (Revelation 11:15), not as the Lamb, but as "the Lion of the tribe of Judah" (Revelation 5:5). In this the people of God can take comfort.

SHEPHERD KING

People don't always stay in the pigeonholes that our stereotypes build for them. Example: some Americans were surprised that a peanut farmer from Georgia could become president of the United States. Is that the stuff of which presidents are made? Harry Truman also rocked millions back on their heels when he came from humble beginnings to win the Oval Office. Presidential candidates are stereotypically wealthy and prestigious professional people.

We are thrown a bit off balance, it seems, when someone becomes what we never expected. Israel was surprised when David, a mere shepherd boy, became king. How could a gentle shepherd hope to rule and lead a nation?

Significantly, David is described as a man after God's own heart. We note with interest that in our text Isaiah pictures God as a *shepherd king*, ruling with a strong hand, yet feeding his flock, gathering his lambs, and gently leading the vulnerable ones. He is Lord of lords, but he is also the Good Shepherd who leads us beside still waters and makes us lie down in green pastures. His name is wonderful! —R. W. B.

CONCLUSION

Winston Churchill agreed to deliver a speech to the students at the boys' school he had once attended as a youngster. The subject of his address was to be the secret of his success. When the hour came for his much-heralded address, the statesman mounted the podium, noted the topic for the day, spoke only five words, and then returned to his seat. His message? "Never, never, never, give up!"

Indeed, the secret of success in most important matters is simply perseverance—refusal to give up. The difference between perseverance and defeat is often the conviction that victory is just around the corner.

The people of God are comforted, and they comfort one another, with the certainty that God is faithful. No matter how dark the moment seems, he will eventually bring his promised deliverance. His greatest deliverance has already come in Jesus, and it will be brought to completion in his final return.

Discovery Learning

This page contains an alternate lesson plan emphasizing learning activities. Classes desiring such student involvement will find these suggestions helpful. The next page is a reproducible activity page to further enhance discovery learning.

LEARNING GOALS

As a result of studying Isaiah 40:1-11, the adult will be able to:

1. Recall or paraphrase expressions from Isaiah 40:1-11 that indicate comfort.

2. Explain how Isaiah's prophecy can comfort us today.

3. Plan to share the comforting truths in personal ministry to those who need comfort.

INTO THE LESSON

The first four sessions in this study have titles beginning with the words, "A Time of...." On the wall at the front of your classroom, display a clock and the heading, "A TIME OF—." Have also the words COMFORT, ENCOURAGEMENT, JOY, and RIGHTEOUSNESS AND PEACE prepared so you can display them with the respective studies.

As class members arrive and are seated, greet each one and ask, "Are you comfortable?" Have a few throw pillows available; if anyone mentions discomfort from the "too-hard" seats, offer him or her a pillow. As you get your class members thinking about and discussing physical comfort, ask, "What do we usually think about when we are discussing 'being comfortable'?" Then add the label COMFORT as you make the transition from physical comfort to spiritual comfort, the essence of today's text.

INTO THE WORD

The opening portion of Handel's *Messiah* is based on Isaiah 40:1-5. Bring a recorded version of this oratorio to class and play this section for your students. (Perhaps a class member would bring a small sound system for the occasion.) Direct your class members to follow the verses in Scripture as the passage is sung. (If using such a recording is not feasible, have a good reader read the text aloud.)

Provide paper and pens for the following activity. Working individually, your students are to examine today's text to find comforting truths that are contained in it. Instruct them to condense each truth to three or four words. For example, "hard service completed" (v. 2) and "word stands forever" (v. 8).

Be prepared with your own list. Here are several you might include: "sin is paid for" (v. 2); "glory will be revealed" (v. 5); "all will see" (v. 5); "Lord has spoken" (v. 5); "Word stands forever" (v. 8); "Here is your God!" (v. 9); "Lord comes with power" (v. 10); "Reward is with him (v. 10); "He tends his flock" (v. 11); "He carries them close" (v. 11).

Allot five minutes for your students to prepare. Then read the text aloud one verse at a time, pausing for students to read the comforting words they found in each.

Give each student a copy of the following antiphonal devotional reading. Divide your students into two groups. One group is to read the parts of the "discouraged," and the other the parts of the "comforters." It would be ideal, but not necessary, for the two groups to face each other. After allowing a short time for your students to skim through the reading, lead them in reading it aloud.

Discouraged: "The struggle with the devil is so long and so hard."

Comforters: "But your hard service will soon be over."

Discouraged: "The sins of the nation are so many."

Comforters: "But her iniquity can be pardoned."

Discouraged: "God seems so far away."

Comforters: "But the glory of the Lord will be revealed!"

Discouraged: "Oh, how can we be sure?"

Comforters: "The mouth of the Lord has spoken it!"

Discouraged: "Human beings are like grass that withers and fades and dies."

Comforters: "But the word of our God—with its truth and its hope—stands forever."

Discouraged: "But the city of God is surrounded by vicious and evil warriors."

Comforters: "Look! God comes with a strong hand, and his arm will rule!"

Discouraged: "We are like feeble sheep, wandering, helpless, hungry."

Comforters: "He will feed his flock like a shepherd; he will gather you with his arm and carry you in his heart."

Discouraged: "But—"

Comforters: "The Word of our God stands—*forever!*"

INTO LIFE

Ask your students to identify some church members and friends they know who are struggling. These might include those who are sick, people facing problems in a personal relationship, one who is out of work, etc. Urge the students to communicate comforting words to these persons this coming week by phone, by note, and by visit. Plan to do the same yourself!

Paralyzed or Energized?

When we experience serious discouragement, it is not uncommon to find ourselves somewhat paralyzed emotionally. However, there are some constructive steps a person can take to deal with such discouragement.

Think of a situation that causes you or someone you know to be discouraged. Write it in the box below. Then consider each of the steps that follow and write one or two suggestions on how you could apply each step to the situation you have named.

● **First, make a clear distinction between the temporary and the permanent.**
Check your vocabulary. Do you often use the words never and always? These words speak of permanence, and they are self-defeating.

● **Second, remember to do only what you can do today.**
Discouraged people are usually anxious people. They worry a lot. When we are anxious, we are attempting to solve tomorrow's possible problems today. Jesus teaches us to focus on what can be done today. (See Matthew 6:31.)

● **Third, deliberately remember instances of God's faithfulness in the past.**
We must allow the intellect to override the emotions. Emotionally we are unable to reconstruct positive experiences, but intellectually we can affirm them. Read Deuteronomy 7:9; Psalm 89:1; and 1 Peter 4:19.

● **Fourth, focus on those realities that do not change.**
The God who delivered his people still does. Consider Isaiah 40:8; Malachi 3:6; Hebrews 1:12; 13:8; and James 1:17.

God's Promise of Deliverance

Unit 1. The Coming of a New Day
(Lessons 1-5)

A TIME OF ENCOURAGEMENT

LESSON 2

WHY TEACH THIS LESSON?

"You blockhead, Charlie Brown! Can't you do anything right?" We read it in the Sunday comics and smile. Do we laugh because it is funny, or because it is familiar? Haven't we all been—at least occasionally—where Charlie Brown always seems to be?

Sometimes it concerns our walk with the Lord. Old habits refuse to die. New disciplines are hard to develop. Old friends challenge our faith. Attempts to share our faith seem to fail miserably. Maybe we should just quit!

Our tendency to feel that way is exactly the reason your students need this lesson. We all need the reminder that God's "salvation will last forever, [his] righteousness will never fail!"

INTRODUCTION

A. THE WAY OUT IS UP

The smallest obstacles sometimes can thwart living creatures. For example, it is said that a bumblebee can be held captive in an open tumbler. The bee will bounce around the sides of the glass until it dies. The only way of escape, so it thinks, is horizontally through the transparent glass near the bottom of the container. It either cannot or will not look up and escape through the opening at the top.

People also can be held prisoner by things they at first view as small and inconsequential matters—a habit that they should break, but don't; an attitude that should be corrected, but is allowed to continue and harden. Unnecessarily, they remain captives to these things. Either they do not know there is a way out, or, having been told about it, they don't believe it will work for them.

Judah's downward slide away from God may have begun with what some might regard as "little" things—failure to observe and remember God's blessings in the past, disrespect for elders, or disregard of a bothersome law that restricted one's pursuit of pleasure. In time, these "little" things formed a life-style that forged spiritual shackles the people could not break. By the time of Isaiah's prophetic ministry, Judah was faced with a future filled with real problems. There was nothing make-believe about them. God's judgment was coming upon them; captivity and slavery lay ahead. They would find themselves in the pit of despair. When that time came, Isaiah said, their escape would come from looking up to the Lord. Seeking their own solutions, or just looking down and around, would never lead to their release. The only way out would be up!

The same holds true for many who are battling life's problems today. The way out is still up. To seek a solution apart from God leads to discouragement and failure. Knowing that the Lord of Heaven offers the way of escape provides the encouragement that is needed to persevere, even during the darkest of times.

DEVOTIONAL READING
ACTS 27:14-26

LESSON SCRIPTURE
ISAIAH 51:1-8

PRINTED TEXT
ISAIAH 51:1-6

LESSON AIMS

This lesson is designed to help the student:

1. Identify elements of encouragement from Isaiah 51:1-6.

2. Explain how Isaiah's message can encourage us today.

3. Plan to share those encouraging truths from Isaiah in personal ministry to someone who is discouraged.

KEY VERSE

My salvation will last forever, my righteousness will never fail.

—Isaiah 51:6

Lesson 2 Notes

Note

Since the fall of the ten northern tribes, which comprised the nation known as "Israel" during the years of the divided monarchy (931-721 B.C.), the southern kingdom of "Judah" was sometimes known by both names. (See Isaiah 48:1.) Israel, of course, was the original name of the nation—all twelve tribes.

What Do You Think?

The people of Judah were urged to look at their heritage, the founding of their nation. God's covenant with Abraham and his mighty acts in Israel's history would be a source of encouragement to them in their suffering and a reassurance that his promises for the future were valid.

How do those same facts encourage Christians today? What additional facts and events can provide us with encouragement for our own future and the promises of God to us?

What Do You Think?

If anyone had reason to be discouraged and to give up, Abraham and Sarah did. Yet, it was out of their barrenness that God produced a nation. When Joseph was a slave in Egypt, his situation looked rather hopeless. His faithfulness ultimately resulted in great blessing for himself and

B. Lesson Background

In the chapters preceding Isaiah 51, several themes are seen. One is the greatness of God. The Lord, Isaiah insisted, is more powerful than all false gods and idols combined. A second theme is Israel's unfaithfulness. It was Israel's unfaithfulness that would bring God's judgment, which would take the form of the Babylonian captivity. In stark contrast to Israel's unfaithfulness is the faithfulness of God. God would remain faithful to his promises. Someday he would deliver the people from their captivity.

Eventually Babylon, the chosen instrument of God's judgment against Judah, would fall. Its fall would demonstrate to everyone the impotence of the false gods and idols. After that, Judah/Israel would be restored as a nation, and the people would receive abundant blessings of the Lord.

Intertwined with the message of the fall and restoration of Israel are Isaiah's prophecies regarding the Servant of the Lord. This Servant will be the subject of the second unit of lessons in this quarter's study (lessons 6-9). The Servant's identity and mission will be considered in detail at that time.

The words of this lesson's Scripture text, written by Isaiah more than one hundred years before the Babylonian captivity actually occurred, were intended for that future generation of God's people who would suffer as captives in Babylon. The prophet's words would come as an encouragement for the captives to remain faithful in the midst of those dark days. They were to understand that the Lord had not forgotten Israel. His promises of a great and glorious future would surely come to pass.

I. THE FOUNDATION OF THE FAITHFUL (ISAIAH 51:1-3)

A. Remembering Their Beginnings (v. 1)

1. **"Listen to me, you who pursue righteousness and who seek the Lord: Look to the rock from which you were cut and to the quarry from which you were hewn.**

The prophet was directing God's message to a dispirited people. The command for them to *listen* is repeated three times in this chapter (vv. 1, 4, 7). This was a divine "wake up call." The Lord was calling his chosen people to look at their glorious past to learn lessons about the future he had in store for them.

The call was given to those who *pursue righteousness.* The phrase is further defined as those *who seek the Lord.* Righteousness is defined by the nature and character of God. In this context, following righteousness is contrasted with pursuing the passing, temporary things of this world (v. 6).

Look to the rock … to the quarry was a call for those who would seek the Lord in the Babylonian captivity to look back at their past history, especially at their beginning. They would be reminded of their humble origins and of their growth into a great multitude of people. From such lowly beginnings they had become a mighty nation. And how had this come about? There was but one explanation—the blessing of God. Israel as a people was a creation of God. The people could no more claim credit for their beginning and their development as a nation than a lifeless statue could claim to have given itself form out of a shapeless rock. The purpose for this reflection on their past history is seen in verse 3.

B. Recalling Their Ancestors (v. 2)

2. **"Look to Abraham, your father, and to Sarah, who gave you birth. When I called him he was but one, and I blessed him and made him many.**

A review of Israel's past would lead one all the way back to Abraham and Sarah. The entire nation issued from these two, who were beyond the age of having a child by natural means when God's promise that they would have a son was fulfilled in them. Read Genesis 12:1-7 and 17:1-21 for a review of how this beginning took place.

He was but one. God called Abraham out of Ur of the Chaldees before he had any children. God promised to bless him, and he fulfilled his promise (Genesis 12:2; 24:1, 35). Not only did God give Abraham material blessings, but he also *made him many.* He made Abraham "a father of many nations" (Genesis 17:5).

The point is this: if the Lord could begin with one man and make a great nation, surely he could begin again with a faithful remnant of the exiles (who numbered in the thousands—Ezra 2:64) and cause his people to flourish once again. Truly God's track record is one of the greatest incentives to faith.

C. RECEIVING FORMER BLESSINGS (v. 3)

3. "The LORD will surely comfort Zion and will look with compassion on all her ruins; he will make her deserts like Eden, her wastelands like the garden of the LORD. Joy and gladness will be found in her, thanksgiving and the sound of singing.

The Lord will surely comfort Zion . . . he will make her deserts like Eden. Literally, the text reads, "The Lord has comforted Zion: he has comforted all her waste places; and has made her wilderness like Eden." This future condition of God's people was so certain that Isaiah could speak of it as if it had already been accomplished. Indeed, in the mind of God it was as good as done!

At the time of Judah's fall to the Babylonians, great destruction would take place in the land. Because virtually all of the people would be removed to other lands, much of Judah would be uninhabited and untended. *Desert* in Scripture refers to being deserted, not necessarily to the arid regions we know as deserts today. One can only imagine what the land would look like after seventy years of neglect. Ezekiel described the abandoned land as a "desolate land" and the cities as "lying in ruins, desolate and destroyed" (36:34-36).

Like Eden. The land's desolate condition would change. Isaiah said that the land would once again flower and bloom and be fruitful—so much so that he compared it to the Garden of Eden in the very beginning. The prophet Joel used this imagery in describing the land of Judah before the ravages of the Babylonian invasion occurred (2:3). Ezekiel, like Isaiah here, prophesied that the land would once again be "like the garden of Eden" (36:35). Such would be the blessings God would bestow on the land when the Babylonian captivity ended and the exiles returned home.

The sound of singing. Music stops when a land is afflicted, for music is associated with times of happiness, joy, and peace (Isaiah 24:8). By saying music would be found again in Zion, Isaiah was prophesying that Judah's affliction would end and the people would live happily in their homeland. Thus the thought of this verse reinforces the message contained in verses 1 and 2—the people in captivity should take heart; God had not forgotten them; brighter days lay ahead. This would all come to pass for those among God's people who would look to him in faith and continue to trust in him, even though the days of their captivity were very dark.

TOO GOOD TO BE TRUE?

These may be momentous times. Israel and Palestine (PLO) have signed a peace treaty of sorts—a covenant of mutual acknowledgment. Much of the world is skeptical, however. Considering the hatred that has manifested itself in violence for decades between these peoples, it is understandable that one might wonder how long this compatibility will continue. By the time you read this, they could be fighting again.

his family. King Jehoshaphat of Judah, when faced with overwhelming enemy forces, prayed, "O our God, . . . we have no power to face this vast army that is attacking us. We do not know what to do, but our eyes are upon you" (2 Chronicles 20:12). He was reminded by the prophet, "The battle is not yours, but God's" (2 Chronicles 20:15).

What desperate situations have you seen or experienced that God turned to victory? What are some situations in which you are still waiting for the victory? How can we encourage and support one another in such circumstances? How do these passages— as well as today's text—help in this?

God's promise to transform Zion (Isaiah 51:3) is pictured by visual 2 of the visuals packet.

WHAT DO YOU THINK?

When life looks desolate and bleak, it is not easy to believe that beauty and joy are in our future. How can we live with anticipation of the "best" when we are experiencing what seems to be the "worst"? How do we keep our focus on the trustworthy promises of God's word instead of on the fickle feelings of our emotions? (See Hebrews 11:1, 2.)

Judah in exile, to whom Isaiah's prophecy was directed, likely received his promises of peace and restoration with anything from guarded optimism to outright incredulity. Sometimes good news seems too good to be true. The prophet foretold a time of "joy and gladness . . . thanksgiving and the sound of singing." The prospect of a return to good old days of peace and prosperity must have seemed incredible.

Could the shepherds, centuries later, truly grasp the implications of the good news brought by God's angel: "Today in the town of David a Savior has been born to you: he is Christ the Lord"? Did they dare to believe what the heavenly host proclaimed: "Glory to God in the highest, and on earth peace to men on whom his favor rests"? (Luke 2:11, 14). At least they mustered enough hope to seek out the Christ child, as did sages from the East. Wise men still seek the Savior.   —R. W. B.

II. THE FUTURE OF THE FAITHFUL (ISAIAH 51:4-6)

A. THE LORD'S RIGHTEOUS PROMISES (v. 4)

4. "Listen to me, my people; hear me, my nation: The law will go out from me; my justice will become a light to the nations.

Listen to me. The Hebrew term here is a stronger term than that used in verse 1. More than mere listening, it is a call to give one's undivided attention. The previous section promised the restoration of Judah after the captivity. Verse 4 and those that follow in our text look to something greater than the return of the land to abundance and prosperity. They describe the glorious future when the Lord would send forth his *light to the nations.* This, too, was a part of the original promise of blessing to Abraham (Genesis 12:2, 3).

The law here refers to the gospel of redemption, not the law of Moses. This law, or instruction, would *go out* from God to all nations. (See Isaiah 2:4; cf. Isaiah 42:4.)

Earlier, Isaiah had spoken of a time when the glory of the Lord would be revealed, and said that "all mankind" would see it (Isaiah 40:5). This was fulfilled in the coming of the Messiah, Jesus. Simeon, the aged resident of Jerusalem, sang at Jesus' coming, "For my eyes have seen your salvation, which you have prepared in the sight of all people; a light for revelation to the Gentiles and for glory to your people Israel" (Luke 2:30-32).

B. THE LORD'S UNIVERSAL PROMISES (v. 5)

5. "My righteousness draws near speedily, my salvation is on the way, and my arm will bring justice to the nations. The islands will look to me and wait in hope for my arm.

The prophet continues to speak of the great day of the Messiah's coming, and he describes it as being *near.* In other prophecies as well, Isaiah makes it appear as though the coming of the messianic kingdom would immediately follow the restoration of Israel. In fact, the events would be separated by more than five hundred years. The prophets received God's messages and delivered them to his people. It is obvious that not all was divulged to the prophets in this process. (See 1 Peter 1:10-12.) From God's standpoint, the coming of the Messiah was near, just as it was certain. And so God could say through Isaiah, *my salvation is on the way.* In this statement we are reminded once again that the Lord's timing is not man's. Peter reminds his readers that "with the Lord a day is like a thousand years, and a thousand years are like a day" (2 Peter 3:8).

My righteousness refers to the great plan that God would put into effect with the Messiah's coming. That plan consists of two parts. The first is his righteous plan to redeem his people through Christ. This thought is touched on by the apostle Paul in his statement, "I am not ashamed of the gospel, because it is the power of God for the salvation of everyone who believes: first for the Jew, then for the Gentile. For

HOW TO SAY IT
Isaiah. Eye-ZAY-uh.

WHAT DO YOU THINK?

Verses 5 and 6 clearly look beyond the Jews' return to Israel and view the great "day of the Lord" when Jesus returns in power and glory. Written some 2700 years ago, the prophet says that day is "near." How can it have been "near" so long ago and not have come by now? What is the significance of this wording, and how does it provide encouragement to us while we yet wait for that great day?

in the gospel a righteousness from God is revealed, a righteousness that is by faith from first to last, just as it is written: 'The righteous will live by faith'" (Romans 1:16, 17).

The second part of God's righteousness has to do with the punishment of those who resist his will and reject his offer of grace through Christ. If God's righteousness is seen in the salvation of those who accept his offer of pardon, it is seen no less in the punishment directed to those who despise his gracious offer and who, in so doing, show that they despise him who makes the offer.

The expression *my arm* refers to the strength or might by which the Lord would accomplish his purposes. For many, the result will be judgment and punishment, but not for all. For those who believe the great news and accept the Christ, God's arm will bring blessing and salvation. (See 2 Thessalonians 1:5-10.)

The islands are the most distant lands. Even peoples scattered to the farthest reaches of the earth will be blessed by this great act of God. These peoples will *wait on the Lord*. This means that these distant peoples will look to God for deliverance and will accept the salvation that he offers. The record in the book of Acts reveals with what readiness the Gentiles received the gospel of Christ when it was preached to them. (See Acts 11:21; 13:48; 14:1; 17:4; 18:8-10, etc.)

C. THE LORD'S EVERLASTING PROMISES (v. 6)

6. "Lift up your eyes to the heavens, look at the earth beneath; the heavens will vanish like smoke, the earth will wear out like a garment and its inhabitants die like flies. But my salvation will last forever, my righteousness will never fail."

God's people are called to look up *to the heavens,* that is, to the vast expanse of the sky. They are also to look down on the *earth.* The material universe seems to us to be stable, dependable, that which will just go on and on.

In truth, however, it is not permanent. Isaiah states that the *heavens will vanish like smoke.* This presents a picture of the vast universe disintegrating and disappearing like smoke that is blown away by the wind.

The prophet changes the metaphor when describing the fate of the earth, though the truth he is conveying is the same. He says *the earth will wear out like a garment.* The figure of a garment is used similarly by the psalmist when he writes, "They [the heavens and earth] will perish; . . . they will all wear out like a garment. Like clothing you will change them and they will be discarded" (Psalm 102:26; see also Hebrews 1:11).

The entire created universe will not last forever. It is only a matter of time until it will not exist as we know it. This material universe does not provide a lasting foundation for anyone. Security must be found elsewhere. Jesus' admonition in the Sermon on the Mount sets forth a similar concept: "Do not store up for yourselves treasures on earth, where moth and rust destroy, and where thieves break in and steal" (Matthew 6:19).

The *inhabitants* of the earth *will die like flies* or "like gnats." The meaning is that humanity is just as frail and finite as the smallest insect. Mankind is subjected to the same law of perishableness as the physical universe; our physical bodies shall die. It is readily apparent, therefore, that anyone who trusts in the flesh as though it were permanent is foolish indeed.

Over against the temporal nature of all things related to the physical universe stands God, the One who is eternal. And he offers us *salvation.* Though we die in the flesh, by God's gift we may live eternally. We can have full confidence in the promises of God, for he is the righteous one. He said through Isaiah elsewhere, "The grass withers and the flowers fall, but the word of our God stands forever" (40:8).

WHAT DO YOU THINK?

The circumstances of life change so rapidly that we dare not put our confidence in these things. Verse 6 of our lesson text makes it abundantly clear that there is no permanence in this material world. The daily news is a constant reminder that it is foolish to seek lasting security here. Our only source of confidence and lasting joy in life is to be found in the righteousness and salvation of the Lord (Isaiah 51: 6, 8). We must place our trust in the One who remains, when all else perishes (see Hebrews 1:10-12).

Those who suffer take great comfort and encouragement in that truth. How about those of us whose lives are predictably routine? How can we keep the vision of the Lord's coming salvation even through the mundane events of life? How can such a vision change the mundane to vibrant?

PRAYER

PRAYER

Our Father, the spiritual darkness around us seems almost overwhelming at times. In our discouragement your faithfulness sustains us. Strengthen our trust in your great promises. Build in us a faith that lives for the coming of your glorious kingdom. In the name of Jesus the King we pray. Amen.

THOUGHT TO REMEMBER

The hope of God's glorious tomorrow gives one courage and strength to walk through today's darkness.

DAILY BIBLE READINGS

Monday, Dec. 4—Encouraged to Trust (Exodus 14:10-18)

Tuesday, Dec. 5—God's People Liberated (Isaiah 41:11-16)

Wednesday, Dec. 6—Joy of Being Forgiven (Matthew 9:1-8)

Thursday, Dec. 7—Cheered by a Friend (Matthew 14:13-27)

Friday, Dec. 8—God's Support in Prison (Acts 23:1-11)

Saturday, Dec. 9—Comfort From an Unexpected Source (Acts 27:21-25)

Sunday, Dec. 10—God Is With His People (Isaiah 43:1-7)

The verse following our text gives a practical application that may be drawn from God's truth contained here in verses 1-6: "Do not fear the reproach of men or be terrified by their insults." God's enemies will come to nothing, and he will remain faithful to his promises. Let us take courage, therefore, and remain faithful to him.

HOPE AND CAUTION

How old is Earth? Some scientists speculate that the age of our planet is millions, even *billions*, of years. Some Christians, on the other hand, would measure the earth's age in thousands of years. Archeology, geology, and carbon-dating notwithstanding, the exact age of the universe is known only to God. And God has not revealed to us the birth date of the universe.

God has, however, outlined the events of creation, and he has described the end-time demise of the heavens and the earth. Through Isaiah he indicates that the world may simply die of old age, like a worn-out garment. Other Scriptures predict more cataclysmic events: "The earth . . . and the works that are therein shall be burned up" (2 Peter 3:10, KJV).

Whatever the details, the material world will someday cease to be; it is temporal. But we have God's promise that salvation and righteousness "will never fail." The spiritual world is everlasting. Let us rejoice because of this truth, and let us be prepared for that day. Peter concludes rightly that we should be holy and godly, and "look forward to the day of God" (2 Peter 3:11, 12).

—R. W. B.

CONCLUSION

Everyone sat spellbound by the courage of the circus animal trainer. Armed with nothing more than an ordinary wooden chair and a small whip, he stepped into a cage filled with ferocious tigers.

Once inside the cage, he barked orders at the huge animals and cracked his whip. The tigers growled ominously and pawed the air. But at the trainer's command, these great wild cats perform—jumping through flaming hoops and over barrels.

Suddenly the unexpected happened—all of the lights in the arena went out. The trainer was trapped in the cage with the tigers.

No one knew for sure what to expect. When the lights were restored moments later, the trainer was standing with whip and chair in hand in the same place where he had been when the lights went out. Each animal seemed just as much under his control as before. The audience gasped and then erupted in a standing ovation.

When interviewed later, the trainer was asked if he was afraid when he was stranded in the dark with the animals. He admitted to being more afraid than ever before. "After all," he told the reporters, "I knew the cats' night vision was much better than mine. I was at their mercy."

He then explained how he was able to maintain his composure. "I remembered," he added, "that the tigers didn't know that I couldn't see them! I just cracked my whip and talked to them until the lights came on. They never knew the advantage they had over me."

In life, when surrounded by the forces of darkness and evil, we who are God's children may feel overwhelmed and at the mercy of our enemy. But this we know and are assured of: he who is in us is greater than he who is in the world (1 John 4:4). We have the advantage.

Isaiah encouraged Judah in exile to look through their dark and depressing situation to the glorious future God had in store for them—their return to their homeland. May we look to Christ, the light of the world, and find assurance for our eternal future in the presence of God.

Discovery Learning

This page contains an alternate lesson plan emphasizing learning activities. Classes desiring such student involvement will find these suggestions helpful. The next page is a reproducible activity page to further enhance discovery learning.

LEARNING GOALS

Having participated in this study of Isaiah 51:1-6, each adult disciple will:

1. Identify elements of encouragement from Isaiah 51:1-6.

2. Explain how Isaiah's message can encourage us today.

3. Plan to share those encouraging truths from Isaiah in personal ministry to someone who is discouraged.

INTO THE LESSON

(If you are using the clock and title idea suggested in lesson 1, add the label "ENCOURAGEMENT" for this week's session.)

Recruit an artistic member of your class to prepare a life-sized paper head. On the front have a face drawn (eyes, nose, mouth). On the back of the head include a pair of eyes. Attach the head to a stick or a ruler.

As class begins, show the head—front and back—and ask, "What is this person able to do?" ("He can look back as well as ahead.") When you receive the answer, display two signs you have prepared with print large enough to be seen by all: **"LOOKING BACK: The Foundation of the Faithful"** and **"LOOKING AHEAD: The Future of the Faithful."** Display these respectively to the left and right at the front of your room. Identify the two ideas as being the basic outline of today's text, Isaiah 51:1-6.

INTO THE WORD

Write the following Scripture references on triangular pieces of paper shaped like pennants, one reference per piece. Attach each piece to a different pencil so that they look like flags. The references are Genesis 2:8, 9; Genesis 12:1-7; Psalm 102:25, 26; Isaiah 24:8; Jeremiah 31:33, 34; Joel 2:3; Luke 2:30-32; 2 Peter 3:8.

Distribute these eight "flags" to eight of your students, one flag for each. Have each of these students take a moment at this time to find the Scripture that is identified on his or her flag and read it silently to become familiar with its content.

After they have done this, invite one of your better readers to stand before the class and read aloud the six verses of today's Scripture text. After this reading, ask the reader to read the text aloud once again, going slowly this time. During this second reading, those who are holding the "flags" are to "flag the reader down" when the reader

reads a phrase of the lesson text that relates to a passage held by a flag holder. Each time the text reader is "flagged down," have the flag holder read his or her passage and note how it relates to what the text reader has just read.

Before the class session, print the following headings on separate strips of paper, using letters large enough to be read by all in the class: "Remembering Their Beginnings," "Recalling Their Ancestors," "Receiving Former Blessings," "The Lord's Righteous Promises," "The Lord's Universal Promises," and "The Lord's Everlasting Promises." Then roll up each strip .

At this point in the session, hand these six rolled phrases to six class members and have the strips read randomly. The phrases relate to the two posters that you displayed earlier at the front of the room. Ask your class first to decide which three of the phrases relate to "Looking Back" and which to "Looking Ahead." Then ask the class to decide which phrase goes with each verse of today's text. As the matches are made, mount each strip under the correct heading and in verse order. Point out that the six phrases and the six verses contain six reasons to be encouraged in the Lord.

INTO LIFE

Divide your class into groups of four students each. Provide each group with a pen and a sheet of paper, at the top of which is written, "Be encouraged, Christian, because—" Have each group write down as many reasons for encouragement as they can that are related to the verses of the lesson text, and ask them to give the verse number. Then let the groups share their suggestions. Here are two examples: "you are standing on the Rock" (v. 1); "God keeps his promises" (v. 1).

Distribute small pieces of stationery. Ask students to review the reasons for encouragement (above).Each person is to think of one person who could use one of those messages and then write an encouraging note to that person. Urge the students to mail the notes this week.

Read verse 3 of the text aloud. Emphasize the last clause: "joy and gladness shall be found therein, thanksgiving, and the voice of melody." Note that you have been discussing reasons we have for joy and singing. Ask the class members to identify songs, hymns, and choruses that are expressions of joy and encouragement to them. Suggest that they use these in their own devotional times this coming week.

The Rock From Which You Were Cut

The Lord's message to the exiles in Babylon was to remember the "rock" from which they had been "cut." That "rock" is God. Look up the Scriptures on each of the "rocks" below. What does each say about God, and how might that have brought hope to the exiles?

Rock of Ages

"… and that rock was Christ" (1 Corinthians 10:4). The ultimate fulfillment of Isaiah's prophecy is found, not in the return of the exiles to Jerusalem, but the coming and/or the return of Christ. Match each of the following verses from Isaiah 51 with the corresponding New Testament verse that describes its fulfillment.

1. Isaiah 51:4   ____ Matthew 5:11, 12

2. Isaiah 51:6   ____ Revelation 7:16, 17

3. Isaiah 51:7   ____ Hebrews 1:10-12

4. Isaiah 51:8   ____ Acts 13:46-48

5. Isaiah 51:11   ____ Matthew 6:19, 20, 33

God's Promise of Deliverance

Unit 1. The Coming of a New Day
(Lessons 1-5)

A TIME OF JOY

WHY TEACH THIS LESSON?

The first two lessons of this quarter were written more than a hundred years in advance for a generation not yet born, the generation of Jews who would experience the Babylonian captivity. The message to them was that their suffering was nearing an end; deliverance was near.

The message of today's text was addressed to Isaiah's contemporary generation. In a time of political unrest, they too were promised deliverance—but not soon. Things would get worse before they got better. Still, in the end, "the people walking in darkness [would see] a great light" (Isaiah 9:2).

This situation may more closely approximate the feelings of your students today. In our current climate of moral decline and political and economic uncertainty, things may well get worse before they get better. We will find joy if we look to the "Wonderful Counselor, Mighty God, Everlasting Father, Prince of Peace" (Isaiah 9:6).

INTRODUCTION

A. A TIME FOR CHILDREN

Christmas is a special time, particularly for children. Some parents may bemoan the impact of commercialism and its constant appeal to their children. Yet, when all is said and done (and spent!), they delight in watching their little ones anticipate and enjoy Christmas morning. The Christmas story itself, which highlights the birth of God's own Son, possesses an appeal that captures a child's imagination

In spite of the fact that it has continued to keep children at the heart of its observance of Christmas, our society has become an increasingly difficult place for children to live and grow up. The impact of the nation's moral and spiritual decline has wreaked havoc in the lives of countless innocent children, particularly through the breakup of their families.

The Scripture text for today is one of the most stirring messianic prophecies in all of the Old Testament. It describes through impressive titles and elevated language the Child whose birth is the reason for genuine celebration at Christmas. We should remember, however, that this prophecy was delivered during a difficult period for children in Judah's history. Ahaz, king of Judah at the time, had sacrificed some of his own children in the fire as part of his devotion to pagan gods (2 Chronicles 28:1-4). Because of the king's blatant disobedience, other children were seized as captives by invading nations (vv. 5, 8, 17-19; 29:9).

Perhaps it was only fitting, then, that Ahaz should have been the recipient of the prophecies concerning Immanuel (Isaiah 7:14) and the child promised in today's text. Both prophecies were foretelling the coming of Jesus Christ, the King who encouraged little children to come to him and rebuked anyone who hindered them.

May the children in our families and our neighborhoods know not only that Christmas is for them, but that Christ is as well.

B. LESSON BACKGROUND

The hope and joy promised in Isaiah 9:1-7 must be considered against the backdrop of the gloom and misery present in Judah when Isaiah spoke this message.

DEVOTIONAL READING
LUKE 1:46-55

LESSON SCRIPTURE
ISAIAH 9:1-7

PRINTED TEXT
ISAIAH 9:1-7

Dec
17

LESSON AIMS

As a result of this lesson, students should:

1. Describe the hope generated by this prophesy for Isaiah's contemporaries and later readers.

2. Explain the significance of light and darkness in spiritual imagery.

3. Share the light brought by the child described in verse 6.

KEY VERSE

For to us a child is born, to us a son is given, and the government will be on his shoulders. And he will be called Wonderful Counselor, Mighty God, Everlasting Father, Prince of Peace.

—Isaiah 9:6

OPTION

Use the reproducible map activity on page 150 as you present this background information. The correct answers for the blanks follow:

1. *Naphtali*
2. *Zebulun*
3. *Aram*
4. *Damascus*
5. *Samaria*
6. *Jerusalem*
7. *Assyria*

WHAT DO YOU THINK?

One of the problems the people of Judah experienced was that they began to question God's faithfulness and the validity of his word. When God's word is rejected, something must fill the void. Isaiah tells us in chapter 8 that the people eventually strayed so far from God as to consult mediums and spiritists. This is not unlike the current interest in New Age teaching. We are living in an era in which technology has become an extremely significant aspect of life every day. It provides great benefits to us, but it cannot meet our need in the spiritual dimension. It tends to leave us cold and calculating, insensitive and indifferent. As a result, people are searching elsewhere for personal meaning.

Is this good news or bad news? That is, does it suggest an openness to the gospel since people are searching, or does it suggest it will be more difficult to get a fair hearing with the gospel? Explain your answer.

Either way, what are some specific ideas that can help in sharing the gospel in this climate?

Judah was being threatened by an alliance between the northern kingdom of Israel and Syria, and King Ahaz and his people were terrified.

Isaiah (accompanied by one of his sons) approached Ahaz and told him not to fear the alliance, for it would not stand. He urged the king to trust God to provide deliverance for Judah. The nation's problems were spiritual in nature, not political. Isaiah then challenged the king to ask God for a sign to verify Isaiah's message. But the unbelieving Ahaz refused to ask, at which point Isaiah uttered the virgin birth prophecy found in Isaiah 7:14. Instead of turning to God, Ahaz preferred to seek help from Assyria. In no uncertain terms Isaiah told Ahaz that the Assyrian military machine would eventually turn on Judah and leave behind extensive damage (Isaiah 7:18-25). The Lord would, in effect, hide his face from his people (8:17).

The final verses of chapter 8 describe conditions that would exist in Judah as a result of the Assyrian invasion. The people would actually consult mediums and spiritists for assistance rather than "the law" and "the testimony" (vv. 19, 20). Instead of looking inwardly and assessing their own guilt, they would curse God and the king (v. 21). The people would be engulfed in spiritual darkness, and their land would be turned into a curse. However, God, whom they were cursing, would not forever turn his back upon his people.

I. A TRANSFORMED LAND (ISAIAH 9:1-5)

A. FROM DARKNESS TO LIGHT (vv. 1, 2)

1. Nevertheless, there will be no more gloom for those who were in distress. In the past he humbled the land of Zebulun and the land of Naphtali, but in the future he will honor Galilee of the Gentiles, by the way of the sea, along the Jordan—

Nevertheless indicates a link with the material at the close of chapter 8. So also does the word *gloom*, which appeared in 8:22. In the time of affliction, the message of hope was proclaimed. A dramatic change from the depressing scenario of disobedience and despair was on the horizon. Those who heard the message probably understood it to mean relief from oppression by the Assyrians. Prophecy can have more than one fulfillment, however, and we shall see that Isaiah also had in mind the later deliverance from sin by the power of Christ.

Zebulun and *Naphtali* were mentioned first in Isaiah's description of future events. These were two of the twelve tribes of Israel, neither of which was of great significance in the nation's history. This was due in part to their geographical location. Zebulun and Naphtali were neighboring tribes situated within the northernmost sector of Israel, with the Sea of Galilee serving as part of Naphtali's eastern border.

These two tribes were far removed from the influence of Jerusalem, which under David became the political and religious center of the nation. Residents of Zebulun and Naphtali felt the pagan influence of the Phoenicians immediately to their north, as well as from within these tribes because of their failure to remove the Canaanites completely during the conquest (Judges 1:30, 33). Furthermore, armies invading Israel would tend to come from the north, meaning that tribes such as Zebulun and Naphtali would be among the first to experience any hardship that would occur. In the time of Isaiah it was they especially who suffered during the Assyrian invasion under Tiglath-Pileser (2 Kings 15:29).

All of these factors contributed to a feeling of contempt in which the more central and southern tribes held the northerners. This was reflected in the title, *Galilee of the Gentiles*. The latter part of this verse describes the great contrast between the turmoil that Zebulun and Naphtali had suffered and the blessing that God had in store for these once-maligned territories.

2. The people walking in darkness have seen a great light; on those living in the land of the shadow of death a light has dawned.

So certain is the accomplishment of God's word that Isaiah speaks as though he were standing in the day of the fulfillment of God's promise. How was this formerly despised region of Zebulun and Naphtali to be honored? The answer is given by Matthew, who quotes this verse (Matthew 4:15, 16) after recording that Jesus settled in the town of Capernaum (which was located in the territory of Naphtali). Thus, this area that held a long-entrenched reputation as a place of "darkness" (spiritual as well as political) became the residence of the "light of the world." The *land of the shadow of death,* where much suffering inflicted by invaders had occurred, became host to Life personified.

This illustrates the Scriptural principle that God's ways are far different from man's. He tends to use people, places, and objects of little value in the eyes of the world to accomplish his purposes. It was as unlikely that Jesus should have made Galilee his headquarters as it was that he should have made a stable in Bethlehem the place of his birth.

The central message of visual 3 of the visuals packet is that the light that dispels the shadow of death (Isaiah 9:2) came to earth in the incarnate Son of God.

CARRY THE LIGHT

I'm afraid of the dark. Actually, I fear what is *in* the dark. The bogeymen of childhood no longer frighten me, but the darkness of ignorance and sin hides scores of modern monsters that are very threatening. Lurking in the darkness of secularism are doubt and fear. Humanism is casting dark shadows into every corner of our culture. Homosexuals have come out of their closets, and they have brought the darkness of their perversions with them. The midnight madness of carnal corruption seems to engulf us.

Jesus said that the doers of evil love darkness (John 3:19, 20). He also said, "I am the light of the world. Whoever follows me will never walk in darkness, but will have the light of life" (John 8:12). In so saying he showed that he is the light prophesied by Isaiah, the light that shined upon those "in the land of the shadow of death."

It is the Christian's privilege to reflect the light of Christ. Twila Paris has written a challenging song, *Carry the Light.* It asks, "Who will tell the children . . .? Who will preach the Gospel . . .?" The answer is an imperative: "Carry the Light!"

—R. W. B.

B. FROM GRIEF TO JOY (v. 3)

3. You have enlarged the nation and increased their joy; they rejoice before you as people rejoice at the harvest, as men rejoice when dividing the plunder.

The prophet sees God's people multiplied and rejoicing in the days of the "great light," like people rejoicing in the days of a bountiful harvest, or when dividing the spoil taken from a conquered enemy. Jesus most certainly increased the nation by creating an entirely new nation in which both Jews and Gentiles could be included (Ephesians 2:14-17; 1 Peter 2:9). Perhaps this gave added significance to Jesus' appearance in an area that was scornfully known as "Galilee of the Gentiles." From many nations believers in Jesus have joined the "holy nation" and have added their testimonies to the company of the joyful.

C. FROM OPPRESSION TO DELIVERANCE (vv. 4, 5)

4. For as in the day of Midian's defeat, you have shattered the yoke that burdens them, the bar across their shoulders, the rod of their oppressor.

Isaiah elaborated further on the effects of the light in eliminating the people's darkness. Their oppression and enslavement would cease. *The yoke, the bar,* and *the rod* were all items used to control animals, so that they might do the bidding of their masters. Israel was reduced to such a condition under the Assyrian onslaught, and it is likely that those who heard these words spoken would have thought in terms of deliverance from the Assyrians.

WHAT DO YOU THINK?

Isaiah said, "The people walking in darkness have seen a great light." Yet today people are still walking in darkness. Paul writes, "For you were once darkness, but now you are light in the Lord. Live as children of light" (Ephesians 5:8). This means that we are to recognize the darkness for what it is, and live in stark contrast to that darkness. To his followers Jesus said, "You are the light of the world" (Matthew 5:14).

What is our responsibility as Christians living in a spiritually darkened world, and how can we fulfill our responsibility as children of the light? What are some specific things we can do to shine Jesus' light on our darkened community?

WHAT DO YOU THINK?

Isaiah prophesied of one who would break the "yoke that burdens them, the bar across their shoulders, the rod of their oppressor." The immediate reference was to Assyria, but the greater reference was to Jesus, who proclaimed *"freedom for the prisoners" and "release [for] the oppressed" (Luke 4:18, 19). Sadly, many have not taken advantage of the freedom he offers. We see all around us people still held captive to sin. What are some ways you see evidence of this captivity and a need for the freedom Isaiah prophesied? Why is it so many people who are thus enslaved do not seem to recognize it? How can we be more aggressive in proclaiming this released in a way that helps people see their need for it?*

The reference to *the day of Midian's defeat* brought to mind the victory that God gave Israel over the oppressive Midianites during the days of Gideon (Judges 7:19-25). This incident would have held special meaning for the tribes of Zebulun and Naphtali, since it occurred in their general vicinity.

The removal of the Assyrian menace would have been a marvelous event to witness. Yet, at best it could deal with only part of Israel's misery, and not the main part at that. Another form of oppression lay at the root of Israel's woes. This was the tyranny of sin. See Isaiah's indictment against the people (Isaiah 1:1-8). Sin was the yoke, bar, and rod that was degrading the nation and leading it to destruction. Israel never could be really free until it was rid of this greater burden.

There is only one way anyone can have this yoke broken and this burden lifted. God alone has the power to accomplish such a deliverance. It is as impossible for man to do this as it was for Gideon to conquer Midian in his own strength.

JOY TO THE WORLD

Serendipity is a happy word. A serendipity is an unsought fortunate discovery. It is finding a quarter in a public telephone change cup, or getting an unexpected promotion, or receiving an inheritance from an unknown relative. If Hebrew vocabulary had a counterpart, it surely would appear in this text. Isaiah was given a joyous message of hope for his people, when all seemed hopeless!

God's prophets did not often have good news to announce. For the most part, they issued warnings of gloom and doom. Isaiah, however, was privileged to tell of the coming of the Messiah, who would bring peace and joy and hope. He predicted a brighter future for Judah, and for all people of all times and all places.

Countless people live in quiet desperation. Disappointment, discouragement, and depression foster unbearable personal pain. Psychiatrists, analysts, therapists, and ministers carry huge counseling loads, trying to help clients find a life that is tolerable.

For all who despair, Christ is joy. He is the reason for this joy-filled season. We who believe in him "are filled with an inexpressible and glorious joy" (1 Peter 1:8), for he has broken sin's shackles and has brought us salvation.

—R. W. B.

5. Every warrior's boot used in battle and every garment rolled in blood will be destined for burning, will be fuel for the fire.

One does not destroy military supplies when a battle is imminent. To burn the boots, along with the soldiers' garments *rolled in blood*, would indicate the battle is over. It is an assurance of victory.

This verse also reinforces the fact that the real battle facing Israel was not an ordinary battle, but was spiritual in nature, aimed at addressing Israel's real problem. Thus, vast armies and man-made weapons of war were useless. God had another strategy in mind. His primary and most powerful weapon was to be a Child.

HOW TO SAY IT

Ahaz. AY-haz.
Canaanites. KAY-nan-ites.
Capernaum. Kuh-PER-nay-um.
Naphtali. NAF-tuh-lye.
Phoenicians. Fih-NISH-unz.
Tiglath-Pileser.
   TIG-lath-pih-LEE-zer.
Zebulun. ZEB-you-lun.

II. A TRIUMPHANT LAD (ISAIAH 9:6, 7)

A. HIS ACCOLADES (v. 6)

6. For to us a child is born, to us a son is given, and the government will be on his shoulders. And he will be called Wonderful Counselor, Mighty God, Everlasting Father, Prince of Peace.

Here was the glorious climax of Isaiah's picture of future deliverance and joy. He had described the conditions of the transformed land and its people, the defeat of the oppressor, and the nature of the accompanying conflict. Now he turned his prophetic spotlight on just whom God planned to use to bring these magnificent things to pass. While the distraught King Ahaz was preoccupied with alliances, battle tactics, and political maneuvers, God had Israel's future resting squarely upon the shoulders of a Child.

Every child is *born;* this Child was, in addition, to be *given.* The stage had been set for the coming of One who would secure for Israel (and for mankind) deliverance from sin, which would indeed multiply the nation and increase its joy. No greater commentary on this thought can be found than the timeless proclamation of John 3:16.

The government will be on his shoulders. Rather than describing his rule as a burden he must carry, this phrase more likely referred to an insignia (such as a key) that sometimes was laid upon the shoulder of a ruler to symbolize authority. (See Isaiah 22:22.)

The most striking feature of this passage is the series of names or titles that are associated with the Child. While it is true that there is no record of Jesus' actually being called by any of these names, it is also true that there is no record of his ever being called "Immanuel" either. These titles should be taken as indicative of the characteristics of the promised Child. In other words, he would be worthy to receive such honors.

Wonderful Counselor. Elsewhere Isaiah says the "Lord Almighty" is "wonderful in counsel" (Isaiah 28:29). Thus this description indicates the Child is divine in nature.

Wonderful is an apt description of one who is God as well as man. Thus some scholars make *Wonderful* and *Counselor* separate descriptions. The Messiah would indeed be "wonderful" in his nature. "Wonderful" describes the circumstances of his birth, death, resurrection, and ascension. His teaching "amazed" those who heard it (Matthew 7:28). The name *Counselor* is likewise well suited to the One who is wisdom itself. It is he who says, "Counsel and sound judgment are mine; I have understanding and power" (Proverbs 8:14).

With either translation, *Wonderful Counselor* or *Wonderful* and *Counselor,* the Child's divinity is indicated. So there is little practical difference between the two interpretations.

Mighty God. Here the Child's divine character becomes even more apparent. The Hebrew term used for God (*El*) appears also in the name "Immanu-el" (God with us.) The phrase itself appears in Isaiah 10:21 as another name for the Lord. (See also Jeremiah 32:18, "the Lord Almighty.")

Everlasting Father or "Father of eternity" highlights the promised One's gentleness and tenderness. He would possess these fatherly qualities eternally. It is not possible to find adequate fulfillment of a description of this magnitude in anyone other than Jesus Christ. No other one could show us the mighty God and at the same time exemplify the kind of tenderness that any human father would do well to emulate.

Prince of Peace is perhaps the title most heralded at Christmas, mainly because at Jesus' birth the heavenly host announced peace on earth. Jesus created peace by triumphing over "powers and authorities" (Colossians 2:15) and by defeating the devil (Hebrews 2:14, 15). The battle of Calvary was the most intense struggle in the history of the world, despite the absence of conventional weapons of warfare. The Prince of Peace paid the price of peace, which was his own blood (Colossians 1:20). This peace remains the only true and lasting peace, for it is peace with God.

B. HIS ACHIEVEMENTS (v. 7)

7. Of the increase of his government and peace there will be no end. He will reign on David's throne and over his kingdom, establishing and upholding it with

WHAT DO YOU THINK?

The search for peace in our world is unending. Unfortunately, most people are looking in all the wrong places. For them, peace is defined as the cessation of conflict, whether it be between individuals or nations. However, such a state is only conditional. The circumstances or conditions that currently exist make peace possible, but if there is any change in those circumstances, peace may vanish very quickly. Real peace is possible only when justice and righteousness are in the land. "The way of peace they do not know," stated Isaiah, "there is no justice in their paths" (Isaiah 59:8).

How can we teach them "the way of peace"? What can we say, or what can we do, to demonstrate the peace that Christ promised in John 14:27?

justice and righteousness from that time on and forever. The zeal of the LORD Almighty will accomplish this.

Of the increase of his government and peace there will be no end. Earthly governments usually expand through war, but the kingdom portrayed here thrives by means of peace, justice, and righteousness. The Messiah's kingdom shall have no end, either in time or extent.

The mention of the *David's throne* is another signpost marking this passage as messianic. David had been promised an everlasting kingdom (2 Samuel 7:12-16), a promise fulfilled in his greatest descendant, Jesus Christ. (Compare Luke 1:31-33.) The Messiah's kingdom would be firmly established. Furthermore, it would be upheld and characterized by justice and righteousness, for ever. *The zeal of the Lord Almighty will accomplish this.* God's "jealousy" for his own honor, which involves his people's final triumph over the forces of evil, will cause all that is promised here to be fulfilled.

CONCLUSION

A. CHRISTMAS LIGHTS

While Christmas is ideally a season of joy and celebration, a quick reality check will tell us that some amount of darkness envelops the lives of many people. Because of a serious illness, a financial crisis, a death in the family in the past year, or a similar experience, these persons may find the sounds of seasonal tunes and greetings of "Merry Christmas!" shallow and even a bit offensive.

As Christians we must remember that we are more than followers of the Light of the world; we *are* the light of the world (Matthew 5:14). We possess the power to dispel darkness. We must be especially sensitive to the concerns of those whose condition is reminiscent of the people in our text for today. These also have been "walking in darkness," and their residence has become "the land of the shadow of death." The light of a visit, a card, a meal, or a gift can have an impact far beyond the Christmas season.

Someone has observed, "In Christ we move from P.M. to A.M." We who are his followers are called to have the same effect on others.

B. THE KINGDOM OF KINGDOMS

If Jesus Christ is the King of kings, then his church deserves to be regarded as the "Kingdom of kingdoms," or the greatest of all kingdoms. Many earthly kingdoms have attempted to establish justice and peace, but the methods they have used to achieve these often have been anything but just and peaceful. The kingdom of Jesus seeks justice, peace, and righteousness. Unlike the world, the church believes that only in a relationship with God through the Child promised by Isaiah can these become realities. Without God they are noble ideals, but remain like the carrot on the stick, ever out of reach.

Whenever the church has failed to sound a distinct message on behalf of Jesus Christ, it has lost the kind of impact it was meant to have in the world. When it has allowed the world to define peace, justice, and righteousness, it has failed to be the bearer of good news of great joy.

The hostility we see toward the Christian message today is in essence no different from that of Ahaz in Isaiah's day, Herod in Jesus' day, or Communism in this century. Psalm 2:2 reminds us, "The kings of the earth set themselves, and the rulers take their stand and the rulers gather together against the Lord and against his Anointed One." Let us remember that Ahaz, Herod, and Communism have come and gone; of the increase of Christ's government and peace, there shall be no end.

Discovery Learning

This page contains an alternate lesson plan emphasizing learning activities. Classes desiring such student involvement will find these suggestions helpful. The next page is a reproducible activity page to further enhance discovery learning.

LEARNING GOALS

As a result of this study of Isaiah 9:1-7, each adult learner will:

1. Describe the hope generated by this prophesy for Isaiah's contemporaries and later readers.

2. Explain the significance of light and darkness in spiritual imagery.

3. Share the light brought by the child described in verse 6.

INTO THE LESSON

(If you are using the clock/label idea from lesson 1, remember to add the "Joy" label.)

Provide paper and pens for your students and ask each one write the numbers 1 through 27 down the left side of his or her sheet. After they have done that, tell them that you are going to read aloud a list of twenty-seven words. As you read each word, the students are to put a plus or minus sign on their sheets to indicate whether each word has a positive or negative connotation. Read this list clearly, but not too slowly: *gloom, distress, afflict, humbled, light, shadow, death, dawned, yoke, burdens, rod, oppressor, warrior, battle, blood, burning, government, wonderful, counselor, mighty, everlasting, prince, peace, increase, throne, justice, forever.*

After you have completed the reading, ask your students to look over their lists of symbols. Ask, "Where are most of the pluses and where are most of the minuses?" They will indicate that most of their first symbols are minuses and that only at the end is there a significant number of pluses. Mention that these words are taken directly and in order from today's text and that the pattern of minuses and pluses reflects the nature of the content. Isaiah first describes the sad state of affairs, especially among the northern tribes of Israel, and only then tells of the glorious future as the Messiah's light comes to that very area.

INTO THE WORD

Refer to a map of the Holy Land in the time of Isaiah as you present the historical and geographical information included in the "Lesson Background" section and in the commentary on today's text. This will be important for the students to get an understanding of today's text. Such a map should show the kingdoms of Judah and Israel, the location of the areas occupied by the tribes of Zebulun and Naphtali, and the nation of Aram (Syria) to the north.

Option: Make copies of the map on the next page and have the students fill in the missing geographical information as you present the material. (Refer to a the marginal note on page 144 to help the students get their maps labeled correctly.)

Have your students write the following statement on the back of the sheets used in the opening activity: "A Transformed Land: from _____ to _____ (vv. 1, 2); from _____ to _____ (v. 3); from _____ to _____ (vv. 4, 5)."

The lesson outline provides a sample of appropriate terms, but expect learners to suggest others. (Have them give reasons.) Having these verses read aloud in several versions may encourage a variety of answers as well as help the students' understanding of the verses.

For your consideration of verses 6 and 7, display seven unlit candles in simple candleholders. Have an eighth candle already lit for the purpose of lighting the other candles. Then darken your room as much as possible.

Use these candles for a reverent, worshipful reading of verse 6 in the following manner. Ask seven class members to come forward one at a time and light a candle as you slowly read the seven phrases relating to verse 6:

"To us a child is born."

"To us a son is given."

"The government will be on his shoulders."

"He will be called Wonderful Counselor."

"He will be called Mighty God."

"He will be called Everlasting Father."

"He will be called Prince of Peace."

Once the verse is read and all the candles lit, turn the lights on again. Use the commentary section to explain the significance of each phrase. Separate each relevant candle from the rest as you discuss each phrase.

Then read verse 7 aloud. Ask how many put a minus sign for the word *government* in the initial class activity. Probably many did. Ask if they would change that minus for the context of verse 7. Ask them to explain why.

INTO LIFE

Close with a prayer circle. Darken the room and have seven class members hold the candles and thank God for each of the seven truths of verse 6. If those who pray need direction, be prepared to hand them a slip of paper with the appropriate clause and prayer directive. For example, "To us a child is born"; thank God for the marvel of the incarnation: God became flesh and lived among us.

Map It Out

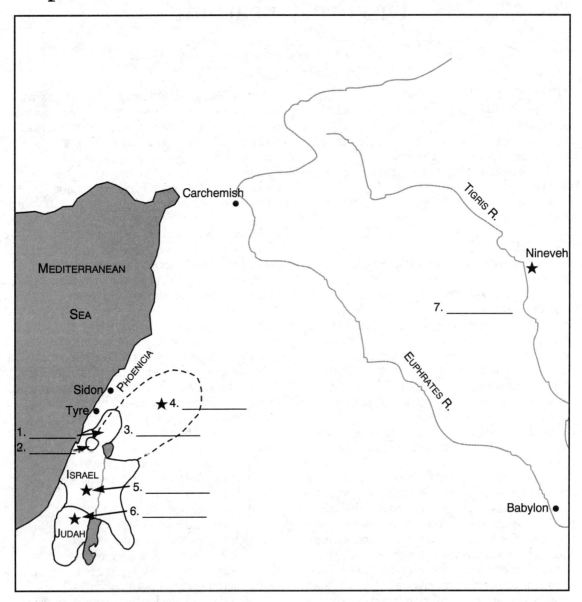

Identify the following:

1. _____ and 2. _____ Two of the twelve tribes, mentioned in today's text (Isaiah 9:1).

3. _____ Israel's neighbor to the north and ally against Judah (also known as Syria) (Isaiah 7:8).

4. _____ Capital of Syria (Isaiah 7:8).

5. _____ Capital of Israel (Ephraim) (Isaiah 7:9).

6. _____ Capital of Judah (Isaiah 7:1).

7. _____ The nation God would use to punish Israel and Judah (Isaiah 7:17).

God's Promise of Deliverance
Unit 1. The Coming of a New Day
(Lessons 1-5)

A TIME OF RIGHTEOUSNESS AND PEACE

LESSON 4

WHY TEACH THIS LESSON?

Christmas can be at once both the "most wonderful time of the year" and one of the most troubling. While Christians thrill to the retelling of that old story of Jesus' birth, they are bothered by the commercial suggestion that "Christmas spirit" is expressed in spending—or comes from a bottle. Groups of Christians gather to praise and worship the Christ of Christmas; groups of demonstrators assemble to ban the display of a manger scene from yet another piece of public land.

Today's lesson helps your students focus on the wonderful aspects of Christmas. The wonder of leader who judges rightly, of a lion lying down with a lamb, of angels announcing good news to shepherds. These are the wonders of Christmas. These and the peace that comes to those on whom his favor rests. Allow these wonders to encourage your students today.

INTRODUCTION

A. THE CHRISTMAS PRESENCE

Today's lesson falls on the day before Christmas, "Christmas Eve." By now, many households have had a Christmas tree up for a number of days or even weeks. All that is missing are the presents that will be placed under the tree.

One of the most enchanting and heartwarming Christmas traditions is a brightly and beautifully decorated tree. Many persons have joyous memories of family members trudging through the snow to find just the right tree. Today the varied lights and ornaments available for decorating the tree produce a dazzling display.

Let us now consider the tree mentioned in today's lesson text from Isaiah 11. From the standpoint of appearance, it hardly seems worth comparing with the richly adorned trees that we have come to associate with Christmas. The tree of which Isaiah spoke was but a mere "stump" (v. 1).

Let us not be fooled by appearances, however. Isaiah's ordinary stump sent out an extraordinary shoot, the "Branch" who would grow to become "beautiful and glorious" (Isaiah 4:2). It should not surprise us, therefore, to learn that the announcement of the birth of the One who was that Branch was first made to lowly shepherds, or that he was born amid humble surroundings.

Every person, no matter what his or her status in life, can take encouragement from the fact that Jesus was born into the simplest of surroundings. Those surroundings help to draw our attention to the real message of this season. Christmas has never depended upon the *presents* one receives, but only on the *presence* of Jesus.

B. LESSON BACKGROUND

In last week's lesson, we saw the importance of considering the context of a Scripture passage. Isaiah's prophecy of a "great light" (Isaiah 9:2) was spoken

Dec
24

DEVOTIONAL READING
HEBREWS 8:6-12

LESSON SCRIPTURE
ISAIAH 11:1-9; LUKE 2:1-20

PRINTED TEXT
ISAIAH 11:1-6; LUKE 2:10-14

LESSON AIMS

As a result of this lesson, students should:

1. Describe the changes Isaiah and the angels (Luke 2) predicted as a result of the Christ's coming.

2. Contrast the purpose of Christ's coming with the world's concept of Christmas.

3. Plan ways the congregation, Bible school class, and/or individuals can demonstrate the truth about Jesus' mission.

KEY VERSE

The wolf will live with the lamb, the leopard will lie down with the goat, the calf and the lion and the yearling together; and a little child will lead them.
—Isaiah 11:6

only after he had painted a vivid picture of the darkness produced by Israel's sin (8:19-22). Likewise, the prophecy in today's lesson text of a coming "Branch" is related to what precedes it. It was the climax to a series of messages using trees (or a similar type of vegetation) to symbolize nations.

Following the prophecy of the Child who would reign upon David's throne (9:6, 7), Isaiah returned to the theme of judgment, addressed chiefly to the kingdom of Israel and its irresponsible leadership (vv. 8-17). As early as 9:18, he was laying the groundwork for the prophecy to appear in chapter 11: "Surely wickedness burns like a fire; it consumes briers and thorns, it sets the forest thickets ablaze, so that it rolls upward in a column of smoke." Israel was going to be overrun by the Assyrians; the devastation inflicted on the land would be most severe. And God would use the Assyrians to chastise the kingdom of Judah as well.

With chapter 10, verse 5, Isaiah's oracle of judgment takes a sudden turn eastward and comes down with full force upon the Assyrian empire. Assyria, whom God had chosen to use as an instrument to punish his people, has become intoxicated with a desire to ravage as many nations as possible, including Judah with its capital city, Jerusalem (v. 11). Assyria's lust for conquest has gone out of control. God will not stand for such a proud heart (v. 12), and he promises to rise up and put a stop to the Assyrian war machine. The divine judgment that will fall upon Assyria is the subject of verses 15-19. Note the imagery Isaiah uses in verse 19 to describe the outcome of that judgment: "And the remaining trees of his forest will be so few that a child could write them down."

In verse 20, the prophet turns his attention once again to Israel, in order to compare its destiny with the fate of Assyria. Here his words carry a tone of optimism and hope, in anticipation of what the beginning of chapter 11 will promise. In 10:20-22, Isaiah refers to a "remnant" of Israel who will return to God following his judgment carried out by the Assyrians upon Israel. And although Judah will suffer greatly at the hands of the Assyrians, God's people are not to fear them. God will rescue his people (vv. 24, 25).

God's people needed to remember that he is the Master Forester, with the power to uproot and plant trees (nations) as he desires. Within one century from the time of Isaiah, the curtain fell on Assyria, ending her role in the history of empires. For his people, however, God had other plans.

The second part of our lesson text comes from a very familiar portion of Scripture. In fact, Luke's account of the birth of Jesus has become so familiar that we may fail to appreciate the astonishing content of the angel's message to the shepherds. May we in this season recapture the sense of wonder the shepherds felt when they received the good news of the Savior's birth.

OPTION

Use the reproducible activity, "Isaiah and the Trees" to explore some of this background material. See page 258.

I. THE PROMISED MESSIAH (ISAIAH 11:1, 2)

A. HIS HUMAN SIDE (v. 1)

1. A shoot will come up from the stump of Jesse; from his roots a Branch will bear fruit.

In chapter 10 mighty Assyria was compared with a forest that was to be cut down by God's judgment, never again to rise (vv. 17-19, 33, 34). Israel, too, was cut down as a result of the judgment of God, but there was hope for Israel's future—the time would come when new life would spring up from that which appeared dead. A tender *shoot* would grow *from the stump of Jesse*. The *stump of Jesse* refers to the house of David, for there is but one Jesse mentioned in Scripture, and that is David's father.

The nation eventually recovered from the devastation brought on by the invasions of the Assyrians and later the Babylonians. Clearly, however, an individual is spoken of in this verse, and that one is Jesus Christ, who was David's greatest descendant. The New Testament attests to this. (See Revelation 22:16; compare Romans 15:12.) When Jesus was born, Herod was king of Judea; and the line of David, once the line of nobility, was reduced to common life. From an ancient family whose glory was all but gone arose One more glorious than David had ever been.

B. HIS HEAVENLY SIDE (v. 2)

2. The Spirit of the LORD will rest on him—the Spirit of wisdom and of understanding, the Spirit of counsel and of power, the Spirit of knowledge and of the fear of the LORD.

After indicating that the Messiah would be descended from the human line of David, Isaiah began to focus upon those divine qualities that would distinguish him from all others and would prove the Messiah to be the perfect ruler.

The Spirit of the Lord will rest on him. Isaiah was clearly referring to how God would equip the Messiah for his task. Certainly leaders throughout the Old Testament (such as the judges) were given the Holy Spirit for specific purposes, but the Spirit would *rest on* or continually lead the promised Branch. Thus did Jesus possess the Spirit "without limit" (John 3:34).

The qualities that would be manifested in the Messiah through the power of the Spirit are named in a series of pairs. The first is *wisdom* and *understanding*. The One who described himself as "greater than Solomon" (Matthew 12:42) possessed wisdom "without limit." This embraces intellectual power and the ability to perceive moral truth.

The terms *counsel* and *power* bring to mind last week's Scripture text, which indicated that the promised Child was to be called "Wonderful Counselor" and "Mighty God." The Messiah would have practical knowledge, enabling him to instruct and guide his people, together with the power to execute his decisions. Concerning the final pair, *knowledge* and *the fear of the Lord,* the prepositional phrase *of the Lord* can be understood as applying equally to both the knowledge and the fear. To fear God and to know him were at the heart of Old Testament religion. Proverbs 1:7 says, "The fear of the Lord is the beginning of knowledge." For Jesus to have possessed these two qualities distinguished him as the truly godly man and as the sum total of what the Old Testament described as a righteous individual.

II. THE PRIORITIES OF MESSIAH'S REIGN (ISAIAH 11:3-5)

A. IMPARTIAL JUDGMENT (v. 3)

3. And he will delight in the fear of the LORD. He will not judge by what he sees with his eyes, or decide by what he hears with his ears.

He will delight in the fear of the Lord. The Hebrew text literally reads, "And his smelling [will be] in the fear of the Lord." Desiring something or finding delight in it was often expressed by means of the symbolism of smelling. It may be compared with the intensely competitive athlete who speaks of "smelling victory." Old Testament sacrifices were said to provide a "an aroma pleasing to the Lord" (Leviticus 1:17, for example), indicating his approval of them. The phrase, therefore, describes the Messiah's high degree of commitment to pleasing God.

Isaiah then highlighted the Messiah's work as judge. It is interesting, in light of the preceding explanation of "smelling," that Isaiah mentioned two other senses, seeing and hearing. For the Messiah to judge accurately he would have to know more than what was available by means of the *eyes* and *ears.* Being empowered by God's Spirit, he would be able to discern the hearts of people (1 Samuel 16:7; John 2:24, 25). His judgment would be just (John 5:30).

WHAT DO YOU THINK?

The description in Isaiah 11:2-4 of the Messiah includes characteristics long considered desirable in any leader: wisdom, understanding, knowledge, strength of character, impartial judgment, and the fear of the Lord. Each of these qualities is absolutely essential to Christian leadership. A church is unlikely to rise above the level of the character and commitment of its leadership. (See Matthew 20:24-28 and 23:1-12.)

In the world, however, these qualities are not always thought of as important. Many seem to be more impressed with shrewdness than with wisdom and understanding, with positional power rather than strength of character, and with corporate and political influence rather than with impartial judgment.

What do you think would happen if national leaders were selected according to these standards? If business and industry leaders were so chosen? What can Christians do to raise these ideals as standards for our political and corporate leaders?

WHAT DO YOU THINK?

Isaiah stated that the Spirit of the Lord would rest upon the Messiah (11:2), enabling him always to exhibit the qualities of wisdom, understanding, knowledge, and the fear of the Lord. Christians are promised the gift of that same Holy Spirit (Acts 2:38) and are challenged to bear the "fruit of the Spirit" (Galatians 5:22, 23). Paul tells us to be "filled with the Spirit" (Ephesians 5:18).

To what extent, then, ought the characteristics with which Isaiah described the Messiah be present in the Messiah's followers? Why are they seen more in some than in others? Can we develop them to a greater degree in our lives, or is their presence totally dependent on the Spirit? Explain. If we can develop them, how?

WHAT DO YOU THINK?

One of the characteristics of the Messiah's ministry was his compassion for the needy. Jesus fulfilled this in his life as he responded to people's physical and material needs. But he did not limit his response to those needs. He was able, instead, to identify the whole need of persons.

What happens when that perspective is not maintained in relief efforts today? What has been the result when programs have responded only to physical needs? Is a church that responds only to non-physical needs correcting the imbalance of such programs, or is such an approach equally flawed? Explain.

CIRCUMSTANTIAL EVIDENCE

Good mystery writers keep readers off balance by leading them wrongly to believe that various innocent characters committed the crime (usually murder), until a surprise ending reveals "whodunit" (usually someone the reader never suspected).

Sometimes readers are led on "wild goose chases" by circumstantial evidence. A character is seen at the scene of the crime; her fingerprints are discovered on the murder weapon; or his car is identical to the one supposedly driven by the killer. None of these bits of evidence is proof sufficient to convict a defendant in court. Smart judges and juries regard such evidence as inconclusive.

True justice requires consideration of more than incriminating appearances. The Messiah prophesied by Isaiah "does not look at the things man looks at. Man looks at the outward appearance, but the Lord looks at the heart" (1 Samuel 16:7). His justice is perfect. And his followers are cautioned: "Judge not according to the appearance, but judge righteous judgment" (John 7:24, *King James Version*). Christians must overcome personal biases. Circumstantial evidence is not trustworthy.   —R. W. B.

B. COMPASSION FOR THE NEEDY (v. 4a)

4a. But with righteousness he will judge the needy, with justice he will give decisions for the poor of the earth.

Throughout history the *poor* have been victims of injustice and oppression. They have been discriminated against in favor of the wealthy and powerful. The Messiah, however, would not side with the rich against the poor; he would see to it that the poor received impartial judgment. The humble and downtrodden would receive from him consideration equal to that accorded any others.

In the Sermon on the Mount, Jesus referred to the "poor in spirit" and the "meek" as those who would be "blessed" (Matthew 5:3, 5). There may be a reference here to these persons. But the main idea of the verse is that Jesus would be a friend of the poor, the oppressed, the downtrodden, and would treat them with fairness.

C. CONDEMNATION FOR THE WICKED (v. 4b)

4b. He will strike the earth with the rod of his mouth; with the breath of his lips he will slay the wicked.

The Hebrew word for *rod* is used in the Old Testament to describe a tool of chastisement or punishment. Isaiah used the word when he was speaking of Assyria, the "rod" of divine anger (10:5). The rod *of his mouth* in the verse before us suggests that the very words of Christ will bring judgment upon *the wicked*. He will speak with authority, and what he says will be carried into effect instantly. In the last day, his spoken word will seal the eternal destiny of all the nations (Matthew 25:31-46).

D. RIGHTEOUSNESS AND FAITHFULNESS (v. 5)

5. Righteousness will be his belt and faithfulness the sash around his waist.

Isaiah concluded his description of the Branch's personal characteristics by saying that *righteousness* (already mentioned in verse 4) and *faithfulness* would be as a *belt* or *sash* tied *around his waist*. In ancient times a man who was about to engage in an activity that required physical exertion and freedom of movement would gather up his loose outer garment and tuck it under his belt so his garment would not hinder him. All of Jesus' actions were characterized by commitment to his Father's righteous purpose and faithfulness to truth. (Compare Ephesians 6:14.) These were always as close to him as the belt or sash around his waist, and they characterized his nature.

III. THE PEACE OF MESSIAH'S KINGDOM (ISAIAH 11:6)

6. The wolf will live with the lamb, the leopard will lie down with the goat, the calf and the lion and the yearling together; and a little child will lead them.

Isaiah's fondness for images taken from the created world produced a wide range of striking word pictures throughout his book. This verse contains one of the most memorable of them. It served to emphasize the degree of change that the Messiah of whom he has been writing would bring about through his labors. Animals that no one would dream of placing in pairs were pictured as living in a state of harmony and bliss. Supervising this incredible transformation of character would be a little child.

How should this scene be understood? It is important to observe the manner in which the New Testament interprets Isaiah's imagery. For example, the changes of land features that are described in Isaiah 40:3, 4 are declared fulfilled in the ministry of John the Baptist (Luke 3:1-6). There the language of Isaiah is viewed as symbolic of the impact that John the Baptist's ministry would have. Perhaps the same could be said of the verse before us now. The changes wrought in people's lives through the gospel of Jesus Christ and the once-impregnable barriers that have crumbled by the power of his love have produced friends and comrades among people whose animosity at one time seemed permanent.

At the same time, there is something to be said for a view that sees verse 6 of our text as a portrayal of conditions under the reign of the Messiah, when the gospel shall have accomplished its full effects in all the nations, when "the earth will be full of the knowledge of the Lord" (Isaiah 11:9). The Scriptures indicate that the created world is waiting "on tiptoe" (Romans 8:19, J. B. Phillips) for its liberation from bondage (8:21). The establishment of peace between animals that have long been bitter enemies may be included in Isaiah's prophecy, thus constituting part of the restoration of a sin-cursed world to divine wholeness.

IV. THE PROMISE HAS COME! (LUKE 2:10-14)

The final portion of our printed text is taken from Luke's timeless account of the birth of Jesus. This was he of whom the prophet Isaiah had spoken nearly seven hundred years earlier, and of whom we have been studying in the preceding portion of our Scripture text. To lowly shepherds tending their flocks at night in a field near Bethlehem came the wonderful news of the Messiah's birth.

A. A SAVIOR FOR ALL (vv. 10, 11)

10, 11. But the angel said to them, "Do not be afraid. I bring you good news of great joy that will be for all the people. Today in the town of David a Savior has been born to you; he is Christ the Lord.

The words *do not be afraid* make up one of the most important watchwords in the Gospels. The same angelic command was issued on the morning of Jesus' resurrection (Matthew 28:5). Thus the ministry of Jesus to the world was introduced and climaxed with the banishment of fear.

Good news. The good news was that a *Savior* had been *born* to them. It was he who would "save his people from their sins" (Matthew 1:21). Through his death and resurrection Jesus made it possible for *great joy* to come to *all the people.* Both the empty cross and the empty tomb are signs that he is the Savior and that he reigns as *Christ the Lord* (Acts 2:36).

The mention of the *town of David* (Bethlehem) here and in verse 4, plus the reference to the "house and line of David" in verse 4, testified to the important link between David and Jesus. Luke was identifying this newborn child as the One who would fulfill such prophecies as those we have been studying.

WHAT DO YOU THINK?

Isaiah paints a picture of the Messiah's kingdom when his reign is complete. It is a picture of tranquillity, trust, and peace—of a world without fear. When we come to Christ in faith, trusting him implicitly, we should begin to exhibit those same qualities in our relationships. We must model to the world the kind of character and values that encourage integrity and mutual concern. We must return good for evil, kindness for indifference, and love for hatred. In short, we must be like Jesus!

To what extent can we as individuals and as a church exhibit a semblance of such a state? If we displayed more of those characteristics, what would it do for our witness to the world? What can we do to be sure we more perfectly display the character of the Messiah and of the kind of kingdom he will ultimately rule?

Isaiah's description of the Messiah's peaceful reign is illustrated by visual 4 of the visuals packet.

WHAT DO YOU THINK?

The angel said the good news of joy was for "all the people" (v. 10), but then the group of angels announced peace "to men upon whom [God's] favor rests" (v. 14). How would you explain this apparent contradiction? How is this good news for all if the peace is restricted to people who win God's favor? How do we find God's favor? How do we help others find God's favor?

PRAYER

Father, may we in this season of giving remember to receive the gift that you placed in Bethlehem's manger. Thank you for sending just the gift we needed. In his name we pray. Amen.

THOUGHT TO REMEMBER

"May we keep Christmas in our hearts, that we may be kept in its hope."   —PETER MARSHALL

DAILY BIBLE READINGS

Monday, Dec. 18—No Love, No Kinship (1 John 4:1-12)

Tuesday, Dec. 19—Love Perfected (1 John 4:13-21)

Wednesday, Dec. 20—Memory With Hope (Genesis 9:8-17)

Thursday, Dec. 21—Immanuel, God With Us (Isaiah 7:10-17)

Friday, Dec. 22—Preparation of Zechariah (Luke 1:5-17)

Saturday, Dec. 23—Announcement to Mary (Luke 1:26-38)

Sunday, Dec. 24—A Marvelous Birth (Luke 2:1-7)

B. A SIGN FOR THE SHEPHERDS (v. 12)

12. "This will be a sign to you: You will find a baby wrapped in cloths and lying in a manger."

The angel gave the shepherds a way by which they would know the message was true. At one and the same time it would unmistakably identify which baby born in Bethlehem that day was the Messiah. (It would seem that in a small town the size of Bethlehem few babies would have been born on any given day.) It would not have been unusual to find a baby *wrapped in cloths* (King James Version: "swaddling clothes"). This was the ancient practice, equivalent to the modern mother's wrapping her newborn in a receiving blanket. However, the sight of a new baby obviously cared for with love and tenderness yet cradled in the feeding box of animals would be so unusual as to make identity of the Christ child absolutely certain.

If it had been our responsibility to organize such a monumental event, it is not likely that we would have arranged it in the way described by Luke. Surely we would have treated the holy Child in a manner befitting his nature. But this only proves how different God's ways are from man's (Isaiah 55:8, 9). Every detail in the birth event was unmistakably God's own work, designed to bring "glory to God in the highest."

C. A MESSAGE FOR THE AGES (vv. 13, 14)

13, 14. Suddenly a great company of the heavenly host appeared with the angel, praising God and saying, "Glory to God in the highest, and on earth peace to men on whom his favor rests."

The wondrous news of the birth of God's Son was so exciting that Heaven's angels could not keep silent. It was impossible for only one of them to announce it! But the real impact of the coming of Jesus was to be experienced on earth. The familiar *King James* phrase, *peace on earth, good will toward men,* is not found in our text. The Greek is literally "peace to men of good will." The angels were announcing the arrival of peace "in men"—that is, peace that an individual can possess if one chooses to order one's life according to God's *good will* or *purpose.*

During this season, "peace on earth" is treated as a highly noble and desirable ideal that is somehow in the power of man to attain. This is a perspective in direct opposition to what the angels declared in the fields near Bethlehem. Jesus came for the very reason that man cannot achieve real peace through his own agenda. Without Jesus Christ, peace will remain ever in the realm of elusive possibility. With him, any person, even in the throes of the most severe tribulation, can possess a peace that "transcends all understanding" (Philippians 4:7).

CONCLUSION

We know the Christmas story so well; we have heard it so often! But is it so familiar to us that we lose our sense of wonder at the events of that remarkable night in Bethlehem? Consider the surroundings: a smelly stable, the usual farm animals, common shepherds, a simple peasant couple, a manger filled with hay. And lying on that hay in the feed trough was Jesus, in the middle of it all. The stable became a sanctuary.

The circumstances of our lives may not always be pleasant. Misfortune, even calamity, may intrude upon us. If Jesus is enthroned in our hearts, however, even the dire situations we face will undergo change. If the Savior is at the center of our lives, turmoil will give way to peace, sadness will turn to joy, and despair will be replaced by hope. Jesus makes the difference.

Discovery Learning

This page contains an alternate lesson plan emphasizing learning activities. Classes desiring such student involvement will find these suggestions helpful. The next page is a reproducible activity page to further enhance discovery learning.

LEARNING GOALS

As a result of studying and comparing the two texts in this lesson, the learner will:

1. Describe the changes Isaiah and the angels (Luke 2) predicted as a result of the Christ's coming.

2. Contrast the purpose of Christ's coming with the world's concept of Christmas.

3. Plan ways the congregation, Bible school class, and/or individuals can demonstrate the truth about Jesus' mission.

INTO THE LESSON

As students arrive, ask some of them about their Christmas trees. How long have they had theirs up? Do they prefer live or artificial trees? How do they decorate their trees—lights, bulbs, tinsel, all the above? How long do they usually display their trees? Does the tree come down the day after Christmas, closer to New Years Day, or when? Why does the Christmas tree have to come down at all? What is different about Christmas that we put trees in our homes? What other differences are apparent at Christmastime?

From this discussion, observe that there are even bigger differences in our world because of Christmas—that is, because Christ came. These are not just external differences of decoration, but differences in our lives. Today's lesson texts tell us about some of the changes—the differences—that came when Jesus came to earth.

OPTION

Bring a small Christmas tree and some decorations. Have the class help you decorate the tree while you discuss the topics suggested above.

INTO THE WORD

If you are using the "clock" idea (see p. 133), put up the RIGHTEOUSNESS AND PEACE label. Then display the following outline on the chalkboard or on a poster.

I. The Promised Messiah (Isaiah 11:1, 2)

II. The Priorities of Messiah's Reign (Isaiah 11:3-5)

III. The Peace of Messiah's Kingdom (Isaiah 11:6)

IV. The Promise Has Come! (Luke 2:8-14)

Divide the class into four groups, assigning each group one of the four points of the outline. Each group is to read its assigned text and note the changes predicted as a result of Christ's coming. Allow five to eight minutes.

When the groups have finished, ask one good reader to read Isaiah 11:1-6 aloud. Have another read Luke 2:8-14. Then have each group reporter tell what the group discovered from its text.

Take a few minutes to discuss how many of those changes are apparent in our society today. Why are they not all apparent? (Some are predictive of end times, the culmination of the Messiah's mission; Isaiah 11:6, for example. Others are conditional, requiring a response from individuals. The angels promised peace not to the whole earth generally, but "to men on whom his favor rests.")

OPTIONS

Choose one of the following activities to make the transition from the Bible study to the application activity:

• Ask, "How are these promises different from what the world seems to expect—at Christmas or any other time?" As you discuss this, observe the contrast between the hectic pace of our commercial Christmas with the "peace" anticipated in the Scripture texts. Note that Christmas, emptied of its religious significance, has no power to change our secularized society. It is only the *Christ* of Christmas who can effect real change.

• If you have access to a VCR, a television, and the "Peanuts" video *A Charlie Brown Christmas* (© 1965, United Feature Syndicate), play the final five minutes, from the time Charlie Brown asks, "Isn't there anyone who knows what Christmas is all about?" and Linus retells the story from Luke 2. Discuss the change the real meaning of Christmas makes, as illustrated by the tree in the video.

INTO LIFE

Observe how every year at Christmas people seem more willing to help people in need than at other times of the year. The Salvation Army receives more donations, churches distribute fruit baskets and canned goods and the like to the needy, and many individuals have Christmas traditions that include serving at a homeless shelter or some similar ministry. But what about the rest of the year? Aren't the changes mentioned in our texts for today supposed to last longer than our Christmas trees?

Together plan a way your class or individuals from your class can be involved in a long-term way to make a difference in people's lives as you share in Christ's mission.

Isaiah and the Trees

This is the time of year many people use a tree to symbolize something of their beliefs about Christmas. Isaiah also used trees as symbols—sometimes of hope and joy and sometimes of judgment and destruction. Identify the use of the tree symbol in each of the following passages.

Isaiah 6:11-13

Isaiah 7:2

Isaiah 10:17-19

Isaiah 10:33, 34

Isaiah 11:1

Isaiah 44:23

Isaiah 53:2

Isaiah 55:12

Isaiah 60:21

God's Promise of Deliverance
Unit 1. The Coming of a New Day
(Lessons 1-5)

A TIME FOR
SHARING GOOD NEWS

LESSON 5

WHY TEACH THIS LESSON?

With all the activity of our modern pace of living, its easy to be overwhelmed, to lose perspective, to forget our *purpose* in living. Sometimes just keeping up with life is all we seem to be able to manage. In that, however, is tragedy, for that is the way we lose our distinctiveness in the world.

This lesson provides an opportunity to recall our purpose as Christians. We live to be a testimony to the Lord's power and grace, to be a "display of his splendor" (Isaiah 61:3). Challenge your students to keep that in mind as they put into practice the truths of this lesson.

INTRODUCTION

A. THE REASON FOR ALL SEASONS

The days after Christmas are frequently characterized by a kind of letdown from the flurry of activities leading up to Christmas Day itself. When the holidays have passed, many who made the effort to "put Christ back into Christmas" will slip back into their former routines. Perhaps they wish that somehow the "spirit of Christmas"—the feelings of love, joy, peace, and goodwill—could last all year.

As Christians we know that such a wish *can* come true, because Christmas is much more than a season or a spirit; it is God's good news concerning the Savior. Because he himself is the very source of life, his influence cannot be confined to any one month or segment of the year. Jesus is not just the reason for the season; he is the reason for living itself.

More than seeing Christ put back into Christmas, the world needs to see him put into daily life on a consistent basis. That responsibility falls squarely on the shoulders of us who are called to overcome the darkness with his light in his name.

B. LESSON BACKGROUND

Today's lesson is taken from the second part of Isaiah's prophetic writings (chapters 40-66). The important themes that characterize Isaiah's prophecies in chapters 1-39 are present with equal power in chapters 40-66. Among them are the "bad news" of God's judgment on Israel and the "good news" of his deliverance and salvation. These themes are prominent in the chapters preceding the printed text for this lesson. Isaiah 57 and 58 dwell on various sins and abuses in Israel that produced her sad condition. Chapter 59 contains Isaiah's declaration that the burden of responsibility in addressing Israel's plight lay with Israel. The Lord's arm never had been too short to save his people, nor his ears too dull to hear their cries (v. 1). The people's iniquities had separated them from God (v. 2).

Following Isaiah's summary of Israel's sins, God is pictured as surveying his chosen nation's desperate condition. Isaiah 59:16 describes what he saw. There was no one to champion the cause of the weak and innocent against the oppressors in

DEVOTIONAL READING
ROMANS 15:15-21
LESSON SCRIPTURE
ISAIAH 60, 61
PRINTED TEXT
ISAIAH 60:1-4; 61:1-4

Dec
31

LESSON AIMS

As a result of this lesson, students should:

1. Describe the good news brought by the Lord's anointed.

2. Explain how the gospel is a fulfillment of that good news.

3. Share the good news of Christ.

KEY VERSE

The LORD has anointed me to preach good news to the poor....to bind up the brokenhearted, to proclaim freedom for the captives and release from darkness for the prisoners. —Isaiah 61:1

WHAT DO YOU THINK?

Isaiah 57—59 describes the darkened spiritual condition of the people of Israel in Isaiah's day. The sins of which Israel was guilty

may be summed up by saying the nation had shown disregard for God's moral and ethical laws and was spiritually sick as a result. One might make the same assertion of our own society. What parallels, if any, do you see between Israel (Judah) in Isaiah's day and our own country?

TEACHER

Use the passages indicated below to stimulate this discussion. Compare the sinful behavior described in each with our society.

57:1-4 (A loss of moral and spiritual conscience)

57:5-7 (Widespread immorality and idolatry)

57:10, 11 (Spiritual poverty and godlessness)

58:3-7 (Blatant hypocrisy)

59:1-11 (A lack of integrity and justice)

59:12, 13 (A rebellious spirit and treacherous behavior)

WHAT DO YOU THINK?

Admitting that things are not as they ought to be in our society, many turn to remedies that are inadequate to treat the real sickness. They are convinced that more money, more social programs, more law enforcement, more education, or more legislation will provide a remedy. Why do these seem to prove inadequate again and again? How can God's solution be brought into our situation? Do we need a modern-day Isaiah? If so, describe how such a person would execute his ministry. If not, then what do we need?

Israel, much less anyone to deliver Israel from its pagan enemies. So God pledged himself to do for his people what they were unable to do for themselves. After God's "enemies" and "foes" had been punished, penitent Israel would be saved by the coming of the Messiah (vv. 18, 20). Isaiah takes no note of periods of time, and his prophecy of the deliverance of Israel blends into a vision of triumphant deliverance and continuing spiritual life in the Messiah's kingdom (v. 21).

The beginning of chapter 60 elaborates on the glorious results of the execution of God's plan of human redemption. The beginning of chapter 61 focuses on the unique individual who would bring the plan to fulfillment.

I. THE BENEFICIARIES OF GOOD NEWS (ISAIAH 60:1-4)

A. THE LORD'S PEOPLE (VV. 1, 2)

1, 2. "Arise, shine, for your light has come, and the glory of the LORD rises upon you. See, darkness covers the earth and thick darkness is over the peoples, but the LORD rises upon you and his glory appears over you.

The people whose sins separated them from God (Isaiah 59:2) are now encouraged to bask in the divine light that has arisen to dispel their darkness. Their former pitiful condition is described in 59:9: "So justice is far from us, and righteousness does not reach us. We look for light, but all is darkness; for brightness, but we walk in deep shadows." It is a scenario reminiscent of that found in the text of our lesson two weeks ago: "The people walking in darkness have seen a great light; on those living in the land of the shadow of death a light has dawned" (Isaiah 9:2).

The source of this wondrous light is captured in the phrase, *"the glory of the Lord."* Although there is a sense in which "the whole earth is full of [God's] glory" (Isaiah 6:3), Isaiah also predicted a time when the glory of God would be "revealed" to all mankind (Isaiah 40:5). Such exalted language as this must find its true fulfillment only in that historic moment recorded in John 1:14: "The Word became flesh and made his dwelling among us. We have seen his glory, the glory of the One and Only, who came from the Father, full of grace and truth."

See, darkness covers the earth. Not just Israel, but the whole earth and all the nations were enshrouded in spiritual darkness. Upon Israel, however, a glory dawned, coming from God himself. In this glory Israel was to stand, and then the results indicated in the following verse would occur.

B. THE NATIONS OF THE WORLD (VV. 3, 4)

3. "Nations will come to your light, and kings to the brightness of your dawn.

When Isaiah announced the coming of God's light to dispel sin's darkness, he went on to describe the light's global impact. The *nations* would be astonished by the glory radiating from Israel and they would be drawn to it. Isaiah had spoken earlier of the conversion of the Gentiles in coming to Jerusalem: "In the last days the mountain of the Lord's temple will be established as chief among the mountains; it will be raised above the hills, and all nations will stream to it" (Isaiah 2:2; see also verses 3, 4).

Among those turning to the light of the Lord would be *kings*. In Old Testament times, kings, even those who ruled God's people, often corrupted or openly opposed the worship of God. The psalmist observed, "The kings of the earth take their stand and the rulers gather together against the Lord and against his Anointed One" (Psalm 2:2). The New Testament records Herod the Great's attempts to destroy the Christ child, whom he saw as a threat to his kingship (Matthew 2:16-18).

Isaiah predicted a radical transformation in the attitude of kings toward the Lord. In so doing, he touched on the power of the gospel to change even the most proud and rebellious individuals. The apostle John, in his description of the new Jerusalem, saw the consummation of Isaiah's prophecy: "The nations will walk by its light, and the kings of the earth will bring their splendor into it" (Revelation 21:24).

POWER OF LIGHT

Has anyone ever discovered why flying insects are attracted to light? Moths destroy themselves flying through flame. A modern device attracts winged insects to its light and exterminates them on contact.

Bright lights attract human interest, too. Neon lights, strobes, lasers, and even candlelight—they all have peculiar fascination, particularly when seen against stark darkness.

Isaiah heartened Judah (and us) with his prophecy of the coming light—"the glory of the Lord" (v. 1). The "light of the world," Jesus Christ, appeared in the black midnight of man's sin and despair. He showed us the way out; indeed, he was, and is, the only way out. In him is forgiveness and hope.

This "light" continues to attract all nations, for, as Jesus predicted, "But I, when I am lifted up from the earth, will draw all men to myself" (John 12:32). In Christ we see the great light of God. And when we follow that light, we do not fly to our destruction, but to our salvation.
          —R. W. B.

4. "Lift up your eyes and look about you: All assemble and come to you; your sons come from afar, and your daughters are carried on the arm."

Here Isaiah uses one of his many touching word pictures to elaborate on the procession of peoples streaming toward Zion. Zion is compared to a mother looking about with joy as her family gathers around her. Earlier Zion's condition was so bad that it was likened to blindness (59:10). Because of the appearance of the true Light, however, Zion's standing has reversed dramatically. Everywhere she looks there is evidence of God's goodness and blessing.

Your daughters are carried on the arm, or "on the hip." This was the common manner of carrying children in the Near East. Elsewhere Isaiah pictures the Gentiles carrying Zion's sons in their arms and her daughters on their shoulders (49:22).

The symbolism of this is very powerful. Whereas Israelites had been forcibly taken from their homeland by Gentiles, now, as the nations flock toward Zion, they bring with them her children who had long been scattered. While Gentiles (such as the Persians) did assist Israelites in returning home following the Babylonian captivity, Isaiah's language again directs our attention to a fulfillment of far greater impact. His words paint an inspiring picture of the collapse of the barriers that once separated Jew and Gentile. This reconciliation was a result of the death of Jesus Christ at Calvary (Ephesians 2:14-18).

II. THE BEARER OF GOOD NEWS (ISAIAH 61:1-4)

A. COMPELLED BY DIVINE POWER (v. 1a)

1a. The Spirit of the Sovereign LORD is on me, because the LORD has anointed me.

In chapter 61, Isaiah turns his attention to the specific individual who would accomplish all of the marvelous things described in chapter 60. Most important for our understanding of this passage is the fact that Jesus, in a synagogue service at Nazareth, applied Isaiah's words to himself (Luke 4:16-21). Verse 21 of Luke's account records that Jesus declared, "Today this scripture is fulfilled in your hearing." Clearly, Jesus was pointing to himself as the one who could lay claim to Isaiah's words and speak them as his own.

WHAT DO YOU THINK?

In view of the "darkness" that covers our society and the world community, the need for the "light" described by Isaiah (60:1) seems even more acute. John identifies Jesus as "the true light that gives light to every man" (John 1:9). Jesus spoke of himself as the light of the world (John 8:12). We need to penetrate our culture with the gospel so that the light of Christ may shine in the spiritual darkness there. Many Christians, however, are so intimidated by the indifference and antagonism of the non-Christian world that they retreat into their sanctuaries or small groups and find their security there. Others associate with groups whose aggressive tactics hardly reflect the spirit of Jesus. How can we find a position between those extremes, neither so timid as to be unnoticed or so aggressive as to be obnoxious? What specifically can this class do this week that would be a positive expression of that light?

WHAT DO YOU THINK?

On the next page is a discussion question to help your class apply the principle of verses 1 and 2 in light of Jesus' use of the passage in Luke 4:16-21.

Visual 5 of the visuals packet conveys the good news that lives broken by sin can be repaired by God's anointed One.

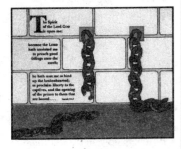

WHAT DO YOU THINK?

In Luke 4:16-21, Jesus identifies himself as the one described by Isaiah in 61:1, 2. If the church is to carry on the mission of Christ in the world, then these verses ought to sharpen the focus of its ministries. Over the years one of the problems with the church has been its tendency to lose its clear sense of mission and to substitute in its place the maintenance of the institution. Measuring a church's effectiveness by the number of people present for programs, the size of budgets, and the investment in real estate, we change our focus from the needs of people to the needs of the organization.

Compare the three or four programs or ministries that seem to get the most attention and support in your church with the mission expressed in Isaiah 61. What strengths do you see? What suggestions might you offer to improve your church's ministry focus?

The Spirit of the Sovereign Lord is on me. In Old Testament times God gave his Spirit to many persons whom he called to serve him in various ways. Such expressions as the one that follows are found in the Old Testament: "The Spirit of God came upon him [Saul] in power, and he joined in their prophesying" (1 Samuel 10:10). For other examples see Exodus 31:3; Numbers 24:2; Judges 3:10; 6:34; 11:29; 13:25. Upon his Son, however, God poured out his Spirit more abundantly. Speaking of the Messiah, who would arise from the line of David, Isaiah earlier said the Spirit of the Lord would rest upon him continually (Isaiah 11:2). Elsewhere, Jesus affirmed his unmeasured possession of God's Spirit (see John 3:34).

The Lord has anointed me. Among the Jews, a person was set apart for divine service by the act of anointing, which involved the pouring of oil on the person's head. Kings were thus consecrated to office (1 Samuel 16:1, 13) as were priests (Leviticus 8:12). There is one instance of the anointing of a prophet (1 Kings 19:16). From the Hebrew word for *anoint* comes the *Messiah*, or "anointed one." God himself anointed the Messiah (Psalm 45:7), and the writer of Hebrews testifies that Jesus is the Messiah (Hebrews 1:8, 9). This anointing was not with oil, but with the Holy Spirit (Acts 10:38.)

B. COMMITTED TO REBUILDING PEOPLE (vv. 1b-3)

1b. ...to preach good news to the poor. He has sent me to bind up the brokenhearted, to proclaim freedom for the captives and release from darkness for the prisoners.

Jesus' ministry was to include *the poor,* the unfortunate, the needy. His *good news* was not limited to a few, but included all persons. *He has sent me.* "God sent his Son" (Galatians 4:4), but the Son did not come into the world by compulsion. He came of his own will and desire when he was sent (see Philippians 2:5-7). Isaiah then listed the things the Messiah would be sent to do. The first of these, "*to bind up the brokenhearted,*" portrayed him as someone with a heart for people, particularly those whose lives were badly in need of repair. In another passage, Isaiah captured the Messiah's gentleness with the promise, "A bruised reed he will not break" (Isaiah 42:3). Jesus' ministry to the brokenhearted is clearly seen in the record of his life.

The next two phrases focus on the freedom the Messiah would proclaim and grant to the imprisoned. The words *"proclaim freedom"* call to mind the language contained in the regulations concerning the Israelites' jubilee (Leviticus 25:10). This special year occurred every fifty years, at which time land was to be returned to the family that had originally owned it, and those in bondage were to be set free.

When Jesus quoted this passage in the Nazareth synagogue and applied it to himself, he was declaring the institution of a new kind of jubilee. Just as the New Covenant is better than the Old, so is the new jubilee far superior to the old. The jubilee inaugurated by Jesus accomplished goals that were similar to those of the old one, but on a much grander scale. Jesus made it possible for mankind to return to its original owner—namely, God himself. He came to bring freedom from sin to those long held captive in its tyranny. Today Christians are called to *proclaim freedom* in Jesus' name to all the world.

2. ... to proclaim the year of the LORD's favor and the day of vengeance of our God, to comfort all who mourn.

The fact that the Messiah would *proclaim the year of the Lord's favor* also indicates that Isaiah had in mind a new kind of jubilee that the Messiah would bring to pass. Jesus came to proclaim God's "year of favor," that is, a period of time during which God's favor (grace) would be given to those who repented and turned to him. The word *favor* provides a link to the message of the angels to the shepherds on the night Jesus was born. Perhaps the announcement of "peace to men on whom his *favor* rests" constituted a declaration that the *year* (time) prophesied by Isaiah had come.

In contrast to this was the further announcement of *the day of vengeance of our God.* Some think that the comparatively much shorter time period for God's wrath (*day* as opposed to *year*) highlights the fact that in the Messianic era, grace would predominate over wrath. This is certainly at the heart of the gospel message, but it should not make us lax regarding the fact that a day of vengeance is inevitable. For now, those who *mourn* in repentance of their sins can still find the *comfort* of forgiveness (Matthew 5:4; James 4:9).

GOD'S NEW YEAR

Today is New Year's Eve. Many persons around the world will be reflecting on the year just ending. For some, those thoughts will be happy; for others, the dominant feeling will be that of regret. Regardless, all will look forward to the new year with the hope that it will be a good year.

Isaiah announced a new "year of the Lord"—a year (or era) of God's favor. The remnant of Judah, who, some 150 years later were in captivity in Babylon, may have interpreted this prophecy to mean that they would be released from captivity and allowed to return to their homeland to restore their holy city and national heritage. Good news, indeed!

Students of the New Testament see in the announcement a second prophecy—one fulfilled by the coming of Christ (Luke 4:21), who ushered in the present era of peace and possibilities. The most recent "year of God's favor" began when in the fullness of time "God sent his Son" (Galatians 4:4, 5).

Is it possible to find a third meaning in Isaiah's prophecy? The New Testament tells of Christ's return in terms of *day* rather than *year.* We read that God "has set a day when he will judge the world with justice" (Acts 17:31). The Jerusalem restored by the returning remnant of Judah can hardly be compared to the "new Jerusalem, coming down out of heaven from God" (Revelation 21:2), to usher in the ultimate "year of the Lord."

—R. W. B.

3. ... and provide for those who grieve in Zion—to bestow on them a crown of beauty instead of ashes, the oil of gladness instead of mourning, and a garment of praise instead of a spirit of despair. They will be called oaks of righteousness, a planting of the LORD for the display of his splendor.

In this verse Isaiah uses a number of striking images to describe the impact of the Messiah's ministry. To those who mourn in repentance for their sins, promises signaling divine favor were given. These mourners would receive *a crown of beauty instead of ashes.* The term *crown of beauty* actually refers to a coronet or turban, an ornamental covering for the head signifying joy and gladness. This would replace the ashes that were sprinkled on one's head during a period of mourning.

Similar is the expression, *the oil of gladness instead of mourning.* The pouring of oil on someone was associated with times of celebration (Psalm 23; Ecclesiastes 9:8). Because of the Messiah's ministry the tears of those who mourn would be wiped away and replaced by joy.

The next figure, *a garment of praise instead of a spirit of despair,* calls to mind other references in Isaiah to clothing as symbolic of one's characteristics and attitudes. (See Isaiah 11:5; 59:16, 17.) Sackcloth was the traditional dress for those in grief or mourning. The prophet here points out that a spirit of praise would characterize people in the day of the Messiah's coming. No more would a drooping, feeble spirit characterize the people of God. Released from the bondage of sin and restored to wholeness, they would praise God for his grace bestowed upon them.

OPTION

The reproducible activity page 166 contains an activity that identifies 22 prophetic statements in today's text. Use this activity to explore the prophecies and their fulfillments.

WHAT DO YOU THINK?

In Isaiah 61:3, the prophet describes God's redeemed people as "oaks of righteousness, a planting of the Lord for the display of his splendor."

What does this imagery suggest to you? Do you know someone whom you would describe as an "oak of righteousness"? If so, describe that person. If not, describe what such a person would be like if there were one?

What does it mean to be "for the display of his splendor"? Describe the person whose life displays God's "splendor." Is that description an accurate one for your church? Why or why not?

PRAYER

Father, thank you for those who faithfully taught us the gospel and helped us to grow in Christ. Help us to renew our enthusiasm for sharing the gospel and winning the lost to Jesus. In his name. Amen.

THOUGHT TO REMEMBER

"So send I you to bind the bruised and broken,
O'er wand'ring souls to work, to weep, to wake,
To bear the burdens of a world a-weary—
So send I you to suffer for my sake."
—E. Margaret Clarkson

DAILY BIBLE READINGS

Monday, Dec. 25—Heavenly Choir (Luke 2:18-20)

Tuesday, Dec. 26—A Bright Future (John 6:41-47)

Wednesday, Dec. 27—The Glory of Christ (2 Corinthians 8:16-24)

Thursday, Dec. 28—Receive Your Brother (Philemon 10-18)

Friday, Dec. 29—Honest Reasoning (Luke 5:1-11)

Saturday, Dec. 30— Infirmities Healed (Luke 5:12-15)

Sunday, Dec. 31—God's Glory in Evidence (Isaiah 60: 15-22)

Those who accept the Messiah's good tidings are identified by the figure *oaks of righteousness*. The Speaker of verse 1, who would preach, bind up, proclaim liberty, etc., is the One who states that these persons are righteous. Although this righteousness is their own, it comes from God (Isaiah 60:21). The New Testament indicates that this righteousness is credited to us through faith in Jesus Christ (Romans 3:22). In other words, this righteousness is a gift (Romans 5:17). Consequently, we become the trees of God's planting, designed to bring forth fruit that is in keeping with the righteousness that he has bestowed upon us. As trees of righteousness, we will bear righteous fruit, and this will be to the glory and honor of God. Using a different figure, but with the same thought in mind, Jesus said, "Let your light so shine before men, that they may see your good deeds and praise your Father in heaven" (Matthew 5:16).

C. COMMITTED TO REBUILDING PLACES (v. 4)

4. They will rebuild the ancient ruins and restore the places long devastated; they will renew the ruined cities that have been devastated for generations.

Now Isaiah's emphasis shifts to a consideration of the work to be done by God's renewed people, "for the display of his splendor" (v. 3). At first glance this language may seem to refer to the return of the Jews from captivity in Babylon and the rebuilding of Jerusalem and Judah that followed. But in light of the context, both preceding and following this verse, it is clear that we must look for something in line with a messianic interpretation and with Jesus' application of the opening words of the chapter to himself. Help is obtained by examining Acts 15:13-17, where James was speaking about the inclusion of Gentiles into the church. James stated that the prophets were in agreement with this action, and then he quoted from Amos 9:11, 12 to illustrate. Acts 15:16 is especially noteworthy: "After this I will return and rebuild David's fallen tent. Its ruins I will rebuild, and I will restore it."

The rebuilding of ruins was associated with the activity of the church in expanding her outreach and bringing the gospel message to others. That rebuilding process is still going on through the faithful witness of committed followers of Jesus. All around us each day are people whose lives *have been devastated*. They need to hear and know that "the year of the Lord's favor" has not yet run out. The Rebuilder and Repairer of broken lives is still "on call."

CONCLUSION

According to today's Scripture text, the Messiah came to earth because he was sent by the Lord God with a particular mission to fulfill. Throughout his ministry he never lost sight of this task: "For I have come down from heaven not to do my will but to do the will of him who sent me" (John 6:38).

On the day of his resurrection, Jesus appeared to his disciples and spoke these words to them: "Peace be with you! As the Father has sent me, I am sending you" (John 20:21). While this passage is not usually referred to as Jesus' Great Commission, it is filled with meaning for disciples of Jesus today. Jesus says that his disciples are sent by him just as he was sent by the Father. We who have received the marvelous benefits of the Messiah's ministry are also sent to share the same good news with others.

How is this done? One answer to this question lies in a study of Isaiah 61, which states the objectives of the Messiah's ministry. If Jesus' mission was aimed toward the brokenhearted, the prisoners, the mourners, and the devastated ones, then so must ours be. Each of us likely has contact with persons who fall into these categories. Perhaps their lives have consisted of one round of bad news after the other. Let us commit ourselves to sharing God's good news with them.

Discovery Learning

This page contains an alternate lesson plan emphasizing learning activities. Classes desiring such student involvement will find these suggestions helpful. The next page is a reproducible activity page to further enhance discovery learning.

LEARNING GOALS

After today's lesson, each adult will be able to:

1. Describe the good news brought by the Lord's anointed.

2. Explain how the gospel is a fulfillment of that good news.

3. Share the good news of Christ.

INTO THE LESSON

Bring some daily newspapers to class. As you read headlines from them, have your learners raise their hands and show "thumbs up" or "thumbs down" based on whether the article appears to be good or bad news. Typically there will be more bad than good news.

INTO THE WORD

Read aloud the clauses of today's text as listed here. Have students respond to each by showing thumbs up for good news or thumbs down for bad news. Discuss any over which there is disagreement.

1. "Arise, shine, for your light has come."
2. "The glory of the Lord rises upon you."
3. "See, darkness covers the earth and thick darkness is over the peoples."
4. "But the Lord rises upon you and his glory appears over you."
5. "Nations will come to your light."
6. "Kings [will come] to the brightness of your dawn."
7. "[Zion], lift up your eyes and look about you: All assemble and come to you."
8. "Your sons come from afar."
9. "Your daughters are carried on the arm."
10. "The Spirit of the Sovereign Lord is upon me."
11. "The Lord has anointed me to preach good news to the poor."
12. "He has sent me to bind up the brokenhearted."
13. "[He has sent me] to proclaim freedom for the captives ."
14. "[He has sent me to proclaim] release from darkness for the prisoners."
15. "[He has sent me] to proclaim the year of the LORD's favor."
16. "[He has sent me to proclaim] the day of vengeance of our God."
17. "[He has sent me] to comfort all who mourn."
18. "[He has sent me] to provide for those who grieve in Zion."
19. "[He has sent me] to bestow on them a crown of beauty instead of ashes, the oil of gladness instead of mourning, and a garment of praise instead of a spirit of despair."
20. "They will be called oaks of righteousness, a planting of the Lord for the display of his splendor."
21. "They will rebuild the ancient ruins and restore the places long devastated."
22. "They will renew the ruined cities that have been devastated for generations."

Have your learners form groups of three or four. Ask one third of the groups to read Isaiah 60:1-4; 61:1-4, and determine which of these prophesies were fulfilled in the Jews' return from captivity (538 B.C.) Another third should read the same text and determine which prophecies were fulfilled with the coming of Christ, his death on the cross, and his resurrection. The final third should determine which await fulfillment in the return of Christ.

Allot five to eight minutes for this activity, and remind the class that a prophecy may have more than one fulfillment. When time is up, have someone from each group report the group's ideas to the class.

OPTION

Use the reproducible activities on page 166 for a variation on this activity and the application activity below.

INTO LIFE

Focus on the prophecies that have been fulfilled in Christ and that will be fulfilled at his return. Ask the class to suggest some some practical situations in which various parts of the good news may be especially welcome, and how can we share the good news in those situations. (For example, the "brokenhearted" [61:1] may be those grieving a loss; visits to funeral homes and sending sympathy cards to the bereaved are ways to share good news in such cases.)

Ask, "If we do these things, how will it be true that we might 'be called oaks of righteousness, a planting of the Lord for the display of his splendor'" (61:3)? Observe that such deeds glorify Christ, and that is what he has called us to do (Matthew 5:16).

Close with a challenge to act on these ideas and a prayer for God to be glorified as you do.

Prophecy and Fulfillment

Read Isaiah 60:1-4; 61:1-4. Then indicate whether each of the following prophecies was fulfilled in the Jews' Return from Captivity (R), the Birth and Ministry of Christ (B), or in the Second Coming of Christ (S). Mark the appropriate letter in the blank before each statement.

____ 1. "Arise, shine, for your light has come."

____ 2. "The glory of the Lord rises upon you."

____ 3. "See, darkness covers the earth and thick darkness is over the peoples."

____ 4. "But the Lord rises upon you and his glory appears over you."

____ 5. "Nations will come to your light."

____ 6. "Kings [will come] to the brightness of your dawn."

____ 7. "[Zion], lift up your eyes and look about you: All assemble and come to you."

____ 8. "Your sons come from afar."

____ 9. "Your daughters are carried on the arm."

____ 10. "The Spirit of the Sovereign Lord is upon me."

____ 11. "The Lord has anointed me to preach good news to the poor."

____ 12. "He has sent me to bind up the brokenhearted."

____ 13. "[He has sent me] to proclaim freedom for the captives ."

____ 14. "[He has sent me to proclaim] release from darkness for the prisoners."

____ 15. "[He has sent me] to proclaim the year of the LORD's favor."

____ 16. "[He has sent me to proclaim] the day of vengeance of our God."

____ 17. "[He has sent me] to comfort all who mourn."

____ 18. "[He has sent me] to provide for those who grieve in Zion."

____ 19. "[He has sent me] to bestow on them a crown of beauty instead of ashes, the oil of gladness instead of mourning, and a garment of praise instead of a spirit of despair."

____ 20. "They will be called oaks of righteousness, a planting of the Lord for the display of his splendor."

____ 21. "They will rebuild the ancient ruins and restore the places long devastated."

____ 22. "They will renew the ruined cities that have been devastated for generations."

Prophecy in Practice

Choose two or three phrases from the prophecies fulfilled in Christ (above) and write them on the chart below. For each one, suggest a situation in which that good news needs to be shared or a person who needs to hear it. What can you do to meet that need?

GOOD NEWS	SITUATION IN WHICH THE GOOD NEWS IS NEEDED

God's Promise of Deliverance

Unit 2. The Ministry of the Suffering Servant
(Lessons 6-9)

THE SERVANT'S CALL

LESSON 6

WHY TEACH THIS LESSON?

For one who follows Christ, who seeks to be "like Christ," perhaps nothing could be more important than a description of Christ. It is not a description of his physical appearance that we need (we have no complete description of what the Lord looked like), for we are not called to be like him in that fashion. Instead, we need a description of his ministry, his activities, his priorities.

This we find in the Servant Songs of Isaiah. Written seven hundred years before Christ appeared in his human body, these songs describe his ministry as he "became flesh and made his dwelling among us" (John 1:14). These songs were an encouragement to the exiles in Babylon, as they identified with the suffering servant. As they submitted to God's will, the songs assured them, they would see God's deliverance. Jesus, too, did God's will (John 6:38), and through that brought deliverance from sin. We Christians can learn from both the exiles and the example of Christ. We, like the exiles, can identify with the servant and apply these songs to ourselves because we know the ultimate Servant and have identified with him and with his purpose.

This lesson, then, becomes a challenge to participate in the ministry of Christ. Do not allow your students to leave its message in the past, either with Judah in captivity or with Jesus in Galilee and Jerusalem. It's for today, in your town, in your life.

INTRODUCTION

A. "CALLED TO SERVE"

"This Is a Service Organization," read the sign in front of the church building. For that congregation the words were much more than a slogan. A drug rehabilitation center, an orphanage, a nursing home, a lunch-hour Bible study for businessmen, and a halfway house for troubled youth were just a few of the expressions of these believers' commitment to meeting the needs of people in the name of Christ. When I asked the minister what inspired the church's many ministries, he replied, "We believe that when God calls us, he calls us to serve."

When those believers answered that call, they joined a great host of saints whom God has raised up to accomplish his purposes on earth. Throughout the history of God's kingdom on earth God has honored his children by inviting them to share in the unfolding of his will. In Isaiah 42 we are introduced to the One who personifies this biblical concept of servanthood.

B. LESSON BACKGROUND

The Servant Songs of Isaiah (42:1-4; 49:1-6; 50:4-9; 52:13—53:12) belong to a section of the book of Isaiah (chapters 40—55) that has as its backdrop the Babylonian captivity of the nation of Judah. In this setting the exiled Judean nation is portrayed as the "servant of the Lord."

Some Bible students understand the servant to be the Messiah, and see the servant's mission fulfilled only in Jesus Christ. No one could doubt that these passages speak of Christ or that he is their ultimate fulfillment. The New Testament

DEVOTIONAL READING
JOHN 7:37-44

LESSON SCRIPTURE
ISAIAH 42:1-9

PRINTED TEXT
ISAIAH 42:1-9

Jan
7

LESSON AIMS

As a result of studying this lesson, each student should:

1. Describe the role of the Lord's "servant."

2. Compare that role with that of Christ.

3. Choose a ministry individuals or the class can support to participate in the ministry of Christ.

KEY VERSE

Here is my servant, whom I uphold, my chosen one in whom I delight; I will put my Spirit on him and he will bring justice to the nations.   —Isaiah 42:1

WHAT DO YOU THINK?

Ancient Israel had difficulty accepting and fulfilling its role as servant of the Lord. The nation seemed to have a limited understanding of what it meant to be God's chosen people. God chose them and blessed them above all peoples, but it was not because of their goodness or special merit. Nor were they chosen so that they alone would live forever in God's favor. God chose them and cared for them because he would be faithful to his covenant with Abraham and bring to fulfillment his promise of blessing for the whole world (Genesis 12:1-3; Deuteronomy 7:7, 8; 9:5, 6).

What evidence do you see that the church as a whole or certain Christians individually have the same difficulty? If Christians generally understood what it means to be the "servant of the Lord" today, what differences would be seen in the church? in our communities? in the homes of Christians?

Visual 6 of the visuals packet is based on Isaiah 42:1-4.

affirms as much in such passages as Matthew 12:15-21. At the same time, prophecy often has more than one fulfillment. The promise to Abraham (Genesis 12:2, 3 was fulfilled first in Isaac (Genesis 17:19), but ultimately in Christ (Galatians 3:14). Thus we may view the servant passages as speaking first of the nation of Israel, specifically the faithful among the exiles in Babylonian captivity. From that perspective we will also note that they find their ultimate and complete fulfillment in Jesus Christ.

According to the prophet, the Babylonian captivity (586-538 B.C.) would serve three purposes. First, by it God would punish Judah for her sins. In a manner typical of God's dealings with his people, he would use a hostile nation as an instrument of his judgment upon his people's apostasy. Second, the Babylonian captivity would purge Judah of her idolatry. Throughout her national history Judah had been drawn to idol worship. After a series of more limited judgments, God would use the Babylonian captivity to demonstrate, once and for all, the catastrophic consequences of following false gods. The third and final purpose for the captivity would be to prepare the Israelite nation to become a "light for the Gentiles" (42:6; 49:6). By dispersing his people among the nations God would position them to become a universal witness to the message of the one true God.

In the Servant Songs of Isaiah God intended to minister to his exiled nation. The songs provided the captives with reassurance that through obedient submission to the divine will their suffering would serve a purpose that would reach far beyond their own race and their own generation. These prophecies ultimately anticipated a period in the future when Jesus himself would emerge from Israel as God's Servant, whose sufferings would save the world.

I. GOD COMMISSIONS HIS SERVANT (ISAIAH 42:1-4)

A. THE SERVANT CHOSEN BY GOD (v. 1a)

1a. "Here is my servant, whom I uphold, my chosen one in whom I delight.

Here is my servant. With these words God announced his selection of Israel as the servant he would raise up to accomplish his purposes on earth. The Hebrew term translated "servant" means "one who performs some deed in obedience to the command of another." In the Bible and throughout the ancient world the word was often used as a formal title for an officer of the royal court. (See for example, 2 Kings 3:11, where the same term is translated "officer," and 22:12, where it is "attendant.") The title "servant" implied both honor as the king's representative and at the same time complete subservience to the king's command. In similar fashion the Christian's service to the heavenly King brings honor to God's servants and expects submission to his commands.

Abraham, Moses, and David were among important biblical personalities who were referred to as God's "servants" as they performed deeds at his command. In the book of Isaiah the term *servant* is used once to describe the prophet himself (20:3), but most commonly it refers collectively to the nation of Israel (41:8; 44:2, 21; 45:4; 48:20). The exiled Israelite nation, as they submitted to God's commands and performed his will, would become a faithful remnant (see 46:3) and function as his servant.

My chosen. In Old Testament times servants rarely initiated their own positions. Whether in a royal court or the household of a common citizen, those who served were normally *chosen* or commissioned by their superiors. This explains why in this verse, and in many others, the title *servant* is accompanied by the term *chosen* (41:8; 44:2). As with the role of being God's servant, being his *chosen* one brought with it a balance of privilege and responsibility. For the people of Israel, the privilege consisted of their being selected, lovingly and graciously, from among the nations to be a special people to God. Their responsibility included the challenges of representing the one true God among the nations and of being held to the higher standards expected of such a position. Our relationship with Christ is likewise a position of great privilege and serious responsibility.

B. THE SERVANT EMPOWERED BY GOD'S SPIRIT (v. 1b)

1b. "I will put my Spirit on him and he will bring justice to the nations.

In the New Testament the Spirit of God (Holy Spirit) is described as abiding in the believer as a permanent resident, producing "fruit" of character and service. In the Old Testament God's Spirit (God's empowerment) is said to have related to his people in a different manner. The Spirit is described as an external force or power that came "upon" individuals to equip them temporarily for some specific service. In such fashion Jephthah and Samson were empowered with courage or strength by God's Spirit (Judges 11:29; 14:6) without necessarily becoming "spiritual" people. The same is true for the effect that the Spirit would have upon the nation of Israel. The prophet simply meant that God would equip his people to perform the task to which he commissioned them.

C. THE NATURE OF THE SERVANT'S MINISTRY (vv. 2, 3a)

2, 3a. "He will not shout or cry out, or raise his voice in the streets. A bruised reed he will not break, and a smoldering wick he will not snuff out.

By studying the Servant Songs we gain insight into the way God works in his world. We see that God accomplishes his will through spiritual influences of sacrifice and grace, rather than through aggressive, coercive, and manipulative tactics such as lie behind much of human achievement. This is the emphasis of these verses as they describe the servant's ministry. Israel would not assume a posture of self-promotion but one of genuine humility. Rather than exploiting the weakness of broken humanity, the servant would show compassion toward those whose lives were broken and nearly extinguished. Rather than attempting to force God's justice and impose his peace, the exiled Israelite nation would patiently wait for God to accomplish his will in his own way and in his own time. As they endured the sufferings of the Babylonian captivity and were then subsequently restored to their homeland, this generation of exiled Judeans would bear witness to all peoples that they who submit to the one true God will eventually receive his vindication and reward. It was the nation's task to bring the world to God by means of a spirit of obedience and grace. Later, Jesus Christ, the Lord's Servant par excellence, would say, "But I, when I am lifted up from the earth [am crucified], will draw all men to myself" (John 12:32). The Servant would compel people to righteousness, not by driving them, but by drawing them with the irresistible power of his sacrificial love.

D. THE GOAL OF THE SERVANT'S MINISTRY (vv. 3b, 4)

3b, 4. "In faithfulness he will bring forth justice; he will not falter or be discouraged till he establishes justice on earth. In his law the islands will put their hope."

The phrases *bring forth justice* and *establishes justice* appear three times in this brief song (vv. 1, 3, 4). They spell out the goal of the servant's ministry. The *justice* was not some punishment that God was prepared to enforce upon the nations. It was rather a new *justice*, which he was prepared to offer them. It was a verdict, a truth, revealed by his *law* (notice the parallel between *justice* and *law* in verse 4) and leading to a new basis for interpersonal and international relationships. This truth was that there is but one true God who rules his world by righteousness and justice (v. 6). As the nations embrace this truth they will learn to live together in equity and peace.

How to Say It

Babylonian. Bab-uh-LOW-nee-un.

Jephthah. JEF-thuh (th as in thin).

Pisidia. Pih-SID-ee-uh.

Option

The reproducible activity on page 174 will provide your learners an opportunity to compare the characteristics of the "servant of the Lord" in Isaiah with Jesus' description of kingdom leadership.

What Do You Think?

Two of the greatest enemies of effective Christian service are fear of failure and discouragement in the presence of adversity. These twin killers destroy confidence and weaken endurance. When we focus on our own inadequacies, we set up a self-defeating context for our service. God reminds us that we serve him "who created the heavens" and "spread out the earth" and who gives "breath its people" (v. 5). He also affirms that he will take hold of his servant's hand (v. 6). How does this promise of God encourage you? What have you attempted in his name because you knew he had hold of your hand? What will you attempt with that confidence?

The verbs *bring forth* and *establish* mean to "decree" or "proclaim." The servant role of Israel was to be, therefore, much like that of a prophet who would carry God's liberating message to the world.

II. GOD ASSURES HIS SERVANT'S SUCCESS (ISAIAH 42:5-9)

A. The God Who Sends the Servant (vv. 5, 6a)

5, 6a. This is what God the Lord says—he who created the heavens and stretched them out, who spread out the earth and all that comes out of it, who gives breath to its people, and life to those who walk on it: "I, the Lord, have called you in righteousness; I will take hold of your hand.

This is what God the Lord says. These words seem to indicate the beginning of a new prophetic utterance, independent of the Servant Song in verses 1 through 4. The theme of Israel's role as God's representative among the nations, however, is continued in these verses. First, God who commissioned the servant is described. He might have been identified as the God who raised up Abraham or who brought Israel out of Egypt. But, since the ministry of the servant was to be universal, God is described in terms of two of his roles that equally affect all peoples and all nations: that of Creator and Provider. God's claim to control the events of history is established by virtue of the fact that he made the world and continually gives life to all of its inhabitants. He who *spread out* (literally, "beat out") the earth as a smith shapes a bowl from a lump of silver is capable of shaping history as well. He who *gives breath* to humanity can raise a nation from its ranks to accomplish his purposes and fulfill his will.

I, the Lord, have called you in righteousness. It seems that the prophet continues to speak of the captive Israelite nation collectively and the role they would play in teaching the peoples of the earth about the one true God. The phrase *in righteousness* refers not to the qualifications of the Lord's chosen one but to the purpose of the Lord's calling. In this usage the expression should be rendered "unto righteousness" or, even better, "unto justification." The basic idea behind the term employed here is "to render normal." The Lord's people were to have a part in "normalizing" relations between God and the peoples of the earth. The God who called his people to this mission would also *hold* and *keep* them as they participated in its unfolding.

B. The Universal Ministry of the Servant (v. 6b)

6b. "I will keep you and will make you to be a covenant for the people and a light for the Gentiles.

From the beginning, God's election of Israel as his chosen people had a universal goal. One of the promises God made to Abraham when he first called him was that through him all families of the earth would be blessed (Genesis 12:3). Though the ultimate fulfillment of that promise would await the coming of Christ (Acts 3:25, 26; Galatians 3:8), the prophet makes it clear that this generation of exiled Israelites would play a role in moving this part of God's unfolding plan toward its goal.

Israel's intercessory role in the conversion of the nations is characterized in two ways. First, Israel is described as *a covenant for the people.* (See also Isaiah 49:8.) In biblical times covenants reconciled or bound one party to another. In this case God was one party and the non-Jewish nations were the other. Israel, or more particularly the exiled Judeans, would have a part in the reconciliation of the two. The way this would be accomplished is suggested by the phrase *a light for the Gentiles.* By this expression the prophet probably meant that as the foreign nations witnessed Israel's patient submission to the will of God and the positive benefits that came of it, they would be convinced that the God of Israel is, indeed, the one true God.

There is a truth here that is applicable to the Christian. God uses people to spread his truth to the world. As was the case for ancient Israel, our relationship with God as it is witnessed by those around us has the power to enlighten people spiritually and invite them to seek the true and living God. By submitting to his will and living according to his precepts, we can help to mediate a reconciliation between a lost world and the saving God.

C. THE DELIVERANCE THAT COMES THROUGH THE SERVANT (v. 7)

7. "... to open eyes that are blind, to free captives from prison and to release from the dungeon those who sit in darkness.

These metaphors of the spiritual enlightenment and liberation that the nations would experience as they learned the truth taught by Israel's exile and subsequent return to Canaan had special meaning to the Judean captives. They themselves were liberated from their *prison* of captivity by the mighty hand of God as he conquered Babylon and secured their release through Cyrus in 538 B.C. Even as God used Cyrus to liberate them from a physical, political bondage, God would use them in the liberation of the nations from the bondage of spiritual darkness. Sin binds a soul in the darkest prison of all—a prison of guilt and alienation from God. It is from such bondage that Jesus came to deliver mankind.

D. THE TRUTH REVEALED BY THE SERVANT'S WORK (vv. 8, 9)

8, 9. "I am the LORD; that is my name! I will not give my glory to another or my praise to idols. See, the former things have taken place, and new things I declare; before they spring into being I announce them to you."

Here we see the culmination of the prophet's message to the nations. From the beginning of this chapter he has been speaking of the role that would be played by the faithful remnant of the Israelite exiles (God's servant) in the enlightenment and the liberation that God would bring to the nations of the earth. He now defines the great spiritual truth that forms both the basis and goal of that spiritual deliverance: there is but one true God and Yahweh (*the LORD*) is his *name* (v. 8). Indeed, this truth constitutes the goal of all of God's revelation to mankind. This is the truth God wanted the Egyptians to learn from the ten plagues (see Exodus 7:5; 8:22). Isaiah repeatedly says that this truth would be learned from God's punishment and subsequent restoration of his people. (See Isaiah 49:23, 26.)

Monotheism (the worship of one God to the exclusion of all others) is a concept that is taken for granted by most modern Westerners, but not so the peoples of the ancient world. Predominantly polytheists (those who worship many gods), the people surrounding tiny Israel made gods of virtually all objects and forces of material creation. It would be difficult for them to abandon their *idols,* but such would be required if they were to embrace the one true God (see Exodus 20:1-5). It is likewise essential for us to abandon any object, person, ambition, or ideology that might function as a god in our lives if we are to worship God as he intends and deserves to be worshiped.

Before they spring into being I announce them to you. This final statement is meant to stand as proof of the claim that Jehovah alone is God. In the previous chapter (41:22, 23) he challenged the false gods to declare the future ahead of time as proof that they truly were gods. Only One who is in control of history can declare what will be before it happens. By declaring the fate of his exiled people ahead of time and then bringing it to pass, God demonstrated that he is the Sovereign Lord of the universe.

WHAT DO YOU THINK?

As a group, list some things your congregation could do to serve God in the manner suggested in Isaiah 42:6, 7.

How might you be "a light for the Gentiles"? How could you help "open eyes that are blind"? In what ways could you help to "free captives" and "release . . . those who sit in darkness?"

(Put these phrases into contemporary settings and discuss how your church might be a "service organization" in your ministry area.)

WHAT DO YOU THINK?

Isaiah 42:18-25 reveals that Israel deliberately chose not to hear God's call or to see the great privilege and responsibility he had given them. Israel became as spiritually blind and deaf as other nations. The people's self-interest and disobedience left them with no testimony and vulnerable to the very nations to whom they were supposed to have been a witness.

To what extent do you think the church faces the same danger? What steps can we take to be sure we do not ignore God's call but, instead, focus on the mission to which he has called us?

PRAYER

Father in Heaven, thank you for honoring us with the privilege of participating in the unfolding of your will. When you call us may we answer as willing servants, ready to do your bidding. In Jesus' name. Amen.

THOUGHT TO REMEMBER

God accomplishes his will through spiritual influences of sacrifice and grace. We serve him best when we so live.

DAILY BIBLE READINGS

Monday, Jan. 1—Song of Victory (Isaiah 42:10-17)

Tuesday, Jan. 2—Israel—Deaf and Blind (Isaiah 42:18-25)

Wednesday, Jan. 3—Israel's Redemption (Isaiah 43:1-7)

Thursday, Jan. 4—Israel, the Lord's Witness (Isaiah 43:8-13)

Friday, Jan. 5—God as Redeemer (Isaiah 43:14-21)

Saturday, Jan. 6—The Greatness of his Power (Ephesians 2:1-10)

Sunday, Jan. 7—Jesus' Power (Matthew 12:22-32)

HAPPY NEW YEAR!

New Year's Day may be my favorite holiday. I like new beginnings—new years, new weeks, new days. I even get excited over the beginning of new months, despite the inevitable bill-paying. In fact, that is one reason I like "day 1"—I can balance accounts, clean the slate, and start budgeting all over again.

Solomon was a cynical mid-lifer when he said, "There is nothing new under the sun" (Ecclesiastes 1:9). He was suffering from boredom and frustration, disillusioned by his own mortality. Often we forget to embrace the newness of ordinary events, such as the dawn of each day, or the first day of each week. Much excitement surrounds the first day of the year, but the same kind of excitement can be generated over any new start, any fresh beginning.

Isaiah spoke of "new things." Today is the first Sunday of a new year and the first day of a new week. It is an appropriate time for reflection, repentance, renewal, and resolution. New beginnings are possible with God. "If anyone is in Christ, he is a new creation; the old has gone, the new has come" (2 Corinthians 5:17).   —R. W. B.

CONCLUSION

In Matthew 12:17-21 the gospel writer tells us that what Isaiah predicted of the servant (Israel) was ultimately fulfilled in Jesus' life and ministry. This reveals to us another capacity of prophetic literature. It is the power of the Word of God to leap beyond its historical, contextual meaning to anticipate the unfolding of God's will in ways that perhaps even the prophet himself never could have anticipated. Not only would Israel serve as God's servant, but, in a deeper and fuller sense, another Servant, One "whose origins are from old, from ancient times" (Micah 5:2), would arise to accomplish God's eternal purposes. What God began in creation and continued in Israel was completed through the ministry of Jesus Christ.

Other New Testament Scriptures reveal that Isaiah's prophecy concerning the Lord's Servant pointed to Christ Jesus for its ultimate fulfillment. When the Jews in Antioch of Pisidia railed against Paul and Barnabas's preaching of the gospel, the two took that message to the Gentiles. In doing so, they stated that their action was governed by divine directive and offered as proof Isaiah's prophecy in 42:6 and 49:6 (see Acts 13:46, 47). In the preaching of the gospel, therefore, was the ministry of the Lord's Servant continued: light was given to the Gentiles, the light that brings salvation to all persons everywhere.

Wherever his gospel is proclaimed today, Christ, the Lord's Servant, continues to be the light of life to those who are lost in sin's darkness.

"WHO SAID LIFE WAS FAIR?"

Life's Not Fair, but God Is Good! The title of Robert Schuller's book speaks to the frustration experienced by many of God's people as they struggle to understand and accept the injustices of our existence. The rich get richer, the poor get poorer. Drunk drivers, drug dealers, prostitutes, pornographers, and rapists go free after only a "slap on the wrist" administered by our judicial system. Babies die—millions of them—before they are even born. Good people get sick; hard workers lose their jobs. People live longer, but many without quality; and some die without dignity. Life is not fair.

But God is good! Through his prophet God announced that his justice would be established in the earth (v. 4). His Servant, the Messiah, would bring to fulfillment God's eternal purpose. His purpose of redemption—a plan of salvation for the righteous and judgment for the wicked—that's more than fair.

"Will not the Judge of all the earth do right?" asked Abraham before Sodom was destroyed (Genesis 18:25). The implicit answer is yes; of course, he will! Perfect justice is inherent in God's nature. That truth will be understood when the Servant Christ returns as the ruling King.   —R. W. B.

Discovery Learning

This page contains an alternate lesson plan emphasizing learning activities. Classes desiring such student involvement will find these suggestions helpful. The next page is a reproducible activity page to further enhance discovery learning.

LEARNING GOALS

As a result of this study, the adult student will:

1. Describe the role of the Lord's "servant."
2. Compare that role with that of Christ.
3. Choose a ministry individuals or the class can support to participate in the ministry of Christ.

INTO THE LESSON

At the front of the classroom, display the letters of the word *servant* vertically on the chalkboard, a poster, an overhead projection, or some other means.

Ask the learners to form an acrostic. Ask them to suggest words related to being a servant starting with each letter of the word *servant*. Give them a minute or two to think; then ask for suggestions. Write several words next to each letter as they are suggested, leaving room for the following. After a few words have been suggested for each letter, say, "I'd like to go back over the list and suggest some additional terms. Maybe you have not identified these with being a servant before, but today's lesson will explain how they are relevant. Then list the following (*without* noting the verse numbers): **S**pirit-filled (v. 1); **E**lect (v. 1; *elect = chosen*); **R**ighteous (v. 6; references to *justice* in vv. 1, 3, and 4 also suggest righteousness); **V**aluable (implied in vv. 1-4); **A**pproved (v. 1); **N**ot discouraged (v. 4); **T**enderhearted (v. 3).

INTO THE WORD

Have a good reader read the text aloud, Isaiah 42:1-9. Then divide the class into small groups (three to five members in each). Half the groups are to review the text and see how many of the ideas in your original acrostic can be found in this passage. (Probably some will be there and some will not.) The remaining groups will review the text to see where to find the ideas added at the end of the acrostic activity (listed above; note verse numbers cited).

After a few minutes, ask for reports from one of the groups with the first assignment and one with the second. Allow the other groups (if any) to suggest additional insights if they want. Then have all the groups discuss, "What was the servant's mission?" (The earlier discussion related more to the servant's nature and character.) As the groups report on their findings, note how Israel fulfilled this mission first and how Christ fulfills it even more completely. (Information in the commentary section will prove helpful in this.)

OPTION

The lesson writer uses the following sentences in his development of today's lesson. Read each aloud, in the order given, and ask your adults to match the idea with a verse of the text. If a wrong "match" is chosen, indicate the error but ask, "How do you see the idea of this statement as related to the verse you have identified?" Verse numbers are given, but, of course, do not read those.

• "As the foreign nations witnessed Israel's patient submission to the will of God and the positive benefits that came of it, they would be convinced that the God of Israel is, indeed, the one true God" (v. 6).

• "For the people of Israel, the privilege consisted of their being selected, lovingly and graciously, from among the nations to be a special people to God" (v. 1).

• "God accomplishes his will through spiritual influences of sacrifice and grace" (v. 3).

• "Predominantly polytheists (those who worship many gods), the people surrounding tiny Israel made gods of virtually all objects and forces of material creation" (v. 8).

• "Rather than exploiting the weakness of broken humanity, the servant would show compassion toward those whose lives were broken and nearly extinguished" (v. 3).

• "Sin binds a soul in the darkest prison of all—a prison of guilt and alienation from God" (v. 7).

• "Since the ministry of the servant was to be universal, God is described in terms of two of his roles that equally affect all peoples and all nations: that of Creator and Provider" (v. 5).

• "The prophet simply meant that God would equip his people to perform the task to which he commissioned them" (v. 1).

You may prefer to add other statements from the lesson.

INTO LIFE

Observe that while Israel and Jesus Christ both fulfilled the prophecy of today's text, we too can play a role in its fulfillment. As we participate in the mission of Christ, we become much like the servant in this passage. Ask the class to work in groups to use the information from the Bible study activity to create a list of characteristics and actions of the Lord's servant today. After five minutes, ask for reports and compile a master list on the chalkboard.

Then focus on the "actions" mentioned above. From them, choose a ministry or project your class can initiate to participate in the ministry of Christ.

Isaiah and Jesus on Servant Leadership

Servant leadership and the leadership styles of the world are vastly different. Complete the following chart to discover how Scriptural standards of servant leadership differ from worldly leadership standards and practices.

BIBLICAL STANDARDS	CONTRASTING WORLDLY PRACTICES
1. What characteristics of servant leadership are suggested in Isaiah 42:1-4? v. 2. v. 3. v. 4.	1. What contrasting characteristics are obvious in the world?
2. How did Jesus describe servant leadership in Matthew 20:24-28. v. 26. v. 27. v. 28.	2. How did Jesus describe worldly leadership in Matthew 20:25.

Paul on Leadership

Listed below are the qualifications for elders and deacons from 1 Timothy 3:1-13; Titus 1:6-9. Next to each, write "I" if it matches (exactly or is similar) to a characteristic of the Servant of the Lord in Isaiah 42. Write "J" if it matches something from what Jesus said in Matthew 20:24-28. (This is a composite list; repeated items are only listed once.)

____ Able to teach
____ Above reproach
____ Blameless
____ Can encourage others with sound doctrine
____ Can refute those who oppose the truth
____ Children believe; are not "wild and disobedient"
____ Desires the task
____ Gentle (not violent)
____ Has a good reputation outside the church
____ Holds deep truths of the faith with clear conscience
____ Holy and disciplined
____ Hospitable
____ Husband of but one wife
____ Loves what is good

____ Manages his own family well
____ Not a lover of money
____ Not a recent convert
____ Not given to drunkenness
____ Not over-bearing
____ Not pursuing dishonest gain
____ Not quarrelsome
____ Not quick tempered
____ Respectable
____ Self-controlled
____ Sincere
____ Temperate
____ Tested and proven
____ Upright

God's Promise of Deliverance
Unit 2. The Ministry of the Suffering Servant
(Lessons 6-9)

THE SERVANT'S MISSION

LESSON 7

WHY TEACH THIS LESSON?

In this the second of the Servant Songs of Isaiah, we see the purpose for which God called his Servant then and for which he calls his servants even today. He said to his Servant, "I will also make you a light for the Gentiles, that you may bring my salvation to the ends of the earth." Our lesson writer affirms, "Christians today can participate in the ministry of God's Servant as they proclaim the good news that Jesus saves."

Not only is it true that "Christians today *can* participate," but they must! Issue that challenge as your lesson comes to a conclusion today.

INTRODUCTION

A. THINGS ARE NOT ALWAYS AS THEY SEEM

There is a Chinese parable about an old man who lived with his son in a tiny cottage. One night the old man's horse—the only horse he had—wandered away, and his neighbors all came to say how sorry they were about his misfortune. "How do you know this is ill fortune?" he replied.

A week later the horse came home, bringing with him a whole herd of wild horses. The neighbors then congratulated him on his good fortune. The old man smiled and asked, "How do you know this is good fortune?"

The man's son began to ride the new horses. One day he was thrown from a horse, and the fall left him with a crippled leg. Right on cue the neighbors approached the old man to express their regrets over his bad luck, but the old man asked, "How do you know it is bad luck?"

A few days later a Chinese warlord came by and conscripted all able-bodied men for a bloody war, but the old man's son, being crippled, was passed over in the draft. Once more the neighbors came to congratulate the old man on his good luck, and once more he replied, "How do you know this is good luck?"

The story ends there, though it could have gone on forever. The point of the parable is that things are not always as they seem. In the long run, some immediate circumstance, good or bad, may ultimately lead to a most unexpected outcome.

Today's text was written to a people who were convinced that their immediate circumstance was the worst of fortunes. The message of the prophet, however, enabled them to see that their temporary suffering would lead to a glorious future. Unlike the Chinese parable, however, which pictured a life driven by fate, this prophetic message declared that Israel's negative circumstance would be turned into something good by the power of a sovereign God.

B. LESSON BACKGROUND

The text of this lesson comprises the second of the four Servant Songs of Isaiah. These songs were written to encourage that generation of Judeans who were exiled to Babylon (586-538 B.C.). The destruction of Jerusalem and the subsequent deportation of her citizens to Babylon had long been foretold by the prophets as the means by which God would punish his people for their idolatrous ways. The Servant Songs, however, revealed to these exiles that their suffering would be more

DEVOTIONAL READING
MALACHI 3:1-5
LESSON SCRIPTURE
ISAIAH 49:1-6
PRINTED TEXT
ISAIAH 49:1-6

Jan
14

LESSON AIMS

This lesson should enable the students to:

1. List what God does to prepare and support his servants as they do his will.

2. Explain that Christians are called to be faithful servants sharing the good news of Christ.

3. Commit to praying for missionaries—especially those supported by the local congregation.

KEY VERSE

I will also make you a light for the Gentiles, that you may bring my salvation to the ends of the earth.

—Isaiah 49:6

LESSON 7 NOTES

than punitive. Their suffering would "restore" Israel by paying the penalty of the nation's apostasy and thereby paving the way for the reestablishment of the state of Israel in the land of promise. These repentant exiles would "save" the nations by becoming a living illustration of the truth that those who submit to the true and living God will, in due time, find their vindication and reward. As the nations witnessed the obedient suffering of the exiled Judeans and the positive benefits it brought to the Israelite nation, they too would desire to know the God who brought this to pass.

I. THE SERVANT'S REFLECTIONS (ISAIAH 49:1-4)

Whereas in the first Servant Song (Isaiah 42:1-4) God was the speaker, in the second, the speaker was the servant (the exiled Judeans).

A. THE SERVANT'S CREDENTIALS TO MINISTER ON GOD'S BEHALF (vv. 1-3)

1. Listen to me, you islands; hear this, you distant nations: Before I was born the LORD called me; from my birth he has made mention of my name.

Listen . . . hear this. In the first three verses of the song, the servant spoke of his call to servanthood and the credentials that qualified him to speak authoritatively on God's behalf. This language bears some resemblance to other texts in Scripture that record prophetic calls. For example, of the prophet Jeremiah it was also said that he was commissioned from before birth and had his mouth equipped to speak for God (Jeremiah 1:5, 9). To the *islands* and *distant nations* the servant affirmed his calling, because that which God would accomplish through his servant Israel would take place before the eyes of the nations and would ultimately be for their benefit.

Before I was born the Lord called me. Interpreters disagree over the exact intent of this statement. Some suggest that it is poetic hyperbole, an exaggeration for the sake of emphasis. It seems better, however, to regard it as an actual statement of fact. In a manner similar to the commissionings of Jeremiah and Paul, God consecrated Israel to his service before Israel was even born. (See Jeremiah 1:5; Galatians 1:15; Isaiah 44:2, 24; 46:3.)

From my birth is literally "from the inward parts of my mother." This reference to mother and child could refer to God's actual use of Abraham and Sarah to produce the chosen people. (Compare Isaiah 51:2.) Above all it is clear from the prophet's language that Israel's appearance on the world scene was no accident, but was the unfolding of the predetermined will of God.

As noted in the previous lesson, these Servant Songs are also messianic. That is, in addition to describing Israel, they describe the ultimate Servant of the Lord, Jesus the Messiah. In that, the prophecy is its own fulfillment. It speaks of one who was commissioned before birth, and that One of whom it speaks has yet to be born!

Isaiah punctuated the fact that God was in control of these events by placing *the Lord* in the emphatic position in the Hebrew text. This great work was the Lord's doing, not man's. Only God can determine the future and announce it before it comes to pass.

2. He made my mouth like a sharpened sword, in the shadow of his hand he hid me; he made me into a polished arrow and concealed me in his quiver.

He made my mouth like a sharpened sword. With these words the prophet began to describe Israel's role as the spokesperson of the Lord. God's word (spoken through the servant) was like a *sharpened sword* and a *polished arrow* in its power to announce and execute the will of God. In similar fashion Ephesians 6:17 speaks of "the sword of the Spirit, which is the word of God." (See also Hebrews 4:12.) Israel would proclaim the authoritative word of the King of Heaven and earth. It would constitute a sharp and penetrating word as it announced judgment upon the Babylonians and liberated Israel from her bondage.

The references to the Lord's servant being hidden *in the shadow of his hand* and *in his quiver* are of particular interest. At one level this language undoubtedly refers to God's protection of his people during their years of captivity. The stories of Daniel and his companions illustrate how God vindicated those who remained faithful to him during the exile. (See Daniel 1, 3, 6.) It is possible, however, that the prophet had an additional thought in mind. This may be his way of saying that the word of judgment that God would announce through Israel would come quickly and unexpectedly as a blow from a concealed weapon. Israel, like a sheathed sword or a quivered arrow, was hidden away until the time came for it to become an instrument of God's will. Certainly no one expected the defeated and devastated Israelite nation to have any power to bring about the destruction of mighty Babylon. But God, who is the Lord of history, in his own time and in his own way unsheathed the sword of his servant's word to announce Babylon's doom and to bring about the return of his people from their captivity. Sacred history reveals that God has made a habit of taking that or those whom men think obscure or unimportant and using them as the instruments of his will.

3. He said to me, "You are my servant, Israel, in whom I will display my splendor."

You are my servant, Israel. This is but one of several places in chapters 40-55 of Isaiah where the servant is identified as *Israel* (see 41:8, 9; 44:1, 2; 48:20). In the literary and historical context of chapters 40-55, "Israel" (Jacob) most specifically refers to the penitent Judean exiles who learned the sad lessons of the exile and who, as a faithful "remnant" of the nation of Israel, obediently endured their suffering as they expectantly waited for the Lord's deliverance. (Compare 46:3-13; also 43:1-13; 44:1-5; 49:8-13.) The idea of the "servant" as one (group) from the nation whose action saved the nation is an important theme in the Servant Songs (49:5; 52:13—53:12) and ultimately anticipated the vicarious suffering and death of Jesus Christ (Acts 8:30-35; 1 Peter 2:21-25).

The word *splendor* is often translated "glory." The Old Testament concept of "glory" carries with it the idea of "honor," "beauty," or "brilliance." With reference to God it often manifested itself in the form of a brilliant, radiating light that evoked a sense of awe in those who beheld it. In this text the prophet suggests that the servant Israel would function like a mirror to reflect God's splendor to the world. This analogy is an important one and is particularly instructive to the modern church. A mirror is nothing in itself. It can only reflect the light that strikes it. In similar fashion, the church has no glory of its own. It serves only to reflect the glory of God revealed in his Son. The church is what God intended it to be when it reflects glory rather than receives it.

The Living Word

The fragment of the Isaiah scroll pictured in visual 7 of the visuals packet is one of the Dead Sea Scrolls, the first of which was discovered in 1947 in a cave a few miles south of Jericho.

HOW TO SAY IT
Achan. AY-kan.
Cyrus. SIGH-russ.
Hagar. HAY-gar.
Zerubbabel. Zeh-RUB-uh-bul.

PRENATAL DESTINY

If our first grandchild is a boy, he surely is destined to be a sports fan, for my son-in-law is not only an avid sports spectator but a participant as well. If our grandchild is a girl, she surely will be a brilliant student and a gifted musician, like her mother!

Neither of these predictions necessarily will come true. Most gifts and interests are possibilities for both males and females, especially since today's children are being "freed" from gender-specific stereotypes. We may have a granddaughter who plays ball, or a grandson who plays piano, or twins (wouldn't that be grand!) who both do all things well. We can only guess what their personal inclinations may be.

God's call of Israel to be his servant nation had to do with more than genetic traits and parental predispositions. It was by divine design that Israel would be the agent to

NOTE (v. 4)

Observing that these Servant Songs refer to Christ as well as to Israel, some students may be bothered by the suggestion that the Servant "misunderstood" his ministry. Certainly Christ had no such misunderstanding! The words find fulfillment, however, in that virtually everyone else in Jesus' day did misunderstand. The disciples' gloom, fear, and doubt after the crucifixion until they were finally convinced of his resurrection are evidence enough of their misunderstanding. But what appeared to have been a defeat became instead the instrument of deliverance.

WHAT DO YOU THINK?

In verse 4 the Lord's servant acknowledged his doubts concerning his usefulness in accomplishing the mission to which he had been called. The servant felt that he had labored "in vain" and spent his strength for nothing. In spite of it, there were no results. Few things are more discouraging.

What situations tend to make you feel this kind of discouragement—that your work, even for the Lord, is futile? How do you pull yourself out of this kind of discouragement? What can Christians do to be aware of one another's frustrations and share the encouragement of our faith with one another? How does the servant's declaration that "what is due me is in the Lord's hand, and my reward is with my God" help bolster our faith in God's service today?

carry out God's eternal will for the human race. Even before God's nation was born, he promised Abraham that it would be so. In Canaan as sojourners, in Egypt as slaves, in Judah as a people, in Babylon as exiles, and back in Judah as only a remnant—God's chosen servant was brought along toward its ultimate destiny. Through Israel all the nations of the earth would be blessed, for Israel was to be progenitor of the Messiah.

As "new Israel," Christians have inherited the destiny of God's chosen. Jesus calls us, and those who follow him are to be servants of his salvation.　　—R. W. B.

B. THE SERVANT'S MISUNDERSTANDING OF HIS MINISTRY (v. 4)

4. But I said, "I have labored to no purpose; I have spent my strength in vain and for nothing. Yet what is due me is in the LORD's hand, and my reward is with my God."

For the expression *but I said,* one might substitute "but I thought to myself." Israel is speaking. The people are reflecting upon their recent history, and the statement reveals that they misunderstood what happened to them and how God could use it to accomplish his purposes in his world. It was part of a consistent pattern of "deafness" and "blindness" that the servant demonstrated toward the role of God in the Babylonian captivity (see Isaiah 42:18-25). As the exiles looked back over more than fifty years of captivity, they saw only shame and humiliation. The servant Israel's presence in Babylon appeared to be just the opposite of what he had been called to become. The one who was called to be the sharp sword of the Lord and the mirror of his glory was instead an outcast among the nations. Stripped of their freedom and their dignity, these exiled Judeans felt helpless to achieve their own agenda, much less accomplish the work of the Lord. The redundant language punctuates their sense of futility—*to no purpose...in vain...for nothing.* The words for "no purpose" and "vain" are actually the same term, and the same one that is used so often in Ecclesiastes, where it describes a life that is completely empty and meaningless. Measured by circumstance alone, the servant's life appeared to have served no purpose.

It was faith, and faith alone, that enabled the servant to find meaning in life when there appeared to be none. This is what he meant when he said, *Yet what is due me is in the Lord's hand, and my reward is with my God.* With these words the servant expressed his unshakable confidence that God who promised him vindication was capable of bringing it to pass.

These words of the servant illustrate the capacity of faith to empower life. While faith expects much of the believer, it also supplies much to the believer. It enables us to see life as something far more than a trip through time controlled by chance or circumstance. We can see it rather as a pilgrimage, a spiritual journey with an eternal destination. The events along the way, positive or negative, do not dictate life's meaning. They are part of a process controlled by the will of a sovereign God, which unfolds in our lives as we submit to him by faith. For us, as for the servant, faith can give meaning to life even in its most empty hours.

BY FAITH, NOT BY SIGHT

Laborers who work diligently with few or no visible results have to be admired. Egyptians who first labored to build the pyramids did not live long enough to see the project completed. Though they could observe progress year-to-year, they could only imagine what the finished structures would look like.

Assembly line workers usually see only a small part of the product they work on. Soldiers risk limbs and life in battle, as they advance into enemy territory or stand off enemy attacks, even though they do not know how things are going in the larger war effort. Teachers, social workers, and other "people persons" often work with little visible proof of their effectiveness. All of these folk are motivated by some degree of faith that they are making a contribution in the advancement toward a significant goal. Reflecting on his situation, the Lord's servant began to feel that he had labored in vain. His confidence in God, however, carried him through. He stated, "Surely the justice due to me is with Jehovah" (v. 4, *American Standard Version*).

Christians often must do kingdom work without perceptible positive results. But "we live by faith, not by sight" (2 Corinthians 5:7). Jesus taught that a significant portion of gospel seeds scattered never produce fruit (Matthew 13:1-23). Yet we must keep believing that our "labor in the Lord is not in vain" (1 Corinthians 15:58).

—R. W. B.

II. THE PURPOSE OF THE SERVANT'S CALLING (ISAIAH 49:5, 6)

A. THE SERVANT'S MINISTRY TO ISRAEL (vv. 5, 6a)

5, 6a. And now the LORD says—he who formed me in the womb to be his servant to bring Jacob back to him and gather Israel to himself, for I am honored in the eyes of the LORD and my God has been my strength—he says: "It is too small a thing for you to be my servant to restore the tribes of Jacob and bring back those of Israel I have kept.

This passage has long been a problem for Bible students because of a variation in the Hebrew texts. In the original Hebrew, the word *not* is identical in sound and almost identical in written form with the expression *to him*. In some manuscripts, the phrase *gather Israel to himself* is rendered *though Israel be not gathered*. The *King James Version* of the Bible followed that reading, creating an apparent contradiction in what the prophet has otherwise been saying. The Dead Sea Scrolls and most ancient versions suggest that the former reading, *gather Israel to himself*, is correct (and it is so translated in most of the more recent Bible versions). Thus, this phrase simply affirms what the text elsewhere says—that the servant's goal was to restore Israel to her preexilic status as an independent state in Palestine.

A far more difficult issue here is how to interpret the meaning of the important term *servant* in verses 5 and 6. The most obvious answer is supplied in verse 3, where Israel is clearly identified as the servant. As most interpreters have noted, however, the expression *and now* at the beginning of verse 5 suggests a break with what has preceded it. Further, it is noted in these verses (5, 6) that the servant's task was to bring back or restore Israel. If the servant was Israel, how could Israel restore Israel?

Commentators have gone in at least three directions in their attempts to solve this interpretive difficulty. Some suggest that the servant here was not Israel, as in verse 3, but rather the prophet Isaiah who delivered God's liberating word concerning the restoration of Israel (see Isaiah 20:3). Others suggest that the reference was to Cyrus the Great, the Persian king whom God would actually use to accomplish Israel's liberation (see Isaiah 44:24—45:4). While either of these interpretations is possible and is within the range of meanings assigned to the term *servant* by the prophet Isaiah, there is another interpretation that is possible, and perhaps preferable, in the immediate context.

As suggested in the comments on verse 3, in Isaiah 40—55 "Israel" sometimes refers to the exiled Judeans, or, even more specifically, to those among them who constituted a faithful "remnant" of penitent believers who accepted God's judgment upon their apostasy and who obediently suffered through the captivity in faith that God would eventually restore them (Isaiah 46:3-13; also 1:27, 28). This notion has the support of the opening lines of the section in Isaiah devoted to the servant of the Lord (40:1, 2) and also best explains the primary meaning of the final Servant Song (52:13—53:12) in its immediate, historical context, namely,

WHAT DO YOU THINK?

Rising above his frustration, the servant realized he was "honored in the eyes of the Lord" and that "God has been my strength." To what extent does that apply to Christians—are they "honored in the eyes of the Lord"? If so, how? How is that demonstrated? And when is the strength of the Lord apparent? How can one know whether he is acting in the strength of the Lord or doing things in his own power? Of course, when I act on my own, I eventually fail, but how can I see that coming before reaching the failing point, and turn things over to God and his power instead?

WHAT DO YOU THINK?

The servant's call to "bring my salvation to the ends of the earth" is still at the top of the Lord's agenda. No congregation of Christians will ever be what Christ intended until they begin to act on his command to "go and make disciples of all nations." This means not only giving generously to cross-cultural mission causes and church-planting efforts, but also sending out its own to the lost of the world.

How can your class or individuals in your class increase your efforts in this task? How can you encourage your church to give more to missions? To take an active role in planting new churches? To recruit people from the congregation to enter missionary service or some other vocational Christian service? to be more active in sharing your faith in your community?

PRAYER

Father, grant us the courage to complete the mission to which you have called your church. May we have the patience to wait upon you to fulfill your promises and to accomplish your will in your own time. In Jesus' name. Amen.

THOUGHT TO REMEMBER

Human extremity is God's opportunity.

DAILY BIBLE READINGS

Monday, Jan. 8—*God Is Everywhere* (Psalm 139:7-14)

Tuesday, Jan. 9—*God Is All-Knowing* (Psalm 33:13-22)

Wednesday, Jan. 10—*God Is All-Powerful* (Jeremiah 32:17-22)

Thursday, Jan. 11—*The Source of Mercy* (Psalm 130)

Friday, Jan. 12—*The Promise of Peace* (Isaiah 26:1-8)

Saturday, Jan. 13—*Message of Salvation* (Isaiah 48:9-16)

Sunday, Jan. 14—*Message of Joy* (Isaiah 48:17-22)

that the servant (the penitent Judean exiles) would suffer for the entire nation, paving the way for their restoration to Canaan.

This is but one example of the larger Old Testament concept of the "one (or few) for the many," which is behind such texts as Abraham's bargaining for the citizens of Sodom (a few righteous being able to save the evil many, Genesis 18:16-33) and the furor over the sin in Israel's camp (Achan's sin resulting in judgment for the army of Israel, Joshua 7). The idea behind the one for the many is that the righteousness (or sin) of an individual member of the community has the power to benefit (or harm) the entire community. Other examples of this may be found in the Old Testament system of sacrifice, where the slaughter or release of unblemished animals had the power to "make atonement" (remove the consequences) for the sins of the entire nation (Leviticus 16). In similar fashion the death of the high priest had the capacity to clear the guilt of the manslayers who had been exiled to the cities of refuge (Numbers 35:25, 28).

B. THE SERVANT'S MINISTRY TO ALL THE WORLD (v. 6b)

6b. I will also make you a light for the Gentiles, that you may bring my salvation to the ends of the earth."

God's election of Israel to be his chosen people was never an end in and of itself. It was rather a means to a greater end that had implications for the whole world. (See Genesis 12:3; 22:18; 26:4; 28:14.) Though the complete fulfillment of this universal mission was not accomplished until the coming of Christ and the spread of his church (Luke 2:32), this generation of exiled Judeans would yet participate in its gradual unfolding by bearing witness to what can happen to a people who submit to the Lord God of the universe. The vindication and restoration that followed their suffering are held out as a promise of what God will do for all peoples who bow before him.

Paul and Barnabas quoted this part of verse 6 to explain their turning to the Gentiles after the Jews had rejected their message in Antioch (Acts 13:47). There is a sense in which the ministry of the Servant, begun in Israel and fulfilled in Jesus Christ, continued on in the work of the early church. Not only was Jesus of Nazareth the personified Servant of the Lord, but also his followers could be identified with God's Servant as they spread the gospel, which brought light to the nations. In the same way, Christians today can participate in the ministry of God's Servant as they proclaim the good news that Jesus saves.

CONCLUSION

The pages of Scripture are full of the stories of people who misunderstood what God was seeking to do in their lives. Abraham misunderstood how God was going to provide him a son through Sarah; so Abraham produced another son through Hagar instead. In his suffering, Job thought God was unjustly punishing him for some sin he had not committed, when in reality God was permitting his faith to be tested. Jacob thought his life had been a struggle against men, when all along he had really been wrestling with God. Jonah resisted, then resented his mission to Nineveh because he mistakenly thought only Israel should be saved. Paul mistakenly believed that Christianity posed a threat to the worship of the one true God and thought it his duty to persecute the church.

All of these incidents illustrate the danger of hastily drawn conclusions about the will of God for human life. As today's lesson indicates, the servant too misunderstood the purpose of what God had brought about in his life. As those who seek to serve God today, we should faithfully follow his will as revealed in Scripture and wait patiently for him to disclose the meaning of the individual events of our lives.

Discovery Learning

This page contains an alternate lesson plan emphasizing learning activities. Classes desiring such student involvement will find these suggestions helpful. The next page is a reproducible activity page to further enhance discovery learning.

LEARNING GOALS

Following today's study, each adult will:

1. List what God does to prepare and support his servants as they do his will.

2. Explain that Christians are called to be faithful servants sharing the good news of Christ.

3. Commit to praying for missionaries—especially those supported by the local congregation.

INTO THE LESSON

Before class, write the words of Isaiah 49:6b on index cards, one word per card. ("I will also make you a light for the Gentiles, that you may bring my salvation to the ends of the earth.") Make one set of cards for every four to six people you expect to attend your class.

If your class meets around tables, put a set on each table. If not, make one set available before anyone has arrived. As your students enter your classroom, invite them to begin arranging the cards in proper order. (Do not tell them the reference just yet.) As the group gets larger, suggest that a couple of people take a new set and begin to arrange them. Keep starting new groups to accommodate people as they arrive. Your goal is to have each student in a group of four to six people when everyone has arrived.

Announce the reference and read it from your Bible. Give the groups a minute to rearrange their cards.

INTO THE WORD

Since your class is already in small groups, give each half of the groups one of the following assignments.

1. "Read Isaiah 49:1-6. From this passage, list as many truths as you can about what God does for his servant and what God wants his servant to do. Note the verse number with each one." These groups should come up with something like the following:

What God does for his servant: "He has called me" (v. 1). "He knows and calls me by name" (v. 1). "He has sharpened my tongue for truth" (v. 2). "He hides me in his hand" (v. 2). "He calls me his servant" (v. 3). "He will reward me for my work for him" (v. 4). "He formed me in the womb" (v. 5). "He sees me as glorious" (v. 6). "He is my strength (v. 6).

What God wants his servant to do: "He expects me to restore Israel" (v. 6). "He expects me to be light to the Gentiles (v. 6). "He makes me his vessel of salvation to the ends of the earth (v. 6).

2. "Read Isaiah 49:1-6. From this passage, list as many general facts as you can—except for those about what God does for his servant or what God wants his servant to do. Note the verse number with each fact." Such ideas as the following should be noted:

"God expects all nations to heed his servant" (v. 1). "God uses his servant as an arrow" (v. 2b). "God is glorified in the servant" (v. 3). "The servant acknowledges his feelings of futility" (v. 4a). "The servant's role to save Israel is the lesser of his roles" (v. 6a).

Give the groups about ten minutes to work; then ask for one of the groups with the first assignment to report. List their findings on the chalkboard. Allow other groups with the same assignment to supplement the report. Then take a report from a group with the second assignment, writing their ideas on the board and supplementing with ideas from other groups.

Discuss the following questions as review and reinforcement of this study. (1) What was the task of God's servant Israel? (2) What did God do to prepare his servant? (3) What did God do to support his servant? (4) How does the task God gives the church differ from the task of God's servant Israel?

INTO LIFE

Verse 6 is the heart of today's lesson. The servant's task was to spread the light of God's salvation to the whole world. Christians today are to join in that task. Help your class memorize verse 6b as a way the Holy Spirit can daily urge each to fulfill his or her servant's task.

Ask each group to arrange their index cards from the opening activity as described below.

"Arrange the verse on two lines. The word *that* begins the second line, and should be offset to the left. Point out the parallels: *I* (God) is over *you* (servant); *light* is over *salvation*; *for the Gentiles* is over *of the earth*." (The verse is printed below with the parallel elements emphasized.)

I	will also make you a	**light**	*for the Gentiles,*
that **you**	may bring my	**salvation**	*to the ends of the earth.*

Ask for volunteers to say the verse aloud; then have the class read the verse together two or three times. Have one half of the class say the first line, and the other half the second line. When general familiarity is gained, close the session by reminding your students of their privilege and duty to be God's servants.

You Are My Hiding Place

"In the shadow of his hand he hid me" (Isaiah 49:2). What does it mean to be hidden by God? Hidden in the Scriptures below are a variety of expressions used in the Bible to describe how God "hides" his people. Look up the Scriptures cited and note next to each phrase the relevant Scripture passages. (Some passages will be used with more than one phrase, and some phrases will have more than one Scripture reference.)

Psalm 17:8, 9   Psalm 32:7
Psalm 27:5   Psalm 143:9
Psalm 31:20

HE HIDES US FROM…   *HE HIDES US WITH (OR IN)…*

Accusing tongues   His dwelling

Our enemies   Himself ("in you")

The intrigues of men   The shadow of his wings

Trouble   The shelter of his presence

The wicked   Songs of deliverance

         His tabernacle

Don't Hide the "Light"

"I will also make you a light for the Gentiles, that you may bring my salvation to the ends of the earth" (Isaiah 49:6). How can you help in sharing this light of salvation with the people around you? Use the letters of the word *light* to start five words or phrases that describe an action you can take this week to share this light with a friend, co-worker, relative, or someone else who needs to hear the gospel of Jesus Christ.

L _____

I _____

G _____

H _____

T _____

God's Promise of Deliverance

Unit 2. The Ministry of the Suffering Servant

(Lessons 6-9)

THE SERVANT'S STEADFAST ENDURANCE

`LESSON 8`

WHY TEACH THIS LESSON?

Pornography. Abortion. Misrepresentation of Christian ideals. These are just a few of the reasons for teaching this lesson! No, these issues will not actually be addressed in today's lesson, but the fact that they are prevalent in the world is ample reason to study this Servant Song from Isaiah 50. The servant was being challenged and accused. But he set his face "like flint" to endure the challenges, encourage his fellows, and continue his ministry. He knew that God was the one who justifies, so no one could lay a charge against him. Your learners need to know the same thing.

INTRODUCTION

A. "SHOULD A MAN LIKE ME RUN AWAY?"

Our world is full of fleeing people. Rather than face life's challenges and endure life's hardships they run from them. "Move on" is their motto—to a new school, a new job, a new town, a new "life." They respond to difficulty with a new forwarding address.

In striking contrast to this fleeing spirit stand the strong words of Nehemiah, the wall builder of old Jerusalem: "Should a man like me run away?" (Nehemiah 6:11). These words were offered in response to a threat raised against him by the enemies of God's people. Wanting no strong Jerusalem, they resisted all of his efforts to reconstruct its walls. Refusing to be distracted by their interruptions or deterred by their opposition, Nehemiah remained true to his calling and completed the task that God assigned him. Aware of who he was and, more importantly, of who God was, Nehemiah simply refused to quit.

This same spirit of faithful devotion to God's calling was displayed by the servant of the Lord in today's text. In spite of rejection and persecution, the servant was determined to see his task through to the end God desired.

B. LESSON BACKGROUND

The third of the four Servant Songs of Isaiah is the subject of this lesson. Though the speaker in this song is not identified, the language and context suggest that he is the servant of the previous two songs (42:1-4; 49:1-6). As noted in the two previous lessons, there is some debate over who the servant is in these texts. The broader context of Isaiah 40—55 favors an interpretation that the title "servant" refers to the nation of Israel (see 41:8; 44:2, 21; 45:4; 48:20; 49:3) or, more particularly, to that generation of penitent Judean exiles who obediently endured the suffering of the Babylonian captivity and became the faithful remnant from whom God would rebuild his nation (see Isaiah 10:20-22). This particular song begins to explore the servant's faithfulness to his calling in spite of persecution from those who opposed him.

DEVOTIONAL READING
HEBREWS 12:1-11
LESSON SCRIPTURE
ISAIAH 50:1-11
PRINTED TEXT
ISAIAH 50:4-11

Jan 21

LESSON AIMS

This lesson should encourage students to:

1. Explain how God's servant responds to adversity or challenge.

2. Suggest ways God supports his servants today, as well as how Christians can support one another.

3. Plan to monitor personal efforts to be steadfast and faithful.

KEY VERSE

Because the Sovereign LORD helps me, I will not be disgraced. Therefore have I set my face like flint, and I know I will not be put to shame. —Isaiah 50:7

Lesson 8 Notes

I. THE SERVANT ENDURES PERSECUTION (ISAIAH 50:4-6)

A. The Servant Is Instructed by God (v. 4)

4. The Sovereign Lord has given me an instructed tongue, to know the word that sustains the weary. He wakens me morning by morning, wakens my ear to listen like one being taught.

The servant (the faithful remnant) was speaking either to his fellow Judean exiles or, perhaps, as in the case of the previous Servant Song (49:1-6), to the nations at large. He began by describing how the Lord prepared him to speak a comforting word to those who were weary of suffering, even as he was.

The first words out of the servant's mouth revealed his understanding of who controlled his life and of at least one of the purposes that his suffering had served. The servant saw himself as a pupil, enrolled in the "school of hard knocks." Experience had been his teacher. It was not an experience dictated by chance, but one shaped by the unfolding will of *the Sovereign Lord*. His suffering was not accidental; it was providential. It was used by God to equip him to minister to his fellow exiles.

The servant's suffering resulted in a *an instructed tongue* (literally, "a tongue of pupils"). The idea behind this unique expression is that before the servant could become a teacher, he first had to become a student. He was to speak not only what he had been told, but also what he had personally experienced. Taught daily (*morning by morning*) by the captivity that those who wait upon the Lord will eventually find their strength, the servant was uniquely qualified to speak an appropriate *word* to the *weary*.

Among other things, this text teaches the unique value of knowledge gained by experience. This kind of knowledge has at least two advantages over theoretical knowledge. First, it is typically more empathetic toward the student. The teacher has already gone where he or she wishes to take the pupil. Second, it is frequently more respected by the student. It has been authenticated by life, tried and proved true in the real world. It seems that God had this in mind when he sent his Son to earth. The author of Hebrews in 2:10-18 declared that Jesus was uniquely qualified to be the supreme messenger of God's truth because, unlike the angels, he came to earth and spoke as a human to humans: "Because he himself suffered when he was tempted, he is able to help those who are being tempted" (v. 18). There is also a sense in which Christians, after the model of Christ, are prepared by suffering to minister more effectively to their fellow humans. (See 2 Corinthians 1:3, 4.)

A Word Aptly Spoken

Shopping for greeting cards can take a long time. One reason is that many cards make interesting reading; more important, however, searching for just the right verse or sentiment to fit the recipient and the occasion deserves careful consideration. And that translates into time. Card creators must be gifted in anticipating our needs, reading our minds and hearts, as it were, and in writing perfect expressions of thoughtfulness.

Saying the right words to the right person at the right time is a gift. Friends with that kind of intuition and initiative are very special. For one who is on the receiving end of such communication, there is great comfort and encouragement. And those who speak (write, send) the messages experience great satisfaction and blessing, too. "A word aptly spoken is like apples of gold in settings of silver" (Proverbs 25:11).

Israel the servant was given the ability to speak "the word that sustains the weary"—a word aptly spoken for the discouraged and downtrodden exiles in captivity. This honor and opportunity has been passed on to Christians, the church, God's servant in this age.

Morning by morning, he wakeneth mine ear to hear.

The gospel is the *right word*, the lost are the *right audience*, and now is the *right time*. "And how good is a timely word!" (Proverbs 15:23).　　　　—R. W. B.

B. THE SERVANT IS OBEDIENT IN SPITE OF PERSECUTION (vv. 5, 6)
5, 6. The Sovereign LORD has opened my ears, and I have not been rebellious; I have not drawn back. I offered my back to those who beat me, my cheeks to those who pulled out my beard; I did not hide my face from mocking and spitting.

Not every child of God who suffers profits from the experience. Some are broken by suffering. Others are embittered by it. In this verse the servant expressed the attitude that enabled him to turn suffering into a springboard for spiritual growth. This same attitude enables the believer today to grow spiritually as a result of enduring life's hard blows.

The Sovereign Lord has opened my ears. The servant was able to remain faithful in the face of suffering because, by faith, he saw it as God's will that he should suffer. He believed God was in his suffering, using it as a stimulus to his spiritual awakening. Earlier Isaiah characterized the servant (Israel) as spiritually "blind" and "deaf," having failed to learn from the Lord's chastening (Isaiah 42:18-25). This passage confirms that what Israel had not learned from previous plagues, famines, and invasions, they finally did learn from the destruction of their nation by the Babylonians: that God would hold his people accountable for their rebellion against him (see v. 24). Accepting his suffering as the Lord's chastening, the servant did not recoil against it but obediently submitted to it, hearing its message and learning its truth as for the first time (50:4, 5). Smarting from his suffering, the servant submitted to God, as if saying to him, "I hear you." There is a sense in which the servant's experience illustrates the claim that sometimes God has to get our attention before he can instruct us.

Of course, it was not God who actually *beat* the servant's *back* or *pulled out [his] beard*. These cruel acts, meant to be humiliating as well as painful, were perpetrated against Israel by their Babylonian oppressors. Recognizing this, the reader can understand how the servant could both nobly endure the suffering that his adversaries inflicted upon him and then later condemn them and pronounce their doom (v. 11). He could endure it because he knew God was using it to awaken him spiritually and instruct him. Yet he could condemn his oppressors because they persecuted him for their own evil and vindictive reasons. For this they should and would be held accountable.

HEARING AIDS

Communication fails more often, it seems, because of poor listening skills than because of poor speaking skills. Ask almost any wife. Some complain that their husbands won't talk to them, but most accuse their mates of *not listening*.

Actually, the fault of poor listening habits is not gender related; females probably are just as guilty as males. Good listeners are hard to find. Effective counselors, successful salespeople, and happily married couples have learned the great importance of intentional listening. It is a gift in some persons, yet a skill that can be developed by anyone to *everyone's* benefit.

God gave servant Israel "an instructed tongue, to know the word that sustains the weary" (v. 4). He also gave him the gift of discernment through listening: "The Sovereign Lord has opened my ears" (v. 5). Both speaking and listening were essential to the servant's mission.

Successful communication continues to require clear speaking and attentive listening. God's people are advised to "be quick to listen, slow to speak" (James 1:19). The emphasis is upon hearing. As many have cleverly observed, that is why God gave us two ears, but only one mouth!

WHAT DO YOU THINK?

The Lord's servant said, "I have not been rebellious; I have not drawn back" (v. 5). How different from the prevailing mindset of our time! We are living in a time when the pursuit of personal happiness has been elevated to the supreme good. The assumption is that if only one can escape pain, suffering, hardship, and restricted freedoms, that person will be happy. Such a view is based on the false notion life's circumstances produce happiness. The person who knows real joy—lasting joy—in life is the person who loves God, trusts him, and learns to grow through life's circumstances, whatever they may be.

Does this mean we should never draw back or look to escape any difficulty? Why or why not? If not, how do we know when to seek release and when to endure?

HOW TO SAY IT
Baal. BAY-ul.
Nehemiah. NEE-heh-MY-uh.
Pharaoh. FAIR-o or FAY-ro.
Zechariah. Zek-uh-RYE-uh.

WHAT DO YOU THINK?

The resolve of the Lord's servant to stand by his convictions and to accomplish his purpose in the face of rejection or persecution is expressed in his statement that he had set his face "like flint" (v. 7). We are living in times of change, not only material change, but social and spiritual change as well. Christian standards of morality and ethical behavior, so long upheld by the majority in our society, are characterized by many as archaic. We are being told that the Christian understanding of marriage and family is no longer tenable.

How can a Christian or a church stand by the moral truths of Scripture without appearing to be hard, unloving, and unforgiving? In other words, how does one take a stand against immoral practices without taking a stand against the immoral people God has called us to save?

WHAT DO YOU THINK?

Some change, of course, is good. For example, methods that once were expedient may no longer be effective. Yet some church leaders seem to set their faces like flint every time a new idea or program is proposed. Suggest some criteria by which to judge when a change is good and when it ought to be opposed.

Christians must listen with their *hearts*, too, ever sensitive to nonverbal expressions of pain and unspoken cries for help. "Open my ears, Lord, and teach me to listen."

—R. W. B.

II. THE SERVANT'S CONFIDENCE IN THE LORD'S HELP (IS. 50:7-9)

A. THE SERVANT BELIEVES THAT GOD WILL DELIVER HIM (v. 7)

7. Because the Sovereign LORD helps me, I will not be disgraced. Therefore have I set my face like flint, and I know I will not be put to shame.

The confidence that the servant expressed did not come from within but from above. It grew out of a faith that God would not abandon him to his foes. This faith was well founded. The pages of Scripture are filled with the accounts of persons who have stood up for God in the face of opposition and found him to be "an ever-present help in trouble" (Psalm 46:1). Moses before Pharaoh, Elijah before Ahab and the prophets of Baal, and Daniel and his companions before the Babylonians are familiar examples of well-placed faith in God's power to protect his children.

Therefore *I will not be disgraced*. With these words the servant's expectations of God are clarified. The servant did not envision help in the form of freedom from suffering. Rather, he expected help to enable him to endure suffering. The sting was taken out of the blow and the humiliation out of the abuse because the servant knew that the situation ultimately would not stand, it would not carry the day. The servant was able to endure because he understood that the future was not in the hands of the ruthless; it was in the hands of the Sovereign Lord of the universe.

The same resource that God provided his servant is available to the struggling saint today. The power of suffering to undo us is overcome by the realization that God will not allow us to suffer more than we can endure, and that he has prepared a destiny for us where suffering no longer can intrude to rob us of our joy.

I set my face like flint. This metaphor of resolve describes the determination of the servant to carry out his task in spite of all obstacles and opposition. He was not the first to do so. Throughout the history of Israel many who answered God's call faced opposition and even persecution in their efforts to serve him. Sometimes this opposition came from a foreign source, such as a belligerent king or a hostile foe. In the case of Israel's prophets, opposition often came from the Israelites themselves. As the prophets proclaimed a message that God's people did not want to hear, they were persecuted by kings and commoners alike. In preparing Ezekiel to go to the rebellious house of Israel to speak his words to them, God had to make the prophet's face "harder than flint" to withstand the opposition he would receive from his countrymen (Ezekiel 3:8, 9). It is possible, therefore, that at least part of the persecution the servant faced likewise came from his own countrymen.

B. THE SERVANT CHALLENGES HIS ENEMIES TO COMPETE AGAINST GOD (vv. 8, 9)

8, 9. He who vindicates me is near. Who then will bring charges against me? Let us face each other! Who is my accuser? Let him confront me! It is the Sovereign LORD who helps me. Who is he that will condemn me? They will all wear out like a garment; the moths will eat them up.

The language of these verses is that of the law court. The servant envisioned himself as the accused in a legal tribunal. The exact identity of his *accuser* is unclear. The adversary could be those who are described in verse 6, the Babylonian oppressors of the Judean exiles; or the adversary could be skeptical Jews who remained unconvinced that God was about to do a great thing through his servant (the faithful remnant of Israel), as verses 10 and 11 may imply. The fact that the adversary came to *bring charges* and *condemn* rather than physically harm the servant would seem to favor the view that these were fellow exiles who were slow to believe that anything good would come out of Israel's suffering in the Babylonian captivity.

It seems that the remnant's claim to servanthood had not gone unchallenged. To all appearances the faithful exiles seemed more abandoned by God than chosen by him. Here they were, helpless captives of a pagan nation, without their temple and without their land, broken and humiliated by their devastating defeat. In the minds of many Judeans, the stigma of their captivity was so great that they would never live it down. Never again would they be worthy to bear the title, "the chosen people."

This same claim was made against them even after they returned to the promised land. The prophet Zechariah was later to answer that objection by relating a vision he had from God. It depicted Satan accusing Joshua (the high priest of the postexilic community) of being defiled by the captivity and disqualified to preside over the temple worship. It was the Lord himself who came to Joshua's defense, purifying him and pronouncing him qualified to lead the worship of the restored nation (Zechariah 3:1-10).

In similar fashion the *Sovereign Lord* was *near* to justify the servant. He functioned as the servant's legal advocate. Though many, including some skeptical Jews, did not think the faithful remnant worthy to represent God, the Lord did. He declared them innocent and defended them against their detractors.

The wording in verse 9 is dramatic, emphasizing the Lord's role in the proceedings. (The drama of the verse is seen better in the *King James Version:* "Behold, the Lord God will help me.") The servant's confidence swelled because he had a Vindicator who was more than a match for any would-be accuser. What adversary would dare approach to challenge him now? If they dared to accuse him, they would only grow old trying to make the charge stick, wasting away like a moth-eaten *garment.*

With similar words the apostle Paul expressed the confidence of the Christian: "If God is for us, who can be against us? ... Who will bring any charge against those whom God has chosen? It is God who justifies. Who is he that condemns?" (Romans 8:31-34).

III. THE SERVANT EXTENDS THE CALL OF GOD (ISAIAH 50:10, 11)
A. THE SERVANT ENCOURAGES THE GODLY (v. 10)
10. Who among you fears the LORD and obeys the word of his servant? Let him who walks in the dark, who has no light, trust in the name of the LORD and rely on his God.

In this verse the servant addressed his fellow exiles or those who feared the Lord. In the Old Testament the fear of the Lord was the Hebrew equivalent to our idea of piety or being sincerely religious. To fear the Lord meant to live reverently before God. It meant to live by a world view that saw God at the center of all of life. The ethics, the values, the priorities of the person who feared God were all shaped by the belief that there is one true God who made all things and to whom all are accountable.

It is important to note here that the prophet equated the person who *fears the Lord* with one who *obeys the word of his servant.* Reverence expects obedience. Though worship is one way in which a believer expresses reverence for God, the ultimate test of a believer's reverence for God is submission to his will. By calling for obedience to the servant's word, the prophet was equating the message that the servant delivered with the very will of God. As noted in the comments under verses 8 and 9, not all of the Jews accepted the notion that God was active in the remnant's suffering and that he was going to use them to provide release for the captives and restoration to the state of Israel. By placing these two phrases side by side,

PRAYER

Heavenly Father, we are thankful for the Christ who was willing to deny himself and suffer on our behalf. Give us the strength to bear the burdens of servanthood with the confidence that You will sustain us and receive us to yourself. In Jesus' name. Amen.

THOUGHT TO REMEMBER

Those who serve God do so often at the cost of opposition and persecution. God will not abandon those who suffer in his name.

DAILY BIBLE READINGS

Monday, Jan. 15—God's Faithfulness (Isaiah 49:7-13)

Tuesday, Jan. 16—God Does Not Forget (Isaiah 49:14-18)

Wednesday, Jan. 17—God's Restoration (Isaiah 49:19-26)

Thursday, Jan. 18—God Reaches Out to All People (Isaiah 56:1-8)

Friday, Jan. 19—God Against Idolatry (Isaiah 57:1-13)

Saturday, Jan. 20—God Ready to Heal (Isaiah 57:14-21)

Sunday, Jan. 21—God Chooses Compassion (Isaiah 58:1-14)

the prophet meant to equate reverence for God with acceptance of the prophet's explanation of the servant's (the faithful remnant's) mission.

Commentators differ over the meaning of the phrases, *who walks in the dark, who has no light.* It is not clear in the Hebrew text whether these phrases refer to the servant or to the fellow exiles he was addressing. It seems more probable that the language describes those whom the servant was addressing. If this is the correct interpretation, the darkness could describe the exiles' lack of enlightenment concerning all that God was going to achieve through his faithful remnant. The exiles had yet to accept the proclamation that the glory of the Lord would be revealed through the servant's patient endurance of his suffering and his subsequent vindication and restoration. They saw no end to their misfortunes and had no hope for the future.

The key to finding such a hope is expressed in the invitation that the prophet extended to *trust in the name of the Lord and rely on his God.* These phrases are essentially two different ways of saying the same thing. To trust in the Lord's name means to place confidence in or *rely on* God. It means to take God at his word.

In this same way Christians find hope. Our hope, like the servant's, rests in the promises of God. Though our present circumstance may not suggest that we have a glorious future, God's Word yet declares it. We step out of the darkness of fear and despair when we trust in God's promises and take him at his word.

B. THE SERVANT WARNS THE UNGODLY (v. 11)

11. But now, all you who light fires and provide yourselves with flaming torches, go, walk in the light of your fires and of the torches you have set ablaze. This is what you shall receive from my hand: You will lie down in torment.

This final verse of the chapter is in the form of a prophecy of judgment. It is filled with a kind of irony that is typical of many prophetic threats of punishment. The idea is that the opponents of the servant would be destroyed by the very arguments that they used against him. The *fires* they kindled and the *light* in which they walked was their belief that they could have a secure future only by carving one out for themselves. And this they would do by accommodating themselves to their pagan captors, their beliefs and life-style. They had built an ideological and ethical fire that said, "When in Babylon, do as the Babylonians do." They warmed themselves in its false sense of security. The sad irony is that by identifying with the pagan Babylonian nation, they would end up suffering its fate—destruction and sorrow.

This final warning balances God's grace with his justice. Though the invitation to deliverance is generous and merciful, those who reject it will have to answer to God.

CONCLUSION

In Philippians 3:12-14 the apostle Paul describes the Christian life as a race, and calls the church to run it to the finish. It is clear from his words that the race of life is not a sprint; it is a distance run. It requires great endurance to "press on toward the goal to win the prize for which God has called me heavenward in Christ Jesus" (Philippians 3:14).

Paul was an outstanding example of one who was committed to finishing the race of life. In spite of stoning, beatings, shipwrecks, and imprisonment he continued to "press on toward the goal." Like the servant of today's lesson he offered his back to those who beat him (cf. v. 6) and bore his suffering with grace, knowing ultimately that he would be vindicated by the Lord. Paul understood that when it comes to the race of life, it is not how fast the Christian runs but how far.

Discovery Learning

This page contains an alternate lesson plan emphasizing learning activities. Classes desiring such student involvement will find these suggestions helpful. The next page is a reproducible activity page to further enhance discovery learning.

LEARNING GOALS

After this study, an adult student of the Word will:

1. Explain how God's servant responds to adversity or challenge.

2. Suggest ways God supports his servants today, as well as how Christians can support one another.

3. Plan to monitor personal efforts to be steadfast and faithful.

INTO THE LESSON

Put the following letters on sheets of paper, one letter per sheet: A, A, E, H, M, N, O, R, T, T, T, W. Display them randomly at the front of your classroom, but in such a manner that you can rearrange them for correct wording. Tell your class that if they "belong to the right club," they will figure out the three-word phrase these letters can be rearranged to form. (The phrase is "No matter what.")

Let students guess either the whole phrase or individual words. After a short time, if they need help, move the first letters of the three words—N, M, W—into place and continue. Give more letter placement clues as necessary. Emphasize that today's study is a reminder of this basic truth: God's servants endure no matter what comes.

Prepare the following descriptions of three members of God's "No-Matter-What Club." Recruit three members to read them, giving one clue at a time until someone guesses who each is.

Paul: 1. No matter what, even if I am imprisoned, I will do right. 2. No matter if close friends forsake me, I will be true to God. 3. No matter if I should be threatened with death, God still rules my life. 4. No matter what happens to me, I will preach the gospel in Asia and Europe.

Joseph: 1. No matter what, even if I am imprisoned, I will still do right. 2. No matter if those as close as brothers rise up against me, I will finish my job. 3. No matter if I am falsely accused, I will persist in righteousness. 4. No matter what, I will save my family in Egypt.

Nehemiah: 1. No matter what, I want to do the right thing for God. 2. No matter if men falsely accuse me to the authorities, I will be true. 3. No matter, if I have to carry a weapon while I work, I will continue. 4. No matter what, the wall will be built to God's glory!

INTO THE WORD

Divide your class into groups of three or four students each. Tell the groups that the theme of this lesson is the steadfast endurance of the Lord's servant. Give each group a sheet containing the following questions and have them examine today's text for answers:

1. What support does God give to his servant to help him remain faithful to his task?

2. List three or four circumstances that often interfere with endurance. What response to each can be found in the text?

3. By what slogans, suggested by the text, can the servant of God be encouraged to endure?

Allot about ten minutes for the groups to work. As they share their answers, list them on the chalkboard. Expect some of these ideas (and others) for question 1:

a. God's servant can endure because God is there every morning (v. 4).

b. Your enemies will grow old, weaken, and die (v. 9).

c. No servant of God will ultimately be ashamed (v. 7).

d. God's servants will speak the right word when you need it (v. 4).

e. God is your constant companion (v. 8).

Expect some of these ideas (and others) for question 2:

a. Fatigue (being weary) makes endurance more difficult; an encouraging word will sustain God's servant (v. 4).

b. Opposition makes endurance especially difficult; a determination to learn from difficulty will help (vv. 5, 6).

c. Accusations and false charges can wear down the servant; God is the one who vindicates (v. 8).

For sample slogans, "One person and God are a majority," is close to the thought of vv. 7 and 8. "Set your jaw and stiffen your lip—God is your helper!" is based on v. 7.

INTO LIFE

Make copies of the first activity on the next page (190) for learners to mark on their own and to keep for daily encouragement.

OPTION

Give each of the groups you established earlier one of the three Bible names from the opening activity. Ask each group to compare the principles of endurance discovered in today's lesson with the life of the group's assigned character. Then the group should answer these questions:

1. How did Paul (or Joseph or Nehemiah) demonstrate these same traits?

2. In what situations are Christians called on to demonstrate the same traits?

Self-check of My Steadfast Endurance

Mark each statement with A for *always*, U for *usually*, O for *often*, S for *sometimes*, N for *never*. Decide how you are doing!

_____ I speak helpful words to people who are hurting.

_____ I am daily aware of God's presence.

_____ I listen carefully to God's Word.

_____ I learn from experience to depend on God.

_____ I endure slander and abusive language from others without retaliating in kind.

_____ I act on the conviction that God will give his approval of me in spite of present difficulty.

_____ I am committed to being God's servant.

_____ I refuse to accept solutions that are not consistent with God's Word.

_____ I am determined to follow God *no matter what!*

Walking in the Light

"Who among you fears the Lord and obeys the word of his servant? Let him who walks in the dark, who has no light, trust in the name of the Lord and rely on his God" (Isaiah 50:10). In what darkness have you found it especially necessary to "trust in the name of the Lord and rely on [your] God"? What counterfeit lights (v. 11) are offered by some today? How can we show that the light of the gospel is the only true light for our darkened world?

DARK SITUATIONS	WORLDLY "LIGHTS"	HOW GOD'S LIGHT IS BETTER

God's Promise of Deliverance
Unit 2. The Ministry of the Suffering Servant
(Lessons 6-9)

THE SERVANT'S VICTORY

LESSON 9

WHY TEACH THIS LESSON?

The moving description of the Suffering Servant of Isaiah 52 and 53 has inspired poets and songwriters for decades. The inescapable comparison of the description here with that of the crucifixion of Christ in the Gospels is compelling. Who could read this and not be filled with both sorrow and joy—grieving for the afflicted servant and yet exuberant that "by his wounds we are healed"!

This lesson should evoke an emotional response from your students. Closing your time together with some praise songs would be quite appropriate.

At the same time, the proper response to this lesson is not emotional only, nor should the lesson be used merely to focus inward. While praise for the salvation the Lord has given *us* through the Suffering Servant is appropriate, it is not the only focus. Inherent in the context is the demand to tell *others*. The Servant came "to justify many" (v. 11), not just a few. As Philip began at this Scripture and told the Ethiopian eunuch "the good news about Jesus," challenge your students to begin here and tell the good news whenever they can.

INTRODUCTION

A. "A TALE OF TWO SERVANTS"

"Who is the prophet talking about?" asked the Ethiopian eunuch upon reading from the fifty-third chapter of Isaiah (Acts 8:34). His confusion is understandable. In the book of Isaiah, the servant is identified with the prophet himself (20:3), and with the Israelite nation, or, more particularly, with that generation of Israelites who suffered through the Babylonian captivity and remained faithful to God (41:8; 44:2, 21; 45:4; 48:20; 49:3). Philip answered the eunuch's question by telling him "the good news about Jesus" (Acts 8:35).

The answer offered in this lesson will be one that seeks to be consistent with both the book of Isaiah and the later statements of the New Testament. In Isaiah, the servant is collectively the repentant Israelite exiles who faithfully suffered through the Babylonian captivity and who became the righteous remnant through whom God would restore the Israelite nation (49:5; 46:3). Yet the words of this text describe a Servant who suffers in a manner and for a purpose that is ultimately beyond that of the exiled Israelites. He is One not identical to Israel, but One who came out of Israel and died to save the world—Jesus Christ (Acts 8:34, 35).

If this answer seems confusing or contradictory to the student, he or she should be aware that Old Testament prophecy is sometimes given to dual or multiple applications or "fulfillments." For example, the expression, "out of Egypt I called my son" (Hosea 11:1), referred historically to God's calling Israel out of Egypt in the Exodus; at the same time, the expression anticipated prophetically Jesus' being taken to Egypt so as not to be killed by Herod, and his subsequent return to Israel (Matthew 2:15). In other words, the "son" in Hosea was Israel, but, as the Gospel of Matthew informs us, the "son" was also in a fuller and unique sense Jesus (Matthew 2:15). A similar phenomenon, it seems likely, is at work in this Servant Song from Isaiah.

DEVOTIONAL READING
REVELATION 3:14-21
LESSON SCRIPTURE
ISAIAH 52:13—53:12
PRINTED TEXT
ISAIAH 53:1-6, 10-12

LESSON AIMS

After studying this lesson a student should:

1. Explain how God can bring salvation from suffering and victory through defeat.

2. Conclude that the prophecies of Isaiah were fulfilled in Christ's death and resurrection.

3. Praise and thank God for sending Jesus to be our Servant Savior.

Jan 28

KEY VERSE

After the suffering of his soul, he will see the light of life and be satisfied; by his knowledge my righteous servant will justify many, and he will bear their iniquities.
—Isaiah 53:11

B. LESSON BACKGROUND

Today's text is taken from the fourth and final of the Servant Songs of Isaiah (52:13—53:12). The first two songs acquainted us with the servant's call and his mission. Last week's lesson on the third song introduced us to another aspect of the servant's ministry, which is more fully developed in this final song. It is the unique and compelling concept that the servant's suffering would accomplish the Lord's purposes and save his people. This suffering, which in a limited and somewhat symbolic way referred to the struggles of the exiled Israelites, ultimately anticipated the vicarious suffering of the Messiah for the sins of all humanity.

I. THE APPEARANCE OF GOD'S SERVANT (ISAIAH 53:1-3)

A. AN UNLIKELY SAVIOR (vv. 1, 2)

1. Who has believed our message and to whom has the arm of the LORD been revealed?

Who has believed our message? Isaiah prophesied to an unbelieving people (see 30:9-11; 42:23). In light of what follows, it seems that his complaint centered on the people's rejection of his prophecy concerning what God would accomplish through his suffering servant. As both Jesus and Paul revealed in their quotations of this text, these opening questions were meant to imply that few believed (John 12:38; Romans 10:16). The questions addressed the unbelief of the people toward the unlikely prospect that God was going to achieve his purposes through the suffering and defeat of his servant. It was hard for both the nations and even some Israelites to understand how *the arm of the Lord* (the power of God) could be *revealed* through Israel's humiliating defeat and subjugation at the hands of the Babylonians. Harder still was it for Jew and Gentile alike to believe that victory over sin and death would be achieved through the death of the Messiah. "We preach Christ crucified," Paul wrote, "a stumbling block to Jews and foolishness to Gentiles" (1 Corinthians 1:23). To the lost, the death of Christ remains an unbelievable solution. Like Naaman, who expected some great show of God's power, the world's answer is always in the spectacular. The willing sacrifice of a humble servant is not "good enough." But "the foolishness of God is wiser than man's wisdom, and the weakness of God is stronger than man's strength" (1 Corinthians 1:25).

2. He grew up before him like a tender shoot, and like a root out of dry ground. He had no beauty or majesty to attract us to him, nothing in his appearance that we should desire him.

He grew up before him like a tender shoot, and like a root out of dry ground. The comparison of the servant to a *tender shoot* and a *root* has messianic overtones. By use of these terms, Isaiah prophesied the rise of the Messiah (Isaiah 11:1-5). The main thrust of this verse, however, is clarified in the latter half of it. *He had no beauty or majesty to attract us to him.* The servant was as unattractive and unappealing to men as the formless shoot of the scrub brush that springs up in the desert. The thought is that on the basis of *appearance,* there was nothing that would recommend the servant to men as a champion and savior. In Psalm 118:22, 23 a similar idea is expressed regarding Israel: "The stone the builders rejected has become the capstone; the Lord has done this, and it is marvelous in our eyes." (See also Matthew 21:42 where Jesus applies it to himself.) In Deuteronomy 7:7 Israel, the nation God chose, is described as the least significant of all peoples, and in Ezekiel 16:1-7 the citizens of Jerusalem are characterized as an abandoned baby, whom only the Lord pitied. The point of all these texts is that Israel was an unlikely candidate to be the people of God through whom he would

Visual 9 of the visuals packet illustrates Isaiah 53:6. Display it when you come to that verse.

All we like sheep have gone astray

achieve his purposes on earth. If such favor for Israel in general was unlikely, it was even more so for that generation of exiles who endured the humiliation of the captivity.

What has been said of Israel is even more true of Jesus Christ, the ultimate Suffering Servant of the Lord. He was born to peasants in an insignificant town, and a feeding trough was his bed. He wrote no book, ruled no nation, commanded no army, owned no house, lived the life of an itinerant preacher, and died like a common criminal. His whole appearance on earth was not of the kind to which people normally gravitate in search of a Savior. "Who would have believed" that God would come to save us in such a One?

B. A REJECTED SAVIOR (v. 3)

3. He was despised and rejected by men, a man of sorrows, and familiar with suffering. Like one from whom men hide their faces he was despised, and we esteemed him not.

The point of these poignant words is that not only did the servant's appearance make him an unlikely savior, it even repulsed those who looked upon him. The key to understanding the source of this repulsive appearance is found in the words *sorrows* and *suffering*. These words can also mean "pains" and "wounds." They describe the effects that his suffering had upon his appearance (vv. 4-6). The language remembers the observation near the beginning of the song: "his appearance was so disfigured beyond that of any man" (52:14).

For the servant Israel this refers to the wretched state of the exiles (Isaiah 42:22). In her humiliated defeat at the hands of the Babylonians, Israel was *despised and rejected by men*, as Lamentations 2:15 clearly shows. Though this verse is not directly quoted in the New Testament and applied to Christ, it is yet a fitting description of how men would reject him in his humiliating death. When we understand that Christ's death was made necessary because of our sins, our guilt and shame make it even more difficult for us to look upon the Suffering Servant.

II. THE SUFFERING OF THE SERVANT (ISAIAH 53:4-6)

A. BURDENS BORNE (v. 4)

4. Surely he took up our infirmities and carried our sorrows, yet we considered him stricken by God, smitten by him, and afflicted.

The people of God at first misunderstood the suffering of the servant. As the latter part of the verse suggests, they thought it was something God had sent merely as punishment for sin. This understanding of servant Israel's suffering was correct as far as it went, as the prophet's earlier statements make clear: "Who handed Jacob over to become loot, and Israel to the plunderers? Was it not the Lord, against whom we have sinned? For they would not follow his ways; they did not obey his law" (Isaiah 42:24). What the Israelites now realized was that God used the servant's suffering for an additional purpose—their emotional and physical healing.

Interestingly, the New Testament quotes only the first half of the verse and applies it to Jesus' healing ministry. Matthew states that this part of the Servant's role was fulfilled by Jesus in his being sent to heal the sick (Matthew 8:16, 17). This further illustrates the phenomenon that an Old Testament prophecy may have one meaning in its own context yet find a fulfillment of a different type in the life of Christ.

At the same time, however, it is clear from what follows that Christ's sufferings were borne for mankind, and that his sufferings were the remedy for all the ills that come upon flesh.

WHAT DO YOU THINK?

The Suffering Servant was assumed to have been "stricken by God." Why else, after all, would he be suffering so much? Since the time of Job people have made the assumption that suffering must be related to guilt or foolishness, or both?

Why is that such an easy conclusion to draw in the midst of suffering (either our own suffering or that of someone else)? How does this passage refute that notion? (Consider also Luke 24:25-27; John 9:1-3; Philippians 3:10, 11.) How would you answer someone who complained, "I don't know what I've done, but I must have made the Lord angry at me—or else why would I be suffering so much"?

WHAT DO YOU THINK?

Most people do not like to admit guilt. They will make excuses or fix blame on someone else. For them, verses like Isaiah 53:6 and Romans 3:23 are hard to take. It may be difficult for a person to admit that he or she has sinned against God, but it is a necessary step if one would be free of sin's guilt and penalty. How can we get people to admit the truth of their guilt so we can also lead them to accept the truth that we have a Savior to take away that guilt? "Speaking the truth in love," as Paul says (Ephesians 4:15), must surely be part of it—but how do you do that? Suggest some specific actions or statements.

WHAT DO YOU THINK?

In modern society, suffering is generally viewed as a form of weakness rather than strength. It makes little sense to us that anything of real worth can be achieved through suffering, so we desire to avoid it, if at all possible. Yet it was promised of the servant that "after the suffering of his soul" he would "see the light of life and be satisfied" (v. 11).

To what extent do you think that applies to Christians today? That is, is our suffering actually good for us? Why or why not? What, then, should be our response when suffering comes?

B. A SACRIFICE FOR SIN (vv. 5, 6)

5, 6. But he was pierced for our transgressions, he was crushed for our iniquities; the punishment that brought us peace was upon him, and by his wounds we are healed. We all, like sheep, have gone astray, each of us has turned to his own way; and the LORD has laid on him the iniquity of us all.

In this powerful passage we are allowed to behold the nature of the servant's suffering: *for our transgressions; for our iniquities*. The preposition *for* (used twice in verse 5; also in verse 8) means "because of," "on account of." The emphasis in these texts is that the servant paid the penalty for sin. The first of the two words the prophet uses to describe sin is particularly instructive. The word *transgressions* literally means "rebellions." At the heart of the biblical concept of sin is the idea of rebellion against God. Motivated by pride, the sinner chooses to place his or her will above God's and thereby to rise up against him.

The punishment that brought us peace was upon him, or "was borne by him." As many commentators note, it is difficult to see how this could refer to Israel. Yet, as Isaiah proclaimed at the beginning of the section in which the Servant passages are found (Isaiah 40—55), the suffering of the captivity was in some sense a payment for Israel's sins: "Speak tenderly to Jerusalem, and proclaim to her that her hard service has been completed, that her sin has been paid for, that she has received from the Lord's hand double for all her sins" (Isaiah 40:2). In other words, the same God who brought the Babylonian captivity as a punishment of Israel's sins, now, in consideration of the suffering that the exiles endured, considered their sin paid for and announced their pardon. What this text suggests is what Isaiah 53 confirms.

This does not suggest by hard work or self-deprecation one can atone for his own sin any more than animal sacrifices, accepted by God in the Old Covenant, could actually take away sin (Hebrews 10:1-4). This was a figurative atonement, a part of the role of the "schoolmaster" of the law (Galatians 3:25, KJV) to lead us to Christ.

While the suffering of the penitent exiles paid for the sins of Israel in a figurative manner, the suffering of Jesus on the cross paid for the sins of all mankind in a literal sense. He was sinless, yet he suffered for sin (Hebrews 4:15; 1 Peter 2:22), not his own sin, but ours. He suffered in our place. He was wounded even to death, as verses 8 and 9 make clear, and it was all for us, not for any sin he had committed. He offered himself as a sacrifice, and his sacrifice made atonement for our sins. Rebellious and wandering sinners though we are, we can be restored to God and have peace with him because upon Jesus is laid *the iniquity of us all*. (See Romans 3:25; 2 Corinthians 5:21; 1 John 2:2; 4:10.)

"ALL WE LIKE SHEEP"

The Bible often uses the metaphor of sheep to describe the Lord's people. Christ himself is called the Good Shepherd. The idea of being protected, guided, fed, and cared for like helpless woolly lambs is a warm and cozy thought. Snuggling down in the shelter of the shepherd's love is a comforting analogy. Psalm 23 and John 10 are favorite texts for all Christians, because they assure us that the Lord is our Shepherd, and he is willing to give his very life for our safety and salvation.

Another aspect of the sheep metaphor, however, is disquieting, to say the least. Sheep are prone to go astray, to go their own way, as it were; thus the need for constant shepherding. And despite the vigilance of the shepherd, sheep often choose wrong and dangerous paths.

Isaiah compares man's spiritual waywardness with the straying of sheep. We are inclined to wander off the narrow way that leads to abundant life. Whenever we insist on going our own way, disregarding the directions and leadership of the Good Shepherd, we sin and place our souls in serious jeopardy. Hear his voice and follow him.

—R. W. B.

III. THE VINDICATION OF THE SERVANT (ISAIAH 53:10-12)
A. THE LORD'S WILL ACHIEVED (vv. 10, 11)

10, 11. Yet it was the LORD's will to crush him and cause him to suffer, and though the LORD makes his life a guilt offering, he will see his offspring and prolong his days, and the will of the LORD will prosper in his hand. After the suffering of his soul, he will see the light of life and be satisfied; by his knowledge my righteous servant will justify many, and he will bear their iniquities.

The opening line of this verse informs us that *it was the Lord's will* that the Servant should suffer. The Servant's suffering was not accidental, it was providential. In the context of Isaiah, this means that the suffering that the penitent exiles endured in their captivity was not simply the result of international politics or military aggression. It was the unfolding of the divine will. Their suffering was more than punishment. God was also going to use it as a means by which to pave the way for Israel's restoration to Canaan. This is how the *will of the Lord will prosper* in the servant's *hand.*

In the same way, the death of Jesus was no an accident of political forces. Jesus came to earth for the very purpose of dying a sacrificial and atoning death. (See, for example, John 12:27.) It was God's will that, by Jesus' death, he would "be just and the one who justifies those who have faith in Jesus" (Romans 3:26).

Though the Lord makes his life a guilt offering. The Hebrew text is unclear as to whether the Lord or the Servant is doing the offering. Most translations take it to mean that the Lord is doing it, and that seems to fit best with the idea expressed in the preceding clause. As applied to Jesus, either idea is appropriate. The New Testament affirms that God purposed Christ's death on the cross (Acts 2:23) and that Christ willingly offered himself for the sins of all the world (John 10:17, 18).

The backdrop to this language is the Old Testament system of sacrifice. The *guilt offering* referred to by Isaiah is described in Leviticus 5:14-19. The text prescribes the offering up of a ram from the flock in order to achieve the forgiveness of the person guilty of the sin. The idea is that God accepts the life of the sacrificial animal as a substitute for the life of the sinner. The consequences of the sin are thus atoned for, and the sinner is spared the "wages of sin" (death). The new and compelling idea that Isaiah 53 adds to this sacrificial concept is the startling revelation that the Lord will offer a person (the Servant), not an animal, for sin.

It is obvious how this applies to Christ. Speaking of Jesus, the author of Hebrews says, "He did not enter by means of the blood of goats and calves; but he entered the Most Holy Place once for all by his own blood, having obtained eternal redemption" (Hebrews 9:12). Jesus literally gave up his life as a sacrifice for the sins of all humanity.

Less obvious is how this sacrificial idea applies to the servant identified as "Israel" in the book of Isaiah. The answer seems to be that God accepted the suffering of the penitent exiles as a sacrifice for the collective sins of the Israelite nation. Thus, God's servant (the repentant exiles) would *justify many* (the entire nation of Israel) and make it possible for them to be restored to God. It is also possible that by *many* the prophet meant to include the Gentiles. Of the servant the Lord said, "I will also make you a light for the Gentiles, that you may bring my salvation to the ends of the earth" (49:6). As was noted in last week's lesson, this "salvation" would occur as the nations witnessed what God did through the penitent exiles and came to believe in him.

PAIN AND GAIN

Paul Brand and Philip Yancey have written a book entitled *Pain: the Gift Nobody Wants.* In it they relate the startling statistic that the people of the United States

WHAT DO YOU THINK?

Isaiah 53 was written some seven centuries before Christ and yet that it offers a vivid description of what took place at Calvary! What does that tell you about God—about his foreknowledge, about his control of world events, about his power? What does that do for your faith? How will your life reflect that this week?

PRAYER

Thank you, merciful Father, for sending your Son to suffer and die in our place, that we might have victory over sin and death. Help us to give of ourselves sacrificially that others may know of your saving grace. In Jesus' name, amen.

THOUGHT TO REMEMBER

The message of the Servant Songs ultimately anticipates the message of the cross. The Sovereign Lord of the universe can turn suffering into salvation and defeat into victory.

DAILY BIBLE READINGS

Monday, Jan. 22—A Righteous Remnant in Israel (Zephaniah 3:8-13)

Tuesday, Jan. 23—Children of Light Produced (Ephesians 5: 6-14)

Wednesday, Jan. 24—Gratitude for What God Has Done (1 Peter 1:3-9)

Thursday, Jan. 25—Faith Produces Good Works (Galatians 5:1-12)

Friday, Jan. 26—Rising Above Persecution (Acts 5:33-42)

Saturday, Jan. 27—God's Ultimate Authority (Revelation 21:22-27)

Sunday, Jan. 28—God Reigns (Isaiah 52:7-15)

---

spend $63 billion per year on pain relievers. The irony is that, while we have greater ability to manage pain, it seems increasingly difficult for us to find activities and experiences that make us feel good. We have lost sight of the interdependent relationship of pain and pleasure. Simply put, to have a rainbow there has to be a little rain. A Chinese philosopher points out that in order to feel the exquisite sensation of scratching, one must first endure the discomfort of a big itch.

If gain follows pain, it follows that the greater the pain the greater the gain. And no greater pain has ever been experienced than the torture of Christ on the cross. The physical torment was very real, but the spiritual dimensions of the agony were greater still. No pain ever achieved greater gain. By his sacrifice we are justified—perceived by God to be righteous in spite of our transgressions.

His pain was—and is—our gain!

—R. W. B.

B. THE SERVANT GLORIFIED (v. 12)

12. Therefore I will give him a portion among the great, and he will divide the spoils with the strong, because he poured out his life unto death, and was numbered with the transgressors. For he bore the sin of many, and made intercession for the transgressors.

This final Servant Song concludes with a prediction of the Servant's victory. Normally suffering and death lead to defeat. But in a paradox only God could construct, these very symbols of defeat are made the means to victory for the Servant and all people. Rather than overpowering the enemy, the Servant passively submits to him (v. 7). Instead of beating them, he is beaten by them. Instead of taking lives, he gives his own. And the God who "works in mysterious ways" turns that which appears to be a humiliating defeat into a glorious victory.

For the people of Isaiah's day this meant that the humiliation of the Babylonian captivity would ultimately lead to the restoration of a glorified Zion in the land of Canaan. For those of us this side of Calvary, the prophet's words hold even greater promise. They anticipate the death, burial, and resurrection of Jesus Christ, by which all humanity may find forgiveness of sins and the promise of eternal life.

CONCLUSION

When John the Baptizer saw Jesus coming to the Jordan, he announced his arrival by saying, "Look, the Lamb of God, who takes away the sin of the world!" (John 1:29). There are other words he might have chosen. He might have said, "Look, the Son of David, who has come to restore the kingdom to Israel!" or, "Look, the Master Teacher, who has come to proclaim the truth of God!" or, "Look, the Great Physician, who has come to heal the sick!" or, "Look, the Great Reformer, who has come to show us a new way to live!" He might have said any of these, for they were all true. But he reached instead for the very purpose for which Christ had come and said, "Look, the Lamb of God, who takes away the sin of the world!"

This, the most powerful and compelling of the Servant Songs, anticipates better than any other Old Testament prophecy the significance of Christ's coming. In some way the suffering of the servant Israel led to God's redeeming the nation from the bondage of the Babylonian captivity. But that pales in comparison to the sacrifice of Jesus Christ, God's ultimate Servant, at Calvary. There the very Son of God offered himself as the sacrificial Lamb. Allowing himself to be slain he paid the penalty for the sins of all mankind so that we all might be brought back to God.

Discovery Learning

This page contains an alternate lesson plan emphasizing learning activities. Classes desiring such student involvement will find these suggestions helpful. The next page is a reproducible activity page to further enhance discovery learning.

LEARNING GOALS

As a result of this lesson, a student will:

1. Explain how God can bring salvation from suffering and victory through defeat.

2. Conclude that the prophecies of Isaiah were fulfilled in Christ's death and resurrection.

3. Praise and thank God for sending Jesus to be our Servant Savior.

INTO THE LESSON

On the next page are the words to a song based on the printed text for this lesson. During the week before class, give a copy to a talented singer. Ask that singer to practice these lyrics to the tune of "Joy to the World" and to come prepared to sing them, or to lead the class in singing them, as today's session begins.

When it is time to begin, have your soloist sing. Or distribute copies of the song and have your singer lead the class in singing.

INTO THE WORD

When the song is finished, have a class member read Isaiah 53:1-12 aloud to the class. Then lead a discussion of these questions:

1. What is the general mood of this passage of Scripture? (It is gloomy, dealing as it does with the suffering of the Lord's Servant.)

2. Why might the tune selected for the paraphrasing of the text possibly be considered inappropriate? (It is a joyous, upbeat tune, which is normally associated with a happy event.)

3. Why might the tune be considered appropriate? (The suffering and death of Christ, the ultimate Servant of the Lord, brought true joy to the world!)

Write the following nine Scripture phrases on slips of paper, one phrase per slip. Do the same with the nine Scripture references in the following paragraph. Distribute the phrases and references randomly. (The references match the phrases in the order given.)

Phrases: (1) "He did not open his mouth," v. 7.
(2) "He was numbered with the transgressors," v. 12.
(3) "By his wounds we are healed," v. 5.
(4) "He grew up … like a tender shoot," v. 2.
(5) "We all, like sheep, have gone astray," v. 6.
(6) "[He was] with the rich in his death," v. 9.
(7) "A man of sorrows, and familiar with suffering," v. 3.

(8) "[He] made intercession for the transgressors," v. 12.
(9) "My righteous servant will justify many," v. 11.

References: (1) Matthew 26:62, 63; (2) Luke 23:32; (3) Mark 15:15; (4) Matthew 2:23; (5) Psalm 119:176; (6) Matthew 27:57-60; (7) John 11:35; (8) Luke 23:34; (9) Romans 3:24.

Have the holders of the Scripture references find and read their verses aloud. As each is read, let the holder of a matching phrase from Isaiah 53 read it aloud. Comment as desired, showing especially how this great Servant Song finds its ultimate fulfillment in Jesus, the Servant Messiah.

OPTION

If have not already done so, distribute copies of the reproducible activity page 198. Direct the students' attention to the "Check It Out" activity at the bottom of the page. Give them a few minutes to complete the activity; then review to be sure everyone found the verses from which the various expressions in the song came.

INTO LIFE

If you have not yet given each member a copy of the song on page 198, do so at this time. Sing the song together. Point out to your students that singing these truths to the tune of "Joy to the World" can be a marvelous reminder of how God's Servant, who suffered and died, has given us reason to rejoice.

You might ask if any in your class would like to compose a stanza for this hymn based on verses 7-11, which were not used in the hymn sung today. Promise those who agree to do so that you will have the class sing their stanzas next Sunday. That would be excellent review and reinforcement.

OPTION

Many preachers and teachers have pointed out that we can legitimately substitute our own names for the pronouns *our* and *we* in Isaiah 53:5. And to a great extent we can personalize much more that appears in the chapter. Distribute index cards and felt-tip pens, and ask the students to write the words to Isaiah 53:5, 6, substituting their own names for the personal pronouns (and adapting the grammar as necessary). Ask them to keep this card someplace handy so they can ponder its truth daily (perhaps in personal devotions) this week.

Joy to the World

The verses below, based on Isaiah 53:1-12, can be sung to the tune of "Joy to the World."

Who has believed our strong report?
To whom is he revealed?
For he shall grow
Up as a tender plant
And root out of dry ground,
And root out of dry ground,
And root, and root, out of dry ground.

He has no form nor comeliness,
No beauty of desire.
He is despised,
Rejected of men ,
A man of sorrows full,
A man of sorrows full.
We hid, we hid our faces from him.

He surely bore our griefs and pain.
Although we did not know
His wounds and his bruises
Were taken for our sins.
He suffered for our peace,
He suffered for our peace,
And by his stripes we are healed.

All we like sheep have gone astray;
We turned to our own way.
The Lord gave him
Our sins and shame.
And by his death he saves,
And by his death he saves,
And by his death he saves all men.

Joy to the world because he poured
His soul out unto death.
He stood with men
Of transgression.
He bore the sin of men,
He bore the sin of men,
He makes the plea to God for us.

Check It Out

Look over the lyrics to the song above and compare them with the Scripture text, Isaiah 53:1-12. Each time you find an idea drawn from the text, write the verse number next to the phrase. For example, line 1 ("Who has believed our strong report?") is taken from verse 1: "Who has believed our message...." Write a *1* next to the first line.

Use a concordance to find New Testament references to the fulfillment of several of the images in the song. Write the references in the space below.

JONAH FLEES FROM GOD

LESSON 10

WHY TEACH THIS LESSON?

Choice. The very word has become almost sacred in our culture. From the brand of soup we buy to the church we attend, we want choices. We want to compare our options and get the best deal. Some even want the ability to choose life and death!

Unfortunately, many of our choices are wrong. In that, Jonah represents all of us! But God has a way of taking our bad choices, teaching us a lesson from them, and then allowing us to choose better. We see this pattern in Jonah. May this lesson help your students see it in their own situations.

INTRODUCTION

A. FISH STORY?

During the depression of the 1930s a stuffed whale was transported by a freight car and exhibited in many cities of the United States. The man in charge of the exhibit carefully pointed out that while the mouth of the whale certainly was large enough to envelop a man, the opening in the whale's throat was not large enough to allow the man to pass into the whale's stomach. To that exhibitor, the biblical account of Jonah was a "fish story"—unreliable, untrue.

To the discerning, however, the exhibitor's attempts to discredit the biblical account of Jonah don't hold water. The book of Jonah says that God prepared "a great fish" to swallow Jonah to preserve the prophet's life. The person who believes in the Creator God has no difficulty believing that he could accomplish this.

Instead of "a fish story," the account of Jonah is a story of God's love and human responsibility. It speaks of God's relationship to his chosen people and the rest of the world. Specifically, it emphasizes God's love for all people and his desire for all to be saved from the terrible consequences of wickedness. And, in a forceful manner, it depicts the importance of carrying out God's assigned tasks, even if a task is unpleasant or difficult.

B. LESSON BACKGROUND

Little is known of the prophet Jonah. Our principal source of information concerning him is the book that bears his name. Additional personal information about him is found in the notice given in 2 Kings 14:23-25. From this brief reference we learn several things.

First, the identity of the prophet is confirmed. The twenty-fifth verse of 2 Kings 14 corroborates the statement of identification given in the opening verse of Jonah—he was the son of Amittai. From the reference in 2 Kings we discover that Jonah was from the town of Gath Hepher. Joshua 19:10-16 indicates that this town was in the part of the land that had been assigned to the tribe of Zebulun. Gath Hepher was situated about three miles northeast of Nazareth, the town where Jesus, centuries later, grew to manhood. Jonah, therefore, was a prophet of the northern kingdom, the kingdom of Israel, as opposed to the kingdom of Judah to the south.

DEVOTIONAL READING
JONAH 2:2-9

LESSON SCRIPTURE
JONAH 1, 2

PRINTED TEXT
JONAH 1:1-4, 10-15, 17; 2:1, 10

LESSON AIMS

After studying this lesson, students should:

1. List both good and bad choices recorded in Jonah 1 and 2.

2. Suggest ways to measure choices against the will of God.

3. Examine some recent choices and take steps to reverse any that may not have been consistent with God's will.

Feb
4

KEY VERSE

But Jonah ran away from the Lord and headed for Tarshish.
—Jonah 1:3

It's easy to condemn Jonah for trying to evade his responsibility. After all, he had a clear and direct command from God—how could he have run away? Yet are not many Christians doing the same thing? When asked to perform some ministry task, they may respond by saying, "It's not my job," or, "Isn't that what the preacher is hired to do?" or, "I am too busy." Jesus' penetrating question: "Why do you call me, 'Lord, Lord,' and do not do what I say?" (Luke 6:46), is challenging.

Yet aren't there times when each of these responses is valid? How does one determine when a request for help in ministry should be treated as a call from God to serve and when it may be—even should be—passed off?

HOW TO SAY IT

Amittai. Uh-MIT-eye,
     or AM-uh-tie.
Gath Hepher. Gath HE-fer.
Jehu. JEE-hew.
Jeroboam. Jair-o-BO-um.
Nazareth. NAZ-uh-reth.
Nineveh. NIN-uh-vuh.
Phoenician. Fih-NISH-un.
Tartessus. TAR-teh-sus.
Zebulun. ZEB-you-lun.

The reference in 2 Kings also gives us some indication, although nothing definite, of the time of Jonah's prophesying. Jeroboam II, who is named in these verses as the king of Israel, ruled from about 789 to 748 B.C. The lands that he restored to Israel in fulfillment of Jonah's prophecy (v. 25) were those east of the Jordan, which were taken from Israel during the reign of Jehu (2 Kings 10:32, 33), most probably near the close of that king's reign (about 815 B.C.). So this prophecy of Jonah would have been delivered some time after 815 B.C. It may be deemed certain that the prophecy was given some time before Jeroboam's conquests, either near the end of the reign of his predecessor or about the beginning of Jeroboam's reign. If Jonah flourished in the reign of Jeroboam II, he was a senior contemporary of the prophets Amos and Hosea.

During this time Israel had its battles with Syria to the north. But a far more potentially dangerous foe lay farther to the east—the nation of Assyria, whose capital city was Nineveh. From the Assyrian inscriptions, we learn that Jehu, the great-grandfather of Jeroboam II, had been forced to pay tribute to Assyria. The people had been required to pay that tribute continually ever since. On that basis alone we can understand the animosity that a citizen of Israel would feel toward Assyria. Furthermore, the Assyrians were a strong, fierce, warlike people, noted for their cruelty. Jonah was a good patriot and lover of Israel. The combination of these factors, it would seem, led him to respond the way he did when God called his prophet to take a very important message to that pagan nation.

The dominant purpose of the book of Jonah seems to be to expose and rebuke in Jonah the tendency to bigotry, and to show that God, the Creator of all, has a tender, compassionate care for every living person.

I. THE CALL (JONAH 1:1-4)

A. NINEVEH'S NEED (vv. 1, 2)

1. The word of the LORD came to Jonah son of Amittai:

We are not told the manner in which God communicated with Jonah, whether audibly or by means of a dream or vision. But there was no question in Jonah's mind that God was the one giving him the commission recorded in the following verse.

2. "Go to the great city of Nineveh and preach against it, because its wickedness has come up before me."

Most of God's prophets delivered his messages to the people of Israel. Jonah, however, was directed to *go to … Nineveh*, Assyria's capital city, which was about 750 miles northeast of Israel. (See the map on page 150.)

Nineveh was called *great*, it seems, because of its size and the influential place that it held as the capital of the dominant nation in the regions east of Israel. Jonah 4:11 tells us that Nineveh was home to one hundred twenty thousand young children. The entire population of the city may have been as large as six hundred thousand.

Preach against it, because its wickedness has come up before me. God was fully aware of the wicked life-style of the Ninevites, and Jonah himself was not unaware of their reputation. Unpleasant as the task may have seemed to Jonah, he knew what his responsibility as a prophet of God was. He was to be God's agent to help the Ninevites change—for the good.

We today have been commissioned to take the gospel of God's grace to the world. Sometimes we are hesitant to warn people of the danger that awaits them if they live wicked lives. Perhaps we are afraid we will offend them; or perhaps we fear an unpleasant response from them, and that will lead to our being rejected by them. Whatever the reason for our reluctance, we need to remember that God's message of warning is always for man's ultimate good. That should spur us on to do the work he has commissioned us to do.

B. THE MAJOR PROBLEM (v. 3)

3. But Jonah ran away from the LORD and headed for Tarshish. He went down to Joppa, where he found a ship bound for that port. After paying the fare, he went aboard and sailed for Tarshish to flee from the LORD.

God told Jonah to go east to Nineveh. Instead the prophet went in the opposite direction. It is believed that *Tarshish* was Tartessus, a Phoenician city on the south coast of Spain, some two thousand miles west of Israel!

Jonah's intention was to *flee from the Lord.* This may mean that Jonah imagined he could flee to a place where God would be unaware of his presence. Yet it seems almost incredible that a prophet would not be aware of God's omnipresence. Years before, David had written, "Where can I go from your Spirit? Where can I flee from your presence?" (Psalm 139:7). Thus some students point out that the phrase is more accurately translated "flee from *the presence of* the Lord" (cf. *King James Version, New American Standard Bible)* The expression "to be..." or "to stand in the presence of a king" is often used to mean "acting as the king's official minister." (See Genesis 41:46; 2 Kings 3:14; Luke 1:19.) Elijah used the phrase in 1 Kings 17:1 ("whom I serve" is literally "in whose presence I stand") of his office as a prophet of God. The phrase here, then, may mean that Jonah was renouncing his office as the Lord's prophet so he would not have to carry out the mission he was given. He would no longer stand "in the presence of the Lord" as his servant.

Joppa was a Mediterranean seaport about fifty miles from Gath Hepher. There Jonah boarded a ship that would take him where he wanted to go.

Although much of the narrative in the book of Jonah centers around the prophet, the Lord is the key figure of action in the book. The purpose of this opening scene will have been achieved if the reader inquires how God is going to proceed. But we will be missing much if we ask only how the Lord will frustrate Jonah's plan to flee. This is not just a biblical "cops and robbers" account about how God gets his man. It has to do with the fulfilling of a specific commission from God.

There are a several important truths that may be learned from God's dealings with Jonah, not the least of which is that we should carefully consider our devotion to God, the demands of Christian discipleship, and our willingness to serve him.

THE GOD AND RUN CLUB

Young faces pictured on milk cartons and on the backs of carpet-cleaning ads tell a tragic story. Some of these youngsters were abducted by strangers with evil intent. Others have been "kidnapped" by noncustodial parents after bitter divorces. Many, especially the teens, are simply runaways—kids who leave home and family for one reason or another. Thousands of teens run away from home every year, most of them seeking freedom from control.

Jonah tried to run away from God to avoid the distasteful task of preaching to the Ninevites. Like a teen fleeing the control and discipline of parents, Jonah tried to hide from the chief authority figure of life, the omnipotent God.

The spiritual descendants of Jonah are legion. Among the children of God, countless runaways turn up missing every year. They want Christianity without a commission, discipleship without discipline, freedom without faithfulness.

Our heavenly Father is loving, but never permissive. He guides us, not with *suggestions,* but by *commandments.* His authority is supreme, and his children must submit to him. As Jonah learned, one cannot hide from God; we run from him to our own peril.
                                                                        —R. W. B.

C. GOD IN CONTROL (v. 4)

4. Then the LORD sent a great wind on the sea, and such a violent storm arose that the ship threatened to break up.

The verb *sent* in the Hebrew text here has a stronger meaning than the reading of our text suggests. It actually means "cast" or "threw." It is the same word that is used of King Saul's casting a spear at David, and later at Jonathan (1 Samuel 18:11; 20:33). It denotes a hard throw as opposed to a gentle toss such as a parent tossing a sponge ball.

To picture what type of *storm* the Lord caused to arise, think of what happens when a large stone is thrown into the water. Only the water relatively close to the stone is disturbed to any large degree. So it seems that the Lord "threw" this storm only where this particular ship was sailing and that the sea around was calm. This would explain the sailors' conviction that this storm was far beyond what was natural (v. 7). Added to the destructive force of the fierce wind was the terrible weight of the driven water, which threatened to destroy the ship. God was making life exceedingly difficult on that one ship in that spot at that time.

II. THE TESTING (JONAH 1:10-15, 17)

The intervening verses (vv. 5-9) describe the terror experienced by the seamen on the ship and the steps they took to avert disaster. Apparently they all agreed that they would be saved only by divine intervention, so each of these pagan crewmen frantically cried out to his god, all the while throwing the cargo overboard.

Suspicion was raised toward Jonah's being in some way connected with this disastrous situation when the chief officer found him below deck sleeping instead of calling upon his God. That suspicion was strengthened when the sailors decided to cast lots to find out who was responsible, and the lot fell on Jonah. Upon interrogation by the sailors, Jonah identified himself and told them that he worshiped "the God of heaven, who made the sea and the land" (v. 9). At some point, he also told them he was running away from God (v. 10), though when he did so is not recorded. Perhaps he made some reference to it when he boarded the ship, or he may have confessed it when they questioned him after the storm came up.

A. POINTED QUESTION (v. 10)

10. This terrified them and they asked, "What have you done?" (They knew he was running away from the LORD, because he had already told them so.)

To this point the sailors had had a general suspicion that there was something supernatural about the storm. But now Jonah's confession convinced them that the wrath of the Most High God was coming upon them. *What have you done?* This was not so much a question of inquiry as it was of wonder—"How could you provoke the wrath of so powerful a God?" Implied also is the question, "And how could you involve us in your guilt?" Distressed as the seamen were, apparently some kind of respect, or perhaps fear, caused them to be careful how they treated this person who had such powerful connections!

Here again we see that God was in control. He wanted the people of Nineveh to be brought to repentance. He wanted Jonah to be his messenger, but Jonah had acted in self-interest. Jonah needed to face the truth about himself in God's eyes.

The sailors were looking for more than Jonah's name when they asked his identity. His purpose for being on the ship, his country of origin, and the identity of his God were all important parts of the cause of the problem they all faced. Many times one's relationship to God is the key factor in the development *and* in the resolution of a problem.

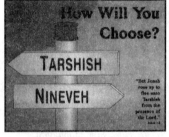

One's freedom to choose to obey or disobey God's commands is the theme of visual 10 of the visuals packet.

Isn't it entirely possible that our efforts to avoid responsibilities by excuses, finding other things to do, or just closing our eyes to a situation, grieve God as much as did Jonah's flight? What do you suppose would happen if God made direct and obvious corrections in our man-made plans today? Would God's mission for the church be accomplished more thoroughly and more quickly by more people?

B. PAINFUL SOLUTION (vv. 11-15)

11. The sea was getting rougher and rougher. So they asked him, "What should we do to you to make the sea calm down for us?"

The situation was becoming dire, for the turbulence of the sea was increasing. Feeling certain that Jonah was responsible for their plight, the sailors also felt that he must make some sort of restitution to appease Jehovah so he would not destroy them all. Because Jonah was the prophet of Jehovah, perhaps these men felt Jonah could reveal Jehovah's will in this regard, so they asked him, *What should we do to you?*

12. "Pick me up and throw me into the sea," he replied, "and it will become calm. I know that it is my fault that this great storm has come upon you."

It would seem that Jonah spoke these words under divine direction, for it was God's plan to have Jonah rescued by a great fish he had prepared. At the same time, however, Jonah recognized his *fault* in this matter and assumed the responsibility for it. He was willing to sacrifice himself so that all the persons on board the ship would be spared. Speaking as God's prophet, Jonah assured the sailors that if they threw him into the sea, the troubled waters would *become calm.*

13. Instead, the men did their best to row back to land. But they could not, for the sea grew even wilder than before.

Whether it was because these sailors (undoubtedly pagan) were of tender heart or they stood in awe of Jonah because of his relation to Jehovah, whose mighty power was being proved to them, they were reluctant to throw Jonah overboard. So they tried their best to row the ship to land. But the wind, which was coming from shore, was too strong for them to make any headway.

14. Then they cried to the LORD, "O LORD, please do not let us die for taking this man's life. Do not hold us accountable for killing an innocent man, for you, O LORD, have done as you pleased."

No longer calling upon their own gods, these pagans called upon *the LORD,* Jehovah, the God of Jonah. They recognized his hand in all that had happened—the storm, the falling of the lot on Jonah, the sentence the prophet pronounced on himself. Now, as they finally prepared to carry out what they understood to be the divine sentence, they pleaded that Jehovah would not hold them guilty of murder. Undoubtedly, this explains their reluctance to throw Jonah into the sea earlier. Who would want to be guilty of murdering the special servant of such a powerful God as the one who had sent this fierce storm on them?

15. Then they took Jonah and threw him overboard, and the raging sea grew calm.

The scene ends with Jonah's being thrown into the sea, followed by the immediate calming of the sea. The experienced seamen knew immediately that the storm was over. God was at work.

MAN OVERBOARD!

Pirates used to make prisoners and incorrigible crew members "walk the plank." It was a prearranged (and premature) burial at sea. These days, incidents of people being intentionally drowned in the sea are few. Everything possible usually is done to rescue a "man overboard."

WHAT DO YOU THINK?

When the sea stopped raging after the sailors threw Jehovah's prophet overboard, the sailors expressed a new appreciation for the power of Jehovah. Without being thrown into the sea, we too can give testimony to God's power by the way we conduct ourselves every day. Name some specific ways our lives can testify for the power of God.

(If you need to prompt the discussion, offer these ideas: If we are unjustly criticized, if illness strikes, if economic conditions turn against us, how can we be a testimony for God's power?)

WHAT DO YOU THINK?

How close we feel to God at any particular moment is affected dramatically by our prayer lives. This seems reasonable. Can a husband and wife experience a sense of unity and harmony if they never talk to each other? How, then, can we expect to feel close to God, to really sense his presence in our lives, if we do not communicate with him? Some people pray only when they are in trouble (like Jonah in the fish). Suggest some ways to develop a consistent and effective prayer life, a life of prayer in both good times and bad.

PRAYER

Help us, our heavenly Father, to search the Scriptures to know what You want us to do. Then help us, by Your power, to do it. In Jesus' name. Amen.

THOUGHT TO REMEMBER

"[Jonah] found that desertion, however possible, can never be satisfactory. God's authority is not to be run away from." —J. E. Henry

DAILY BIBLE READINGS

Monday, Jan. 29—Israel's Disobedience Recalled (Psalm 78:1-8)

Tuesday, Jan. 30—God's Care for His People (Psalm 78:9-16)

Wednesday, Jan. 31—Faithlessness Disapproved (Psalm 78:17-31)

Thursday, Feb. 1—God's Steadfast Love (Psalm 78:32-41)

Friday, Feb. 2—Easy to Forget (Psalm 78:42-55)

Saturday, Feb. 3—Davidic Dynasty (Psalm 78:67-72)

Sunday, Feb. 4—An Unproductive Flight (Jonah 1:5-10)

Jonah's situation was unique. Many sailors' lives were at risk because of his disobedience. Apparently he experienced great remorse for his sin, for he penitently confessed it to the sailors; and he actually requested that he be thrown overboard.

Retribution for sin is not always as swift as in Jonah's case, but God does have ways to get our attention. Earthquakes, hurricanes, and other "acts of God" remind us of who is in control, and can bring us to our knees in gratitude and/or repentance. At least they should! —R. W. B.

C. GOD CARES (v. 17)

17. But the LORD provided a great fish to swallow Jonah, and Jonah was inside the fish three days and three nights.

Many efforts have been made to discredit this account of *a great fish* because man has never observed a fish such as is mentioned here. The biblical record is that God specially *provided* a great fish to swallow Jonah, to keep him from drowning or being digested, and to give him time to think about the predicament his disobedience had got him into. Who is man to say what God can and cannot do?

In this episode, God's care for both the pagan seamen and his unwilling prophet is demonstrated. The fact that God is at work for our good at all times (Romans 8:28) is a promise illustrated here.

III. THE DELIVERANCE (JONAH 2:1, 10)

A. PRAYER (v. 1)

1. From inside the fish Jonah prayed to the LORD his God.

The following verses (2-9) indicate the sentiments Jonah felt and expressed to God at this time, among which were fear, admiration, thanksgiving, and recommitment. One can only imagine the specific words of his prayer. We may be certain, however, that it was a heartfelt communication with God about his situation. Can we pray otherwise or even less and still expect God to help us?

B. DELIVERANCE (v. 10)

10. And the LORD commanded the fish, and it vomited Jonah onto dry land.

What an unpleasant way to be brought back to the starting point! Now that Jonah was back on dry ground, we would expect that he would be ready to obey the Lord wholeheartedly. Next week's lesson will show that Jonah still had some lessons to learn on that subject. But it will also show that his prayer was not the kind that some people make while in a hospital bed: "If I get well, I'll be in church every Sunday"; or, "I'm going to give a tithe of all my income"; or, "I'm not going to refuse to serve the next time!"

CONCLUSION

From childhood up, people who attend Bible study classes are taught the story of Jonah and the "whale" (from the unfortunate translation of Matthew 12:40 in the *King James Version*). The emphasis normally is on God's power, evidenced in Jonah's miraculous preservation in and rescue from the "belly of the whale." This emphasis is proper.

There is more to be learned from this account, however. Although the circumstances of our lives are different from Jonah's, we are no more excused from obeying God's directions than he was.

We may not be named to carry out a specific task as Jonah was, but there is no question that every Christian has work to accomplish for God, which no one else on earth is to do. This lesson reveals God's displeasure when his servants try to evade their responsibility.

Discovery Learning

*This page contains an alternate lesson plan emphasizing learning activities. Classes
desiring such student involvement will find these suggestions helpful. The next page
is a reproducible activity page to further enhance discovery learning.*

LEARNING GOALS

As a result of this study, adults will:

1. List both good and bad choices recorded in Jonah 1 and 2.

2. Suggest ways to measure choices against the will of God.

3. Examine some recent choices and take steps to reverse any that may not have been consistent with God's will.

INTO THE LESSON

Bring to class several items in similar yet different pairs. You might bring two cans of soup, one tomato and one vegetable. Perhaps you could bring two neck ties, one striped and one solid (or with an exotic pattern).

If you can get a copy of the Koran (check your public library), bring that also. If not, make a paper book cover for another book and write "Koran" in large letters on it.

Begin by asking the students how many prefer [hold up one item—perhaps the tomato soup] and how many prefer the similar item [e.g., vegetable soup]. Do the same with each of the "choices" you have to display. Comment on the importance of choice in our culture, noting that these choices are morally neutral, matters of personal preference.

Observe that some choices are not at all neutral. Hold up the Koran (or reasonable facsimile) and your Bible. Discuss the importance of making a right choice between these two books, both of which are believed by some to be divinely inspired.

Of course, most of our choices are not between such dramatic extremes. Still, they involve doing God's will. Note that today's lesson will help us determine how to make right choices in some of those areas.

INTO THE WORD

Have five copies of the entire text of Jonah 1 and 2 available for readers whom you have recruited during the week before class. Have each copy highlighted appropriately for each of five parts to be read: narrator, God, shipmaster, sailors, and Jonah. The narrator reads all the words not spoken by the others, including preface words to their dialogues. Provide a name tag on a neck cord for each reader to wear to identify his or her part. Have the group stand in front of the class and read the entire text.

Place these two column headings on your chalkboard: *Choices God Made* and *Choices Men Made*. Divide your class into two groups. Have one group examine Jonah 1 and 2 and list the choices God made; the other group is to list the choices men made. After five minutes let the groups report their findings. Write them under the appropriate headings on the chalkboard. As each entry is offered, ask for a Bible verse that confirms it.

It may prove profitable to let the groups alternate in offering their findings. Occasionally ask, "Do you others have a related choice to the one given by the other group?" For example, the first group may note, "God chose Jonah to be his preacher to Nineveh"; to which the second group could respond, "Jonah chose not to do what God commanded" (from verses 2 and 3, respectively, of chapter 1. Though lists may vary significantly, choices may run all the way from "God chose to attempt to convert the wicked Ninevites" to "God chose to rescue Jonah from the fish's stomach."

Focus on the *Choices Men Made* column. Look at each one and ask, "Was this a good choice or a bad choice?" Discuss reasons for each evaluation. For example, when Jonah chose to go to Tarshish, that was a bad choice because it was opposed to God's word (will).

INTO LIFE

Write each of the following five phrases on a separate strip of paper and attach each to the wall:

"Escaping to Tarshish"

"Sleeping Through the Storm"

"Flying Head Over Heels Into the Deep"

"Sitting in the Fish's Belly"

"Praying in a Dark Place"

Ask your students to do one of the following: "Describe how a Christian occasionally gets into one of these Jonah-like predicaments." Discuss how one determines when he or she is in one of these situations and how to choose to do right.

Distribute writing paper and tell the students, "Pick the situation (from the strips mentioned above) that best characterizes you and your Christian life. Write down what choices got you there, and how you ought to have chosen. Then write an action plan of at least three specific steps you can take do God's will." Do not share these publicly, but allow the students time for personal reflection. Close with prayer.

Choices—Good and Bad

Read Jonah 1:1—3:3 and list the choices some person(s) made in each of the verses cited on the chart below. In column 2, note whether the choice was right (+) or wrong (–). Of course, it is possible to do the right thing for wrong reasons, or to do the wrong thing out of ignorance and an attempt to do right. So in the third column, note the apparent motive (if discernible) of the one(s) making the choice. Then, in the final column, evaluate the motive.

CHOICE	RIGHT/ WRONG	APPARENT MOTIVE	EVALUATION
1:3			
1:5			
1:5			
1:13			
1:15			
1:16			
2:1			
3:3			

My Choices

Is there some decision you need to make. In the space below, list your alternatives, motives, and possible results of each choice. Is there some clear word from the Lord that relates? If so, note the appropriate Scripture reference(s). Try to evaluate your motives in the pending decision.

God's Love for All People
(Lessons 10-13)

GOD SHOWS MERCY

LESSON 11

WHY TEACH THIS LESSON?

"What kind of people ought you to be?" Peter asks (2 Peter 3:11). Sometimes the best answer to that question is an example. We ought to be people like David, "a man after God's own heart." Or we ought to be like Mary of Bethany who sat at the feet of the Master. She, Jesus said, had chosen "what is better." We ought to be like Paul. We ought to be like Esther.

More often, however, we find we are a lot like Jonah. He is not usually at the top of anyone's list of role models. Jonah is known for his disobedience, as we saw in last week's lesson. This week we see him obey, but he's not happy about it.

He is like the little boy who kept standing when his father had told him to sit. Finally the father became more emphatic and more persuasive, and compelled the boy to sit down. "I may be sitting on the outside," the toddler declared, "but inside I'm still standing up!"

Jonah is one of the most surprising characters in the Bible. Who would have thought a prophet of God could display such bigotry and hatred of another people? Today we see Jonah at his worst—wishing for the death and destruction of his enemies. We can almost hear the whine in his voice when he complains that God was being too gracious. And then he wants to die just because the vine that had shaded him withered. "Is this any way to act?" we wonder. And while we have to admit the surprising truth that God's prophets weren't perfect, maybe we will open our hearts to admit that we aren't perfect, either! If so, this lesson will have achieved its purpose.

INTRODUCTION

A. WE MUST CHANGE

Not everyone immediately accepts an idea that is new. Few people are willing to admit that their minds are that closed, however. So they give other reasons (excuses): "I'm too busy"; "I've had my turn; let somebody else do it"; "Somebody else can do it better than I can." These are among the responses given by many who are asked to take part in the church's ministry. Sometimes a person accepts an assignment and then just doesn't fulfill it because "something came up."

The fact is that some people are just not willing to step out from the familiar and do what needs to be done to further the Lord's work. This reluctance is widespread, in spite of the Bible's teaching to the contrary.

Perhaps the greatest challenge to the teacher of this lesson will be to get the members of the class to identify ways in which people today demonstrate the attitudes of Jonah. When people see the "Jonah" in themselves and determine to change, a new day can dawn in their lives, creating a new wave of interest and participation in the life-saving ministry of Christ's church. Personal participation is essential if the student expects to benefit from what the church, under God's direction, is doing.

B. LESSON BACKGROUND

Last week's lesson provides the background for this one. The first part of the account of Jonah—his futile attempt to flee God's presence, his being swallowed by a

DEVOTIONAL READING
GENESIS 18:20-33
LESSON SCRIPTURE
JONAH 3, 4
PRINTED TEXT
JONAH 3:1-5, 10; 4:1-5, 11

LESSON AIMS

This lesson should help students:

1. Describe the response of Nineveh to Jonah's preaching and the response of Jonah to God's mercy.

2. Contrast God's attitude with that of Jonah.

3. Express compassion for the lost by working to bring God's message of reconciliation to them.

OPTION

Use the reproducible activity, "Matched Sets," on page 214 to illustrate the surprising nature of Jonah.

Feb
11

KEY VERSE

I knew that you are a gracious and compassionate God, slow to anger and abounding in love, a God who relents from sending calamity.   —Jonah 4:2

WHAT DO YOU THINK?

The message Jonah proclaimed to the people of Nineveh was not of his own devising; it came from God. Christians too have a message from God that is to be delivered to the people of their generation. We must be thoroughly acquainted with the Bible if we are to present God's message accurately to the people of our day. At the heart of this message is God's love, mercy, and grace, all of which find their highest expression in the atoning death of God's Son on our behalf. Part of the message, however, deals with man's response to God's grace, and this includes the need to repent of sin and to turn from it. Warning of certain judgment for rejecting God's gracious offer is part of the message also.

How well is this message being communicated to our world? to your community? Why do some people refer to Christians who try to share this message as "Bible thumpers"? Is there a way to be aggressive about sharing the message of the Bible without coming across in this negative stereotype? If so, how? If not, how should we respond?

OPTION

Use the reproducible activity, "Desires and Responses," on page 214 to compare Jonah's commission and message with those given to Christians.

specially prepared fish, and his unusual escape from it—is dramatic and powerful. The second half of the account (this lesson) is equally powerful.

Today's text emphasizes Jonah's attitude while carrying out and viewing the results of the mission God gave him. Jonah's attitude needed to be changed. Our study will reveal God's efforts to effect that change in his prophet.

I. A SECOND CHANCE (JONAH 3:1-5, 10)

A. THE UNCHANGING WORD (vv. 1, 2)

1, 2. Then the word of the LORD came to Jonah a second time: "Go to the great city of Nineveh and proclaim to it the message I give you."

God spoke to the fish that had swallowed Jonah, and the fish vomited him upon the dry land. We are not told where Jonah was when the Lord gave him his commission the *second time,* nor when it came. It may well be that *the word of the Lord came to Jonah* while he was on that beach pondering his terrifying, yet amazing, experience. Patiently the Lord dealt with his disobedient prophet. In his first commission, God had instructed Jonah to "preach against" Nineveh because of the people's wickedness (1:2). In the second, Jonah was told that he was to *proclaim* the *message* that God would give him.

Christ gave his disciples the commission to take his gospel into all the world. There should be no misunderstanding about his wishes in this regard. We know that God wants the world to be redeemed, and yet many Christians are reluctant to speak to others about Christ. Many members of the church are more than willing, if not anxious, to have the "professionals" do that kind of work. Is there any doubt that there is a direct correlation between how well we know the Bible and how willing we are to teach it to another? Many reasons can be given to show the value of daily study of the Bible. Not the least of them is that in so doing we will be better equipped to fulfill this commission that the Lord Jesus has given to us all.

Nineveh was a grossly wicked city. God alone knew the fateful results if a word of warning and the opportunity to repent were not given to it. So he would not release Jonah from the duty that was his. And what shall we say about the great urban centers of our land? More and more voices are being raised concerning the escalating signs of the spiritual and moral decay that is occurring there. Shall we ignore it, hoping it will go away? Shall we, like Jonah, flee from any responsibility to bring change? At the very least we must pray that God will raise up people who will take Christ's message of hope and life to these influential yet troubled places. And as he does, we must be ready to support those persons in any and every way we can.

B. OBEDIENCE (v. 3)

3. Jonah obeyed the word of the LORD and went to Nineveh. Now Nineveh was a very important city—a visit required three days.

With the results of his effort to evade God's commission still fresh in his mind, Jonah would not flee. This time he would do as he was commanded.

A very important city. The Hebrew text literally reads "a city great unto God." The exact meaning of this expression is unclear. Perhaps included in it is the thought that God regarded Nineveh with interest because of the part it would play in carrying out his purposes.

A visit required three days. This phrase, literally "a three-day walk," is a description of the size of the city. Some think it means the city was large enough that it took three days to walk straight across it; others, that it was a three days' journey in circumference; still others, that it took three days to walk through the city, traversing the main streets and marketplaces. Of these, the second seems most probable, though the translation in the *New International Version* would suggest the third. This much we can be safe in saying: Nineveh was a very large city, and the task given Jonah would have been overwhelming were not God directly involved in it.

The evangelization of the world is a formidable undertaking, even in these days of rapid transportation and instantaneous communication. Nevertheless, we have the responsibility, under the same God to whom Jonah was accountable, to take the first step with every intention of continuing the "three-day walk" in sharing the gospel of Christ with everyone.

The enormity of the task should cause all Christians to be more responsible and generous in their support of world evangelization through missionaries. Going one step further, all should be seeking and encouraging capable young Christians to consider the challenge of taking the gospel into all the world as their life's work.

C. PROCLAMATION (v. 4)

4. On the first day, Jonah started into the city. He proclaimed: "Forty more days and Nineveh will be overturned."

Heedless of the danger he faced, Jonah entered the capital city of this enemy of his nation and began to sound God's warning. Again, the time reference is expressed as a "walk," a day's journey. He did not travel one whole day before beginning to preach, however. Instead, he preached as he made his way from one gathering place to another during the day. We learn from Isaiah 36:11, 13 that there would have been people in this Assyrian city who would have understood the language Jonah spoke. Word of his message, therefore, would have spread among the citizens of Nineveh.

The message was one of warning, of doom. Nineveh would be *overturned*. Its destruction would be like that of Sodom and Gomorrah. (The same word, though translated "overthrow," is used of that event in Genesis 19:21, 25; Deuteronomy 29:23.) If these were the only words spoken by Jonah, they were impressive enough to cause the people to believe and to repent of their sins and to hope that God would not carry out the announced destruction. Some, however, think that Jonah would have elaborated on this statement, specifying Nineveh's sins and telling them that the destruction would not come if they repented. In light of Jonah's attitude and subsequent actions, he probably was not even considering the possibility that the people would repent. He appears to have been more interested in delivering the message of doom and making a hasty retreat! Unfortunately, most of us know or have known people who delight in being bearers of bad news.

D. RESULTS (vv. 5, 10)

5. The Ninevites believed God. They declared a fast, and all of them, from the greatest to the least, put on sackcloth.

Jonah must at least have told the people that *God* would be the source of the impending destruction. When they heard Jonah's message, they *believed God*. Putting faith to action, citizens from all walks of life were moved to repentance, with fasting and putting on sackcloth.

Verses 6-9 record that when the king heard of Jonah's preaching, he put off his royal garments and put on sackcloth and sat in the dust (or ashes). Expressing grief by sackcloth and ashes was practiced by various peoples of the Middle East. The king and the nobles took the lead in this citywide revival, proclaiming that every person, and even all livestock, should neither eat nor drink, but wear sackcloth in the hope that God would not carry out the threatened destruction.

10. When God saw what they did and how they turned from their evil ways, he had compassion and did not bring upon them the destruction he had threatened.

HOW TO SAY IT

Nineveh. NIN-uh-veh.
Tarshish. TAR-shish.

WHAT DO YOU THINK?

As Jonah was needed to carry God's message to Nineveh, the need for messengers to take the gospel to a lost world today is great. Too often the values of the world influence the thinking of those in the church. Entering the ministry or mission work is not seen as a way to "get ahead" in life, so many Christian parents discourage their children from going in this direction. But those who do commit their lives in service to Christ can testify that they are the recipients of an abundance of the Lord's blessings. At a time when the demand for Christian workers is increasing, it is crucial for the church, and especially Christian parents, to encourage people to share in this ministry.

How many people from your own church have entered missionary service? What are some things your church can do to encourage more participation? How can your class encourage more people to be involved in missions?

OPTION

Why not set a goal to recruit a certain number of people to enter the mission field over the next three or four years, and then work to meet that goal?

God, never out of touch with the world, saw the deeds of Nineveh as indications that they were turning away from their harmful and evil ways. So God did not follow through on the threats that had been made about the city. The key factor was the change in the people's conduct. Because *they turned from their evil ways,* God withheld the threatened destruction.

God promises blessing or punishment according to the principle stated in Jeremiah 18:7-10. In each case, God's actions are conditional—they are called forth by the actions of people. This is an unchanging truth concerning God's nature. If, as in the case of the Ninevites, people change and obey God, his threatened punishment will be withheld.

SAVING THE CITY

The book of Jonah seems to be a Cliff's Notes version of what must have been a much longer epic. Only two short verses are given to Jonah's preaching and Nineveh's extraordinary response. His sermon, especially, was abbreviated. It would seem that he said more than, "In forty days Nineveh will be destroyed."

In any case, when an entire city of many thousands repents simultaneously in such a short time—that is phenomenal. We could wish that saving cities would happen like that today! Urban evangelism is the greatest challenge for the church today. A formerly rural society has become "citified." Evangelistic methods must change to reach the highly educated, economically privileged, and very private people of the new culture in this technological era.

The cities, however, are made up of more than those in the "uptown." There are also the teeming masses of economically underprivileged in the "downtown." These too need the gospel of Christ.

Accommodating culture without compromising God's message is the balancing act that Christians must perfect to save our cities. What would Jonah's approach be to the cities of today?

Lord, help us!   —R. W. B.

II. UNEXPECTED OUTCOME (JONAH 4:1-5)

A. ANGER EXPRESSED (vv. 1, 2)

1. But Jonah was greatly displeased and became angry.

For disobeying the direct command of the Lord, Jonah had been thrown into the raging sea and had been swallowed by a great fish. For three frightful days and nights he lived in the belly of that fish. From there he cried to God, and God heard his cry and rescued him. Oh, how thankful Jonah was for the Lord's salvation! (See Jonah 2:2-9.) How strange, therefore, and how selfish for him to think that he could be a recipient of God's grace but that that same grace should not be extended to other sinners who, like himself, had repented of their evil deeds!

Jonah had obeyed God by finally going to Nineveh and delivering the message God had given him to speak. Clearly, however, Jonah's heart was not in it. Assyria was the enemy of Israel, and Jonah wanted Nineveh to be destroyed (Compare verse 11.) When that didn't happen, Jonah was displeased, and his displeasure grew into anger.

2. He prayed to the LORD, "O LORD, is this not what I said when I was still at home? That is why I was so quick to flee to Tarshish. I knew that you are a gracious and compassionate God, slow to anger and abounding in love, a God who relents from sending calamity.

By this statement Jonah showed that his thinking was not lined up with God's where the people of Nineveh were concerned. Jonah wanted them wiped off the face of the earth, and he knew that God would be merciful and spare them if he went and preached to them. So, he explained, that was the reason he had fled to

Visual 11 of the visuals packet is a reminder of God's loving and compassionate nature.

Tarshish after receiving God's first call. Jonah's manner of expression suggests that he felt he had been justified in disobeying God. He saw nothing wrong with putting his will above God's will regarding who should receive God's mercy and who should not.

B. HOW WRONG CAN YOU BE? (vv. 3, 4)

3, 4. "Now, O LORD, take away my life, for it is better for me to die than to live." But the LORD replied, "Have you any right to be angry?"

It is better for me to die than to live. Perhaps Jonah felt this way because of wounded vanity, since he had predicted a destruction that was not going to be carried out. It may be that he felt like a traitor, since he had had a part in sparing Nineveh from destruction. Whatever the reason, he had much to learn about the kind of attitudes God wants his people to have in their hearts.

God's response to Jonah's fierce anger was tender kindness. His question called for Jonah to examine his own heart and life to see how graciously God had dealt with him. Couldn't Jonah see that that same grace and mercy could be extended to persons of another nationality or race as well?

In many instances, honest searching of our hearts reveals that the problems we attribute to God or others are actually in us.

C. JONAH STILL UNCONVINCED (v. 5)

5. Jonah went out and sat down at a place east of the city. There he made himself a shelter, sat in its shade and waited to see what would happen to the city.

Jonah left the city and made a *shelter* in which he could live while he *waited to see what would happen to the city.* The shelter would have been a tent-like structure made of interlaced scrub branches, which did not entirely keep the sun off Jonah. It seems that he still clung to the hope that Nineveh would be destroyed. Did he misinterpret God's question in verse 4? Did he mistakenly think God meant by it that Jonah was too hasty in his judgment—that because God did not bring destruction upon Nineveh immediately did not mean that he would not bring it at all?

Verses 6-10 are omitted from our text, but they contain information necessary for our understanding of the conclusion of this account.

As Jonah sat in his Spartan structure, God showed mercy to him once again by preparing a special plant that grew quickly up over Jonah's shelter and provided shade for him. The shade served to "ease his discomfort" (v. 6), both of body and spirit, and Jonah was very glad for the relief it brought him. The next morning, however, after Jonah had come to depend on the shade, God prepared a worm that attacked the plant, causing it to wither as quickly as it had grown.

The next agent God used in his effort to instruct Jonah was the east wind. The combination of the blazing sun and the scorching wind made Jonah want to die. At this point God spoke to him about his feelings for the plant that had been destroyed. Jonah openly admitted his anger at the loss of it, for it had been a blessing to him. God then came to the heart of the matter, attempting to get Jonah to have a better understanding of God's love for human beings. Jonah had pity on, that is, he was loath to lose, a senseless plant, which he neither planted nor caused to grow, a plant that made its appearance in a day and departed just as quickly. From there God drove home the lesson with unanswerable force.

A KIND KIND OF GOD

J. B. Phillips is the author of a classic little book entitled, *Your God Is Too Small.* In it he explores some of the erroneous conceptions people have about God. Some, for

WHAT DO YOU THINK?

Things did not go the way Jonah expected or wanted, either with the city of Nineveh or with the vine that provided shade for him in the blistering heat. Similarly, our prayers are not always answered in the way we would like. The Christian life is a life based on trust—trust that God will always do what is best for us. We may think we know what is best for us, but God, in fact, knows what we need. (See Isaiah 55:8, 9; Romans 8:28.)

If Jonah had kept that in mind, how do you think he would have responded? How should our belief in that fact find expression in our lives? Cite a specific example if you can.

WHAT DO YOU THINK?

Underlying the entire account of the book of Jonah is the truth that God's love is universal. Jonah's reaction to the possibility of Nineveh's salvation was an expression of the attitudes and perspectives of his own people, who wanted to build a wall around God's love and mercy and claim them only for themselves. This book stands as a testimony against all who make exclusive claims regarding God's love and mercy.

What walls are present today that exclude, or seem to exclude, some people from God's grace? How can your church tear down some of these walls? How can your class get involved in tearing them down? How can individuals help tear them down?

example, imagine that God is some kind of celestial cop, vigilant to catch his creatures in wrongdoing. Others may picture God as a grandfather type, permissive and indulgent, a regular softy. We usually assign to God human characteristics, for they are all we know. With our material, finite minds we cannot accurately conceive of a spiritual being.

Phillips, of course, urges us to expand our thinking and stretch our imaginations to believe in the God of the Bible. Jehovah not only exists above and beyond the material universe, but he also is with us here and now. Justice and mercy, grace and truth are inherent elements of his being.

Jonah knew, at least in part, what God is like—"gracious and compassionate … slow to anger … abounding in love" (4:2). But his God was too small if he believed that Jehovah would exclude Nineveh, or *any* people, from his love and grace.

Peter describes God as "not wanting anyone to perish" (2 Peter 3:9). Do we have such a compassionate spirit? Do we feel personal responsibility for sharing the gospel with unreached people groups? Do we take global, cross-cultural evangelism seriously? Our God is big enough and kind enough to love the whole world and every generation.

—R. W. B.

III. FINAL QUESTION (JONAH 4:11)

11. But Nineveh has more than a hundred and twenty thousand people who cannot tell their right hand from their left, and many cattle as well. Should I not be concerned about that great city?"

The Hebrew word translated *be concerned about* is the word for "pity." If Jonah could become fondly attached to a plant of little worth that had grown up without his help, wasn't it fitting for God to look upon the people of Nineveh in the same way? The difference was that this *great city* was God's; he had permitted it to grow into a great power, and he sustained it. Therefore, he had all the more reason to be concerned for the people there.

Another reason God gave for his desire to spare Nineveh was the fact that living in the city were a hundred and twenty thousand persons who could not *tell their right hand from their left.* This is generally taken to mean small children, those who were innocent of serious wrongdoing. Given this number of such children, it is estimated that the total population of the city was around six hundred thousand. Even the presence of *many cattle* in Nineveh evoked God's compassion.

This verse gives us a glimpse of the heart of God and reveals his tender mercy over all his works. It teaches us that God loves all people and that he is displeased with the narrow-minded attitude that would lead anyone to exclude those of another race or nationality from his kingdom.

We don't know how Jonah responded to God's final question. More important to us, however, is whether *we* understand the depth of God's love for mankind and how wide is his mercy. Are we willing to do what we can to see that all persons, across town and around the world, learn of them?

CONCLUSION

Jesus said, "Go into all the world and preach the good news to all creation" (Mark 16:15). That is our mission, just as Jonah's mission was to go to Nineveh. Christ's commission was intended, not for preachers or missionaries alone, but for all of his followers. We are to make known the gospel; we are to spread the word of God's concern for all mankind. The message of the book of Jonah is that God's love knows no ethnic nor racial boundaries. It is inclusive. Let us do all we can to fulfill our mission, and rejoice when lost souls anywhere turn to him to experience his mercy and find eternal life.

Discovery Learning

This page contains an alternate lesson plan emphasizing learning activities. Classes desiring such student involvement will find these suggestions helpful. The next page is a reproducible activity page to further enhance discovery learning.

LEARNING GOALS

With this study, adult learners will:

1. Describe the response of Nineveh to Jonah's preaching and the response of Jonah to God's mercy.

2. Contrast God's attitude with Jonah's.

3. Express compassion for the lost by working to bring God's message of reconciliation to them.

INTO THE LESSON

Use the first activity, "Matched Sets," on the reproducible page (page 214) to introduce the lesson. Use the page as a worksheet for the students to complete individually or cut apart the phrases and tape each one to an index card. Make several sets of the cards so the students can work in small groups.

The class will probably match four pairs easily but may be confused about the last one. (The last line of the exercise is a match straight across from the left to the right column.) Point out that this just doesn't seem reasonable, but it is exactly what happened, as we will see in today's lesson.

OPTION

Separate cards with the left-column phrases from the one from the right column. (Use only the first four pairs.) Read aloud one of the cards from the left column and then one, chosen at random, from the right (resulting in a mismatched expression). Read all four "pairs" this way, allowing the class to enjoy the humor of the erroneous pairing. Then read the cards for the last pair. Observe that while that sounds like another mismatched pair, it is not. It expresses a true event, as we will see in today's lesson.

INTO THE WORD

Have a good reader read aloud Jonah 3 and 4. Then discuss the following questions:

1. How did Jonah expect Nineveh to respond to his message? (See 4:2.)

2. How did the Ninevites respond? (3:5-9.)

3. How did God respond to the Ninevites' repentance? (3:10.)

4. How did Jonah respond to God's grace? (4:1-3.)

5. How did God respond to Jonah's bad attitude? (4:4-11.)

6. We are not told how Jonah responded to the Lord's rebuke. How do you suppose he responded? Why?

Make copies of the following list of events from Jonah 3 and 4, and give one to each student. Ask the students to rate each event as surprising (S) or not surprising (NS). Students may work individually or in pairs.

1. The size of the city of Nineveh.

2. Jonah's message to Nineveh.

3. The fact that the Ninevites believed God.

4. The king's decree.

5. Inclusion of the animals in the fasting and wearing of sackcloth.

6. God's repenting of the evil he had planned for Nineveh.

7. Jonah's displeasure at God's change of plans.

8. Jonah's waiting to see what would happen.

9. God's provision of a vine to provide shade for Jonah.

10. The elimination of the vine that had shaded Jonah.

11. Jonah's death wish.

12. God's last loving statement on Nineveh (4:11).

After a few minutes, review each event. Is there consensus on whether each one is surprising? What would the students have expected in the cases where they were surprised? Is it a happy surprise or sad? How do these surprises encourage or discourage the students in their attempts to serve the Lord?

INTO LIFE

Make copies of "Desires and Responses" on page 214 for your students. Allow about ten minutes for the learners to complete the activity; then discuss their findings.

Observe that Jonah's call was to a large group, a whole city, and not just to individual friends and neighbors. While we have a great responsibility to the individuals around us (we need to practice "life-style evangelism"), perhaps there is also a group your class can work to reach.

• Is there a section of town that seems to have been ignored by the church, an area in desperate need of the gospel?

• Could your class participate in a two- to four-week mission trip—possibly to join a missionary supported by your church? Perhaps you could begin planning now for a summer trip.

• Is there some other identifiable group your class could help, either directly or by prayer and financial support of a missionary?

Make plans to follow through on one of these activities to share the gospel.

Matched Sets

Listed below in the left-hand column are a variety of individuals in different situations. To the right are listed some expected responses to those situations. Draw a line from the situation to the expected response.

SITUATION	RESPONSE
A football player who scores a touchdown.	Waves her hand so people can see what's on her finger.
A woman who receives a diamond engagement ring.	Cries and mourns the loss of a pet.
A politician who has just won an election.	Celebrates in the end zone.
Angels in heaven when a sinner repents.	Thanks the people who helped in the campaign and promises that great things are ahead.
A child whose dog has been hit by a car.	Rejoice that the lost one has been found.
A preacher whose message ignites a massive revival.	Sits and pouts his misfortune.

Desires and Responses

The first two gauges below illustrate God's desire for Nineveh and for the world today. In the second set of gauges, draw a needle (an arrow) to represent Jonah's desire for Nineveh. On the second, draw a needle to represent where the real desire of most Christians seems to be. (Illustrate where their actions would register on the scale, not just where their words might register.) Use another color to draw a needle that illustrates your own desire. (Again, consider actions, not just intentions.)

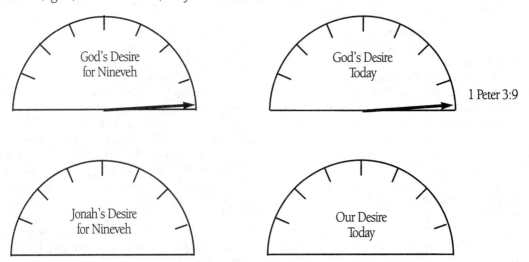

God's Desire for Nineveh

God's Desire Today

1 Peter 3:9

Jonah's Desire for Nineveh

Our Desire Today

What can you do to make the gauge of **your** desire to register more like the one showing God's desire?

THE LOYALTY OF RUTH

LESSON 12

WHY TEACH THIS LESSON?

Jonah never met Ruth. She lived centuries before his time. But if somehow he could have met her, perhaps it would have changed his perspective.

Jonah hated the Ninevites. Perhaps he hated all Gentiles. To Israel belonged the glory of a relationship with the Almighty. Let all other peoples be condemned and destroyed! Let them be like Sodom and Gomorrah! They are all wicked and sinful anyway.

At least, that seems to have been his attitude. So how would he have reacted to the presence of a Gentile woman of sterling character? What would have been his response to a noble Gentile woman who renounced her own pagan gods to identify with the God and the people of Israel?

And what will be our response to the example of such a woman? This lesson will force us to ask—and answer—that question.

INTRODUCTION

A. Skeletons in the Closet

What king of Israel and Judah was greater than David? The prophets viewed his kingdom as Israel's golden age—the model for the coming messianic glory. They called the Messiah "Son of David" or simply "David" (Jeremiah 30:9, for example). David was described as a man after God's own heart (1 Samuel 13:14).

David's life certainly had its darker side. This is seen in his adultery with Bathsheba and in the deterioration within his own family as a result of rape, murder, and rebellion among his children. But there was another skeleton in David's closet. His great-grandmother was a Gentile. Her name? Ruth, the Moabitess.

Ruth, however, has become the personification of loyalty and fidelity, a powerful example for all generations in developing character and godly values. Her commitment and conduct lifted her from the category of a skeleton in the closet to that of a respected role model.

Ruth's transformation arose from a series of promises she made to Naomi. Central among these was her vow, "Your people will be my people and your God my God" (Ruth 1:16). Arising from this foundational commitment to Naomi and to Naomi's God, she struck out on a new path that changed her life forever and contributed significantly to Israel's future. What a wonderful skeleton to have in one's closet!

B. Lesson Background

This lesson and the next are based on the book of Ruth. This biblical short story, made up of four chapters, takes its title from the main character of the story, Ruth of Moab. In the Hebrew Bible this book is one of five books known as the Scrolls. (The others are the Song of Solomon, also known as Song of Songs, Lamentations, Ecclesiastes, and Esther.) These five books are a part of the third section of the Hebrew Bible and are read at special occasions during the Jewish year. In our English Bible, the book follows Judges, which provides its historical setting. This connection is seen in the opening statement of the book, "In the days when the judges ruled."

DEVOTIONAL READING
PSALM 119:59-72
LESSON SCRIPTURE
RUTH 1
PRINTED TEXT
RUTH 1:1-8, 16-18

LESSON AIMS

After this lesson, a student should be able to:

1. Summarize the characteristics of Ruth evidenced by her actions.

2. Describe how Ruth can be a model of godly behavior.

3. Determine to improve a relationship (perhaps with a mother-in-law) by following Ruth's example of godliness.

KEY VERSE

Don't urge me to leave you or to turn back from you. Where you go I will go, and where you stay I will stay. Your people will be my people and your God my God.
—Ruth 1:16

Feb
18

LESSON 12 NOTES

The story of Ruth touches us because it gives us realistic glimpses of life in Judah prior to the time of the kings. It teaches the qualities of courage, duty to family, fear of God, honor, loyalty, and love. The main characters (Naomi, Ruth, and Boaz) display these noble traits even under stress. The book also warns God's people against dismissing foreign people simply because they are foreign. It shows that conversion, even by enemies, is possible and can bring blessing in unexpected ways. As we shall see, a foreigner became an ancestress of King David himself, and she was the very model of what an Israelite wife should be.

Literary analysis shows us the artistic quality of the book as a short story making use of a semi-poetic style, wordplay, symmetry, character development, and dialogue. Theological subtleties abound. Though God as a character does not speak in the book as he does in the books of Judges and Samuel, his providential mercy lies behind the entire story and remains prominent in the minds of all the characters. Though we are hearing a tale of simple villagers in an agricultural setting, we find much to teach us about God's ways among his people and the qualities he values.

As the story opens, a severe famine has come to Judah during the time of the judges. Elimelech and Naomi, along with their two sons, Mahlon and Kilion, leave their home in Bethlehem and journey to Moab where, presumably, food was available. There the family settles. In time, however, Elimelech dies. The two sons marry women of Moab, and within ten years Naomi's two sons also have died. Naomi decides to return to Bethlehem and seek help from her family, and her daughters-in-law offer to go with her. She tries to dissuade them by saying that she can offer them no help. Orpah turns back, but Ruth will not leave her mother-in-law. The two women come to Bethlehem at harvest time.

Ruth gleans in the fields of Boaz, a man of prominence who was related to Elimelech. Ruth's hard work and determination stand out. Boaz treats her kindly when he hears the sad story of Ruth and Naomi. Naomi later advises her how to behave toward Boaz at the threshing floor (chapter 3). Boaz promises to handle Naomi's and Ruth's affairs with honor. The next day he calls the village court into session (chapter 4) and confronts the "kinsman-redeemer" with Naomi's deplorable situation. The man agrees to redeem Elimelech's land, but refuses to marry the foreigner Ruth. Boaz seizes the opportunity to redeem the land and to marry Ruth to continue the family line. A son, Obed, is born to Boaz and Ruth; so Naomi finds joy in her advanced years. The story ends with a genealogy running from Perez, son Judah, through Boaz and Ruth to King David. The same, or similar, genealogies appear in Matthew 1, Luke 3, and 1 Chronicles 2:5-15.

We notice movement in the plot development geographically, from Judah into Moabite exile and back to the safety of the promised land. Also the character development moves from Elimelech as the dominant person to Naomi, to Ruth, then to Boaz, and finally to David. The tension in the plot moves through deepening danger and distress to emerging hope, and finally to a bright future.

NOTE

The kinsman-redeemer was a close relative charged with the responsibility of representing and protecting one who was poor, widowed, or orphaned. (See lesson 13.)

I. A FAMILY COPES WITH TRAGEDY (RUTH 1:1-5)

A. FAMINE IN BETHLEHEM (vv. 1, 2)

1. In the days when the judges ruled, there was a famine in the land, and a man from Bethlehem in Judah, together with his wife and two sons, went to live for a while in the country of Moab.

The opening statement of the book of Ruth identifies the time frame as *the days when the judges ruled.* Judges sometimes presided over court cases, but their most important duty was to organize and lead their people in war against an enemy. They were sometimes called "saviors."

OPTION

It is somewhat surprising that this Hebrew family was able to live peaceably in Moab, as Israel and Moab were bitter enemies, both before and after the time of Ruth. To explore Moab-Israelite relations, use the reproducible activity "Friend or Foe" on page 222.

The era of the judges stretched from the time of Joshua and Caleb to the monarchy of Saul. The books of Judges and 1 Samuel describe this period of Israel's history. The genealogy at the end of chapter 4 suggests the second generation before Samuel as the generation of Boaz and Ruth.

Bethlehem is located about six miles south of Jerusalem. Ephrath and Ephrathah are other names for the town (Genesis 35:19; Micah 5:2). Thus the members of the family in this account are called Ephrathites (v. 2). Another town called Bethlehem was located in the territory of the tribe of Zebulun (Joshua 19:15), so this one is specified as the one *in Judah*. For the *country of Moab* the Hebrew text has the "fields of Moab," which means the pastoral territory of that country. Moab lay just east of the Dead Sea.

The cause for the *famine* that came on the land is not stated, but drought or warfare was the probable cause. Southern Palestinian farmers lived on the margin of subsistence, so that several bad harvests in a row could make life difficult for them. Towns such as Bethlehem, situated on the eastern side of the Judean watershed, would receive significantly less rain than those on the western side; so they were especially susceptible to drought conditions.

2. The man's name was Elimelech, his wife's name Naomi, and the names of his two sons were Mahlon and Kilion. They were Ephrathites from Bethlehem, Judah. And they went to Moab and lived there.

The name *Elimelech* signifies "my God is king." Nothing more is known of this man other than what is recorded here. Seemingly, Elimelech had done all that he could to keep the wolf of hunger from his door, but it was a losing battle. When it became apparent that conditions were not going to improve immediately, he took his wife and two sons to *Moab.*

The fact that the Moabites accepted Elimelech and allowed this foreigner to live among them in peace speaks well of him. The period of the judges was a time of social and moral degeneration in Israel, a time when "everyone did as he saw fit" (Judges 21:25). However, at the time when many were doing their own thing, there were others seeking to walk in the ways of God. It would seem that Elimelech and his family were among the latter.

GOTTA KEEP MOVIN'

The moving van is a familiar sight to all of us, for ours is a mobile society. Moving is neither good nor bad of itself, but the motivations and results are often negative. We are a restless people. Many of us are without roots, family ties, or close friends.

Sometimes, of course, people move for very practical reasons. Elimelech and Naomi moved their family to Moab to escape a famine. Work, income, food, and shelter—chasing the necessities still keeps people on the move. Ruth's in-laws were by no means transient or vagrant. Once they were settled in Moab, they stayed at least ten years. When the land of Judah once again was productive and prosperous, Naomi chose to return to familiar surroundings and reestablish her home there.

Christians today must rediscover the church-family values of fellowship, loyalty, and faithfulness. "Church shopping" and "church hopping" have hurt the body. The spirit of community has suffered. Let us remember and return to our religious roots and be glad we are part of the family of God. —R. W. B.

B. DEATH IN THE FAMILY (vv. 3-5)

3. Now Elimelech, Naomi's husband, died, and she was left with her two sons.

The story moves along swiftly at this point, and embellishing details are omitted. How much time passed before the death of Elimelech we are not told. Nor are we told how Naomi, now a widow away from her own country, survived. We presume that the people of Moab were hospitable toward her and her sons.

HOW TO SAY IT

Bathsheba. Bath-SHE-buh.
Boaz. BO-az.
Elimelech. E-LIM-eh-leck.
Elisha. Ee-LYE-shuh.
Ephrath. EF-rath.
Ephrathah. EF-rah-tah.
Ephrathites. EF-ruh-thites.
hesed (Hebrew). HES-ed.
Kilion. KIL-e-on.
Mahlon. MAH-lun.
Moabitess. MO-ub-ITE-ess (strong accent on ite).
Naomi. Nay-O-me, Nay-O-my, or NAY-o-my.
Orpah. OR-pah.
Perez. PEE-rez.
Zebulun. ZEB-you-lun.

WHAT DO YOU THINK?

Elimelech took his family to Moab because of a crisis situation. Perhaps the Hebrew laws of redemption and the Jubilee Year, when property ownership was returned to the original family, gave him confidence that he could go and someday return and, to some extent at least, pick up where he left off (Leviticus 25:23-28).

If a former church member—who had sold his home and moved away because of a job change or some other "crisis"—were to return, would your church be able to offer any kind of assistance in getting the person resettled and active in the church? Why or why not? What kind of help might be offered if the church was able? To what extent ought the spirit of the Old Testament laws of redemption, including the Jubilee Year, be practiced in the church today?

4a. They married Moabite women, one named Orpah and the other Ruth.

The sequence of the biblical text makes it seem that Naomi's sons took Moabite wives after their father's death. Taking these wives suggests their intention to remain permanently in Moab. From verse 10 of chapter 4 we learn that Ruth was the wife of Mahlon.

4b, 5. After they had lived there about ten years, both Mahlon and Kilion also died, and Naomi was left without her two sons and her husband.

It is uncertain whether the *ten years* is marked from the time when Elimelech and his family entered Moab until the death of the sons, or only from the time of the marriages of the sons until their deaths. The former seems preferable.

The author continues to make a long story short, omitting details. Up to this point in the narrative, the emotions of the characters are not described. Think, however, of the sorrow Naomi felt at the loss of her mate and then of both her sons. And think of the hardship she faced as a result. She was destitute in a foreign culture. In ancient patriarchal society a woman seldom functioned apart from a male agent, whether her father, brother(s), husband, or son(s). Naomi's situation suddenly turned desperate: she was a widow in a foreign land away from the support of near family and clan structure. With her sons dead, she was left with only her two daughters-in-law. And since these two Moabite women themselves now were widows, they might be expected to return to their own parents and relatives for the support that they could give them. But what was Naomi to do?

II. NAOMI GOES HOME (RUTH 1:6-8)

A. GOOD NEWS FROM HOME (v. 6)

6. When she heard in Moab that the LORD had come to the aid of his people by providing food for them, Naomi and her daughters-in-law prepared to return home from there.

With details at a minimum, we can only wonder how long the famine lasted in Judah or how Naomi heard, *in Moab,* that it had ended. One detail is made plain, however, and that is the source of relief: *the Lord had come to the aid of his people.* One can only imagine the prayers that must have been offered by God's people for relief from the famine, but surely they were many.

The expression used here, literally, *the Lord had visited his people,* usually designates God's punishment. Here, of course, it refers to God's blessing. The term in Hebrew primarily means "to review, take note of, inspect" and secondarily "to take action appropriate to the results of the inspection." The Lord, so to speak, had reviewed his people's condition and had taken steps to improve it. Crops were growing on the farmlands again, giving hope of harvest. This was taken as God's blessing upon his people.

The impression is given that Naomi's daughters-in-law were in close contact with her, perhaps even living with her. Together, they began making preparations to return to Naomi's homeland.

B. GOING HOME (v. 7)

7. With her two daughters-in-law she left the place where she had been living and set out on the road that would take them back to the land of Judah.

Naomi left her home of many years in Moab and began the journey back to Judah. No doubt she had mixed feelings prompted by fear of the uncertain future that lay before her. She may have wondered if anyone from her family or her husband's family would remember her or bother to help. Regardless, there was no future for her in Moab, so she must push on in faith.

Naomi's character commanded such respect and love from her Moabite daughters-in-law that they wanted to stay with her, even though to do so meant they would have to leave their native land. And so Orpah and Ruth joined Naomi for the walk to Bethlehem. The strength and courage of all three is remarkable.

THINKIN' 'BOUT HOME

For most of us, *home* is still a nostalgic word. We remember the warmth and love of family togetherness, the laughter and joy of childhood experiences, and the closeness and security we felt in times of trouble. Our senses continue to flash back memories of the smells and tastes of home-cooked meals, the feel of blankets "tucked in" at night, the sounds of clocks and radios, and the sights of Mother's apron, Dad's saw or fishing pole, or sunlight streaming through a window, illuminating the imaginary world of our personal toylands.

Sometimes we yearn to go home, to return to that safe place of refuge from the toils and cares of adult life, to find again the family and friends who gave us such contentment in our youth.

During the years she spent in Moab, Naomi must have thought often about going home. No doubt she reminisced about good people and good times in Bethlehem, and longed for the comfort and security of native customs and celebrations. We are not surprised to read that she "set out on the road … back to the land of Judah" (v. 7).

Christians are comforted by thoughts of going to their spiritual home, the heavenly place prepared by the Lord for the faithful. Terry Toler expressed it musically:

I'm thinkin' 'bout home,
Thinkin' 'bout goin' home;
Dreamin' 'bout leavin' here …
Thinkin' 'bout home.

—R. W. B.

C. NAOMI'S KINDNESS (v. 8)

8. Then Naomi said to her two daughters-in-law, "Go back, each of you, to your mother's home. May the LORD show kindness to you, as you have shown to your dead and to me.

This verse and verses 9-15, which are not included in the printed text, give indication of Naomi's kind and generous spirit. She was old and would do what she must, but her daughters-in-law were young. Their lives were before them. They could still find husbands and build families. So Naomi urged them to turn back and remain with their people. Both girls protested that they would go with her. After more persuasion by Naomi, however, "Orpah kissed her mother-in-law goodby" (v. 14). Naomi then turned to Ruth and encouraged her also to return to her people.

Ruth's response to her mother-in-law is recorded in verses 16 and 17. Her words of devotion to Naomi are among the most beautiful in the Bible. They form an expression of affirmation and dedication that has lived for centuries.

III. RUTH'S LOYALTY (RUTH 1:16-18)

A. RUTH'S VOW (vv. 16, 17)

16, 17. But Ruth replied, "Don't urge me to leave you or to turn back from you. Where you go I will go, and where you stay I will stay. Your people will be my people and your God my God. Where you die I will die, and there I will be buried. May the LORD deal with me, be it ever so severely, if anything but death separates you and me."

WHAT DO YOU THINK?

Nearly all of us have heard verses 16 and 17 recited at a wedding. It may surprise us to find these words were spoken by a woman to her mother-in-law and not to a husband (nor a man to his wife). Has this been inappropriately pulled out of context, or is this a valid part of a wedding ceremony? Why do you think so?

WHAT DO YOU THINK?

When Naomi accepted Ruth's declaration of lifelong loyalty, she also accepted the offer of help implied in Ruth's statement of commitment. That may have been difficult. To admit that one needs help is considered by some a confession of inadequacy. We are an independent people, and many persons cherish their independence to a fault. How does this resistance to admit inadequacy stifle spiritual growth? To be specific, how does it affect one's relationship to God and how does it affect our ability to minister to one another as the members of the body of Christ? How does refusing another's help affect the spiritual growth of one denied the opportunity to help us?

See Galatians 6:2.

PRAYER

Merciful Father, we thank you for the steadfast love you have for us. May our love for you and for one another remain strong and loyal always. Through Christ we pray. Amen.

THOUGHT TO REMEMBER

Remember God's wish, "I desired mercy [hesed], not sacrifice" (Hosea 6:6).

DAILY BIBLE READINGS

Monday, Feb. 12—A Forefather's Generosity (Genesis 50: 15-26)

Tuesday, Feb. 13—Provision of Food (Exodus 16:9-21)

Wednesday, Feb. 14—God's Care for the Earth (Psalm 104: 10-18)

Thursday, Feb. 15—Bread for the Poor (Psalm 132:11-18)

Friday, Feb. 16—God's Faithfulness (Psalm 145:11-20)

Saturday, Feb. 17—Loyal Commitment (2 Timothy 2:1-7)

Sunday, Feb. 18—Naomi's Considerate Behavior (Ruth 1: 9-15)

WHAT DO YOU THINK?

The lesson writer suggests loyal love (hesed) is the most significant element of any meaningful relationship. Do you agree? Why or why not?

Ruth's reply has the character of a personal plea, a confession, and an oath. She was so moved by the love she had experienced from Naomi that she begged her not to press her to go home. She could not face a future apart from this trusted friend. She vowed to go with Naomi no matter where she might travel. She confessed her commitment to Naomi's people and to Naomi's God. There is a three-fold commitment here. Ruth pledged herself and her future to Naomi as a person who could be trusted, to Naomi's people and their social customs, and to Naomi's God and his goodness. Ruth's commitment to Naomi's God equaled a rejection of the religious tradition in which she had been reared. Ruth's sense of loyalty to Naomi led her to make life-altering alignments that cut to the very core of her heart. Something about Naomi's manner of life and her trust in God drew Ruth to her decision. Her entire future hung on this decision.

The last clause of Ruth's vow took the form of the familiar self-curse seen elsewhere in the Old Testament (1 Samuel 20:13, for example). This was the ancients' strongest form of affirmation similar to what a person today would mean by saying, "May God strike me dead if...!"

Ruth was making an irrevocable pledge, meant to be lifelong and beyond. Even when she died she would be buried where Naomi was buried. Seldom have words of such determination and strength of purpose been spoken. They are a marvelous testimony to the character of Ruth.

B. NAOMI'S RESPONSE (v. 18)

18. When Naomi realized that Ruth was determined to go with her, she stopped urging her.

The strength of Ruth's declaration proved her loyalty and her determination. She would not take "no" for an answer. Naomi's sensitive perception told her not to pressure Ruth further. Ruth's decision was made as much for Ruth's good as for Naomi's welfare. Ruth's act of sacrifice became her means for development and making a contribution to God's purposes.

The last verses of chapter 1 describe Naomi and Ruth's arrival in Bethlehem, and the stir it caused. Soon the townsfolk knew of the sorrow Naomi had experienced during the years since she had last seen her friends there.

CONCLUSION

The Hebrew term *hesed* is one of the Old Testament's most powerful terms describing God's divine nature. The *New International Version* employs at least a dozen different English words to convey the meaning of this Hebrew term. Primary among these are kindness, love (often unfailing love or great love), and mercy.

When Naomi urged her daughters-in-law (Orpah and Ruth) to return to their families, she pronounced a benediction of God's "kindness" (*hesed*) upon them, even as they had shown to their deceased husbands, her sons (Ruth 1:8). Later in the account (Ruth 3:10) another mention is made of Ruth's "kindness" (*hesed*).

Orpah returned to her people, but Ruth refused to leave her mother-in-law. When Ruth spoke her vows to Naomi, she was expressing her love, loyalty, and concern for her. She was committing herself wholly to the interests and welfare of her deceased husband's mother. Ruth possessed and practiced *hesed*.

Hesed has been defined as "covenant love," such as that of friend with friend, marriage partners with each other, and child of God with God. *Hesed* is the quality that makes all of these relationships possible. Without loyal love, these relationships go sour or they are broken altogether. May this divine quality characterize each of us.

Discovery Learning

*This page contains an alternate lesson plan emphasizing learning activities. Classes
desiring such student involvement will find these suggestions helpful. The next page
is a reproducible activity page to further enhance discovery learning.*

LEARNING GOALS

This study will enable the class members to:

1. Summarize the characteristics of Ruth evidenced by her actions.

2. Describe how Ruth can be a model of godly behavior.

3. Determine to improve a relationship (perhaps with a mother-in-law) by following Ruth's example of godliness.

INTO THE LESSON

As class members arrive, have on display a collection of large boxes taped or tied shut. Begin class by asking, "What does a stack of boxes make you think of?" Once someone says, "Moving," mention that today's study is a "moving" lesson in both the geographical and emotional sense of the word. (Or just write the word *moving* on your chalkboard and discuss its meanings as students arrive.)

A map of Israel during the time of the judges, showing the location of Moab also, will aid your learners' understanding of this lesson.

INTO THE WORD

Before class obtain twenty opaque sheets (8 1/2 by 11 inches) and number them one through twenty. On half sheets of paper (5 1/2 by 8 1/2 inches) print in large letters the following twenty words, one word per sheet: *adequacy, Bethlehem, Bethlehem, Boaz, faith, fame, family, famine, Hebrew, joy, Judges, Kings, Mahlon, Moab, Moab, Moabitess obscurity, solitude, sorrow, superstition.* Tape the numbered sheets as liftable flaps to the front wall of your classroom or to the chalkboard. Arrange them in numerical order in five rows of four each. Tape the twenty words under the flaps, one word per flap.

To begin, have your learners count off by fours. Have the "ones" skim chapter one, the "twos" skim chapter two, etc. Allow three minutes for this. Then hold up to your class a strip on which you have written "FROM ____ TO ____." Tell your learners that you want them to find the ten pairs of words under the flaps that represent ten "moving" experiences (from ____ to ____) in the book of Ruth. Ask a volunteer to choose two numbers from one through twenty; then show the words under those two flaps. Re-cover the words and have another volunteer choose two numbers from one through twenty. Continue doing this until all the matches are made.

Here are the pairs of words to be found. A brief explanation accompanies each: (1) from *Bethlehem* to *Moab*, the original move of Naomi's family; (2) from *famine* to *adequacy*, the reason for the move of Naomi's family to Moab; (3) from *joy* to *sorrow*, Naomi's change from her delight in her family to her loss of husband and sons; (4) from *family* to *solitude*, Naomi's situation; (5) from *Moab* to *Bethlehem*, Naomi's return home (6) from *Moabitess* to *Hebrew*, Ruth's change of national identity; (7) from *superstition* to *faith*, Ruth's religious change; (8) from *Mahlon* to *Boaz*, from Ruth's first husband to her second; (9) from *obscurity* to *fame*, Ruth's move from remote Moabitess to grandmother of King David; (10) from *Judges* to *Kings*, the historical setting of the book of Ruth.

Have a volunteer read Ruth 1:1-19a aloud to the class. Then lead the class in discussing the following *why* questions: (1) Why did the family move to Moab? (2) Why was Naomi's predicament so dire when her sons died? (3) Why did Naomi decide to return to Bethlehem? (4) Why did Naomi urge her daughters-in-law to return to their homes in Moab? (5) Why did Ruth decide to accompany Naomi to Bethlehem?

Develop an acrostic on the word *loyalty* to emphasize Ruth's character and choices. Here are samples: L (love for another); O (obedience); Y (yielding to another's best interests); A (attachment to principle); L (lifetime decision); T (total commitment); Y (yearning for relationship). Relate each word or phrase suggested to the concept to what is seen in Ruth's relationship to Naomi or to God.

INTO LIFE

Suggest that each of us would probably like to move closer to Ruth's standard of godliness. Review the "loyalty" acrostic and ask for ideas about how each quality can be expressed within the church today. (For example, "yielding to another's best interests" might be expressed by changing the style of music in the worship services—or not changing it—to be more effective in evangelism instead of following one's own preference.) Try to get suggestions for individual participation as well as suggestions for the church as a body.

Finally, ask the class to look over the suggestions in an introspective way. Ask them to evaluate individually whether any relationship in their lives is not in harmony with one or more of the suggestions. Don't ask them to share this information with the class, but distribute index cards for them to write an action plan to improve that relationship by following Ruth's example.

Friend or Foe?

Elimelech took his family to Moab. That sounds like a simple enough statement. Yet it is a surprising statement when one knows the history of Moab-Israelite relations. Look up the following Scriptures and write a brief note about what each says about how these two nations got along.

Exodus 15:13-15

Numbers 22:1-6

Numbers 24:17

Numbers 25:1-4

Deuteronomy 2:9

Joshua 24:8, 9

Judges 3:12-30

Judges 11:16-18

1 Samuel 12:9

1 Samuel 14:47

1 Samuel 22:3, 4*

2 Samuel 8:11, 12

2 Kings 1:1; 3:4-27

*How is the incident in 1 Samuel 22:3, 4 different from all the others cited here? Do you suppose the fact that David's father was the grandson of Ruth the Moabitess (Ruth 4:21, 22) may account for this difference? Why or why not?

Unfailing Love

Ruth's character was noted by the quality of kindness (Hebrew, *hesed*: unfailing love, similar to the Greek *agape*). It is the kind of love that will not quit, even when sorely challenged and pressured. It is a rare quality today, but sorely needed. Consider some relationship that is being pressured in your own life. What can you do to demonstrate *"hesed"*?

RELATIONSHIP	SOURCE OF STRESS	PLAN TO SHOW HESED

THE KINDNESS OF BOAZ

LESSON 13

WHY TEACH THIS LESSON?

"The Lord helps those who help themselves." Probably all of us have heard that said often. It might come as a surprise to some, then, to learn the statement is not in the Bible. The Scriptures instead teach that God helps those who cannot help themselves. (Romans 5:6, for example.) Still, diligence is demanded (Hebrews 6:10-12). It seems clear that God will not do for us what he expects us to do.

Today's lesson illustrates both of these truths. It was by God's providence that Ruth chose the field of Boaz in which to glean. Another would not have been so kind (Ruth 2:22). Another would not have been capable of fulfilling the role of kinsman-redeemer. Another would not have been able to continue the messianic line. These were matters beyond the ability of Ruth or Naomi or even Boaz to control. God was shaping the future to his own purposes.

Still, what if Ruth had not gone to glean at all? What if she had not been known for the kindness she had showed to Naomi (Ruth 2:11, 12)? Certainly God was at work—he was at work in and through the life of one who had devoted herself to do right and to put her hope in him. He was at work through one who was diligent to do what she could.

Divine providence and human effort work together. Let this lesson challenge your students to follow Ruth's example, blending diligence with total reliance on the providence of God.

INTRODUCTION

A. HELP NEEDED

Imagine for a moment that you live in a country in which the only civil government that exists is that which functions on the village level. There are no national controls, no taxes, no government bureaucracy, and no national military forces. Every family manages its own affairs without outside interference. This is how things were in Israel during the time of the judges. The last verse in the book of Judges states, "In those days Israel had no king; everyone did as he saw fit" (Judges 21:25).

Life was uncertain in the days of the judges. With the death of Joshua, strong central leadership over the tribes soon disappeared. Animosities developed, and on occasion fighting broke out among the tribes. Read chapters 19-21 of Judges for the details of how eleven of the tribes of Israel nearly annihilated the tribe of Benjamin when it tried to defend one of its villages where a murder occurred.

Ever present was the danger of raids by bandits who would attack villages without warning. These raiders would seize crops, property, women, and children. To defend themselves against such attacks, a cluster of villages might coordinate their defense efforts.

During these times Israel was subjected also to invasion by the peoples round about them. Whenever Israel's situation became dire, God raised up a Spirit-filled leader to rally groups of citizen soldiers to attack the enemy. We know these mighty warriors as "judges." Such God-directed leaders might not hold any official position within the village power structure, but they were recognized as God's leaders in times of emergency.

DEVOTIONAL READING
RUTH 2:14-20

LESSON SCRIPTURE
RUTH 2—4

PRINTED TEXT
RUTH 2:1, 8-12; 4:13-17

LESSON AIMS

After this lesson the student should:

1. Explain how God protected Ruth and Naomi through Boaz the kinsman-redeemer.

2. Conclude that God still protects and redeems us.

3. Express hope for the future because of reliance on God.

KEY VERSE

The Lord bless him!… He has not stopped showing his kindness to the living and the dead.
—Ruth 2:20

Feb
25

HOW TO SAY IT

Boaz. BO-az.
Elimelech. Ee-LIM-eh-leck.
Menahem. MEN-uh-hem.
Moabite. MO-ub-ite.
Moabitess. MO-uh-BITE-ess.

OPTION

Use the reproducible activity, "My Redeemer," on page 230 to explore the connection between the "kinsman-redeemer" and Jesus Christ.

Just as the nation at times needed the strong leadership the judges provided, and the villages needed protection against raiders, even so there were the weak in Israelite society who needed protection from those who might take advantage of them. It becomes clear that in a society such as Israel's in the time of the judges, the family unit was of vital importance. In the family one enjoyed protection and the provision for physical and spiritual needs. The untimely loss of a husband and father dealt a devastating blow to the welfare of the remaining members of the family. They then looked to the extended family for help and protection. In today's lesson we read of an instance when such help was requested and received.

B. LESSON BACKGROUND

Last week's lesson told of a Hebrew family from Bethlehem in Judah who moved to the country of Moab to escape a famine. There the husband and father, Elimelech, died. The widow, Naomi, was left with her two sons. The two sons married Moabite wives, but both sons died also.

The widow Naomi decided to return to her home in Bethlehem, and her two widowed daughters-in-law determined to return with her. Naomi urged both to return to their families in Moab. One did so, but the other, Ruth, would not. So the two women came to Bethlehem: Naomi, bereft of husband and sons, embittered (Ruth 1:20, 21); Ruth, a young widow, a stranger in a foreign land, perhaps fearful of her reception by the citizens of Bethlehem.

The two women were in financial straits when they arrived in Bethlehem, but hard work was no stranger to this young Moabitess who was devoted to her mother-in-law. Barley harvest was just beginning, and Ruth set about to find food for their table.

I. BOAZ AS KINSMAN (RUTH 2:1)

1. Now Naomi had a relative on her husband's side, from the clan of Elimelech, a man of standing, whose name was Boaz.

The word translated *relative* primarily means "known," "well known," "an acquaintance." Its usage here, and in the feminine form in Ruth 3:2, denotes a person with whom one is intimately acquainted, thus one's *relative*. In Ruth 3:9–4:14, however, the Scripture uses a special expression in both noun and verb forms to describe the relation of Boaz to Naomi and Ruth. That term is translated "kinsman-redeemer" in our version. In Israelite society in the time of the judges, the kinsman-redeemer had the responsibility to maintain his extended family. It was his duty to represent and protect the family's poor, widows, and orphans. Also, he was to buy back ancestral land that had passed from the family's possession. While the term *kinsman-redeemer* is not used here of Boaz, his responsibility toward Naomi and Ruth is implied by the statement that he was *from the clan of Elimelech*.

The expression *a man of standing* is translated "mighty warrior" in Judges 6:12; 11:1. In 2 Kings 15:20 the phrase is used of the heads of households who were taxed by King Menahem so Israel could pay the tribute imposed by the Assyrians. We conclude, therefore, that Boaz was a man of some wealth, vigor, and good reputation, a man of full standing as the head of a family in Bethlehem.

The name *Boaz* literally means, "in him is strength." We usually think of strength in terms of physical might or fighting prowess. However, it is measured in other ways as well. The position as redeemer and protector in Israel's society required a man of many unusual qualities. Boaz was such a man. He directed his estate with efficiency. He showed respect for the law and customs of his people. He took charge of difficult situations. He was resourceful, as was shown in his dealing with the kinsman-redeemer who was a closer relative than he to Naomi and Ruth.

He showed respect for those working for him. He was generous and kindhearted. He rose above bigotry. He showed concern for Ruth's reputation. He was careful not to embarrass Naomi or Ruth. The Scripture thus describes Boaz as a man of moral strength and nobility of character.

II. THE KINDNESS OF BOAZ (RUTH 2:8-12)

Verses 2-7, which are not included in the printed text, describe how Boaz and Ruth met. Naomi accepted Ruth's proposal that she go to the fields and gather grain. The field Ruth chose to glean in happened to belong to Boaz, Naomi's relative. Boaz came from the town and greeted the workers cordially. Noticing Ruth, he inquired of his overseer as to who she was. The overseer identified her as the Moabite girl who had come back with Naomi from Moab, and he stated that she had worked hard all day with only a brief rest. Boaz then approached Ruth and spoke to her. His kindness to her at this first meeting was based on the fact that already he had heard about Naomi's plight and Ruth's dedication to her (v. 11).

A. BOAZ PROVIDES PROTECTION (vv. 8, 9)

8, 9. So Boaz said to Ruth, "My daughter, listen to me. Don't go and glean in another field and don't go away from here. Stay here with my servant girls. Watch the field where the men are harvesting, and follow along after the girls. I have told the men not to touch you. And whenever you are thirsty, go and get a drink from the water jars the men have filled."

The term *daughter* is used here as a term of respect. At the same time it suggests Boaz was probably of mature age, older than Ruth. He was, in effect, giving fatherly advice to this one who was gleaning in his field.

Don't go and glean in another field. At harvest time the reapers went through the grainfields and cut down the standing grain with hand sickles. They were followed by those who gathered up the cut grain and tied it up in bundles or sheaves. After these came the ones who would pick up the sheaves and carry them, perhaps on a wagon or a cart, to the threshing floor. There the grain would be separated from the straw and chaff.

When picking up the cut grain to tie it in sheaves, some was invariably dropped or missed. Or some might fall out of a sheaf as it was loaded on to the cart. The law permitted those who were needy the right to *glean* the fields and pick up this grain (Leviticus 19:9, 10; 23:22). Even a whole sheaf, if it was overlooked on the first pass, was to be left for the gleaners (Deuteronomy 24:19). Ruth was gleaning in Boaz's field, and as an indication of his concern for her welfare he urged her to stay in his field near where his *servant girls* were working. Seemingly, these girls were the ones who were tying up the sheaves of grain.

I have told the men not to touch you. Some versions render this "molest" or "harm" or "bother." As long as Ruth stayed in Boaz's fields, she would be under his protection. Another expression of his kindness and concern for Ruth was his permission for her to drink of the water reserved for the workers. Normally, gleaners were not given such a privilege.

And that was not all. Boaz continued to extend special favor toward Ruth by sharing his lunch with her (v. 14) and by instructing his harvesters to allow her to take grain from the sheaves. He even instructed them to pull some grain out of the bundles for her (vv. 15, 16).

B. RUTH RESPONDS (v. 10)

10. At this, she bowed down with her face to the ground. She exclaimed, "Why have I found such favor in your eyes that you notice me—a foreigner?"

WHAT DO YOU THINK?

Some people say, "God helps those who help themselves." Others say, "No—just 'let go and let God!'" Ruth's example seems to support the former. Instead of waiting for God to supply their needs, Ruth went out and gleaned in the harvest fields. God's providence then took over to bless her and Naomi in a remarkable way.

Does this suggest a mandate for us to do on our own all that we can? What dangers may be inherent in such a philosophy? Are there times when one ought not to do for himself in this way? Why or why not? If so, when? When we are active, how can we be sure we are going the right direction to be blessed by God's providence and not opposing what God would rather do in our lives?

The kindness Boaz showed to the foreigner Ruth stands as an example for all generations. Visual 13 of the visuals packet depicts one of his acts of kindness.

WHAT DO YOU THINK?

Ruth provided for the needs of Naomi and her by gleaning in the fields. This was a common practice, sanctioned by the Old Testament law to allow the poor to provide for themselves.

Compare this practice with the modern forms of government sponsored welfare and social programs. How are they similar? How are they different? Do you think a program with similar goals and intent could be set up to provide for the poor of today's urban culture? What about in rural areas? Why or why not?

WHAT DO YOU THINK?

Ruth and Naomi accepted the kindness and generosity of Boaz, apparently without any reluctance. By contrast, some people today become embarrassed when offered some kindness from another. Perhaps they see it as an indication of insufficiency. They may try to act as though they have no need.

Why is this a dangerous practice? In what sense is the person who can never accept a kindness from another depriving himself? How is the potential giver deprived? What would have been the result if Ruth and Naomi had refused any help?

She bowed down with her face to the ground. This act was in accord with the customs of people in that time and in that part of the world. By prostrating herself before Boaz, Ruth was showing very high respect for him. She was overwhelmed by the kindness of this man whom she now met for the first time. Her act of obeisance was an expression of beautiful humility and modesty, and by it she demonstrated her profound gratitude for the provisions Boaz was generously making for her.

As *a foreigner,* Ruth could have never imagined that she would receive such preferential treatment as Boaz was bestowing on her! She was surprised, amazed, and bewildered.

C. BOAZ ANSWERS GRACIOUSLY (vv. 11, 12)

11. Boaz replied, "I've been told all about what you have done for your mother-in-law since the death of your husband—how you left your father and mother and your homeland and came to live with a people you did not know before.

Boaz had received a full account of this young widow's life since her bereavement. Whether he had learned it from his servants or his neighbors in town we are not told. And he had witnessed with his own eyes how this young Moabitess was toiling in the field to provide food for her mother-in-law and herself. Boaz had also taken note of Ruth's bravery in leaving her parents and her native land to come and become a part of a people whom she had never known before. He had good reason to respect this young woman. Being the man of noble character that he was, he wanted to help her.

12. "May the LORD repay you for what you have done. May you be richly rewarded by the LORD, the God of Israel, under whose wings you have come to take refuge."

Boaz acknowledged that in the long run only God can truly reward courageous living. Sensitive humans may recognize goodness in others sometimes, but they might not. God alone fully knows the intent behind actions and words, and He will reward those who are compassionate, caring, and committed to serving and helping others.

Boaz recognized that Ruth had done more than change her residence. She had left behind the idolatry of her native people and had come to faith in the living God. This was a decision reached at the deepest level of the heart and involved attitudes, values, and ways of thinking and ways of responding to people and situations. She had cast her lot with Naomi's people and with their God. His response was to wish God's own *reward* for her kindness and her faith.

Psalm 91:4 picks up the same expression as Boaz used in the last part of this verse—as does the familiar hymn "Under His Wings." By the use of this beautiful and picturesque phrase, Boaz recognized that Ruth's strongest redeemer was the God of Israel in whom she had placed her trust.

MERCY FOR THE MERCIFUL

"You get what you pay for" is a common expression among consumers. It is generally expected that higher priced goods and services will be superior in quality. When we pay "top dollar," we expect the best in products and labor. And though it doesn't always work out that way, the principle generally holds true.

Such a reciprocal dynamic is definitely at work in spiritual matters. Solomon suggested it: "Cast your bread upon the waters, for after many days you will find it again" (Ecclesiastes 11:1). Jesus was more explicit. He said, "Blessed are the merciful, for they will be shown mercy" (Matthew 5:7). Whatever you give, you receive in kind; and the more you give, the more you receive.

That's the way it worked for Ruth. She selflessly ministered to Naomi, then received generous and merciful treatment from Boaz.

Of course, *receiving* mercy must not be the primary motivation for *giving* mercy. Ruth struck no bargain with God when she chose to be a blessing to her mother-in-law. She pledged her loyalty on the "regardless" level. Likewise, whatever we do for God should not be done to earn personal reward, but to honor him and to help others. Then rich rewards and personal happiness will be ours.

—R. W. B.

III. THE REWARDS OF KINDNESS (RUTH 4:13-17)

Chapter 3 records how Ruth acted on Naomi's advice to put herself into the hands of Boaz, her kinsman-redeemer. She thereby showed her trust in him to act honorably in her behalf and in behalf of her dead husband.

In the background of this episode was the "law of the brother-in-law" (levirate), which required the brother of a man who had died childless to marry the deceased's widow and raise up children for him (Deuteronomy 25:5-10). It is clear here in Ruth that the kinsman-redeemer was to take over this responsibility in the absence of a brother of the deceased.

Boaz indicated to Ruth that he was willing to fulfill the role of kinsman-redeemer to her. There was a member of Elimelech's family, however, who was a closer relative to Naomi, and thus to Ruth, than Boaz was. If that man desired to accept the responsibility of kinsman-redeemer to Naomi and Ruth, he was to be given the first opportunity to do so (3:12, 13).

Without delay, Boaz met at the city gate with the closer relative and ten elders of the city. The negotiations that followed revealed Boaz's resourcefulness, but they also underscored his true concern for Naomi and Ruth and the continuation of the names of their deceased husbands in Israel. When the closer relative declined to fulfill the role of kinsman-redeemer for the two women, Boaz made it officially known that he would accept that responsibility. He purchased all that had belonged to Elimelech, Naomi's deceased husband, and their two deceased sons; and he took as his wife, Ruth, the widow of one of the sons (4:1-12).

A. GOD BLESSES BOAZ AND RUTH (v. 13)

13. So Boaz took Ruth and she became his wife. Then he went to her, and the LORD enabled her to conceive, and she gave birth to a son.

God blessed the union of Boaz and Ruth, and Ruth gave birth to a son. From the opening pages of Scripture God's covenant promises focused on the gift of children. Seth, born to Adam and Eve after Abel was slain, extended God's blessings into the future. Abraham's hope lay with Isaac. Hannah's earnest and faithful life was rewarded with the birth of Samuel. Every new generation was a sure sign of God's keeping his promise never to forsake his people.

B. GOD BLESSES NAOMI (vv. 14, 15)

14, 15. The women said to Naomi: "Praise be to the LORD, who this day has not left you without a kinsman-redeemer. May he become famous throughout Israel! He will renew your life and sustain you in your old age. For your daughter-in-law, who loves you and who is better to you than seven sons, has given him birth."

God had blessed Naomi with a daughter-in-law who risked everything for her, and with a son-in-law redeemer/protector/kinsman. The greatest gift of all, however, was an infant grandson to carry on Elimelech's line of descent. Again the underlying theme of future hope emerges. Since Naomi herself would have no more children, this child would bring her joy and happiness and be a comfort in her old age.

WHAT DO YOU THINK?

Boaz showed great kindness to Ruth in protecting her and in fulfilling the role of kinsman-redeemer. He understood the law of God that required a close relative of a deceased man to care for his widow and to raise up children to keep the deceased's name alive in Israel. Boaz would obey the law, thus doing what was right. At the same time, a potential kinsman-redeemer declined to fulfill the role, fearing he would jeopardize his family inheritance (4:6).

What do you suppose made the difference? Why would Boaz redeem the land and the other man would not? Was it just the fact that he was "in love" with Ruth and the other man was not? Or was there something more noble about Boaz? If so, what? How can we develop the kind of character that Boaz demonstrated?

(Consider Galatians 5:22, 23; Matthew 7:21-23; John 14:15.)

WHAT DO YOU THINK?

The book of Ruth contains several valuable lessons for us today. For example, we see the blessings that result from the unconditional loyalty of one human being to another. We see how kindness to another is rewarded. We see God's providence at work, even in very sad circumstances.

How does the message of Ruth encourage you in your service for Christ? What hope for the future does it inspire within you?

PRAYER

Holy Father, we honor you as our divine protector and redeemer. Help us to emulate you in these ways as we relate to all other persons. Through Christ we pray. Amen.

A THOUGHT TO REMEMBER

"Be kind and compassionate to one another" (Ephesians 4:32).

DAILY BIBLE READINGS

Monday, Feb. 19—Gleaning the Field (Ruth 1:19—2:7)

Tuesday, Feb. 20—Befriended and Protected (Ruth 2:13-23)

Wednesday, Feb. 21—Aggressive Behavior (Ruth 3:1-13)

Thursday, Feb. 22—Giving Encouragement (Ruth 3:14-18)

Friday, Feb. 23—Nearest Kinsman Declines (Ruth 4:1-6)

Saturday, Feb. 24—Making a Formal Claim (Ruth 4:7-12)

Sunday, Feb. 25—Blessed Descendants (Psalm 128)

C. GOD BLESSES OBED (vv. 16, 17)

16, 17. Then Naomi took the child, laid him in her lap and cared for him. The women living there said, "Naomi has a son." And they named him Obed. He was the father of Jesse, the father of David.

The duty of nurturing the child fell not to Boaz and Ruth only. It also became Naomi's joyful responsibility. The community also participated in this joyful occasion by naming the baby *Obed.* This was an acceptable Hebrew name that means "servant." No reason is given for the choice of this particular name, but the townsfolk may have been thinking of the service of love and duty that he would render to his grandmother Naomi.

God blessed Obed in several ways. He had parents of noteworthy character, and a loving and grateful grandmother. The community in which he grew up seems to have been a caring and supportive one. Perhaps the greatest blessing, however, is the fact that his own grandson was David, the great king of Israel.

UNPREDICTABLE POTENTIAL

Great-grandmothers have little way of knowing how great their descendants might become. Consider the ancestors of Alexander the Great, Napoleon, and George Washington. Little did they know these fellows would make history! The ancestors of Newton, Pasteur, Marconi, and Edison had no idea that their descendants would make discoveries and inventions that would change the world. How could the forebears of Florence Nightingale, Abraham Lincoln, Martin Luther King, Jr., and Mother Theresa know what great contributions their offspring would make to humanity? They may have dreamed of it, but they could not have predicted it.

Naomi did not suspect that many generations later Jesus, the Christ, would be born to the wife of her descendant, Joseph (Matthew 1). Mary gave birth to *Immanuel,* God incarnate. Little Obed was truly a temporal blessing to his grandmother, but beyond that he became progenitor of One who brought eternal blessing for all mankind.

Who knows what your great-grandchildren and their great-grandchildren will achieve and contribute to mankind? Perhaps through you, too, generations to come will find salvation in Christ. Pray that you and yours will remain faithful.   —R. W. B.

CONCLUSION

In our day many persons believe that the events that occur are strictly the result of natural or human causes. Believing that blind forces of fate control what happens in life, these persons become uncertain, perhaps even terrified, of what the future holds.

The book of Ruth shows, however, that there is another power at work in our world. It is the power of God. Although that power itself is invisible, its results may be seen. Those who see with the eyes of faith know that these words of the apostle Paul are true: "And we know that in all things God works for the good of those who love him, who have been called according to his purpose" (Romans 8:28). The power of God works in the lives of godly people. We have seen that in our lessons from Ruth. Naomi's godly character had a profound influence on her daughter-in-law Ruth, the Moabitess. Ruth loved Naomi and she came to love Naomi's God. It is obvious that Boaz loved God.

Although Naomi and Ruth had experienced great personal tragedy and sadness, the Almighty worked through their kinsman-redeemer, Boaz, to accomplish his will, to replace their sadness with joy, and to secure a happy future for them all. The kindness of Boaz, when thus seen, has a powerful message for our skeptical age. Who holds the future? God does.

Discovery Learning

This page contains an alternate lesson plan emphasizing learning activities. Classes desiring such student involvement will find these suggestions helpful. The next page is a reproducible activity page to further enhance discovery learning.

LEARNING GOALS

Participating in this session will equip the students to:

1. Explain how God protected Ruth and Naomi through Boaz the kinsman-redeemer.

2. Conclude that God still protects and redeems us.

3. Express hope for the future because of reliance on God.

INTO THE LESSON

Hold up several store coupons or manufacturer's coupons (the kind shoppers use to save money) and ask, "What is the common word associated with the use of these?" When someone responds, "redeem" or "redemption," read from a major dictionary its complete definition for the word *redeem*. Note the first definition is "buy back" (*Webster's New Collegiate Dictionary*, Merriam-Webster). Observe that while we commonly think of ourselves as "redeeming" the coupons, we actually *have them redeemed*. The store redeems the coupons—that is, they "buy back" the coupons by discounting the amount charged for the appropriate items. A later listing under *redeem* in your dictionary (5, b, 2 in *Webster's New Collegiate*) will probably give something like "convert into something of value (~ trading stamps)" as a definition. Still, it is the store that gives the coupon value, not the shopper. Thus, it is the store that actually redeems the coupon.

INTO THE WORD

Discuss how clarifying this principle helps us understand the concept of "redemption" in Scripture. For example, if one has thought of redeeming coupons as something he does by getting something of value for them, it might have been difficult to understand how the Lord redeems us—what does he buy with us? Instead, the Lord gives something of value—his own life—to redeem us, to buy us back from sin's control.

Today's lesson will show another biblical example of redemption. Its intent, in the Old Testament law, was to provide for the widows and orphans in society. A second benefit, however, was to illustrate the redemptive role of the coming Messiah.

Make copies of the first activity on page 230, and distribute the copies to your students. Have them read the lesson text and then work individually or in small groups (three or four) to complete the chart. Then discuss.

Copy the following word-find puzzle on a large poster board for group use. (Or make individual copies to give your students.) Have the class find the following words, which highlight Boaz's character: *careful, discreet, generous, gentle, gracious, honest, kind, loyal, meek, perceptive, protective, respected, spiritual, wealthy, wise.*

A	E	B	D	I	S	C	R	E	E	T
E	V	I	T	C	E	T	O	R	P	S
S	I	M	R	C	W	L	S	D	R	E
U	T	E	E	I	F	U	P	G	B	N
O	P	H	S	E	O	F	I	J	Y	O
I	E	E	P	R	K	E	R	K	F	H
C	C	D	E	L	E	R	I	M	R	Q
A	R	N	C	N	L	A	T	O	F	P
R	E	I	T	T	C	U	S	U	R	
G	P	K	E	X	N	Y	A	Z	L	Z
U	V	W	D	W	E	A	L	T	H	Y
L	A	Y	O	L	G	B	O	A	Z	N

As the words are found, ask your group to suggest verses of the text related to each. Discuss how God used each characteristic to equip Boaz to be the kinsman-redeemer for Ruth and Naomi.

INTO LIFE

Ask the class to consider how each of the adjectives from the word-search puzzle relates to Jesus, our Redeemer. Discuss how his role in each of these areas gives confidence for our future. Use the reproducible activity "Under His Wings," on page 230, in combination with this activity.

OPTION

If there is time, observe that these characteristics (the adjectives from the word-search puzzle) are appropriate to us as well. Provide several concordances and have the students look up passages that command or encourage these characteristics in all Christians.

My Redeemer

The role of the kinsman-redeemer, in the Old Testament law, was to provide for the widows and orphans of one's family. A second benefit, however, was to illustrate the redemptive role of the coming Messiah. Look up the Scriptures below and write a statement comparing the role of Boaz as kinsman-redeemer to the role of Christ as Redeemer.

	BOAZ	CHRIST
The Need for Redemption	Ruth 3:1, 2	Colossians 1:13, 14
The Willingness of the Redeemer	Ruth 3:12, 13	John 10:17, 18
The Inability of Another to Be Redeemer	Ruth 4:6	Acts 4:12
The Price of Redemption	(Not Stated)	1 Peter 1:18, 19
The Benefit to the Redeemed	Ruth 4:10, 13-17	Galatians 4:4-7

Under His Wings

"May the Lord repay you for what you have done. May you be richly rewarded by the Lord, the God of Israel, under whose wings you have come to take refuge" (Ruth 2:12).

Compare the blessings Ruth received, having taken refuge under his wings, with the blessings Christians receive today—and expect in the future.

Ruth 2:14	Matthew 6:31-33
Ruth 2:15, 16	Ephesians 3:20
Ruth 3:11	Matthew 21:22
Ruth 4:9, 10	Galatians 3:13, 14
Ruth 4:13	Ephesians 5:25-27

Spring Quarter, 1996

Theme: Teachings of Jesus

Special Features

Lessons

Unit 1. Teachings About the Kingdom of Heaven

Unit 2. Teachings About God

Unit 3. Teachings About Living

About these lessons

The lessons of the Spring Quarter are based on texts taken from the Gospels of Matthew, Luke, and John. Unit 1 is a study of five of Jesus' parables, each of which considers a different truth concerning the kingdom of Heaven. The four lessons of Unit 2 focus on the nature of God and Christ. Unit 3 has four lessons, all dealing with teachings taken from the Sermon on the Mount and with emphasis on living a Christian life-style.

Mar 3

Mar 10

Mar 17

Mar 24

Mar 31

Apr 7

Apr 14

Apr 21

Apr 28

May 5

May 12

May 19

May 26

Your Teacher!

by Edwin V. Hayden

Teacher! What pictures, thoughts, and emotions does the word call to your mind? The impressions should be associated pleasantly with home, school, and Sunday school at its various levels. Someone there led you through the adventures of learning to tie your shoes, to read, to know Jesus, to enjoy songs and poetry, to share with others the things you enjoyed, to appreciate the works and the Word of God, to earn and manage money, to respect the intimacies of family living, and all the other things that have brought lasting joy and solid accomplishment.

Among your favorite teachers, no doubt, were the ones who loved you, loved the material they taught, and exercised imagination and enthusiasm in bringing you and the subject matter together. Your parents were probably your most effective, as well as your earliest, teachers.

You may, however, be among the unfortunate ones to whom *teacher* is not a love-inspiring word; hence, it does not immediately draw you to Jesus as Master Teacher. If so, you stand to gain the greatest benefit from this quarter's study of the "Teachings of Jesus." He is what the best of teachers strive to be, and he teaches what the wisest of persons still need to know.

JESUS OUR TEACHER

In the Gospels Jesus is referred to most often as Master or Teacher. Occasionally he is called rabbi, which refers to Jewish teachers. He heralded God's kingdom, but his activity is called "teaching" almost three times as often as it is called "preaching."

This quarter's lessons present major aspects of his teaching about the kingdom of Heaven (lessons 1-5), about God (lessons 6-9), and about living as citizens in God's kingdom (lessons 10-13). He invited his disciples to "learn from me" (Matthew 11:29). His lessons are taught by his example as well as by his words. Our lessons of Jesus' "teachings about" various subjects point to his words more than his example, but the person and works of Jesus cannot be excluded from any study of his words. He demonstrated before he described.

TEACHINGS ABOUT THE KINGDOM OF HEAVEN (UNIT 1)

MARCH

The five lessons to be studied in March exemplify a teaching method used most effectively by Jesus—the parable, or story based on circumstances familiar to the hearers, but setting forth eternal truths the people needed yet to learn. The texts point to these facts about the kingdom of Heaven: it centers in God as the divine King; it is made up of citizens who choose to live under God's authority; and the citizens are responsible for definite commitments in relation to their King.

Lesson 1. Parable of the Sower (Matthew 13:1-9, 18-23). The blessings of God's kingdom are available equally to all who hear the gospel as good seed broadcast by a faithful messenger. Growth and fruitfulness from the sowing depend on the soil into which the seed falls; that is the hearer. God's kingdom, then, is made up of those who receive the gospel into good and honest hearts, permitting it to produce the works of God.

Lesson 2. Parable of the Unforgiving Servant (Matthew 18:21-35). As God forgives and welcomes penitent sinners to his kingdom, so he requires that the ones welcomed shall forgive their fellow citizens of any wrong that has been done between them. Jesus taught this in the story of a servant who was forgiven a huge debt by his royal master and then dealt harshly with a fellow servant who owed him a pittance.

Lesson 3. Parable of the Vineyard Workers (Matthew 20:1-16). God's generous mercy will be extended to all mankind on God's own terms. He gives to everyone what he needs—grace—not merely what he has earned. In Jesus' story of the laborers, each was paid a full day's wage to cover his daily needs, even though most of them did not work a full day to earn such a wage.

Lesson 4. Parable of the Three Servants (Matthew 25:14-30). God's kingdom will offer to each citizen unlimited opportunities to serve to the extent of one's willingness and capacity. Jesus taught this through a story of stewards entrusted with their master's assets, and who, afterward, were dealt with according to their faithfulness, or lack of it, in conducting their master's business.

Lesson 5. Parable of the Great Feast (Luke 14:15-24). People who think they have an "inside track" to God's kingdom by reason of their lifelong association with things religious are in special danger of becoming careless and preoccupied with other matters, and therefore of losing out entirely. This Jesus taught in his story of guests who reneged on their early acceptance of a great man's invitation to his feast, and so were replaced by strangers invited at the last minute.

TEACHINGS ABOUT GOD (UNIT 2)

APRIL

Who and what kind of being is the King in Heaven? The four lessons for April deal with that question. They do not try to prove that God exists. They demonstrate it. The teacher is Jesus, who could say, "No one knows the Father except the Son and those to whom the Son chooses to reveal him" (Matthew 11:27). Jesus revealed the Father much more fully by what he was than by what he said.

Lesson 6. The Living Lord (Luke 24:13-27). Our Easter lesson brings us to the afternoon of Resurrection Day, and the risen Lord in conversation with two otherwise unknown disciples. To them he unfolded the Scriptures showing that Messiah's suffering death and triumphant resurrection were in God's plan from the beginning. His way is a matter of death and life, with life finally and eternally victorious.

Lesson 7. The Loving God (Luke 15:1-10). Criticized for being too receptive of social and moral outcasts, Jesus responded that he was doing as the loving heavenly Father does, rejoicing at the finding and rescue of that which was lost. His critics themselves would rejoice similarly, he said, at the rescue of one of their sheep that strayed.

Lesson 8. The Good Shepherd (John 10:1-18). Jesus was like God not only in his care for the lost; he himself was the one in whom "all the fullness of the Deity lives in bodily form" (Colossians 2:9). Thus he fit David's declaration, "The Lord is my shepherd" (Psalm 23:1). Not only would he seek the one lost sheep until he found it; he would lay down his life to save the flock or any of its members. In saying, "I am the good shepherd," he was saying he was God on earth.

Lesson 9. The True Vine (John 15:1-17). As God is the source of all life through creation and provision, so Jesus is he who makes spiritual life possible to his followers by their vital contact with him. This lesson is conveyed by means of the figure of a branch that flourishes or withers, depending on whether it draws its life forces through a firm, natural relationship with the plant. Jesus not only gives and sustains one's spiritual life, but he makes his followers to be like himself in their character.

MAY | *TEACHINGS ABOUT LIVING (UNIT 3)*

Our four lessons for May are found in Jesus' great Sermon on the Mount, as recorded in Matthew 5–7. Sometimes called the "Constitution of the Kingdom," it describes the life and character of those who follow Jesus, draw their spiritual being from him, and thus become more like him. Persons not acquainted with him nor committed to him cannot achieve the life-style he describes in these chapters.

Lesson 10. Teachings About Happiness (Matthew 5:1-12). The "Blesseds," or "Beatitudes," with which the Sermon opens hold up a joy-filled experience that everybody fervently desires, but few attain because they are looking in the wrong places, like looking for roses on broomsticks. Many persons expect the blessings of God while denying the God who blesses. Jesus shocks his hearers into listening and remembering, while assuring the earnest seekers of truth that the love of God will bring joys that they are neither expecting nor seeking.

Lesson 11. Teachings About Loving Your Enemies (Matthew 5:38-48). Right relationship with God will lead us naturally into becoming more like God in his attitude toward mankind in general—toward our friends and our enemies as well as toward ourselves. Here again Jesus taught first by example, in extending mercy to all, in dying for those who approached him as enemies, and in praying for forgiveness for his persecutors. His followers will go with him in this direction also. It is a direction requiring great courage in the follower.

Lesson 12. Teachings About Riches and Anxiety (Matthew 6:19-21, 24-34). This lesson brings us to Jesus' teaching about material possessions and their influence on one's attitude toward life as a whole. One's ownership of things is temporary at best, Jesus taught. Wealth will go off and leave us, or we will go off and leave it. We need, therefore, to be focused on what is eternally meaningful, and to have our trust firmly established in him who provides for both time and eternity. Doubt and fear must yield to faith.

Lesson 13. Teachings About Prayer (Matthew 6:5-15). A fitting climax to Jesus' teaching comes with a study of the Christian's communication with God, both privately and in company with others. That communication is the lifeline of our relationship with God. Jesus taught about prayer both by praying and by describing the attitudes and expressions that are appropriate to prayer. These are modeled in the Lord's prayers and in "The Lord's Prayer."

The kingdom, and the power, and the glory belong to God. Thus, our Teacher's instruction focuses on him from first to last. He demands that we have that same focus.

Jesus the Master Teacher

by Henry E. Webb

They called him "Rabbi." This was a title of respect, and Jesus accepted it. The title meant "teacher," and it pointed to one of Jesus' major activities. For centuries the Jewish people were instructed to hold their teachers in high esteem. Because the law was the holiest object in the life of the people, those who taught from the law or expounded on its provisions were naturally held in high regard.

A TRAVELING TEACHER

We usually think of a teacher as one who gives instruction in a school where there are classrooms and a library and where everything operates on a schedule.

In Jesus' day there were few formal schools of this type. Jesus' classroom was the world. There was no formal schedule; his students (called "disciples") lived with him day and night, week in and week out. When Jesus said, "Follow me," he was inviting a person to be a part of his school and join his band of traveling students. Acceptance meant leaving family and occupation.

Without faith in Jesus, one would hardly abandon his normal activity or business to become a full-time follower. One had to believe that Jesus could impart some valuable insights to justify the investment of time and energy that discipleship demanded. Some, in fact, declined Jesus' invitation. Others, however, had faith in him and became his disciples.

THE NATURE OF GREAT TEACHING

Jesus was an exciting teacher! Often he had to teach outdoors because no building could hold the crowds that came to hear him. How can we account for the multitudes that were drawn to him?

(1) Jesus' teaching was directed at the *major issues of life*. He discussed hypocrisy, lying, anxiety, and many of the other problems that plague people every day. He addressed the issues of life after death, relationships, and the ways a person can approach God. He took no interest in obscure interpretations of rabbinic traditions, which preoccupied the religious teachers of the day. Jesus bypassed the trivial to deal with the timeless. All humans in every age struggle with the problems that Jesus discussed.

(2) Jesus utilized *concrete imagery*. At times he taught by means of parables, simple stories told in concrete terms that even the unlearned could readily understand. To illustrate the various receptions people give the word of God's kingdom, Jesus told a story of a farmer whose seeds fell on different types of soil, an occurrence easily visualized by every person who heard him speak. When he told of a father who welcomed home a son who was a prodigal sinner, all who heard him felt as never before the power and tenderness of God's love. Concrete pictures such as these are worth hundreds of words of abstract theory.

(3) Jesus was a master in the *use of questions*. The Gospels record more than a hundred questions that he posed. Some of Jesus' questions were clearly rhetorical: "Is not life more important than food, and the body more important than clothes?" (Matthew 6:25). While the answer to such a question is obvious, posing the question opens for discussion the important subject of human priorities.

Jesus sometimes used a question to drive home a point: "Do people pick grapes from thornbushes, or figs from thistles?" (Matthew 7:16). The skillful use of questions is an effective way not only to open a topic for discussion but also to maintain interest and keep the attention of students at an optimum level.

(4) Jesus dealt with theological issues in *language people could understand*. Theology is the study of God, and we all need to learn about him. Many theologians, however, confuse people. In contrast, Jesus taught about his Father in such a positive and simple way that anyone could understand.

A DIFFERENT KIND OF RABBI

God's law given through Moses was often at the center of Jesus' teaching, and always loomed in the background. Jesus, however, was not an ordinary expositor of the law. He differed from the rabbis in that he saw the deeper meaning of the law, while they mostly were concerned with outward conformity to its precepts. Since he was the Son of the Author of the law, he knew the law's intent. He could speak with genuine authority about its purpose and aims, opening treasures of meaning that other teachers missed entirely.

Jesus was forthright to affirm that he had come to fulfill the law (Matthew 5:17). Nobody could ever suggest, however, that Jesus failed to keep or obey the law. Rather, it was in obeying the law perfectly that he fulfilled it, thus making it possible for all persons to be freed from the penalty that breaking the law demanded.

THE PURPOSE OF TEACHING

Fundamentally, a teacher is one who imparts knowledge. Jesus did this as he instructed his disciples concerning the kingdom of Heaven, his own nature, and his oneness with his Father in Heaven. Learning is at the very heart of discipleship. Knowledge is most useful when it makes a difference in the way we live. "Now that you know these things," Jesus once said, "you will be blessed if you do them" (John 13:17).

Jesus not only imparted knowledge, important as that is. First and foremost, he was concerned with people's relationship with God. We are to love him with all our being, and we are to seek his kingdom above all else. After that is Jesus' emphasis on how people deal with each other, and on the values people adopt to guide them through life. The joys and sorrows, the satisfactions and the hurts of life are located primarily in the realm of human relationships. Here one finds both love and hate, right and wrong, benevolence and crime. In the realm of morality human beings rise to God-like beauty of character or stoop to the level of demons. Nobody ever probed the mysteries of ethical motivation as Jesus did in the Sermon on the Mount—yet in terms so simple that even the unlearned person can comprehend.

The teachers of Jesus' day insisted that mere compliance with the law was adequate ethical behavior. Jesus went deeper. He indicated that it was right to obey the law in all that it commanded in matters of ceremony and human conduct. However, he showed that the focus of ethical behavior rests on the vital considerations of motive and intent. Jesus' insight centered on the sources of human conduct.

Two millennia have passed since he taught, and Jesus' teaching is still relevant to the critical issues that every human confronts. Cutting away the chaff of legalistic tradition, he exposes the underlying motives of pride and greed that cause mayhem in the life of family and society. The Master Teacher is always on target. Those who hear him are always confronted with vital themes that deal with life's central issues.

THE PERSONAL DIMENSION

Finally, we must not fail to note that teaching is a highly personal activity. It was particularly so with those teachers who lived every day with their disciples, but it is also true of others. What a teacher is is as important to teaching as what the teacher says; the force of personality reinforces (or detracts from) the spoken lesson.

We can sense the appeal of Jesus' personality by the way little children were drawn to him. Such winsomeness is a trait not usually found in adult teachers, but it is one that all should seek to develop. The attracting power of God's truth is only enhanced when it is presented through a winsome personality. Let the love of God shine through you!

PARABLE OF THE SOWER

LESSON 1

WHY TEACH THIS LESSON?

The Parable of the Sower seems an appropriate one with which to begin a study of Jesus' parables and other teachings. Its message addresses the need to listen carefully, to heed the lessons of the Word of God. It is a familiar story, and in that there is the danger of taking it for granted, assuming it offers nothing new to the Bible student. Such an attitude makes the heart hard, like the path in the parable. One should, instead, approach this parable in humility and an attitude of self examination. A person who was once good soil and received the Word gladly—even producing a crop, may since have become unproductive. Perhaps the weeds have grown up in it and choked out the Word. Or maybe that "good soil" has been allowed to lie fallow, with no seed planted there in a long time. Use this lesson to recall your students to aggressive Bible study, hearing the Word afresh and understanding it—and putting it into practice.

INTRODUCTION

A. HEAR! HEAR!

Because her hearing is severely impaired, a veteran missionary resident in our retirement home is seldom able to enjoy the biblical preaching and teaching she so greatly loves. She searches for a teacher who speaks with a voice she can hear and understand.

A more common hearing problem is addressed by Jesus in the parable before us today. (See also Mark 4:1-20; Luke 8:4-15.) It afflicts even persons who can hear small sounds, but do not know what to do with the sounds that come to them. They seem not to be aware of what they hear, so as to understand and respond. Conversation is lost on them, except as an opportunity to say what is on their own minds. In church or Bible school they may attend but not pay attention. They have not learned to listen.

Listening is a skill not sufficiently taught in churches, schools, and colleges. The students who will become public speakers and teachers are instructed in their craft, but the hearers are not taught how to listen. It is a lack that Jesus addressed in his story leading to its logical conclusion, "Consider carefully how you listen" (Luke 8:18).

B. LESSON BACKGROUND

Jesus' ministry in Galilee was nearing its height in popular acclaim, with great crowds gathering to hear him and to benefit from his miracles. Not everyone was pleased, though, with what they saw and heard. The nation's religious leaders felt threatened by his popularity and therefore stubbornly opposed him. His words were examined for traces of false doctrine, leading to charges of blasphemy. His deeds, especially his miracles of healing, were scrutinized for wrongdoing, resulting in charges of Sabbath violation.

Even among his admirers were many who were not prepared to understand and follow the teaching he urged upon his disciples. The multitudes were fascinated, but not ready to accept the hard teachings.

DEVOTIONAL READING
MATTHEW 13:10-17

LESSON SCRIPTURE
MATTHEW 13:1-23

PRINTED TEXT
MATTHEW 13:1-9, 18-23

LESSON AIMS

This study should help the student:

1. Retell and explain the parable of the sower.

2. Compare and contrast the listeners represented by the unproductive soils with the listeners represented by the good soil.

3. Accept responsibility for listening with understanding and for responding to Christian teaching.

VISUALS FOR THESE LESSONS

The Adult Visuals/Learning Resources *packet contains classroom-size visuals designed for use with the lessons in the Spring Quarter. The packet is available from your supplier. Order no. 392.*

KEY VERSE

The one who received the seed that fell on good soil is the man who hears the word and understands it. He produces a crop.

—Matthew 13:23

LESSON 1 NOTES

Display visual 14 from the visuals packet (not shown) as you begin the lesson. The poster provides a chronological listing of the parables of Jesus (with parables studied this quarter highlighted).

WHAT DO YOU THINK?

Jesus had already been teaching on the day he gave the parables in Matthew 13. He was openly challenged by the scribes and Pharisees, and his family had come "to take charge of him," believing him to be "out of his mind" (Mark 1:20). No one would have blamed him if he had got in the boat and sailed away for a break. Instead, he got in the boat and taught some more.

How does a person know when to take a break and when to press on in the Lord's work? How can we follow the Lord's example without falling victim to burnout?

Display visual 1 from the visuals packet as you begin to discuss the parable. The visual illustrates all four types of soil.

But he that received seed into the good ground is he that heareth the word, and understandeth it; which also beareth fruit.

Matthew 13:23

I. PEOPLE AND PROCEDURES (MATTHEW 13:1-3a)

1. That same day Jesus went out of the house and sat by the lake.

The *day* already had been marked by stress and conflict. Jesus had been teaching, perhaps in the house belonging to Simon Peter and Andrew (Mark 1:29), in the town of Capernaum on the northern shore of the Sea of Galilee. On this day some of the scribes and Pharisees had demanded a supernatural sign to establish Jesus' right to teach as he did. He rebuked the demand and offered a sign that they would see only later—the sign of the prophet Jonah, whose three days inside the great fish would become a symbol of Jesus' time in the tomb before rising on the third day.

The *day* also had seen the arrival of Jesus' earthly family, perhaps by a day's journey from Nazareth. The Lord had declined to receive them, preferring rather to serve his spiritual family of believers (Matthew 12:38-50).

Did Jesus seek rest and relaxation as he went alone to sit beside the lake, or did he anticipate the gathering of a crowd larger than any he could address in the house? In any event, his day of teaching was far from over.

2. Such large crowds gathered around him that he got into a boat and sat in it, while all the people stood on the shore.

This was to be a teaching session, so Jesus did not stay on the shore where eager seekers for miracles would press upon him, and where he would be in danger of being pushed into the water. Besides, where on the shore could he sit in the manner of teachers in the synagogue (Luke 4:20), as the multitude *stood* to be taught? On an earlier occasion Jesus taught from a similar arrangement (Luke 5:1-3). He may even have used the same *boat* each time. It would be hard to find better acoustics than in speaking from open water to the slope of the shoreline. The Lord of lands and lakes—the great lover of all mankind—knew how to bring them all together in glorifying their Maker!

3a. Then he told them many things in parables, saying:

Matthew 13 records seven parables, some very brief, out of the many things Jesus taught concerning the kingdom of God. Four of the seven deal with growing things and seem to apply to his hearers generally. Three deal with priorities in value and apply especially to his disciples.

Parables (the word signifies a comparison, or casting one thing alongside another) are stories of common matters involving common people, but illustrating eternal truths. In telling them Jesus dealt with subjects so familiar to his hearers that they became interested and involved. The story-comparisons served a purpose for three different groups in Jesus' audience. First, the Lord's *critics* could find no solid ground in the parables for accusations against him. Second, the parables formed a test of the moral state of his hearers. The *crowds* could listen and remember, then perhaps listen again and learn, if they had interest in spiritual things and were willing to exert the effort to understand the parables. If not, their lack of interest would be readily apparent. The *disciples*, who were interested, could seek out applications for their immediate instruction and spiritual growth. So Jesus explained why he taught in parables (vv. 10-17) and provided his own commentary on certain of the stories (vv. 18-23, 36-43).

II. THE PARABLE (MATTHEW 13:3b-8)

A. SOWER, SEED, AND SOWING (v. 3b)

3b. "A farmer went out to sow his seed.

The parable gets its name from the older translations of this verse, "A *sower* went forth to sow." At planting time, a *farmer* is a sower. Later he is a cultivator. When the crop is ripe, he is a harvester.

Sowing grass seed, including small grains such as wheat, rye, and barley, is very different from planting larger seeds, such as corn and beans. The larger seeds are placed in the soil and covered. For the smaller seeds, the ground may be prepared for sowing by loosening the surface. The seed is broadcast—scattered by handfuls so as to be spread evenly over the area. Light raking afterward may help the seed to penetrate the soil and take root.

In Bible lands the farmers did not live on separate farms. They lived among others in villages, and *went out* to work their unfenced fields. Autumn seeding would be done for the spring and early summer harvest of barley and wheat. It is suggested that the events before us took place in October and that a seed-sowing workman may have been visible in the background as Jesus spoke. The *farmer* in Jesus' parable is replaced almost immediately by Jesus' emphasis on the seed and the soil.

WHICH SEED WILL GROW?

In Shakespeare's play *Macbeth*, the character Banquo consults a trio of fortune-telling witches with these words: "If you can look into the seeds of time, And say which grain will grow and which will not, Speak then to me." It's a good question. Which seed will grow and which will not? Perhaps all of us at one time or another have wished we could look into the future. It may be we desired information that would help us choose the right career move, the best investment, or the perfect mate.

When thinking about sharing their faith with others, Christians are often tempted to ask the question, "Which seed will grow?" Yet the question never appears in Jesus' parable of the sower. The sower's responsibility was to sow seed, not test soil.

None of us knows for sure which seed will grow and which will not. Sometimes our witness will bear fruit by leading someone to Christ. Sometimes it will not. It is possible to influence people whose response to Christ will be made many years and many miles from us. Our job is to sow the seed and trust God to bring the increase.
—C. B. Mc.

B. SEED-PROOF SOIL (v. 4)

4. "As he was scattering the seed, some fell along the path, and the birds came and ate it up.

Paths, packed hard by the feet of people and burdened beasts, led alongside, and even through, the unfenced fields. Some of the scattered seed would fall on the pavement-like surface, where it would lie unprotected until it was picked up and eaten by hungry birds.

C. SHALLOW SOIL (vv. 5, 6)

5. "Some fell on rocky places, where it did not have much soil. It sprang up quickly, because the soil was shallow.

This is not ground that is littered with loose stones. That can be productive. Here, rather, is shallow soil over layers of limestone. Seed here would be warmed by heat reflected by the underlying rock, and would spring up quickly.
6. "But when the sun came up, the plants were scorched, and they withered because they had no root.

Attention shifts naturally here from the seed to the sprouts from the seed. The same sun that warmed the seeds into life would dry the thin soil and wither the almost rootless plants.

D. CROWDED SOIL (v. 7)

7. "Other seed fell among thorns, which grew up and choked the plants.

Sixteen different kinds of thorn-bearing plants have been identified in Palestine, and their seeds would be present in the soil. No farmer or gardener needs to be

WHAT DO YOU THINK?

The typical farming methods of Jesus' day made the indiscriminate sowing of these various soils common. Today's methods more efficiently sow the seed on the good soil, with little of it going into unproductive ground. Sometimes that involves making good ground out of bad (through cultivation, irrigation, fertilization, etc.).

How much, if at all, should that instruct our "broadcasting" of the gospel? Should we try to identify good ground and sow the seed there, or should we sow it more generally and let the seed, as in this parable, fall where it may? Should we do something before (or after) we sow the seed to make the soil more productive? If so, what?*

Do any of the other parables in Matthew 13 help us in this? How does the warning against throwing pearls to pigs (Matthew 7:6) apply? What about Paul's use of the farming metaphor in 1 Corinthians 3:6-9?

*NOTE

The next three questions will help you explore this issue further with your class.

WHAT DO YOU THINK?

Many people are unresponsive to the Word of God. Their hearts are like the path in the parable. They may exhibit some superficial interest in spiritual matters, but they quickly resist if we try to press them about faith, repentance, and obedience to the Lord. It may be that only an occasion of personal crisis can cause them to "break up [their] unplowed ground" (Hosea 10:12).

What can and should we do for such people? How do we maintain a witness to the gospel without hardening their hearts further? How do we maintain a relationship with them so we will know when they may be open to the gospel? Is there anything we can do to till this hard ground? If so, what?

WHAT DO YOU THINK?

God looks for a response that involves all the heart, all the soul, and all the mind (Matthew 22:37). If a believer has come to the Lord on the basis of a vivid emotional experience, is that person doomed to fall away like the seed that sprouted in stony ground? What, if anything, can we do to help these shallow hearers develop into good hearers of the Word? How can we encourage them to engage in a study of the Word that will stimulate their thinking? How can we challenge them to move beyond a commitment that rises or falls with the ever-fluctuating levels of human emotion so that they will have something to keep them steadfast when trials, discouragements, and doubts arise? Suggest some specific ways.

reminded that noxious weeds seem always more vigorous than the desirable growths.

E. PRODUCTIVE SOIL (v. 8)

8. "Still other seed fell on good soil, where it produced a crop—a hundred, sixty or thirty times what was sown.

The ground where seed found lodging to sprout and grow with adequate rootage, moisture, and light produced the harvest for which the total investment of seed and labor was made. An Iowa farmer who harvested no more than a hundred bushels of corn for every bushel of seed he planted would not be pleased with the crop, but harvests vary with different kinds of grain as well as different growing conditions. Jesus' estimates are accurate to the local circumstances. Genesis 26:6, 12 reports that when Isaac planted crops in Gerar, God blessed him with a hundredfold harvest. Christians must remember that in every instance God gives the increase (1 Corinthians 3:6, 7).

Visitors to Galilee near Capernaum have reported seeing the four kinds of soil mentioned by Jesus, all within a very limited area. It would be impossible to control closely where the broadcast seed would fall, and also impossible to see from the surface where the rock lay close to the surface, or where the seeds and roots of thorny growths were already in the ground.

III. THE POINT (MATTHEW 13:9, 18)

9. "He who has ears, let him hear."

This is the point of the whole parable. Jesus was talking to his hearers about hearing. The sentence construction is emphatic. Luke's account of the parable says that the Lord raised his voice to emphasize the admonition: "When he said this, he called out, 'He who has ears to hear, let him hear!'" (Luke 8:8). Listen and think about what you hear.

18. "Listen then to what the parable of the sower means:

The intervening verses, 10-17, contain Jesus' response to his disciples when they asked him privately why he had begun to address the crowds in parables rather than in plain and literal terms. The plain teachings and the explanations, he said, were for them rather than for the general public. Hardhearted persons were not presently prepared to hear, see, and understand his message. If they would understand the parables, the understanding would come later with remembering, pondering, and observing the truth of what was said. For now, the explanation of the parable would be given to none but the Lord's faithful followers.

IV. THE APPLICATION (MATTHEW 13:19-23)

The Parable of the Sower becomes immediately a lesson about the kinds of soil into which the seed fell. The different soils were the different hearers of the Word.

A. HEARERS WITHOUT UNDERSTANDING (v. 19)

19. "When anyone hears the message about the kingdom and does not understand it, the evil one comes and snatches away what was sown in his heart. This is the seed sown along the path.

The hard-packed pathway represents the hearer whose mind is focused on other, and perhaps opposing, interests. This hearer may listen only to scoff at the speaker or the message. To such a hearer, completely absorbed with self and the world, the kingdom message makes no sense. This person may even have heard and rejected the gospel so many times that rejection has become a habit. *The evil one*—Satan (Mark 4:15)—has ready access to this person's mind and removes the message.

Lest we too readily assume that we are not that hardhearted, we might well measure the time it takes for a Bible lesson or sermon to disappear from our own mind or memory. Then practice listening with deliberate purpose to share the message with someone else.

B. HASTY HEARERS (vv. 20, 21)

20, 21. "The one who received the seed that fell on rocky places is the man who hears the word and at once receives it with joy. But since he has no root, he lasts only a short time. When trouble or persecution comes because of the word, he quickly falls away.

The Lord seems here to be describing the kind of excitable person who is easily impressed by promises—and just as easily depressed by disappointment. This person may be "tossed back and forth by the waves, and blown here and there by every wind of teaching" (Ephesians 4:14). The church that offers "Help, healing, and hope" will attract such a one, but may finally cause rejection of the message altogether because it led this person to expect more of health and happiness than is consistent with Christian teaching and experience. Such a person's early zeal and enthusiasm may lead to burnout and desertion, especially if the person's zeal is not sufficiently applauded by fellow Christians.

Not thoroughly "rooted and established in love" (Ephesians 3:17), this hearer still lives and serves in Christ long enough to experience trouble and persecution because of his or her faith. The same heat of hardship that strengthens the mature Christian destroys the shallow one.

C. TOO BUSY HEARERS (v. 22)

22. "The one who received the seed that fell among the thorns is the man who hears the word, but the worries of this life and the deceitfulness of wealth choke it, making it unfruitful.

The hearer represented here may be a solid citizen, involved in community affairs. He likes what he hears of the gospel and concludes that Christ can add to his satisfying life. He may be able to wedge some church activities into his full schedule. For a time it may seem that he does rather well at worshiping both God and money (Matthew 6:24). But then some emergency arises to demand all-out commitment one way or the other. Unable finally to put the kingdom of God foremost above either the fearful worries of poverty or the fleeting pleasures of wealth, the too busy hearer lingers half-alive in Christ, incapable of producing either the fruit of the Spirit (Galatians 5:22, 23) or the reproductive fruit of evangelism.

D. FRUITFUL HEARERS (v. 23)

23. "But the one who received the seed that fell on good soil is the man who hears the word and understands it. He produces a crop, yielding a hundred, sixty or thirty times what was sown."

The good-ground hearer is normal! Such a person does not have the faults that characterize the others. He or she listens and lets the truth soak in, then acts according to it. This one will "hear the word, retain it, and by persevering produce a crop" (Luke 8:15). Honesty forbids that the hearer should claim to receive the message and then neglect to follow it. Patience is found in one's willingness to undergo the period of growth and development through good times and bad, allowing God to work on his own schedule to produce his fruits of character and influence. The *good ground* is not all equally productive, but is acknowledged *good* if it produces to its capacity.

WHAT DO YOU THINK?

The listeners represented by the thorny ground attempt to follow Christ while still clinging to the treasures and values of this world. These persons need to hear the New Testament equivalent of Elijah's challenge to the Israelites on Mount Carmel: "How long will you waver between two opinions? If the Lord is God, follow him; but if Baal is God, follow him" (1 Kings 18:21). Perhaps James 4:4, which equates friendship with the world with spiritual adultery and becoming God's enemy, will help. Strong words may be required to awaken "thorny-soil hearers" to the foolishness of their choking out spiritual blessing and power by pursuing the things of this world.

Suggest some specific actions to help "thorny-soil hearers" develop into good hearers of the word.

WHAT DO YOU THINK?

Sometimes, even the "good-soil listeners" need a little help. In a large auditorium, having a high quality sound system may be important. For those with special hearing problems, special listening devices installed in designated areas may be required. What are some other ways the church can make sure everyone who wants to hear the Word can hear it clearly? What equipment, policies, or staff requirements may be helpful? What can the worshipers themselves do to make it easier for themselves and others to hear? Whose responsibility is it to make a person a good-soil listener, the church or the hearer? Why?

PRAYER

We are grateful, dear God, for the capacity to receive your word. May we treasure the ability, and protect it, and use it to your glory, for Jesus' sake. Amen.

THOUGHT TO REMEMBER

"Consider carefully how you listen" (Luke 8:18).

DAILY BIBLE READINGS

What is the significance of the multiplied harvest? Is it the spreading of God's word from each one to many others? If so, it is not enough that "each one win one." How many persons have you helped to win to Christ? And how many were involved in winning you? On a harvest report, what would be the record for your acreage?

THE POWER OF A SEED

Seeds are simple but powerful objects. They vary in size from the dustlike seeds of the epiphytic orchids—thirty-five million of which weigh only one ounce—to the forty-four pound seed of the double coconut that grows in the Seychelles Islands in the Indian Ocean. Some of the smallest seeds have the power to produce very large plants.

The most massive living thing on earth is the General Sherman tree in California's Sequoia National Forest. Standing 275 feet tall, it has a girth of just over eighty-three feet and contains enough timber to make five billion matches. Its estimated weight, including roots, is 2,756 tons. Yet a sequoia tree starts from a tiny seed that weighs only 1/6000th of an ounce.

God's Word is also a powerful seed. When we open our hearts to his Word, we become fertile ground for that seed. Like the good ground in the parable, we become fruitful and effective. God's Word produces an abundant harvest of righteousness in our lives. How receptive is the soil of your heart to the seed of God's Word?

—C. B. Mc.

CONCLUSION

A. DEMONSTRATION

Just as the time of growth and harvest revealed the kinds of soil that Jesus described, so the months of his developing ministry revealed the kinds of hearers in his audiences. There were the rulers of the people, hardened by prejudice so that any impression made by his words was a negative impression. Satan made short work of the gospel with most of them.

There were the eager short-time followers who thronged Jesus to receive his words and his miracles. Once they would have made him king, but they turned away when he refused to be their kind of king (John 6:60-66).

There was the rich young ruler, who was seriously interested in life eternal, but had too much in this present life to make the exchange.

Then there were various kinds of good ground among the apostles and their contemporaries. We don't know much about most of them. And the same is true about any effort to identify "soil samples" among our own contemporaries. Most important is the quality of our own hearing and response to the Word.

B. BROADCASTING

How is the Parable of the Sower to become clear to people who have no experience with seeds and soils and growing things? Perhaps there is a helpful linking word, *broadcasting*. The gospel message, like the seed, is broadcast (spread abroad) with little awareness of where it may land or which tiny bit may sink in and bring results. The messenger broadcasts in faith, and the hearer must listen responsibly. There are hardened hearers, mentally and emotionally deafened by the noise and repetition of commercial promotion. There are excitable hearers, swept one way and then another by the most recent emotional appeal. There are preoccupied hearers, absorbed with business, pleasure, and daily problems, so they have scant time for serious contemplation. And there are still thoughtful hearers, who listen carefully, consider thoughtfully, and respond appropriately. Any of us can increase his or her own responsiveness by the spiritual exercises of prayer, Bible study, and thoughtful conversation with others about God and his purposes.

Discovery Learning

This page contains an alternate lesson plan emphasizing learning activities. Classes desiring such student involvement will find these suggestions helpful. The next page is a reproducible activity page to further enhance discovery learning.

LEARNING GOALS

As a result of participating in today's lesson, a student will be able to:

1. Retell and explain the parable of the sower.

2. Compare and contrast the listeners represented by the unproductive soils with the listeners represented by the good soil.

3. Accept responsibility for listening with understanding and for responding to Christian teaching.

INTO THE LESSON

Have the students work in pairs to name several qualities or characteristics of a good listener. After two minutes ask for their results. Write their answers on a chalkboard, poster paper, or overhead transparency. Here are some possible answers: acting interested, caring, being empathetic, maintaining good eye contact, giving feedback, being willing to get involved, allowing adequate time, and not interrupting. (Other responses are possible, and all answers should be accepted).

Make the transition into the study of today's Bible text by explaining that listening is a critical issue in our response to the gospel and to the will of God every day.

INTO THE WORD

Ask for a volunteer to read Matthew 13:1-9 aloud.

Explain Jesus' use of parables as you feel it necessary for your class.

Ask another volunteer to read Matthew 13:18-23.

After the second reading divide the class into three groups, assigning each group a type of soil: the path (vv. 4, 19); the rocky soil (vv. 5, 6, 20, 21); and the thorny soil (vv. 7, 22). Tell the class that each of these types of soil represents a different type of hearer of the gospel of Christ. Ask each group to determine the qualities or characteristics lacking in the hearer that its soil represents. They can consider items in the list developed at the beginning of class and any other qualities they can think of. Examples are, the *hard-packed soil* lacks understanding and does not give adequate time to listening; the *rocky soil* lacks commitment and endurance; and the *thorny soil* lacks proper priorities and is not committed. Encourage each group to discuss the qualities of its soil (hearer) in the context of listening to the gospel, not only initially but also on a continuing basis.

After allowing seven minutes for discussion, have a spokesperson from each group summarize the group's conclusions for the entire class. Accept each response and be ready to probe where necessary. (For example, "So what are the priorities of those identified as thorny soil?")

Move into a discussion of the hearers represented as *good soil* by reading Matthew 13:8, 23 and asking this question: Is the secret to being "good soil" the absence of the negative qualities of the other soils? Lead the discussion to the conclusion that these hearers of God's Word have sincerity of heart, patience, a desire to apply God's truth personally, a willingness to change, and endurance.

INTO LIFE

Jesus points out that the good soil is productive, bringing forth a harvest. Ask the students to work in pairs to make an acrostic using the word *listen*. The words chosen should be qualities appropriate for the Christian who has heard, understood, and applied the Word of God in his or her life. The following is an example:

A PERSON WHO HEARS THE GOSPEL AND RESPONDS IN FAITHFUL OBEDIENCE WILL BEAR FRUIT SUCH AS:

L love, learning
I   interest in others, initiative
S sanctity (holiness), Spirit-led living
T trust in God, telling others
E enthusiasm, evangelism, endurance
N needs-meeting, nurturing others

As students share their entries, write them on the chalkboard, poster paper, or overhead transparency. Encourage a variety of responses and accept them all (even if oddly phrased).

Ask the class members to reflect on the following: In what way, if any, have you demonstrated the qualities or characteristics of any of the four soils of the parable? Encourage specific responses. Guide the discussion toward the realization that each person is responsible for how he or she listens to God's Word.

Conclude the session by having the same pairs of students share their answers to the following question: In what way this week will I improve how I listen to God's direction and bear fruit for him?

Soil Samples

Read Matthew 13:1-9, 18-23. Then note the activities in the left column of the chart below. In the context of hearing the Word in Sunday morning services of your church, which "soil" is characterized by each activity? Put a mark in the appropriate column. Then add one more activity that fits each soil type.

ACTIVITY	PATH	STONY	THORNY	GOOD
Staying up late on Saturday to watch television or visit with friends				
Following along on a printed outline of the speaker's message				
Skipping Sunday School and attending worship only				
Maintaining several responsibilities during the worship service				
Taking notes on the message				
Reducing time spent in Bible study for more "relationship-building"				
Doing so much Sunday afternoon that worship is quickly forgotten				
Asking oneself, "What will I do about the truths I am hearing?"				
	✔			
		✔		
			✔	
				✔

Broadcasting

How is the Parable of the Sower to become clear to people who have no experience with seeds and soils and growing things? Perhaps there is a helpful linking word, *broadcasting*. To the sower, broadcasting meant spreading abroad the seed with little awareness of where it may land or which tiny bit may sink in and bring results. To us, *broadcasting* is a media term, referring especially to radio or television.

Today's messenger "broadcasts" the Word in faith, and the hearer must listen responsibly. There are hardened hearers, mentally and emotionally deafened by the noise and repetition of commercial promotion. There are excitable hearers, swept one way and then another by the most recent emotional appeal. There are preoccupied hearers, absorbed with business, pleasure, and daily problems, so they have scant time for serious contemplation. And there are still thoughtful hearers, who listen carefully, consider thoughtfully, and respond appropriately. Any of us can increase his or her own responsiveness by the spiritual exercises of prayer, Bible study, and thoughtful conversation with others about God and his purposes.

How does changing the metaphor from a farming to a media illustration help you to understand the parable better? What implications does it suggest for our broadcasting of the gospel today?

How can every Christian be a "broadcaster," taking the Word to new "markets" every day?

PARABLE OF THE
UNFORGIVING SERVANT

LESSON 2

Mar
10

WHY TEACH THIS LESSON?

"Seventy times seven?" Are you serious? The traditional rendering of Matthew 18:22, Jesus' reply to Peter's query, "How often do I have to forgive," is mind boggling. Even the *New International*'s "seventy-seven" seems excessive.

And it would be if we weren't in so much need of forgiveness ourselves. Keep Peter's question in mind as you present this lesson on the "Unforgiving Servant." Observe that the need to forgive the smaller debt, the 100 denarii, is the "seventy times seven" (seventy-seven times). In comparison, it suddenly seems not to be excessive at all. If your students see that, this lesson will have been a success.

INTRODUCTION

A. OF DEBTS AND DEBTORS

A newborn baby boy was found to have a serious defect in his heart. Rushed by helicopter to a children's hospital many miles away, he underwent radical surgery, followed by intensive care. When the infant was discharged, the hospital's receptionist wanted to know if his father was prepared to pay the bill immediately—a total of more than a hundred thousand dollars!

"Look," said the young father, "I'll make monthly payments on it as long as I live, and after that I don't care."

Debt—the obligation to pay for a benefit already received—is variously viewed. Some people spend without considering anything beyond the present benefit. They seem not to recognize that other people must bear the losses of unpaid debt. Others, on the other hand, limit their expenditures to what they can pay for immediately. Even they, however, face the continuing obligation noted in Romans 13:8: "Let no debt remain outstanding, except the continuing debt to love one another."

This brings us to another kind of obligation, or debt, incurred when we offend, injure, or mistreat another person, including God himself. But how do we pay that debt? Money can be returned, or property damage can be paid for, but how shall we unsay hurtful words, or unbruise a black eye, or undo a thoughtless, sinful act? Those are the debts that we never can pay. They remain unpaid until they are forgiven. So the Lord teaches us to pray, "Forgive us our debts, as we also have forgiven our debtors" (Matthew 6:12). In today's lesson he speaks of wiping out social, emotional, and moral obligations in terms of canceling money debts.

B. TO FORGIVE IS DIVINE

"To forgive what he (or she) did to me is just impossible. It's too much to expect of any human being." Most of us have heard something like that more than once. Perhaps we have said it ourselves. And it is not all wrong. The essayist Alexander Pope was never more right than when he wrote, "To err is human, to forgive divine." The first clause is a short form of Romans 3:23: "For all have sinned, and fall

DEVOTIONAL READING
EPHESIANS 4:25—5:2
LESSON SCRIPTURE
MATTHEW 18:21-35
PRINTED TEXT
MATTHEW 18:21-35

LESSON AIMS

This study should help the student:

1. Retell and explain the parable of the unforgiving servant.

2. Compare the forgiveness from debt offered by a king to the forgiveness offered by God through Jesus.

3. Make a prayerful beginning toward forgiving someone who has wronged us.

KEY VERSE

Do not judge, and you will not be judged. Do not condemn, and you will not be condemned. Forgive, and you will be forgiven.
—Luke 6:37

LESSON 2 NOTES

short of the glory of God." The second clause is a short form of Psalm 103:8-13, which includes this: "The Lord is compassionate and gracious, slow to anger, abounding in love. . . . As far as the east is from the west, so far has he removed our transgressions from us."

Forgiveness is a quality of God, who cannot tolerate wickedness, but who can remove it by forgiving the penitent sinner. That divine quality was fully expressed in Jesus, whose mission was to bring God's forgiveness to mankind (Romans 8), and who prayed for his murderers, "Father, forgive them, for they do not know what they are doing" (Luke 23:34). That divine quality of forgiveness enables the child of God, through the indwelling Holy Spirit, to do what is humanly impossible, even as the dying evangelist Stephen prayed, "Lord, do not hold this sin against them" (Acts 7:60).

That is not to say that non-Christians can never forgive offenses against them. Through the influence of teaching and example the human tendency of those who do not know the Lord Jesus is sometimes overcome by the divine quality of forgiveness. Occasionally, however, the appearance of forgiveness is simply tolerance of evil by one who doesn't care. Genuine forgiveness requires a person to recognize evil for what it is, to reflect the divine abhorrence of any wickedness, and yet to throw the mantle of patient love over the confessing offender.

C. LESSON BACKGROUND

Jesus' public ministry in Galilee had passed its peak of popularity. No longer was he addressing the multitudes and demonstrating his deity by many miracles. His closest disciples were now convinced of his deity, as indicated by Peter's confession (Matthew 16:13-20), and by the transfiguration event and Heaven's confession (Matthew 17:1-8). Now he was teaching the Twelve concerning his coming death and resurrection, with the attendant difficulties they would face (Matthew 16:21-28).

Some stresses and tensions had become evident among the apostles. They were arguing about position and preference among themselves, while Jesus was urging humility and care for others (Matthew 18:1-10). Recognizing differences of opinion—even hard feelings—among his followers, the Lord set forth a plan, which the offended person was to follow in reestablishing a right relationship (Matthew 18:15-18). The offender might not even know that he had committed any offense; or he might be a habitual offender, who apologized repeatedly for repeated offenses.

I. HOW MANY TIMES? (MATTHEW 18:21, 22)

21. Then Peter came to Jesus and asked, "Lord, how many times shall I forgive my brother when he sins against me? Up to seven times?"

The teaching session before us began with a personal question. Had Peter become the object of jealousy and unkind remarks because following his confession he had received Jesus' compliment (Matthew 16:17, 18), or because he was one of the "inner circle" witnessing the transfiguration? (Matthew 17:1-4). No indication is given regarding the reason for Peter's question.

Jewish tradition of a later date declared that the extent of required forgiveness was three times. If this was the teaching of the spiritual leaders in Jesus' day, Peter undoubtedly felt that he was being quite generous in offering to forgive an offender *seven times.*

22. Jesus answered, "I tell you, not seven times, but seventy-seven times.

Seventy-seven times—or even seventy times seven (that is, 490), as some translations render it—was not intended as a precise number. To make a tally of injuries would violate the principle of 1 Corinthians 13:5: "[Love] keeps no record of

WHAT DO YOU THINK?

Peter wanted to put limits or conditions on forgiveness. "How many times?" he asked. And don't we also tend to limit or put conditions on forgiveness? How is each of the following statements a reflection of the desire to limit forgiveness?

• "I'll forgive him if he gets down on his knees and begs for forgiveness."

• "I'll forgive her if she proves to me she is really sorry for what she has done."

• "I'll forgive him, but first I want to make him 'squirm' a little bit."

• "I'll forgive you this time, but don't let it happen again."

Visual 2 illustrates Jesus' response to Peter in verse 22. It uses the alternate translation "Seventy times seven" noted in the commentary, so a word of explanation might be necessary.

wrongs." It would also misrepresent the infinite grace of God, which is the theme of Jesus' ministry.

This teaching of personal forgiveness for personal offenses should not be applied, however, to public affairs of criminal justice. (See Romans 13:1-7.) Unlimited judicial clemency for habitual crimes is no part of Jesus' program.

II. THE PARABLE (MATTHEW 18:23-34)

What began as a conversation between Jesus and Peter became immediately a teaching session directed first to all the apostles and then to all who would become followers of the Christ.

A. A FORGIVEN DEBTOR (vv. 23-27)

23. "Therefore, the kingdom of heaven is like a king who wanted to settle accounts with his servants.

The discussion of unlimited forgiveness introduces the subject of the infinities of God. It leads Jesus to tell a parable about *the kingdom of heaven*. Couched in terms of this world, the parable deals with a royal relationship with citizen-slaves. It deals with a king-sized debt, kingly compassion, and kingly judgment. It is an awesome story.

Luke 19:12-27 and Matthew 25:14-30 tell of noblemen who left their countries for an extended period of time, during which they entrusted their business to responsible servants. Upon their return they demanded an accounting of the servants' business activities. An occasion for taking account might occur, however, without an owner's prolonged absence (See Luke 16:1, 2.) Such an occurrence might be compared with our experience at the end of the month, or when one's job performance comes up for review. The accounting that took place in the parable for our study in this lesson was of this type.

24. "As he began the settlement, a man who owed him ten thousand talents was brought to him.

A man so debt-ridden, or guilt-ridden, might have been reluctant to come; but come he must. One estimate of the man's debt is that it was enough to pay a thousand Roman soldiers' daily wages for a hundred years. This debtor was no unimportant person. He could have been a high official, such as a governor, appointed by the king to rule over a great part of his domain and to bring into his treasuries the revenues of one of the provinces. (Compare Daniel 2:48, 49.) Let us consider, then, our responsibility to God for handling the spiritual treasures of Heaven! Our unpayable debt to God gives point to the parable.

25. "Since he was not able to pay, the master ordered that he and his wife and his children and all that he had be sold to repay the debt.

Whatever the man may have done with his king's money, it was gone, and he was as helpless to pay his vast debt as we are helpless to pay God for our used-up blessings and our sins.

The sale of a man and his family, along with whatever possessions he may have, to satisfy his debts is a fact recognized—not necessarily approved—in Leviticus 25:39-41; Nehemiah 5:4, 5; and 2 Kings 4:1. The last passage quotes the plaint of a widow: "My husband is dead . . . now his creditor is coming to take my two boys as his slaves."

26. "The servant fell on his knees before him. 'Be patient with me,' he begged, 'and I will pay back everything.'

In desperation the debtor prostrated himself before his king and begged for a delay in judgment. Even so, his pride prevented an honest confession of helplessness. Instead, he made the ridiculous promise to pay all if only given enough time.

WHAT DO YOU THINK?

The lesson writer says, "This teaching of personal forgiveness for personal offenses should not be applied, however, to public affairs of criminal justice." Do you agree or disagree? Why? What other exceptions, if any, do you think there are to the principles here? Explain.

WHAT DO YOU THINK?

In Jesus' parable the debtor promised the king, "I will pay thee all." This illustrates the common misunderstanding of sin and our ability to deal with it. It seems to be terribly difficult for the worldly minded person to appreciate the magnitude of our indebtedness to God because of our sins. Such a one would never imagine himself to be the debtor in the parable, owing more money than most of us ever dream of having. How can the magnitude of one's sin be made clear so that the need for a Savior is obvious? Do you think Christians sometimes obscure the magnitude of sin for fear of "offending" someone? Why or why not? What steps can be taken to be sure we do not do this?

HOW TO SAY IT
denarii (Greek). dih-NAIR-ee-eye.

WHAT DO YOU THINK?

Thinking of God's forgiveness of us should help us to forgive those who wrong us. Unfortunately, we are too often like the unforgiving servant of the parable. We may find it especially difficult to forgive when the effects of an offense remain with us. How would you maintain a forgiving spirit even in the following circumstances?

• The reckless act of another has left you with a physical scar.

• The unkind behavior of someone has created a recurring painful memory for you.

• The hurtful action has caused the loss of a friend, either through death or alienation.

WHAT DO YOU THINK?

How can prayer help remove bitterness that remains in a heart as a result of a wrong done? How would you pray for yourself in such a case? How might you pray for your offender?

It reminds us of the pride of man trying to establish his own terms for gaining God's approval. Pressed to the limit he will beg desperately and promise anything—anything but complete dependence on God's mercy.

27. "The servant's master took pity on him, canceled the debt and let him go.

Pity for the man's hopeless condition, including his failure even to recognize his hopelessness, led the king to grant more than was asked—a total cancellation of the debt. Thus the king accepted to himself the loss it represented and paid the debt. In like manner, God, through Christ, paid the penalty for our sins. Instead of selling the man into slavery, he *let him go.*

A country doctor who canceled all bills owed to him was complimented for his unselfishness. He responded that it had been a totally selfish act; he was tired of his debtor friends' avoiding him on the street. God—represented by the king in this parable—recognizes forgiveness as the only way to maintain friendly relations with those who have committed offenses. Not selfishness, however, but divine compassion is the motivating force of God's forgiveness.

B. AN UNFORGIVING CREDITOR (vv. 28-30)

28. "But when that servant went out, he found one of his fellow servants who owed him a hundred denarii. He grabbed him and began to choke him. 'Pay back what you owe me!' he demanded.

Like some people who are "converted" through a traumatic experience, this man was frightened and made marvelous promises, but he was not truly converted. Instead, he used his newly found freedom to "lord it" over another of his king's servants. Proverbs 30:21-23 says the things the earth cannot tolerate "a servant who becomes king." This servant suddenly thought he should reign. The same pride that prevented his asking forgiveness prevented also his granting forgiveness to another.

By one estimate the amount the first servant had owed the king was more than a million times greater than the *hundred denarii* that he was owed by his fellow servant. Yet his actions in demanding payment were violent and merciless. They portray the attitude of one who expects a merciful God to overlook his sins, but is unforgiving toward another child of the same Savior.

29, 30. "His fellow servant fell to his knees and begged him, 'Be patient with me, and I will pay you back.'

"But he refused. Instead, he went off and had the man thrown into prison until he could pay the debt.

By action and by words, the hapless small debtor made the same plea this merciless creditor had made to his king. One might expect the similarity to stir sympathy in the one now making the demand. But reason was as far from him as was mercy. The small debt was not enough to justify selling the victim into slavery. A debtor's prison was chosen as the alternative.

What did he gain by it? Nothing but a strange satisfaction of his own arrogant pride and lust for power. It is the same satisfaction sought and gained by the one who says, "I'll never forgive that kind of treatment from anybody. They don't get away with walking all over me!"

Not many of us have opportunity to exercise the kind of royal generosity found in the forgiving king, but we can do small favors and forgive small injuries. That is where the meaningful tests of Christian living begin.

C. NO MERCY FOR THE MERCILESS (vv. 31-34)

31. "When the other servants saw what had happened, they were greatly distressed and went and told their master everything that had happened.

Others of the king's servants were shocked and distressed by the rough treatment accorded to one of their colleagues by another. They acted properly in laying the matter before their lord for correction. Romans 12:19 recommends that Jesus' followers in similar manner leave acts of punishment to God. But there is a difference—he does not need to be told what has happened.

32, 33. *"Then the master called the servant in. 'You wicked servant,' he said, 'I canceled all that debt of yours because you begged me to. Shouldn't you have had mercy on your fellow servant just as I had on you?'*

Here is the central point of the parable. God's infinite mercy demands that his people also be merciful.

The king lost no time in addressing the problem. He called the culprit into his presence and pronounced judgment. The sin he condemned was not dishonesty and financial default; it was the man's despising and rejecting the king's example in dealing with a debtor. The man had asked for time to pay, and the king had canceled the debt. The man's victim had asked for time to pay, and the man had cast him into prison.

Just as I had on you. This is a parable of the kingdom. It speaks of God's infinite mercy in Christ, and that mercy is the basis of God's requirement that his children be merciful to one another. Elsewhere the Scripture speaks directly of the requirement for mutual forgiveness: "Be kind and compassionate . . . forgiving each other, just as in Christ God forgave you" (Ephesians 4:32; see also Colossians 3:12, 13). That principle was flagrantly violated by the forgiven but unforgiving debtor/creditor.

MEASURE FOR MEASURE

In Shakespeare's *Measure for Measure,* the severe and upright Lord Deputy, Angelo, presides over the case of a poor young man condemned to death because he seduced his sweetheart before they were able to wed. The man's sister, Isabella, approaches Angelo and pleads for her brother's life. While admitting his wrong, she asks that Angelo have mercy and rescind the stern sentence of death for her brother's crime. The unbending Angelo is deaf to Isabella's plea, declaring, "Your brother is a forfeit of the law, and you but waste your words."

Isabella responds with this beautiful appeal: "Alas! alas! Why, all the souls that were were forfeit once; and he that might the vantage best have took found out the remedy. How would you be, if he, which is the top of judgment, should but judge you as you are? O, think on that; and mercy then will breathe within your lips, like man new made."

Can one who has received God's mercy be so unfeeling as to refuse to show mercy to others? God has chosen not to punish us as we deserve, but by his grace through Christ to forgive the magnitude of our transgressions. Because we are condemned prisoners set free from Hell, God's mercy, grace, and love should flow to others from us like persons "new made." —C. B. Mc.

34. *"In anger his master turned him over to the jailers to be tortured, until he should pay back all he owed.*

Anger describes the judicial and punitive emotion of God, a king, or a judge. *Jailers* could add affliction to confinement. *Torture* was not used by Jews or Romans as punishment for debt, but an Eastern despot would use it to make a debtor reveal where he had hidden assets that could be applied toward payment. In this case the sentence was of indefinite duration. Earlier the servant had escaped being sold into slavery, only now to be sentenced to endless punishment.

How shall we explain the reactivation of the forgiven debt? Does God's computer include a memory file that can be used at any time to call up deleted material? Or is his forgiveness truly complete? Let us remember that the offender was not

WHAT DO YOU THINK?

Some charge the master in this parable with being unfair. They allege that, having forgiven the debt, he should not later have been permitted to demand payment.

What do you think? Is he unfair? If so, does that mean God is unfair? Does this suggest God can recall his forgiveness once it is granted?

How would you answer the critic who says this passage proves God is unjust?

PRAYING TO FORGIVE

O, our great and gracious God, you have made us in your image, and we praise you. We have marred that likeness in many ways, but especially in our failure to forgive as you have forgiven us. May we see again your perfect likeness in Jesus our Lord, and may we learn from him to forgive. Free us, please, from any unforgiving spirit that hinders our being fully forgiven and offering acceptable praise in his name. Amen.

THOUGHT TO REMEMBER

"Be kind and compassionate to one another, forgiving each other, just as in Christ God forgave you" (Ephesians 4:32).

DAILY BIBLE READINGS

Monday, Mar. 4—Warning Against Wrong Teaching (Matthew 16:5-12)

Tuesday, Mar. 5—Declaring One's Belief (Matthew 16:13-20)

Wednesday, Mar. 6—Sharing a Vision (Matthew 17:1-13)

Thursday, Mar. 7—Healing a Child (Matthew 17:14-21)

Friday, Mar. 8—Paying the Tax (Matthew 17:22-27)

Saturday, Mar. 9— Determining Greatness (Matthew 18:1-14)

Sunday, Mar. 10—Handling a Grievance (Matthew 18:15-20)

punished for old debt; he was punished for the new offense of withholding mercy from another. Given the example of grace and mercy, he had chosen instead the way of law and punishment. So to the way of law and punishment he was returned. It is, of course, impossible to depict our infinite God fully in human terms.

III. A SOLEMN WARNING (MATTHEW 18:35)

Jesus made his own application of the human story to the divine reality.

35. "This is how my heavenly Father will treat each of you unless you forgive your brother from your heart."

If one is looking for the unpardonable sin, here is where it will be found. It is in the heart of one who prays, "Forgive us our debts, as we forgive our debtors," while harboring malice and plotting revenge for some perceived insult or injury. Such a one belittles God, who offers pardon for king-sized transgressions, while the unforgiving one closes the gates of Heaven against himself by nursing a king-sized rage over his neighbor's pint-sized offenses.

Judgment frequently arrives in early installments to the unforgiving one, as the body, mind, and spirit suffer the erosions of an acid disposition. Hence Jesus' requirement that forgiveness must come from the heart. God knows, and our own bodies and spirits know, exactly how much or how little it means when we say, "I forgive." The unforgiving are, by the very nature of their attitude, incapable of receiving forgiveness (Matthew 6:14, 15).

HOW GOD FORGIVES

In Ephesians 4, Paul describes our new life in Christ. Among the qualities he mentions are kindness and compassion. He calls on us to demonstrate those qualities by forgiving each other, just as God forgave us (4:32). God forgives us completely. How can this be described?

The prophet Micah painted a word picture of God's removal of Israel's sin. He said that God would hurl their iniquities "into the depths of the sea" (7:19). Imagine all your sins, every wrong you have ever done, buried in the depths of the sea!

The deepest place in the ocean is the Marianas Trench, southwest of Guam in the Pacific Ocean. This undersea depression reaches a maximum depth of 36,201 feet, nearly seven miles. By comparison, the world's tallest building, the Sears Tower in Chicago, rises 110 stories from the street. So deep is the Marianas Trench that it would take a stack of twenty-five Sears Towers to reach from the ocean floor to the surface above the trench.

Anything dropped into the ocean at such a depth would be covered with so much water it would never again see the light of day. That's how God forgives; and that's how he calls us to forgive others—deeply, completely, permanently.   —C. B. Mc.

CONCLUSION

Jesus spoke his parable in reply to a question from the apostle Peter: "How often should I forgive"? The answer in brief was this: "As often as God forgives you." Consider the night when Peter boasted to Jesus, "Even if all fall away on account of you, I never will" (Matthew 26:33). Within a few hours, three times he vehemently denied knowing Jesus. Moments later Peter was weeping, and within hours Jesus was dying. Immediately after the Lord's resurrection, however, Peter was included by name in an invitation to meet Jesus in Galilee (Mark 16:7). Then in Galilee the Lord made a special point of accepting Peter's acknowledgment of personal devotion, and giving to Peter a shepherd's appointment over his flock (John 21:15-17). Peter knew what he was talking about when he preached Christ as Savior, To "give repentance and forgiveness of sins to Israel" (Acts 5:31). He was not counting the sins, nor worrying whether there would be enough forgiveness to go around.

Discovery Learning

*This page contains an alternate lesson plan emphasizing learning activities. Classes
desiring such student involvement will find these suggestions helpful. The next page
is a reproducible activity page to further enhance discovery learning.*

LEARNING GOALS

As a result of today's lesson, a student will be able to:

1. Retell and explain the parable of the unforgiving servant.

2. Compare the forgiveness from debt offered by a king to the forgiveness offered by God through Jesus.

3. Make a prayerful beginning toward forgiving someone who has wronged us.

INTO THE LESSON

As far in advance of class time as possible, ask two class members to be prepared to engage in a short, friendly debate on how debt should be handled. Ask one to present the view that debt should be avoided entirely. Romans 13:8 (especially from the *King James Version*); Proverbs 22:7, 26, 27; and Psalm 37:21 may be cited as evidence for this view. Ask the other to take the view that buying things on credit is the normal way of doing business in today's society. Deuteronomy 15: 8; Ezekiel 18:18; and Matthew 5:42 could be cited on this side of the issue. Introduce the debate and allow each debater to speak for three minutes. Allow for brief rebuttals.

Ask, "How do we handle the debt incurred when we offend or are offended by someone? Is there a difference in the way we handle our financial debt and our interpersonal debts? Are we as eager to repay those debts as we are our financial debts?" Use the reproducible activity "Debts and Forgiveness" on page 252 to explore this issue with the class. Observe that financial credit is generally a mutually beneficial arrangement. The lender earns interest on the loan and the borrower gets the use of the money sooner than if he or she had saved up. The situation is very different with interpersonal debts!

INTO THE WORD

Use the second reproducible activity, "Forgiving One Another" to explore biblical passages that relate to forgiveness. After about seven minutes discuss their findings.

Give each class member a blank sheet of paper (or use the back side of the reproducible page). During the first part of this study activity, the class members are to work individually. Ask them to read Matthew 18:23-27 and list ways the events of the parable parallel our forgiveness by God in Christ. Answers should include these or similar thoughts: the servant was totally unable to repay his debt, and we cannot pay for our debt of sin; the servant's debt

would lead to slavery, and our sin leads to spiritual slavery; the king canceled the debt, and our sin-debt is canceled or paid for in Christ; the result is freedom. After four or five minutes, ask students to work in groups of three to share their answers with one another. Allow about two minutes for this sharing.

Now read verses 28-30 aloud to the class. Point out that ten thousand talents was an enormous amount of money in that day. It could have paid the wages of a regiment of 1000 soldiers for over eighty years! The one hundred denarii owed by the other man was equivalent to about three months wages for one man.

Discuss, "How could the first servant treat his fellow servant so cruelly after receiving such grace? What was he thinking and feeling—or *not* thinking and feeling?"

Next, read verses 31-35 aloud to the class. Summarize the study by stating the point of the parable: God's infinite mercy demands that his people also be merciful.

INTO LIFE

Ask for volunteers to act out the following three scenes:

• A husband comes home from work late again, and the wife is angry because he did not call her.

• A person driving his new car has just been hit from behind by another driver.

• A worker who has just been fired by an unfair boss is telling a friend, who is trying to be sympathetic.

After each scene has been played, ask the class to comment. What attitudes were expressed? What insights to our own behaviors do these give us?

Ask one or two of the pairs to replay their roles with the offended party attempting to maintain a spirit of forgiveness. Take note of the difficulty many persons have in forgiving those who offend them. Point out also that the results—physical, emotional, social, and spiritual—of a person's unforgiving spirit can be profound and severe. (See the comments in the second paragraph under verse 35, page 250.) Everyone benefits from godly forgiveness.

Ask each student to think of some personal relationship in which he or she needs to give forgiveness. Ask them to commit themselves to taking whatever action is needed to see that forgiveness is offered in a Christlike spirit. Conclude the class with prayer, asking the Lord for guidance in those situations. Allow a time of silent prayer, encouraging the class members to begin praying for the will and ability to forgive others as God has forgiven them.

Debts and Forgiveness

The word *debt* is used both of money owed through some kind of credit transaction and of offenses committed against another person. Compare the two on the chart below.

	MONEY	OFFENSES
How is this kind of debt incurred? (Is it intentional or unintentional? What kind of terms are arranged, if any? Why would a person incur such a debt?)		
Why would another person allow this kind of indebtedness against him or her?		
How is this debt repaid?		
What is the relationship between the two parties when the debt is repaid?		
Under what conditions can this debt be forgiven?		
What is the relationship between the two parties when the debt is forgiven?		

Forgiving One Another

Look up the following Scriptures. What does each say about forgiveness?

Matthew 6:12-15

Matthew 18:21, 22

Luke 17:3, 4

Romans 12:19-21

1 Corinthians 13:5

Ephesians 4:32

Colossians 3:12, 13

PARABLE OF THE VINEYARD WORKERS

WHY TEACH THIS LESSON?

"Me first! Me first!" It's the cry of the child, who has not learned the grace of honoring others above oneself (Romans 12:10). Unfortunately, age alone does not always teach that grace. The adult may be more subtle, but his heart can still cry "Me first!"

James and John suffered from this immaturity. "Give *us* the first seats in your kingdom," they requested (Mark 10:35-37). The rest of the apostles were no different (Luke 9:46; 22:24). Perhaps some of your students have the same problem.

It is seen today in an attitude that suggests some people are beyond the reach of God's grace. We, apparently, are somehow more deserving. The idea is ludicrous—and we would never state it so bluntly. But our attitude reveals it. When the notorious sinner is converted, do we rejoice or withdraw? Like the disciples in Jerusalem when Saul of Tarsus tried to join them, we too often withdraw.

When the twelve-hour laborers in today's lesson complained about the grace shown to the one-hour workers, they were displaying symptoms of this very same condition. When God extends grace, the response of his children should be one of joy, not jealousy. It's a hard lesson to learn, but one we all need. That is the reason this lesson is offered.

INTRODUCTION

A. WHAT WOULD YOU SAVE?

"You must leave your home within the hour and take with you only what you can carry!" Faced with that choice, what would you take?

Thousands of families have had to make that choice in recent years as they have been faced with hurricanes, floods, or fires. What have these people carried away with them? Usually not "big-ticket" items, such as entertainment centers, though these may have occupied much of their time and attention. Instead, the number-one item was frequently the family photo album—not very expensive, but priceless because it never could be replaced and it was personally treasured. When it comes time to make ultimate decisions, amazing changes may take place regarding one's priorities. Then, what is usually first suddenly becomes last, and what is usually last suddenly becomes first.

Jesus was always dealing with ultimate values in his teachings about the kingdom of Heaven, where moth and rust do not corrupt, and where tornado, flood, or fire do not destroy. That kingdom has its own set of values, which often contrast sharply with those recognized in this world.

B. LESSON BACKGROUND

The parable in today's text was spoken by Jesus after the one in last Sunday's lesson. Both illustrate the grace of God. Last week we learned of God's

DEVOTIONAL READING
MATTHEW 19:23-30
LESSON SCRIPTURE
MATTHEW 19:23—20:16
PRINTED TEXT
MATTHEW 20:1-16

LESSON AIMS

This study should help the student:

1. Describe evidence of the parable workers' envy and the landowner's generosity.

2. As in the parable, contrast our response to being treated fairly with our response to seeing others being generously rewarded.

3. Rejoice with everyone who receives God's generous gift—forgiveness and eternal life.

KEY VERSE

So the last will be first, and the first will be last.
—Matthew 20:16

LESSON 3 NOTES

WHAT DO YOU THINK?

This parable is prefaced with a promise and a warning. The promise is that everyone who has left family or possessions for the Lord's sake will be rewarded (Matthew 19:29). The warning is, "Many who are first will be last, and many who are last will be first" (Matthew 19:30). This warning is repeated at the conclusion of the parable also (Matthew 20:16).

What connection, if any, do you see between the promise and this parable? In what ways does the parable affect your expectation from the promise? In what ways does the promise help you understand the parable?

mercy, expressed in forgiveness; this week God's mercy is seen in generosity to the poor. In both, our minds are stretched to see the dimensions of the divine kingdom.

Today's story was told during a stressful time in Perea shortly before Jesus' death. The religious leaders did not like his rebukes of their pretensions to superior wisdom, character, and authority. His own disciples were still displaying some selfish ambitions.

Matthew 19 records a series of related events. Verses 13-15 tell of the Lord's blessing little children as examples of the humility that should characterize his followers. Verses 16-26 tell of the rich young ruler who desired eternal life, but not enough to make it his first priority. Verses 27-30 relate a conversation in which Peter wanted to know what reward would be coming to him and the others because, in leaving all to follow Christ, they had done as the rich young man had not. The Lord assured them of rewards on earth and in Heaven, but warned that "many who are first will be last, and many who are last will be first" (v. 30). The parable in today's lesson develops that theme.

I. A PERSISTENT EMPLOYER (MATTHEW 20:1-7)

A. EMPLOYING UNDER CONTRACT (vv. 1, 2)

1. "For the kingdom of heaven is like a landowner who went out early in the morning to hire men to work in his vineyard.

The introductory *for* links the narrative firmly to the warning just spoken.

Obviously, the *landowner* in this parable owned and managed a considerable estate. The *vineyard* is important only as background for the owner's concern to harvest its grapes before the autumn rains came and ruined the crop.

Since the working day occupied some twelve hours from sunrise to sunset, the landowner went *early* to the marketplace, where he could expect day laborers to be looking for employment. He would hire workers for this day's needs.

2. "He agreed to pay them a denarius for the day and sent them into his vineyard.

The agreement seems to have involved some negotiation, and assumed the force of a binding contract. A *denarius* was a Roman silver coin accepted as the daily wage for a soldier or laborer.

There are, of course, rewards other than money for one who works for God and men. One is the deep satisfaction of being useful. For the Christian, there is joy in serving Jesus!

LOOKING FOR WORKERS

In studying the parable of the vineyard workers, our attention usually centers on the wages the landowner paid to the laborers. But let us concentrate for a few moments in the fact that the Master gives out work as well as wages.

Genesis 2:15 says that God put Adam in the Garden of Eden "to work it and take care of it." Man was created to do something, not simply to pass his days idly. The Bible extols the value and dignity of work.

The apostle Paul encouraged the Corinthians to "give yourselves fully to the work of the Lord, because you know that your labor in the Lord is not in vain" (1 Corinthians 15:58). To the Ephesians Paul wrote that Christian leaders are "to prepare God's people for works of service, so that the body of Christ may be built up" (Ephesians 4:12). The New Testament speaks of the work of the gospel, the work of evangelism, the work of preaching, the work of teaching, the work of leading. There is plenty of work to do in the kingdom. No matter when a person comes to Christ, or what abilities that person possesses, there is work that he or she can, and should, do.

HOW TO SAY IT

Denarius. dih-NAIR-ee-us.
Perea. Peh-REE-uh.

Work that one does to make a difference in other people's lives brings satisfaction and joy. Our Lord honors us by allowing us to experience the special joy that comes through sharing in the most important work in the world.   —C. B. Mc.

B. EMPLOYING WITH A PROMISE (vv. 3-5)

3, 4. "About the third hour he went out and saw others standing in the marketplace doing nothing. He told them, 'You also go and work in my vineyard, and I will pay you whatever is right.'

It was about nine o'clock when the landowner, still needing help to harvest his grapes, went looking for more workers. How did the men feel about their idleness? Did they know that other workers had already been hired? Anyway, this time there was not dickering over their wage. Whatever they received would be better than nothing. They showed a meaningful faith in their employer, and acted on it.

5. "So they went. He went out again about the sixth hour and the ninth hour and did the same thing.

Here is reflected the urgency expressed in Jesus' reference to his Father's harvest: "The harvest is plentiful but the workers are few. Ask the Lord of the harvest, therefore, to send out workers into his harvest field" (Matthew 9:37, 38). So at midday and again in mid-afternoon the lord of this harvest repeated his search for workers, with the same results as previously.

C. EMPLOYING THE UNEMPLOYED (vv. 6, 7)

6. "About the eleventh hour he went out and found still others standing around. He asked them, 'Why have you been standing here all day long doing nothing?'

The landowner would need to be desperate for help to go seeking for workers one hour before quitting time. Perhaps he was not looking for workers so much as he was expressing concern that the laborers he had seen earlier had been employed. As for the laborers, they may well have been desperate enough for work to pursue job-hunting at that hour. In the hand-to-mouth existence of many of the population of Palestine in that day, the day's wage was just about the day's need. Having given up hope of earning enough for their daily needs, these workers still hoped for something, even a little. And perhaps they could make a good enough showing in an hour to be hired sooner the next day.

7. "'Because no one has hired us,' they answered. "He said to them, 'You also go and work in my vineyard.'

Who, if anyone, was at fault in the workmen's predicament? Had they been job-hunting seriously all day? Such questions are left unanswered. Anyway, the landowner accepted their explanation and sent them to work. There is not even the mention of payment to these workers. Either the workers were tired of loafing and would welcome the activity, even without the assurance of pay, or they simply had enough faith in the landowner to believe he would treat them fairly. Such faith, as we will see shortly, would have been well founded, and is typical of the faith we can have in our heavenly Father. "God is not unjust; he will not forget your work and the love you have shown him" (Hebrews 6:10).

II. A GENEROUS EMPLOYER (MATTHEW 20:8-10)

8. "When evening came, the owner of the vineyard said to his foreman, 'Call the workers and pay them their wages, beginning with the last ones hired and going on to the first.'

Deuteronomy 24:14, 15 directs, "Do not take advantage of a hired man who is poor and needy.... Pay him his wages each day before sunset, because he is poor

WHAT DO YOU THINK?

What do you suppose was the response of the workers hired last when they received a full day's wage? If the gracious pay they were given represents God's grace, how does that suggest we ought to respond to the grace God has given us? Is such a response common today? Why or why not? How can we encourage one another to express a proper sense of gratitude for the blessings of God's grace?

WHAT DO YOU THINK?

From childhood we learn to voice the complaint, "That's not fair!" when our rewards are not as large as we think we deserve, or the punishments are greater. Thus, when we read the parable of the workers in the vineyard, we may find ourselves sympathizing with the day-long workers.

It is a sign of spiritual maturity when we can acknowledge that God is just and wise, that his wisdom and his ways are far above us (Isaiah 55:8; Romans 11:33-36), and that we must humbly submit to his arrangements as far as blessings and rewards are concerned. How can we reach that level of maturity? What can the church do to help young people mature in this way and resist the selfish and demanding mind-set of the world?

WHAT DO YOU THINK?

Visual 3 assumes each worker was paid the same amount (one denarius) and compares that with the amount of labor done. Display the visual and discuss the questions on it.

Group	Gross Pay	Hours	Hourly Rate
1	$60.00	12	$5.00
2	$60.00	9	$6.67
3	$60.00	6	$10.00
4	$60.00	3	$20.00
5	$60.00	1	$60.00

Visual 3

and is counting on it." Bread for the evening meal in the laborer's home might be bought with that day's wages. The servant who had acted as *foreman* in the field now became the paymaster.

The last … to the first. For purposes of the parable, the all-day workers had to know how much the one-hour workers were paid.

9. "The workers who were hired about the eleventh hour came and each received a denarius.

We can only imagine the feelings of these men. They had received no assurance of payment, and had worked for only an hour before sundown, yet they received payment for a full day's labor! We should not expect them to be quiet about it.

What could have been the employer's motives in directing such generosity? He must have been thinking more of the workers' need than he was of his own gain. If reward was involved, it was reward for their faith and willingness to work without assurance of payment, rather than for what they were able to accomplish. Romans 4:4, 5 shows the similarity of this situation and the grace of God regarding our salvation: "Now when a man works, his wages are not credited to him as a gift, but as an obligation. However, to the man who does not work but trusts God who justifies the wicked, his faith is credited as righteousness." So the last are first, and the first, last. But don't wait for an eleventh-hour call that may not come.

10. "So when those came who were hired first, they expected to receive more. But each one of them also received a denarius.

What about the workers who were called at the third, sixth, and ninth hours of the day? The purpose of the parable was served by considering the payment given to the one-hour workers and the all-day laborers. That purpose would have been clouded by noting that the half-day workers could compare their per-hour payment with those ahead of them in the line. If the landowner's intent in giving the last ones hired a full day's wage so they could meet their daily needs, then we might assume he had acted similarly with all the rest. Probably all the workers received the same pay because they all had essentially the same need.

They expected. The expectation of those who worked all day was based rather naturally on comparisons that would come out to their advantage. Some of their neighbors had received a day's wage for an hour's work; at that rate, they may have reasoned, they should receive two weeks' wage for their day's work! Conveniently forgotten was the firm commitment they had negotiated in the morning.

III. A JUST EMPLOYER (MATTHEW 20:11-16)

A. PRESUMPTUOUS COMPLAINT (vv. 11, 12)

11, 12. "When they received it, they began to grumble against the landowner. 'These men who were hired last worked only one hour,' they said, 'and you have made them equal to us who have borne the burden of the work and the heat of the day.'

The workers' complaint was brought not against the paymaster but against the owner who had directed the manner of payment. Their objection was centered not in what the landlord had done to them, but in what he had done for someone else. They were saying, "These who have done so little to earn it have been made equal to us who have done so much. We worked not only all day, but in the blistering heat of noon, while they enjoyed the relative cool of late afternoon."

What was the offensive quality? Why, the amount of money paid to those who had worked only one hour, of course. No factor other than money seemed worthy of consideration by these all-day workers. That was made rather plain in the morning's bargaining for a contract. Thoughts about the satisfaction of being useful, or gratefully participating in God's provision, had no place in their thinking.

You made them equal to us who are really superior! So complained the Pharisees when Jesus spent time with sinners. So cries the athlete on learning that another has been given an equally favorable contract. So wails the church worker who finds another recognized for unimpressive service. The elder brother in Jesus' parable of the prodigal son utters this same complaint when the prodigal returns home and is given a celebration feast (Luke 15:25-32).

Human nature does not take kindly to equal treatment for lesser personages, but that is the way of God's kingdom.

NEWCOMERS

When Israel entered Canaan under the leadership of Joshua, the people were instructed to drive out the idol-worshiping peoples who inhabited the land, to have no dealings with them. Through the centuries, the Jews maintained separateness from the people of other nations, to greater or lesser degrees. By the first century A.D., however, the line of separation was quite distinct.

When the gospel was first preached to Gentiles, some Jewish Christians had difficulty accepting them as brethren in Christ. This in spite of the fact that the gospel plainly declares that all persons, whether Jews under the law or Gentiles outside the law, are in need of God's grace, his mercy, his forgiveness, which no one merits.

The apostles and elders of the Jerusalem church met to consider this issue. The discussion boiled down to this: "Are we going to let those people into our church?" Their Holy Spirit-inspired answer was, "Yes, we are."

Like the workers in the parable, some members of a church may feel resentment toward new converts to the Lord's kingdom. They may say, "I sure liked our church a lot better before all these strangers showed up." If your church is seeing the addition of "strangers" or "newcomers," thank God that lost people are coming to know Christ, and rejoice that the Lord's work force is being strengthened.

—C. B. Mc.

B. PROMISES ARE KEPT (vv. 13, 14)

13. "But he answered one of them, 'Friend, I am not being unfair to you. Didn't you agree to work for a denarius?

The one addressed may have been the spokesman for the group, or simply the most persistent complainer. The singular and personal response, however, applied equally to each one.

Friend, here, translates the Greek word for comrade. Jesus used this word when he addressed Judas in Gethsemane (Matthew 26:50). It is a term of indifference, not a term of affection.

I am not being unfair to you. The bargainers had established their price, and that price was paid. They had no right to complain. The landowner had not reduced his payment to them in order to overpay the workers who came to his vineyard later.

14. "'Take your pay and go. I want to give the man who was hired last the same as I gave you.

The interview was ended, and the plaintiff was dismissed. He should take his money and go. Let him make the most of it. Even a denarius or a dollar is more or less valuable, depending on the way it is used. So also even God's blessings are enhanced or reduced by the way they are received and used. We are reminded of the parables of the pounds and of the talents with their indication of rewards based on levels of faithful performance (Luke 19:11-27; Matthew 25:14-30). Even in today's parable there is nothing to encourage faithlessness or delay in response to the Lord's invitation. Each worker went to work when he was summoned.

WHAT DO YOU THINK?

What are some dangers that are inherent in the habit of envying the prosperity of others? How can we avoid or break this habit?

PRAYER FOR UNDERSTANDING

Thank you, O God, for the wisdom with which Jesus taught the deep truths of Heaven from the common experiences of earth. Be patient, please, with our slowness to understand; also with our greater slowness to put into practice the truths we do understand. May we be faithful workers in your vineyard, fully assured of your promises and rejoicing in your grace, through Christ Our Lord. Amen.

DAILY BIBLE READINGS

Monday, Mar. 11—God's Concern for the Poor (Deuteronomy 24:10-15)

Tuesday, Mar. 12—A Disappointing Harvest (Isaiah 5:1-7)

Wednesday, Mar. 13—God's Right to Choose (Romans 9:14-24)

Thursday, Mar. 14—A Day Fixed for Judgment (Acts 17:24-34)

Friday, Mar. 15—A Way to Behave (Leviticus 19:9-14)

Saturday, Mar. 16—A Sad Decision (Matthew 19:16-26)

Sunday, Mar. 17—A Change of Mind (Matthew 21:28-32)

People who insist on justice will receive justice, and no more. They are slow to appreciate mercy, generosity, or grace, all of which seem to them like injustice. It is hard for them to see that any of us are blessed, not because we are good, but because the Lord is good.

C. PRIORITIES ARE ESTABLISHED (vv. 15, 16)

15. "'Don't I have the right to do what I want with my own money? Or are you envious because I am generous?'

Two questions, answered automatically in their context, are addressed first to the grumbling day laborers, then to the apostles, to the Jewish faultfinders, and to Jesus' total audience, then and now.

Human organizations and secular governments have come increasingly to challenge the common law that recognizes an owner's *right* to do as he wishes with his property. Regulations and restrictions of various kinds now apply. But Jesus spoke in a simpler time of the more natural application of common law. More importantly, he was teaching about the kingdom of heaven and God's right to rule in it. Those who believe in God as Jesus revealed him still acknowledge his total authority there, even in matters they cannot understand. They will say with the patriarch Job, "Though he slay me, yet will I hope in him" (Job 13:15).

The second of the two questions, *Are you envious because I am generous?* focuses on God's right to dispense grace and salvation on his own terms. Those terms are clearly set forth to be accepted or rejected by any and every person. God never gives less than he has promised. In the matter of salvation, he gives infinitely more than anyone has a right to expect.

16. "So the last will be first, and the first will be last."

Jesus had said this previously to his disciples in the conversation that led to the parable of the vineyard workers (Matthew 19:30); the principle appears again as the conclusion to which the parable led. The *last* and *first* might be people, with the greatest being the ones who have been servants of all. The *last* and *first* could be in items of importance, with small-coin offerings being more significant than large gifts. (See Luke 21:1-4.) In all things God will make the final determination, often reversing the order recognized by the world.

CONCLUSION

If we find the parable of the vineyard workers a bit difficult to understand and apply, we are in very good company, beginning with the disciples to whom it was first delivered. It warned against presumptions of importance, but shortly afterward the apostles James and John were applying for positions of preference in the coming kingdom (Matthew 20:20-28). The other apostles objected, and Jesus had to remind them all that "whoever wants to be first must be your slave" (v. 27). Demonstration came in time, as Paul, last to become an apostle, came to labor "harder than all of them" (1 Corinthians 15:8-10).

Reversal of the orders is seen dramatically in Jesus' parable of the rich man and the beggar Lazarus (Luke 16:19-31). "If you think you are standing firm, be careful that you don't fall" (1 Corinthians 10:12).

Let the charter member of a church learn to welcome most earnestly the newest convert. Let the one who has labored most fruitfully in former years seek out and encourage the one whose fruitful labors lie mostly in the future. And let every Christian build on that number-one priority that will not be reversed, because it comes from God in the first place: "Seek first his kingdom and his righteousness, and all these things will be given to you as well" (Matthew 6:33).

Discovery Learning

This page contains an alternate lesson plan emphasizing learning activities. Classes desiring such student involvement will find these suggestions helpful. The next page is a reproducible activity page to further enhance discovery learning.

LEARNING GOALS

As a result of participating in today's lesson, students will be able to:

1. Describe evidence of the parable workers' envy and the landowner's generosity.

2. As in the parable, contrast our response to being treated fairly with our response to seeing others being generously rewarded.

3. Rejoice with everyone who receives God's generous gift—forgiveness and eternal life.

INTO THE LESSON

Distribute copies of the reproducible activity "It's Only Fair!" from page 260. Give the class a couple of minutes to look over the situation described there, and then discuss the following questions:

Do you agree with Marilee? Why or why not?

What would you do if you were the sales manager?

After a few minutes, point out that this fictional situation is similar to the one in the parable we will study today.

INTO THE WORD

To establish the background for today's Scripture text, point out that Peter expressed interest in receiving what he thought he deserved for being a follower of Jesus. Read Matthew 19:27-30 and explain that Jesus told the Parable of the Vineyard Workers to enlarge on his comment in verse 30: "Many who are first will be last, and many who are last will be first."

Ask a class member to read Matthew 20:1-16 aloud to the class. Before the reading, instruct the class to listen for elements of *trust*, *envy*, and *generosity* in the Parable of the Vineyard Workers. After the text has been read, explain that Jesus made the point that there is a vast difference in the way God deals with us in his kingdom and the way people expect to be treated in this life.

Now discuss the elements of the parable that class members listened for: (a) trust (the workers recruited at the third, sixth, and ninth hours trusted the man to pay them "whatever is right"—and the workers hired at the eleventh hour trusted the man to treat them right with no mention of pay at all); (b) envy (the jealousy of the all-day workers); and (c) generosity (the vineyard owner gave all the servants what they needed, a full day's wage, though many had not worked for it).

Remind the class that Peter desired to receive what he deserved (Matthew 19:27). Jesus responded by teaching that God gives us much more.

Observe that *generosity* is essentially the same as what the Bible calls *grace*. God gives us *what we need*, rather than what we deserve. God's grace is seen most plainly in the death of his Son. We were lost in sin, unable to save ourselves. God knew our need and sent his Son to die for us, even though we did not deserve such love. (See Romans 5:8; Ephesians 2:1-10.)

Have your class divide into groups of four or five students each. Ask each group to work together to paraphrase this parable with an emphasis on *need* instead of *reward*. (Note that a denarius would just about cover the laborer's daily needs for himself and his family.)

After a few minutes, ask for volunteers to read some of the paraphrases. Discuss, "How does seeing each worker get his needs supplied equally—instead of each worker being paid the same for different work—reduce our tendency to envy?

Read verse 16 aloud. Point out that this should be understood not so much as the first get sent to the end of the line and the last to the head, but that the first and the last are treated equally. In terms of reward, or in meeting needs, the first equals the last and the last equals the first. Discuss the implications of that view. Conclude with the observation that God graciously gives us everything we need, no matter when, how, or where we enter his kingdom. And in the end, those who accept his Son as their Savior receive eternal life.

INTO LIFE

Distribute copies of "Absolute Standards or Relative?" from the reproducible page 260. Give students about five minutes to fill in their responses; then discuss. Note that the Christian understanding of absolute values is the reason we appreciate God's grace. We realize we have been forgiven so much we have no room to complain when another is forgiven. In one sense, none of us has worked the whole day; we all depend on the generosity of the Master to reward us as if we had!

Finally, have each class member think of a response to this question: "What adjustments do I need to make in my thinking to more fully appreciate God's grace?" Ask them to meditate on that for a minute or two; then conclude the session with prayer.

It's Only Fair!

Marilee went to the computer store bright and early Saturday morning. She had shopped around, so she knew what she wanted. She had compared prices and features and was ready to deal on a computer system. She negotiated what she believed to be a good price and went home happy about the good deal she got.

Later that morning Fred went to the same store. He had just been to a computer exposition at the convention center, so he knew the manufacturer's next generation machine was just about to be released, which would slash the prices on all the "old" models. He paid an even lower price, about $150 lower, than Marilee had paid.

That afternoon Karen went to the same store. She had an ad from a competitor and challenged the sales manager to beat the price. He did, and Karen got her system, identical to Marilee's, for $400 less than Marilee paid.

Saturday evening, Marilee spoke to Karen. When she found out what Karen had paid for the same system she had bought, she rushed back to the computer store. She angrily demanded that the sales manager give her a $400 refund. "After all," she said, "it's only fair!"

Do you agree? Why or why not?

What would you do if you were the sales manager?

Read Matthew 20:1-16. Does this change the way you view Marilee's situation? Why or why not?

Absolute Standards or Relative?

The laborers who worked all day in the parable had a relative view of morality. Fairness was defined by comparing their situation with others. The master had an absolute view: fairness was established by the standard set and agreed to.

To what degree is the debate between absolute and relative standards causing problems today?

Where?

How do you see these problems expressed?

How can a Christian make a case for absolute standards without being labeled "intolerant"?

How can taking an absolute view help us appreciate what we have and to rejoice with—not envy—others who may have even more?

PARABLE OF THE
THREE SERVANTS

WHY TEACH THIS LESSON?

The Parable of the Talents is surely one of the best known of Jesus' parables. It is also one of the least applied! God has entrusted much to every Christian. Yet, in the average church, twenty percent of the members serve in eighty percent of the ministries.

There is a little of the lazy servant in almost all of us. Use this lesson to help your students expose and cast out the lazy servant from their lives. Encourage each one to identify and develop some talent they have that can help to build up the kingdom of God.

INTRODUCTION

A. WEIGHTY MATTERS

A remarkable word—*talents*—runs through the parable before us today. It comes from the Greek *talanton* and enters our language with two separate, but related meanings, both reflected in Jesus' story found only in Matthew 25:14-30.

A *talent* seems to have been first a unit of weight, applied principally to precious metals. In New Testament times a talent of silver was worth approximately six thousand denarii. Since a denarius was considered a fair day's wage, it would take a working man in those days almost twenty years to earn a full talent!

The other significance of *talent* appears in the parable with the distribution of moneys to responsible servants, each according to his *ability* (v. 15). The master considered each man's intelligence, energy, aptitude, and character. The most capable servant was trusted with the most money. He was *talented* in both ways.

Our lesson title emphasizes people. The money or the ability is but the tool with which the person does his work in relation to his opportunities. On that he will be judged.

B. LESSON BACKGROUND

Shortly after Jesus' final ministry in Perea (last week's parable was given during that time) he entered Jerusalem, welcomed by a throng present for the Passover festival. For two days he taught in the temple, opposed but not attacked by the Jewish leaders. On the afternoon of the second day he went with his disciples to the Mount of Olives (Matthew 24:3), where he taught them many things in preparation for his death and resurrection. He emphasized the responsibilities that would be theirs after his departure.

Jesus spoke of the coming destruction of Jerusalem, which occurred in A.D. 70. He spoke of his coming again—the certainty of the fact and the uncertainty of the time. He spoke of the need for faithfulness on the part of his people. Then came three great teachings recorded in Matthew 25, all dealing with the judgment at his coming again. The parable of ten bridesmaids (vv. 1-13) taught

DEVOTIONAL READING
MATTHEW 25:1-13
LESSON SCRIPTURE
MATTHEW 25:14-30
PRINTED TEXT
MATTHEW 25:14-30

Mar
24

LESSON AIMS

This study should prepare the student to:

1. Contrast the responses of the faithful servants with the response of the lazy servant.

2. Conclude that using money and ability pleases God and builds up his kingdom.

3. Choose a talent to develop in building God's kingdom.

KEY VERSE

For everyone who has will be given more, and he will have an abundance. Whoever does not have, even what he has will be taken from him.
—*Matthew 25:29*

LESSON 4 NOTES

OPTION

Introduce the study of this parable with a comparison of this one with the parable of the ten virgins, which immediately precedes it. Use the reproducible activity, "Be Prepared," on page 268.

WHAT DO YOU THINK?

The Master assessed each servant's abilities and distributed the talents accordingly. How might this fact reassure a Christian who does not possess some talent he or she feels would be desirable? (See 1 Corinthians 12:11.)

WHAT DO YOU THINK?

The servants who received five talents and two talents seem to have taken immediate action to put their master's money to work. By contrast, so much work in the church is left undone as a result of procrastination! We may say that someday we are going to serve, but that "someday" is slow to come. Meanwhile, that area of service suffers because we are not already there investing our talents.

God expects prompt obedience. How can we motivate ourselves to give it? How can we encourage others—to "spur one another on toward love and good deeds" (Hebrews 10:24, 25)?

the need for watchfulness in preparation for his arrival. The parable of three servants (vv. 14-30) urged diligence in working for him until he comes. In vivid description of judgment itself (vv. 31-46), Jesus showed that caring for those he loves is a requisite of loving service to him. The parables develop the warning: "Therefore keep watch, because you do not know the day or the hour" (Matthew 25:13).

I. SERVANTS RECEIVE AND RESPOND (MATTHEW 25:14-18)

A. ASSIGNMENTS ACCORDING TO ABILITY (vv. 14, 15)

14. "Again, it will be like a man going on a journey, who called his servants and entrusted his property to them.

Again. This word relates to the warning that Christ's coming in judgment will be sudden and unannounced (v. 13). The subject—*it*—is the kingdom of heaven (v. 1).

Travel to distant places was common, but a long journey took a long time. A wealthy man would need to arrange for his business interests to be carried on during his absence. (Compare Matthew 21:33-41.) This man's possessions included much money, which he wanted to be productive. So he entrusted it to certain of his servants to manage in his absence. This was a customary practice in ancient times. Trusted servants were put in positions of responsibility where they would have control over their master's money to use for their master's profit.

Jesus' teaching here is plain. Soon he was to be separated from his disciples. In the Lord's absence, his business on earth would claim the attention of his servants. Christ has honored his people, then and now, with a great trust, and that should be motivation enough for energetic dedication to the task he has given.

15. "To one he gave five talents of money, to another two talents, and to another one talent, each according to his ability. Then he went on his journey.

The master's acquaintance with his servants enabled him to know each one's capacity to carry out an assignment. The one with superior ability was given enough to keep him busy, and the less capable one was not loaded down with an impossible task. These principles are appropriate to any administrator anywhere: can, and will, this candidate do this job as it should be done?

Three servants are enough to serve Jesus' purposes in the parable. They provide samples for the limitless variety of persons involved in the Lord's business between his giving of the Great Commission (Matthew 28:18-20) and his coming in glory to judge the ones to whom he gave it.

B. ACTIVITIES AND RESULTS (vv. 16, 17)

16, 17. "The man who had received the five talents went at once and put his money to work and gained five more. So also, the one with the two talents gained two more.

Two of the three servants went to work immediately. Both exercised the same faithfulness in using the money entrusted to them, and both achieved the same rate of return. We should not suppose that they achieved the one-hundred-percent gain in a short time, or that they stopped when they reached a certain goal. We know only that each had doubled his master's investment by the time he returned.

We have been entrusted with immeasurable gifts of the gospel and the blessing of our own abilities. Applied faithfully, both of these treasures will increase. Any skill will become greater with exercise, and gospel power will grow with application. Neglected, though, any of these gifts will stagnate or shrink. The time to go into business for the Lord is when we receive the treasure, and the time to close shop is when he comes to call us home.

SOMETHING TO STAKE YOUR LIFE ON

Douglas MacArthur served as a brigadier general in World War I. In October, 1918, the allied forces faced the German stronghold along the Hindenberg Line in France. MacArthur, who commanded the 42nd Brigade, was chosen to advance against the heights of the Hindenberg Line and take a fortified knoll, the Cote-de-Chatillon. This was the toughest link in the enemy's position, the one part the Germans could not yield and still win the war.

On the night of October 12, MacArthur met with his commander, General Summerall, to receive his orders. So crucial was this assignment that Summerall closed by telling MacArthur, "Give me Chatillon, or a list of five thousand casualties."

MacArthur replied, "If this brigade does not capture Chatillon, you can publish a casualty list of the entire brigade with the brigade commander's name at the top."

MacArthur took Chatillon because he was willing to stake his life on his success in carrying out his orders. The successful servants in the parable pleased their master because they were willing to assume some risk for his sake.

Are you willing to enter into the Lord's work wholeheartedly, to take risks, in order to carry out the responsibility he has entrusted to you?   —C. B. Mc.

C. INACTIVITY (v. 18)

18. "But the man who had received the one talent went off, dug a hole in the ground and hid his master's money.

The burying of treasure in the ground was a common means of safe-keeping in ancient times. (Compare Matthew 13:44.) A clay jar would be appropriate for underground storage.

This man committed no crime. He did not use the money as his own or treat it carelessly. He simply took the easiest way of getting out of his responsibility. He is represented in our society, including the church, by those who don't want anyone to know that they can render necessary service. It's easier that way, especially if they can convince themselves and others that they have so little ability that there is no use exercising it.

II. SERVANTS REPORT AND ARE JUDGED (MATTHEW 25:19-27)

A. RETURN AND RECKONING (v. 19)

19. "After a long time the master of those servants returned and settled accounts with them.

The *long time* of the master's absence allows for the accomplishment of the two faithful servants, and emphasizes the other servant's long avoidance of responsibility. It also warned the earliest Christians against expecting an immediate return of Jesus to the earth.

B. PRAISE AND PROMOTION (vv. 20-23)

20. "The man who had received the five talents brought the other five. 'Master,' he said, 'you entrusted me with five talents. See, I have gained five more.'

There is a clear note of joy in the servant's report. With enthusiasm he welcomed his master's return. He recognized that his opportunity had come from his lord; now his accounts were ready for inspection. He rejoiced in giving the report.

21. "His master replied, 'Well done, good and faithful servant! You have been faithful with a few things; I will put you in charge of many things. Come and share your master's happiness!'

The master's approval was related specifically to the man's fulfillment of his given task. He had served well in doing what was asked of him.

Few things . . . many things. We might hesitate to call five talents *a few things,* but the master's total estate obviously was much more. And if the servant expected a

WHAT DO YOU THINK?

In many churches there are people who can testify that at one time they were convinced they could never stand before an assembly of worshipers and speak, but now they do it; there are others who once would have thought it impossible that they could enter a near-stranger's home and share the gospel with that person, but now they do it; there are still others who, in the past, would have denied having any leadership ability, but now they lead in the church.

How can one determine whether he or she is "not talented" for a particular activity or the talent is lying dormant, ready to bloom and grow under the right conditions? How can a person assess what he or she could become capable of doing if that talent is not obvious now?

Visual 4 illustrates verse 21. Display it as you discuss the verses that follow.

WHAT DO YOU THINK?

Do you think it is proper for a person to find motivation for service to Christ in the anticipation of hearing the Master's words, "Well done, good and faithful servant"? Why or why not? Shouldn't our desire to serve be motivated by love instead of hope of reward? Explain.

WHAT DO YOU THINK?

The lesson writer says, "Success at one level brought opportunity at high levels." Have you seen this principle to be true in your own life? If so, how?

Is more work a "reward" for a job well done? Why or why not? What was the "master's happiness" the servants were to share if what they got was more responsibility? How does responsibility in the Lord's work bring joy today?

WHAT DO YOU THINK?

It is noted that Heaven will be a place of service, and not just a place of ease and self-indulgence. The privilege of more service as a reward for good service rendered apparently extends even into the eternal realm. (See Revelation 22:3.) The lesson writer says, "One had better enjoy serving that kind of master, or that kind of reward is no reward at all!" What does that suggest about the kind of people who will enjoy Heaven?

long vacation as reward for his efforts, he was in for a surprise. Success at one level brought opportunity at high levels. Good service brought larger assignments to serve. One had better enjoy serving that kind of master, or that kind of reward is no reward at all!

Your master's happiness. Having participated in the success of the lord's business, the servant would participate with his master in the enjoyment of its benefits.

As a foreshadowing of final judgment, this surely indicates disappointment for those persons who love self-indulgence and only occasionally nod toward piety in the expectation of limitless self-indulgence in Heaven. But for those who fervently love God and thoroughly enjoy serving him, the prospect of limitlessly expanding areas of service is marvelous.

22, 23. "The man with the two talents also came. 'Master,' he said, 'you entrusted me with two talents; see, I have gained two more.' His master replied, 'Well done, good and faithful servant! You have been faithful with a few things; I will put you in charge of many things. Come and share your master's happiness!'

The second servant was equal to the first in faithfulness, performance, commendation, and reward. Having two talents to begin with, he was not expected to produce ten. "Whoever can be trusted with very little can also be trusted with much" (Luke 16:10). In terms of a homely little rhyme,

It's not what you'd do with a million,
If a million should e'er be your lot;
It's what you're doing right now
With the dollar and dime that you've got.

The same principle applies to ability/talents.

C. EXCUSE REJECTED (vv. 24-27)

24. "Then the man who had received the one talent came. 'Master,' he said, 'I knew that you are a hard man, harvesting where you have not sown and gathering where you have not scattered seed.

The one-talent man knew he was in trouble. He resorted to an all-too-human ploy—blaming someone else. It began with Adam and Eve (Genesis 3:11-13). Like Adam (v. 12), this man pointed to his judge. The accusation is pitifully awkward.

I knew. He didn't know his master at all, but saw in him a reflection of his own self-serving traits. (Compare Romans 2:1.) So he called his lord cruel and unreasonable, given to using other people to his own advantage. Assuming that he could expect no mercy if anything went wrong with the investment entrusted to him, the man decided to play it safe by burying the treasure.

Harvesting ... sown ... gathering ... scattered. References to the grain harvest depict a person living from others' efforts, reaping the harvest that others have labored to produce, and gathering from the threshing floor the grain that others have threshed out. To the complainer, his master was a thieving, heartless opportunist.

Almost any of us can become expert in discovering scapegoats on whom we can blame our failures. What did this servant gain by blaming his master? And what can we gain from blaming—outwardly or inwardly—our failures on God?

25. "'So I was afraid and went out and hid your talent in the ground. See, here is what belongs to you.'

Was it fear of punishment if he lost some of his master's money that prevented any productive effort by this servant, or was it fear of doing the wrong thing that kept him from doing anything at all? To prevent such paralyzing fears, the apostle Paul heralded, "God did not give us a spirit of timidity, but a spirit of power, of love and of self discipline" (2 Timothy 1:7). John adds, "There is no fear in love. But perfect love drives out fear, because fear has to do with punishment" (1 John 4:18).

Here is what belongs to you. The third servant could not be accused of any crime. He returned his lord's money, promptly and intact. But he had failed to carry out his assignment as a steward.

26, 27. "His master replied, 'You wicked, lazy servant! So you knew that I harvest where I have not sown and gather where I have not scattered seed? Well then, you should have put my money on deposit with the bankers, so that when I returned I would have received it back with interest.

Wicked and *lazy* contrast directly with the *good* and *faithful* of verses 21 and 23. The man's wickedness consisted in his not exercising the positive goodness found in the others.

You knew. This does not necessarily admit that the man was right in what he said about the master. But if the description had been accurate, that very fact should have impelled the servant to do all he could to placate that kind of a master. So he stood condemned by his own words.

Put my money on deposit with the bankers. If the man himself could not do business profitably in the lord's interest, he should at least get help from those who could and would do so. (If you can't go to others with the gospel, you can at least help to employ the services of someone who will.)

Reproduce or Die

Reproduction is one of the essential functions of every organism. Every living thing must reproduce or cease to exist. The most prolific single-cell animals can reproduce themselves in as little as three hours. In a single day, a lone protozoan can become a great-great-great-great-great-grandparent with 510 descendants. Potatoes reproduce by sprouts that come from the plant's "eyes." The leaves of ferns release spores that are spread by the wind to germinate new plants.

The most prolific warm-blooded animal is the New Zealand white rabbit, which produces five to six litters each year with an average of eight to twelve baby rabbits per litter. From protozoa to the rabbits, the means vary, but the object is the same: reproduce or die.

The church must reproduce or it too will die. The seed of the gospel must be scattered abroad in the hope that it will find lodging in receptive hearts. Only then will spiritual birth occur; only then will there be new believers added to the church.

The Lord has entrusted us with the task of sowing the gospel seed. When he returns, will he find the increase he desires?   —C. B. Mc.

III. SERVANTS REASSIGNED (MATTHEW 25:28-30)

At this point the master's judgment turns from commendation or condemnation to the servants, and becomes instruction to other helpers.

A. Reassignment by Results (vv. 28, 29)

28, 29. "'Take the talent from him and give it to the one who has the ten talents. For everyone who has will be given more, and he will have an abundance. Whoever does not have, even what he has will be taken from him.

The non-serving servant had shown himself unworthy of trust. He had missed his opportunity. Now the money formerly assigned to him would be removed and put in the hands of the one who had shown himself most capable and trustworthy. In this action there appears for the first time a difference in the treatment accorded the two faithfully active servants.

The principle of removing from the "have-nots" and adding to the supply of the "haves"—so repugnant to social planners—is an inescapable fact of life. It applies

A SERVANT'S PRAYER

We thank you, our God, for offering us a partnership in your kingdom, and for providing us with what we need for faithful service. Give us, we pray, a clearer view of our responsibility and a new sense of joy in fulfilling our assignments. In Jesus' name. Amen.

THOUGHT TO REMEMBER

"As long as it is day, we must do the work of him who sent me. Night is coming, when no one can work" (John 9:4).

DAILY BIBLE READINGS

Monday, Mar. 18—Greatest Commandments (Matthew 22:34-40)

Tuesday, Mar. 19—Greatness Seen in Serving (Matthew 23:1-12)

Wednesday, Mar. 20—Hypocrisy Condemned (Matthew 23:13-26)

Thursday, Mar. 21—The Pain of Rejection (Matthew 23:29-39)

Friday, Mar. 22—Unpredictable Event (Matthew 24:36-44)

Saturday, Mar. 23—Punishment for Unfaithfulness (Matthew 24:45-51)

Sunday, Mar. 24—Poor Preparation (Matthew 25:1-13)

alike to material substance and to physical, mental, and spiritual growth. Matthew 13:12 applies it to the hearers of Jesus' parables—those who understood would gain in knowledge, and those who lacked understanding would go away empty. Learning becomes progressively easy as one learns, and spiritual—or even physical—development accelerates with advancement. This does not excuse prosperous Christians from being generous to those in need (James 1:27; 1 John 3:17), materially or spiritually. That is an important part of their own development!

At the same time, we must realize that the money given to the servant still belonged to the master! The servant was a steward. His responsibility was to increase his master's holdings. So while it was a reward for the servant to receive the additional talent, it was also in the master's best interest to have a responsible steward handling the talent and not the unfaithful one.

What God has entrusted to Christians, whether it be financial holdings or special abilities or something else, is to be used for his glory. He gives more to the faithful because the faithful glorify him more with it.

B. REJECTION AND REMORSE (v. 30)

30. "And throw that worthless servant outside, into the darkness, where there will be weeping and gnashing of teeth.'"

The same attendants who took the one talent from the lazy servant and gave it to the industrious one were instructed to evict the wretch from the master's presence, where alone in the darkness he could weep and wail over the stupidity that cost him his great opportunity forever.

This agrees with Jesus' other teachings concerning judgment, in which angels are shown to be attendants in the heavenly court. Angels are to accompany the Lord at his coming in glory (Matthew 16:27; 24:30, 31; 25:31), and angels are to carry out the Lord's judgments (Matthew 13:39-42). The hopeless state of the condemned—cast out, shut out from God's presence forever in burning darkness—is everywhere the same.

CONCLUSION

A. WHAT DID I DO WRONG?

Did the unprofitable servant of Jesus' parable complain, "What did I do wrong?" or, "Don't blame me; I didn't do anything"? That, of course, is just what was wrong with what he did. He did nothing with what his master had given him to use. He fell under the judgment of James 4:17: "Anyone, then, who knows the good he ought to do and doesn't do it, sins."

This servant knew the purpose for which his talent was given, and he thwarted that purpose. Do we not similarly thwart the purposes of God's goodness when we use his gifts for our own pleasure, complaining that it is just too much for anyone to expect us to spend our time, our money, and our energy for Christ and his church? Where did we get all those good things anyway? And for what purpose?

B. FAITHFUL OR FEARFUL

The faithful servants were commended; the fearful one was condemned. Faith and fear are not natural companions. Jesus impressed that on his disciples one stormy night on the Sea of Galilee: "Why are you so afraid? Do you still have no faith?" (Mark 4:40). Revelation 21:8 includes the "cowardly" along with liars, murderers, and other evildoers in the lake of fire, the second death. But to Christians in the most frightening circumstances the Lord has promised, "Be faithful, even to the point of death, and I will give you the crown of life" (Revelation 2:10).

"Faithful servant . . . enter."

Discovery Learning

This page contains an alternate lesson plan emphasizing learning activities. Classes desiring such student involvement will find these suggestions helpful. The next page is a reproducible activity page to further enhance discovery learning.

LEARNING GOALS

As a result of participating in today's lesson, a student will be able to:

1. Contrast the responses of the faithful servants with the response of the lazy servant.

2. Conclude that using money and ability pleases God and builds up his kingdom.

3. Choose a talent to develop in building God's kingdom.

INTO THE LESSON

Before class write the word *talents* vertically on a chalkboard or poster in the front of the classroom. When the students arrive, ask them to suggest some talents they have, or wish they have, beginning with each letter of the word. Here are some suggestions:

T teaching
A art, acting
L listening, leadership
E empathy, evangelism
N needlepoint
T talking in public without notes
S singing, sewing

Mention that today's lesson will help us to explore how the talents we have can be used in Christ's kingdom.

INTO THE WORD

As far in advance of class time as possible, ask four class members to prepare to act out the parable of the three servants recorded in Matthew 25:14-30.

Ask the class members to follow along in Matthew 25:14-30 as the four actors present the parable, with you providing needed narration. When the four are finished, lead the class in applause for their talents.

Give each class member a sheet of paper on which you have copied the following five questions (minus the answers shown here), and with space allowed for answers. Ask your class members to answer briefly these questions about the parable:

1. In what way is the man's traveling to a distant country and leaving his business in the care of others like the kingdom of Heaven?

(Jesus would soon go to Heaven and entrust the work of the kingdom to his disciples until his second coming.)

2. On what basis did the master give his servants differing amounts of money?

(The distribution was based on their abilities. See verse 15.)

3. In what ways did the "good and faithful" servants qualify for the master's commendation?

(Apparently they went to work immediately, using what they were given. They did what was asked of them. The implication is that they continued to work till their master returned. They were productive.)

4. What do you think might have been the true motive of the "wicked and slothful" servant?

(Perhaps he wanted to avoid responsibility. He was more concerned about his own comfort and convenience than he was about pleasing his master.)

5. In what ways are Christians now in the role of the servants?

Encourage the class members to share their responses to questions one through four. Discuss them briefly. Emphasize the fact that faithfulness and productivity are equated.

The fifth question provides the transition to life application. Discuss their responses at this time. Point out that we have a variety of God-given gifts and talents and the priceless gospel entrusted to us while Jesus is away. We are to be productive in evangelism, stewardship, and spiritual growth until he returns. The proper use of all he has given us, time, money, abilities is pleasing to him and helps to build his kingdom.

INTO LIFE

Using our talents and other resources responsibly is part of being prepared for the Lord's return. Explore this concept with your students by using the reproducible activity "Be Prepared" on page 268.

After you discuss this activity, refer the class to the list of talents you developed earlier (the acrostic). Give the following instructions: "Choose one of these talents—or another not listed here—that you have and enjoy. Write down two or three ways you could employ that talent more effectively to help build the kingdom of God."

Allow two or three minutes for writing; then ask volunteers to read what they have written. Encourage each one to use his talents in the ways he has suggested.

Close the session with prayer for the Lord's guidance as the class members use their talents for him.

Be Prepared!

There are two parables in Matthew 25 that develop the theme of being ready for the Lord's return. One is detailed in our lesson text, vv. 14-30. The other precedes it, in verses 1-13. Compare the two parables on the chart below.

FIGURE	PARABLE OF THE VIRGINS (vv. 1-13)	PARABLE OF THE SERVANTS (vv. 14-30)
Who represents Christ?		
Who are his followers?		
What is the followers' responsibility?		
How are the responsible followers rewarded?		
How are the irresponsible followers punished?		
What is the message for believers today?		
What would be the result if most believers made a greater effort to obey?		

What similarities do you observe between these two parables?

What differences?

Taken together, what is the basic message of these parables?

THE PARABLE OF THE GREAT FEAST

LESSON 5

WHY TEACH THIS LESSON?

The refusal of the invited guests to attend the banquet in Jesus' parable probably seemed unusual at the time. Such banquets were major social events and were not taken lightly.

We, however, live in an age when such behavior seems normal. It is an age of preoccupation. Our lives and our schedules are so crowded we might easily pass up an invitation to dinner—even a sumptuous one. Business, school, church, and social activities so clutter our calendars it's hard to tell one from another. And that is the danger.

Your students, like all adults in our culture, face a thousand and one demands on their time. Use this lesson to call them back to that which is most important. Responding to Christ's call is our first priority. Having done that, extending that call to others is the one activity for which we dare not be too busy.

INTRODUCTION

A. BANQUET TIME

If you were among those brought up in the "clean plate" tradition at home, you will not soon forget your first banquet and learning that you were not required to eat all your vegetables before accepting the dessert. You came to understand that an oversupply of rich food is an expected part of the celebration at weddings, political rallies, fund raising events, and receptions for notable visitors.

Big dinners are not limited to any one time, place, or circumstance. They are perhaps more notable among people whose daily fare is not plentiful, but banquets can be exciting events even among royalty (Esther 5; Daniel 5:1-4; Matthew 22:1-14). So they are mentioned prominently throughout the Bible, from Abraham's hospitality toward heavenly messengers (Genesis 18:1-8) to the "marriage supper of the Lamb" in Heaven itself (Revelation 19:9).

It is not surprising, then, that when God's Son came to dwell among men, he attended feasts in the homes of the well-to-do as well as quiet dinners in the homes of his friends (Luke 10:38-42). Neither is it surprising that he used these occasions as opportunities for teaching.

B. LESSON BACKGROUND

Two of Jesus' banquet parables are so much alike that they are sometimes thought to be two reports of the same event. Luke 14:15-24 says that a man made a great supper, invited many, and made one servant his agent in notifying the guests, who excused themselves more or less politely and were replaced by others who would accept last-minute summonses to the dinner.

Matthew 22:1-14 says that a king invited many to the marriage celebration for his son and sent notifications through groups of servants, who were treated roughly

DEVOTIONAL READING
LUKE 14:7-14
LESSON SCRIPTURE
LUKE 14:1-24
PRINTED TEXT
LUKE 14:15-24

Mar
31

LESSON AIMS

This study should equip the student to:

1. List the reasons the parable's guests gave for not attending with Jesus' response to their choices.

2. Explain the invitation Christ extends and name ways people might respond to that invitation.

3. Suggest some ways to extend Christ's invitation in an attractive way that will be accepted instead of refused.

KEY VERSE

Then the master told his servant, "Go out to the roads and country lanes and make them come in, so that my house will be full." —Luke 14:23

NOTE

Visual 14 of the visuals packet lists Jesus' parables in chronological order. Refer to it and note the difference between "The Great Feast" (Luke 14:16-24) and "The Wedding Garment" (Matthew 22:1-14).

WHAT DO YOU THINK?

Jesus compared his kingdom with a great supper. Consider the following aspects of hosting a banquet. How does each help us to understand the kingdom?

• People gain great enjoyment in coming together to eat.

• Hosting such a supper requires tremendous preparation.

• The guests come by invitation.

What other comparisons can you think of?

and contemptuously by those who had been invited; whereupon the king punished the offenders and replaced them at his feast with other guests.

The account in Matthew relates to a time of public conflict in Jerusalem during the final week of Jesus' ministry. Luke's account relates to an earlier and somewhat less stressful occasion. The settings account for the differences in details and nature of the stories. Jesus occasionally set forth the same principles at different times and places.

Chapter 14 of Luke begins with the account of a prominent Pharisee's Sabbath dinner, which Jesus attended and where he was "carefully watched" by the Pharisee and others, apparently with the purpose of finding some way to discredit him. Verses 2-6 tell that a man suffering with dropsy appeared in the Pharisee's house, and that Jesus healed him, after first noting the intent of the Pharisees and lawyers to accuse him of thus violating the Sabbath. Clearly, Jesus had observed the persons around him as they had been observing him!

Verses 7-11 record Jesus' good-natured advice to the guests who had crowded to the most honorable seats at the table, noting that they might be embarrassed by being asked to give way to latecomers higher on the guest list.

Verses 12-14 follow with similar advice to the host, that he should make up his guest list from among those who were poor and needy, rather than those who could be expected to reward him with returned favors. If he would do so, the greater reward would come "at the resurrection of the righteous."

I. WHAT BANQUET? (LUKE 14:15)

15. When one of those at the table with him heard this, he said to Jesus, "Blessed is the man who will eat at the feast in the kingdom of God."

The fellow diner obviously was interested in the Lord's reference to rewards in the resurrection. Some Bible students think that this man was expressing approval of Jesus' advice as to the kind of behavior that would please God, rather than what would yield material advantage now. Others think that the speaker was a self-righteous Pharisee who was fully convinced that he would have a favored place at the table in Heaven, where the approved ones would "take their places at the feast with Abraham, Isaac and Jacob in the kingdom of heaven" (Matthew 8:11). At least his comment sparked interest in the discussion and provided Jesus a great starting point for his parable. The ones first invited to the feast might not share in it, after all.

II. PREPARATION AND INVITATION (LUKE 14:16, 17)

16. Jesus replied: "A certain man was preparing a great banquet and invited many guests.

Jesus' response was made to the one who spoke up, but clearly it was intended for all.

A certain man. The man, not otherwise identified, obviously possessed great resources and authority. In application, it is God himself, preparing limitless blessing for those who accept his invitation.

A great banquet. The story of a banquet was surely appropriate at a dinner party, where the invitation and conduct of guests had already been mentioned. Preparation for this feast seems to have been going on for some time and to be continuing. Even so, God had been engaged for centuries in the preparation of men's salvation.

Why does one prepare a dinner and invite guests? That could be asked concerning the Pharisee who hosted this dinner. Did he owe invitations to others who had entertained him? Did he wish to impress people by a display of hospitality? Did he enjoy the company of his guests? Did he want to put them under obligation for future favors? Did he want to feed people who were hungry, in body, mind, or spirit?

God, our ultimate host, loves us, wants to supply our needs, and desires our company. For hundreds of years, through the patriarchs, the law, and the prophets, he had been issuing his invitation to the Jewish people.

CELEBRATE

People love to celebrate. From ancient times people of every culture and nation have had their festive celebrations, and these celebrations have been accompanied by lavish feasts. The oldest North American day of celebration, Thanksgiving, dates from 1621. In that year the Plymouth colonists, rejoicing over the first corn harvest, joined with the neighboring Indians as all brought food and shared their bounty. Now, families in the United States gather every fourth Thursday in November around tables of turkey, dressing, cranberries, and other delectable foods, to enjoy and give thanks for God's bountiful provisions. Canada adopted Thanksgiving as a national holiday in 1879. It is celebrated there on the second Monday in October.

People love to celebrate. The list of holidays celebrated around the world takes five pages of small type in the *Encyclopedia Britannica*! Of all the things people might celebrate, salvation in Jesus Christ is the greatest. Perhaps that is the reason the Lord often referred to the kingdom of Heaven in terms of a banquet. While Christianity involves the death of our sinful selves, being part of God's family is not a perpetual funeral, but a feast.   —C. B. Mc.

17. "At the time of the banquet he sent his servant to tell those who had been invited, 'Come, for everything is now ready.'

Those who had been invited. It seems that all who were invited accepted the invitation. However, the precise time of the feast had not been set. The summons to "come and get it" waited until everything was ready. Esther 5:8 and 6:14 reveal a similar pattern.

Why should only one servant be mentioned as bearing the last-minute summons to the guests who were expected to fill the host's great banquet hall? (Compare verses 21-23.) Perhaps one responsible servant was charged with directing many others who must go to the homes of the guests throughout the city.

When we apply the parable to God's long preparation and invitation to his people, and when we learn that he sent his Son "when the time had fully come" (Galatians 4:4, 5), and when we observe that Jesus took on the "nature of a servant" (Philippians 2:7), the mystery tends to disappear. God's one and only Son becomes the sole authoritative voice to say, "Come!" That does not rule out the necessity for many messengers to carry his invitation.

III. PREFERRING SOMETHING ELSE (LUKE 14:18-20)

Up to this point Jesus' parable followed a common course, telling of customs familiar to his hearers. Now the parable moves away from the norm of human experience. Although it is possible, it is rather unlikely that all the guests invited to a feast would find other things more enticing and decide not to come. But this deviation is necessary to add force to the truth Jesus makes concerning the realities of heaven.

A. FIELDS (v. 18)

18. "But they all alike began to make excuses. The first said, 'I have just bought a field, and I must go and see it. Please excuse me.'

They all alike. Had they all changed their minds about accepting the invitation, so that now they were looking for, or inventing, excuses for getting out of the appointment?

Visual 5 depicts an invitation and a variety of excuses for refusing. Display it in connection with verses 18-20. You might even refer to it to introduce the discussion question that follows in this column.

WHAT DO YOU THINK?

The invited guests who made excuses for not attending the host's banquet represent people today who refuse to accept God's invitation. How are the excuses of a banquet guest similar to the excuses people have for not accepting the gospel invitation? Consider the following excuses, stated or implied in the parable:

- *Possessions*
- *Family*
- *Inconvenience*
- *Lack of respect for the host*
- *Other excuses?*

How can we address these excuses to help people respond to the gospel?

Jesus' hearers may have smiled at the thought of a man's buying real estate without first seeing it. It is not so unusual, though, for even a careful buyer to be fascinated with an important new purchase. And real estate is important! We are reminded of Jesus' earlier reference to a new convert's faith being choked out by the cares of this world, and by the deceitfulness of riches (Matthew 13:22).

The land buyer's apology was at least politely worded: "Please excuse me." Would his reasoning appear as sound to the host as to him?

B. FACILITIES (v. 19)

19. "Another said, 'I have just bought five yoke of oxen, and I'm on my way to try them out. Please excuse me.'

The humor here is heightened by the fact that there were *five yoke of oxen*, that is, ten draft animals in teams fitted for heavy pulling. And the man said he was on his way right now to see how well they would work! Can anyone believe that he would have made such a purchase if he had had any serious doubts about the quality of these animals? And if he had bought them, he certainly could have tried them out at another time.

C. FAMILY (v. 20)

20. "Still another said, 'I just got married, so I can't come.'

Another. This implies that the pattern of excuses from the guest roster could be extended indefinitely. The ones quoted are representative samples. The blunt, covers-it-all nature of the third man's statement, however, heightens the comic aspect of this dinner time commentary.

Deuteronomy 24:5 cites a bridegroom's exemptions from certain duties in ancient Israel in order to establish the pattern of marital joys, but nothing is said about avoiding festive celebrations with one's friends. Surely marriage, family, and home are high in the order of divine priorities. But would attending the host's great supper damage the family relationship?

Jesus' purpose in the parable becomes evident at this point. He was talking about God's invitation to the spiritual feast provided through the gift of his only Son. He was talking about the invited guests' response to that invitation. And immediately after the parable we find this plain statement: "If anyone comes to me and does not hate his father and mother, his wife and children, his brothers and sisters—yes, even his own life—he cannot be my disciple" (Luke 14:26). Christ is more important than kin. First Corinthians 7:29-35 agrees in warning that marriage might come between the believer and service to the Lord.

Just why did the guests go back on their commitment to be present for the feast? They named other interests that seemed more important at the time. The items they named were important, but their real reasons could have been things they would have been ashamed to name. And in every instance they could have come if their desire to do so had been strong enough. Basic to their decision was their attitude toward the host. They did not respect him enough to give first place to his wishes. And that is what determined his response to their excuses.

"NO EXCUSE, SIR"

Visitors to the United States Army post at Fort Benning, Georgia, were observing a training exercise involving recruits of the Army's famed airborne troops, the Green Berets. The most striking thing about these young soldiers was their "esprit de corps," their spirit of comradeship, enthusiasm, and devotion to their cause.

The guests watched as a platoon of Green Beret trainees parachuted into a large field, then quickly assembled into fighting formation in front of the grandstand where the guests were seated. It was a blustery day, and the wind caught the parachute of one young private, slamming him hard into the ground on the far end of the field. Though he had suffered a severely sprained ankle, the soldier rose to his feet and attempted to run to his place in the formation. Limping with great effort across the field, he was the last man to take his position. The private obviously was injured; nonetheless, the sergeant in charge loudly demanded why he was the last man to arrive. Though it was clear to the civilian guests that the soldier had good reason to be late, he nevertheless answered his sergeant with the words, "No excuse, Sir."

When the invitation comes for us to be part of God's kingdom and to be used in his service, may we do our best to obey the Master in whatever he calls us to do and, in the spirit of that young soldier, offer no excuses.   —C. B. Mc.

IV. PLACES TO BE FILLED (LUKE 14:21-23)

A. BY HUNGRY PEOPLE NEARBY (v. 21)

21. "The servant came back and reported this to his master. Then the owner of the house became angry and ordered his servant, 'Go out quickly into the streets and alleys of the town and bring in the poor, the crippled, the blind and the lame.'

Having received the invited guests' negative responses, the faithful servant reported their rejections to his master. That gentleman's reaction was predictable in one who had gone all out to provide a banquet for his friends and found that they did not respect him enough to set aside other activities for the evening. Disappointed and angry, he still would not sit alone at home and let the banquet food go to waste. He would find other guests—the kind who did not have fields and oxen and weddings to occupy their attention—the kind whom Jesus had advised his pharisaic host to invite to his next dinner party (v. 13). Bring the *poor*, bring people limping along on crutches; lead, and be prepared to feed, the ones unable to see— those persons who could not return the invitation. Bring them from the city streets and alleys where they made their homes and searched for discarded scraps of food.

These are the kinds of people who had turned most eagerly to Jesus in their need when he was rejected by the religious establishment. Having little or no holdings in the present world, they had time to learn about the kingdom of Heaven.

B. BY HUNGRY PEOPLE FARTHER AWAY (vv. 22, 23)

22, 23. "'Sir,' the servant said, 'what you ordered has been done, but there is still room.' Then the master told his servant, 'Go out to the roads and country lanes and make them come in, so that my house will be full.

The story moves farther from material probabilities toward spiritual realities. To scour a city for prospective guests and to bring them into the banquet hall would take time, but the accomplishment is made and reported.

There is still room . . . that my house will be full. Here is the thrust of the parable, not in the material limits of an evening in a banquet hall, but in the outreach of a generous and loving God, who would have all men to be saved, and who is not content as long as there is a vacancy in his "many rooms" (John 14:2).

The invitation, therefore, is to be taken beyond the city to outlying areas (beyond Jerusalem and Judea to Samaria and the ends of the earth—Acts 1:8), where the roadways and the paths are to be searched and people to be found.

Make them come in. It will not be easy for the peasant poor to believe that an invitation to a grand banquet in town, right now, is something more than a cruel joke. So they must be compelled by the most earnest persuasion and consistent demonstration of the master's genuine care for every man, woman, and child. This is the spirit of Christ's church. His "ambassadors take the invitation: "We implore you on Christ's behalf: Be reconciled to God" (2 Corinthians 5:20).

WHAT DO YOU THINK?

This parable may be seen as a warning to the one who said, "Blessed is the man who will eat at the feast in the kingdom of God" (v. 15). This one, so sure of himself, just might not make it! Instead, the feast will include those who were despised by the elite of the day, "the poor, the crippled, the blind and the lame" (v. 21).

Do you see this as a warning for Christians today? If so, what is the warning? How should we respond?

WHAT DO YOU THINK?

God wants all persons to be saved and to enter his heavenly home. But many do not listen. Like the poor in the parable, we need to "make [or "compel"] them come in." For some, that may require blunt warnings of judgment. Paul said, "Knowing therefore the terror of the Lord, we persuade men" (2 Corinthians 5:11, KJV). Jude 22, 23 suggests that some persons will respond better to an emphasis on God's love and benevolence.

How does one know which approach to take in sharing the gospel invitation? How can you make the invitation appealing to someone you know who needs to respond to it?

The tragedy of rejecting the gospel is depicted in these words of Luke 14:24. It is a tragedy worse than any automobile accident, airplane crash, or natural disaster—no matter how many casualties. No earthly tragedy can compare with the loss of a soul through rejection of the gospel. On the other hand, every such tragedy is made even worse by the fact that many of the victims face a Christless eternity because they have rejected God's invitation!

What kind of response does the impending tragedy for those who refuse God's invitation demand of Christians? How can your church increase its efforts to respond to this need? How about your class? How about you?

PRAYER OF AN INVITED GUEST

All praise to you, O God, for the glorious love that provides blessings beyond imagination. We thank you for your invitation to share in your glory. We pray your forgiveness for the times when we have forgotten you in our absorption with lesser things. Give us a winsome faith, we pray, to extend to others your invitation to your banquet table in Heaven. Through Jesus our Lord. Amen.

THOUGHT TO REMEMBER

All things are ready; come to the feast!

V. PERMANENCE OF CHOICE (LUKE 14:24)

Traces of humor added a light touch to the earlier parts of Jesus' parable of the feast. These disappear as the parable concludes in a statement of final judgment. **24. "'I tell you, not one of those men who were invited will get a taste of my banquet.'"**

The parable closes with the banquet host announcing his decision concerning the guests who have rejected his invitation to dine at his table; but here a transition occurs. The word *you* is plural, and so it seems that Jesus is directing this statement to all who were present at this meal in the Pharisee's home. These words ring with the judgment of God on Israel's religious leaders and the presumptuous nationals who assumed that, as God's chosen people, they had no further need to honor God with their life choices. Particularly intolerable was their rejection of God's Son, who came to announce and establish the kingdom that had been prepared and prophesied through the ages. To them it would happen as to the guests who didn't want to come to the host's banquet: "The kingdom of God will be taken away from you and given to a people who will produce its fruit" (Matthew 21:43).

Nothing in the parable indicates that the invited guests were bad people. They offended the host, not by their morals, but by their indifference to him and his preparations for them. The depth of that offense is reflected in the emotion that burns in those final words.

The absentees would miss out, not because they were excluded, but because they chose not to come. They said they couldn't come, each for his own reason. The host's final message to them was, "It shall be as you have said."

CONCLUSION

A formal invitation to almost any kind of event will probably conclude with a request for a reply. The request will be made with the letters RSVP, which abbreviate a phrase borrowed from the French, *répondez s'il vous plaît*—"reply, if you please." The host or hostess wants to know how many places to reserve for how many people.

On what basis does one reply? Several kinds of questions will influence a person's decision: Who is offering the invitation? What advantage could I gain, either by attending or by staying away? Do I have any conflicting prior commitments? Is there something else I would rather be doing at the time?

The first and last questions probably influence our decisions more than we realize. They are vital in respect to activities involving the church. The stranger comes or not, depending on who extends the invitation and how enjoyable the experience is perceived to be. The church member participates or not, depending on what he or she thinks of God in relation to the other elements involved.

Church members, like the invited guests in Jesus' parable, have said yes to the Lord's formal RSVP. However, that does not guarantee they will show up when the time comes to render service or even to attend the services. New or compelling personal affairs may get in the way of their full participation in God's banquet.

How does such a person answer questions about the matter? Usually by giving reasons that can be made to seem important. Seldom does one admit having a preference to do something else with his or her time and assets. Almost never will one say plainly, "I just don't care that much about God and my Savior."

What is God to say about it? "I invited him (her) to my banquet in Heaven, and he said yes. Now, however, he has decided that he is more interested in something else, and he won't come. I'll have to get along with others less occupied with things of this present world. But in the place marked with his name at my table, there will be a full plate and an empty chair."

Discovery Learning

This page contains an alternate lesson plan emphasizing learning activities. Classes desiring such student involvement will find these suggestions helpful. The next page is a reproducible activity page to further enhance discovery learning.

LEARNING GOALS

As a result of participating in today's lesson, students will be able to:

1. List both the reasons the parable's guests gave for not attending and Jesus' response to their choices.

2. Explain the invitation Christ extends and name ways people might respond to that invitation.

3. Suggest some ways to extend Christ's invitation in an attractive way that will be accepted instead of refused.

INTO THE LESSON

Open the session by asking your students how they decide whether or not to attend an event to which they have been invited. Write their responses on a chalkboard or poster at the front of the room.

Expect answers such as the following: Acceptance depends on who is extending the invitation, perceived advantages of attending, conflicting commitments, cost, whether the activity is enjoyable, other things they would rather do. Then ask, "Which of these reasons would have the most bearing on your decision?"

INTO THE WORD

Briefly summarize Luke 14:1-14, the background for today's text. (See pages 269, 270.)

Have a volunteer read Luke 14:15-24 aloud to the class. Make it clear that the invitation to the dinner had been extended previously, according to the custom of that day. The servant was notifying those who already had accepted the invitation that it was time to come. All the expense and effort regarding the purchase and preparation of the food already had been made. For them to refuse at this point was a show of disregard for the host.

Give each student a copy of the reproducible activity page 276 and have them complete the first column. Don't wait too long before reviewing what should be in the spaces on the chart. This is difficult enough that some students may prefer to fill the charts in as you review. Help the students make the following associations:

- The host (v. 16)—*God*
- The banquet (v. 16)—*Heaven, salvation*
- Those who accepted the first invitation (v. 16)—*Israel*
- The call to come (v. 17)—*to accept Christ*
- His servant (v. 17)—*Jesus*
- Those who refused to come (vv. 18-20)—*Jews, especially the leaders, who rejected God's Son*

- Second group invited (v. 21)—*the truly humble in Israel*
- Third group invited (vv. 22, 23)—*the Gentiles*

Point out that the people of Israel had professed allegiance to God for many centuries, but when he sent his Son (the Messiah) to announce the coming of the kingdom of God, Israel as a whole and the rulers especially, rejected him.

INTO LIFE

To apply this parable to our lives, ask, "What does this parable teach about a person's refusing God's invitation extended through Christ?" (Read and discuss verse 24.) Have the class complete the second column of the chart now. Again, give just a few minutes for those who want to work independently. Then discuss the chart and help the students see the following associations:

- The host (v. 16)—*God*
- The banquet (v. 16)—*Heaven, salvation*
- Those who accepted the first invitation (v. 16)—*Those who make a profession of faith in Christ*
- The call to come (v. 17)—*to get involved in ministry, service; perhaps the "final call" at the second coming*
- His servant (v. 17)—*Jesus; perhaps the church*
- Those who refused to come (vv. 18-20)—*Nominal Christians who refuse to get involved*
- Second group invited (v. 21)—*people who truly appreciate the grace of God—perhaps those with a shady past who are not accepted by "respectable" church members*
- Third group invited (vv. 22, 23)—*the same as above*

In the parable the respondents' reasons for not attending the host's banquet are seen to be empty pretexts. Many today who have accepted Christ have allowed worldly interests to have priority in their lives, and they offer flimsy excuses for not doing as God wishes.

Ask the class to name some things that Christians allow to crowd God out of their lives. List them on your chalkboard. In this connection have your students consider Demas, who was a co-worker of the apostle Paul (2 Timothy 4:10). Ask what his example teaches us about priorities in life.

Close the session by allotting a minute or so for the students to ponder the list on the chalkboard to see if they are allowing any of these things to become too important in their lives. Ask, "Do you need to make any adjustments regarding the priorities in your life? If so, what adjustments will you begin to make this week?"

Parable of the Great Feast

One of the advantages of teaching in parables is that the lessons live beyond their first application to speak afresh to new generations. This is clearly seen in the parable of the Great Feast, Luke 14:1-14. Spoken in response to a banquet attender—probably a Pharisee—who seemed pretty sure of himself and his salvation, it warned the Jews in general and the religious elite in particular that the kingdom was not for them only. In fact, some of them might not make it!

The chart below shows how the parable first applied to Israel and then how it applies to our modern situation. Read the parable and complete the chart.

FIGURE	FIRST APPLICATION	MODERN APPLICATION
• The host (v. 16)		
• The banquet (v. 16)		
• Those who accepted the first invitation (v. 16)		
• The call to come (v. 17)		
• His servant (v. 17)		
• Those who refused to come (vv. 18-20)		
• Second group invited (v. 21)		
• Third group invited (vv. 22, 23)		

THE LIVING LORD

WHY TEACH THIS LESSON?

Easter Sunday traditionally sees a greater attendance than usual in most churches. This makes it one of the best opportunities for the Bible teacher. These "C-E" Christians (Christmas and Easter) need to be challenged to greater commitment—and so do all of us. What better way to do that than with a confrontation with the risen Christ?

Today's lesson introduces us to two disciples who were not very good Bible students. They were "foolish" and "slow of heart to believe all that the prophets have spoken" (Luke 24:25). Jesus challenged their preconceptions, false expectations, and ignorance by explaining the Scriptures.

The same symptoms are present in many of your own students. The same cure is still the solution.

INTRODUCTION

A. NOT WAS, BUT IS!

Who and what was Jesus?

A Christian can't answer that question as it is presented. The living Lord is not a has-been, to be described in the past tense. The testimony of the Holy Spirit, reported by the apostles and other inspired men, is couched in an unchanging present. That testimony is vital: "No one can say, 'Jesus is Lord,' except by the Holy Spirit" (1 Corinthians 12:3).

The apostle Paul affirmed the resurrection as the central fact in establishing Jesus' identity. Jesus "through the Spirit of holiness was declared with power to be the Son of God by his resurrection from the dead" (Romans 1:4).

"Resurrection from the dead!" Those four words compress the bad news/good news core of the gospel. "Christ died for our sins according to the Scriptures" (1 Corinthians 15:3). The four Gospels detail the bad news of that death, which left even the material world in quake-torn darkness. Jesus' death was necessary as the atonement for our sin. Its necessity saves it from the ultimate tragedy of being without meaning, but does not provide genuine relief. That relief awaited the dawn of the third day, when Christ "was raised . . . according to the Scriptures" (1 Corinthians 15:4). The good news of resurrection provides hallelujahs that begin with the final chapters of the four Gospels, continue as a theme for the book of Acts and the New Testament epistles, and furnish a background for triumphant Revelation. So Jesus is the Lamb of God—"the Living One; I was dead, and behold I am alive for ever and ever!" (Revelation 1:18).

B. LESSON BACKGROUND

Our studies in March dealt with five parables teaching about the kingdom of Heaven. Through the month of April we will consider four lessons that teach about God, as living, and loving, and caring, and life-sustaining. These qualities are presented not only in the words of Jesus, but especially in his works and his being. In this lesson, the lesson for Easter, we find "The Living Lord" in Jesus, risen from the dead.

DEVOTIONAL READING
LUKE 24:1-12
LESSON SCRIPTURE
LUKE 24:1-36
PRINTED TEXT
LUKE 24:13-27

Apr
7

LESSON AIMS

This study should enable a student to:

1. Summarize Jesus' conversation with the disciples on the Emmaus road.

2. Explain how God's Word (prophecy) reveals truths about Jesus—to the two and to us.

3. Express trust in the testimony of God's Word concerning Jesus.

KEY VERSE

Beginning with Moses and all the Prophets, he explained to them what was said in all the Scriptures concerning himself.

—Luke 24:27

Before there could be a resurrection, there had to be a death—a real, stone-cold death. Jesus spent much time and effort in teaching his disciples that he must die at the hands of his enemies, but that he would rise again. Luke 19:28—22:46 details the events of Jesus' final week, and 22:47—23:49 tells of his arrest, trials, and crucifixion.

Luke 23:50-56 tells of Jesus' burial. Two believing members of the Jewish high court (Nicodemus and Joseph of Arimathea) took his body down from the cross, prepared it hastily for burial before the Sabbath began at sundown on Friday, and laid it in the new tomb belonging to one of them (John 19:38-40; Matthew 27:59, 60). The tomb was sealed by the Roman authority and soldiers were posted to guard it (Matthew 27:62-66).

The burial of Jesus was observed by women who had followed him and supported his ministry. They left the place and spent the Sabbath at rest according to the Jewish law (Luke 23:56). They were back at the burial place early on the first day of the week, however, and found the stone closure rolled away from the opening, and the tomb empty. Two men "in clothes that gleamed like lightning" were present to tell them that Jesus was alive, and the women carried the message to his apostles. Peter and John (John 20:3-10) came to the tomb and found it as reported (Luke 24:1-12).

At this point Luke introduces the Emmaus incident, mentioned also in Mark 16:12, 13: "Afterward Jesus appeared in a different form to two of them while they were walking in the country. These returned and reported it to the rest."

I. THE LORD WALKS WITH MEN (LUKE 24:13-16)

A. IMPORTANT NEWS DISCUSSED (vv. 13, 14)

13. Now that same day two of them were going to a village called Emmaus, about seven miles from Jerusalem.

The *two* were followers of Jesus, and probably numbered among the 120 mentioned in Acts 1:15, but they are not mentioned otherwise in Scripture. They had been in Jerusalem enough to know the events of recent days there. Their walk to *Emmaus* took place on the day of Jesus' resurrection, evidently some time after noon.

The two evidently were friends, or perhaps members of the same family. It seems reasonable to infer that they lived in Emmaus. (See verses 28, 29.)

We know nothing about Emmaus except what appears here. The village was about seven miles from Jerusalem, and most Bible students think it was northwest of the city.

14. They were talking with each other about everything that had happened.

There was much news for the two to discuss. In fact, the events of those days in and around Jerusalem have been the subject for discussion among many of the world's people ever since. Virtually everyone in Palestine in those days knew at least something about Jesus, but there was much disagreement as to who he really was. Many had seen his mighty works and heard his amazing words, but very few understood fully what they had seen and heard. When they reported it, they were not believed. Even among the closest witnesses and believers there were many unanswered questions. How could things come to such an end for such a one as Jesus? The pieces just didn't seem to fit together. The travelers' conversation was surely not boring; neither was it trivial small talk.

B. SHARED EXPERIENCE (vv. 15, 16)

15. As they talked and discussed these things with each other, Jesus himself came up and walked along with them.

HOW TO SAY IT

Arimathea. Air-uh-muh-THEE-uh (th *as in* thin).
Cuza. KEW-za.
Cleopas. KLEE-uh-pass.
Emmaus. Em-MAY-us.
Magdalene. MAG-duh-leen *or* Mag-duh-LEE-nee.
Nicodemus. NICK-uh-DEE-mus.

Visual 6 illustrates a verse that comes after our printed text, but it represents the climax toward which the text is leading. The opening of the disciples' eyes was the purpose of this event—and of your class meeting today.

And their eyes were opened, and they knew him; and he vanished out of their sight.

The intensity of their discussion would have made it easy for almost anyone to approach, either from behind them or by an intersecting path, without being noticed. Jesus joined them as an interested listener to their discussion.

Mark 16:9-11 and John 20:11-18 tell that Jesus had appeared that morning to Mary Magdalene. Matthew 28:9, 10 tells of his appearing to other women. But this is the first appearance of the risen Lord mentioned by Luke. Even after the resurrection Jesus associated readily with common people. When thought and conversation center on him, we are most likely to enjoy his presence.

16. But they were kept from recognizing him.

Others also were slow to recognize Jesus after the resurrection. Mary Magdalene mistook him for the gardener at the tomb (John 20:14-16). That evening he had difficulty persuading the eleven apostles that it was really he, and not just a ghost, before them (Luke 24:36-43). Later in Galilee, fishermen/apostles recognized Jesus on the shore only after he had directed them to a miraculous catch (John 21:4-7).

The language here suggests these two were deliberately prevented from recognizing the Lord. His appearing in "a different form" (Mark 16:12) supports that conclusion. If they had recognized Jesus immediately, they might have been so excited by the discovery that they would have been unable to receive the teaching they so greatly needed and the Lord desired to give.

II. THE LORD LISTENS TO MEN (LUKE 24:17-24)

A. ABSORPTION WITH CURRENT EVENTS (vv. 17, 18)

17. He asked them, "What are you discussing together as you walk along?" They stood still, their faces downcast.

The lively discussion between the two disciples would have been evident to the most casual observer. *Discussing together* here translates a word depicting a back-and-forth exchange like the volleying of a ball in a tennis match. In it we can hear a frequent "on the other hand," probably emphasized with gestures. Their *downcast* expressions showed they clearly were disturbed by what they were talking about. Jesus' question stopped them in their tracks.

18. One of them, named Cleopas, asked him, "Are you only a visitor to Jerusalem and do not know the things that have happened there in these days?"

The name *Cleopas* appears in Scripture only here and in John 19:25. There is no evident connection between the two. The companion of Cleopas is nowhere identified or described. The two could not understand how anyone even visiting briefly in Jerusalem could be unaware of what had happened there. And what else could they be talking about? That was the theme of the day!

A MATTER OF PUBLIC RECORD

"Are you only a visitor to Jerusalem and do not know the things that have happened there in these days?" Cleopas asked the stranger on the Emmaus road. The question reveals an important fact that fortifies the credibility of the New Testament accounts of the crucifixion and resurrection of Jesus. These events were not the product of a closely held myth that time and distance made more plausible, but were widely known in the city where they took place.

Fifty days later amid the miraculous manifestations of the Holy Spirit on Pentecost, Peter stood in Jerusalem to proclaim the good news about the risen Lord. "Men of Israel, listen to this: Jesus of Nazareth was a man accredited by God to you by miracles, wonders and signs, which God did among you through him, *as you yourselves know*" (Acts 2:22). Peter appealed to the common knowledge of his listeners as independent confirmation of his message that Jesus had risen from the dead.

WHAT DO YOU THINK?

Unbelievers have challenged the truth of the resurrection by suggesting the disciples so much expected a resurrection that they imagined the sightings. Some say that because Jesus had foretold his death and resurrection, his followers were ready to believe it with the slightest provocation.

The fact that several of Jesus' followers were slow to recognize him when he appeared to them after his resurrection argues against such a claim. It is clear they did not expect to see him after his death! How does that confirm your faith in the resurrection? How can it help you in your witness for the Lord?

WHAT DO YOU THINK?

The two on the way to Emmaus were amazed that the stranger could have been unaware of the recent events in Jerusalem involving Jesus of Nazareth. After telling King Agrippa the facts concerning the death and resurrection of Christ, the apostle Paul told Festus, "I am convinced that none of this has escaped his notice, because it was not done in a corner" (Acts 26:26). Jesus was no obscure prophet.

How does this confirm your faith today? How does it help you answer the critic who claims Jesus was but a mythical character, not a real historical person?

A person can lie about the shape of the St. Louis arch, but he won't get away with it in St. Louis. One can lie about the size of Big Ben, but she can't get away with it in London. Of all the places in the world where no one could have got away with saying that the death and resurrection of Jesus did not occur, that place was Jerusalem. These earthshaking events were a matter of public record.

—C. B. Mc.

B. BAD NEWS OF CANCELED HOPES (vv. 19-21)

19. "What things?" he asked.

"About Jesus of Nazareth," they replied. "He was a prophet, powerful in word and deed before God and all the people.

Jesus did not pretend to be ignorant; the two must put into words what they were thinking. And they did it marvelously. Luke has recorded briefly what is probably a summary of statements by both men. The subject was identified accurately as the man *Jesus* who grew up in *Nazareth* of Galilee. He is the proper center of all our life, thought, and behavior. They acknowledged him properly as a supremely great spokesman for God, but they fell short of affirming his messiahship. They saw in him a perfect balance of power in what he said and what he did. They found in him also a complete integrity, as seen by God and also by men, whether in personal contact or before a multitude. In his life on earth, he showed himself to be Lord, and that they properly acknowledged. What a confession!

20. "The chief priests and our rulers handed him over to be sentenced to death, and they crucified him.

As Jews, Cleopas and his friend recognized the responsibility of the politically oriented *priests* and the recognized religious *rulers* of the Jews for delivering Jesus to the Roman authorities and persuading them to execute Jesus in the Roman style. They told it as it was. It was bad news, overshadowing all the good news of Jesus' life, character, and influence.

21. "But we had hoped that he was the one who was going to redeem Israel. And what is more, it is the third day since all this took place.

There is a dismal past tense in *hoped.* Their hope was shattered when Jesus died. That was at least partly because they expected the wrong things of their Messiah. They expected him to redeem the nation Israel, apparently by a military deliverance from Rome. For that kind of Messiah to die, betrayed by his own people and executed by the authorities he was supposed to overthrow, just could not happen!

Three days was time enough for the incredible facts to soak in and be accepted as final. If it all had been a horrible nightmare, they would have awakened before now. Did they know that Jesus had predicted his resurrection after three days? If so, the time was up!

C. GOOD NEWS OF RESURRECTION (vv. 22-24)

22, 23. "In addition, some of our women amazed us. They went to the tomb early this morning but didn't find his body. They came and told us that they had seen a vision of angels, who said he was alive.

Luke 8:2, 3 mentions women whom Jesus had "cured of evil spirits and diseases: Mary (called Magdalene) from whom seven demons had come out; Joanna the wife of Cuza, the manager of Herod's household; Susanna; and many others. These women were helping to support him out of their own means." Luke 24:10 provides a similar list, adding "Mary the mother of James," as being those who witnessed the burial of Jesus, and then returned to the tomb early on the first day of the week. There they saw and heard the angels who said, "Why do you look for the living among the dead? He is not here; he has risen!" (Luke 24:5).

WHAT DO YOU THINK?

"But we had hoped...." What disillusionment is expressed in these words! The disillusionment of these two came from two sources. First, they had wrong expectations of Jesus. They expected a political kingdom, but Jesus' kingdom is *"not of this world."* Second, they were ignorant of the truth. Jesus was alive, not dead as they supposed.

What causes disillusionment among Christians today? How often are wrong expectations and ignorance at the root of it? How can we reassure disillusioned Christians?

Cleopas and his friend identified themselves as being "companions" of Jesus' followers (v. 24). They had even been present with the apostles, apparently, when the women reported that the tomb was empty. But, like Peter and John, to whom the women brought the same report, these two were not convinced. They were sufficiently impressed, though, to discuss it between themselves and to report it to this interested stranger.

THE WITNESS OF THE WOMEN

Because of the Jewish culture of the first century, the resurrection accounts in the New Testament are given a special credibility as a result of the women's part in them. If the resurrection were a hoax, the perpetrators of it would *not* have made women the primary witnesses.

In that time and place the testimony of women was regarded as invalid. Describing the Jewish legal system, the first-century Jewish historian Josephus says, "Put not trust in a single witness, but let there be three or at the least two, whose evidence shall be accredited by their past lives. From women let no evidence be accepted, because of the levity and temerity of their sex." While we would disagree with this ancient bias against female witnesses, the fact remains that the bias was a strong part of that culture. Yet all four Gospels say that the women were first to discover the empty tomb, and the Gospel record indicates that it was to women that Jesus first showed himself alive after his resurrection.

If the disciples of Jesus fabricated the story of his resurrection, would they have made women the primary witnesses under the circumstances? Hardly. The best answer as to why the New Testament has the women as the first witnesses of Jesus' resurrection is that it really happened just that way.   —C. B. Mc.

24. "Then some of our companions went to the tomb and found it just as the women had said, but him they did not see."

Here is evident reference to Peter and John, with whom Cleopas and his friend felt a close association. John 20:1-9 and Luke 24:12 tell of their visiting and entering the empty tomb, where they observed the grave clothes neatly abandoned. There they were almost, if not entirely, convinced that Jesus had risen. Jesus actually appeared to Peter some hours later (Luke 24:34; 1 Corinthians 15:5). The women's account was supported by all the evidence, but to Cleopas and his friend it still came short of being fully proved.

We may be grateful for the skepticism with which the first reports of Jesus' resurrection were met. His disciples were not easily convinced. They had to be shown. But when provided with proof beyond question, they committed themselves and all they possessed to spreading the ultimate good news. How silly, in contrast, is the "scholarship" of persons who come along thousands of years later with fabricated theories to explain how the gospel story was started, believed, and followed for centuries without being true!

III. THE LORD TEACHES THE TRUTH (LUKE 24:25-27)

A. LACK OF UNDERSTANDING REBUKED (vv. 25, 26)

25. He said to them, "How foolish you are, and how slow of heart to believe all that the prophets have spoken!

"How could you possibly not know about this?"

Now it was Jesus' turn to express amazement that these good friends did not know or understand the Scriptures with which they were supposedly familiar. They were not hardheaded, stupid fools. They were just slow to catch on to the meanings of messianic Scriptures. They had accepted popular political ideas about the

---

WHAT DO YOU THINK?

The writer says, "We may be grateful for the skepticism with which the first reports of Jesus' resurrection were met." Do you agree or disagree? Why?

Some have suggested that Jesus' disciples were ignorant, superstitious, gullible people and would have been eager to believe reports that he had risen from the dead. How does their skepticism obvious in the gospel accounts disprove this suggestion? In what ways does that confirm your faith in the resurrection?

WHAT DO YOU THINK?

What do you suppose Cleopas and his friend first thought when Jesus said, "How foolish you are, and how slow of heart to believe all that the prophets have spoken"?

Within minutes, of course, he had their attention riveted on the Scriptures and their hearts burning with excitement. When, if ever, would you recommend such an opening in discussing spiritual matters today? What dangers may be associated with it? What positive results can be expected? What factors, besides the words, play a role in how well such an expression is accepted?

WHAT DO YOU THINK?

What these disciples needed was a careful study of the Scriptures. It's the same thing the Jewish leaders needed, but refused (John 5:39). It's the same thing we need today.

What kind of commitment to careful Bible study do you think most Christians have? How can Christians be challenged to more careful study? Do you think more consistent Bible study among all believers would help to bring oneness to all believers in Christ? Why or why not? What other conditions must be present for Bible study to be effective?

PRAYER

Thank you, Lord Jesus, for the blessed privilege of walking with you on the way home. Thank you for listening to my concerns and uncertainties, then rebuking me as I need it, and teaching me your word and your way. Amen.

THOUGHT TO REMEMBER

"Whoever wants to save his life will lose it, but whoever loses his life for me will find it" (Matthew 16:25).

DAILY BIBLE READINGS

Monday, Apr. 1—Before Pilate and Herod (Luke 23:1-12)

Tuesday, Apr. 2—Sentenced to Death (Luke 23:13-25)

Wednesday, Apr. 3—Nailed to the Cross (Luke 23:26-38)

Thursday, Apr. 4—Wonderful Promise (Luke 23:39-43)

Friday, Apr. 5—Death of a "Good Man" (Luke 23:44-49)

Saturday, Apr. 6—Buried (Luke 23:50-56)

Sunday, Apr. 7—The Resurrection (Luke 24:1-12)

Messiah rather than study what God's messengers said. The *prophets* here included all the inspired Old Testament writers—Moses, David, and Solomon, as well as those known as prophets, such as Isaiah, Jeremiah, Micah, and Daniel.

What really is the basis of our religious beliefs and practices, and our daily choices? Is it a conviction arising from our own careful study of what the Bible says, or do we simply rest upon the tradition in which we were reared? Could we be guilty of a foolishness similar to what Jesus found in these friends?

26. "Did not the Christ have to suffer these things and then enter his glory?"

The Messiah had to *suffer*—even die—on the way to his *glory*. The clearest indication is in Psalm 22, portraying crucifixion from the viewpoint of the crucified, and Isaiah 53, with its extended description of the Servant's suffering for the sins of others. Then, "He was cut off from the land of the living. . . . He was assigned a grave with the wicked, and with the rich in his death" (Isaiah 53:8, 9). The glory, however, was to follow. God would not abandon him to the grave, nor let his Holy One see decay (Psalm 16:10, 11).

New Testament writers show the theme fulfilled in Jesus (Philippians 2:5-11), and trace that same course for those who would follow him: "If we died with him, we will also live with him; if we endure, we will also reign with him" (2 Timothy 2:11, 12).

B. THE SCRIPTURES EXPLAINED (v. 27)

The walk from Jerusalem to Emmaus would take some two hours. Were Cleopas and his friend halfway there when Jesus joined them? We may be sure that he did most of the talking as they went on. Perhaps they slowed their pace and wished that they had longer to be with this stranger.

27. And beginning with Moses and all the Prophets, he explained to them what was said in all the Scriptures concerning himself.

The Lord was talking about Jesus of Nazareth, the Messiah, but his hearers didn't yet know who was talking. Afterward they said, "Were not our hearts burning within us while he talked with us on the road and opened the Scriptures to us?" (Luke 24:32). The written Word of God was explained to them by the living Word. They weren't bored by the lecture!

Beginning with Moses, that is, the part of the Scriptures written by Moses. Jesus surely mentioned Satan's bruising of the woman's offspring (Genesis 3:15), and the symbolism of the Passover lamb (Exodus 12), and the promise of the coming prophet to whom the people must give heed (Deuteronomy 18:15, 18). He surely noticed David's prophetic references and Isaiah's promise of the virgin-born ruler (7:14) and the serving messenger (61:1-3). He may have mentioned the ruler coming from Bethlehem (Micah 5:2), the son called out of Egypt (Hosea 11:1) and many others.

Jesus had profound respect for the Old Testament Scriptures, but he did not hesitate to declare to the Jewish leaders, "You diligently study the Scriptures because you think that by them you possess eternal life. These are the Scriptures that testify about me" (John 5:39). The life is in the living Lord.

CONCLUSION

Readers of Luke 24 are introduced to unknown walkers on their way to an unknown village. They benefit from the introduction because of an hour spent with the risen Lord. Is there a better claim to fame than to be numbered among those who walk with the resurrected Savior? In him there is no such thing as a nobody. And there is room in the company of Cleopas for any who will earnestly consider and accept the claims of the living Lord.

Discovery Learning

This page contains an alternate lesson plan emphasizing learning activities. Classes desiring such student involvement will find these suggestions helpful. The next page is a reproducible activity page to further enhance discovery learning.

LEARNING GOALS

As a result of participating in today's lesson, a student will be able to:

1. Summarize Jesus' conversation with the disciples on the Emmaus road.

2. Explain how God's Word (prophecy) reveals truths about Jesus—to the two and to us.

3. Express trust in the testimony of God's Word concerning Jesus.

INTO THE LESSON

Distribute copies of the reproducible page 284. Give students about two minutes to solve the puzzle, "Sorting It Out" ; then ask for someone to reveal the solution. The correct answer is "Christ the Lord is risen." There is nothing surprising about that statement, especially in a Sunday school classroom on Easter Sunday. But it was big news to the men in our lesson!

INTO THE WORD

Have the class members read Luke 24:13-27 silently. When they have finished, refer them to the second activity, "Order, Please," on the reproducible page distributed earlier. Ask them to arrange the statements chronologically without looking at the text. (The correct order is 1, E; 2, H, 3, J; 4, A; 5, C; 6, F; 7, I; 8, B; 9, K; 10, D; 11, G.)

Review by discussing the following questions:

• Who were these two disciples? (*One was named Cleopas, but the name of the other is not given. All that is known is in this text.* Apparently they were closely associated with the Twelve—vv. 22, 23. Could the one not named have been one of the Twelve? It's possible, but not likely. The two most likely lived in Emmaus, and the apostles were all from Galilee, except Judas Iscariot.)

• What were the two disciples discussing on their way to Emmaus? (*The events associated with Jesus' death and reports of his resurrection.* Discuss what that conversation must have been like—the excitement; the wanting to believe but apparent inability to do so, the gestures, etc. It must have been a lively and engrossing discussion.)

• Why did they not recognize Jesus? (*Apparently the Lord prevented them from it. Mark says he appeared "in a different form."* Discuss why Jesus would not want to be recognized. Would there have been any conversation and teaching if they had immediately recognized him, or just a very emotional reunion?)

• What was wrong with the disciples' description of Jesus? (*They identified him only as a "prophet." He was, and is, much more.* They had believed he was the Messiah, but now they did not [v. 21]. Perhaps they had even believed Jesus was the Son of God [Matthew 16:16]. If so, they had changed their view on that, too. The crucifixion had dashed all their hopes and crushed their faith.)

• What had kept the two disciples from understanding why Jesus had to die and that he would be raised again? (*Though the text does not say, they probably were looking for a political leader to set up an earthly kingdom, just as others were.* [See Mark 10:35-45; Luke 19:11; John 6:15; Acts 1:6.]

• Why were they now so sad and skeptical? (*Their inaccurate expectations had not been met, so they became sad and lost hope.* So today, when one's expectations are based on mistaken interpretation of Scripture, one may miss the wonderful blessings of God!)

INTO LIFE

Give the class a copy of the following list of Old Testament Scriptures. Have them look up each reference and read what each one says about the Messiah. Jesus probably cited at least some of these in explaining his mission to the two disciples!

Genesis 3:15

Psalm 16:10

Psalm 22:1

Psalm 22:16

Isaiah 53:5

Ask, "What problems in the world do you believe may be symptoms of the world's not believing the Bible?" Make a list of their answers, and discuss how Christians may be able to address these issues with Scriptural solutions. Naturally, this could become a very long list. Keep this discussion brief, however, as the next question is also significant.

Ask, "What problems in the church do you believe may be symptoms of Christians' not believing or understanding the Bible?" Point out that we, like the two on the road to Emmaus, may approach Bible study with preconceived notions that are not consistent with the Bible's real message. Discuss how we can strip away such false expectations and get to the truth—and then act on it.

Conclude by reading verse 27 aloud. Urge the class members to study God's Word regularly and make it the sole basis of their faith in Jesus.

Sorting It Out

Jesus chided the two on the road to Emmaus for not understanding the prophetic message about him. "How foolish you are, and how slow of heart to believe ... the prophets," he said.

Remove the letters of that statement—in order—from the grid below. The remaining letters will reveal a message that they needed, as we need yet today, to know.

HOCWFOOHLISHYORUAREIANDS

HOWTSLOWOTFHEHARETTOBLE

LORIEVDETIHESPRROPIHESTESN

Write the solution below.

Order, Please

Read Luke 24:13-27. Then arrange the statements below in chronological order. Try to do it without looking at your Bible.

_____ A. Cleopas asked, "Are you only a visitor ... and do not know the things that have happened?"

_____ B. "We had hoped that he was the one who was going to redeem Israel."

_____ C. Jesus asked, "What things?"

_____ D. Jesus said the disciples were "foolish ... and slow of heart to believe ... the prophets."

_____ E. Two disciples began walking to Emmaus.

_____ F. The disciples referred to Jesus a "a prophet, powerful in word and deed."

_____ G. Jesus explained the Scriptures about himself.

_____ H. Jesus joined the two disciples on the road.

_____ I. The disciples told how Jesus was crucified.

_____ J. Jesus asked the disciples what they were discussing.

_____ K. The disciples related the women's report of seeing angels at the empty tomb.

Check the Scripture and see how well you did. Getting the Scriptural facts straight is important, as Jesus told the two disciples!

THE LOVING GOD

LESSON 7

WHY TEACH THIS LESSON?

Seeking the lost. It's as natural as searching for an animal that has wandered away. It's as common as looking for a coin that has been dropped and has rolled out of sight. It happens every day.

Seeking the lost? Who, me? That's the preacher's job! That's what we pay him for, isn't it? That requires special training!

Somehow, when it's to our own advantage, seeking the lost is natural. But when it is for the Lord, some people back off fast. But if we really had a heart like our Father's, we would rejoice in the finding of the lost. It would *be* to our advantage to see the lost saved. It is hoped that this lesson can share that concept with your students and enlist them in the seeking and the celebrating!

INTRODUCTION

A. INTRODUCING THE FATHER

"Dad, this is the work crew I have been telling you about. Fellows, meet my father." That's a plain introduction. There shouldn't be anything hard about it.

Jesus had been working for years at just that kind of introduction; but on the evening before he must leave to go back home, one of his crew said they would be satisfied if only the Lord would show his Father to them (John 14:8). Jesus had just been talking about preparing lodgings for them in His Father's house, and providing the way for them to get there. By his words, works, and character Jesus had revealed his Father to them; he had assured them that he was not only *like* his Father, he was totally one *with* him. A more thorough introduction would be impossible.

That introduction, extended to all mankind, was the purpose for which Jesus came into the world. He had come to give eternal life; and "this is eternal life: that they may know you, the only true God" (John 17:3).

The essential character of the Father in Heaven is love (1 John 4:8). It was love that led him to give his one and only Son for the salvation of mankind (John 3:16). It is love that impels him to seek out and invite sinners to the eternal banquet he has prepared for them (Luke 14:15-24). That searching and rejoicing love is the central quality of the Father to whom Jesus introduces us in Luke 15.

B. LESSON BACKGROUND

The teachings recorded in Luke 14 and 15 are closely tied in time and subject. They were given during Jesus' later ministry in Perea, east of the Jordan, before he went to Bethany to raise Lazarus from the dead (John 11).

The subject discussed in Luke 14 and 15—the conflict between the religious leaders' proud superiority and Jesus' ministry among the people they despised—is not limited, however, in time or in location. That conflict had surfaced many months earlier in Galilee when Jesus accepted Matthew's invitation to a dinner with many of his disreputable friends (Luke 5:27-32). It was the conflict between Jesus and those who "were confident of their own righteousness and looked down on everybody else" (Luke 18:9). That conflict reached a final severity in Jerusalem when Jesus told those leaders that tax collectors and prostitutes would precede

DEVOTIONAL READING
LUKE 15:11-24
LESSON SCRIPTURE
LUKE 15:1-10
PRINTED TEXT
LUKE 15:1-10

Apr 14

LESSON AIMS

This study should prepare the student to:

1. *Compare the lost coin and the lost sheep parables.*

2. *Explain how Christians today might be like the various people in the parable.*

3. *Name ways to seek and to encourage the lost.*

KEY VERSE

I tell you, there is rejoicing in the presence of the angels of God over one sinner who repents.
—Luke 15:10

HOW TO SAY IT

Akha. AH-kuh.
Caesarea. Sess-uh-REE-uh.
Cornelius. Kor-NEE-lih-us
   or Kor-NEEL-yus.
denarius. dih-nair-ee-us.
drachma. DRAK-ma.
Perea. Peh-REE-uh.

WHAT DO YOU THINK?

The Pharisees were eager to keep themselves separate from "sinners," and they criticized Jesus for not taking the same attitude. Paul, in fact, warns: "Do not be misled: 'Bad company corrupts good character'" (1 Corinthians 15:33).

What, then, should be our attitude toward and conduct with "sinners"—those who practice homosexuality or adultery, those who indulge in excessive use of alcohol, or those who engage in criminal activity, for example? How can we follow Jesus' approach without being "misled" as Paul warned?

OPTION

Use the reproducible activity "Lost, Lost, Lost!" on page 292 to compare the three parables in Luke 15.

them in God's kingdom because those disreputable people had repented at the preaching of John the Baptist, and the priests and rulers had rejected it (Matthew 21:31, 32).

I. RECEIVING THE "WRONG PEOPLE" (LUKE 15:1-3)

1. Now the tax collectors and "sinners" were all gathering around to hear him.

Tax collectors were Jews employed by the Roman authorities to collect the duties imposed by Rome. They were despised as traitors to their own nation and for making themselves rich by charging more than they were authorized to collect (Luke 3:12, 13). *Sinners* were those people who for any of several reasons were outside the Jewish religious community. Persons of loose morals and bad behavior, and irreligious persons would be included.

These were not welcomed in the synagogues. But Jesus welcomed them, and they came from great distances to hear him. Having come with that purpose, they listened attentively to what he had to say. Church people should bring the same serious purpose to their church attendance—to hear the Word of God.

2. But the Pharisees and the teachers of the law muttered, "This man welcomes sinners and eats with them."

Pharisees. The name derives from a word meaning "separated." They were zealous keepers and advocates of the Mosaic law. Jesus came into conflict with their legalism, which emphasized outward conformity to ceremonies and practices, often to the neglect of spirit and purpose. The joyous love of God was foreign to them.

Teachers of the law were the scribes who made hand-lettered copies of the Scriptures. Their interest in the Scriptures led naturally to their being teachers of the law. Their skills and interests made them natural partners with the Pharisees, and therefore critical of Jesus' departures from legalistic tradition.

Luke's language here describes the critics' complaint as a continuous grumbling among themselves against Jesus. *This man welcomes sinners and eats with them.* In the thinking of the scribes and Pharisees, to welcome any contact with a sinner would seem like approval of the sin; it would defile the person accepting the sinner's company, and would bring condemnation.

He *eats with them.* Here was the chief complaint against Jesus. Eating with another person still indicates a measure of acceptance and intimacy that is not found in casual conversation, or even social visiting in another's home. The idea is strong in the roots of our word, *companion,* which comes from the Latin for bread eaten together. When the apostle Peter was rebuked by the Jewish Christians in Jerusalem for being too friendly with the Gentile household of Cornelius (Acts 11:2, 3), the chief complaint was that he had eaten with them.

What determines our choices of dinner companions? Business advantage? Social advancement? Convenience? The advancement of Christ's kingdom? How comfortable are we with Jesus' way of doing things, such as making up our guest lists among the homeless? (See Luke 14:12-14.)

3. Then Jesus told them this parable:

Jesus did not need to be informed about what the Pharisees and teachers were thinking and saying among themselves. He knew, just as on other occasions (Luke 5:22; 6:8). We must never think that our God does not know what we are doing, or saying, or thinking, or suffering. He knows all too well our dissatisfaction with his way of doing things.

The *parable* that follows, occupying the rest of chapter 15, is actually three parables in one, each emphasizing the concern of the loving God for that which is lost, and his joy at the recovery of such a one. The first two (verses 4-10) are not the kind of stories we usually identify as parables, but still provide commonplace comparisons with eternal truth.

II. JOY AT FINDING A LOST SHEEP (LUKE 15:4-7)

Jesus' parable dealt with matters familiar to his audience. But many today may not grasp the full meaning in the imagery he used. How many of us have owned or tended sheep?

Here we need the Bible to help us understand the Bible! We might start with Psalm 23, and learn to depend on the Lord as Shepherd for leading, protecting, and the finding of daily nourishment. We need to ponder the Good Shepherd who lives with and protects his sheep, even to laying down his life for them (John 10:1-18). Jeremiah 31:10-20 and Ezekiel 34:11-16 will instruct us both in the shepherd's care for his flock and in God's care for his people. We need that instruction, too, in order to understand the church leader's responsibility among the people he serves (Acts 20:28-31; 1 Peter 5:1-5).

A. CARE FOR ONE IN A HUNDRED (v. 4)

4. "Suppose one of you has a hundred sheep and loses one of them. Does he not leave the ninety-nine in the open country and go after the lost sheep until he finds it?

One of you. If Saul of Tarsus, a rigid Pharisee (Acts 26:5), was also a maker of tents (Acts 18:3), we may suppose that some of the Pharisees and teachers of the law now facing Jesus were keepers of sheep. At least they lived among shepherds enough to appreciate their intimate involvement with their flocks. These men might be heartless in their application of the law toward their fellowmen, but they had a tender feeling toward their animals. Jesus made his appeal to that tender spot. His hearers' response, in feeling if not in words, would indicate the nature of God and answer their grumblings against himself.

And loses one of them. The loss of one percent of any possession would not seem important until the owner recognizes the individuality and the peculiar value of what is lost. The good shepherd calls his sheep by name (John 10:3), and does not regard any as a mere statistic. So it is with God.

Any lost item may assume a peculiar quality. Almost any of us will become disturbed and spend important time looking for relatively unimportant items. When, on the other hand, the lost item is not replaceable, as an heirloom or a child, the concern takes on a whole new aspect. With God, no person is replaceable.

Leave the ninety-nine in the open country. Jesus raised no questions about the shepherd's putting the flock at risk by leaving them in the open pasture land. That was not an issue in the parable. Jesus' focus was on finding the lost. The search for a missing child may leave the rest of the family feeling neglected, but they will be cared for when the emergency has been met.

Go after the lost sheep until he finds it. The search acknowledges only one purpose, and is not complete until it is successful. The parable is not truly understood until we feel the wrench of lostness as it applies to a person out of contact with Christ, "the Shepherd and Overseer of your souls" (1 Peter 2:25).

B. CELEBRATING THE RETURN (vv. 5, 6)

5, 6. "And when he finds it, he joyfully puts it on his shoulders and goes home. Then he calls his friends and neighbors together and says, 'Rejoice with me; I have found my lost sheep.'

Celebration begins with the recovery of the lost sheep. Luke 15 is filled with happy endings, except for those persons who refuse to join in Heaven's rejoicing (Luke 15:25-30).

OPTION

The reproducible activity "Sheep and Shepherds" on page 292 will help your students read for themselves what the Bible teaches about the role of the shepherd in protecting the sheep.

WHAT DO YOU THINK?

Recall the last time you misplaced something and had to search for quite some time before you found it. What emotions did you feel? Panic? Frustration? What?

What was the real value of that item? How does it compare to the value of a human soul? Why do you think we do not display more concern for lost souls than we do for lost car keys or some other item? How can we more fully appreciate—and act on—the value of the lost souls all around us?

Visual 7 illustrates the joy of the shepherd who has found his sheep (v. 6).

Rejoice with me; for I have found my sheep which was lost.
Luke 15:6

WHAT DO YOU THINK?

If we do not fully appreciate the condition of the lost, how can we appreciate the wonderful state of the redeemed? Is the response of your congregation when someone accepts the gospel anything like the celebration of the shepherd with his friends? Why or why not? How many Christians do you know who express the joy of their own salvation? Could it be that many of us just don't understand how bad it is to be "lost" and how good it is to be "saved"? What changes would take place in our worship and our evangelistic efforts if most Christians demonstrated a full appreciation for what it is to be saved and how tragic it is for even one to be lost? How can we start to make some of those changes?

The laying of the lost one on the shepherd's shoulder provides a natural, vivid, and tender detail. Even if the lost one was able to walk, the carrying would provide comfort and assurance, besides speeding the return home. Back home, the celebration goes beyond personal gladness to become a neighborhood party. "Come and celebrate with me!" Such rejoicing has to be shared.

The Lord did not say how the shepherd's invitation might have been accepted by the neighbors, or how many would join in the celebration. Some might come because they were glad the sheep was found; some because they were glad the shepherd felt so good about it; some for a "good time." And some would stay at home, talking about the shepherd's foolishness in going to so much trouble over one sheep.

The neighbors' responses would certainly depend on their regard for the shepherd. The ones who loved him most would join most heartily with him in his rejoicing. And that brings us to the conclusion Jesus presented.

CARRIED TO SAFETY

Most of us have heard or read of accounts of dogs that have shown great courage in protecting human beings or in rescuing them from life-threatening situations.

One such dog was a Chesapeake Bay retriever owned by the Homme family of Livingston, Montana. One day in 1978, Mrs. Homme was washing dishes as she watched her five-year-old son, Kenny, who was playing in the backyard. Suddenly Mrs. Homme noticed that Kenny was gone. She ran outside and heard Kenny shouting for help from a surging creek in back of their house. The boy had fallen down an embankment and into a creek swollen from recent rains.

The Hommes' dog, Chester, was already in the water trying to save the boy. As the dog swam toward Kenny, the water swept the child into a culvert. Chester fought the raging current for ten minutes before finally reaching the boy. Kenny grabbed Chester's fur twice but lost his grip both times. Finally Kenny was able to climb onto the dog's back, and Chester carried him out of the culvert to shore.

Mankind was drowning in the surging current of sin, headed toward the endless tunnel of Hell. Had Jesus not entered this world to carry us to safety, we surely would have perished in the flood. —C. B. Mc.

C. HEAVEN'S REJOICING (v. 7)

7. "I tell you that in the same way there will be more rejoicing in heaven over one sinner who repents than over ninety-nine righteous persons who do not need to repent.

Up to this point Jesus' argument had been developed in the minds of the hearers as they supposed themselves to be be the shepherd. Such a one would surely find pleasure in possessing a sizable flock, safe and sound; but *rejoicing,* beginning with the shepherd and involving his neighbors, would attend the recovering of one that had been lost.

The Lord spoke now on his own authority, declaring that the loving God feels the same way about people. He is pleased with dependable good behavior on the part of any, but his greater rejoicing—shared with the angels in Heaven and his loving friends on earth—attends the return of a penitent sinner to his care and presence.

Righteous persons who do not need to repent might include persons such as the parents of John the Baptist, "upright [i.e., righteous] in the sight of God, observing all the Lord's commandments and regulations blamelessly" (Luke 1:6), or Cornelius of Caesarea, devout and generous (Acts 10:1, 2); yet even these would acknowledge their need of constant care, guidance, and correction from their heavenly Shepherd. It seems clear that Jesus was thinking of the Pharisees, scribes, and persons like them, those who were "confident of their own righteousness" (Luke 18:9) and recognized no need for repentance. God has no pleasure, of course, in such pride. These persons are represented in the older brother of the returned wanderer (Luke 15:25-32), who may have been as virtuous as he thought he was, but had no loving rapport with his father and refused to share with him in celebrating the wanderer's return.

III. JOY AT FINDING A LOST COIN (LUKE 15:8-10)

To emphasize the point he was making, Jesus continued his parable and changed the scene and the actors. The person suffering the loss and celebrating the return is no longer a man outdoors but a woman at home. The loss is not a living creature wandering astray, but a lifeless possession misplaced. The course of action is the same, and the conclusion the same.

A. CONCERN FOR ONE IN TEN (v. 8)

8. *"Or suppose a woman has ten silver coins and loses one. Does she not light a lamp, sweep the house and search carefully until she finds it?*

The *silver* piece mentioned here was a Greek coin called a drachma. It seems that the drachma was equivalent to the Roman denarius, which amounted to a day's wage for a soldier or laborer. The fact that there were *ten* coins may have no special significance. This simply may have been the woman's (perhaps widow's) available household funds. One student of customs in Bible lands has pointed out, however, that a woman's marriage dowry could include coins worked into a dress or a circlet around the head. These would establish her status as a married woman and would remain as her possession even if the marriage were dissolved by divorce. The loss of one coin in such case could seriously mar the symbolism as well as the value of her possession.

Members of the Akha tribe in the hills of northern Thailand in 1992 showed special interest in this passage from Luke. There an Akha woman in tribal costume wears a headdress including a circlet of nine silver coins. This identifies her marriage status, and the loss of even one coin from the circlet would be a great embarrassment. It would also reduce the "good" odd number nine to the "bad" even number eight. In any such circumstance the loss of one coin would be regarded very seriously.

In a modest house familiar to Jesus' hearers the candle and broom would be appropriate tools for an all-out search. If the house had any windows, they would have been few and small. Most likely it would have a dirt floor.

As in the case of the shepherd, the search would continue until the lost was found.

B. CELEBRATING THE FIND (v. 9)

9. *"And when she finds it, she calls her friends and neighbors together and says, 'Rejoice with me; I have found my lost coin.'*

In the preceding parable a man experienced the loss; here it is a woman. Jesus didn't want to leave out anyone as He exhorted all to join with Him and the Father in seeking and saving the lost.

Did the woman accept responsibility in speaking of the *lost coin*? Perhaps so, but the loss was hers, whether by carelessness, by accident, or by the act of another person. Similarly, God experiences the loss in his family and seeks the return of the absentee, whatever or whoever caused the departure.

C. HEAVEN'S REJOICING (v. 10)

10. *"In the same way, I tell you, there is rejoicing in the presence of the angels of God over one sinner who repents."*

WHAT DO YOU THINK?

For most of us the loss of a single coin would be a minor problem. But what if we were to lose fifty dollars or so, which is closer to the value of the coin in the parable? What if we lost the equivalent of a full day's wages? If, as some scholars believe, the coin was part of the woman's dowry, and therefore was a symbol of her married status, how much would she have prized that coin? What does that suggest about God's attitude toward individual sinners? Maybe we can't save everyone, or even large numbers, but what does this parable suggest about the need to be diligent to save even one person at a time? What can we do this week to apply this principle?

WHAT DO YOU THINK?

Christians sometimes dampen their enthusiasm for Heaven by fretting over questions such as these: "How will we know each other there?" "How will we feel if loved ones are missing from Heaven?" "How will we escape the embarrassment of remembering our earthly sins?" How does the picture here of the rejoicing that goes on in Heaven help you to allay those concerns? (See also Revelation 21:4.) How might this picture help you to encourage another to accept Christ?

PRAYER OF A RELUCTANT REJOICER

Help us, please, our loving God, to see your world and your people as you see them—their lostness when separated from you, and their loveliness when they come home. May we learn to share your concern over anyone who strays and your celebration at that person's return. In Jesus your Son. Amen.

THOUGHT TO REMEMBER

Friends of the Good Shepherd will rejoice with him when a lost sheep is brought home.

DAILY BIBLE READINGS

Monday, Apr. 8—The Importance of One (Matthew 18:10-14)

Tuesday, Apr. 9—Lost Sheep Returned (1 Peter 2:18-25)

Wednesday, Apr. 10—Sinners Called to Repentance (Luke 5:27-32)

Thursday, Apr. 11—Sought and Saved (Luke 19:1-10)

Friday, Apr. 12—Freely Restored (Luke 15:11-24)

Saturday, Apr. 13—Petty Self-Righteousness (Luke 15:25-32)

Sunday, Apr. 14—Contending Loyalties (Luke 16:1-13)

Like verse 7, this verse speaks of the joy in Heaven over one sinner who repents and returns to God's family. Unlike verse 7, there is no comparison here with any other circumstance. Does Jesus mean to say that the angels themselves rejoice when a sinner is converted? Perhaps so. There are Scriptures that indicate the angels' interest in our salvation. (See Matthew 18:10; Luke 2:10-14; 1 Peter 1:12; Revelation 3:5.) The main point of Jesus' teaching in this chapter, however, is that God, in whose presence the angels dwell, seeks sinners and rejoices when one who was lost is found.

Contrary to some popular opinions, Heaven is not dull. It is characterized by celebration of God's victorious goodness, now and forever. Don't stay away!

LOST FOREVER

The English mathematician and physicist Sir Isaac Newton gave the world many of its most important scientific discoveries. He invented calculus, advanced the field of optics, and devised the laws of motion and of universal gravitation. The publication of his works marked an epoch in the history of science.

Newton authored one manuscript that the world will never see, however, for it was accidentally destroyed. While teaching at Cambridge University, Newton once left his rooms and forgot that a burning candle remained on his desk. It is thought that his pet dog overturned the candle and set the papers on fire. By the time Newton returned to his rooms, the manuscript had been consumed in the flames.

The parables of the lost sheep and the lost coin are two of several stories Jesus told about lost objects, all designed to convey God's concern for lost people. The loss of money, property, or even a valuable scientific manuscript may make us poorer, but nothing can compare with the tragedy of a soul eternally lost. Understandable, then, is the rejoicing in Heaven when one sinner returns to God. —C. B. Mc.

CONCLUSION

A. THE REST OF THE STORY

Our loving God cares for the lost. He rejoices when they are found. His people are expected to share in his rejoicing. This is the message spoken and demonstrated by Jesus to answer the objections raised against his spending time with the people who did not qualify for approval in the synagogue. To the lost sheep the shepherd stands in the relationship of God to a lost sinner. To the lost coin the searching woman likewise stands in the relationship of God to a lost sinner. But that relationship is more forcefully represented in a father who permitted his younger son to take his inheritance to waste it far from home, and then welcomed the lad with extravagant celebration when he came home (Luke 15:11-24). Jesus' reply to his critics was not complete, however, until he identified them as the stay-at-home son who refused to join in that celebration (Luke 15:25-32).

We have seen the character and concern of the loving God as shown in Christ, who came "to seek and to save what was lost" (Luke 19:10). We must determine how we are going to relate to him in those concerns. That is the rest of the story.

B. DRAW YOUR OWN CONCLUSIONS

Jesus' skill as a teacher is uniquely demonstrated in the questions he asked, bringing out from others the principles, conclusions, and judgments they would not accept if he presented them. His questions, explicit and implied, were the vehicle for his teaching that we are considering in this lesson. How shall we respond to him? To which will we give more attention: a lost wallet or a lost neighbor? Draw your own conclusions.

Discovery Learning

*This page contains an alternate lesson plan emphasizing learning activities. Classes
desiring such student involvement will find these suggestions helpful. The next page
is a reproducible activity page to further enhance discovery learning.*

LEARNING GOALS

As a result of participating in today's lesson, a student
will be able to:

1. Compare the lost coin and the lost sheep parables.

2. Explain how we might be like the various people in
the parable.

3. Name ways to seek and to encourage the lost.

INTO THE LESSON

During the week before class, recruit two of the class
members to be ready to act out the two "seeking and
finding" roles of Jesus' parables in Luke 15:1-10. Suggest
that they be creative, dramatizing the stories as the text allows. Tell them that they will perform their roles during
the Bible study part of the session.

To begin this session, distribute sheets of paper on which
you have copied a large circle and the following labels: 1.
"crooks" and prostitutes; 2. government officials; 3. general public; 4. close friends and followers; 5. others.

Ask the students to make pie charts showing how they
think Jesus would divide his time among those groups if
he were here today (a larger piece of "pie" means more
time). Not all five groups have to be used.

Ask, "How much of the "pie" did you allot for group
1? Discuss how much time Jesus would spend with this
group. As class members share their points of agreement
or disagreement, encourage as many as possible to get involved in the discussion. The point is to get everyone
thinking about the context of these parables of Jesus.

INTO THE WORD

Have everyone read Luke 15:1, 2 silently: then ask this
series of questions:

Who were these people who came to hear Jesus? (See
comments under verse 1.)

Why were the Pharisees and scribes upset? (*They believed that it was sinful to associate with sinful people and that
by eating with such persons Jesus gave approval to their sins.*)

Use the question labeled "What Do You Think?" on
page 286 to discuss the issue of keeping separate from
the world vs. getting involved in people's lives.

Tell the class that the two short parables of Jesus that
form our lesson text bear on this subject. Introduce the
class member who at this time will portray the shepherd
seeking one lost sheep. Next, introduce the class member to portray the woman searching for her lost coin.

When she has finished, express appreciation for both
performances.

Have a volunteer read Luke 15:3-10 aloud to the class.
Then ask the class members to work in pairs to develop
three questions the Pharisees and scribes might have
wanted to ask concerning the parables. (Examples:
Weren't the ninety-nine sheep in danger in being left
alone? Isn't God happy that there already are good people? Why would the woman spend so much time and effort over a little coin?) After several have shared their
questions, point out that all such questions miss Jesus'
point. Then ask, "What is Jesus' point?" (The loving God
is seeking his lost people, and their return is cause for
great joy.)

OPTION

Use the reproducible activity "Lost, Lost, Lost!" on
page 292.

INTO LIFE

Give each student a copy of a chart like the one shown
below. By circling a number from one to five, each student
indicates to what extent he or she identifies with the "characters" in today's text. (One means "I'm not at all like this
one," and five means "I'm very much like this one.")

The tax collectors/sinners	1	2	3	4	5
The Pharisees/scribes	1	2	3	4	5
The lost sheep	1	2	3	4	5
The shepherd	1	2	3	4	5
The woman who lost the coin	1	2	3	4	5
The friends/neighbors	1	2	3	4	5

When all have completed their charts, divide the class
into groups of three or four students each. Ask each person in each group to take thirty seconds to explain his or
her highest scores (for example, why he or she identifies
with the shepherd, the friends/neighbors, etc.).

Mention that today's text has to do with seeking the
lost and restoring them to fellowship with God. Divide the
class into two groups: the "Search Party" and the "Cheer-
ing Section." Have the class members in the former group
discuss ways Christians today can reach out with the
gospel to those lost and dying in sin. Have those in the
other group discuss ways to help new Christians feel welcome in the church. After five or ten minutes let all share
their conclusions. Close with the prayer that each class
member will become involved in both efforts.

Lost, Lost, Lost!

There are actually three parables in one in Luke 15. Use the chart below to compare the three and to see the common message.

TEXT	VERSES 4-7	VERSES 8-10	VERSES 11-32
What was lost?			
How was it found?			
What was the response when it was found?			
What is unique about this parable (compared with the other two)?			
What is the central idea?			

Sheep and Shepherds

Look up the following Scriptures and summarize what each says about the care of a shepherd for his sheep.

Psalm 23

Jeremiah 31:10-20

Ezekiel 34:11-16

John 10:1-18

Teachings of Jesus

Unit 2. Teachings About God

(Lessons 6-9)

THE GOOD SHEPHERD

LESSON 8

WHY TEACH THIS LESSON?

'Twas a sheep, not a lamb, that strayed away
   In the parable Jesus told;
A grown-up sheep that had gone astray
   From the ninety and nine in the fold.

Out on the hillside, out in the cold,
   'Twas a sheep the Good Shepherd sought;
And back to the flock, safe in the fold,
   'Twas a sheep the Good Shepherd brought.

Many of us have heard the Parable of the Good Shepherd since we were very young. That's no reason to dismiss it as a children's story. We all have a tendency to wander off and not to follow the Shepherd. Use this lesson to challenge your class—and yourself—to a new commitment to the Lord.

INTRODUCTION

A. FOLLOW WHAT LEADER?

Do you remember the old game called "Follow the Leader"? The leader liked to choose a course or perform feats that others couldn't accomplish, and so they would have to fall out. Proud indeed was the one who could not be thrown off the track, and so might become the next leader for the group. The game was good to develop some abilities, but it could be unkind to some.

Even without that game, we will probably always be following leaders. In that, we resemble sheep, whose tendency to move in flocks of followers is well known.

What leader shall we follow? That question is best answered in today's lesson, introducing Jesus as the Good Shepherd, who not only leads by direction and example, but gives his very life to caring for those who elect to follow him.

B. OF SHEEP AND SHEPHERDS

Domestic sheep need a great deal of care. They are virtually helpless against wild beasts, including wolves and big cats. They are subject to disease and to wandering far from sources of food and water. In unfenced areas they need the constant care of shepherds, who come to know the animals by name through daily association.

Scripture abounds in references to God's people as his sheep needing and receiving his care: "We are his people, the sheep of his pasture" (Psalm 100:3); "The Lord is my shepherd; I shall not be in want" (Psalm 23:1). The prophets Isaiah (40:11), Jeremiah (23:1-4), Ezekiel (34:1-19), and Zechariah (11:17) expand on the theme of God's shepherding of his people, his expectation that his religious leaders will exercise the same care, and his rebuke to those who care more for themselves than for their flocks.

C. LESSON BACKGROUND

Our lesson today continues the story that occupied John 9: the healing of a man born blind, with the discussion that followed it. John 9:39-41 tells that certain

DEVOTIONAL READING
JOHN 10:31-42

LESSON SCRIPTURE
JOHN 10:1-30.

PRINTED TEXT
JOHN 10:1-18

LESSON AIMS

This lesson should enable the student to:

1. Explain the significance of the parable's sheep-related statements.

2. Describe the shepherd/sheep relationship we can have with Jesus.

3. Express a commitment to follow the Good Shepherd.

Apr
21

WHAT DO YOU THINK?

Since sheep are weak and foolish creatures, the sheep metaphor may not seem very complimentary. But it is accurate. Think of the following attributes of sheep. How are we like them in relation to our Good Shepherd, Jesus?

• *Weakness.*

• *Lack of natural defenses.*

• *Tendency to wander.*

• *Inability to find good food and water.*

• *Susceptibility to disease.*

KEY VERSE

I am the good shepherd. The good shepherd lays down his life for the sheep. —John 10:11

OPTION

Your students who do cross-word puzzles will enjoy the repro-ducible activity on page 300. Use it to introduce the lesson or as a review to be completed after class. The solution follows.

ACROSS	DOWN
2. Thief	1. Kill
3. Voice	4. Opens
5. Calls	6. Listen
7. Steal	7. Sheep
10. Pasture	8. Figure
11. Saved	9. Destroy
12. Father	13. Nothing
17. One	14. Cares
20. Authority	15. Command
21. Gate	16. Life
23. Name	18. Enter
24. Wolf	19. Abandons
25. Shepherd	22. Pen

WHAT DO YOU THINK?

How do Christians today rec-ognize the voice of the Shepherd? What other voices are calling to them today? How do we distin-guish between all the conflicting voices calling to us?

Pharisees who were following Jesus with varying degrees of interest objected to his suggestion that they were spiritually blind. He responded by talking about the Good Shepherd in contrast to sheep-stealers and hired hands, and the Pharisees didn't see what he meant (John 10:6). When he finished, some of them thought he was crazy; but some of them disagreed, arguing that a crazy man couldn't give sight to a man who was born blind (John 10:19-21). So we look at what Jesus said that caused his hearers to argue as they did.

I. THIEVES AND THE SHEPHERD (JOHN 10:1-5)

A. THE INTRUDER VS. THE OWNER (vv. 1, 2)

1, 2. "I tell you the truth, the man who does not enter the sheep pen by the gate, but climbs in by some other way, is a thief and a robber. The man who enters by the gate is the shepherd of his sheep.

The *sheep pen* was typically a walled enclosure providing nighttime protection for several flocks at a time. The walls could be of rock, high enough to keep wild animals from leaping over, and topped with thorns to keep thieves from climbing them. The *gate* was the one opening to the pen. It was guarded by a watchman, usually one of the shepherds, who would sleep in the opening.

Penalties for sheep-stealing were written early into the law of Moses (Exodus 22:1). The *thief* comes to steal by surprise or in secret. The *robber* comes with violence openly, as marauding bands of Midianites plundered Israel in the time of Gideon (Judges 6:1-6). The owner-shepherd of any flock in the fold could come openly to the gate to be recognized and admitted.

B. THE SHEPHERD KNOWN AND FOLLOWED (vv. 3, 4)

3. "The watchman opens the gate for him, and the sheep listen to his voice. He calls his own sheep by name and leads them out.

The shepherd comes each morning to the sheep pen and is admitted by the *watchman*. The gate is opened by the watchman's getting out of it. Most sheep pens did not have an actual hinged *gate* to open. Once the gate is "open," the shepherd starts to call out his own sheep *by name*. He does not even need to enter the pen. The sheep recognize his voice, respond to their names, and come out of the pen to follow him.

To the leader of men it is surely not less important to know and call by name those whom one would lead. It is a skill sometimes used by charlatans, but priceless when it expresses a genuine regard for the person.

4. "When he has brought out all his own, he goes on ahead of them, and his sheep follow him because they know his voice.

Once a shepherd's flock is outside the pen, he *goes on ahead* of it and leads on to the places of pasture, shade, and water, talking as he goes.

In the church the true shepherd leads by example, doing what the sheep have not yet learned to do (1 Peter 5:3); also by teaching, saying what the sheep do not yet know or believe. The false teacher, on the other hand, will lead the flock astray (Acts 20:30), or say only those things the people already know or wish to hear (2 Timothy 4:3).

RECOGNIZING THE MASTER'S VOICE

Imagine being able to tell your computer to program your VCR, pay the phone bill, schedule a lunch date, or fetch your electronic mail. Such technology will be widely available at work and at home in the near future. Already AT&T has begun installing computerized voice recognition systems that can recognize words like "collect" and "person to person" about as well as a human operator can.

Though a computer that recognizes human voices will bring revolutionary changes to the way we work and transact business, a more revolutionary change takes place when a person learns to recognize the voice of Jesus in his or her own life. The Lord said that his sheep would know his voice and would follow him. Later on in the Gospel of John (14:25, 26 and 16:12-14), Jesus promised that the Holy Spirit would guide his apostles to record his teaching for future generations of believers. When we read the New Testament, we do something far more amazing than a computer that understands human speech. We hear the very voice of Jesus directing our lives in the way of eternal life.   —C. B. Mc.

C. STRANGERS ARE REJECTED (v. 5)

5. "But they will never follow a stranger; in fact, they will run away from him because they do not recognize a stranger's voice."

The sound of the voice that has accompanied care, security, and provision makes the difference between the sheep's following confidently and running away. The leader in the church needs to be around long enough to build confidence in a familiar, caring voice.

These first five verses clearly establish Jesus as the shepherd, in contrast to the false prophets, false messiahs, and heartless religious leaders (Matthew 23) who had taken advantage of the people.

II. TEACHING NOT UNDERSTOOD (JOHN 10:6)

6. Jesus used this figure of speech, but they did not understand what he was telling them.

In failing to see the point, the Pharisees showed the dimness of their spiritual vision (John 9:39-41). How many times do we need to hear or read a Bible teaching before we really understand it and make it a part of ourselves? Jesus often felt the need to repeat and to explain.

III. THE DOOR AND THE INTRUDERS (JOHN 10:7-10)

From being the shepherd of the flock, Jesus becomes the one through whom all others must come to establish their claims.

A. WRONG ENTRANCE AND REJECTION (vv. 7, 8)

7. Therefore Jesus said again, "I tell you the truth, I am the gate for the sheep.

I am the gate. The sheep would come through him for protection and would go through him to find pasture. Those who would claim the right to lead and feed their flocks must come through him. Later he said plainly, "I am the way and the truth and the life. No one comes to the Father except through me" (John 14:6). That is echoed in the words of the apostle Peter, "There is no other name under heaven given to men by which we must be saved" (Acts 4:12).

8. "All who ever came before me were thieves and robbers, but the sheep did not listen to them.

Anyone else who claimed the authority Jesus did was claiming too much. The heroes of the Old Testament did not make such claims. But robbery was not foreign to some described in Jeremiah 23:1: "'Woe to the shepherds who are destroying and scattering the sheep of my pasture!' declares the Lord." Ezekiel 34:1-19 provides a fuller description of the same kind of rogues.

The situation became even more serious with the end of the Old Testament prophetic period, when the dominant teachers added their interpretations and adjustments. They gave such authority to their interpretations as sometimes even to overrule Scripture. Jesus charged the teachers of his own time with making

WHAT DO YOU THINK?

The picture of the Shepherd guarding the sheep from thieves and robbers is very clear in the parable, but how do we apply it? Our Shepherd is in Heaven, unseen to our physical eyes. The thieves and robbers don't usually announce themselves as the bad guys. What can a Christian do when he or she sees some of the flock being carried off by "thieves"? What if those sheep believe they are following the Shepherd? Who's to say they are wrong? By what or whose authority?

Scripture ineffective by their traditions (Matthew 15:3-9). And by their treatment of the recently healed blind man (John 9:22, 34), the Pharisees before Jesus at that moment demonstrated the truth of his charge.

The sheep did not listen to them. The common people were paying less and less attention to the clerical establishment—a fact that rendered that establishment intensely jealous of Jesus' popularity.

B. WHAT IS THE PURPOSE? (vv. 9, 10)

9. "I am the gate; whoever enters through me will be saved. He will come in and go out, and find pasture.

Entrance into the state of salvation is through Jesus Christ as Lord—trustful faith in him, turning to him and his way in repentance, confession of him as Lord and Savior, burial with him in baptism, and the new life as his follower.

The safety of the sheep pen is not enough. Christ is also the *gate* through which one walks each day to feed one's spirit on Scripture and Christian fellowship; also to exercise oneself and grow in following Jesus as Shepherd.

I AM THE GATE

In 1846, the American explorer John Charles Fremont named the five-mile-long strait at the entrance to San Francisco Bay. He called it the Golden Gate. The famous Golden Gate Bridge spans that strait to connect San Francisco on the south with Marin County on the north. Begun in 1933, the bridge opened in 1937. Its center span is suspended from two towers 746 feet high. It reaches 4,200 feet across the strait, 220 feet above the water. It is one of America's most remarkable engineering feats and remains one of the longest suspension bridges in the world.

Jesus said he is the gate that spans the greatest gulf that ever existed: the eternal chasm between sinful men and a holy God. "Whoever enters through me will be saved" was his promise (John 10:9). He is the bridge, the entrance way into the kingdom, our golden gate into heaven.   —C. B. Mc.

10. "The thief comes only to steal and kill and destroy; I have come that they may have life, and have it to the full.

The sheep-stealer would have no interest in the animal except to get what he could for its wool and its carcass. The false teachers' interest was to claim and count followers and to exercise control; thus depriving them of the life Jesus came to give. Such "leaders" have been known literally to murder persons unwilling to conform to their patterns. Jesus' enemies were even then plotting to kill him.

The fullness of life to which the Lord Jesus provides access is notable first for its extent. It is everlasting (John 3:16). It abounds also in quality. He is the source of all light and life. It is full in outreach, encompassing fellowship with the family of God in all times and in all the earth. It is full of purpose and meaning, extending to partnership with the Almighty in his work. Is there, in fact, any meaningful direction in which the Christian life does not extend beyond human limits? That is the reason, after all, for John's writing his Gospel: "These are written that you may believe that Jesus is the Christ, the Son of God, and that by believing you may have life through his name" (John 20:31).

IV. THE GOOD SHEPHERD (JOHN 10:11-18)

A. CARING SHEPHERD, COWARDLY HIRED HAND (vv. 11-13)

11. "I am the good shepherd. The good shepherd lays down his life for the sheep.

The good shepherd. The one perfect and ideal Shepherd had been prefigured in Psalm 23, Ezekiel 34:23, and this from Isaiah 40:11: "He tends his flock like a

WHAT DO YOU THINK?

John 10:10 indicates that we should enjoy a "full" life in Christ. What does that mean? How is it different from the popular notion of grabbing all the "gusto" because "you only go around once in life"? With what should our lives be "full"?

Visual 8 is a classic portrayal of the Good Shepherd and the lengths to which he will go to "lay down his life for the sheep."

shepherd: He gathers the lambs in his arms and carries them close to his heart; he gently leads those that have young."

There are physical risks in protecting a flock from wild animals and vicious men (Genesis 31:39; 1 Samuel 17:34-36). Shepherds sometimes die in the attempt; and Jesus gave this "last full measure of devotion" to his ministry for mankind. This fact had been emphasized in Jesus' teaching, but it was not yet understood even by his closest friends. That would happen only after his death.

The giving of life, however, did not begin and end with physical death. The shepherd's life—his time, interests, and life-style—was given to his flock from the day he became a shepherd. It was even more so for Jesus, whose self-giving is spelled out in Philippians 2:5-8. Beginning with his surrender of heavenly glory for earthly limitations, it includes the acceptance of humble and menial service in the path of obedience all the way to the cross. His was a lifetime of life-giving.

12, 13. "The hired hand is not the shepherd who owns the sheep. So when he sees the wolf coming, he abandons the sheep and runs away. Then the wolf attacks the flock and scatters it. The man runs away because he is a hired hand and cares nothing for the sheep.

Not every *hired hand* displays the spirit condemned here, one that is interested only in his pay and his perks. Many hired shepherds care genuinely for the flock, just as many hired baby-sitters care for their charges and will protect them hero-ically in emergencies. What the Lord seeks among his people are servants who love and care for the people who belong to the Lord.

There are, however, mercenary spirits in the church, saying and doing what is popular for material gain, or looking around for a congregation where they can be most comfortable. The fault lies in putting their own advantage above the welfare of the Lord's flock.

The *wolf* is a major threat to the flock, killing some and scattering the rest to suffer all kinds of harm. Concerning God's human flock, Jesus warned against false prophets who "come to you in sheep's clothing, but inwardly they are fero-cious wolves" (Matthew 7:15); and Paul warned elders in the church at Ephesus to guard against the intrusion of "savage wolves" who will come and "will not spare the flock." They will "distort the truth in order to draw away disciples after them" (Acts 20:29, 30). It takes courage for any shepherd to stand up against well-disguised wolves.

B. SHEPHERD KNOWS AND IS KNOWN (vv. 14, 15)

14, 15. "I am the good shepherd; I know my sheep and my sheep know me—just as the Father knows me and I know the Father—and I lay down my life for the sheep.

Three special qualifications identify the Good Shepherd. First is his perfect knowledge of each member of his flock, answered by the sheep's recognition of him as the shepherd. The knowledge in each instance includes awareness, recogni-tion, and acquaintance, as one knows a friend so as to talk truthfully *about* him and to talk comfortably *with* him. Paul counted this knowledge of Christ as more valu-able to him than anything or all things beside (Philippians 3:7-11).

Next among the Good Shepherd's qualifications was his perfect intimacy with God as his Father. That included Jesus' complete awareness of the Father's will and a total eagerness to perform it. So his every word or deed was accomplished with divine awareness, authority, and approval.

The third and crowning qualification was this: the Good Shepherd continually lays down his life for the sheep, in days of labor and nights of prayer, as well as in

PRAYER OF A FAULTY FOLLOWER

Thank you, our eternal God, for sending your Son to be our Good Shepherd, leading in the way of life by his willing death. Help us, we pray, to follow him more faithfully in his way of life, abundant and eternal. Amen.

THOUGHT TO REMEMBER

"The Lord is my shepherd; I shall not be in want" (Psalm 23:1).

WHAT DO YOU THINK?

Peter charged the elders of the church to "be shepherds of God's flock" (1 Peter 5:2). How much of what Jesus says about himself in this parable applies to elders and other church leaders today? List and explain as many specific points as you can.

DAILY BIBLE READINGS

Monday, Apr. 15—Sheep Without a Shepherd (Mark 6: 30-34)

Tuesday, Apr. 16—Encourage One Another (Hebrews 10:19-25)

Wednesday, Apr. 17—God's Resurrecting Power (Hebrews 13:17-21)

Thursday, Apr. 18—Corrupt Leadership (Ezekiel 22:23-31)

Friday, Apr. 19—God Knows His Own (2 Timothy 2:14-19)

Saturday, Apr. 20—Genuine Security (John 10:23-30)

Sunday, Apr. 21— Authenticated by Works (John 10:31-42)

sacrificial death for them. "Greater love has no one than this, that he lay down his life for his friends" (John 15:13).

C. WELCOMES THE LARGER FLOCK (v. 16)

16. "I have other sheep that are not of this sheep pen. I must bring them also. They too will listen to my voice, and there shall be one flock and one shepherd.

The Good Shepherd could not limit his care to the sheep presently in one protective enclosure. That enclosure was obviously the Jewish people who would hear and follow him. Non-Jews also would hear his invitation and come under his care. That had already started to happen in Samaria (John 4:39-42). It would go forward as the gospel was preached to Cornelius (Acts 10), then in Antioch (Acts 11:19-23), and then throughout the Roman Empire. Gentiles became part of the Lord's *one flock*. That oneness is made very clear in Acts 15:1-34 and Ephesians 2:13-18, and it is built entirely on their common loyalty to the one Good Shepherd, Jesus Christ.

D. GIVES HIS LIFE FOR THE SHEEP (vv. 17, 18)

17, 18. "The reason my Father loves me is that I lay down my life—only to take it up again. No one takes it from me, but I lay it down of my own accord. I have authority to lay it down and authority to take it up again. This command I received from my Father."

God's love for his one and only Son was never conditional, but there were special occasions when God's pleasure was made known. Matthew 3:17 and 17:5 mention it in connection with Jesus' baptism and his transfiguration. Philippians 2:9-11 emphasizes it in response to Jesus' willing obedience in going to the cross: "Therefore God exalted him to the highest place and gave him the name that is above every name."

Matthew 26:53 emphasizes the voluntary self-sacrifice, noting that legions of angels were available to rescue Jesus from execution if he requested it. His was the *authority* and the ability to choose his course. That *command*—that commission, like a military officer's command over his troops—was bestowed by the Father. Our Shepherd is good beyond comparison, and beyond description, even in the words of his own choosing.

CONCLUSION

The teaching before us resulted in a division among the Pharisees who heard it, some being more than ever determined to follow their traditions in opposition to Jesus, whom they called insane and demon-possessed. Some on the other hand were drawn to follow Jesus, saying that a demon could never speak as Jesus spoke, nor produce a miracle like healing a man born blind (John 10:19-21).

Our Good Shepherd does indeed create division when he comes as owner of the sheep and calls his own to follow him. If he would limit himself to works of mercy and words of wisdom, all kinds of sheep would feed at his trough. But when he claims sole authority and asserts that none can come to the heavenly Father except by following him, multitudes will choose to follow other leaders, more comfortably adjusted to the world around them. But the world around them is doomed to ultimate destruction.

John recalls another time when followers of Jesus decided that he demanded too much and turned away. Then Jesus asked the apostles if they would also go away, and Peter responded, "Lord, to whom shall we go? You have the words of eternal life" (John 6:66-69).

In choosing your leader, check his credentials and see where he is going. The Good Shepherd still offers the only lasting and abundant life.

Discovery Learning

*This page contains an alternate lesson plan emphasizing learning activities. Classes
desiring such student involvement will find these suggestions helpful. The next page
is a reproducible activity page to further enhance discovery learning.*

LEARNING GOALS

After participating in this lesson, a student will be able to:

1. Explain the significance of the parable's sheep-related statements.

2. Describe the shepherd/sheep relationship we can have with Jesus.

3. Express a commitment to follow the Good Shepherd.

INTO THE LESSON

Make copies of the crossword puzzle on page 300 and give one to each student. Ask the students to try to complete these without looking at their Bibles first. Then have them turn to John 10 to finish.

After a few minutes, provide answers for anyone who needs some. (See page 294.) Point out that the words in the puzzle will be important ones to understand as you work through the lesson today.

INTO THE WORD

Ask the class for volunteers to read John 10:1-18 two verses at a time. With everyone studying the passage, ask, "What does this passage tell us about the *shepherd*?" Write the word *shepherd* on the chalkboard or poster board; then, as students respond, write their answers in a column under the word. (Possible answers: *he enters by the gate; he leads; he knows the sheep by name; he is good; he is willing to die for the sheep; he has authority from the Father.*)

Ask a second question, "What does this passage tell us about the *sheep*?" Write the word *sheep* and then list the students' responses in another column on the chalkboard or poster board. (*They are in danger; they know the shepherd and listen to his voice; they follow him; they don't follow others.*)

Summarize this study by pointing out that we are like sheep spiritually, weak and in need of a shepherd who will feed, guide, and protect us.

OPTION

Review the Scripture passage by playing a game fashioned after the TV game show, *Jeopardy*. On large sheets of paper, print each of the following answers on one side and the questions on the other.

1. He lays down his life for the sheep. (Who is the Good Shepherd?)

2. He kills and destroys the sheep. (Who is the thief?)

3. The place where the sheep stay overnight. (What is the sheep pen?)

4. The one from whom the sheep will run. (Who is the stranger?)

5. They know the shepherd's voice. (Who are his sheep?)

6. The type of life possessed by those who follow the Good Shepherd. (What is full life?)

7. He opens the gate for the shepherd. (Who is the watchman?)

8. He catches and scatters the sheep. (What is the wolf?)

9. As grass for sheep, it is our spiritual food. (What is the Bible?)

10. The promise to those who enter through the gate. (What is salvation?)

Divide the class into two or three teams, with each team selecting a leader to "buzz in." As you show and read each "answer" sheet, the leaders signal when they think their group has the correct "question" (or the groups could take turns answering). Remember, in *Jeopardy* you give the answer and the players must respond with the appropriate question. Give one point for each correct "question." Display the back of the sheet when the correct question is given by your contestants or when you have to tell them what the correct question is.

INTO LIFE

List the following Old Testament passages on the chalkboard, with an overhead projector, or on a handout: Psalm 23:1-4; Psalm 100:3; Isaiah 40:11; Isaiah 53:6, 7; Ezekiel 34:1-16, 22-24; Jeremiah 31:10; and Micah 2:12.

Read each passage (or ask a volunteer to read) and then ask, "What spiritual insights does this passage give you about our spiritual lives? What kind of behavior does it suggest is appropriate for us 'sheep'?" Lead the class to see that God has frequently pictured himself as our shepherd. He leads, guides, and protects us. He meets our needs. We belong to the One who created us. His care is loving and gentle. Our sin has caused us to go astray; the shepherd must save us. God will protect us from evil shepherds; Jesus is the Son of David who will be the Good Shepherd and bring all God's sheep together. But we must submit to him as our shepherd and commit ourselves to following him.

After a few moments for reflection, ask for volunteers to tell of the differences Jesus has made in their lives as the Good Shepherd who gives life more abundantly. Allow several minutes of sharing and then conclude with prayer.

Sheep Crossword

Try to complete the puzzle without looking for answers in your Bible first. If you get stuck, look up John 10 and read the verse given for each clue.

ACROSS

2. Synonym for robber (v. 1)
3. The sheep listen to the shepherd's (v. 3)
5. What the shepherd does so the sheep will come out of the pen (v. 3)
7. What the thief comes to do (v. 10)
10. The sheep find this under the shepherd's care (v. 9)
11. The one who enters by the gate, Jesus, will be _____ (v. 9)
12. He knows Jesus just as Jesus knows his sheep (v. 14)
17. How many flocks the Shepherd wants (v. 16)
20. Jesus has this to lay down his life and take it up again (v. 18)
21. Jesus is both the shepherd and this (v. 7)
23. The shepherd even knows this about each sheep (v. 3)
24. Predator of sheep (v. 12)
25. The one who enters by the gate (v. 2)

DOWN

1. The thief comes to do this (v. 10)
4. The watchman does this for the shepherd only (v. 3)
6. The sheep do this to the shepherd's voice (v. 3)
7. The shepherd's charges (v. 2)
8. Jesus used a _____ of speech that the people did not understand (v. 6)
9. The thief comes to do this (v. 10)
13. This is how much the hired hand cares for the sheep (v. 13)
14. The hired hand _____ nothing for the sheep (v. 13)
15. What Jesus received from his Father to give him his authority (v. 18)
16. Jesus came to bring this (v. 10)
18. It must be done through the gate (vv. 1, 2)
19. What the hired hand does when the wolf approaches (v. 12)
22. Where the sheep are kept (v. 1)

I am the good shepherd. The good shepherd lays down his life for the sheep.—John 10:11

THE TRUE VINE

LESSON 9

WHY TEACH THIS LESSON?

"Grapevines are cultivated to produce grapes." This statement by our lesson writer today should come as no surprise to anyone. Today's lesson, then, serves more as a reminder of things already known than an adventure into new territory.

Reminders are important. Peter wrote, "I will always remind you of these things, even though you know them and are firmly established in the truth.... I think it is right to refresh your memory" (2 Peter 1:12, 13). This lesson will refresh the memory of your students and encourage them to be about the business of bearing fruit.

INTRODUCTION

A. WHO PULLED THE PLUG?

"Come home, please! Now!"

The frantic tones of the wife's voice on the telephone brought a day's work at the office to a halt as the husband rushed to the rescue at home. Through the open door to the basement came the smell of death—death of a winter's supply of roasts and steaks in the family's now-warm freezer chest. Removal and disposal of the mass decay was a long and memorable task. Meanwhile the family's playful puppy, at home in the basement, showed a continuing interest in the electric cord which he had apparently pulled free from its outlet several days previously.

Nothing works when it is deprived of its vital power! This fact is more familiar to many modern city dwellers than is the ageless principle of growing things. Nothing lives and grows unless it has a vital connection with sources of energy in light, moisture, and nutrition. In bushes, vines, and trees, life requires roots in the ground, bringing nutrients to standing trunks, which supply branches and leaves, flowers and fruit. All must grow together.

The spiritual life of mankind is equally dependent on a vital connection with its source in God, through his Son, Jesus Christ our Lord. The Lord himself said so, in terms familiar to fruit growers everywhere.

B. GRAPES OF PROVISION AND JUDGMENT

In Scripture the grapevine became a symbol for Israel itself, as God's vine, transplanted from Egypt to a place prepared for it. The nation failed to produce the expected spiritual fruit, however; and God, in judgment, permitted it to be trampled down (Psalm 80:8-16; Isaiah 5:1-7; Jeremiah 2:21; Hosea 10:1, 2). Jesus also spoke judgment on men who withheld the proper return from God's well-prepared vineyard (Mark 12:1-12).

C. AFTER SUPPER CONVERSATION

Events of Jesus' final week moved swiftly. It was the Passover season, and the Lord made careful arrangements to observe the feast with his apostles. Near the end of the supper he used the ceremonial bread and fruit of the vine in establishing a memorial Communion to be observed by the church in time to come. Lingering at the table, Jesus spoke to the apostles about his departure to prepare a place for them in his Father's house. At last he gave the order to leave (John 14:31).

DEVOTIONAL READING
JOHN 15:18-27
LESSON SCRIPTURE
JOHN 15:1-17
PRINTED TEXT
JOHN 15:1-17

LESSON AIMS

This study should prepare the student to:

1. Compare the image of grapevines bearing fruit with a Christian's fruit bearing.

2. Explain the importance and results of remaining in Jesus, the true Vine.

3. Establish a plan for increasing personal fruitfulness in Christ.

Apr
28

KEY VERSE

I am the vine; you are the branches. If a man remains in me and I in him, he will bear much fruit; apart from me you can do nothing.   —John 15:5

The Lord's next recorded words provide the text for our study. Were the words spoken while the group was still in the upper room, seeing and smelling the "fruit of the vine"? Or was the group walking through the city toward Gethsemane, perhaps passing near the temple with its great ornamental golden vine, heavy with clusters, over the door?

I. THE VINE AND ITS CARE GIVER (JOHN 15:1-3)

1. "I am the true vine, and my Father is the gardener.

Jesus wove literal fact and symbolic comparison so skillfully that there is little need for explanation. He spoke literally of himself and his Father in Heaven. He spoke figuratively of the vine and the gardener who labored to make the vine productive.

Jesus had spoken of himself as "light" and "life" and "Good Shepherd" (John 9:5; 14:6; 10:14). Now he speaks of the *true vine* in contrast with Israel in its disappointing performance and in contrast with such material figures as were seen nearby.

2. "He cuts off every branch in me that bears no fruit, while every branch that does bear fruit he prunes so that it will be even more fruitful.

In me describes the relationship of the believer to his Lord. In his epistles Paul uses the phrase, "in Christ," nearly one hundred times. Believers are baptized "into Christ Jesus" (Romans 6:3; Galatians 3:27). "If anyone is in Christ, he is a new creation" (2 Corinthians 5:17), "created in Christ Jesus to do good works" (Ephesians 2:10).

Fruit. Grapevines are cultivated to produce grapes. Grapes are produced, not on the stalk, but on the branches. The unfruitful branch is cut off and discarded (Matthew 7:16-20). The Lord's living branches are expected to produce "the fruit of righteousness that comes through Jesus Christ—to the glory and praise of God" (Philippians 1:11). The fruit of the Spirit includes "love, joy, peace, patience, kindness, goodness, faithfulness, gentleness and self-control" (Galatians 5:22, 23), reflecting him whose we are and in whom we live.

As a gardener removes the unfruitful branches and then clears the fruitful branches of hindrances to their becoming even more fruitful, so God allows to Christians the cleansing disciplines of sorrow, disappointment, and trial. He sometimes uses his pruning knife to remove excesses of luxury and pleasure that hinder the believer's spiritual development. The most joyous and effective servants of the Lord may be those who have least of the world's "good life."

LEAVES OR FRUIT?

Matthew 21 records an unusual event in the last week of Jesus' earthly ministry. Walking from Bethany into Jerusalem, the Lord passed a fig tree. He examined it and found that it was full of leaves, but had no fruit. Jesus said it would never bear fruit, and it withered and died.

The tree wasn't exactly a lazy fig tree. It was full of leaves. It was busy. It was doing something. It had absorbed light from the sun. It had taken in carbon dioxide from the surrounding air. It had drawn up water and nutrients from the soil. And it had done something with all these resources. It had used them to build its own roots, stems, branches, and leaves. But it was missing the one thing God had created it to produce: figs! It was full of activity, but no fruit.

Churches and people also can be very busy and still produce no fruit. What happens as a result of the ministries and programs carried on by your church? Do they result in changed lives, in the salvation of lost people, and in the making of disciples? Are you producing leaves or fruit?

—C. B. Mc.

3. "You are already clean because of the word I have spoken to you.

The sharp blade of Jesus' teaching had been at work on the apostles for about three years, cutting away at their worldly pride and ambition, convincing them to

WHAT DO YOU THINK?

What is the "fruit" that Christians are expected to bear? (See Philippians 1:11; Galatians 5:22, 23.) Do most of the Christians you know bear fruit? Why or why not? Is there something the church can do to make more of its members fruitful? If so, what? If not, what will it take to get unfruitful Christians to bear fruit?

I am the vine,
ye are the branches.
He that abideth in me,
and I in him, the same bringeth
forth much fruit;
for without me ye can do nothing.
John 15:5

Use visual 9 to dramatize the fruit-bearing responsibility we have. It quotes verse 4 of the text.

leave all else and follow him. They still had much to learn, but they were on their way. The same cleansing word, conveyed through Scripture, is available to all who will hear, believe, and obey.

II. THE VINE AND ITS BRANCHES (JOHN 15:4-6)

A. CONNECTED AND FRUITFUL (vv. 4, 5)

4. "Remain in me, and I will remain in you. No branch can bear fruit by itself; it must remain in the vine. Neither can you bear fruit unless you remain in me.

Remain in me. Jesus was asking the disciples to keep on living in him even after his going back to be with his Father. This was said within the hour after Jesus had provided the most meaningful instrument for remaining in him—the memorial bread and fruit of the vine, through which his people were to enjoy fellowship with him until he comes again (1 Corinthians 11:26). Paul acknowledged the remaining, as he wrote, "Christ lives in me" (Galatians 2:20).

The branch cannot bear fruit on its own power; neither can it bear fruit that is foreign to its own vine. A grapevine does not bear figs (James 3:12), nor a Christian produce the works of the devil. "Whoever claims to live in him must walk as Jesus did" (1 John 2:6).

5. "I am the vine; you are the branches. If a man remains in me and I in him, he will bear much fruit; apart from me you can do nothing.

Jesus was talking directly to the apostles, but his statement applies also to "those who will believe in me through their message" (John 17:20). The reference is clearly to believers as individuals, related directly and intimately to Jesus as the vine.

The verse emphasizes, both positively and negatively, what has been said. The fruit-bearing capacity of the one living in Christ is amazingly great. For one who relies on his own power, there is no capacity at all.

ATTACHED TO THE VINE

Against their dad's orders, two brothers were playing football on the lawn next to their dad's tomato patch. "Go long," the quarterback called, as he rifled a pass just beyond the outstretched fingertips of his receiver. It was a beautiful diving catch, but the downfield brother landed on the tomato plants.

Frantically the boys reset the stakes and retied the plants, but that still left the half dozen tomatoes they had broken off. To cover their crime, the pair worked a little magic with clear adhesive tape.

For close to a week their dad was none the wiser. But in time the atrophying tomatoes begged for a closer examination, which revealed that the dying fruit was not really attached to the vine. The ruse was up, and the two deceivers were brought to justice.

Jesus' analogy of the branches and the vine shows that unless we are connected to him, we cannot bear fruit and eventually we will die. Are you really connected to him, or are you just taped up for show? —C. B. Mc.

B. FATE OF THE UNFRUITFUL (v. 6)

6. "If anyone does not remain in me, he is like a branch that is thrown away and withers; such branches are picked up, thrown into the fire and burned.

When any person, for whatever reason, fails to live continually in vital relationship to Christ, that person is thrown away from God's fruitful vine and gradually loses even the appearance of spiritual life. This should serve as a solemn warning to anyone who supposes that he or she has no real need for such ongoing relationships as prayer, Bible reading, Communion at the Lord's table, and encouragement with the Lord's people (Hebrews 10:19-27). How else can a person sustain a meaningful life in Christ? The withering may be so gradual as to be for a time unnoticed, but it occurs with fatal certainty.

WHAT DO YOU THINK?

What does it mean to "remain" in Jesus? How does the believer remain in him? What factors or practices influence this remaining? Is it possible not to remain in him once one is in Christ? If so, how does that happen? If not, why would he give this warning?

Such branches are picked up.... Matthew 13:41, 42 names angels as having the task of bringing together the scattered single branches and consigning them to the flames. They are worthless, even as fuel.

Note the progressive fate of the branch that lacks a continuing vital attachment to the vine. It is fruitless; it is cut off; it withers; it is bundled up with others like itself; it is cast into the fire and burned. Can the process be halted and reversed? Only if the branch goes back to its beginning, with an eager strengthening of attachment to the true vine!

III. VITAL CONNECTION (JOHN 15:7-11)

A. REACHING AND GLORIFYING GOD (vv. 7, 8)

7. "If you remain in me and my words remain in you, ask whatever you wish, and it will be given you.

Here is a great promise based on a great condition, and leading to a great disappointment in the careless and inattentive: "When you ask, you do not receive, because you ask with wrong motives, that you may spend what you get on your pleasures" (James 4:3).

Jesus' disciples must not only live in Christ; they must have Christ living in them. His teaching must come to life in the thoughts, words, and actions of the believer. A believer's prayer will be like Jesus' prayer in Gethsemane: "Not my will, but yours be done" (Luke 22:42). The asking will be in harmony with the divine will expressed through Jesus, and God will respond to the prayer. The response may not follow the immediate plans of him who prays, but it will honor God's loftier purpose. The Father will give what is asked in the name—the whole person—of Jesus (John 16:23).

8. "This is to my Father's glory, that you bear much fruit, showing yourselves to be my disciples.

God the Father is glorified in what Jesus the Son says and does. God is also glorified in what the Son accomplishes through the disciples he has taught: "Let your light shine before men, that they may ... praise your Father in heaven" (Matthew 5:16). Fruit bearing does not make one a follower of Jesus, but it does reveal who is a follower. "By their fruit you will recognize them" (Matthew 7:20).

BEARING FRUIT

Hungry? Could I interest you in the ripened ovary of a seed-bearing plant, together with the edible fleshy accessory parts? What's that? Fruit. From insects to humans, many living things depend on fruits as an important part of their diet. We eat them raw. We cook them, dry them, can them, squeeze them into juice, and boil them into jellies and preserves.

Being food is, however, only a secondary function of fruits. Their principal role is in reproduction. Fruit protects the developing seeds and aids in their distribution. Fruit is part of God's plan for ensuring that each kind of fruit-bearing plant will continue to exist. It is evidence that a plant is alive and will have a life in the future.

The New Testament often speaks of spiritual fruit. Righteousness, truth, and benevolence are all mentioned as fruit. In Galatians 5:22, 23 Paul names the fruit of the Spirit: love, joy, peace, patience, kindness, goodness, faithfulness, gentleness, and self-control. Spiritual fruit is evidence of Christ's life in us and a preview of the life he will lead us to live in eternity.   —C. B. Mc.

B. LIVING IN THE POWER OF LOVE (vv. 9, 10)

Love, the first fruit of the Spirit (Galatians 5:22), identifies the followers of Christ: "By this all men will know that you are my disciples, if you love one another" (John 13:35).

WHAT DO YOU THINK?

"Without me you can do nothing" (v. 5). "If you remain in me and my words remain in you, ask whatever you wish, and it will be given you" (v. 7). If a believer's life is not showing positive results, does this mean he or she is not remaining in Jesus? What is the responsibility of other Christians who witness such an ineffectiveness in a brother or sister? Can one challenge a fellow believer to remain in Christ without "judging"? What would you do if you suspected a fellow believer was not "remaining" in Christ?

9. "As the Father has loved me, so have I loved you. Now remain in my love.

God had publicly declared his pleasure in Jesus as his Son whom he loves (Matthew 3:17; 17:5). Jesus' life was a constant expression of self-forgetful love for all mankind, but he maintained a special affection for certain friends (John 11:5), and his closest companions (John 13:23). John 13:1 declares that Jesus, "having loved his own who were in the world, he now showed them the full extent of his love."

Love is the bonding agent for the union of vine and branch. As nutrient-carrying moisture must flow throughout a plant for it to live, so love must be continually received from Christ and returned to Christ for the believer to bear fruit.

10. "If you obey my commands, you will remain in my love, just as I have obeyed my Father's commands and remain in his love.

Obey my commands. The language indicates something more than a reluctant conformity. The word *obey* can also be translated *keep*, suggesting the work of a guard, protecting a treasure. The divine precepts are to be thus respected. First John 5:3 says it: "This is love for God: to obey his commands. And his commands are not burdensome."

Obedience is surely a part of that protective regard for our Lord's commands. If we love, we will obey; and when we obey, love is expressed and developed. Obedient love is the bond of "remaining," whether between the heavenly Father and the Son (John 14:31), or between the Son and his follower. It is not a sullen conformity!

C. EQUIPPED FOR JOY (v. 11)

11. "I have told you this so that my joy may be in you and that your joy may be complete.

How different this is from the popular idea that religion—especially a religion of obedience to divine commands—is a killjoy operation! In fact, it is designed to provide *joy*, lasting and complete. How strange that Jesus should introduce it on the eve of his death! Yet joy provides a theme for the rest of the Lord's farewell discourse (John 16:20-24).

The promised joy begins in Jesus himself, whose chief pleasure lay in doing his Father's will (Hebrews 12:2). He prayed that he might convey that joy in full measure to his disciples (John 17:13). Real joy comes out of real loving. Joy grows with loving obedience.

IV. LOVE AS THE LINK (JOHN 15:12-17)

A. COMMAND AND DEMONSTRATION (vv. 12, 13)

12, 13. "My command is this: Love each other as I have loved you. Greater love has no one than this, that he lay down his life for his friends.

Jesus issued more than one command, but the love command was first in importance (Matthew 22:34-40), as covering the whole law, and as being newly taught by himself (John 13:34). Paul summarized it in Romans 13:8: "Let no debt remain outstanding, except the continuing debt to love one another, for he who loves his fellowman has fulfilled the law."

Christians are to keep on loving, as they keep on living in Christ: "May the Lord make your love increase and overflow for each other and for everyone else" (1 Thessalonians 3:12). Their example is Christ. The apostles were yet to see the ultimate demonstration in Jesus' laying down his life on the cross, not only for his friends, but also for his enemies. Yet they had seen him lay down his hours and days, his rights and interests, in serving them and others. "This is how we know what love is: Jesus Christ laid down his life for us" (1 John 3:16).

WHAT DO YOU THINK?

We can have an abiding sense of joy in the midst of the most severe trials, because we know we shall gain victory over death even as Jesus did. But verses 10 and 11 of our text indicate that fullness of joy comes from loving, obeying, and serving Jesus. How does obedient service bring joy? Do you think most believers actually believe it does? Why or why not? And if service brings joy, why do so many Christians complain of burnout? What happened to the joy in their service?

WHAT DO YOU THINK?

Our love for one another is to be of the same quality as Jesus' love for us. Do you think we come up to this standard in our church? If not, why not? Do we "lay down our lives for our brothers"? (1 John 3:16) Do we really make sacrifices of time and effort on one another's behalf, reflecting Jesus' loving sacrifice? Do we assume that we love one another because we exchange hugs and handshakes and verbal greetings on Sunday? Are we there when a brother or sister suffers a death in the family? Are we available when a fellow believer needs a listening ear and an uplifting word? Are we willing to share our money and possessions to provide for another Christian who is in need? What areas do we need to work on to better show real love for one another?

WHAT DO YOU THINK?

Jesus said, "You are my friends." How does the idea of being a friend of Jesus challenge our behavior? Consider the following aspects of friendship. How do we practice each of these in regard to being Jesus' friend?

• A friend is someone with whom we can be ourselves.

• A friend is someone with whom we share something of importance.

• A friend is someone we want to introduce to other friends.

PRAYER OF A NEEDY BRANCH

Thank you, Father, for the love that ministers to us with a pruning knife when it is necessary to remove hindrances to our fruitfulness in you. May our praise be expressed in the fruits of righteousness and love that Jesus enables us to bear in his name. Amen.

THOUGHT TO REMEMBER

Joy crowns the life that is built on, and in, Jesus as Lord.

DAILY BIBLE READINGS

B. FRIENDSHIP AND ITS FRUITS (vv. 14-16)

14, 15. *"You are my friends if you do what I command. I no longer call you servants, because a servant does not know his master's business. Instead, I have called you friends, for everything that I learned from my Father I have made known to you.*

Jesus has a right to regard any of his followers as *servants*—literally slaves, bought with the price of his life's blood (1 Corinthians 6:19, 20). Yet he laid out his plans before the apostles as a master does not do with slaves, but reserves for his *friends*. That gave them a higher motivation—grateful love—to serve him well. We cannot lay claim to all the apostles' intimacies and privileges with Jesus, but we can go far beyond the slaves' compulsions, to serve him with a friend's love and devotion.

16. *"You did not choose me, but I chose you and appointed you to go and bear fruit—fruit that will last. Then the Father will give you whatever you ask in my name.*

The apostles' friendship with Jesus was initiated by him. He *chose* and called them, mostly one by one, but they accepted the invitation and followed.

Appointed you. The appointment is described in Luke 6:12-16. Mark 3:13-15 shows that the appointment was accompanied by special powers to be used in producing fruit that would last. The apostles were to prepare for the establishment of the church, lead it through its earliest years, and provide the Scriptures for its continuance through the ages. To that end they worked "signs, wonders and miracles" (2 Corinthians 12:12) in response to special prayers for special purposes in the name of Christ. Yet Paul's "thorn in [his] flesh" stayed with him in spite of persistent prayer (2 Corinthians 12:7-9). He was more fruitful because of it.

C. ESTABLISHING THE LINK (v. 17)

17. *"This is my command: Love each other."*

The apostles' power in prayer was not to be used selfishly, but in continuing care for other members of the Lord's body—other branches in the true vine. Every act of obedience to any other command must harmonize with the command to mutual love, patterned according to the love of Christ. Only this can sustain the living relationship of branches in the true vine.

CONCLUSION

A. "I AM WITH YOU"

The Lord who taught that his followers must remain in him promised also that he, through his Holy Spirit, would remain with them and in them for ever: "Christ in you, the hope of glory" (Colossians 1:27) is the basis, and "I am with you always, to the very end of the age" (Matthew 28:20) is the pledge to the loving, obedient branch in God's vine.

B. THE OTHER SIDE OF THE COIN

The positive aspects of life in Christ, bonded by love and committed to keeping his Word, become negative aspects in relation to God's enemies. Immediately after his command to "love one another" as those who live in him, Jesus warned that the world will hate you if you do! (John 15:18—16:4). The world does not take kindly to having its sin revealed and rebuked, by word or by example. It hated and crucified Jesus when he claimed more than the world was willing to grant. It will hate also his people who press those claims in his name. Loving and living in Jesus is a matter of choice. That choice excludes while it includes. Its **FAITH** is spelled "Forsaking All I Take Him."

Discovery Learning

This page contains an alternate lesson plan emphasizing learning activities. Classes desiring such student involvement will find these suggestions helpful. The next page is a reproducible activity page to further enhance discovery learning.

LEARNING GOALS

As a result of participating in today's lesson, a student will be able to:

1. Compare the image of grapevines bearing fruit with a Christian's fruit-bearing.

2. Explain the importance and results of remaining in Jesus, the true Vine.

3. Establish a plan for increasing personal fruitfulness in Christ.

INTO THE LESSON

Recruit a couple of your class members to perform the following skit. Don't worry about props; your adults can pantomime the action and everyone will understand.

The husband walks to center stage, which is supposed to be in his living room, and turns on the TV. He stands there expectantly for a moment; then his expression turns to confused disappointment. He tries the switch a couple more times. Finally he turns to the wife, who is off to the side (in the kitchen?), and calls, "Honey, the TV's broken. You'd better call the repairman."

The wife enters. "It's broken? What happened?"

"I don't know. I just tried to turn it on and—nothing!"

The wife looks around the TV. "Well here's the trouble!" she says. "It's not plugged in!"

Thank your actors and lead in the applause for their efforts. As they are being seated, ask, "Why wouldn't the TV work." Obviously, it has to be connected to the power to function properly.

Make the transition into the lesson by noting that Christians have to be connected to the power to function properly, too. In Jesus' words, we are branches that have to be connected to the Vine to bear fruit.

INTO THE WORD

Ask the class to listen for the points Jesus makes as you read the text. Then read John 15:1-8 aloud. Have students call out points while you write them on a chalkboard or poster board. Possible points include the following:

- Jesus is the source of what we need to be fruitful and joyful.
- Branches that do not bear fruit are cut off.
- Productive branches are pruned by the gardener/God.
- Pruning produces greater fruitfulness.
- The Word prunes/cleans us.
- We cannot be productive apart from the vine.

- Remaining branches bear much fruit and receive all they need.
- God is glorified when we bear much fruit.
- Fruit bearing is a demonstration of being a disciple.

OPTION

Provide the class with a list of points and ask them to find the verse or verses that support each. Use the reproducible activity "Bearing Fruit" on page 308.

Divide the class into small groups of three or four people. Assign each group one of the following questions: (1) How does God "prune" us to bear more fruit? (2) How do we remain in Christ? (3) What does the branch (disciple) receive from the vine (Jesus)? (4) What fruit can we produce that will glorify God? After several minutes of group discussion, ask for a spokesperson from each group to summarize the group's answers for the entire class.

Now read John 15:9-17. Ask half of the class to count the number of times some form of the word *love* is used. Ask the other half to count how often some form of *obey* or *command* is used. Discuss the relationship between obedience and love. How is that related to fruit bearing?

INTO LIFE

Give each small group a set of six index cards. The cards, prepared before class, should have the following phrases written on them, one phrase on each card:

- Loving God.
- Obeying God.
- Experiencing joy.
- Loving others.
- Being Jesus' friend.
- Bearing fruit.

Ask each group to work together to place the cards in the order in which the events happen in the Christian life. Students will probably be puzzled, perhaps even frustrated. Help them realize that all these are interrelated and all are important. In fact, there is no one way in which these happen. Point out that one Christian's experience may be different from another's, but emphasize that these experiences all continue together, and all are to be treasured.

Offer time for personal reflection as described in the box on page 308. You can distribute copies of the page or just give oral instructions. After several minutes of contemplation, ask for volunteers to share their thoughts.

Bearing Fruit

Read John 15:1-8. Then study the list below. Next to each point, write the number(s) of the verse(s) from the passage that teach that truth.

Then look over the list again. After each statement, write a practical implication that can be drawn from that truth. (The first one has been done for you as an example.)

• Jesus is the source of what we need to be fruitful and joyful.
   Verse:
   Practical Implication: I need to maintain my fellowship with him through prayer, Bible study, and contact
                           with his people.

• Branches that do not bear fruit are cut off.
   Verse:
   Practical Implication:

• Productive branches are pruned by the gardener/God.
   Verse:
   Practical Implication:

• Pruning produces greater fruitfulness.
   Verse:
   Practical Implication:

• The Word prunes/cleans us.
   Verse:
   Practical Implication:

• Remaining branches bear much fruit and receive all they need.
   Verse:
   Practical Implication:

• God is glorified when we bear much fruit.
   Verse:
   Practical Implication:

• Fruit bearing is a demonstration of being a disciple.
   Verse:
   Practical Implication:

Spend a few moments in silent meditation to consider what you can do to experience a greater level of remaining, obeying, loving, fruitfulness, or joy. In the space below specify one thing you will do this week in order to remain in Christ and bear more fruit.

TEACHINGS ABOUT HAPPINESS

LESSON 10

WHY TEACH THIS LESSON?

No generation of recent memory has needed the admonition of Romans 12:2 more than the present one. "Do not conform any longer to the pattern of this world...." What better pattern to follow than that of the Beatitudes? These verses in Matthew 5 describe someone who in no way is shaped after "the pattern of this world." In fact, the world would call much of the advice here just plain crazy!

Since "the foolishness of God is wiser than man's wisdom" (1 Corinthians 1:25), however, that's okay! When your students see the utter disharmony of today's text with the world's standards, they will have begun to see life as God wants them to live it.

INTRODUCTION

A. PURSUIT OF HAPPINESS

"Pursuit of Happiness" is named, along with "Life" and "Liberty," in the American *Declaration of Independence* among the "unalienable Rights" with which the Creator has endowed all men alike. None of us would deny that right to anyone, any more than we would deny to anyone the right to chase the end of a rainbow in search of gold. We would note, however, that the pursuit of what most people regard as happiness in selfish indulgence is a primary source of misery rather than of well-being. The pursuit of happiness has led many to flit from one spouse to another; to cheat and steal in efforts to become rich; to ingest drugs in order to feel good, and so on and on, all because "I have a right to my happiness."

With Jesus, happiness was never a goal to be sought. It was, instead, a secondary result of seeking a right relationship with God. He said of himself, "I seek not to please myself but him who sent me" (John 5:30).

In that context, the Beatitudes (named from the Latin *beatus,* or *blessed*), may be considered a thesis on happiness. The Greek *makarios* has been translated "happy" as well as "blessed." In Matthew 5:3-12, however, most English language translations of the Bible render it "blessed."

Blessed implies a favorable judgment from Heaven. Psalm 1, for example, begins, "Blessed is the man who does not walk in the counsel of the wicked.... But his delight is in the law of the Lord," and concludes, "The Lord watches over the way of the righteous, but the way of the wicked will perish." Scripture everywhere shows divine approval of the qualities described by Jesus. That approval bears fruit, moreover, in the utmost of well-being and eternal joy.

B. LESSON BACKGROUND

Are Matthew's record of the "Sermon on the Mount" (Matthew 5—7) and Luke's account of the "Sermon on the Plain" (Luke 6:12-49) two reports of the same event? Many Bible scholars think so, and they wrestle with differences between

DEVOTIONAL READING
PSALM 1:1-6
LESSON SCRIPTURE
MATTHEW 5:1-12
PRINTED TEXT
MATTHEW 5:1-12

LESSON AIMS

This lesson should help the student to:

1. Match each Beatitude with its promise.

2. Compare other biblical beatitudes with the ones in Matthew 5.

3. Strengthen Beatitudes already present; establish habits that will develop Beatitudes not so evident.

May
5

KEY VERSE

Rejoice and be glad, because great is your reward in heaven.
—Matthew 5:12

LESSON 10 NOTES

Visual 10 shows a hillside overlooking the Sea of Galilee. The setting for Jesus' sermon must have been very much like this.

Seeing the multitudes,
he went up into a mountain
and he opened his mouth,
and taught them.
Matthew 5:1

WHAT DO YOU THINK?

The idea of being "poor" in any sense of the term may trouble some of us. We live in a society in which the quality of life is judged by the amount of money and possessions one has. Jesus' call to be "poor in spirit" challenges us to admit that we are weak, insecure, and, from a moral standpoint, prone to fail.

Why is it so hard for some people to admit the poverty of their own unaided condition? Do you think secular "self-esteem" philosophies help or hinder a person in coming to admit this need? Why? What can the church do to promote both a healthy self-esteem and a biblical concept of our need for a Savior?

the two. A respectable number of us, on the other hand, consider the two passages to be accounts of separate events, taking place several months apart. Now we shall consider Matthew's record.

Jesus had been preaching, teaching, and healing for about a year in Galilee and had become so famous that throngs of people were coming—many by several days' journey from all directions—to see, hear, and benefit from his ministry (Matthew 4:23-25). Among them were many who expected a politico-military Messiah to lead in rebellion against Roman rule in Palestine, and they wondered if their kind of Messiah had come. Some would even force Jesus to become their king (John 6:15). The time had come to spell out plainly—especially to his followers—that he was not that kind of king, and his was not that kind of kingdom. He would expect his disciples to be the kind of people he was—exactly the reverse of the cruel, power-hungry, and luxury-loving rulers so familiar in places of authority around them.

I. THE TEACHER AND HIS HEARERS (MATTHEW 5:1, 2)

1, 2. Now when he saw the crowds, he went up on a mountainside and sat down. His disciples came to him, and he began to teach them, saying:

The traditional "Mount of the Beatitudes" (Horns of Hattin) is a low hill, perhaps lowered by centuries of erosion, several miles southwest of Capernaum. Jesus probably expected to be followed by the crowd, and he chose a place where he could be seen and heard.

The Lord seated himself in the manner of Eastern teachers. Thus his message had to be conveyed in words; lively dramatics were impossible. That is good for us, since we can read his words, and not dramatic gestures. Yet his very presence provided a vivid demonstration of his message.

His committed followers, including the twelve who were to be called apostles, gathered around him, probably also seated on the ground. At the outset Jesus talked directly to these men, no matter how many others may have come within the range of his voice as he continued. We are constantly amazed at the ability of any teacher under such circumstance to address large crowds without mechanical or electronic help. The listeners must have given quiet attention!

The Sermon on the Mount has been called the constitution of the new covenant. At least it describes the citizens of Heaven's kingdom. The law of the old covenant had been given to Moses alone on a high and inaccessible mountain; this was given publicly on a mountain known only for the loftiness of its Teacher and his teaching. Jesus did not, and does not, expect strangers, not knowing or committed to him, to adopt the life-style he described. Many would consider it foolishness. First they must know and be drawn to him; then they can accept his direction.

II. THE CHARACTER THAT BLESSES (MATTHEW 5:3-9)

The blessed life is described first in the believer's relationship to God and the character growing from it.

A. A SENSE OF SPIRITUAL NEED (v. 3)

3. "Blessed are the poor in spirit, for theirs is the kingdom of heaven.

The heavenly *kingdom* belongs, Jesus says, to the one who comes as a beggar to its gate! *Poor* translates a word used of a destitute condition, hopeless in itself. In it we hear echoes of the tax collector in the temple, bowed and pleading, "God, have mercy on me, a sinner," and going home "justified" (Luke 18:13, 14). The blessed ones claim no spiritual assets; they acknowledge a spiritual need. Thus acknowledging, they are in a position to receive and accept Heaven's wealth. Paul caught this idea; he acknowledged that his standing as a law-abiding Pharisee was worthless in relation to his need for Christ and life eternal (Philippians 3:4-11).

After Jesus' introductory description of the most blessed of all persons, we are prepared to understand better the following items. Humility, purity, pity, and the rest of the character traits here grow naturally in the soil of dependence on God.

The acceptance of material poverty for the sake of spiritual values will also bring its blessing, as Jesus promised to the disciples who had surrendered homes and businesses to follow him (Luke 18:29, 30); but that seems not to be the principal thrust of this Beatitude.

POOR IN SPIRIT

Imagine yourself applying for a credit card. A young account executive takes down the information to open your account.

"What is your income?" she asks.

"I don't have any income," you reply.

"No income?"

"That's right. No job, no salary, no income of any sort."

"Well then, what about your assets—stocks, bonds, real estate holdings?"

"I don't have any assets," you answer.

"No assets?"

"Right again. Nothing. Nothing in the bank, nothing stuffed in my mattress at home, and nothing in my pocket. I'm penniless."

"Let's see; what about your liabilities? Do you owe anything?"

"My debts? Oh, yes. I owe trillions of dollars," you respond.

"That's wonderful," she says. "Here's your card. You have unlimited credit, beginning immediately, and you will never see a bill. We've taken care of everything."

Far-fetched? Well, yes, if you're dealing with the bank. But not if you have come to Christ. Jesus said the *poor* in spirit enjoy the benefits of his kingdom. Membership is open by admitting that we own nothing that would make us worthy of salvation, that we have no way of earning God's favor, and that we owe a sin debt we cannot pay. Come to Jesus on those terms, and you're in. He's done for you what you could never do for yourself. To paraphrase the advertisement, "Don't leave home without him."

—C. B. Mc.

B. GODLY SORROW (v. 4)

4. "Blessed are those who mourn, for they will be comforted.

This, too, was addressed to Jesus' disciples, but can have limited application to other people who, having suffered severe loss, learn not to place undue value on what is trivial and transient. Paul is helpful here: "Godly sorrow brings repentance that leads to salvation and leaves no regret, but worldly sorrow brings death" (2 Corinthians 7:10). God's people know the kind of mourning for sin that caused Paul to acknowledge himself chief of sinners, while remembering that God still forgave and employed him (1 Timothy 1:15-17). Our mourning over the sins of others is a little like Jesus' lamenting over the sin and the approaching destruction of Jerusalem (Luke 19:41-44). Our sorrowing in sympathy with suffering neighbors answers the admonition to rejoice with those who rejoice and mourn with those who mourn (Romans 12:15). God's people cannot take lightly the sin-damage that weighs so heavily on the heart of God.

The comfort promised after godly mourning calls to mind the Comforter promised to the apostles after Jesus' going to be with the Father—the *paraclete*, or Companion called alongside to sustain, encourage, and strengthen (John 14:15-18). Just as the Spirit's coming awaited the death and resurrection of Jesus, so God's perfect comfort to his children comes only after they have known godly mourning.

OPTION

Use the reproducible activity "Scrambled Beatitudes on page 316 either to introduce the Beatitudes or as a review.

WHAT DO YOU THINK?

How can the ones who mourn be happy? Isn't that a contradiction of terms? In what sense is there a blessing for the one who mourns the loss of a loved one? ... for one who mourns the condition of the lost? (See James 4:8-10.) ... for one who mourns for the sake of another? (See Romans 12:15.)

WHAT DO YOU THINK?

The writer claims the word meek "describes a strength like that of a well-trained animal brought under control." Our culture, however, seems to equate meekness with weakness and timidity. Why do you think that is so? If you weren't in a Sunday school class, would you take it as a compliment if a co-worker said you were "meek"? Why or why not? How can we restore the good reputation of "meekness"? (See Numbers 12:3; Matthew 11:29.)

WHAT DO YOU THINK?

We live in a society where impurity abounds. How, then, can we achieve or maintain purity of heart? Does the pursuit of purity suggest one should never watch television—at least, prime time television? Why or why not? How does the viewing of violent and/or immoral acts, especially when they are done by the "hero" of the plot, affect our thinking and attitudes about such things?

Job said, "I made a covenant with my eyes not to look lustfully at a girl" (Job 31:1). What would such a covenant include today? What other "covenants" might we need to make with ourselves? (See also Philippians 4:8, 9.)

C. GENTLE STRENGTH (v. 5)

5. "Blessed are the meek, for they will inherit the earth.

Meek—gentle or humble—describes a strength like that of a well-trained animal brought under control so as to serve purposes outside itself. It is the quality of the gentle giant, having no need to prove his power and having no wish to use it for himself. It is the quality of one who has bowed most humbly before God; hence has no terror for any man—Moses before Pharaoh, or John the Baptist before Herod, or Jesus before Pilate—King over all, but giving his all for others.

Psalm 37:11 says, "The meek will inherit the land." The entire psalm is their instruction against being upset by the short-lived prosperity of the wicked, knowing that God will make his own final distribution of his assets. Even now the gentle ones can enjoy God's world as the arrogant and demanding ones can never do. They possess what never could be bought or earned.

D. AN APPETITE FOR GODLINESS (v. 6)

6. "Blessed are those who hunger and thirst for righteousness, for they will be filled.

Psalm 42:1, 2 describes this spiritual appetite: "As the deer pants for streams of water, so my soul pants for you, O God." So the longed-for *righteousness* is a positive relationship with the Almighty. The child of the King has no greater desire than to do his Father's will. "My food," said Jesus, "is to do the will of him who sent me and to finish his work" (John 4:34).

Here is an appetite that can be satisfied most fully in all who possess it. The opportunities are limitless. Isaiah 55:1, 2 expresses the Lord's invitation: "Come, all you who are thirsty, come to the waters; and you who have no money, come, buy and eat!… Eat what is good, and your soul will delight in the richest of fare."

Keen physical hunger and thirst are not common among people who seldom work hard or go long without refreshment. We deaden our appetites with indulgence in the kinds of food that quiets the hunger without giving the body the nutrition it needs. Spiritual appetite, also, increases with spiritual exercise and the avoidance of innutritious spiritual food.

E. PATIENCE IN PRACTICE (v. 7)

7. "Blessed are the merciful, for they will be shown mercy.

Up to this point, the Lord's emphasis has been on attitudes toward God and qualities within the child of God. Now Jesus moves to a practical expression of those qualities in dealing with others. Jesus' compassion in feeding and healing the needy ones around him provides the pattern for this Beatitude. It goes beyond Proverbs 14:21: "Blessed is he who is kind to the needy." It imitates the mercy of God in extending forgiveness when punishment is deserved, providing food for the thankless, and sustaining life in those who deny its source.

F. PURITY WITHIN (v. 8)

The Lord's test of character moves at this point from observable actions to the hidden wellsprings of thought and motive. These are known to God, and they become known to men as the thoughts grow into determination and doing.

8. "Blessed are the pure in heart, for they will see God.

"Above all else, guard your heart," urged the wise king, "for it is the wellspring of life" (Proverbs 4:23). And purity of heart is necessary for standing before God (Psalm 24:3, 4).

Pure translates a word that speaks of cleansing or purging. Jesus rebuked severely those whose passion for cleanness was limited to what could be seen by men. He spoke of such persons as whitewashed tombs, beautiful on the outside but filled inwardly with decay (Matthew 23:27). So he judged the thoughts and intents of the heart, linking hatred with murder, and lust with adultery (Matthew 5:21, 22, 27, 28).

Pure describes also that which is free from foreign substances. The pure heart does not include mixed motives or competing affections. When the pure heart speaks, the hearer does not have to wonder what is really meant. Thoughts, words, and deeds fall into one consistent pattern. Christians are urged to focus their attention on what is good and desirable (Philippians 4:8). It is a pattern not easily preserved in the face of what is offered by the communications media in our society.

To *see God*, though, is worthy of the utmost attention. To recognize, understand, and perceive him who is all-holy, all-just, all-wise, all-powerful, and eternal is reward enough for total effort. And it is impossible to one whose perceptions and senses of value are dominated or scrambled by the thought patterns of this present world. To see God with perfect clarity is not possible in this present world; but there will be plenty of opportunity to clear up the vision, face to face, after all hindrances are removed.

G. CAMPAIGNING FOR PEACE (v. 9)

9. "Blessed are the peacemakers, for they will be called sons of God.

So God's children are to exert themselves in word and deed to prevent and to heal misunderstandings and conflicts, even at the cost of great patience with personal wrong, but always with firmness for truth. "Peace in our time" must not be purchased through the surrender of moral principle, simply delaying more serious warfare. That is the folly of parents who shy away from the tensions of family discipline, and so condemn their sons and daughters to more serious conflict with society and with God.

Genuine *peacemakers* are acknowledged by God to be his children. They show the family resemblance to the "God of peace" in sharing "the peace of God" through Jesus Christ (Philippians 4:7-9). That is achieved through convincing persons to be reconciled—adjusted—to God (2 Corinthians 5:18-21). He cannot change in adjustment to sinful men; so he makes peace by forgiving the penitent ones and claiming them as his children.

MAKING PEACE

Back in 1990, Iraq sent 120,000 troops to take over little Kuwait. Months of negotiations and sanctions failed to dislodge them. Then the United Nations launched Operation Desert Storm. After 89,000 tons of explosives softened up the Iraqi army, ground troops drove it out in a mere one hundred hours; and peace returned.

Peace in the biblical sense is more than the absence of hostility. It is the general well-being that comes with righteousness. To bring lasting peace, sometimes we must confront the sin and evil that cause enmity and strife. Our weapons are not guns and bombs; we have a weapon of divine origin (2 Corinthians 10:4): the Word of God (Hebrews 4:12). —C. B. Mc.

III. EXPERIENCE THAT BLESSES (MATTHEW 5:10-12)

Children of God's kingdom are blessed not only in their character and relationships, but also in their response to what happens to them.

A. HATRED FROM GOD'S ENEMIES (vv. 10, 11)

10. "Blessed are those who are persecuted because of righteousness, for theirs is the kingdom of heaven.

HOW TO SAY IT:
beatus (Latin). BEE-uh-tus
makarios (Greek). muh-CAR-ee-os.

WHAT DO YOU THINK?

The secular world seems to be stepping up its attacks on those who stand up for morality in general and against Christians in particular. Do you see a corresponding blessing coming to those who are thus attacked? If so, what? If not, why not—that is, what has happened to the promise of verses 10-12? What do you expect to see in the next few years, both in terms of secular "persecution" and of "blessing" for the righteous?

God's peacemaking children are warred against by the forces that reject God. The God-hating world would "drive" or "chase" (literal meaning of the word translated *persecute*) them out of its presence. That persecution had begun with Jesus and it would continue. First Peter 2:20-23 and 3:14 speak encouragement to those who endure patiently the unjust punishment that comes to them because of their allegiance to Christ. It identifies them as citizens of his kingdom and sharers in his glory. Having that, they have small use for the world's approval and favors.

11. "Blessed are you when people insult you, persecute you and falsely say all kinds of evil against you because of me.

This, too, is addressed specifically to faithful followers of Jesus. The persecution here described is mostly verbal. It is not true, however, that "words can never harm me." Insults and slander can destroy a career as surely as can violence, and the wounds are slow to heal.

Three qualifications attend the persecution that blesses. It is vicious, it is false, and it comes to the Christian because of Christ. It sounds like the kind of treatment accorded now to "bigoted, narrow-minded religious right-wingers" by people who resist and resent any restriction or rebuke to their flagrant and destructive misbehavior. The experience is not new, nor without solace (1 Peter 4:14).

B. FELLOWSHIP OF GOD'S FRIENDS (v. 12)

12 "Rejoice and be glad, because great is your reward in heaven, for in the same way they persecuted the prophets who were before you."

Here the Lord recommends celebration of what the world would call misery. What a marvelous company was and is that of the prophets! Each in his own time was faithful in delivering God's message, in spite of rejection and mistreatment: "They mocked God's messengers, despised his words and scoffed at his prophets" (2 Chronicles 36:16; compare Hebrews 11:32-40). Each generation seemed to revere the ancient prophets, while rejecting those who brought God's word to themselves (Matthew 23:29, 30; Acts 7:52).

The apostles learned from Jesus, however, and did not wait until after death to enjoy the approval of Heaven. When they experienced persecution—physical and verbal—for the sake of Christ, they left "rejoicing because they had been counted worthy of suffering disgrace for the Name" (Acts 5:41; cf. Philippians 3:10-14).

CONCLUSION

The Sermon on the Mount, beginning with the Beatitudes, is indeed lofty teaching. It is so high, in fact, that many readers consider it wholly unrealistic. The principles here spoken go directly against the currents of both Jesus' time and ours, which measure the "good life" in terms of pride, power, pleasure, and possessions. But that "good life" has always ended in death and self-destruction.

Some would consider the spiritual view itself to be the way of life. Like the materialists, they would make happiness their goal, but they would seek it by a different route. They would grasp the teaching and forget the Teacher. That is to deny the ultimate reality behind the Sermon.

Happiness is not the goal, and to seek it as such is to lose it in utter frustration. God, in his Son Jesus, is the goal and the life. Joy is the experience of life in him, found in obedient faith. And that means down-to-earth being and doing in his name. Before Jesus came down from the mountain after the sermon, he warned against hearing and admiring without doing: "Not everyone who says to me, 'Lord, Lord,' will enter the kingdom of heaven, but only he who does the will of my Father who is in heaven" (Matthew 7:21). Right there is the life-style of the kingdom where joy is unavoidable.

Discovery Learning

This page contains an alternate lesson plan emphasizing learning activities. Classes desiring such student involvement will find these suggestions helpful. The next page is a reproducible activity page to further enhance discovery learning.

LEARNING GOALS

As a result of participating in today's lesson, a student will be able to:

1. Match each Beatitude with its promise.

2. Compare other biblical beatitudes with the ones in Matthew 5.

3. Strengthen Beatitudes already present; establish habits that will develop Beatitudes not so evident.

INTO THE LESSON

Ask the class, "If you can believe the TV commercials, what is happiness, and how can we find it?" As students supply answers, write them on a chalkboard or poster board. Then follow up with, "How do you think the 'experts' of our day define happiness and how to achieve it?" Again, list their answers. Finally, ask, "What seems to be the most prevalent idea of happiness in *your* neighborhood?" List the answers once more.

By now you should have quite a list. Possible items on it include feeling good emotionally, being physically "in shape," or being in control of your own destiny; happiness is found in exercise and diet plans, certain beverages, being accepted by others, money, being "your own person." Make the transition to today's lesson by pointing out that in the Sermon on the Mount Jesus gave some very direct teachings about happiness (Matthew 5–7).

INTO THE WORD

Before class, prepare several sets of index cards as follows: Write each of the eight character statements of Matthew 5:3-10 ("the poor in spirit," "they that mourn," etc.) on index cards, one per card. Do the same for each of the eight promises ("theirs is the kingdom of heaven," "they shall be comforted," etc.) Shuffle each set of sixteen cards, separate the class into the same number of groups as you have sets, and give each group one set. Ask students to match each Beatitude with its promise and then put the pairs in their biblical order as found in Matthew 5. Challenge them to try it with their Bibles closed at first (unless your class is dominated by new Christians with little Bible background). Then have them check the reference to be sure they are accurate.

OPTION

Use the reproducible activity "Scrambled Beatitudes" on page 316 for a variation of this exercise.

After time for study, have someone read the Scripture aloud. Discuss each Beatitude together, one at a time. (See the commentary section for an explanation of each Beatitude.) Point out the meaningful progression of the Beatitudes: realization of poverty prompts sorrow for sin, which leads to humility and denial of self, which is followed by a search for righteousness, etc. (The commentary section will help you with this, also.)

Divide the class into study groups of two to four persons each, and ask them to look up the following passages (write them on a chalkboard/poster board or on a handout): Psalm 1:1; 32:1, 2; 94:12; Proverbs 3:13; Matthew 13:16; Luke 14:13, 14; Romans 14:22; Titus 2:13; James 1:12, 25; 1 Peter 3:14; 4:14; Revelation 19:9. If you prefer, each study group may look up a few of the passages and then report to the class. Ask each group to summarize their findings about being blessed and to develop a definition of what it means to be *blessed.*

After adequate time, ask a spokesperson from each group to share the group's findings. Guide the discussion to emphasize that being blessed is more dependent on our relationship with and obedience to God than on our circumstances. To be blessed is to have a happiness that comes from God and has a sure future reward. Even while suffering, we are fortunate, content, and happy in God!

INTO LIFE

Ask each class member to indicate how he sees himself in each characteristic. Use a scale from 1 ("This just isn't me") to 5 ("Yes, that's me"). Ask them to write each characteristic and then put their rating next to each one.

Allow time for personal reflection and completion. Then ask, "What difference would it make in your life if you more fully developed the characteristic you rated lowest in your life?" Let them think about that for a moment, and discuss it if they will—though that may be an area they will not share in a large group.

Use the same small groups as before and ask each person in the group to tell each of the others in the group what he or she perceives to be each one's strongest Beatitude characteristic and why. Then have each person share one area where he or she feels improvement is needed (in himself, not in the others). The groups should discuss these, offering encouragement and suggestions.

Have each group choose a person to offer the closing prayer.

Scrambled Beatitudes

Read Matthew 5:1-12. Then match the "blessing" half of each Beatitude with its promise half by drawing a line from one to the other. In the blanks before each blessing half, write a number that represents that Beatitude's position in the list (1 for first, 2 for second, etc.).

_____ Blessed are the peacemakers

_____ Blessed are the poor in spirit

_____ Blessed are those who are persecuted because of righteousness

_____ Blessed are the pure in heart

_____ Blessed are those who mourn

_____ Blessed are the merciful

_____ Blessed are those who hunger and thirst for righteousness

_____ Blessed are you when people insult you, persecute you and falsely say all kinds of evil against you because of me

_____ Blessed are the meek

Rejoice and be glad, because great is your reward in heaven, for in the same way they persecuted the prophets who were before you

for theirs is the kingdom of heaven

for they will be called sons of God

for they will see God

for they will be shown mercy

for they will be filled

for they will inherit the earth

for they will be comforted

for theirs is the kingdom of heaven

The Beatitudes and You

Which of the nine Beatitude characteristics do you think you best model? Why?

In what ways have you seen the promised blessing come true in your life?

Which of the characteristics is weakest in your life?

What do you need to do to strengthen this area of your life?

Who can help you in this?

What will you do this week to make some progress in growing in this area?

TEACHINGS ABOUT LOVING YOUR ENEMIES

LESSON 11

WHY TEACH THIS LESSON?

Few issues of life demonstrate just how unnatural the Christian life is more than that of how one responds to one's enemies. In fact, even the response of a Christian is often too natural and not enough Christian! *Love* our enemies? It's contrary to everything we feel. Revenge, or at least justice, seems more in order.

We all know, however, that Jesus commands us to love. This is nothing new to anyone who has been a Christian more than a few months. Knowing and doing, however, seem often to be strangers. So we need a reminder. And along with the reminder, we need motivation.

This lesson provides the reminder. Jesus' teaching on this subject is clearly set forth in the pages that follow. His own example provides some motivation in this regard. How about your own example? Does it also challenge your students to walk the path of the Master? Can you, with Paul, say, "Follow my example, as I follow the example of Christ" (1 Corinthians 11:1)?

Pray for yourself and for your students as you prepare to teach this lesson. The Holy Spirit will provide motivation that cannot be written into any lesson book!

INTRODUCTION

A. MOTHER'S ENEMIES

Mother's Day is properly a celebration of love. Mother love begins naturally as tender affection for the infant offspring. It becomes a bond with the child as a person, loving the mother; then a lifelong relationship, tested and changing as personalities develop. Even after experience gives way to memory, Mother's Day never could be monotonous! Love is like that. But when a child is threatened, whoever poses the threat becomes the mother's enemy.

A Christian mother reveals a special quality, reaching out to other children in church, community, and beyond, with concern that all should know the blessings of a heavenly Father. Her enemies are those who threaten the wider family, especially in the realm of faith, morals, and character. So love and enmity are interwoven on Mother's Day, and so they are in Jesus' teaching on the subject.

B. NO MORE PERSECUTORS?

Last week we heard the Lord's blessing on those who, because they belong to him, will be opposed, slandered, and excluded from positions of influence. They are to rejoice, Jesus said, in their fellowship with him who endured greater persecution. Today's lesson may lead some to suggest that we may do away with enemies by making them our friends. Are we thus to forfeit the blessing we were so recently promised?

There is no danger of that, unless we surrender and join the enemy. And that would do away with all blessing forever. No, our Lord had enemies enough to kill

---

DEVOTIONAL READING
LUKE 10:25-37

LESSON SCRIPTURE
MATTHEW 5:38-48;
LUKE 10:25-37

PRINTED TEXT
MATTHEW 5:38-48

LESSON AIMS

This study should enable the student to:

1. Summarize Jesus' teachings concerning personal responses to evil.

2. Determine ways to demonstrate the love Christians ought to show their enemies.

3. Pray for and show love to someone who has been particularly difficult or unfriendly.

May
12

KEY VERSE

But I tell you: Love your enemies and pray for those who persecute you.

—Matthew 5:44

LESSON 11 NOTES

him, and he still has enemies enough to share with all his followers. That is true in spite of all our love and prayers. The blessing remains, along with the Lord's example and instruction about dealing with those who insist on opposing him and his followers.

C. LESSON BACKGROUND

The Sermon on the Mount presents a direct challenge to all that has gone before. The character traits that are "blessed" in the introductory section stand in stark contrast to the world's standard of values at every point on which they touch (Matthew 5:3-11). There was more to come, relating to the law of Moses and its application. Some would think that Jesus was attempting to destroy the law. Not so. He was defending the law from the deadening interpretations and shallow applications that had destroyed its force (vv. 17-20). In doing so, he spoke with an authority equal to that of the original presentation on that other mountain, Sinai. Six times he quoted popular interpretations of basic laws, and added, "But I tell you—" (vv. 21-44).

Much that Jesus said was associated with purity in heart (Matthew 5:8). Deeds, good or evil, are begotten in thoughts and intentions known at first only to the thinker and to God (Proverbs 4:23; 1 Samuel 16:7). The way to avoid murder, Jesus said, is to avoid anger (Matthew 5:21-26). The way to avoid adultery is to avoid lustful thinking (vv. 27-30). The way to avoid endless conflict is to develop the attitude of Jesus in helpful love rather than prideful retaliation (vv. 38-48). These last *I tell yous* provide our study for this week.

I. ACCEPT ABUSE FOR JESUS' SAKE (MATTHEW 5:38-42)

A. ACCEPT INSULT/INJURY (vv. 38, 39)

38. "You have heard that it was said, 'Eye for eye, and tooth for tooth.'

The quoted law is be found in Exodus 21:23-25; Leviticus 24:19, 20; and Deuteronomy 19:15-21. It prescribed punishments for crimes that had been confirmed by witnesses. Leviticus 19:17, 18 forbids private vengeance for personal offenses, and Proverbs 24:29 urges against it.

Two purposes were evident in the Old Testament law. One was to warn the potential offender that he could expect to be damaged as he damaged another. The second purpose was to limit retaliation and prevent escalating feuds. No person was to be killed for insulting his neighbor. Jesus would control personal retaliation with one tough principle.

39. "But I tell you, Do not resist an evil person. If someone strikes you on the right cheek, turn to him the other also.

Do not fight with the person who insults you. A right-handed blow to the right cheek would be made with the back of the hand. That kind of slap in the face would be a major insult, but not a major injury. And God's person, fully assured of his worth in the sight of the Almighty, is not overly concerned with his standing in the sight of men. (Compare John 13:3-5.) He who loves does not keep books on personal slights and insults (1 Corinthians 13:4-7). Instead of "getting even" for the insult, the follower of Christ is to show his willingness to accept it in double measure! The offender will have failed in his effort to destroy the Christian's composure. Rather than being overcome with evil, the Christian will have overcome evil with good (Romans 12:21). He will have reflected the character of Christ, who "suffered for [us], leaving [us] an example, that [we] should follow his steps. . . . When they hurled their insults at him, he did not retaliate; when he suffered, he made no threats. Instead, he entrusted himself to him who judges justly" (1 Peter 2:21-23).

WHAT DO YOU THINK?

Jesus' command to turn the other cheek to the person who strikes us ranks high among his "hard sayings." If a person should strike us—either physically or verbally—the natural tendency is to strike back in the same manner.

What happens when we retaliate in kind? What does that do for the cause of the gospel? What does forbearance of the evil do for the cause of the gospel? (See Proverbs 15:1.) What kind of attitudes and practices prepare a believer to be able to turn the other cheek in the moment of conflict?

WHAT DO YOU THINK?

The author says, "That kind of slap in the face would be a major insult, but not a major injury." What if it were more injurious? Would that change anything? Why or why not? Try to support your position with Scripture.

B. ACCEPT LEGAL INTRUSION (v. 40)

40. "And if someone wants to sue you and take your tunic, let him have your cloak as well.

Jesus already had advised his followers to settle their differences out of court, even at loss to themselves. Lawsuits would cost much more (Matthew 5:25, 26). The basis for losing one's garments in a lawsuit is found in Exodus 22:26, 27 and Deuteronomy 24:10-13. The light *tunic* and/or the heavier outer *cloak* might be taken as security for a loan, but the creditor was not allowed to keep a poor man's cloak overnight, since it served also as his blanket. Jesus directed his disciples to yield twice as much as was required, giving up the blanket garment also to the claimant. The Christian is fully aware of his legal rights, but he will not press or demand them at the expense of another person. Self is no longer number one with him.

SO SUE ME!

Western society has become one of rampant litigation. Perhaps nowhere is this more evident than in the United States, where eighteen million new lawsuits are filed every year. With only six percent of the world's population, the United States has seventy percent of all the world's lawyers. While much good is done by the legal system—defending the rights of the accused, prosecuting criminals, protecting the victims of negligence and injury—Americans are overrun with lawsuits.

In contrast with the litigious climate of our society, Jesus urged people to go out of their way to come to terms with their adversaries. The chief question for a Christian in conflict is not "How do I get everything that's coming to me?" but "How can I restore this damaged relationship?" —C. B. Mc.

C. ACCEPT POLITICAL PRESSURE (v. 41)

41. "If someone forces you to go one mile, go with him two miles.

Cyrus king of Persia is said to have authorized his couriers to require citizens with horses to help them on their way with government business. Greek and Roman rulers copied the plan with variations. Roman officers in Palestine could demand help from residents for a distance of *one mile*. So Simon of Cyrene was pressed into service to carry the cross of Jesus to the place of execution (Luke 23:26). Such service was commonly rendered grudgingly. But Jesus again directed his followers to do twice as much as was required. The first mile was duty; the second was opportunity. The first was bondage; the second was freedom.

D. ACCEPT MATERIAL BURDENS (v. 42)

42. "Give to the one who asks you, and do not turn away from the one who wants to borrow from you.

The Christian is directed to give *when* asked, but not necessarily *what* is asked. Jesus himself was known to give spiritual gifts rather than the material benefits requested (John 4:13-15). When a lame man looked to Peter and John for money, they gave him healing instead (Acts 3:1-10). That was done in the name of Jesus Christ, who gave his all to us and for us. The directive is to give as one can, according to the real needs and eternal benefit—not necessarily the deserving character—of the recipient.

Lending to the poor in his need is specifically commanded in Deuteronomy 15:7-11. The Jewish people were forbidden to charge interest on loans to one another. Jesus went a step farther: "If you lend to those from whom you expect repayment, what credit is that to you? Even 'sinners' lend to 'sinners,' expecting to be repaid in full" (Luke 6:34). The serious follower of the Lord will be victimized occasionally in his refusal to protect his rights, but he would rather be mistreated many

WHAT DO YOU THINK?

"Give to the one who asks you...." But what about the unscrupulous people who think nothing of taking advantage of the generosity of Christians? What about 2 Thessalonians 3:10? If we give money to anyone who asks, don't we run the danger of supporting a person's drug habit or drinking problem?

Are there precautions we can take to balance the need to help and the need to avoid these bad situations? If so, what? What if the situation defies our safeguards and we are left either to help and risk being taken advantage of or not help and risk turning away someone in genuine need? What is the Christian thing to do then? Why?

Is the responsibility of the individual Christian any different from the responsibility of the church as a whole? Why or why not? If so, how?

WHAT DO YOU THINK?

Apparently some people who call themselves Christians have felt it legitimate to hate certain people. Madalyn Murray O'Hair, the famous atheist, claimed that she received a great deal of hate mail from Christians. Perhaps we have bristled at the sight of Saddam Hussein on television. It could be that reading the militant statements of "pro-choice" or "gay-rights" activists stirs up strong negative sentiments within us. We can hate what they do or what they stand for, but we must love them. Some of them are blind, woefully ignorant, and spiritually lost.

How can we control our emotions so that we do not hate people who are hard to love? How can we show agape-type love to them? (See the commentary on v. 44 for an explanation of agape.*)*

Use visual 11 to illustrate v. 44.

WHAT DO YOU THINK?

What are some of the positive results of praying for those who have offended us?

• How does it help us?

• How does it help those for whom we pray?

• How does it help the situation in which the conflict arose?

• How does it help the church as a whole?

• What other benefits can you think of?

times than to mistreat another human being once. That is following and honoring him who said, "Whatever you did for one of the least of these brothers of mine, you did for me" (Matthew 25:40).

II. LOVE AS GOD LOVES (MATTHEW 5:43-48)

Jesus shows and prescribes the nature of God as the way of real and lasting life.

A. RETURN GOOD FOR EVIL (vv. 43, 44)

43. "You have heard that it was said, 'Love your neighbor and hate your enemy.'

The grand injunction to *love* one's *neighbor* shines out amid a cluster of laws on holy living, from Leviticus 19: "Do not seek revenge or bear a grudge against one of your people, but love your neighbor as yourself" (v. 18). Jesus called it the second greatest commandment of all, exceeded only by the command to love God wholly.

Scripture nowhere commands one to *hate* his *enemy*—especially his personal enemy. Yet the Israelites were forbidden to make peace with the Canaanites as enemies of God (Exodus 34:11-16), and Psalm 109 calls down judgment on the oppressors of the righteous. It would be easy to interpret such passages as approving, if not commanding, hatred of the enemy.

At best, those who were looking for the easy way could search the phrases, "your neighbor," "your brother," and "one of your people" for an interpretation that would excuse them from loving too many. (See Luke 10:29.)

Which of us, moreover, is not influenced somewhat by traditions implying that distaste for *them* is an important part of loving *us*? That wrong concept had to be answered!

KILL THEM WITH KINDNESS

In his book *Through the Valley of the Kwai*, Ernest Gordon writes about a group of American soldiers who encountered some wounded Japanese prisoners at a railway station in Burma. World War II was raging. Had these groups met on the battlefield, they would have tried to destroy each other; but now the prisoners were helpless, packed in railway cars, their uniforms incredibly filthy with mud and blood, their wounds uncared for. Quickly opening their packs, the Americans knelt by their enemies to give them food and water, to clean and bandage their wounds. The Japanese responded with grateful cries of "Aragatto!" (thank you).

Few things in the universe compare with the power that is unleashed when we love an enemy. Unexpected and undeserved kindnesses, gracious acts of mercy, soft answers in the face of wrath have the power to shatter walls of prejudice and enmity. According to Jesus, the best revenge we can exact upon our enemies is to kill them with kindness.

—C. B. Mc.

44. "But I tell you: Love your enemies and pray for those who persecute you,

The *love* here commanded and depicted is not an intense liking. It may, in fact, operate in the face of a strong dislike. The Greek *agape*, used here, is not basically emotional. It has been defined as "active and intelligent goodwill without regard for the response," an inclination to do good, rather than evil, to all persons, no matter how we may feel about them personally. Jesus' directive begins and ends with an appeal to God, who does good to all: *pray for*—call down good on—those who call down evil on you; and pray that God will exercise his wisdom in dealing most helpfully with the offenders. Prayer is a benefit that can be bestowed on even the most reluctant recipient. Between blessing and petitioning, we are directed to do as we ask God to do—to work for the offender's best eternal welfare.

Those who have seriously tried the Lord's program have found that it becomes less difficult. They also find that the feelings of dislike for the enemy tend to fade, and their problem of enmity declines. If enmity continues, it is the other person's problem, not theirs.

B. IMITATING OUR FATHER (v. 45)

45. "…that you may be sons of your Father in heaven. He causes his sun to rise on the evil and the good, and sends rain on the righteous and the unrighteous.

Luke 6:35, 36 extends on the same idea: "Love your enemies, do good to them, and lend to them without expecting to get anything back. Then your reward will be great, and you will be sons of the Most High, because he is kind unto the ungrateful and wicked. Be merciful, just as your Father is merciful."

The basic evidences of God's love are offered alike to all mankind. His children also are to distribute their goodwill without quotas or special directives. Not all recipients, however, are equally benefited by the distribution. The same sunshine and rain that bring good crops to the prudent farmer will produce gullies and brambles for the sluggard. But God's favors and his children's love are still available to all.

C. BE DIFFERENT FROM THE UNGODLY (vv. 46, 47)

46, 47. "If you love those who love you, what reward will you get? Are not even the tax collectors doing that? And if you greet only your brothers, what are you doing more than others? Do not even pagans do that?

Jesus turned for a moment from affirmative to negative motivation. Were his follower/hearers really content to be like "those people" to whom they felt most superior? For his comparison he chose the Jewish *tax collectors* for the Roman government—who frequently became wealthy by lining their own pockets with unauthorized assessments. As betrayers, oppressors, and wealthy crooks, the tax collectors were generally despised. They would be most comfortable in the company of others like themselves—loving those who loved them. For a modern counterpart we think immediately of gangs and "families" who gain power and wealth by violence, while exercising the strongest of love and loyalty within their tight little circles. If we limit our love to our own families and social circles, how is our love more praiseworthy than theirs?

The same principle applies to *greet*. The Greek text uses a word as warm as a smiling bow and as broad as the Hawaiian *aloha*. It could be used on any occasion, but always as an affectionate expression of good wishes.

So how do we conduct our greetings, in the place of worship, for example? Is it an occasion for meeting and visiting with our own family and friends? Do we have a limited hello and handshaking list? If so, how do we deserve more praise in this matter than do worldly people who have words of encouragement for none beyond their own circles, and trade gifts with the same people on every holiday?

CAN WE ALL JUST GET ALONG?

In the spring of 1992, the world watched in horror as South Central Los Angeles reacted to the acquittal of four police officers accused of beating Rodney King. Anarchy spread along the streets as gangs attacked, robbed, and left luckless drivers bleeding on the roadways. Wholesale looting went largely unchecked while more than 3,700 fires raged out of control. Fifty-five people died, and more than three thousand were injured before order was restored.

In what *Time* magazine called the most emotional television moment of 1992, the man at the center of it all, Rodney King, stepped before the cameras and nervously asked, "Can we all just get along?"

HOW TO SAY IT

agape (Greek). uh-GAH-pay.

WHAT DO YOU THINK?

Jesus' call to perfection (v. 48) is in contrast to the excuse often heard for misbehavior: "Oh, well, nobody's perfect!" In 1 John 1:8 and in other places in the New Testament it is made clear that Christians are not immune to sin. Why, then, are we told to "Be perfect"? In what sense, if any, is this possible? If none, then what is the point of this verse? How can we obey Jesus' command to "be perfect"?

It's a good question. One of the strong themes of the Bible is that of "getting along" with our fellowmen. Even when they aren't part of our family. Even when they aren't our neighbors. Even when they differ from us in race, nationality, or political perspective. Even when they are our enemies.

—C. B. Mc.

D. GROWING UP TO GOD (v. 48)

48. "Be perfect, therefore, as your heavenly Father is perfect."

The admonition points to the grown-up status of God's children (v. 45). It is echoed in Ephesians 5:1, 2: "Be imitators of God, therefore, as dearly loved children and live a life of love, just as Christ loved us and gave himself up for us." Paul himself had imitated God in Christ for many years before he wrote confessing that he had not yet reached the goal of complete maturity, but he pressed "toward the goal to win the prize for which God has called me heavenward in Christ Jesus" (Philippians 3:12-14). God was not through with him yet.

God himself is the perfection, the goal toward which all growing is directed, just as he is the holiness toward which all dedication is aimed: "Be holy because I, the Lord your God, am holy" (Leviticus 19:2). The Christian's maturity will follow the pattern of God's perfection, though it will not reach the same level. His saints are common believers who by his grace have become pure in heart and see God.

CONCLUSION

A. "BE GOOD TO MY GRANDCHILDREN"

A closing word for Mother's Day is appropriate. After the day is past—communications have been made and tributes spoken, gifts have been received and flowers have served their mission—what does Mother most desire from her day? Would she not thoughtfully say, "If you really want to honor me, be good to my grandchildren"?

Jesus our Lord did say, many times in many ways, "Love as I have loved you." Neither mother love nor Christian love, in any generation, is a minimum performance, limiting itself to those expressions that are required or necessary. Where love is lacking, the law can require a parent to provide decent housing and food for children. Mother love adds hugs and kisses, dries tears, and shares laughter, games, and stories. Mother love fixes favorite foods and buys pretty dresses. Mother love finds time for talking, listening, and praying together. Those build treasured memories.

B. REJOICING TO RUN

Scripture frequently compares the Christian life to a foot race, to be run with disciplined preparation (1 Corinthians 9:24-27) and patience (Hebrews 12:1, 2) to the goal (2 Timothy 4:6-8).

Who, though, ever enters a foot race grudgingly, as a matter of necessity, dragging through it with the least possible effort? That's not the way it's done!

Jesus was fully aware of the joyless drudgery with which many people face their days, and he provided the answer for it, as we have just seen. We are encouraged to replace "Do I have to?" with "Let me at it!"

"You don't have to do that!"

"Of course, I don't; but what fun is there in doing only what you have to do? That's a drag. The fun is in doing what you want to do, beyond the requirements."

So the joyous runner in life's race is strong enough to accept insults he doesn't have to, and accept legal adjustments he doesn't have to, and walk miles he doesn't have to, and give more generously than he has to, and pray for enemies he doesn't have to—all for the sake of the Lord who made all kinds of sacrifices he didn't have to, for our sakes, and for the joy that was set before him (Hebrews 12:2). That is loving, and living!

Discovery Learning

This page contains an alternate lesson plan emphasizing learning activities. Classes desiring such student involvement will find these suggestions helpful. The next page is a reproducible activity page to further enhance discovery learning.

LEARNING GOALS

As a result of today's lesson, a student will be able to:

1. Summarize Jesus' teachings concerning personal responses to evil.

2. Determine ways to demonstrate the love Christians ought to show their enemies.

3. Pray for and show love to someone who has been particularly difficult or unfriendly.

INTO THE LESSON

Ask the class members to relate specific memories of a mother's love in action. When did their mothers show love in an outstanding, unmistakable, and unforgettable way? Take a few moments to celebrate the love of our mothers (or other caregivers) on this Mother's Day. Lead the class in praising God for our mothers and those who have helped us become who we are, especially in Christ.

Jesus was very aware of the fact that the world does not share our mothers' great love for us as Christians. Today's lesson is concerned with how to respond to those who are hostile toward us.

OPTION

Distribute the word search puzzle from the reproducible page 332. Give the class a few minutes to solve the puzzle, using their Bibles for help.

INTO THE WORD

Read Matthew 5:38-48. Then ask the students to separate into five groups with two to five people in each group. Give each group a card with one of these groups of Scripture references. (If you have more than twenty-five students, form additional groups and give duplicate assignments.)

1. Matthew 5:38, 39; Exodus 21:23-25; Romans 12:21
2. Matthew 5:40; Exodus 22:25-27; Philippians 2:3, 4
3. Matthew 5:41; Ephesians 6:7, 8; Colossians 3:22-24
4. Matthew 5:42; Deuteronomy 15:7-11; Matthew 6:2-4; Acts 20:35
5. Matthew 5:43, 44; Leviticus 19:18; Romans 5:8-10; 12:18-21

Ask each group to take a few minutes to study the Scriptures assigned; then prepare to tell the class what Jesus taught in the verse or verses from Matthew. Finally, determine how the other Scripture passages are related to that teaching, and be prepared to explain that to the class.

Watch the groups as they study. If one seems to be stumped, you may want to help with information from the lesson explanation in this book. When the groups give their reports, be ready to supplement some or all of them with your own comments or thoughts drawn from your preparatory study of the lesson.

These teachings are hard to understand and even more difficult to put into practice. Lead a brief discussion of why Jesus' teachings are so difficult to apply to our lives. Possible answers: *We tend to be selfish; our culture focuses on protecting one's rights; we do not want others to take advantage of us or take us for granted.*

Now read Matthew 5:45-48. We must be different from the world and more like our heavenly Father. Though we will never be perfectly loving and holy as he is, we should be growing toward that perfection. Ask someone to read Philippians 3:12-15. As we become more like Jesus, we love even our enemies. As we demonstrate love for all others, we become more like Jesus (Luke 23:34).

INTO LIFE

Distribute "Putting It Into Practice" from page 332 and have the students complete the activity. Then discuss it.

Or divide the class into groups of three. People of each group are to choose a situation from "Putting It Into Practice" or think of another situation in which a Christian is insulted, slandered, or otherwise mistreated. It may be a situation that has actually has happened or imaginary. Each group is to plan a short skit. Acting as the Christian, one group member will explain how he has been mistreated. The other two will act as the Christian's "good self" and his "bad self." The bad self will stand beside him and suggest all sorts of mean and spiteful ways of getting even. The good self will stand on the other side of him, remind him of Jesus' teaching and suggest right ways of acting. Each skit should be played out to a conclusion, whether good or bad.

After each skit, lead the class in applause and appreciation. When all have been presented, lead a discussion of any insights gained from the presentations.

Ask each class member to think of a person who could be considered his or her enemy. Encourage prayer for that person as a first step in applying the teachings of Jesus. Keeping the groups of three, invite each group to pray together for their enemies and their ability to show love in the name of Jesus Christ.

Bible Word Search

Fill in the blanks from Matthew 5:38-48. Then locate those words on the grid below. Use the word list at the bottom of the page if you need additional help.

"You have ____ that it was said, 'Eye for ____, and ____ for tooth.' But I tell you, Do not ____ an evil person. If someone ____ you on the ____ ____, turn to him the other also. And if someone wants to ____ you and take your ____, let him have your cloak as well. If someone forces you to go ____ ____, go with him ____ miles. ____ to the one who ____ you, and do not turn away from the one who wants to ____ from you.

"You have heard that it was said, 'Love your ____ and ____ your ____.' But I tell you: ____ your enemies and ____ for those who ____ you, that you may be sons of your ____ in heaven. He causes his sun to rise on the ____ and the good, and sends rain on the ____ and the ____. If you love those who love you, what ____ will you get? Are not even the ____ ____ doing that? And if you ____ only your ____, what are you doing more than others? Do not even ____ do that? Be ____, therefore, as your ____ Father is perfect."

P	W	U	Y	G	P	R	A	Y	L	P	L	K	L	R
I	A	O	N	M	I	T	A	X	N	I	E	C	E	T
S	N	G	R	R	E	V	C	G	V	E	O	H	S	T
U	E	S	A	R	I	N	E	E	H	L	T	I	H	M
O	I	O	K	N	O	G	E	C	L	A	S	G	E	I
E	G	N	W	S	S	B	H	E	F	E	I	V	S	L
T	H	E	G	Q	A	T	C	T	R	R	U	P	E	E
H	B	T	W	O	V	T	B	T	E	H	L	J	U	A
G	O	Y	E	T	O	R	S	R	C	O	E	O	S	Z
I	R	T	E	R	O	T	L	A	E	E	U	A	V	I
R	A	E	S	T	R	C	P	K	H	W	F	S	R	E
H	R	Z	H	I	I	K	W	E	S	T	A	R	G	D
G	G	E	K	N	E	Y	E	U	D	Y	O	R	E	V
R	R	E	U	H	E	A	V	E	N	L	Y	O	D	P
S	S	T	K	E	T	U	C	E	S	R	E	P	T	J

Putting It Into Practice

Consider the following situations and suggest a proper response in light of Matthew 5:38-48. Use the back of this sheet to write your responses.

1. Mary's husband Joe is on the phone. He has just announced, out of the blue, that he won't be home for dinner; he's going to a friend's house to watch the ball game on TV. She had planned a special evening together. She says, …

2. Fred was recently elected shop foreman. A co-worker, who also wanted the position, has begun spreading lies about him. Some of his friends have backed away from him, and management has called him in to "answer some questions." On the way to that meeting, he meets the rival co-worker. Fred …

3. Tom is the Sunday school superintendent for his church. He has asked all the Sunday school teachers to give several days advance notice (except in emergencies) when substitutes are needed, but one teacher habitually "forgets" to notify him. On Saturday night the teacher calls; a company function he has known about for *three months* will keep him out of his class the next day. Tom says …

Word List: asks, borrow, brothers, cheek, collectors, enemy, evil, eye, Father, give, greet, hate, heard, heavenly, love, mile, neighbor, one, pagans, perfect, persecute, pray, resist, reward, right, righteous, strikes, sue, tax, tooth, tunic, two, unrighteous

TEACHINGS ABOUT RICHES AND ANXIETY

LESSON 12

WHY TEACH THIS LESSON?

Worry. The very word sounds dismal and bleak—like the way we feel when we give in to worry.

Money. Now there's a word that sounds good! Supposedly, it's the cure to whatever you worry about.

So why doesn't money take away worry? If your class members are like most people, one of the main things they worry about is money! And not necessarily because they don't have it, either. Today's church is the wealthiest church in history. Unfortunately, many of her members have not learned to share. Studies show that the wealthier a person becomes, the less he or she gives to the church—or to any charitable cause.

Obviously, something is needed. It is hoped that this lesson will present the case for trusting in God and not in wealth to such a degree that your members will be more willing to share. If they do, they will find they worry less and trust God more.

INTRODUCTION

A. TREASURING TREASURES

Treasure Island! The very name of Stevenson's adventure story will quicken the pulse of one-time boys familiar with its account of conflict in search for hidden wealth. Long before Stevenson, however, Jesus caught the imagination of sober adults by comparing the kingdom of Heaven to buried treasure so great that the finder would sell all he possessed in order to claim it (Matthew 13:44).

Treasure! What a word! As a noun it speaks of riches, usually stored up or hoarded. It may speak of any precious items highly prized. *Treasure* is also a verb. It speaks of collecting and/or storing up things of value; also cherishing or holding on to what is most appreciated. One does treasure one's treasures.

Matthew 6:19-21 speaks literally of collecting, storing up, cherishing, and clinging to what one values most. In what are we most interested? On what do we spend time and money most freely? What do we collect, store, hide or display, and protect most carefully? With Jesus it was and is the reign and the realm of God.

B. LESSON BACKGROUND

In his Sermon on the Mount Jesus talked immediately about ultimate values, boldly challenging the ideas popularly accepted by his hearers, then and now. Pleasure, prosperity, and power are false gods, he showed. Thoughts and attitudes, he said, are basic to one's acceptance with God. And they are not the thoughts and attitudes popularly encouraged as leading to "success" in the world today.

Jesus spoke first of pure thoughts as the basis of moral behavior (Matthew 5). Then he considered three practices important in religious life—generosity to the poor, prayer, and fasting (Matthew 6:1-18). All such practices, he said, should be done without fanfare, as between the worshiper and God.

DEVOTIONAL READING
LUKE 12:13-21

LESSON SCRIPTURE
MATTHEW 6:19-21, 24-34;
LUKE 12:13-21

PRINTED TEXT
MATTHEW 6:19-21, 24-34

LESSON AIMS

This study should prepare the student to:

1. Explain Jesus' prescription for worrying about food, clothes, and tomorrow.

2. Compare God's provision for birds and flowers with his care for Christians.

3. Identify a way by which one will cease fruitless worrying.

KEY VERSE

Seek first his kingdom and his righteousness, and all these things will be given to you as well.
—Matthew 6:33

May 19

LESSON 12 NOTES

Visual 12 from the visuals packet illustrates today's key verse. Display it as you begin your Bible study.

WHAT DO YOU THINK?

What does it mean to "store up … treasures in heaven"? Salvation is a free gift, isn't it? What can we do here to "store up" a reward there? And does this treasure accumulate—is it possible to store up little or much, depending on the efforts expended?

(See 1 Corinthians 3:10-15; 1 Timothy 6:17-19.)

OPTION

For a fun way to introduce the lesson, distribute the reproducible page 332, and see if your students can "Change Worry to Trust." (A possible solution to the puzzle follows.)

Worry
Worse
Torte
Tooth
Truth
Trust

Then suddenly he turned to material considerations—money, buying groceries, and clothing. The Sermon came down to earth with a thud that must have shocked some of his hearers. The Lord insisted, though, that the Christian's *earth* maintains inseparable ties with *Heaven*.

I. TREASURE IN HEAVEN (MATTHEW 6:19-21, 24)

A. MATERIAL INVESTMENT (vv. 19-21)

19. "Do not store up for yourselves treasures on earth, where moth and rust destroy, and where thieves break in and steal.

Stop accumulating a stockpile of material goods in a place where nothing is ultimately secure. Jesus described that insecurity as it applied to his hearers' preferred investments—costly garments (Joshua 7:21; 2 Kings 5:22, 26) and metal objects such as coins. These could be eaten by moths or by corrosion and become worthless. Swifter destruction can come to present-day material investments through flood, fire, windstorm, or a stock market crash.

Thieves could dig through the clay or rock walls of houses to get around barred doors, and so take anything of value. Modern security measures can hinder the process but can never prevent it. Jesus warns us simply that the material world is no secure depository for wealth.

20. "But store up for yourselves treasures in heaven, where moth and rust do not destroy, and where thieves do not break in and steal.

Start building up a treasury in Heaven, where there is real security. Luke 12:33 gives directions for turning material wealth into heavenly riches through gifts and activities honoring Christ. First Timothy 6:17-19 provides practical instruction for well-to-do Christians, to be rich in good works, sharing generously. "In this way they will lay up a treasure for themselves as a firm foundation for the coming age." The Lord promised rewards, on earth and in Heaven, to those who left the security of homes and businesses in order to follow and serve him (Luke 18:28-30).

Financial investment in eternity is clearly accessible, but not with the idea of buying one's way into Heaven. That purchase price has been paid in the only possible way by Jesus himself. But *treasures* suggests by definition an accumulation beyond what is necessary. Paul made investment in Heaven by forgoing his right to receive living expenses from the Corinthians and financing his work by making tents (Acts 18:1-4; 1 Corinthians 9:3-18). In this he has been joined by the non-preaching elder who explains happily that his occupation is serving the Lord, but he operates a small business to finance it.

21. "For where your treasure is, there your heart will be also.

God is not served with material things as though he were in need of them, since he is himself the source of all things material and otherwise (Acts 17:24, 25). He is, on the other hand, vitally concerned with the persons he has made in his own image, that they should love him and seek him with a whole heart. And that is not possible as long as their attention is fixed on things material and temporary.

WHAT'S IT WORTH TO YOU?

Psychology Today asked more than twenty thousand people what they would be willing to do for a million dollars. Twenty-three percent of the men and twenty-one percent of the women said they would marry someone they didn't love. Twenty-two percent of the men and ten percent of the women said they would tell a lie about a business associate. Twenty-one percent of the men and ten percent of the women said they would steal something. Eighteen percent of the men and ten percent of the women said they would bribe someone or take a bribe. Twelve percent of the men and ten percent of the women said they would divorce their spouses.

What would you do for a million dollars? Is there something more important than money in your value system? Jesus taught that there are some things more permanent than money, and that a wise person will invest himself in something that is more lasting than earthly riches.

—C. B. Mc.

B. SELF-INVESTMENT (v. 24)

Verses 22 and 23 provide an important link between treasure-building and self-commitment. Their theme is singleness of focus and purpose. The Lord warns against blurred double vision, conflicting interests, and uncertainty in one's course. "He is a double-minded man, unstable in all he does" (James 1:8).

24. "No one can serve two masters. Either he will hate the one and love the other, or he will be devoted to the one and despise the other. You cannot serve both God and Money.

Serving two masters is described in language that indicates being slave to separate owners. No one is totally his own master: "When you offer yourselves to someone to obey him as slaves, you are slaves to the one whom you obey" (Romans 6:16). Obedience to competing masters is impossible, since the act of obedience to one is an act of disobedience to the other. The servant has to choose, on the basis of feeling—hating one and loving the other—or on the basis of action—following the command of one and disregarding the other.

Money, or riches, as a master is a tyrant opposed to God in direction and goal. It is not possible to keep *God* and *money* totally separate. A person can serve God *with* money, thus investing in heavenly treasure; or one may use the things of God in serving money, as the politician who attends church regularly for two months before each election, but not otherwise. Jesus sounds again and again the challenge issued by Joshua: "Choose for yourselves this day whom you will serve" (Joshua 24:15); and by Elijah: "How long will you waver between two opinions? If the Lord is God, follow him; but if Baal is God, follow him" (1 Kings 18:21).

Self-dedication in terms of time, energy, influence, and even one's personal rights is what gives meaning to any other investment in God's kingdom. In praising the generosity of Christians in Macedonia, Paul noted that they "gave themselves first to the Lord" (2 Corinthians 8:5).

II. TRUST IN GOD (MATTHEW 6:25-32)

The Christian has chosen to *serve* God rather than riches as his master, so he is to *depend on* God rather than money for his security.

A. UNCERTAINTY ABOUT NECESSITIES (v. 25)

25. "Therefore I tell you, do not worry about your life, what you will eat or drink; or about your body, what you will wear. Is not life more important than food, and the body more important than clothes?

Do not worry. The basic necessities of *life* are not to be matters for uncertainty. The life itself, which God gave in the first place, is infinitely more important than a well-stocked pantry to sustain it. God is not going to let you starve. So, too, the *body* that God made and caused to grow is vastly more important than the clothing that protects it. God will give what is necessary to sustain what he has already bestowed.

Much of our attention to *food* and *clothes* seems to deal, in fact, not with needs, but with likes and dislikes in taste and appearance.

In 1 Timothy 6:6-10 Paul echoes the Lord's warning against becoming entangled in the web of concern for wealth. He urges, "But if we have food and clothing, we will be content with that."

WHAT DO YOU THINK?

How can we tell if we are allowing our money or our possessions, rather than Christ, to be our master? To what degree do you think the following indicate which master we follow? Why?

• Our giving to the Lord and his work

• The general run of our thoughts

• Our possessions

• Our response to special appeals

• The use of our time

• The criteria we use for voting in national elections

WHAT DO YOU THINK?

Most of us have food and clothing enough. And yet we have cause for worry. Natural disasters like wind storms or severe flooding could happen to us. We could lose our jobs—this is common in our time when businesses fail or relocate or cut back on their payrolls. Through accident or illness we could lose the ability to work. Some of us are even now experiencing one of these, or some equally difficult situations. Some would say this Scripture is just too "pollyanna" for today's stressful times!

How would you respond to such a claim? How do we keep from worrying in the face of such circumstances?

HIGH ANXIETY

Upset stomach? Sweaty palms? Tense feeling? Pounding heart? You're not alone. Fears about health, finances, employment, children, career development, marriage, and other problems overwhelm many people. People with jobs worry about their work. People without jobs worry about not working. Parents worry about illnesses or accidents involving their children.

To combat worry, people turn to prescription drugs, seminars, and self-help books. Some of the current advice is to set aside specific times to worry, get more rest, exercise, or eat special diets. Then there is psychological counseling, behavior modification, and group therapy.

With so much to worry about and so many confusing options for treating it, how do we turn off the anxiety alarm? Jesus gave us the key by reminding us that the Creator who put us here is still in charge. In one sense, the common problems that worry us are not our problems. They are God's. He understands us and our needs better than we do. Try as you may, you cannot worry up a better answer to your needs than God can provide.

—C. B. Mc.

WHAT DO YOU THINK?

"Look at the birds of the air." They don't have insurance or savings accounts. They don't have steady jobs. They don't know where their next meal is coming from.

Does Jesus expect us to live like that? Are insurance and savings accounts evidence that we do not trust in the Father's provisions? Why or why not? How do we balance responsible planning and stewardship with "bird"-like expressions of total dependence on the Father?

B. BIRDS AND BASICS (vv. 26, 27)

26. "Look at the birds of the air; they do not sow or reap or store away in barns, and yet your heavenly Father feeds them. Are you not much more valuable than they?

Birds may have been seen fluttering about as Jesus spoke. Clearly, these have no way of accumulating a season's supply of food ahead of time. Neither do they wait in their nests for food to be delivered. Instead, the birds live as God designed them to, finding, eating and/or carrying to their young what God's world makes available to them. Will God feed birds and neglect his own children? By no means! He provides for them also as they live according to the plan he has laid out for them.

Jesus' question, contrasting the worth of birds and of persons in God's sight, is central to his teaching. The biblical account of creation affirms that humankind, made in God's image, was given priority and dominion over the other creatures (Genesis 1:28). Many in our time, though, would dismiss the idea of God and creation, denying any clear distinction between mankind and "other animals," in worth or in moral responsibility. The result is to make men more beastly than the beasts (Romans 1:18-32), working destruction on themselves and all around them. Hear what Jesus says about creation!

27. "Who of you by worrying can add a single hour to his life?

Anxious concern is more likely to shorten life than to lengthen it! Perhaps Jesus was observing the inordinate concern of Greeks, Romans, and other pagans with physical development beyond any purposeful use. First Timothy 4:8 recommends exercise in godliness as infinitely more valuable.

C. CLOTHING AND FLOWERS (vv. 28-30)

28, 29. "And why do you worry about clothes? See how the lilies of the field grow. They do not labor or spin. Yet I tell you that not even Solomon in all his splendor was dressed like one of these.

Time, money, and worry may be overspent on clothing even more than on food.

Again, the Lord's illustrative item may have been visible as he spoke. *Lilies,* of the various kinds growing wild after the winter rains on Galilee's croplands and pastures, are known for their variety and beauty. Let the listeners learn well from observation! The flowers' adornment did not require the gathering of fiber to be spun into thread, woven into cloth, dyed for color, and fashioned into garments. Instead, it came naturally from God's creative provision.

The *splendor* of *Solomon's* court, including what he and his courtiers wore, was proverbial in his own day (1 Kings 10:1-7; 2 Chronicles 9:3-6) and continually through many Oriental traditions. The natural beauty of a small flower was still superior to the most lavish human provision.

30. "If that is how God clothes the grass of the field, which is here today and tomorrow is thrown into the fire, will he not much more clothe you, O you of little faith?

The leaves of lilies are like coarse *grass,* and in rainless months they dry up quickly. Then they become fuel badly needed in Palestine, since it has very few trees. *Fire*—used to heat clay ovens, was generated by burning dry grass and weed stalks in the ovens. From flower to fuel was but a brief journey for the lilies.

The contrast between these short-lived objects and God's faithful children was even sharper than that between birds and men. He who gave so much beauty to the grass would surely not abandon his own spiritual family. To doubt his care and provision, even for one anxious hour, would mark the followers of Jesus as "little faiths" or slight believers. That stands as Jesus' one spoken rebuke in a message of assurance. The disciples had seen enough of God's care surrounding them, and especially in Jesus himself, to support a faith much stronger than they were showing. The Lord's resurrection would go far to correct that deficiency.

D. CONCERNS OF UNBELIEVERS (vv. 31, 32)

31. "So do not worry, saying, 'What shall we eat?' or 'What shall we drink?' or 'What shall we wear?'

These are simple questions about basic necessities. A faith that will prevent anxious concern about these matters will surely be strong enough to prevent our being burdened with questions about the stock market, our television reception, or our standing in the community club.

32. "For the pagans run after all these things, and your heavenly Father knows that you need them.

Untaught Gentiles, having no hope beyond this present life, and no knowledge of a sustaining *heavenly Father,* had reason to be concerned about needs and treasures on earth. These were the only security they knew.

Christians, on the other hand, know an all-caring Father in Heaven, who is aware of their needs and able to supply them. They may cast all their care on him who cares for them (1 Peter 5:7), and they may be free from anxiety as they bring their requests in thankful prayer. Thus assured, they can rest in the indescribable peace of God (Philippians 4:6, 7). Anxious worry on their part would be like *pagan* unbelief!

WHAT'S IN IT FOR ME?

A Florida minister told his congregation that "blessings, benefits, and rewards" would come to anyone who would give ten percent of his income to the church. One member promptly responded with a gift of eight hundred dollars.

Three years later, that member was unemployed. Claiming that he had received no blessings, benefits, or rewards, he sued the church. Before the case could come to trial, a Texas businessman read about it and sent the member a check for eight hundred dollars. The case was dropped.

Was this man wrong to think God refused to bless him? God often rewards faithful stewards with material things, but his blessings are not always counted in dollars and cents. Forgiveness, God's peace and presence in our lives, adoption into the

WHAT DO YOU THINK?

The pagans, Jesus said, "run after" material things. His followers, on the contrary, are to "seek" his kingdom and his righteousness. Besides the obvious difference between the objects of the two pursuits, what point, if any, was he making by contrasting "running after" and "seeking"? Is it possible to "run after" the right things, and thus be wrong because of the improper manner of the pursuit? Explain.

WHAT DO YOU THINK?

What is the connection between putting God's kingdom first and not worrying? Does one lead to the other? If so, which comes first? Do we stop worrying so we can seek his kingdom, or do we seek the kingdom and thus stop worrying? Explain.

THOUGHT TO REMEMBER

No one can serve God and money, but anyone can serve God with money.

DAILY BIBLE READINGS

Monday, May 13—Seeking God's Approval (Galatians 1:6-10)

Tuesday, May 14–Praising God for His Care (Psalm 147:1-11)

Wednesday, May 15—Hope in the Lord (Psalm 39)

Thursday, May 16—A Queen's Appraisal (1 Kings 10:1-7)

Friday, May 17—Confident of God's Watchcare (Psalm 23)

Saturday, May 18—Rewarded for Liberality (Psalm 37:21-26)

Sunday, May 19—Folly of Self-Centeredness (Luke 12:13-21)

family of God, the promise of eternal life—these things have value far exceeding anything that can be bought with earthly currency. 　　　—C. B. Mc.

III. PRIORITY OF HEAVEN (MATTHEW 6:33)

Christians' seeking as for hidden treasure will be quite different from the seeking of unbelievers.

33. "But seek first his kingdom and his righteousness, and all these things will be given to you as well.

God's realm and reign are worthy of your total interest and devoted application. The goal is being accepted as a citizen there, approved of the King. Being right with him—which is *righteousness*—is a part of that grand priority. God's kingdom is first in time, first in importance, first in the citizen's enthusiasm and affection. This is the order established in the model prayer of Matthew 6:9-13: God's glory and his reign, on earth as in Heaven, come first. Afterward are the expressions of dependence for daily bread, forgiveness, and deliverance.

Seeking first the *kingdom* does not mean that the citizen does nothing but worship. He honors God by meeting his obligations to his family (1 Timothy 5:8), his community (Romans 13:1, 2), his neighbors (Luke 6:38), and his employer or employees (Ephesians 6:5-9), among other things. Life's necessities are met, then, as a matter of course. "In God we trust," inscribed on a nation's coinage, must stand as a solemn reminder that ultimate security is not to be found in money.

IV. TOMORROW'S INSURANCE (MATTHEW 6:34)

34. "Therefore do not worry about tomorrow, for tomorrow will worry about itself. Each day has enough trouble of its own."

Today's focus on God's kingdom and our right relationship with him is the one sure way to avoid the distractions of anxious thought about *tomorrow*. The laying up of treasure is always for tomorrow, either on earth or in Heaven. If on earth, there is reason for concern; it won't last. If in Heaven, it is secure and there is reason for contentment. So the right kind of thinking and doing today removes the basis for *worry* about tomorrow. Let each day's responsibilities be met that day. Don't load yourself with tomorrow's burdens today, and don't load tomorrow with today's burdens that piled up while you were distracted with concern for tomorrow.

The popular hymn by Ira Stanphill reminds us that while there are many things I don't know about the future, still "I Know Who Holds Tomorrow." In that I can rest in confidence and in faith.

CONCLUSION

What do you collect as a hobby? Stamps? Classic automobiles? China dolls? Family photos? Your collection may represent a sizable investment in time and money. You may have it insured, but you could not replace it. You could live without it, but you wouldn't enjoy life as much. You may enjoy it as long as you live. Will it then be equally valuable to someone else?

Can you imagine a perfect hobby collection—one without any drawbacks? It would offer keen pleasure in finding and acquiring, without anyone's suffering loss. It would be a joy to keep in order, to show and to share, with friends enjoying it as much as you do. It could not be lost, destroyed, or stolen; hence would need no insurance. It would persuade your best friends to enjoy the same hobby, without in any way diminishing the value of your collection. Nothing to worry about—just enjoyment for you and others.

Well, how about the treasures and truths of God's kingdom, and the gathering of saints to enjoy them with you, forever?

Discovery Learning

This page contains an alternate lesson plan emphasizing learning activities. Classes desiring such student involvement will find these suggestions helpful. The next page is a reproducible activity page to further enhance discovery learning.

LEARNING GOALS

After today's lesson, a student will be able to:

1. Explain Jesus' prescription for worrying about food, clothes, and tomorrow.

2. Compare God's provision for birds and flowers with his care for Christians.

3. Identify a way to cease fruitless worrying.

INTO THE LESSON

Have several jokes and "one-liners" ready on the topic of money or finances. For example: "You know you can't take it with you. Have you ever seen a hearse with a trailer behind it?" "The difference between men and boys is the size of their toys." My favorite bumper sticker says, "I'm spending my children's inheritance."

Begin class by asking people to contribute such funny jokes and sayings, allowing a few minutes for levity.

Make the transition into the lesson by pointing out that the topic for today is money, finances, and the worry that too often comes with them.

OPTION

Use the first activity on page 332.

INTO THE WORD

Ask someone to read Matthew 6:19-21, 24. Handing out sheets of paper, ask pupils to write a poem that summarizes the essence of what Jesus is saying. They can work alone or in small groups for several minutes. (See the first stanza of the poem on page 332 for an example.)

Ask for volunteers to share their poems. Lead the class in applause after each. Point out any especially insightful or meaningful points that are made.

Ask if anyone has any questions about the meaning of this passage. Be ready to define terms and ideas. See the lesson material to prepare for this.

Ask another class member to read Matthew 6:25-32. Guide a discussion by asking the following questions:

• What are the main concerns and worries that Jesus targets? (*Food, clothing, and physical appearance.*)

• Are these bad things? What is the problem? (*They are good, but a problem arises when we worry about them.*)

• Why does focusing on these things lead to worry?

Lead the discussion to an understanding that we can never be satisfied when we focus on possessions. We allow our interest to move beyond need; we develop a desire to be superior to others. This leads to envy and anxiety. We are not comfortable with asking God to make us richer than our neighbors, so we begin to rely on ourselves rather than him. What we have never seems to be enough; we worry about getting more. To those who worry, God says, "Trust me."

Ask, "How does God's care for birds and flowers and the rest of creation assure us of his even greater care for us?" In the discussion that follows, observe that God values humans above the rest of creation (v. 26), so it is natural to believe his care is greater. (Calvary is the definitive statement on that issue!) Discuss the difference between not *worrying* about the future and not *planning* for the future. Might one foolishly fail to plan because he is "not worried" about it? Where do responsibility and dependence meet?

Now ask someone to read Matthew 6:33, 34. Have the class turn poetic once again, summarizing these two verses in rhyme. (See stanza 3, page 332.)

Again, let volunteers share their poems. Commend them, then make sure any questions about the meaning of this passage are answered.

INTO LIFE

Ask each person to think of something he or she tends to worry about, such as wearing the right clothing, relating with a family member, finances, sickness, etc. Without speaking, the class member should write on an index card what he or she worries about most often.

Still silent, class members are to move about the classroom, showing their cards in order to form groups based on general topics of worry (for example, family, health, employment). Be ready to assist those with unique worries, perhaps including them with a related topic or grouping them together as a miscellaneous group. Each group sits together and discusses how individuals can change their focus from worrying to trusting God and seeking his righteousness. Encourage them to be honest, specific, and practical.

If time allows, ask a spokesperson from each group to share the group's ideas with the entire class. Write the recommendations of each group on a chalkboard or poster board as they are reported.

To close, ask each group to spend several minutes in prayer, asking God to help them seek his kingdom and righteousness and cease worrying.

Turn Worry to Trust

Change no more than one or two letters in the word *worry* to form a new five-letter word. Change one or two letters in that word to form a third. Continue in that manner until you have changed your *worry* to *trust!*

WORRY

___ ___ ___ ___ ___

___ ___ ___ ___ ___

___ ___ ___ ___ ___

___ ___ ___ ___ ___

TRUST

If Matthew Had Been a Poet!

Identify the verses from Matthew 6 that support each line of the following poem.

Treasures on earth are insecure,
    Only what's saved in Heaven is sure.
Identify the treasure to locate the heart;
    Serve God, not money, if you want to be smart.

So don't you worry about food and clothes.
    God still feeds the birds, and don't you suppose
You're worth more to him than birds and grass?
    He will never allow your needs to pass.

Seek to be right with God above,
    Make sure it's he alone whom you love,
And all that you need you will receive;
    Seek his kingdom and believe.

On a separate piece of paper, try your hand at an original poem that paraphrases the message of this Scripture passage.

TEACHINGS ABOUT PRAYER

LESSON 13

WHY TEACH THIS LESSON?

"Lord, teach us to pray," Jesus disciples asked one day (Luke 11:1). Thoughtful disciples continue to make the same request. Busy disciples, however, sometimes forget.

Today's pace of life demands a refresher course on prayer. We need to hear again the call to set aside a time for private communication with the Father. In our drive to accomplish more, we are tempted to skip any activities that seem "inactive." But more activity goes on in genuine prayer than most of us realize. Prayer activates the spiritual resources God has put at our disposal.

The model prayer, which is in the center of our focus today, shows us how to do that. Not a formula to be repeated mindlessly, it is a pattern that instructs our own praying. Through considering it once again, your class members will be challenged with the need for prayer to have a vital place in their daily lives. For some, this may be a challenge to a fresh start. For others, it is motivation to keep on in the way they are going. For everyone, it is reassurance that God hears when we pray—when our prayer is as genuine and earnest as is his desire to have us pray.

INTRODUCTION

A. NEEDED INSTRUCTION

It has been reported from battlefields that there are "no atheists in foxholes." Likewise, a poet has written that "lips say, 'God be pitiful,' which ne'er said, 'God be praised!'" Some may suggest, then, that instruction in prayer is not necessary—that these desperate calls for divine help prove that prayer is natural to the human heart. Just the opposite is true. These anguished cries more likely reflect a false sense of security in a groundless appeal to an unknown God. Having never—or seldom—prayed before, these tortured souls are reaching out in fear, not in faith; in panic rather than peace. Genuine prayer is born of a deep relationship between the one praying and his or her Father.

Multitudes may be persuaded that any and all appeals to any superhuman power are equally valid. So one may be prevented from seeking or accepting the very instruction he most greatly needs. Prayer, as described in the Bible, depends on knowing God as he is revealed in the Bible.

Even that, however, is not complete in itself. The people to whom Jesus came were well schooled in the Scriptures. Beyond emergencies they observed times for prayers morning, noon, and evening (Psalm 55:17). Yet when they saw and heard Jesus praying, they sensed a lack and they asked for instruction (Luke 11:1). Observing the prayer habits of those around him, Jesus recognized their need, and he taught them.

HE WHO TAUGHT US TO PRAY NOW HELPS US

During his earthly ministry, the Lord Jesus taught his disciples to pray. Romans 8 reveals that he continues to help us with our prayers. We have the aid of two divine prayer partners.

DEVOTIONAL READING
MATTHEW 7:7-14

LESSON SCRIPTURE
MATTHEW 6:5-15; 7:7-14; LUKE 11:1-13

PRINTED TEXT
MATTHEW 6:5-15

LESSON AIMS

This study should equip the student to:

1. List Jesus' prayer advice and give examples from the model prayer.

2. Identify elements of prayers that please God.

3. Prepare outlines of prayer examples—including the elements Jesus named.

KEY VERSE

When you pray, go into your room, close the door and pray to your Father, who is unseen. Then your Father, who sees what is done in secret, will reward you.

—Matthew 6:6

May
26

LESSON 13 NOTES

Display visual 13 of the visuals packet as you begin the lesson.

WHAT DO YOU THINK?

One of the marvelous aspects of prayer is that it may be offered anywhere. The Bible prescribes no single posture for prayer, nor does it require that we speak aloud. The "room" Jesus prescribes can be under a tree in the backyard, beside the furnace in the basement, or amongst the lawn-care equipment in the garage, or next to our bed at night. Some Christians take prayer walks, communicating silently with God as they move through woods, over meadows, or even along streets. Others have found that behind the wheel of their car they enjoy a relative privacy conducive to effective prayer.

What are some places you have found to be helpful to intimate prayer? What made those places special?

One prayer partner is the Holy Spirit. "We do not know what we ought to pray, but the Spirit himself intercedes for us with groans that words cannot express" (Romans 8:26).

Another prayer partner is the Lord Jesus himself. Romans 8:34 declares that the Lord "is at the right hand of God and is also interceding for us."

As a Christian, you never pray alone. The Holy Spirit, who dwells in the heart of every believer, joins in your prayer. Then, as your prayer and the accompanying prayer of the Spirit reach the court of Heaven, the Lord Jesus turns to his Father and says, "One of our people is praying. Let me join in asking what he is asking."

Of course these partners never pray contrary to God's will (Romans 8:27). If we pray a selfish or wicked prayer, we have no help with that.   —C. B. Mc.

B. LESSON BACKGROUND

Our lesson today grows from three backgrounds. First is its place in the Sermon on the Mount. Today's text was spoken before that of lesson 12. Jesus began the Sermon with blessings of his followers because they exchanged the values of the world for the greater values of God's kingdom (Matthew 5:1-16). Then came the Lord's commentary on popular applications of the Old Testament law. Not outward actions for their own sake, but the wellsprings of action in one's thought and intentions are valuable to God, Jesus said (Matthew 5:17-48). Then he applied that principle to the religious practices of benevolence, prayer, and fasting (Matthew 6:1-18). Of the three, prayer is the one most prominently exemplified and taught by Jesus and his apostles; so today we consider the Lord's teaching on prayer.

A second background will be found in Jesus' own praying, which becomes the basis of Luke's presentation of the model prayer (Luke 11:1-4). The Lord's disciples had observed him at prayer on many occasions, some of which are recorded only by Luke: at his baptism, for example (3:21). See also Luke 6:12; 9:18, 28, 29; 22:31, 32; and 23:34, 46. His disciples knew Jesus at prayer.

A background for application of today's lesson is provided by last week's teaching on riches and anxiety. Philippians 4:6 establishes the link with its warning against anxious care for anything. "In everything, by prayer and petition, with thanksgiving present your requests to God."

I. ON PRAYING ALONE (MATTHEW 6:5-8)

The pronouns *you* and *your* in this passage are singular in the Greek text, indicating one person. This prepares us to accept verses 5 and 6 as teaching about private prayer in contrast to prayers spoken by and for groups of believers worshiping together.

A. SAY IT TO GOD (vv. 5, 6)

5. "And when you pray, do not be like the hypocrites, for they love to pray standing in the synagogues and on the street corners to be seen by men. I tell you the truth, they have received their reward in full.

When you pray. The Lord assumed that his followers would continue in their practice of praying. But they were not to imitate the *hypocrites* (the word signified playactors), pretending to be something they were not. Jesus applied the term most often to the scribes—professional copyists and students of Scripture—and Pharisees, with their passion for outward conformity with the law and the traditions that had grown up around it (Matthew 23).

Standing for prayer (Mark 11:25) was customary at three prescribed hours each day. The worshiper would stand facing toward Jerusalem, with his head covered and his eyes cast down, and would recite a prayer of eighteen petitions, in all some ten times as long as the model prayer Jesus was about to give. What Jesus objected to was the places where the hypocrites chose to be at the time for praying—at busy street corners or at well-filled synagogues, making a public display of their private devotions. Their aim was to receive the admiration of observers. This would be fully accomplished in the performance. They should not expect anything additional from God.

6. "But when you pray, go into your room, close the door and pray to your Father, who is unseen. Then your Father, who sees what is done in secret, will reward you.

The place for personal prayer is like the place for intimate family conversation. Privacy is most appropriate. You address your own personal prayers to *your* Father. The address to *our* Father is proper when several are praying together.

That a literal prayer *room* is not required is seen in Jesus' own example. He found his private place for prayer on the open hillsides before daybreak and after nightfall (Mark 1:35; Luke 6:12; John 6:15). His prayers were directed to "My Father" (Matthew 26:39) or simply "Father" (Matthew 11:25, 26; John 11:41; 17:1).

B. SAY WHAT YOU MEAN (vv. 7, 8)

Here the pronouns *you* and *your* are plural. Jesus seems to have broadened his focus, no longer contrasting his individual disciples with other individual Jews, but contrasting his followers generally with pagan Greeks and Romans.

7. "And when you pray, do not keep on babbling like pagans, for they think they will be heard because of their many words.

The word for *babble* literally means to stammer. Just as one who stammers repeats the same word or words several times, so the pagans used to repeat the same words over and over, sometimes in a chant. A notable example of such paganism may be found in the priests of Baal who chanted for hours in a vain effort to bring fire to their altar on Mount Carmel (1 Kings 18:26-29).

Purposeful insistence, especially in private prayer, is not the same as this babbling sort of repetition (Luke 18:1-8).

8. "Do not be like them, for your Father knows what you need before you ask him.

Pagans, knowing nothing of the living God who *knows* and cares and responds, may be expected to resort to all kinds of mechanisms to catch the attention and turn aside the anger of their insensitive deities. But those who know the living God revealed in Jesus Christ will pray as befits a child approaching the heavenly *Father.*

Thus we bring our expressions of love and our requests to him, though he knows these matters better than we do. In trustful prayer we express our faith, not to make him aware of us, but to develop our awareness of him. So, too, we may discuss with him the state of affairs in the world around us, not as informing him, but to adjust our viewpoint to his will and his way.

II. ON PRAYING TOGETHER (MATTHEW 6:9-13)

The praying of Christians is not limited to private practice. As a family they pray together, and for that also they need instruction. Jesus' teaching pattern has been called the Lord's Prayer, but as a guide to praying by his followers it is appropriately called the Christian's prayer, or the church's prayer. In plan and purpose it is the model prayer.

A. HONOR GOD FIRST (vv. 9, 10)

9. "This, then, is how you should pray: "'Our Father in heaven, hallowed be your name.

This prayer offers an excellent guide for the kind of personal praying already recommended, but is more completely suited to the church's praying together. *This, then, is how you* (plural) *should pray....*

WHAT DO YOU THINK?

Jesus' warning about "babbling" calls to mind the danger of adopting clichés or empty phrases from public prayers. It also warns us against using generalizations such as "Bless all the missionaries," or "Help those who have lost loved ones." If we are not thinking of anyone in particular, are we really praying? Even the Lord's Prayer can be recited vainly.

Suggest some safeguards against vain prayers. How can we pray for the same thing we have prayed about often (see Luke 18:1-8) without the prayer's becoming vain or empty?

WHAT DO YOU THINK?

The literal meaning of the word hallow is to "make holy." Isn't God's name already holy? Why do we need to pray, "Hallowed be your name"? Do you think it is a request or a statement? Why? What personal responsibilities do you think this prayer puts on the one praying it?

Our Father. Those who join in this prayer acknowledge one another as brothers and sisters. At least by suggestion the *our* includes the whole body of Christ in all places and all times.

Father recognizes the relationship noted in Romans 8:14-17, that Christians are adopted children of God, calling him Father and enjoying the rights of inheritance along with Jesus. As our Father, God provides, loves, leads, and chastens his children. Identifying him as *in heaven* indicates his deity as much as his home. He is also with his children on earth.

God's glory fills the first petition of the prayer. This, like the Ten Commandments, begins and is rooted in God. Later petitions and commandments are based on this and are not attainable without it. His *name,* like his person, is to be revered and held sacred. The child of God is to honor the family name by all he is and does. That name must never be profaned—made common or meaningless.

A WILLING FATHER

Jesus taught us to address God as our Father. Imagine yourself a father with young children at a drive-through window. "Welcome to MacRocks. May I help you?" says the young man on the other end of the speaker.

"Yes, I would like three MacRock Funny Meals," you answer.

"Three MacRock Funny Meals. Do you want igneous, metamorphic, or sedimentary rocks?"

"Give me one of each," you say, "and give me some snakes for dessert."

"Do you want rattlesnakes, copperheads, or king cobras?"

"We'll have the rattlers."

An unlikely scene? Of course! No father in his right mind would order rocks and snakes when his children needed something to eat, and no restaurant would offer such a bizarre menu. Likewise our heavenly Father provides for our needs out of a willing heart that desires to give us his good gifts (Matthew 7:9-11).   —C. B. Mc.

WHAT DO YOU THINK?

"Your will be done on earth as it is in heaven." In Heaven, God's rule is absolute. There are no challengers, no half-hearted followers—nothing to detract from the awesome sovereignty of God.

How can his will be done on earth "as it is in heaven"? What do you think this prayer is asking? What personal responsibilities do you think this prayer puts on the one praying it?

10. "'Your kingdom come, your will be done on earth as it is in heaven.

A *kingdom* is the realm and reign of a king—the nation over which he rules and his manner of ruling it. Jesus gave much of his ministry to teaching about God's kingdom, describing it in parables, since human language could not describe literally what the human mind could not imagine. This much we know: it is where God is ruler and we are his subjects. The coming of the kingdom is the beginning and development of that realm. It exists in the world, especially since the birth of the church on the Day of Pentecost. It still needs to *come* to all those who are not yet identified with it. It needs to *come* more fully to immature Christians.

The prayer for God's *will* to *be done on earth* could not be demonstrated more fully than it was by Jesus in Gethsemane, pleading for release from suffering, but adding the overriding prayer for the Father's will, rather than his own, to be done (Mark 14:36). That is not weak resignation; it is earnest desire taking precedence over all other desires, giving oneself and all that one possesses to doing God's will.

B. ASK FOR NECESSITIES (v. 11)

11. "'Give us today our daily bread.

If *daily* needs were not met ultimately by God, who created the world to support its inhabitants, life would be impossible. So today we are dependent for everyday necessities, even though we may have supplies of a few things for a longer term. The acknowledgment relates us to the children of Israel in the wilderness, provided with manna for one day at a time (Exodus 16). We are not encouraged to hoard supplies on earth, where they are subject to mold and decay, but to prefer the bread of life eternal—Jesus Christ our Lord (John 6:48-58). The need in either case is personal, but everyone has the same need. This petition belongs to prayer together, *us* and *our*.

C. FIND FORGIVENESS (v. 12)

12. "'Forgive us our debts, as we also have forgiven our debtors.

Forgiveness is every person's need, as vital to spiritual life as food is for the body. *Forgive* translates a word that speaks of sending away. God is the only one who can so remove the guilt of our offenses against him (Psalm 51:4). Psalm 103:12 says vividly, "As far as the east is from the west, so far has he removed our transgressions from us."

Offenses against God are identified by three different names. The most common word for *sin* is literally "missing the mark"—failing to meet God's rightful expectation. Another, translated "transgression" or "trespass," indicates a false step or blunder by which one violates another's rights. *Debt*, the word used here, speaks of an obligation legally due. In sinning we rob God of his rights and incur an obligation that must be paid by punishment or removed by forgiveness. In Jesus' teaching he compared sins to financial debts. Sins against God created massive debts, removed by his forgiveness. By comparison, human offenses against one another incurred small debts that also must be forgiven (Luke 7:36-50; Matthew 18:23-35). Phillips' translation renders verse 12 literally, "Forgive us what we owe to you, as we have also forgiven those who owe anything to us."

The *Book of Common Prayer* for the Church of England uses *trespasses* in its rendering of this passage, and some churches follow that custom.

Forgive us . . . as we also have forgiven. Here is a sobering reminder that the user of this prayer asks God to forgive him in the same way that he forgives others. Good intentions are not enough. Forgiveness of others belongs *before* the praying (Matthew 6:14, 15): *as we also have forgiven.* Yet Christians do not earn forgiveness by forgiving; they forgive because they have been forgiven (Ephesians 4:32; Colossians 3:13).

D. SEEK GUIDANCE (v. 13)

13. "'And lead us not into temptation, but deliver us from the evil one.'

The prayer moves from dealing with past offenses to prevention of sins in the future. Two elements stand out: the concern that dreads the fall, and the confidence that in his own way God will prevent our falling.

Temptation (testing or trial) comes in two forms. First is the kind of difficulty that develops strength and character as we overcome it. Christians are to welcome that sort of trial, in spite of their human preference for ease (Romans 5:3-5; James 1:2-4). Second is enticement to sin. That temptation, in any form, is Satan's weapon against mankind, and God never engages in it (James 1:13). On the contrary, he promises that he will not allow us to be tempted beyond the means of overcoming it, but will in every temptation provide the way of escape (1 Corinthians 10:13).

The evil one—Satan, the author and agent of enticements to sin. The church, when it joins in prayer, may ask for deliverance from such evils as sickness, poverty, or oppressive tyranny; but it is fitting also to ask for deliverance from the one who lurks in all the areas of life, seeking whom he may devour.

WHAT DO YOU THINK?

James assures us God does not tempt anyone (James 1:13, 14). The prayer, "Lead us not into temptation," then, is not a request that God not lead us into temptation, but that God lead us— which, as he has promised, will not take us into temptation. What personal responsibilities do you think this prayer puts on the one praying it?

TEMPTATION

Genesis 13 tells how Abraham and Lot parted when their pasture lands became too crowded. Abraham let Lot choose the lands he wanted. Genesis 13:10 says that

A LEARNER'S PRAYER

Lord, teach me to pray! Thank you for the open door to your presence. May I have a mind open to your instruction, a heart to understand, a spirit to will, and discipline to do as you direct through Jesus. Amen.

THOUGHT TO REMEMBER

Our Father in heaven, hallowed be your name.

WHAT DO YOU THINK?

How can this be? Jesus says forgive if you want to be forgiven (vv. 14, 15). Paul says forgive because you are forgiven (Colossians 3:13). How can forgiving others be both a cause for and a result of forgiveness from God?

DAILY BIBLE READINGS

Monday, May 20—God Understands Our Hearts (Jeremiah 17:5-11)

Tuesday, May 21—Restraint in Using Words (Ecclesiastes 5:1-7)

Wednesday, May 22—God Cares for His Children (Deuteronomy 32:4-8)

Thursday, May 23—God's Holiness (Isaiah 6:1-8)

Friday, May 24—Prayer for Others (Ephesians 3:14-21)

Saturday, May 25— Conditions for Answered Prayer (2 Chronicles 7:14-22)

Sunday, May 26—How to Pray (Luke 11:1-13)

Lot looked at the plain where Sodom was, then verse 12 records that he pitched his tent near Sodom.

When God's angels came to Sodom, they found Lot at the gate (19:1), the place where city leaders did their business. Lot also owned a house in Sodom (v. 2). He was slow to leave even when the angels told him the city was to be destroyed. The angels almost dragged him and his family out of town (v. 16).

Lot almost perished because he first looked at Sodom, then went near Sodom, then moved into Sodom. This is a model of how temptation and sin work. If you look at sin long enough, you don't mind being near it. Stay near it for a while, and you will get into it. Get into it, and you can't get out without divine help. It's better to stay at the other end of the valley.

—C. B. Mc.

The closing doxology familiar to many who learned this prayer from the *King James Version* does not appear in the oldest manuscripts of Matthew, and so is left out of the *New International Version* and some other newer translations. *For thine is the kingdom, and the power, and the glory, for ever. Amen.* It is a suitable close to the model prayer when being used by groups of Christians, and that may explain how the words became incorporated into the text. David uttered similar words of praise (1 Chronicles 29:11), and Paul echoed them in his final writing (2 Timothy 4:18).

III. ADDED WARNING (MATTHEW 6:14, 15)

Because of the danger attending its possible misuse, one part of the prayer was flagged with comment and warning.

14, 15. *"For if you forgive men when they sin against you, your heavenly Father will also forgive you. But if you do not forgive men their sins, your Father will not forgive your sins."*

This admonition is repeated in Matthew 18:35, where the money debts described in the foregoing parable were equated with sins. Calling the offenses debts, as in Matthew 6:12, or sins, as in the verse before us, makes no difference. He who would be forgiven must be forgiving. So every day becomes judgment day, in which we judge ourselves by the choices we make; and no choice is more important than the determined decision to forgive.

CONCLUSION

Jesus, master teacher and storyteller, used one forceful conclusion, with variations, often and effectively: "Do this!"

When a lawyer identified the greatest of the commandments, Jesus said, "Do this." When the same man identified the helpful neighbor by what he did, Jesus said, "Go and do likewise" (Luke 10:28, 37). He concluded the Sermon on the Mount by identifying the doing hearers of his teachings as wise builders and the nondoing hearers as foolish ones. He had no praise for those who called him Lord, but did not *do* as he directed (Luke 6:46). So too he concluded his teaching on prayer. In case some hearer might miss the "do it" implications in verse 12 concerning forgiveness, he returned to the subject and said it plainly: Forgive, or you cannot be forgiven. Words were not enough. Forgiveness must be from the heart, or it was worthless (Matthew 18:35).

Outward actions for the sake of appearance are worthless. The doing must come from inner purpose. Pray; don't pose as if praying. Pray; don't just say prayers. Revere God; don't just recite respectful words. Give life service, not just lip service, to God's will. Depend on God for what you need; don't just accept his bounties. Follow his guidance, not your own goals, to avoid Satan's snare. And pray earnestly, both for yourself and for your adversary, that forgiveness may be complete.

Discovery Learning

This page contains an alternate lesson plan emphasizing learning activities. Classes desiring such student involvement will find these suggestions helpful. The next page is a reproducible activity page to further enhance discovery learning.

LEARNING GOALS

Participating in this lesson will enable a student to:

1. List Jesus' prayer advice and give examples from the model prayer.

2. Identify elements of prayers that please God.

3. Determine some specific change he can make in his own practice of prayer to pray more like the model Jesus gave us.

INTO THE LESSON

Begin by asking the students where they learned how to pray—either in private or in public. Who taught them, and what are some of their earliest remembrances of praying? Some may tell of a parent or other relative who taught by example. Others may cite a minister or an elder who taught a meaningful lesson on prayer.

Make the transition to the lesson by saying that this final lesson from Jesus' Sermon on the Mount will help us focus on our prayers.

INTO THE WORD

Divide the class into two teams, such as men versus women, or those born in even months versus those born in odd months. Each team is to study today's text, Matthew 6:5-15, and write down words or phrases that describe the prayer Jesus commends. For example: *personal, private, to the point, praising, submissive, dependent, confessing, forgiving, desiring holiness, avoiding Satan.* Ask each team to develop a list of six such words/phrases.

Using a chalkboard or poster board, a person from Team One places spaces on the board, a space for each letter, to represent the first word or phrase on his team's list. Members of Team Two then guess letters. When they name one that fits in the word, it is written in its proper place. This continues till six letters are in place. Team Two then has fifteen seconds to identify the word or phrase. If they fail, leave the incomplete word/phrase on the board and go on with the game.

Team Two then places spaces on the board for their first word/phrase, which Team One gets to solve. The play rotates until all six words/phrases of both teams are used.

If some words/phrases are incomplete, go over the lists again. This time continue the guessing till all of them are complete.

As each word or phrase is identified, discuss how it describes prayer as commended by Jesus.

OPTION

Use the reproducible activity on page 340 to examine the Model Prayer.

This activity can follow either of the activities above. On the board, write the following references from Luke's Gospel. Ask class members to look up the passages and see what they can learn about Jesus' own praying.

- Luke 5:16
- Luke 6:12, 13
- Luke 11:1
- Luke 22:40-46

Ask for volunteers to point out how Jesus practiced what he taught about prayer, or anything else that is notable in the praying of Jesus.

INTO LIFE

Giving each person a sheet of paper, ask each class member to analyze his or her own prayer life on the basis of the words/phrases named in the game. For example: How *personal* are my prayers? How *to the point* are my prayers? How much *confessing of sin* is my prayers?

Invite each person to write a paragraph of analysis, citing both strengths and weaknesses. Ask them to look especially closely at their weaknesses. What specific changes can they make to improve in those areas?

Then spend a few minutes in a general discussion of what we can do to engage in prayer that truly pleases God. Highlight changes that could be made (such as spending more times in prayer, being more specific about needs and worries, being less dependent on memorized phrases and prayers). Think of practices that would be beneficial (such as keeping a prayer journal, always starting and ending with praise, being honest and specific with the confession of one's sin). Suggest the students pay particular attention to ideas that come out of this discussion that may address their own areas of weakness.

Close the lesson with "sentence prayers." Give careful instructions: Everyone is encouraged to contribute one sentence at a time to a group prayer, though he may add another later; each one should try to pray with continuity, so the result will be one long prayer by the group. It is hoped that all will feel comfortable praying, but do not try to force anyone who is reluctant (especially a visitor). Begin the prayer with your own opening sentence expressing praise to God.

His Prayer Is Our Prayer

Use the chart below to examine each phrase or sentence from the Lord's Model Prayer. Determine a general principle from each one; then write a *specific* contemporary statement or request that expresses a prayer for today. (See the example on the chart.)

PHRASE	CONCEPT	CONTEMPORARY PRAYER
Our Father		
In heaven		
Hallowed be your name		
Your kingdom come	Expresses a desire for the expansion of God's reign and influence in the lives of people	O Lord, be my Lord. Rule my heart, my thoughts, and my actions, so that others will see you in me and be led to accept your gift of grace in their lives, too.
Your will be done on earth as it is in heaven		
Give us today our daily bread		
Forgive us our debts, as we also have forgiven our debtors		
And lead us not into temptation		
But deliver us from the evil one		

Summer Quarter, 1996

About these lessons

The letter of James stresses that Christians must put their faith into action. This is seen in the lessons based on James, as various issues of life are considered. The study in Psalms emphasizes God's presence in the world. The psalms praise God for his loving involvement in the lives of people. They call us to praise him and to respond to his presence.

Jun 2

Jun 9

Jun 16

Jun 23

Jun 30

Jul 7

Jul 14

Jul 21

Jul 28

Aug 4

Aug 11

Aug 18

Aug 25

From James to Psalms

by John W. Wade

The lessons for this quarter offer students a rather diverse menu. The first five lessons deal with the book of James, while the remaining eight lessons are taken from the book of Psalms. The central theme of James is the application of the Christian faith to the issues of everyday life. The study in Psalms, on the other hand, deals with such issues as the worship and praise of God, the forgiveness of sins, and commitment to the laws of God.

Someone has labeled this study in James "A Practical Religion." That is not to suggest that the lessons from Psalms will not be practical. To suggest that worshiping God or seeking the forgiveness of sins is somehow impractical would be to betray a serious misunderstanding of worship and sin. When we say James describes practical religion, of course, we don't mean to say that any aspects of the Christian religion are impractical. What we are saying is that James deals plainly with some of the problems that Christians must face in their everyday work and in social contacts. This will be appreciated by students who are looking for help with these very problems.

JUNE | ## JAMES

While this study in James does not cover every verse in the book, it does cover selections from each of the five chapters. The central theme of the book may be summed up in the latter part of James 2:26— "Faith without deeds is dead." In the course of this study, we shall have an opportunity to view this theme from several different angles.

The first lesson, which covers most of the first chapter, deals with trials and temptations that come to everyone, Christians and unbelievers alike. James provides encouragement and guidance for persons who are facing such problems. He informs us that sometimes the Lord allows us to be tempted in order to strengthen us and give us the wisdom to resist future temptations. When we successfully resist temptations, we are promised the "crown of life." However, the first chapter does not deal exclusively with resisting temptations. The chapter closes by presenting some ways in which Christians can live out their faith. They are urged to bridle their tongues, visit the orphans and widows, and keep themselves morally pure.

Lesson 2 deals with the problem of prejudice. James speaks specifically of favoritism toward the wealthy; but the principle he sets forth is that all kinds of biased prejudging are wrong. We live in a society where we face prejudices on every hand: race, religion, social status, and even physical appearance can win favor or disfavor before any other characteristics of a person are known. James sets forth the solution to all of these problems. He urges his readers to observe the "royal law," which requires persons to love their neighbors as themselves. You may use this lesson to challenge your class members to examine their own hearts and evaluate their behavior in the light of this teaching.

The third lesson, based on verses from chapters 2 and 5, presents ways in which a Christian can put his or her faith into practice. James draws on Hebrew history (the examples of Abraham and Rahab) to show how people of faith are justified by what they do. Christians are urged to pray for the sick and afflicted, since "the prayer of a righteous man is powerful and effective" (5:16).

Faith and wisdom receive attention in **lesson 4.** Wisdom is the ability to translate knowledge and information into good actions. Worldly wisdom leads to envy, strife, and confusion; but the wisdom James has in mind is "from heaven" and is pure, peaceable, and full of mercy. Teachers have great responsibilities to teach this wisdom, and so for this reason James warns against assuming this responsibility lightly. Not many ought to be teachers. There is a great need for Christian teachers who will accept the responsibility, however. This lesson should not be used to discourage any who are gifted with the ability to teach.

In **the final lesson** from James, he warns against the "fights and quarrels" that were dividing the congregation. The people were driven by a desire for things. The things they asked for they didn't receive because they asked with the wrong motives. They were warned that "friendship with the world is hatred toward God" (4:4). You will certainly have no trouble relating this lesson to the problems of our society.

PSALMS

You may find the final eight lessons of this quarter more difficult to teach. For one thing, most of your students are not likely to be familiar with many of the psalms chosen as the foundation for these lessons. The very fact that the texts are from the Old Testament will be a "turnoff" to some students, who harbor the mistaken notion that the Old Testament has nothing to say to our generation. Help these students to see that some of the same sins that plague us today have been with the human race since the beginning.

Several of the lessons deal with the subject of worship, which for many people is not very exciting. Lead them to see that precisely because they are not very good at it, they need to study it more. The typical American worshiper has become addicted to spectator sports. When he comes to a worship service, he expects to be entertained; and when he is disappointed, he blames everyone but himself. Help your students to understand that if they expect to get something out of worship, they must put something into it.

This study from Psalms is divided into two units. The first unit, "Praising God," includes lessons 6 through 9. The second unit, "Responding to God," is covered in lessons 10 through 13.

Lesson 6 urges students to praise God as Creator and Sustainer. This lesson is based on Psalm 104. The writer calls our attention to God's vast power as revealed in nature. When he contemplates what this means, he raises his voice in praise. You may want to use this lesson to urge your students to become more concerned about protecting the earth the Lord has entrusted to us; but do not let them become so concerned about the environment that they lose sight of the Creator or fail to regard him with reverence and awe.

Lesson 7 continues the call to praise God because of his involvement in the world he has created. In this lesson the writer turns to God's acts in history, calling attention to the covenant he made with Abraham and continued through succeeding generations. It concludes with praise for bringing Israel out of Egypt and leading them into Canaan. The final verse exhorts them to observe God's laws. You may use this lesson to show how God has blessed us and how he expects us to obey his commandments.

Psalm 34 is the basis for **lesson 8.** The writer praises God for deliverance. His theme is "I sought the Lord, and he answered me; he delivered me." If your class is typical, some members will be hurting from the loss of loved

JULY

ones, problems in their homes, or disappointments in their careers. For them you can show God's consolation, which he offers to those who come to him.

Lesson 9 will help a student realize that God is omniscient, that he knows everything about us—our motives, our thoughts, our actions. There is no place we can hide from his watchful eye. Help your students to see that this need not be frightening. In fact, it can bring us great comfort to realize that we are never outside the range of his love.

Lesson 10 introduces us to the second unit on Psalms. The psalmist relates how he waited patiently for God's deliverance; and when it finally came, he was able to sing the new song that God had put in his mouth. Use this lesson to strengthen the students' trust in God.

Students are likely to be more familiar with Psalm 119, the basis of **lesson 11**, than they are with most of the other psalms studied in this quarter. This psalm is unusual, not only because it is the longest psalm, but also because its structure is extraordinary. Psalm 119 exalts God's law and exhorts its readers to study it and obey it. This lesson gives you an opportunity to stress the importance of Bible study and memorizing Bible passages. ("I have hidden your word in my heart that I might not sin against you," Psalm 119:11).

Psalm 51, the text for **lesson 12**, is also familiar to many students. In it we find David calling out for forgiveness for his great sins against Bathsheba and Uriah. He comes before God humbly with a penitent heart, knowing that he deserves to be punished. But he also comes knowing that God will hear him because God will not despise a "broken and contrite" heart (v. 17). Some members of your class may be carrying a heavy burden of guilt. They need this assurance that God will hear them if they repent.

The writer of Psalm 96, the basis for **the final lesson** of the quarter, urges us to "sing to the Lord a new song." It is a joyous call to worship, but it is more than that. It is a call to share our joy with others who need it so desperately. Give an evangelistic thrust to your lesson. Urge your students to commit themselves to witness to one person in the coming week about the joy they know in Christ.

CONCLUSION

You will find it wise to consult the "Discovery Learning" section of your teacher's manual and the marginal discussion questions, "What Do You Think?" Perhaps you already use these features; but if not, you will find that they have some excellent suggestions for different teaching methods. Using some new and different methods can inject a spark into your teaching that will make these lessons both lively and practical. You will also find the *Adult Visuals/Learning Resources* packet very helpful.

Begin your lesson preparation early, and above all, surround your preparation with prayer that the Lord will use you to reach and move your students.

A Practical Religion
James
(Lessons 1-5)

FAITH AND FAITHFULNESS

LESSON 1

Jun
2

WHY TEACH THIS LESSON?

Our society has lost sight of patience and delayed gratification. We expect things to be "fun." So James's charge to consider our "trials" to be "joy" seems out of place. Even Christians who know better sometimes find themselves complaining about their troubles.

Now, troubles are real and not to be minimized. Don't approach this lesson with a glib attitude about suffering. Some of your students may be carrying burdens of severe financial woes, health problems, prodigal children, open hostility from co-workers, or a variety of others. But these are the people who most need the reassurance and the hope that James offers. Difficult as those trials are, consider it "joy"—not pleasure, joy. God is working even in these hard times for your good (Romans 8:28). This lesson should offer your students that reassurance.

INTRODUCTION

A. HAMMER AND ANVIL

Near the house where I grew up stood a little shop where the town blacksmith worked. My brother and I enjoyed stopping by his shop to watch him work. Sometimes he made horseshoes. Starting with a bar of iron, he would heat it white hot in his forge and then begin beating it into the right size and shape for the horse he was shoeing. Once he had the horseshoe finished, he placed it in the forge and heated it again. Removing it from the forge, he would plunge it into a vat of water or of oil. Sometimes he would repeat this process. "Boys," he would tell us, "it takes a lot of heating and beating to make a horseshoe, and it takes a lot of heating and quenching to make it tough enough to stand the hard treatment the horse will give it."

James had something like this in mind when he wrote about facing and surviving temptations. One who has never faced temptations has not developed the moral stamina to resist them when they come. Only when we have been heated, beaten, and quenched are we strong enough to handle more severe temptations.

B. LESSON BACKGROUND

The writer of this letter identifies himself as "James, a servant of God and of the Lord Jesus Christ" (James 1:1). Most Bible scholars agree that this was the brother of Jesus (Galatians 1:19), a son of Joseph and Mary (Matthew 13:55). He was a leader in the church at Jerusalem (Acts 15:12-21).

Some students suspect a disagreement between James, who calls us to be doers of the word (James 1:22), and Paul, who speaks of salvation by grace and faith, not by works (Ephesians 2:8, 9). But there is no contradiction. James emphasizes the kind of life one lives when he is saved by faith, and so does Paul (Romans 12).

I. JOY THROUGH TEMPTATION (JAMES 1:2-4)

A. REJOICING IN TEMPTATION (v. 2)

2. Consider it pure joy, my brothers, whenever you face trials of many kinds.

James opens his letter with a paradox, a statement that seems to fly in the face of all our experience. How can *trials* or testings be a source of *joy*? Perhaps we can

DEVOTIONAL READING
ROMANS 6:5-14

LESSON SCRIPTURE
JAMES 1

PRINTED TEXT
JAMES 1:2-4, 12-15, 19-27

LESSON AIMS

As a result of studying this lesson, each student should

1. Explain how resisting temptation and enduring trials builds mature faith.

2. List situations in which it is a challenge to do the right thing.

3. Commit to personal right actions—even in troubled times.

VISUALS FOR THESE LESSONS

The Adult Visuals/Learning Resources packet contains classroom-size visuals designed for use with the lessons in the Summer Quarter. The packet is available from your supplier. Order no. 492.

KEY VERSE

The testing of your faith develops perseverance. Perseverance must finish its work so that you may be mature and complete, not lacking anything.

—James 1:3, 4

LESSON 1 NOTES

WHAT DO YOU THINK?

Trials are a proving of our faith under pressure. In each is the opportunity to sin, which makes the term temptation *appropriate, or to grow. As we succeed in resisting the temptations, we build patient endurance and increase our ability to resist. In that we can find joy!*

In fact, some have said faith that has not been tested is not faith at all. Do you agree or disagree? Why?

WHAT DO YOU THINK?

James speaks of "trials of many kinds." What are some of the kinds of trials we face? Suggest some specific benefits that come through each of these trials—benefits that may not come through any other source.

WHAT DO YOU THINK?

"Perseverance," James says, "must finish its work." What do you think is the finished product of this work? What characteristics are evident in one who is "mature and complete"?

Consider Philippians 1:16; Hebrews 10:35-39; 11:39, 40; Revelation 2:10. What do these Scriptures suggest about one's becoming "complete" or "perfect" through perseverance? How can one keep this in view in the middle of trials?

better understand what James is writing about if we understand the difference between pleasure and joy.

Pleasure is passing; joy is lasting. An athlete who trains strenuously for a contest must suffer much pain. He can hardly find pleasure in those long hours when every muscle in his body is aching and he is consumed with fatigue. But even then he can know joy as he looks forward to the contest with the hope of victory.

So it is with trials. As they come upon us, they often bring suffering and strife. The may even become the occasion for our committing sin. (The word can also be translated "temptations.") Yet at the same time we can find joy in them because we know that overcoming them will make us spiritually stronger and better able to resist future trials and temptations. We can also find comfort in the knowledge that no matter how threatening a trial may be, the Lord will not allow us to be tempted beyond that which we can bear. With every temptation God will provide us a way of escape (1 Corinthians 10:13).

THE MANY COLORS OF TEMPTATION

James speaks of "trials of many kinds." The Greek word translated "many kinds" is a word that sometimes means "many colored." Indeed, there are temptations or trials of many colors in our experience.

Confronting our circumstances, sometimes we look at a blank white page. We must make some mark on that austere whiteness; but we hesitate, reluctant to discolor or mar it. As we enter a marriage or a career or even a new school year, we are timid and uncertain. Faith and fortitude are needed.

Often we face rose-tinted prospects. They encourage us to feel we can do no wrong. This color of life may make us try to do more than we can, or to be more than we are, or to depend on good luck more than on a good God.

Often we look at a future that seems to be uniformly black. No lights relieve the darkness; no "gleams of glory" are to be seen. The death of one we love or the closing door of opportunity leaves us gazing into blackness. We need to hold on, hold up, and hold out with faith.

There are also periods when the colors of life are golden and glowing. When we see energetic, reliable grandchildren, when we find some success has crowned years of effort, when God's grace has lifted burdens and opened closed doors, we rejoice and are thankful. Then we need to guard against pride, self-satisfaction, and arrogance. Truly, trials and temptations have many colors.   —J. G. V. B.

B. TESTING DEVELOPS PERSEVERANCE (v. 3)

3. Because you know that the testing of your faith develops perseverance.

One is not born with patience; it is a virtue that must be acquired, and its acquisition does not come easily. Beyond patience is *perseverance*, which might be understood as patience under pressure. Every Christian will have his or her *faith* tested. Sometimes this *testing* comes in the form of physical persecution. At other times it comes in the form of alluring temptations. But more often than not, it comes in the form of subtle pressures, not to surrender our convictions, but to compromise them.

In withstanding these temptations we learn perseverance, the perseverance that will allow us to resist persistent temptations. Just as a refiner's fire burns the dross from gold, leaving it pure, so suffering and surviving temptations is morally purifying.

C. PERSEVERANCE BRINGS GROWTH (v. 4)

4. Perseverance must finish its work so that you may be mature and complete, not lacking anything.

Perseverance is more than the passive acceptance of whatever may befall us. An infant has no perseverance. Every felt need is a crisis, and his cries express his urgent wants. Only as one grows and *matures* is he able to develop this wonderful virtue.

Perseverance and maturity have a symbiotic relationship—that is, each feeds the other and helps it to develop. As we mature, we are able to persevere under more extreme pressure. As we persevere, we develop additional maturity.

II. ENDURING TEMPTATION (JAMES 1:12-15)

A. ENDURANCE BRINGS THE CROWN (v. 12)

12. Blessed is the man who perseveres under trial, because when he has stood the test, he will receive the crown of life that God has promised to those who love him.

To the Beatitudes that Jesus mentioned in the Sermon on the Mount (Matthew 5:1-12) James adds another. The blessings that Jesus promised are enjoyed by those who have reached a high level of spiritual maturity. In the same way, the blessing that James offers is for the spiritually mature, for those who endure to the end. The winner in a race most often is the one who has trained the hardest and disciplined himself the best (1 Corinthians 9:24-27).

In 2 Timothy 4:7, 8, Paul uses similar language to stress the importance of faithfulness to the end: "I have fought the good fight, I have finished the race, I have kept the faith. Now there is in store for me the crown of righteousness, which the Lord, the righteous Judge, will award to me on that day—and not only to me, but also to all who have longed for his appearing." Being a Christian is not some light commitment that may be kept for a time and then laid aside when it becomes heavy or inconvenient. One does not enlist in the Lord's army for six months or a year, but for the duration of one's life or until the Lord returns.

B. THE SOURCE OF TEMPTATION (vv. 13, 14)

13. When tempted, no one should say, "God is tempting me." For God cannot be tempted by evil, nor does he tempt anyone.

Facing up to one's own responsibility for one's sins has never been easy. Evasion started with Adam. He blamed Eve, who in turn blamed the serpent. We have been trying to pass the buck ever since. Certain schools of modern psychology make it easy to blame our infancy or early childhood or our genes for all the problems we create for ourselves by our own misdeeds. But this is a cop out, and it just won't wash with God.

God will allow us to pass through trials, and he may even allow us to be tempted, but he never deliberately tries to entice us to sin.

14. But each one is tempted when, by his own evil desire, he is dragged away and enticed.

A popular television character of a few years ago attempted to excuse his foibles by saying, "The devil made me do it." There is a bit of truth in this statement, for temptations do come from Satan. But he can intrude into our lives only when we leave the door open. He may come in through the door of physical *desire* or he may enter through the door of pride. But in either case, we are responsible for keeping the door closed to his intrusion.

Jesus gave us an example of how to handle temptations. Each time Satan made him an offer, our Lord answered with Scripture. The psalmist said, "I have hidden your word in my heart that I might not sin against you" (Psalm 119:11). The best defense against the evil one is to say no and back it with Scripture.

This verse and the one before it raise a difficulty for some Christians. Hebrews 4:15 says Jesus was "tempted in every way—just as we are." How could that be if God—and Jesus was and is God—cannot be tempted? If temptation is born of our own "evil desires," how could Jesus have experienced it?

WHAT DO YOU THINK?

Verse 12 takes all our trials collectively and views them as one life-long "test." John says no one, even a Christian, is "without sin" (1 John 1:8). If we can have "stood the test" even though we are not "without sin," then what do you think it means to endure this "test"? How should this affect the way we view one another's occasional failings?

WHAT DO YOU THINK?

The life of a sin begins with conception in our mind, fathered by our own lust or desire. If we compare what Jesus said about hatred in relation to murder (Matthew 5:21, 22) or sexual lust in relation to adultery (Matthew 5:27, 28), we conclude that simply mulling over an immoral act in the mind is sin already—even without the overt action. How would you respond to someone who said, "If I've already had the thought in my heart, I go ahead and do the act. If I'm going to be guilty anyway, I might as well"?

Space forbids an extended treatment, but let us make two brief points. First, "temptation" comes in two ways. First is the presentation of a situation that has the potential to cause us to fall. But different people react differently to the same situations. One person is tempted by alcohol and another is not, even though both may be confronted with the same situation. Both are tempted, in one sense, but one is not enticed. Jesus was confronted with every situation that could have become a source of sin for him, but he did not yield. The temptation was offered, but he was not tempted.

Second, the translation *evil desire* is not entirely accurate. The word suggests intense passion, which is certainly consistent with evil desire but is not limited to that. It is the same word Jesus used to describe his intense desire to share the last supper with his apostles (Luke 22:15). Jesus' passion for his ministry became the occasion for his temptations in the wilderness (Matthew 4:1-11). Even a wholesome passion may become an occasion for sin if we are not careful.

C. THE RESULT OF UNTAMED LUST (v. 15)

15. Then, after desire has conceived, it gives birth to sin; and sin, when it is full-grown, gives birth to death.

James compares the origin of sin with conception and childbirth. The life of a child begins at conception, not at birth. In the same way, sin begins when it is first considered, not when it finally is seen in the act. Satan tempts us through our physical appetites and our egos. But usually we do not succumb to his wiles the first time he makes an offer. Only as we allow the idea to take root and grow does it become a visible sin. Jesus made the very important point that a sin conceived in one's heart is just as serious as an overtly sinful act (Matthew 5:21, 22, 27, 28).

The result of allowing a sin to grow and emerge in an overt deed is certain—*death!* As Paul observes in Romans 6:23, "The wages of sin is death." Only by God's gracious forgiveness can that result be avoided.

III. HEARERS AND DOERS (JAMES 1:19-27)

A. IMPORTANCE OF HEARING (vv. 19-24)

19, 20. My dear brothers, take note of this: Everyone should be quick to listen, slow to speak and slow to become angry, for man's anger does not bring about the righteous life that God desires.

In verse 18 James states that God has begotten Christians through the word. Since that is the case, verse 19 stresses the importance of every person's being *quick to listen* to the word. One cannot respond to the word unless one hears it. Many things keep us from really hearing the word—our prejudices, our involvement in things of the world, our unwillingness to make the kind of commitment that God requires of us.

Slow to speak. We usually learn more when we are listening than when we are talking. Some of us become enamored with the sound of our own voices, and as a result we utter a lot of nonsense. Our tongue is off and running before our mind gets in gear.

Slow to become angry. One who speaks quickly is often quick to become angry. Some excuse their quick tempers by acting as if this quality were inborn and uncontrollable. A big part of the problem is that these people have not learned patience.

On every hand we see evidence that anger produces wickedness and violence. A quick loss of temper may cause a person to do physical harm to another person. A slow, simmering anger may lead to a desire for revenge. Our violence-prone society needs to listen to what James is saying here.

WHAT DO YOU THINK?

We have been told that anger must be expressed or it will do severe harm to the person trying to control it. Thus some people scream, curse, or otherwise "fly off the handle" when they are under pressure. If expression of anger relieves one person, it usually leaves others stunned, hurt, or angry. How would you present the case for being "slow to become angry" to someone who claims he must vent his anger to dispel it and to feel better? If anger must be released, how can that be done without violating the caution offered by James here?

21. Therefore, get rid of all moral filth and the evil that is so prevalent and humbly accept the word planted in you, which can save you.

James urges his readers to lay aside their moral filth like a dirty garment. Unless they are willing to do this, they cannot receive the *word* of God that he desires to engraft or implant in their hearts. The word is the good news that offers salvation, but it is also the moral teachings that a saved person must live up to.

22. Do not merely listen to the word, and so deceive yourselves. Do what it says.

Listening passively to the word just won't do. A hearer of the *word* must translate it into a life. The church is crippled today by a great number of members who never make this translation.

23, 24. Anyone who listens to the word but does not do what it says is like a man who looks at his face in a mirror and, after looking at himself, goes away and immediately forgets what he looks like.

Looking in a mirror, a man sees a smudge on his face; but then he forgets what he has seen instead of removing the smudge. He is like the man who hears God's word, *but does not do what it says* to do.

Use visual 1 of the visuals packet to illustrate verses 23 and 24.

HEARING AND DOING

James urged his readers , "Do not merely listen to the word, and so deceive yourselves. Do what it says." His emphasis is on possession and expression, not mere profession. An actor may play the part of a king, a regal possessor of sovereign authority; but he is only a make-believe king, lacking any genuine power. James was concerned lest Christians make a confession of faith without any outcome in works of love, helpfulness, and compassion.

James always insists that word and way must be united. Hanna More (1745-1833) wrote of *Faith and Works:*

If faith produce no works, I see
  That faith is not a living tree.
Thus faith and works together grow;
  No separate life they e'er can know:
They're soul and body, hand and heart:
  What God hath joined, let no man part.

Let us not divide words and works in our lives. While at times we may deceive others, we end up deceiving our own selves!   —J. G. V. B.

B. BLESSINGS FOR THE DOER (v. 25)

25. But the man who looks intently into the perfect law that gives freedom, and continues to do this, not forgetting what he has heard, but doing it—he will be blessed in what he does.

The perfect law that gives freedom is not the Mosaic law. It is the engrafted word of verse 21. It is the new covenant written in the hearts of God's people (Jeremiah 31:31-34). It sets one free from slavery to sin; but only if one both *looks intently into* the word, and also *continues to do this,* keeps on doing what the word says to do. If the word reveals a smudge on his character or way of life, he gets rid of that smudge—and God blesses his doing.

C. DANGERS OF AN UNBRIDLED TONGUE (v. 26)

26. If anyone considers himself religious and yet does not keep a tight rein on his tongue, he deceives himself and his religion is worthless.

We usually think of a doer as one who is busily involved in some activity. But here the doer of the word appears as one who is not using his *tongue*—at least,

WHAT DO YOU THINK?

What methods help you become more of a doer of the word? How could your church be more helpful in this matter?

PRAYER

Dear Father, we know that we must be tested in order to grow spiritually. We pray that you will give us the strength and the patience to rejoice when testing comes. In Jesus' name we pray. Amen.

THOUGHT TO REMEMBER

God will not allow us to be tempted beyond what we can bear.

DAILY BIBLE READINGS

he is not using it recklessly or harmfully, not using it to lie or gossip or stir up dissension. A person who misuses his tongue may *deceive himself* and others into thinking he is *religious* because he never misses a church service or a prayer meeting; but that person is fooling himself, and his *religion* is vain.

D. PURE RELIGION (v. 27)

27. Religion that God our Father accepts as pure and faultless is this: to look after orphans and widows in their distress and to keep oneself from being polluted by the world.

What one believes is important, and James is not denying that. What we believe will in a large measure determine what we do. But James's emphasis is on practical matters, not on theology. James mentions two aspects of *pure religion*: helping *orphans* and *widows*, and keeping oneself morally pure. In the first of these two aspects, he echoes what Jesus said in Matthew 25:31-46. One standard for the final judgment will be how one ministers to the poor and helpless. But helping others does not atone for foul talk or immoral acts. One must not compromise God's standards of holiness.

CONCLUSION

A. LEARNING PATIENCE

A pious old farmer had a cow that was a kicker. She could hardly get through a milking without either kicking him or kicking over the milk bucket. More than once he considered selling her to the butcher. He kept praying to God to give him patience to deal with her, but his prayers seemingly did no good.

Finally he went to his minister with the problem. "Preacher," he said, "I've been praying for months for patience to deal with this critter, but God hasn't answered me."

"Oh," replied his minister, "I think God is answering your prayer all right. He is testing you, and you just haven't passed the exam yet; so he keeps testing you."

B. PURE AND FAULTLESS

In his description of pure and undefiled religion, James does not mention the importance of sound doctrine. Rather, he emphasizes service to others ("looking after the orphans and the widows in their distress") and moral purity ("keeping oneself from being polluted by the world"). This should not lead us to suppose that sound doctrine is unimportant. We need to recognize, rather, that these practical aspects of religion result from receiving God's Word and doing what it tells us to do (vv. 21, 22).

We need to emphasize Christian action today. There is no shortage of places to serve the hurting and the hungry, the angry and the anguished. Yet too many of us have made our Christianity into a spectator sport. We sit on the sidelines and politely cheer others without ever really becoming involved. Many are willing to give of their money without ever giving of their time or of themselves.

We need sermons and we need theology; but we also need examples of what Christian love means. A Mother Theresa ministering to the poor speaks more loudly to the unbelieving multitudes than do a thousand sermons on love.

Even as we serve, we must give attention to our own lives. As we venture out into an unbelieving and morally decaying world, we must take care that unbelief does not erode our faith or that moral corruption does not cause us to become cynical or to compromise our commitment to our Lord.

Discovery Learning

This page contains an alternate lesson plan emphasizing learning activities. Classes desiring such student involvement will find these suggestions helpful. The next page is a reproducible activity page to further enhance discovery learning.

LEARNING GOALS

After this lesson students will be able to:

1. Explain how resisting temptation and enduring trials builds mature faith.

2. List situations in which it is a challenge to do the right thing.

3. Commit to personal right actions—even in troubled times.

INTO THE LESSON

Write the following statement and the possible completions on the chalkboard or from an overhead projector:

The fastest way to grow spiritually is to

- . . . encounter problems and temptations.
- . . . read or listen to God's Word.
- . . . serve the needy.

When you begin class, ask students to form groups of four to six. Have them read and discuss the statements. Which statement do you agree with the most? Why?

After about five minutes for discussion, ask for four volunteers to read excerpts from James 1.

INTO THE WORD

Have a volunteer read James 1:2-4. Groups discuss, "Why should trials bring joy for believers? (v. 2-4)."

Have a volunteer read James 1:12-15. Groups discuss, "Why is the man who perseveres under trial blessed? (v. 12). Trials bring all kinds of temptations. According to James, who is not responsible for temptation? What brings temptation? (vv. 13-15)."

Have a volunteer read James 1:19-22. Groups discuss, "What factors get in the way of receiving God's Word appropriately? (vv. 19-21) How should we receive God's Word? (v. 21)? How should we respond? (v. 22)."

Have a volunteer read James 1:23-27. Groups discuss, "What arguments does James present to show that we need to put God's Word into practice? (vv. 23-27)."

Bring the groups together and ask, "What was the most significant idea you heard in your group?" Allow several to respond.

INTO LIFE

Lead the class to brainstorm responses this question: "What situations make it difficult to obey God?" List the situations on a chalkboard or overhead projector as they call them out. (The goal is to name lots of ideas before discussing them. This encourages greater participation and leads to more ideas for consideration.) After a variety of situations have been listed, eliminate duplicates and group similar ideas. Work together to condense the list to five to ten ideas.

Point out to your class that James 1 moves us from. . .

(A) developing a perspective for handling trials and temptations (vv. 2-15), to. . .

(B) a life-style of obedience (vv. 19-25), to. . .

(C) active participation in serving the needy (v. 27).

Assign various situations from the list to each group. Have them analyze the situation from points A, B, and C to show how faith can be strengthened in that situation.

As a class, summarize the group's discussions to answer this question: "How can trials and temptations make us stronger in faith?" After adequate discussion, introduce this question for discussion: "How can we change our focus from dwelling on our problems to obedience to God?" Again, allow for discussion.

Distribute copies of a personal evaluation you have prepared and photocopied before class. (Use the following statements or the "Trial Analysis" on page 352.) Each class member will need an evaluation form and a pencil:

1. Right now, the greatest struggle I'm facing is . . .

2. This struggle causes me to feel . . .

3. The truth from Scripture I need to remember most during this struggle is . . .

4. One way this test can help me grow is . . .

5. I will seek to obey God in the midst of this struggle by doing the following . . .

Allow five minutes for class members to complete their evaluations. Conclude the lesson in one of these ways:

1. Have students form their groups and allow volunteers to share a struggle. Groups are then to pray for the person's situation in their groups. (No one should be required to share—use volunteers only.)

2. After you describe each idea for prayer, pause for fifteen to twenty seconds to allow students to pray silently:

Ask God to give you wisdom as you seek to grow through your present struggle.

Ask God to help you see his power and promise for you if you live in obedience.

Ask God to help you look beyond yourself to others in need.

You may want to suggest other ideas.

3. Sing together a hymn or chorus such as "Turn Your Eyes Upon Jesus".

Trial Analysis

Select one of the trials listed below. Then imagine you have encountered such a trial in your life. Answer the questions below based upon the situation.(If you are working with a group on this project, determine which trial you want to focus on. Then discuss the related questions.)

- Loss of Job
- Physical Illness or Injury
- Loss of a Loved One

- Financial Difficulties
- Rejection From Friends
- Persecution for Your Faith

1. What kinds of thoughts might you have

- if you respond with bitterness?

- if you respond with fear?

- if you respond with faith in God?

2. By going through this trial, what might you learn about . . .

- God?

- Yourself?

3. How might this trial ultimately make your faith stronger?

4. What might obedience to God look like in the midst of this trial?

FAITH AND RELATIONSHIPS

LESSON 2

WHY TEACH THIS LESSON?

"I now realize how true it is that God does not show favoritism." Thus Peter began his sermon to Cornelius and his gathered relatives (Acts 10:34). Peter stood up against favoritism again at the Jerusalem Conference (Acts 15:7-11). How, then, could he have been guilty later of playing favorites? Paul says, "I opposed him [Peter] to his face, because he was clearly in the wrong" (Galatians 2:11; cf vv. 12-16).

Clearly, we sometimes know better than we do. So we need continual reminders of what we know with encouragement to act in the same way. Probably a poll of your class members would yield a 100% opposition to favoritism. They still need to study this lesson, to encourage one another, and to pray for God's Spirit to empower their application of the truths here. Pray for the Lord's guidance as you prepare to lead them in that quest.

INTRODUCTION

A. OF LAWS AND HEARTS

"You can't legislate morality." That time-honored maxim just isn't so. What is law if not a legislation of morality? Laws against murder and theft are legislated prohibitions against the immorality of taking a human life or taking what belongs to another. Every law is a declaration of what the legislature determines to be moral conduct acceptable to society.

What you cannot legislate are attitudes. Our laws have for many years made discrimination illegal, but still we have problems with prejudice. The laws control the actions, but the heart is unchanged.

Only God can change the heart. He has chosen, however, to use people in that process. The mission of the church—taking the gospel to the world—is a mission of changing hearts. Where laws have failed, the gospel has succeeded.

B. LESSON BACKGROUND

As was mentioned in the first lesson, James, the brother of the Lord, was the author of the book that is called by his name. James had become a leader in the church in Jerusalem. As a leader, he had to guide new Christians as they tried to apply their faith to their daily lives. Since the church had several thousand members, James and the other leaders had to deal with a multitude of problems.

But James was writing for more than the church at Jerusalem. His letter is addressed to "the twelve tribes scattered among the nations," and its inspired advice applies to many beyond the literal twelve tribes of Israel. It has application and value to all Christians in every age.

Today's lesson deals with the problem of favoritism. In our modern society, showing partiality takes many forms. We sometimes are guilty of showing favoritism to a person because of his or her social or economic status, race, or

DEVOTIONAL READING
ROMANS 14:1-12

LESSON SCRIPTURE
JAMES 2:1-13; 4:11, 12

PRINTED TEXT
JAMES 2:1-13; 4:11, 12

LESSON AIMS

As a result of studying this lesson, each student should:

1. Explain what it means to follow the "royal law found in Scripture."

2. Demonstrate how showing preference and being judgmental are both failures to show love.

3. Identify opportunities to demonstrate God's love in action.

KEY VERSE

If you really keep the royal law found in Scripture, "Love your neighbor as yourself," you are doing right.   —James 2:8

LESSON 2 NOTES

language. We may also show prejudice against a person for one of those same reasons. In either case, such action is wrong.

I. SHOWING FAVORITISM (JAMES 2:1-7)

A. THE SIN CONDEMNED (v. 1)

1. My brothers, as believers in our glorious Lord Jesus Christ, don't show favoritism.

The Phillips translation puts this verse in contemporary language: "Don't ever attempt, my brothers, to combine snobbery with faith in our glorious Lord Jesus Christ!"

It is not wrong to have a special concern for members of one's family (1 Timothy 5:8), or for members of God's family (Galatians 6:10). It is not wrong to give respect to one who has earned it by his character and action. *Favoritism* means to show favor for reasons of a very different kind. Some of those reasons will become apparent as our study goes on.

Faith in God and unfair partiality toward certain persons do not go together. If we love and respect God, then we must love and respect those whom he has created. When we reject people simply because they speak a different language, or because their skin is a different color, or because their clothing is patched, then we are, in effect, rejecting the God who made them.

CONSCIOUSNESS OF CASTE AND CLASS

After a church service in India, an American couple was talking with a young Indian Christian about the faith in Jesus that all his followers hold in common. The young man said receiving Communion was difficult for him. He was of a higher caste than some in the congregation. Outside of the church, it was considered wrong for one of his caste to receive food from "untouchables." When one of that caste served the Communion, the young man found it hard to forget what he had been taught.

Like our Indian brethren, we must not let differences of education, social status, wealth, or occupation cause us to draw back from, ignore, or slight our fellow believers. May the ideal expressed in the great hymn by John Oxenham be true of us.

> In Christ now meet both East and West;
> In him meet South and North;
> All Christly souls are one in him
> Throughout the whole wide earth.

> —J. G. V. B.

B. AN EXAMPLE OF THE SIN (vv. 2-4)

2-4. Suppose a man comes into your meeting wearing a gold ring and fine clothes, and a poor man in shabby clothes also comes in. If you show special attention to the man wearing fine clothes and say, "Here's a good seat for you," but say to the poor man, "You stand there" or "Sit on the floor by my feet," have you not discriminated among yourselves and become judges with evil thoughts?

The favoritism that James condemns here is based on a person's economic status. A rich man and a poor man, perhaps both strangers to the congregation, arrive at the home that is hosting the church's worship service. The rich man, readily identified by his *gold ring* and *fine clothes,* is given a choice seat, probably on the best furniture in the house. The *poor man* had to *stand,* or *sit on the floor* at the feet of other worshipers.

A century or so ago, some churches used to charge rent for pews. The rich and the powerful rented the prominent pews. The less affluent had pews in the rear, while the poor had to stand or sit on the floor. It is unlikely that any churches follow

WHAT DO YOU THINK?

Who do you think would receive the warmest reception at your church? The wealthy? The well-educated? Would a stranger be welcomed as quickly as someone introduced as the relative of a member? Would a skeptical but inquiring sinner be as warmly received as a long-term believer?

Often, we don't see ourselves as visitors do. We may think we are treating everyone well when, in fact, we are not. How can a church get an accurate picture of how it treats people who come into her services? What measures can be taken to avoid favoritism. Be specific.

NOTE

A variety of attitudes can be discerned in the congregation pictured on visual 2 from the visuals packet. Use it to stimulate discussion about how we treat those who visit our services. Are we guilty of favoritism?

this practice today, but favoritism is shown in numerous other ways. The rich and the prominent often wield undue influence in making decisions in the church—not because their decisions are wiser or more spiritual, but because of who they are. The values of our secular world all too easily become the values we follow in the church.

C. THE BASIS FOR CONDEMNATION (vv. 5-7)

5. Listen, my dear brothers: Has not God chosen those who are poor in the eyes of the world to be rich in faith and to inherit the kingdom he promised those who love him?

Wealth and position should not merit special privileges within the church. The people told to sit on the floor may be the very persons God honors. God does not measure people by the cut of their clothes, the size of their bank accounts, or the opulence of their dwellings. Rather, God measures people by their faith. In the past he has often used the poor and the weak to accomplish his purposes (1 Corinthians 1:26-29).

This is not to say that God despises the rich just because they are rich, or that he chooses the poor just because they are poor. God's concern is not with what a person has, but with who a person is. A rich person can be just as poor in spirit as an impoverished person; a poor man can be just as devilish as a rich man. What one has in his heart is more important than the clothes that cover his chest.

6. But you have insulted the poor. Is it not the rich who are exploiting you? Are they not the ones who are dragging you into court?

James next points out that the rich, whom they were honoring, were the very ones who oppressed them outside the church. Of course, he is not suggesting that all rich people are oppressors. Some are quite humble and generous. But some rich people cruelly mistreat others, and so we should not honor anyone just because he or she is rich.

Dragging you into court. This refers to the practice of bringing people into court to collect debts. The poor could not afford to hire a lawyer; and besides, the judges were often bought off by the rich. In those days people could be thrown into jail or even sold into slavery for failing to pay their debts.

7. Are they not the ones who are slandering the noble name of him to whom you belong?

James's next charge is even more serious. The rich and the powerful who abuse the poor also misuse the *name* of Christ. They speak it with ridicule or contempt. Not all rich people do this, but as long as some do, it is a mistake to honor anyone just because that person possesses wealth.

II. OBSERVING THE ROYAL LAW (JAMES 2:8-13)

A. COMMENDATION FOR OBEYING (v. 8)

8. If you really keep the royal law found in Scripture, "Love your neighbor as yourself," you are doing right.

The *royal law* is so called because it is sovereign over all other laws. This law quoted from Leviticus 19:18 is one of the two commandments upon which the whole law depends (Matthew 22:37-40). Love of God always comes first, but unless it is followed by the love of one's neighbors, a person has not lived up to God's law. It makes no difference whether the neighbor is rich or poor.

B. CONDEMNATION FOR DISOBEYING (v. 9)

9. But if you show favoritism, you sin and are convicted by the law as lawbreakers.

One might profess that he loved his neighbor as himself, but if he gave preferential treatment to some and not to others, he was violating the law. To some this

---

WHAT DO YOU THINK?

The Christians to whom James wrote were honoring the rich even though it was the rich who were "exploiting" the believers, "dragging [them] into court," and "slandering the noble name" of Jesus. Do you suppose they were trying to make things better for themselves by placating the wealthy? In what ways do believers today make concessions to the world to ease the pressure that may be applied to the church? How can we identify and resist the temptation to make such compromises?

WHAT DO YOU THINK?

In trying to follow the "royal law," some churches have begun some new and innovative ministries. How does each of the following express love for others? What danger of favoritism might be inherent in each one, and what precautions ought the church take to prevent that?

• *Providing food or clothing to the needy*
• *After-school activities for latch-key kids*
• *Child care programs*
• *Support groups for parents, single parents, the newly divorced, the grieving*
• *Singles ministries*
• *English language classes*
• *Reading classes*

Can you suggest some other possibilities? What one new program would you like to see your church start to show love to your neighbors?

WHAT DO YOU THINK?

What, if anything, is the difference between showing favoritism and having a few close friends? Do you think some people are guilty of playing favorites with their friends? What precautions would you suggest for church leaders—or others—to avoid this sin?

WHAT DO YOU THINK?

Why do you think it is so easy for Christians to fall into a judgmental attitude? Do you think Christians are more judgmental with fellow Christians or with unbelievers? Why? How can we practice being more merciful with each group?

might seem like a trivial sin, but not in the eyes of God. Are not all of us, in one way or another, guilty of this transgression? We may openly, even blatantly, show favoritism to some and not to others. Sometimes our favoritism may be subtle, or even unconscious. We need constantly to work at sensitizing ourselves so that we are not guilty of this transgression. No matter how we may regard it, God considers it a sin.

C. OBEYING THE WHOLE LAW (vv. 10, 11)

10, 11. For whoever keeps the whole law and yet stumbles at just one point is guilty of breaking all of it. For he who said, "Do not commit adultery," also said, "Do not murder." If you do not commit adultery but do commit murder, you have become a lawbreaker.

God is a God of absolute righteousness who demands conformity with his will at every point. God's law is a unit; and since the wages of sin is death, even one sin is fatal. We make all kinds of clever distinctions between sins, considering some much more serious than others. We are inclined to minimize our own sins and consider other people's sins much worse. But that is not the way God views the matter. James is making the point that treating people with unjust partiality is a transgression just as surely as adultery or murder is.

D. THE LAW AND JUDGMENT (vv. 12, 13)

12, 13. Speak and act as those who are going to be judged by the law that gives freedom, because judgment without mercy will be shown to anyone who has not been merciful. Mercy triumphs over judgment!

James urges his readers to recognize that they will *be judged* both by their words and by their actions. This is another example of his emphasis on acting as well as hearing and believing. We should live our lives with the knowledge that every act and thought will be a part of the basis for our judgment.

The law that gives freedom. Compare this with "the perfect law that gives freedom" in last week's lesson (James 1:25). We shall be judged by God's truth, by his New Covenant that we know through Christian teaching. We should live every moment with that *judgment* in mind. Even so our living will not be faultless, but our faults can be forgiven by God's *mercy*—but we cannot expect God's mercy unless we are merciful in our dealings with others.

MERCY AND JUSTICE

Shakespeare's drama *The Merchant of Venice* tells of a desperate borrower who pledged to forfeit a pound of his flesh if he failed to repay his loan. He did fail, and the lender went to court to demand his pound.

The debtor could not deny his pledge, but his lawyer urged the creditor not to take the pound of flesh. Eloquently she described the virtue of mercy:

> It is enthroned in the hearts of kings,
> It is an attribute of God himself;
> And earthly power doth then show likest God's
> When mercy seasons justice.

Rejecting the plea for mercy, the heartless creditor continued his demand for justice. The lawyer then turned on him. According to law, this creditor was a criminal because he threatened the life of the debtor. So the one who demanded justice found himself justly condemned.

All of us share that condemnation if we refuse to forgive others. "Judgment without mercy will be shown to anyone who has not been merciful."   —J. G. V. B.

III. EVIL SPEAKING AND JUDGING (JAMES 4:11, 12)

A. EVIL SPEAKING (v. 11)

11. Brothers, do not slander one another. Anyone who speaks against his brother or judges him speaks against the law and judges it. When you judge the law, you are not keeping it, but sitting in judgment on it.

This verse may have reference to the one immediately preceding it, but omitted from our printed text: "Humble yourselves before the Lord, and he will lift you up." Some people betray a lack of humility by running down others. By making others look inferior, they exalt themselves.

On the other hand, James may have been thinking of a larger context in which he was spelling out a number of failings among the brethren: faith without works (1:22), favoritism (2:1), improper talk (3:2), conflicts (4:1). These sins were upsetting the church and threatening to divide it. For example, one conflict was the controversy over letting Gentiles become Christians without first becoming Jews. In that dispute people were speaking evil of their brethren in order to run them down and gain an advantage in the argument. When this dispute finally came to a head, James played a leading role in working out a reconciliation (Acts 15).

In speaking against one another, the people were sitting in judgment upon others. We are reminded of Jesus' admonition: "Do not judge, or you too will be judged" (Matthew 7:1, 2). What they didn't realize was that in judging others they were also judging the law. Apparently this means "the law that gives freedom" that has been discussed earlier in this lesson. When one violated that law by slandering others, he was rejecting the law.

B. EVIL JUDGING (v. 12)

12. There is only one Lawgiver and Judge, the one who is able to save and destroy. But you—who are you to judge your neighbor?

When one sets himself up as a judge, he usurps the position that rightfully belongs to God. The *one Lawgiver* is God. His judgment is always right, and he is able to forgive or to punish. It is highly presumptuous for anyone to take his place. We may dismiss speaking evil as a minor infraction of the law, but assuming the authority of God is far from minor.

CONCLUSION

A. ACTIONS SPEAK LOUDLY

I have a friend who has a wonderful ministry of helping people who are in wheelchairs. With a special van he takes them shopping, to the doctor's office, or on other errands. On Sunday he brings several of them to church. When he first began this ministry, he looked for a church that was accessible to people in wheelchairs. In many churches built several years ago, entrance steps presented formidable barriers. He brought his people to a church where the chairs had to be lifted up several steps to enter the sanctuary. When he arrived, no one offered to give him a hand in getting the chairs up the steps. He concluded that the people in that church did not want people in wheelchairs worshiping with them, and so the next Sunday he visited another church. There he received the same reception.

Finally, he found a church that had only one or two steps. Further, he found many helping hands to move his friends into the building. At the conclusion of the service, he explained his ministry to some of the leaders. They gave him a warm invitation to return. When he returned the following Sunday, he found that a ramp had been installed, allowing easy entrance to the building. In the sanctuary he discovered that a pew had been removed so he had room for the wheelchairs.

WHAT DO YOU THINK?

Is your church accessible to people in wheelchairs? What other unintentional barriers are sometimes present in churches? —in your church? How can we be more careful and remove these barriers?

PRAYER

Dear God and Father of all nations, we come before you confessing that we have sinned in that we have sometimes shown favoritism in our relations with others. Teach us to overcome our prejudices, both those that are obvious and those that we conceal even from ourselves. May we learn to sing again the song we sang as children: "Red and yellow, black and white, They are precious in his sight." In Jesus' name we pray. Amen.

THOUGHT TO REMEMBER

God does not show favoritism, and neither should we.

DAILY BIBLE READINGS

Perhaps the congregations that my friend first visited did not intentionally discriminate against people in wheelchairs, but in their actions they seemed to be saying that they really didn't want to be bothered with them.

B. WHY WE ARE PARTIAL

We have various motives for being partial toward others. Sometimes our partiality grows from our prejudice for or against a person or group. If we are clear-sighted and honest, all of us have to admit that we harbor some prejudices. Such biases, either positive or negative, may stem from experiences, either happy or unhappy, that we have had with other persons or groups. Sometimes we form an opinion about a group when we have had contact with only one or two persons from that group. We project upon an entire group the attributes we observed in only a few members of it. Sociologists speak of this as "stereotyping." Stereotyping simplifies the process of making decisions about others. It's much easier to say, "All _____ are _____ " (you fill in the blanks), than it is to consider each person individually. By taking this action, we play favorites, an action that God labels sinful.

We may have other motives for practicing favoritism. We may give a person the "red carpet treatment" in order to curry favors with him. We may go out of our way to oblige him, or may make complimentary remarks about him (in his presence, of course, and what we say behind his back may be another matter). We do this out of selfish motives, to gain favor in one way or another. We do this to get a job or to hold a job. We do this to gain the favor of the rich and those we consider powerful. "Buttering up" the boss is a time-honored behavioral pattern. Such actions also stand condemned by God, and rightly so.

We stand appalled at the suffering and strife caused in our world today by racial and ethnic hatreds. We have trouble understanding how people can hate one another so intensely. We need to recognize that these hatreds are instilled in the hearts of children from the moment they are born. As parents and grandparents, as teachers and leaders, we need to recognize our responsibility to teach our children in such a way that these hatreds can never take root. If we are to influence our world with the love of Christ, we must find ways to prevent bitter prejudices from developing. And in lives where they have taken root, we must do all we can to eradicate them.

C. GOD'S LAWS

A basic law of the physical world is that for every action there is an equal and opposite reaction. That reaction immediately follows the action. While we cannot break the laws of nature, we can break ourselves upon them. If we should jump from the top of a ten-story building, we would immediately demonstrate the validity of this law (and probably kill ourselves in the process). We would not break the law; we would break ourselves upon it.

The moral law operates in a similar fashion—with one notable exception. When we break a law, the consequences do not follow immediately. God in his infinite mercies spares us and gives us another chance, and another, and another. If, however, we repeat this process long enough, we will have to face the consequences.

God has reserved the power of judgment to himself. Only he is wise enough to mete out final judgment. But we are tempted at times to assume the prerogatives of God and engage in that activity. When we do, we place ourselves under his judgment. That is neither a safe nor a pleasant place to be.

Discovery Learning

This page contains an alternate lesson plan emphasizing learning activities. Classes desiring such student involvement will find these suggestions helpful. The next page is a reproducible activity page to further enhance discovery learning.

LEARNING GOALS

As a result of this lesson, each student should:

1. Explain what it means to follow the "royal law found in Scripture."

2. Demonstrate how showing preference and being judgmental are both failures to show love.

3. Identify opportunities to demonstrate God's love in action.

INTO THE LESSON

Before class write the words *prejudice, favoritism,* and *discrimination* on the chalkboard. To begin, ask class members to form groups of three or four. Provide each group with a sheet of paper and a pencil. Assign each group one of the words on the chalkboard. (If you don't have enough class members to form three groups, ask class members to work in pairs. If you have fewer than six students, ask everyone to focus on the word *prejudice*.)

Ask each group to create a definition for their word and to think of three examples that illustrate the word. Allow groups five to six minutes. Then ask each group to share their definition and examples with the rest of the class.

Ask the entire class, "Why does God oppose the attitudes we just defined?" Allow discussion for one or two minutes. Then say, "One of the challenges to our putting faith into action is dealing with prejudice. We tend to value certain kinds of people, and devalue others. We show favoritism and preference to one kind of person, and we demonstrate prejudice against another. James calls us to overcome favoritism and prejudice by applying the "royal law found in Scripture." Let's focus on this royal law and see how it applies to our prejudice."

INTO THE WORD

Ask for three volunteers: one to read James 2:1-11; one to play the rich man in the passage, and one to play the poor man. As the reader reads, the rest of the class should read in unison the parts in quotations in verse 3 that are said to the rich and poor men. Those playing the roles should then sit down as they are instructed. The reader can continue reading the entire passage.

Discuss these questions: "How would you feel if you were the poor man? What would this event communicate to the rich man? To the church?"

Have the class form their groups again. Ask each group to join together with another group to discuss the ques-

tions below. Provide a copy of the questions for each group, and appoint a discussion leader for each:

1. In what ways did the believers in the illustration "discriminate among themselves?" (v. 4) In what ways did they "become judges with evil thoughts?" (v. 4)

2. Why would someone favor a rich person over a poor person? What does this reveal about such a person's heart?

3. How does James show the unfairness of preferring rich over poor? (vv. 5-7)

4. According to James, what is the "royal law?" (v. 8) How does favoritism (prejudice) violate this law?

5. How might Christians tend to rationalize favoritism/prejudice in their lives and in their churches?

6. How does James show the seriousness of prejudice in 1:9-13 and in 4:11, 12?

Allow about twenty minutes for discussion. Then bring the groups together and ask for their conclusions on questions 5 and 6.

INTO LIFE

OPTIONAL ACTIVITY ON REPRODUCIBLE PAGE 360

Write the following on the chalkboard:

The Royal Law: Love your neighbor as yourself

Ask your class to list several different categories of people who might not naturally feel comfortable in your church. (Students might include: someone from another race or skin color, someone from a different economic class; someone who is homeless; a handicapped person.) List suggestions on the chalkboard.

Then point to one of those listed. Ask, "What are some specific ways we might apply the 'Royal Law' to someone in this situation?" Allow students to brainstorm ideas. Then point to another kind of person on the list and ask the same question. You might do this for several depending upon the time available.

Some of the ideas that might apply to most situations could include: introduce yourself to him; try to make him feel included without feeling uncomfortable or put on the spot; offer to sit with the person; introduce him or her to others; don't "smother" the person with insensitive attention; offer to help her find where she needs to go in the church building; make a contact during the week following his coming to church.

Close with prayer in the original small groups. Encourage students to ask God to give them spiritual power and insight to love all people not just those we prefer.

Getting Practical

Young	Old
White	Black
Poor	Rich
Less educated	More educated
Well dressed	Careless appearance
Highly talented	Minimally talented
Dull personality	Charismatic personality
Civilized	Uncivilized
Unattractive	Attractive

DISCUSS THESE QUESTIONS:

1. To the left are listed some distinctions that can be made among people. Is it wrong to make such distinctions in our minds? If so, why? If not, what causes such distinctions to lead to prejudice?

2. When we prefer one kind of person over another based upon external qualities, we are "judges with evil thoughts" (v. 4). How does this violate the "royal law" described in verse 8?

3. What are some clues we can look for to tell us if we are prejudiced?

4. What can we do to move from favoritism and prejudice to loving all people according to the royal law (v. 8)? Suggest specific steps you can take:

Getting Personal

Consider the questions below and honestly jot down your answers to them:

1. What kinds of people do I tend to favor? What clues tell me this?

2. What kinds of people do I tend to show prejudice against? What clues tell me this?

3. According to James 2:12 and 13, how will God judge me if I am not merciful to people in my judgment?

4. Complete the following prayer:
   God, you know my heart. I need your help in dealing with prejudice regarding . . .

FAITH AND ACTION

WHY TEACH THIS LESSON?

There is much confusion about the relationship between faith and works. Ideas range from the extreme idea that works have no value to the opposite extreme that works provide salvation. This lesson provides the opportunity to help your students come to an understanding of the truth. As for salvation, we are not saved by faith *without* works or by faith *and* works. We are saved by a *faith that works!*

INTRODUCTION

A. FAITH WITHOUT WORKS

When Hudson Taylor, founder of the China Inland Mission, made his first trip to China, he went on a sailing ship. The voyage brought him and his shipmates close to an island in the East Indies where a notorious tribe of cannibals lived. As they neared the island, the wind ceased to blow, and the ship lay motionless in the waters. Then the currents caused it to drift toward the island. As they drew closer, they could see the islanders watching them and anticipating a meal.

Knowing that Taylor was a missionary, the captain of the ship asked him to pray that God would send a breeze to carry them away from the island. "Certainly I will pray that God will send a breeze," responded Taylor, "but first you must set the sails to catch the wind." At first the captain was unwilling to change the sails until the wind started to blow, but as the ship continued to drift toward the island, he finally complied with the missionary's request. Almost as soon as the sails were unfurled, a favorable wind began to blow, and the ship moved to safety.

Taylor was a man of faith, but he realized that prayer is meaningless unless one is willing to work also. His later ministry in China gave a powerful demonstration that he understood what James meant when he said, "Faith without deeds is dead."

B. LESSON BACKGROUND

In today's lesson, as in the two previous lessons, James deals with a practical problem that the church in the first century faced. Faith in God is essential, but a faith that is completely intellectual without any commitment to service is useless.

In the first few months of its existence, the church in Jerusalem certainly understood this. When it became obvious that many of the members were in need, "all the believers were together and had everything in common. Selling their possessions and goods, they gave to anyone as he had need" (Acts 2:44, 45). Faith and works combined to recognize a problem and to solve it.

Had that practice been abandoned and the spirit that had prompted it lost? Some would say yes—if the people had continued to demonstrate their faith by their works, James would not have had to write the admonition that we find in today's lesson. Others would contend that the admonition need not be corrective. Sometimes an admonition is given in order to continue a practice, instead of to initiate it. Paul tells of a visit to Jerusalem in which he was asked to "remember the poor, the very thing I was eager to do" (Galatians 2:10).

If James was written before A.D. 50, as many scholars believe, then these Jewish believers "scattered among the nations" were reading this admonition at the same

DEVOTIONAL READING
GENESIS 22:1-8

LESSON SCRIPTURE
JAMES 2:14-26; 5:7-20

PRINTED TEXT
JAMES 2:14-26; 5:13-16

Jun
16

LESSON AIMS

After studying this lesson, each student should be able to:

1. Explain the link between faith in Christ and service to others.

2. Commit to demonstrating faith by service to others.

KEY VERSE

As the body without the spirit is dead, so faith without deeds is dead. —James 2:26

Lesson 3 Notes

What Do You Think?

Most churches have some plan for meeting material needs among the members. Some typical means are maintaining a food pantry or giving vouchers to a grocery store, maintaining a benevolence fund for distribution as needs arise, establishing an information network for those seeking employment, collecting and refurbishing used furniture for those who need it, and collecting a special offering when a crisis occurs. How does your church meet such needs? Do you think it could or should do more? Why or why not?

What Do You Think?

James says, "If one of you" responds this way to a brother or sister in need.... For James, this was a personal matter.

If you were in charge of your church's benevolence program, what would you do to challenge the personal faith of your fellow church members and encourage personal involvement in ministering to the needy?

What Do You Think?

James wrote in the days before there were government assistance programs for the needy. Do you think it is acceptable for a Christian or a church to refer a needy person to a government relief agency instead of helping from their own funds? Why or why not? Does James's connection of such help with faith rule out secular assistance of any kind? Why or why not?

time that the church in Antioch was preparing to send a relief offering to the church in Jerusalem—where James was an elder (Acts 11:28-30). If it was written later, it may have corresponded to the time Paul was receiving additional relief offerings for the Judean saints (Romans 15:25-27; 1 Corinthians 16:1-4; 2 Corinthians 8, 9).

In any event, James thought it necessary to remind his readers, whether in Jerusalem or among the "twelve tribes scattered among the nations" (James 1:1), that faith cannot be separated from works.

I. WORKS THE TEST OF FAITH (JAMES 2:14-19)

A. A Barren Faith Is Useless (v. 14)

14. What good is it, my brothers, if a man claims to have faith but has no deeds? Can such faith save him?

In this verse James returns to the subject he has dealt with in 1:22-27. Again he emphasizes the importance of practical Christian service. Some may have interpreted the doctrine of justification by faith to mean that Christian service is not required; or perhaps some had just become apathetic in doing what they knew to be right. In either case, it was important that such an error be pointed out and condemned, lest later generations accept it as right. *Can such faith save him?* James raises a rhetorical question, the answer to which obviously is no. A faith that does not lead to good works is clearly not a saving faith.

B. Faith Demonstrated (vv. 15-18)

15, 16. Suppose a brother or sister is without clothes and daily food. If one of you says to him, "Go, I wish you well; keep warm and well fed," but does nothing about his physical needs, what good is it?

To make sure that no one misunderstands the point he is making, James gives his readers an example. To make the example more obvious, he mentions a brother or a sister, not a stranger, who is in need. Of course helping a stranger is no less proper than helping a brother or a sister. Instead of supplying what a person needs, a would-be benefactor may supply only words—pious words, of course: "Go, and may God meet your needs. Praise the Lord!" One can almost hear the sarcasm dripping from James's words as he writes. It would be hard for anyone to miss the point.

There may be occasions when all we can offer or all that are needed are kind words. But James does not have this kind of a situation in mind. He is speaking to a situation in which a person has the means to give substantial help and gives only words instead.

17, 18. In the same way, faith by itself, if it is not accompanied by action, is dead. But someone will say, "You have faith; I have deeds." Show me your faith without deeds, and I will show you my faith by what I do.

A good Christian does not have either faith without works or works without faith. James is saying that the best way for a person to show his faith in Christ is by doing the kinds of things Christ teaches his people to do. That proposition seems fair enough. We can test our own faith by it, but we must exercise care in evaluating other people's ministry by what we see them doing. One person's ministry may be in a public arena that all can see. Another may be called to serve quietly in some obscure spot. Only God knows which one is demonstrating the greater faith.

A Reality Check

For some time a television news program used part of its time for what was called a "reality check." Various claims, assumptions, and emphases made by political or business leaders were examined to see whether things they asserted were actually true. There can be rosy promises or optimistic rhetoric about all an orphanage is doing for neglected, abandoned, or abused children. However, what does an open-eyed inspection of the actual living conditions and treatment of the residents of the institution reveal?

We find James saying that it is one thing to tell people, "Keep warm and well fed," but if we don't really provide heat and nourishment for them, we are offering only words—not deeds. We are devising fantasies instead of realities. I think it was Phoebe Cary (1824-71), now almost a forgotten poet, who wrote:

> When a man can live apart
>   From works, on theologic trust,
> I know the blood about his heart
>   Is dry as dust.

Our faith in Jesus should lead us to bring to men good news about how sin can be forgiven, new life in God begun, and noble and uplifting character formed.

—J. G. V. B.

C. EVEN THE DEVILS BELIEVE (v. 19)

19. You believe that there is one God. Good! Even the demons believe that—and shudder.

The issue being discussed is not the content of one's faith; it is whether one translates his or her faith into action. To illustrate this point, James uses the touchstone of the Jewish faith—the belief in one God: "Hear, O Israel: The Lord our God, the Lord is one" (Deuteronomy 6:4). *The demons* are allies of Satan, opposed to everything Christ stands for. They certainly believe in God, whom they consider the archenemy; but just as certainly they are not going to obey him. For this reason their belief in God leads only to fear and trembling. James challenges his readers to move beyond this level of faith to a faith that produces useful fruit.

II. FAITH AND WORKS TOGETHER (JAMES 2:20-26)

A. THE EXAMPLE OF ABRAHAM (vv. 20-23)

20, 21. You foolish man, do you want evidence that faith without deeds is useless? Was not our ancestor Abraham considered righteous for what he did when he offered his son Isaac on the altar?

Abraham's whole life was a picture of trust in God. The writer of the epistle to the Hebrews extols his faith in some detail (Hebrews 11:8-12). The one incident in the life of Abraham that James chooses to emphasize is God's order for him to sacrifice his son Isaac. It is difficult for us to imagine a greater test of faith than this. Not only was human sacrifice repugnant to Abraham, but God was asking him to sacrifice his only son who could lead to the fulfillment of the covenant; or at least, that is the way Abraham must have looked at it. No matter how difficult this test was, Abraham passed it with flying colors.

22, 23. You see that his faith and his actions were working together, and his faith was made complete by what he did. And the scripture was fulfilled that says, "Abraham believed God, and it was credited to him as righteousness," and he was called God's friend.

Faith and works are not in opposition to one another: they complement one another. Works, in order to be acceptable to God, must be based on faith in him. Faith, if it is to be saving faith, must result in a life committed to works for the glory of God.

The Scripture that James quotes is Genesis 15:6. The previous verse records that God sends Abraham out to look at the starry heavens and asks him to count the stars. He then assures him that his descendants will be as numerous as the stars.

WHAT DO YOU THINK?

James says, "I will show you my faith by what I do." What if I cannot see what a fellow believer is doing—there is no apparent ministry activity beyond attending worship services. Should I assume she has no faith? Should I confront him as a wayward brother? Why or why not?

WHAT DO YOU THINK?

Abraham showed his faith when he obeyed God and offered Isaac. Such an act challenged Abraham at both the intellectual and emotional level. How has your faith challenged you? What kind of actions has your faith produced?

HOW TO SAY IT.
Antioch. AN-tee-ock.
Jericho. JAIR-ih-ko.
Rahab. RAY-hab.

At that time Abraham saw no way the promise could be fulfilled, for he had no children. In spite of this, Abraham believed.

That Abraham's faith was *credited to him as righteousness* does not mean that his obedience atoned for earlier sins. Rather, God, in his infinite wisdom and mercy, chose to count him righteous because he believed God and obeyed him. As Christians we share in God's mercy, for the blood of Christ brings us this same imputation of righteousness if our faith issues in obedience as did the faith of Abraham.

Because Abraham believed God and obeyed him, Abraham *was called God's friend* (Isaiah 41:8). At the invitation of our Lord, we can enjoy a similar friendship if we also trust and obey. To his disciples Jesus said, "You are my friends if you do what I command" (John 15:14).

NO CHART BUT FAITH

Columbus found a world, and had no chart,
Save one that faith deciphered in the skies.

—George Santayana

It is true there was no chart to guide Columbus on his heroic western voyage. There was a conviction that land lay out there beyond the miles and miles of tossing water. Neither he nor any of his crew knew absolutely that this was true until the land finally came into view.

It was the "work" of sailing that made "complete" the "faith" in the reality of the western land. "You see that his faith and his actions were working together, and his faith was made complete by what he did" (James 2:22).

In our lives we must act upon faith in the biblical testimony to Jesus' life, death, and resurrection. We believe in the God "whom no one has seen or can see" (1 Timothy 6:16). We walk and work by faith and not by sight. However, as we obey Jesus and do what he tells us, we become increasingly assured about his salvation. As Jesus asserted, "If anyone chooses to do God's will, he will find out whether my teaching comes from God or whether I speak on my own" (John 7:17). Obedience validates faith.

—J. G. V. B.

B. FAITH WITH WORKS (v. 24)

24. You see that a person is justified by what he does and not by faith alone.

James concludes his argument by affirming once again his basic position that a person is not justified by faith alone. We need to understand, however, that he is not saying one can be saved by works alone. His emphasis throughout this argument is that one cannot be saved by a dead, lifeless, intellectual faith that does not issue in a holy life, given to benevolence.

C. THE EXAMPLE OF RAHAB (vv. 25, 26)

25, 26. In the same way, was not even Rahab the prostitute considered righteous for what she did when she gave lodging to the spies and sent them off in a different direction? As the body without the spirit is dead, so faith without deeds is dead.

James might very well have concluded his argument with verse 24, but he chose instead to strengthen his position by citing another example in which a person was saved by faith demonstrated by works. The example he chose may at first seem inappropriate. Rahab was a prostitute in the city of Jericho. She saved the lives of the Israelite spies who slipped into the city (Joshua 2). James does not hold up her earlier life as a model to be followed by others, but her faith changed her way of life. The point that James makes is that she believed in the God of the Israelites enough to risk her life to save them. From this example one may draw the conclusion that salvation by faith and works is not limited to Israelites, and that conclusion is verified by Jesus' commission to his disciples (Matthew 28:19, 20).

As the body without the spirit is dead, so faith without works is dead also.
James 2:26

Visual 3 reminds us that the possession of faith requires more than mere profession of faith. Display it as you discuss verse 26.

III. PRACTICAL APPLICATION (JAMES 5:13-16)
A. PRAYER AND PRAISE (v. 13)
13. Is any one of you in trouble? He should pray. Is anyone happy? Let him sing songs of praise.

James closes his letter very much as he began it, by dealing with trials and suffering. The term *in trouble* is broad enough to cover any problem or disaster. It certainly includes those who were suffering because of their faith, but it can also include those suffering from illness, poverty, or business loss.

For those who were suffering difficult times, his solution was not to grumble or engage in an extended pity party. Instead, James suggested that they *pray*. Such a prayer might be that the cause of the suffering be removed, or it might be that one would bear the suffering with strength and grace.

Serving the Lord is not always a painful experience. Sometimes it brings joy. Such *happy* occasions should give rise to singing, either as a part of congregational worship or in personal songs as one goes about his or her work. Christianity, more than any other religion, is a singing religion. Some of the world's greatest music has arisen as persons have attempted to express their love of God through music.

B. CARING FOR THE SICK (vv. 14, 15)
14. Is any one of you sick? He should call the elders of the church to pray over him and anoint him with oil in the name of the Lord.

Today we probably offer more prayers for the sick than for persons suffering in any other way. In many congregations it is considered a duty of the elders as well as the minister to visit the sick. *He should call the elders.* Sometimes elders and ministers are criticized because they do not always carry out this ministry, but they may fail because they are not aware of all the illnesses in the congregation. The ill person has a responsibility to inform the leaders of his or her need. Anyone who has experienced an illness knows how encouraging and helpful visits and prayers can be. Jesus encouraged such visits when he said, "I was sick and you looked after me" (Matthew 25:36).

Anoint him with oil. These words have stirred no little controversy. Some have held that the anointing carries almost miraculous powers of healing. Others see it as a medical treatment. The skin of one who has been ill, especially one who has suffered a high fever, may be dry and cracked. The oil is a soothing balm to hasten healing.

15. And the prayer offered in faith will make the sick person well; the Lord will raise him up. If he has sinned, he will be forgiven.

Prayer can open us to receive the power of God. We must not understand this verse in the absolute sense—that God will restore to health every person over whom we pray. Every prayer that we utter must come within the framework of God's will. Jesus in his ministry did not heal every sick person in Palestine. Apparently it was not God's will that all be healed. Even though we don't understand this, yet if we pray with faith we will accept it.

Like the healing, the forgiveness of sins is conditional. Forgiveness requires repentance on the part of the sinner. Serious illness can bring a person face to face with his own mortality. Under these conditions, one is likely to repent and turn to God. Many times, however, those who repent under these conditions soon fall back into their sinful ways. We may be able to prevent this by continuing our encouragement and prayers.

OIL, FAITH, AND HEALING
C. T. Studd was a remarkable British athlete and deeply committed Christian who did missionary work in China, India, Africa, and the United States. In 1885 he was

WHAT DO YOU THINK?

If good works are an evidence of faith, so is prayer. Does your prayer life suggest a strong faith? Why or why not?

We are promised that the prayer of a righteous person will be "effective." If we do not receive what we pray for, is that evidence of a weak faith? Why or why not?

WHAT DO YOU THINK?

As Christians we take great comfort in the fact that Jesus is our high priest and intercessor. We can confess our sins directly and receive forgiveness (Hebrews 4:14-16; 1 John 1:8, 9). Why, then, do you think James says we should "confess [our] sins to each other"? What practical advantages does such confession offer?

WHAT DO YOU THINK?

James links confessing our faults to one another with prayers for healing. Does this suggest illness is God's punishment for sin? Why or why not?

PRAYER

We thank you, O Father, for showing us the way of salvation, a way that requires us to believe in you and to trust in you so that we can walk the path of holiness that you have set before us. Show us the ways by which we can serve you by serving our fellowmen. In the name of our Master, who came as a lowly servant. Amen.

DAILY BIBLE READINGS

Monday, June 10—Faith Tested (Genesis 22:9-14)

Tuesday, June 11—The Least of These (Matthew 25:31-46)

Wednesday, June 12—Blessed by Faith (Galatians 3:6-14)

Thursday, June 13—A Hero of Faith (Joshua 2:1-14)

Friday, June 14—Sustained by Faith (Hebrews 11:29-39)

Saturday, June 15—Futility of Legal Works (Galatians 5:2-12)

Sunday, June 16—Faith and Authority (Mark 6:7-13)

on an extended trip into interior China, walking more than twenty miles a day. One of his feet became infected. In his account Studd wrote, "Though I rested it, it would not heal, but got very puffy and discharged a good deal. So I asked Hogg [one of his companions] if he would anoint me with oil in the name of the Lord. . . . He hesitated at first, but we read James 5 together and prayed about it, and then he said he could see no reason against it, and did so. Since then my foot has got most rapidly better."

Many diverse views are taken of this "anointing" passage in James 5:14. It is true that oil often was used as a medicinal agent in biblical times, as it is today. Christians often combine medical treatment with prayer. Many times God honors the "prayer offered in faith" to "make the sick person well." However, it is still true that "man is destined to die" (Hebrews 9:27). As did our Lord, we submit ourselves to the will of our heavenly Father.

—J. G. V. B.

C. CONFESSION AND PRAYER (v. 16)

16. Therefore confess your sins to each other and pray for each other so that you may be healed. The prayer of a righteous man is powerful and effective.

Much suffering does come as a direct result of a sinful life-style, yet we must recognize that the innocent often suffer through no fault of their own. We know that many illnesses are due in part to the wrong kinds of mental attitudes. When one has cleansed one's soul by the confession of sins, that person's body is given a better chance to regain its strength.

CONCLUSION

The argument about whether we are saved by faith or by good works has gone on for centuries. Jesus had to face this in his ministry. Many of the Jewish leaders, especially the Pharisees, taught that one is saved by observing the law, including the countless regulations they had added to the law of Moses. Often their concern for the law was a cover to hide their greed, a cloak that Jesus on several occasions pulled aside.

When Gentiles became Christians, some of the Jewish Christians began to object. These Judaizers, as they were called, insisted that Gentiles had to conform to the Mosaic law besides being Christians. It was in this context that Paul insisted that salvation is by faith, not works of the law. This issue was discussed at the Jerusalem conference about A.D. 50. At that meeting Paul's view prevailed (Acts 15:1-29).

In his Roman epistle, Paul set forth very emphatically that salvation is by grace through faith. "Where sin increased, grace increased all the more" (Romans 5:20). Some seized upon this as permission to sin freely "that grace may increase" (Romans 6:1). Paul disposed of this idea just as emphatically, insisting that a faith that did not result in a new life was not a saving faith at all (Romans 6:2-4).

In later centuries, some church officials restated the idea of salvation by works. They said a person could have his sins removed by paying money, going on a pilgrimage, or doing some other act of penance. To this error Martin Luther found the answer in Romans 1:17: "The righteous will live by faith." Luther was so devoted to this truth that he had trouble with the book of James. For a time it seemed that James was contradicting Paul. But close study shows that there is no contradiction; the two men were simply emphasizing different parts of the truth that both of them believed: We are justified by faith (Romans 5:1), but faith cannot live without works (James 2:17). So one "is justified by what he does" as well as faith, "not by faith alone" (James 2:24).

Discovery Learning

This page contains an alternate lesson plan emphasizing learning activities. Classes desiring such student involvement will find these suggestions helpful. The next page is a reproducible activity page to further enhance discovery learning.

LEARNING GOALS

Through this lesson you will help students:

1. Explain the link between faith in Christ and service to others.

2. Commit to demonstrating faith by service to others.

INTO THE LESSON

Put the following Scripture references on the chalkboard or on a poster. Do not include the words that follow the references, but leave blank spaces. Ask students to study the Scriptures and make a list of persons and things by which we are "saved" or "justified."

WHO OR WHAT SAVES US?

Romans 8:33	God	Romans 3:24	grace
Matthew 1:21	Jesus	Romans 5:1	faith
Romans 5:9	blood	Romans 8:24	hope
1 Cor. 15:1, 2	gospel	Acts 2:40	selves

If you want this to be done more quickly, assign each reference to one person or pair or group so all the Scripture references can be found at the same time. Students may write the answers on the board as they find them, or call them out and let you write them.

If questions arise about the words *saved* and *justified,* you can point out that these are two features of the same event. When God forgives us, our sins are taken away and we are justified: that is, we are made just or righteous. By the same forgiveness we are saved from sin and Satan and Hell. Everyone who is justified is saved, and everyone who is saved is justified.

Explain that our salvation is accomplished by God and Jesus. The grace that saves us is their grace, their favor that we do not deserve. The blood that saves us is Jesus' blood, shed when he accepted the punishment for our sins so we could be forgiven. God and Jesus provide the gospel, the good news that salvation is available.

Still Peter could say, "Save yourselves." We will not be saved unless we ourselves believe in Jesus. The faith that saves us is *our* faith; the hope that saves us is *our* hope. Today we will see more about our part in our salvation.

INTO THE WORD

Step One: Divide the class into groups of four to six. Ask each group to pick one of the following activities. Copy directions on a card for each group, and be sure each activity is done by at least one group. Supply paper and markers as needed, and allow twelve to fifteen minutes for the work.

Activity A. Read James 2:14-26 and compare it with Paul's statement in Ephesians 2:8, 9. Discuss these questions: (1) Do you see why some people think James's teaching contradicts Paul's statement? (2) Does saying you have faith prove that you really do have it? If not, how do you prove that your faith is real? (3) How do good works give life to faith? (4) Can you show that the teachings of Paul and James are in harmony? Choose one of your group to explain this to the class, and help that person prepare his or her explanation.

Activity B. Read James 2:14-26 and write a modern short story illustrating verses 14-16. Appoint someone as scribe, but brainstorm plot and action together. Have an artist or two sketch illustrations for your story. Or, if you have the visuals packet, have this group start with the picture on visual 3 and write the story it suggests. Or put it in the form of a drama that you can act out for the class.

Activity C. Read James 2:14-26 and then work together to write a short poem about Abraham's action-filled faith, and another poem about Rahab's. For more about Rahab, see Joshua 2:1-21; 6:15-25; Hebrews 11:31. For Abraham, see Genesis 22:1-18; Hebrews 11:17-19.

Step Two: Give three-minute and one-minute warnings for groups to finish their activities. Then let those who chose activities B and C present their projects. Follow with the explanations from groups with activity A.

Step Three: Read James 5:13-16 and briefly discuss how prayer, praise, caring, and confession are practical expressions of faith.

INTO LIFE

Write the words of James 2:24 under the list of things by which we are saved/justified. (See *Into the Lesson.*) Ask the students to work together to build a list of practical ways in which their faith may be complemented by good works this week. Write these ideas under the verse. Be sure they are specific and concrete. You might even wish to choose one item that the class could work together to accomplish, such as providing meals for people in a homeless shelter.

Close with prayer asking God for help.

Faith That Works

Look up the following Scriptures. Then rate Peter's zeal and enthusiasm for the Lord for each incident by placing a dot on the grid below.

1. Matthew 4:18
2. Luke 5:4, 5
3. Matthew 16:13-17
4. Matthew 19:27
5. Luke 22:55-61

6. Luke 22:55-61
7. John 21:17
8. Acts 2:14ff.
9. Acts 4:5-13, 18-20
10. Acts 5:27-29

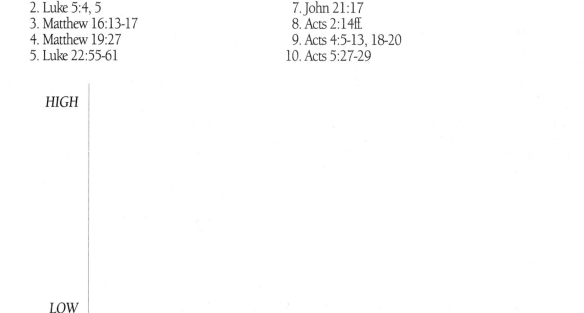

Draw a line to connect the dots. Does the line move generally upward or downward? (circle one)

Very often new converts have a zeal and enthusiasm for their faith that older members lack. As time passes, too often, so does the believer's enthusiasm. James would say that an enthusiastic faith is demonstrated through works.

On the grid above place a dot to represent your own enthusiasm for the Lord when you first accepted Christ (#1). Add more dots to represent several other points in your life since then, including where you are now. (Use a different color from what you used for Peter.) Then draw a line to connect the dots.

If your line has generally moved downward, list some things that could help increase your enthusiasm. If your line has been moving upward, list some things that could help you keep your enthusiasm for your faith on the rise.

THINGS TO DO TO INCREASE AND MAINTAIN YOUR ENTHUSIASM FOR YOUR FAITH

❑ _____
❑ _____
❑ _____
❑ _____

Place a check in the box beside one thing that you plan to do, starting right now, to raise or maintain the level of enthusiasm you have for your faith. Commit to memory Romans 12:11 to help you follow through.

FAITH AND WISDOM

LESSON 4

WHY TEACH THIS LESSON?

Indeed, why teach at all? After reading today's text, you may be asking yourself that very question! "Not many of you should presume to be teachers…" (James 3:1). It is rather presumptuous, is it not, to believe you have the right to stand before a group of faithful, conscientious adults who love the Lord as much as you? What gives you the right to be their teacher?

It's not *what*, but *who*? If God has gifted you to teach, then you must teach! If you teach from the Word of God, then it is not presumptuous at all. James was not discouraging the proper exercise of the practice of teaching, but the schismatic display of arrogance by which some might have taken on the role.

So teach the lesson! Challenge your students to seek that heavenly wisdom by which they, too, will become teachers—or not.

INTRODUCTION

A. WISDOM CAN BE LOST

When Solomon came to the throne of Israel, he was young and inexperienced. In Gibeon, God appeared to him in a dream and offered him whatever blessing he might choose. Solomon might have asked for long life or riches. He asked instead for wisdom to rule his people well. This choice pleased God, who granted him both wisdom and riches, plus long life if he would walk in God's ways.

Solomon demonstrated his wisdom in many ways, and soon his reputation as a wise ruler spread to neighboring lands. The queen of Sheba heard these reports and came to visit. As a result she said, "Not even half was told me; in wisdom and wealth you have exceeded the report I heard" (1 Kings 10:7).

Unfortunately, wisdom is not a once-for-all gift. It can be lost, and that's exactly what happened to Solomon. As he grew older, many things began to distract him—his building activities, his growing wealth and business enterprises, and his many wives and their pagan religions. Solomon's experience was not unique. Most of us have known persons who lived prudently for most of their lives, and then seemed to abandon wisdom in their later years.

Wisdom is a precious gift, valuable to those who possess it and to all those about them. Solomon's example should warn us, however, that such a gift must be guarded and nurtured lest we lose it.

B. LESSON BACKGROUND

In last week's lesson James dealt with faith and works. He said faith that does not lead to good works is not saving faith. Across the centuries the church has had to deal with this problem, and still must cope with it. Thus the admonitions of James are quite relevant.

In this week's lesson James deals with another potential problem. As the church was growing rapidly, too many persons might have wanted to be teachers. Today our problem is just the opposite: we have trouble finding enough teachers! One reason for the difference is that in the early church teachers were given considerable respect. No doubt some were attracted to the office because of the prestige attached to it. At

DEVOTIONAL READING
JOB 28:12-18, 23-28
LESSON SCRIPTURE
JAMES 1:5-8;
3:1-5a, 13-18
PRINTED TEXT
JAMES 1:5-8; 3:1-5a, 13-18

Jun 23

LESSON AIMS

As a result of studying this lesson, each student should be able to:

1. Describe the source, nature, and results of true wisdom.

2. Name ways to demonstrate godly wisdom by God-honoring speech and living.

KEY VERSE

Who is wise and understanding among you? Let him show it by his good life, by deeds done in the humility that comes from wisdom. —James 3:13

LESSON 4 NOTES

times teaching became a lucrative profession, especially if a teacher could attract a large following.

Whatever may have been James's concern about teachers, the standards he set for them are certainly applicable today. A teacher, above all, should be well-grounded in the faith. He or she should lead a life that is a model for students and for others. A teacher's life should exemplify wisdom, wisdom that is based on the Word of God.

I. WISDOM FOR THOSE WHO ASK (JAMES 1:5-8)

A. GOD IS THE SOURCE OF WISDOM (v. 5)

5. If any of you lacks wisdom, he should ask God, who gives generously to all without finding fault, and it will be given to him.

In this chapter, James talks quite a bit about trials and temptations. Thus it is reasonable to suppose that the wisdom he has in mind deals with how Christians may find joy in the midst of trials. Most of us would rather complain about our suffering than rejoice in it. After all, how can one gain much sympathy from others while he is rejoicing in his hardships?

Rejoicing over suffering does not come easy. Indeed, we need to have wisdom, wisdom from God, if we are to rise to that level of Christian maturity. We also need a great deal of wisdom to accept the fact that often we bring suffering upon ourselves by our sins or our foolishness. Such wisdom comes from God through the Scriptures. It is available to those who prayerfully seek it.

OUR INSTRUCTION MANUAL

An instruction manual comes with each new automobile. The vehicle represents the abilities of engineers to plan and to produce an outstanding machine. We look at it from tires to rooftop, from bumper to bumper—the product of the combined knowledge of the people who produced it.

However, the wisdom to use this complex mechanism is detailed in the instruction manual. How do we turn the lights on and off? Where is the hand brake? Where is the control for the turn signals? All these and scores of other instructions are in the Instruction Manual. With them we are able to start and stop, to steer and back up.

James says we need to ask of God to receive wisdom. We have God's instruction manual in the Bible. God's creative ability has given us the whole fabric of humanity: the body, the human associations, the ability to know, love, move, rest, and express our intelligence and affections. God has also told us how to use all this so it will operate with effectiveness. The Instruction Manual is the place we look for the wisdom God gives so liberally and clearly.

—J. G. V. B.

WHAT DO YOU THINK?

If we pray for a sick friend to get well, and he dies, is that evidence that our faith was weak, according to verses 6 and 7? Why or why not?

WHAT DO YOU THINK?

How can I pray "and not doubt" and still say "your will, not mine, be done"? If I say "your will be done," doesn't that confess a doubt in how God will respond? If I have confidence, isn't that arrogantly assuming what I want is God's will? How do you think the issue of doubt or confidence is related to leaving room for God's will?

(Note: is our faith in God or in our prayer?)

B. ONE MUST ASK IN FAITH (vv. 6-8)

6. But when he asks, he must believe and not doubt, because he who doubts is like a wave of the sea, blown and tossed by the wind.

Anyone who comes to God asking a favor must come in faith. "Anyone who comes to him must believe that he exists and that he rewards those who earnestly seek him" (Hebrews 11:6). Throughout this epistle James uses graphic figures to make his points. Such is the case here. A person who doubts is like *a wave of the sea*. Like a wave, the unstable person is driven this way and that, first on a high and then wallowing in the trough of despair.

7, 8. That man should not think he will receive anything from the Lord; he is a double-minded man, unstable in all he does.

One who doubts stands in danger of losing his blessings from the Lord. There are honest doubters like Thomas (John 20:24-29). He was willing to believe, but he needed evidence. God provided it to Thomas, and in his Word he provides it to us.

Some doubters, however, are cynical and even arrogant in their unbelief. The Pharisees, Jesus' most aggressive enemies during his ministry, displayed this kind of doubt. Many of them had witnessed his miracles, but this only entrenched them in their unbelief. Their minds were so closed that no amount of evidence would change them.

Then there are some who just can't make up their minds. *Double-minded* means unstable or wavering. It describes some who were wavering in the face of persecution, but it also describes any person whose faith is not stable regardless of the circumstances.

II. THE POWER OF THE TONGUE (JAMES 3:1-5a)

A. CAUTION TO TEACHERS (v. 1)

1. Not many of you should presume to be teachers, my brothers, because you know that we who teach will be judged more strictly.

Teachers were held in high esteem among Jews. To be called a "rabbi" was to receive a title of honor and respect. It was an honor that was not conferred lightly. For one thing, a teacher had to spend many years in preparation, years that involved hard study and discipline.

The word *presume* is not in the original, which more literally says, "Be not many teachers." The verb for *be* has been translated this way to convey the meaning that is seen in context. James is not discouraging the legitimate exercise of the gift of teaching. But some, without due consideration for the responsibility and accountability involved, might become teachers. This would, indeed, be presumptuous on their part.

From James's warning, we might gather that some had gone after the position of teacher who were not worthy of it or who were not prepared to serve in a responsible fashion. Some desired to become teachers for selfish reasons. In the first century many teachers traveled about, using their skills to take advantage of the people, little caring that their false teaching might lead people astray.

At the same time, James may have been offering a caution, hoping to avoid a problem. Many believe the book was written before the Jerusalem Conference (Acts 15) in A.D. 50. If so, then the church was at that time multiplying at an incredible rate. The need for teachers would have been great. Some might try to fill that need even though they were not qualified to do so.

Some Bible students would date the book of James after the Jerusalem Conference. If they are right, then James almost surely was remembering the presumptuous teachers who had gone to Antioch and stirred up so much trouble (Acts 15:1). These men, the apostles and elders wrote after the Jerusalem Conference, "went out from us without our authorization" (Acts 15:24). They had "presumed" their authority to teach. Were they still causing problems?

James warns all who would be teachers: *you know that we who teach will be judged more strictly.* Teachers must bear the responsibility for what they teach and the impact their teaching has on their students. One who teaches false doctrine that leads souls astray will be accountable when he or she stands before the judgment seat of God.

B. COMPLETE MATURITY (v. 2)

2. We all stumble in many ways. If anyone is never at fault in what he says, he is a perfect man, able to keep his whole body in check.

To *stumble* is to sin or to make a mistake. Mistakes, even honest ones, can lead to unhappy consequences as serious as those of malicious sins. In the immediate

WHAT DO YOU THINK?

The role of teacher is not just a position of status; it creates a relationship. The teacher-to-student relationship is one of influence. If the teacher is wrong about something, that error is compounded by the number of his or her students. Teachers must be very careful about what they teach and what they model by behavior.

How do you think we ought to determine who is qualified to be a teacher in the church? Should we accept any who want to be teachers and leave the responsibility to them—or should the leaders of the church be involved in the decision? Why do you think as you do?

WHAT DO YOU THINK?

To the degree that we all have a sphere of influence, we are all "teachers." How, then, does James's warning apply to teachers who have no "position" as teachers?

context, James has reference to those who would become teachers. Those who make no mistakes in what they say are *perfect,* which means mature or complete. A mark of maturity is that one is in control of oneself. If a person is mature enough to make no mistakes in what he or she says, that person is not likely to make mistakes in what he or she does either.

C. EXAMPLE OF HORSES (v. 3)

3. When we put bits into the mouths of horses to make them obey us, we can turn the whole animal.

A horse weighing several hundred pounds can be controlled by a bit that weighs only a few ounces. In the same way, the tongue can control the whole person. We understand, of course, that the rider actually controls the horse by using the bit. In the same way, the mind is behind the tongue, directing what it says.

D. EXAMPLE OF SHIPS (v. 4)

4. Or take ships as an example. Although they are so large and are driven by strong winds, they are steered by a very small rudder wherever the pilot wants to go.

Compared to the size of a ship, a rudder is very small. Yet it gives direction to the ship even in violent winds. The *pilot* or helmsman can control a ship weighing hundreds or even thousands of tons.

E. THE TONGUE, SMALL BUT MIGHTY (v. 5a)

5a. Likewise the tongue is a small part of the body, but it makes great boasts.

James now applies the two illustrations. The bit and the rudder are both small compared to the size of what they control. In the same way, the tiny *tongue* has tremendous power over the entire person. One who speaks hastily or carelessly or angrily may find himself committed to doing things he should not do.

III. THE FRUITS OF WISDOM (JAMES 3:13-18)

A. WISDOM SHOWN IN A GOOD LIFE (v. 13)

13. Who is wise and understanding among you? Let him show it by his good life, by deeds done in the humility that comes from wisdom.

James may have reference to teachers mentioned in verse 1, but certainly the verse has a more general application. The evidence of wisdom is seen in how one lives. A humble life is clear evidence of wisdom. One who has a great deal of knowledge is tempted to become proud, but true wisdom is not compatible with an arrogant, know-it-all attitude.

B. STRIFE SHOWS LACK OF WISDOM (v. 14)

14. But if you harbor bitter envy and selfish ambition in your hearts, do not boast about it or deny the truth.

A teacher who is arrogant is likely to have *envy and selfish ambition* in his heart. His attitude creates a party spirit among his students. Some copy his arrogance; some rebel against it. It is likely that James had seen some of this in the church.

This problem does not belong exclusively to those who propagate false doctrine. It is quite possible for one who tells the truth to display a narrow, factious spirit that leads to strife. Paul urges us to speak "the truth in love" (Ephesians 4:15). When we confront those who are in error, we must do so with gentleness and humility, always showing love toward the person who is in error. All too often in religious disputes we are more concerned about winning a victory than about advancing the cause of truth.

WHAT DO YOU THINK?

Jesus said, "Out of the overflow of the heart the mouth speaks" (Matthew 12:34). His point seems to be that our speech reveals our heart or our character. Our text's illustrations of the power of the tongue, like the horse's bit and the ship's rudder, seem to make a different point. As the bit dictates direction for the horse and the rudder for a ship, so our tongue (speech) will establish the direction for the entire person (character). Does character determine speech or does speech determine character? How would you explain these two seemingly contradictory passages?

WHAT DO YOU THINK?

James warns of the wrong kind of wisdom, full of envy and selfish ambition. Saul, selected by God to be the first king of Israel, was consumed by his envy and subsequent strife with David. Can you think of other examples of people thought to be wise who were disgraced or discredited because of envy and strife? How would you suggest a person guard against such emotions to show wisdom "by deeds done in the humility that comes from wisdom"?

C. RESULTS OF FALSE WISDOM (vv. 15, 16)

15, 16. Such "wisdom" does not come down from heaven but is earthly, unspiritual, of the devil. For where you have envy and selfish ambition, there you find disorder and every evil practice.

God is not the source of the kind of wisdom that makes one arrogant and contentious. Such wisdom is *earthly* in its origins, arising from selfish desires. These desires are demonic in that they lead to *envy, selfish ambition,* and *disorder,* not to the peace and harmony God desires. Satan has no more effective weapon than strife among Christians. It leads to *every evil practice.*

Over the past two thousand years of its existence, the church has been hampered by discord and division. In some situations it has been necessary for believers to separate themselves from faithless leaders or churches; but all too often strife has been caused by pride and jealousy. No wonder that Jesus prayed for the unity of his followers (John 17:20, 21). The world desperately needs the message of salvation that Christ offers, but it will not hear that message very well as long as we are fighting among ourselves.

D. MARKS OF TRUE WISDOM (vv. 17, 18)

17, 18. But the wisdom that comes from heaven is first of all pure; then peace-loving, considerate, submissive, full of mercy and good fruit, impartial and sincere. Peacemakers who sow in peace raise a harvest of righteousness.

After listing some of the marks of worldly wisdom, James now turns to *wisdom that comes from heaven.* This wisdom is first of all *pure,* that is, it is free from worldly contamination. Since it is free from personal ambition that characterizes worldly wisdom, it is *peace-loving,* free from the strife that so often accompanies the wrong kind of ambition. It is *considerate,* or gentle, willing to go the second mile to avoid conflict. *Submissive* describes one who is willing to listen to others and weigh the evidence. Such a person does not hesitate to change his or her mind in the face of compelling evidence. A person who has heavenly wisdom is able to make decisions without partiality. This recalls what James has written in chapter 2, forbidding Christians to show favoritism.

Seed that is sown produces its own kind of fruit. Those who make peace are sowing the kind of seed that produces righteousness. It is difficult for righteousness to flourish in the midst of strife. But when peace is made without giving up truth or right, there is a climate where righteousness can come to full fruition.

TWO KINDS OF WISDOM

But to every man there openeth
  A high way and a low,
And every man decideth
  The way his soul shall go.

—John Oxenham

Presented in Psalm 1 is the contrast between the man who walks in "the counsel of the wicked" and the one whose "delight is in the law of the Lord." Jesus spoke of the decision that had to be made between the broad road "that leads to destruction" and the narrow road that "leads to life" (Matthew 7:13, 14).

James presents the distinction between the wisdom that is "earthly, unspiritual, of the devil" and the wisdom that is "from heaven." This wisdom is pure, peaceful, gentle. The one wisdom engenders confusion and every evil work, while the other results in mercy, good fruits, and peace.

It takes intelligence to develop a bomb—a knowledge of explosives and wiring and trigger mechanisms. This work of intelligent organization is meant to destroy,

---

Visual 4 illustrates the theme of James 13:13-18. Display it as you discuss these verses.

HOW TO SAY IT

Gibeon. GIB-e-un.
Sheba. SHEE-buh.

PRAYER

Most gracious God and Father, Creator of all true wisdom, may we come before you humbly and hungrily seeking heavenly wisdom, that we may show in our lives that we truly are your children. In our Master's name we pray. Amen.

THOUGHT TO REMEMBER

"The fear of the Lord is the beginning of wisdom; all who follow his precepts have good understanding" (Psalm 111:10).

DAILY BIBLE READINGS

Monday, June 17—Wisdom Granted by God (Job 28: 12-22, 28)

Tuesday, June 18—Messiah's Spirit of Wisdom (Isaiah 11:1-5)

Wednesday, June 19—Surprised by his Wisdom (Matthew 13:53-58)

Thursday, June 20—Wisdom Of Obedience (Matthew 7:21-28)

Friday, June 21—Superior Wisdom in Committed Lives (Daniel 1:17-21)

Saturday, June 22—Faith Begets Wisdom From Above (1 Corinthians 2:1-8)

Sunday, June 23—Folly of Worldly Wisdom (1 Corinthians 3:16-23)

to harm, to maim, and to kill. Its detonation is a victory for hatred, bitterness, and vindictiveness.

On the other hand, it requires wisdom to learn ways of bringing enlightenment to minds yearning for truth, to bring healing to sickly bodies, or to bring harmony where there has been discord. Let us choose and use the wisdom that is "from above."

—J. G. V. B.

CONCLUSION

A. TOO MANY TEACHERS

From James's remarks we conclude that the church may have had an unusual problem: too many teachers! Most churches today wish they had such a problem. We seem always to be in need of more teachers, and we spend a good deal of time and energy recruiting and training teachers for the various teaching ministries of the church.

The problem in James's day, however, is till with us. Teachers must not become teachers for the wrong motives. Teachers without wisdom are worse than no teachers at all! James warned that teachers bear a heavy responsibility. That responsibility applies to their words, what they teach. They must teach sound doctrine, and they must teach it persuasively and with love. But beyond that, they must be a living embodiment of what they teach. Actions speak more loudly than words. A teacher's job is not finished when he or she pronounces a benediction at the end of the lesson. The teaching responsibility—and opportunity—go on seven days a week.

B. WHOSE WISDOM?

We live in an age when knowledge is exploding at an incredible rate. The horizons of information are expanding so far and so fast that no individual can begin to comprehend all that is known. The result is that we are becoming a society of specialists. We know more and more about less and less. This fact alone should not frighten us. After all, God created our vast universe, and any truth that man discovers is God's truth. He endowed us with intellectual powers, and he intends us to use those powers to unlock the secrets of his universe for the benefit of mankind.

The problem is that in this frantic search for knowledge we have almost abandoned our search for wisdom. We have at our fingertips vastly more information than our parents or grandparents possessed, and yet we seem to lack wisdom about how to use this information in matters that are really important. Scientists can tell us how to split the atom, but science does not give scientists the wisdom to know when and under what conditions to unleash the tremendous power of the atom. Genetic engineers hold out the promise of developing better crops and eliminating some of the diseases that have plagued the human race for untold centuries. Yet that science does not provide the wisdom we need to draw up moral guidelines for how and when this knowledge should be used.

Where, then, shall we find this wisdom? Do we need more and larger government research grants to probe the far reaches of our universe? Do we need more scientists directing their skills to unlocking creation's secrets? James gives us the answer. True wisdom comes down from Heaven! It does not come in the form of flashing lights or divinely powered supercomputers. We find heavenly wisdom revealed to us through the Scriptures. It provides the moral standards that allow us to know right from wrong in a society that tries to ignore or obliterate such standards. God's Word tells us what kind of people we ought to be—kind, humble, loving, serving. It also shows us what such a life should be by giving us the divine model—Jesus Christ.

Discovery Learning

This page contains an alternate lesson plan emphasizing learning activities. Classes desiring such student involvement will find these suggestions helpful. The next page is a reproducible activity page to further enhance discovery learning.

LEARNING GOALS

As a result of this study students should:

1. Describe the source, the nature, and the results of true wisdom.

2. Name ways to demonstrate godly wisdom by God-honoring speech and living.

INTO THE LESSON

Distribute copies of "Answers, Please" from the reproducible page 376. Ask the students to work individually to complete the activity. Then discuss the results. Is there general consensus regarding the order? Probably the Bible will not have scored high on anyone's list. (Remember, this is how the world views things.)

Ask, "Why doesn't the world look to the Bible more for answers?" During this discussion, point out that the world is often asking the wrong questions. The world's value system does not appreciate the issues to which the Bible has the answers. These other sources can offer reliable answers to some questions, but those questions are insignificant compared to the questions the Bible can answer.

Move toward the lesson text by asking the class to define and contrast *knowledge* and *wisdom*. Then suggest that knowledge centers on the accumulation of information and facts, while wisdom has more to do with the practical application of what is learned. Ask, "Which is the world more interested in, knowledge or wisdom? Why?"

INTO THE WORD

Ask a volunteer to read James 1:5-8 aloud. Then give a three- to five-minute lecture focusing on the nature of God as *teacher* and our approach to him as *students*. Illustrate your comments on the board or on newsprint by the following outline:

Teacher (God)
      Generous: "gives generously to all "
      Gentle: "without finding fault"
Student (Me)
      Believing: "when he asks, he must believe"
      Focused: "not doubt," not "double-minded"

Emphasize that God takes delight in teaching generously, and that his sensitive Spirit doesn't treat anyone as a "dummy" in the classroom. As students we need absolute confidence in him.

Divide the class into groups of four to six, and assign one of the following projects to each group. Copy the instructions on index cards and provide each group with poster board, markers, and their instructions.

PROJECT 1: INSTRUCTIONS

Read James 3:1-5a. This passage speaks of the accountability of teachers. Imagine your group has been asked to prepare a visual aid for a Sunday school teachers' meeting, using this verse as the theme. Create a poster and slogan that illustrates the potential of a teacher's words for good or for bad.

PROJECT 2: INSTRUCTIONS

Read James 3:13-18 and then write the following captions on a poster: "Earthly Wisdom" and "Heavenly Wisdom." Below each caption list the characteristics of each type of wisdom. Discuss the contrasts together in your group.

After ten or twelve minutes call time. Ask each group to summarize its discussion and display its work.

OPTION

Have all groups work on the activity for James 3:1-5; then use the second reproducible activity, "Wisdom From Above," from page 376.

INTO LIFE

Take a few minutes to brainstorm with your class and develop a list of modern situations where heavenly wisdom needs to be applied. Examples may come from politics, your church life, the businesses and corporations in your area, education, and others.

Be sure each idea is specific. For example, instead of accepting "our church leadership," ask for a specific situation in which the church leaders need to apply God's wisdom, as in calling a new staff member or considering a building or relocation project. List these on the chalkboard or on a poster that everyone can see.

Assign each item to one or more of your class members. Ask them to pray every day in the coming week for God's wisdom for the people involved. Close with a prayer for wisdom for each of your pupils.

Answers, Please

This is the information age. More information is available to people today than ever before. So where does one go for answers today? Examine the following list. Which does the world most often look to for answers? Write a 1 in the blank in front of it. Rank the others from 2-14.

_____ • University	_____ • Library
_____ • TV tabloids	_____ • Bible commentary
_____ • Local newspaper	_____ • High school textbooks
_____ • Pastor	_____ • *Cosmopolitan* magazine
_____ • Parents	_____ • *Wall Street Journal*
_____ • Laboratory	_____ • Bible
_____ • Public broadcasting documentary	_____ • Evening news

Wisdom From Above

We live in an age when knowledge is exploding at an incredible rate. The horizons of information are expanding so far and so fast that no individual can begin to comprehend all that is known. In our search for knowledge we have almost abandoned our search for wisdom. But wisdom is superior to knowledge, and heavenly wisdom is superior to earthly wisdom. Read James 3:13-18, then list the different characteristics of wisdom below the appropriate caption.

EARTHLY WISDOM   *GODLY WISDOM*

In James 1:5 we are told that anyone who lacks wisdom should ask God. Think about an area of your life where you lack wisdom. Then write out your prayer asking God for the wisdom that comes from above. PUSH your prayer—Pray Until Something Happens!

A Practical Religion
James
(Lessons 1-5)

FAITH AND RIGHTEOUSNESS
LESSON 5

WHY TEACH THIS LESSON?

We all know how serious four-letter words can be, but there are a couple of five-letter words we ought also to be wary of. They are *greed* and *pride*. What untold damage these two have done! James blames them for fights and quarrels, misguided prayer, hatred of God, and presumption upon God's grace.

And which of us has not been guilty of both of these vices from time to time. It's hard to see images of the good life splashed across the TV screen and the pages of magazines without wanting what we cannot afford. It's hard to maintain humility when the entire culture pushes us to self aggrandizement.

It's hard, but it's vital. We need God's grace to assist us. Use this lesson to help your students draw near to God and find his grace.

INTRODUCTION

A. SUNK BY GREED

A ship laden with treasure was making its way from a colony to the mother country. In the middle of the Atlantic, the ship sprang a leak. The sailors worked desperately to stop it, but in vain. The order was given to abandon ship.

One of the sailors seized this opportunity to enrich himself with as many gold bars as he could hide in his clothing. Encumbered by the weight as he stepped into a lifeboat, he lost his balance and plunged into the sea. The heavy gold took him swiftly to the bottom. His greed was his undoing.

For their own safety James spoke out against those who selfishly went after things. They desired wealth for the wrong reason, so they could satisfy their lusts.

How timely this warning is now! An observer of our society could not draw a more accurate picture of its problems than James gives us. Daily we are bombarded by advertisements that entice us to buy things. We sacrifice our good name for material possessions, we sacrifice our children for them, and we sacrifice our peace of mind for them. Tragically, we sometimes even sacrifice our lives.

B. LESSON BACKGROUND

In the third chapter, James gave his attention to teachers. He urged them to control their tongues and thereby show wisdom. Those who gained this divine wisdom enjoyed rich blessings, including the blessing of peace.

Chapter 4, in stark contrast, begins not with peace but with war and strife. James depicts a situation in which people seem caught up in the scramble for material things and in the pursuit of worldly pleasures. These people may wear the name *Christian*, but they certainly are not allowing the Lord to direct their lives.

I. THE CAUSE OF CONFLICT (JAMES 4:1-3)

A. STRIFE BEGINS IN LUST (v. 1)

1. What causes fights and quarrels among you? Don't they come from your desires that battle within you?

Fights and quarrels. It is not possible for Christians always to avoid strife. When we stand firm in the faith, we can be certain that Satan will find some way to disturb our

DEVOTIONAL READING
1 CORINTHIANS 3:10-15
LESSON SCRIPTURE
JAMES 4:1-10, 13-17
PRINTED TEXT
JAMES 4:1-10, 13-17

Jun
30

LESSON AIMS

After studying this lesson, each student should be able to:

1. Describe how choosing to serve God necessarily distinguishes a person from the world.

2. Determine to make a specific choice that will honor God and demonstrate he or she is distinctive from the world.

KEY VERSE

Anyone, then, who knows the good he ought to do and doesn't do it, sins.   —James 4:17

peace. But James is not talking about this kind of fighting. He is concerned about the strife that is rooted in lust. The Greek word here translated *desires* may more accurately be translated *pleasures*. The English word *hedonism*, meaning devotion to worldly pleasures, comes from this word. Paul speaks of a civil war that rages within the heart of each one of us between fleshly lusts and our higher spiritual being (Romans 7:15-20). This spills over into conflict with others.

History bears ample testimony to the truth of James's statement. Across the centuries tribes and nations have fought bloody wars for plunder, for power, or for revenge. Historians would be hard pressed to find a war that did not have its roots in these baser motives. On a smaller scale these motives have led individuals to commit acts of violence. We may accumulate vast armaments to deter aggressors, and we may pass laws to protect us from violent persons; but unless we can change the hearts of men and women, we will never see an end to violence.

WHAT DO YOU THINK?

One can hardly imagine that verse 2 is addressed to Christians, but it is! Could the believers actually be fighting and killing one another? Perhaps he is referring to murder by poison—the poison of the tongue (3:8).

If a teacher you respected compared your actions with murder, how would you respond? Why do you suppose James used such stark language here?

B. LUST CAUSES VIOLENCE (v. 2)

2. You want something but don't get it. You kill and covet, but you cannot have what you want. You quarrel and fight. You do not have, because you do not ask God.

The word here translated *want* means strong desire, which in certain situations may be proper. But in this context, clearly it is wrong. Moved by social pressures and lured by clever advertising, we seek this world's baubles. Heightened expectations are hard to satisfy, and when they go unfulfilled we are likely to become frustrated and turn violent. We want these things and we want them now! When we don't get them, we *kill ... quarrel and fight*.

We fail to gain these because we resort to violence to get them. Violence breeds violence, and in the ensuing struggles what we desire escapes us. Our culture tells us that "to the victor belong the spoils." We hold up aggressive people as models for our young people and then wonder why children resort to violence and even murder. Jesus' words, "Blessed are the meek, for they will inherit the earth" (Matthew 5:5), get lost in the din of the struggle.

NOT ASKING

An old story tells of a church in search of a new minister. The officers were using a method that is unwise, generally speaking. A succession of ministers gave "trial sermons," after which a vote was taken to determine which one would be employed. Finally a selection was made. A friend of one of the members asked how this particular choice came about. The reply was, "It wasn't so much how his trial sermon came out. No, our decision came because of how he prayed in public. He asked the Lord for blessings and benefits none of those other fellows knew the Lord had!"

How true are those words in James 4:2! "You do not have, because you do not ask God." These words apply to many things besides prayer. We do not understand or do not enjoy numerous things because we really do not care enough to investigate or explore—in other words, to "ask." What really is a symphony concert? What is the difference between various coniferous trees—the identifying characteristics of pine, spruce, balsam, hemlock, fir?

God was present in the burning bush, but he did not speak to Moses until Moses turned aside to see why the bush burned and was not consumed (Exodus 3:1-4). In many ways God speaks to us only when we "ask." —J. G. V. B.

WHAT DO YOU THINK?

Some people seem to think prayer is a time to address God with our wish list of preferred private blessings. If we are only asking God to meet our selfish desires, as though he were a celestial candy-man, James contends that we will not receive. Yet Jesus said we could "ask whatever you wish, and it will be given you" (John 15:7). How can we ask for personal requests in our prayers without being selfish?

C. IMPROPER ASKING FAILS (v. 3)

3. When you ask, you do not receive, because you ask with wrong motives, that you may spend what you get on your pleasures.

Some do not receive what they want because they do not ask (v. 2). Some, however, ask and do not receive because they *ask with wrong motives*. Because they pray selfishly, God does not give them what they pray for. People whose only concern is to satisfy their own lusts are not likely to pray unselfish prayers. Of course, God hears and answers every prayer, but to a selfish prayer he usually answers no.

II. ALIENATION FROM GOD (JAMES 4:4-6)

A. WORLDLINESS ALIENATES (vv. 4, 5)

4. You adulterous people, don't you know that friendship with the world is hatred toward God? Anyone who chooses to be a friend of the world becomes an enemy of God.

Adulterous people. The oldest manuscripts have the female "adulteresses" here. Even if this is the original reading, we should not understand James to suggest that men are not included. He is using a familiar Old Testament figure. God often described his relationship with his people as a marriage and their unfaithfulness as adultery. God is a jealous God; he does not take lightly the dalliance of his people with other gods.

Thus, the sin James condemns here is not necessarily a sexual sin. At least it is not limited to that. It is unfaithfulness to the Lord. Having once become the "bride" of Christ, how could the believers flirt with the world? But they have. They are guilty of adultery—spiritual adultery.

The *world* here is not the physical world, but the sensual, sinful aspects of the world. Some Christians live in hermitages or monasteries, cut off from that world; but we cannot think this verse suggests that. To withdraw from the world is to reject the Great Commission that commands us to go into all the world. We must live in the world, but live as friends of God.

Many Christians would like to serve God and at the same time dabble in the alluring fruit that Satan offers. James makes it very clear that this arrangement will not work. *Friendship with the world is hatred toward God.* We have no trouble understanding this principle. The difficulty arises when we try to apply it. Satan often tempts us, not to completely reject our Christian standards, but to compromise them. In the process he tries to convince us that God is unfair and even cruel because he demands our absolute loyalty. But we have to choose. "No one can serve two masters" (Matthew 6:24).

5. Or do you think Scripture says without reason that the spirit he caused to live in us envies intensely?

This verse poses a problem. Many versions (e.g., KJV, RSV, NASB) leave the impression that the latter part of the verse is a quotation from the Old Testament, but it is not. Students have found various ways of solving the problem. For example, the *American Standard Version* (1901) divides this verse into two questions. The first asks, "Or think ye that the scripture speaketh in vain?" That may refer to many passages that show the world in opposition to God, as indicated in verse 4. Obviously, the answer is no! The Scripture never speaks in vain. The second question then follows: "Doth the spirit which he made to dwell in us long unto envying?" Again the answer is an emphatic no! In no way can we blame our lust and envy on the Holy Spirit who dwells in us.

Others have solved the problem by taking *the spirit he caused to live in us* to be the Holy Spirit, who is made to dwell in the Christian upon conversion (Acts 2:38). Simply capitalizing the *s* in *spirit* in the *New International Version* would convey this thought. The Scripture does say that God is "jealous" for his people (Exodus 20:5; 34:14; Deuteronomy 4:24; 5:9; 6:15; and others). Thus, when we are flirting with the world, we are arousing the jealousy of the Holy Spirit within us. The problem with this view is that the word for *envy* here has a negative connotation and is never used of God elsewhere; only the milder *jealousy.*

WHAT DO YOU THINK?

James says "friendship with the world is hatred toward God." This is a very sobering thought for people who enjoy many of the comforts of this world. Is an easy life necessarily sinful? How much of the world's pleasures can one enjoy without becoming a "friend of the world" or trying to "serve two masters" (Matthew 6:24)? How can you tell who is a friend of the world and who is God's friend?

Visual 5 of the visuals packet quotes verse 17 of the lesson text. Discuss the picture with your class. What kind of behavior is suggested? How is that related to the themes of greed and pride developed in the lesson today?

Still others would take the spirit to be the natural spirit of man and see this envy (or yearning) as a reference to Psalm 42: "As the deer pants for streams of water, so my soul pants for you, O God" (v. 1). Thus the yearning is for God, not for the world.

B. GOD OFFERS GRACE (v. 6)

6. But he gives us more grace. That is why Scripture says: "God opposes the proud but gives grace to the humble."

Instead of producing lust and envy (v. 5) the Holy Spirit in us *gives us more grace,* more divine favor. This is verified by a quotation from Proverbs 3:34 in the Septuagint, a Greek version of the Old Testament.

Pride is one of the great barriers to receiving God's grace. Those who humbly submit to him God will receive, but he is unyielding to those who arrogantly resist him. "The sacrifices of God are a broken spirit; a broken and contrite heart, O God, you will not despise" (Psalm 51:17).

From time to time Christian scholars have drawn up lists of what they consider the most serious sins, the "seven deadly sins." Pride often heads this list, and for good reason. Pride, which causes persons to elevate themselves and their desires even above God, is the root of most other sins.

III. SUBMISSION TO GOD (JAMES 4:7-10)

A. RESIST THE DEVIL (v. 7)

7. Submit yourselves, then, to God. Resist the devil, and he will flee from you.

In the ancient world (as in ours) submission to anyone was looked upon as weakness. Yet those who submit to God gain strength, strength to resist the devil. With the power of God we can face the evil one, and he will beat a hasty retreat. Peter describes Satan as a roaring lion, but faced by God's power he becomes a paper lion.

In resisting the devil we ought to follow Jesus' example. He used Scripture as his chief weapon. We may be tempted to argue with Satan, but that is a mistake because he is a master of clever argument. When he tried to use his clever arguments against Jesus, our Lord quoted Scripture. That soon put the devil to flight. Of course, to use Scripture we must know it, which is a good reason for stressing the importance of Sunday school and other situations in which we study the Bible.

NOT RESISTING

One of the most enduring of relatively modern legends is that of Faust, the German scholar-magician. This is the story of a man who sold his soul to the devil for twenty-four years of power, knowledge, and pleasure.

This is exactly the opposite of what James tells us in verse 7 of our printed text. He says we are to *resist* the devil, not to enter into an agreement with him. Neglecting our Christian resources, forgetting to pray, forsaking Bible reading, being absent from public worship—all these are ways we diminish our strength to resist the evil one.

The story of Faust first came to general view in England about 1600 with the publication of the drama *Dr. Faustus,* by Christopher Marlowe. In that play the agent of Satan, Mephistopheles, tells Faust how the evil spirits come to tempt and assault men:

> For when we hear one rack the name of God,
> Abjure the Scriptures and his Saviour Christ,
> We fly, in hope to get his glorious soul;
> Nor will we come, unless he use such means
> Whereby he is in danger to be damned.

If we are to resist Satan, we need to eliminate wicked attitudes and actions and encourage those qualities that God's Spirit seeks to instill in us. Instead of hatred, let us

WHAT DO YOU THINK?

James's command to "submit to God" follows his reminder that "God gives grace to the humble" and immediately precedes his command to "resist the devil." What connection do you see between humility and submitting to God? Between submitting to God and resisting the devil? Between humility and resisting the devil? What role do you think "grace" plays in all this?

seek love; instead of pessimism and gloom, joy; in place of unrest and agitation, peace. Thus we resist the devil, who will indeed flee from us.

—J. G. V. B.

B. TURN TO GOD (v. 8)

8. Come near to God and he will come near to you. Wash your hands, you sinners, and purify your hearts, you double-minded.

We must remain close to God if we are to resist the devil successfully. In the parable of the prodigal son, Jesus depicted God as a loving Father who waited for his wayward son and greeted him with love and forgiveness when he returned. This parable gives us assurance that in the same way God waits for us when we return to him from our wandering.

When we do return to God, two things are required of us. We must come with clean hands; that is, our actions must show that we have turned away from sin. We must also come with pure hearts to provide the motivation for our actions.

C. HUMBLE YOURSELVES (vv. 9, 10)

9. Grieve, mourn and wail. Change your laughter to mourning and your joy to gloom.

In this verse, James seems to be addressing Christians who had become careless in their lives and who were devoting too much time and too many of their resources to the pleasures of this world, even sinful pleasures. They should weep over their wickedness and abandon it.

This is not to suggest that a Christian's life should be totally devoid of joy. Quite the contrary. A Christian who gives himself or herself wholeheartedly to the service of the Lord will know joy and satisfaction that this world cannot match.

10. Humble yourselves before the Lord, and he will lift you up.

James sums up his previous admonitions by returning once again to the theme of humility. The emphasis he gives to this matter leads us to believe that the lack of humility was a serious problem among the churches of his day. Pride has been a besetting sin in every age. The rich and the powerful seem to be especially tempted at this point, but even the poor are not exempt.

IV. GOD CONTROLS OUR DESTINY (JAMES 4:13-17)

A. MAN EXCLUDES GOD (vv. 13, 14)

13. Now listen, you who say, "Today or tomorrow we will go to this or that city, spend a year there, carry on business and make money."

In a few words James sums up the attitude of successful business leaders, people who have control of their lives and make their own decisions. Such a person is likely to receive a laudatory write-up in the *Wall Street Journal* or make the cover of *Time*. The executive suites of major corporations are filled with people like this. James is not censuring their ambition, their planning, or their hard work. What he censures is that they order their lives as if they were in complete control—as if God had no place in their plans.

14. Why, you do not even know what will happen tomorrow. What is your life? You are a mist that appears for a little while and then vanishes.

James puts his finger squarely on the problem—life's uncertainty. None of us knows for sure what tomorrow will bring, let alone a year. We sometimes hear this verse read at funerals. It is certainly appropriate there, but we ought to be reminded of it daily.

WHAT DO YOU THINK?

James warns us about presuming too much about the future. "If it is the Lord's will," he reminds us to say. Of course, just saying the words is not enough. We need to have an attitude of submission to God's will. What do you think characterizes one who truly appreciates the uncertainty of life and the future? Do you think it is possible to use "faith" as an excuse to be presumptuous about the future and God's will? Why or why not? How can we cultivate a respect for God's right to change our plans?

THOUGHT TO REMEMBER

"All men desire peace, but very few desire those things that make for peace."

—Thomas a Kempis

DAILY BIBLE READINGS

Monday, June 24—Assured of Innocence (Job 27:1-11)

Tuesday, June 25—Worthy Resolves (Psalm 66:13-20)

Wednesday, June 26—A True Relationship (1 John 2:12-17)

Thursday, June 27—An Expression of Faith (Psalm 138)

Friday, June 28—Blessings of the Righteous (Proverbs 3:27-35)

Saturday, June 29—Trust in God's Grace (Isaiah 55:6-11)

Sunday, June 30—Qualified to Enter God's Presence (Psalm 24:1-6)

B. ACCEPTING GOD'S WILL (vv. 15, 16)

15, 16. Instead, you ought to say, "If it is the Lord's will, we will live and do this or that." As it is, you boast and brag. All such boasting is evil.

A person who plans his or her life without taking God into consideration is, for all practical purposes, an atheist. Such a person may speak eloquently of serving God, but one's actions reveal his true loyalties. The rejoicing and boastings of a self-sufficient person are sinful in the eyes of God.

James is not suggesting that we live aimless lives, driven here and there by the tides of life. His point is that when we do our planning, God should be considered at every step of the way.

C. THE SIN OF OMISSION (v. 17)

17. Anyone, then, who knows the good he ought to do and doesn't do it, sins.

This verse applies specifically to those who ought to include God in their planning, but do not. But it also has broader application. We are quick to condemn the overt sins such as murder, lying, stealing, and adultery, especially if they are not our sins. Often, however, we fail to note the sins of omission—the good deed we didn't do, the kind word we didn't speak. James doesn't make any special allowance for these sins.

NOT DOING

One of the most impressive passages in all the Bible is the dramatic depiction of the judgment scene in Matthew 25:31-46. The Son of man is seen as having come "in his glory, and all the angels with him." For the judgment of "all the nations" he is seated "on his throne in heavenly glory." We are familiar with the sentences of judgment coming from this awesome and ultimate Judge. Those who are sentenced to final doom are those who did not give the Lord food when he was hungry, nor give drink when he was thirsty, nor visit him when he was imprisoned. When they say they cannot remember these failures, the reply comes: "Whatever you did not do for one of the least of these, you did not do for me."

Here the conduct is not evaluated by the wrong things done which should not have been done. Rather, the condemnation is based on the right deeds *not* done that *should* have been performed but weren't. This agrees with James's words found in 4:17 of our lesson today: "Anyone, then, who knows the good he ought to do and doesn't do it, sins."

Have we been silent when we should have spoken, stingy when we should have been generous, self-regarding when we should have been self-giving? Our question to ourselves must be, "Have we done what we could?"

—J. G. V. B.

CONCLUSION

If James had been taking his cue from this morning's newspaper, he could not have more accurately described the present world situation. When the twentieth century began, many optimistically believed the day of world peace had arrived; but, tragically, ours has been the bloodiest, most violent century in all of human history.

Many factors have been blamed for this, among them racism, nationalism, advanced technology, Communism, and religion. Certainly these factors were involved, but James gets to the root of the problem: lust. We lust for things and we lust for power. Until we can find a way to control lust, any thought of peace in our world is a hopeless dream.

The problem is that man in his own strength cannot eliminate lust from his life. Only by yielding to Christ can we hope to overcome the power of greed and desire. That is why it is so essential that our efforts be turned to winning people to Jesus.

Discovery Learning

This page contains an alternate lesson plan emphasizing learning activities. Classes desiring such student involvement will find these suggestions helpful. The next page is a reproducible activity page to further enhance discovery learning.

LEARNING GOALS

After this lesson, each students should be able to:

1. Describe how choosing to serve God necessarily distinguishes a person from the world.

2. Determine to make a specific choice that will honor God and demonstrate that he or she is distinctive from the world.

INTO THE LESSON

Before class, select eight to twelve pictures from magazines that someone might or might not consider to be worldly. You might pictures featuring alcoholic beverages, automobiles, food, fashion jeans, a Bible, cruise ship, mountain vista, and others. Cut out the pictures and glue or tape each one to a sheet of paper. Number the pictures and mount them on the walls around your classroom.

To begin class, ask class members to pair off, preferably with someone not from their family. Give each one a sheet of paper and a pencil. Ask them to move around the room, and look at the pictures. They are to decide if they think what is depicted is worldly. If they both agree, they should write the number of the picture on the paper.

Allow several minutes for pairs to move around and discuss. Then ask them to sit down. They should select one of them to be their spokesperson. Take a tally for each picture regarding how many pairs thought it is worldly. Then write that number in pen on the picture. Note the three items with the most "votes."

Ask the class, "What makes something worldly?" Allow for discussion for several minutes. Then say, "James had a lot to say about worldliness. He sees it as a major obstacle to living for God. He indicates that anyone who is a friend of the world cannot be a friend of God. Let's discover why, and see how we can live as God's friends and servants, and not as friends of the world."

INTO THE WORD

Ask several volunteers to read James 4:1-10, 13-17. Then ask the class, "According to James, what does it mean to be a friend of the world?" Allow several to comment. Then lead a discussion of these questions:

1. Look at James 4:1-3. According to James, what causes fights among Christians?

2. Compare James 4:1-3 with 3:13-18. According to 3:13-18, what causes disorder among Christians? How is that similar to what is said in 4:1-3?

3. James confronts these believers about their envy, selfish ambition (3:16), their desires that battle within (4:1), their covetousness (4:2), and wrong motives (4:3). Consider how he describes such people in 4:4. How is such a person . . .

- an adulterous person?
- a friend of the world?
- an enemy of God?

4. How does choosing to be a friend of the world automatically make one an enemy of God?

5. According to James 4:6-10, how does one move from being a friend of the world to becoming a friend of God?

6. How does choosing to repent of one's friendship with the world affect how we make our plans? See verses 13-17.

OPTION

Make copies of reproducible page 384. Distribute these to the class and have the students work individually or in small groups to complete the activity. Then discuss their definitions.

INTO LIFE

Write these two phrases on the chalkboard:

- bitter envy/covetousness (3:16; 4:2)
- selfish ambition/wrong motives (3:16; 4:3)

Point out that bitter envy and covetousness focus on what we don't have and are consumed with getting. When we succumb to these, we see something that someone has and we are upset that we don't have it. Ask students to think about a time when they have allowed bitter envy and covetousness to control them.

Then emphasize that *selfish* ambition and wrong motives usually focus on getting ahead. We are consumed with pleasure or power and are committed to getting them. As a result, we trample others, put them down, emphasize our importance or our needs, and minimize the value and needs of others. Again, ask students to think about a time when they allowed selfish ambition and wrong motives to control them.

Ask the class, "How should we deal win these destructive dynamics in our heart? James tells us in 4:6-10." Then read the verses. Pause after each verse and ask your students to pray about that verse as it applies to their lives. Have them pray silently.

Ask the students to write down one change they intend to make based upon the Scriptures they just studied.

Friendship With God vs. Friendship With the Word

Read James 3:13—4:17 listed below. Circle any phrase or word that relates to being a friend of the world. Put a box around any phrase or word that relates to being a friend of God. Then when you have completed the passage, write two definitions, each no longer than fifteen words. The first defines *friendship with the world*. The second defines *friendship with God*. Write those in the space indicated below:

What causes fights and quarrels among you? Don't they come from your desires that battle within you? You want something but don't get it. You kill and covet, but you cannot have what you want. You quarrel and fight. You do not have, because you do not ask God. When you ask, you do not receive, because you ask with wrong motives, that you may spend what you get on your pleasures.

You adulterous people, don't you know that friendship with the world is hatred toward God? Anyone who chooses to be a friend of the world becomes an enemy of God. Or do you think Scripture says without reason that the spirit he caused to live in us envies intensely?

But he gives us more grace. That is why Scripture says:

"God opposes the proud
but gives grace to the humble."

Submit yourselves, then, to God. Resist the devil, and he will flee from you. Come near to God and he will come near to you. Wash your hands, you sinners, and purify your hearts, you double-minded. Grieve, mourn and wail. Change your laughter to mourning and your joy to gloom. Humble yourselves before the Lord, and he will lift you up.

Brothers, do not slander one another. Anyone who speaks against his brother or judges him speaks against the law and judges it. When you judge the law, you are not keeping it, but sitting in judgment on it. There is only one Lawgiver and Judge, the one who is able to save and destroy. But you—who are you to judge your neighbor.

Now listen, you who say, "Today or tomorrow we will go to this or that city, spend a year there, carry on business and make money." Why, you do not even know what will happen tomorrow. What is your life? You are a mist that appears for a little while and then vanishes. Instead, you ought to say, "If it is the Lord's will, we will live and do this or that." As it is, you boast and brag. All such boasting is evil. Anyone, then, who knows the good he ought to do and doesn't do it, sins.

My Definition of Friendship With the World	My Definition of Friendship With God

PRAISING GOD AS CREATOR AND SUSTAINER

LESSON 6

WHY TEACH THIS LESSON?

Two kinds of revelation inform us of our Creator. One, which is normally the focus of our studies on Sunday mornings, is called special revelation. This is what instructed the prophets of old and produced the Scriptures that we study to know God's will. This is a message directly inspired by God (2 Timothy 3:16, 17; 2 Peter 1:20, 21).

The other is more common and available to all. It is general revelation by which all people should recognize the Creator (Romans 1:19, 20). This revelation fills us with awe as we consider the vast expanse of the universe—and our God has done all of this.

It is when we combine both forms of revelation that we truly understand God. To see the vast creation may actually fill us with dread. What an awesome God who has done this—and who are we before him? His special revelation answers, especially in his ultimate Special Revelation, the Word made flesh. This awesome God loves us more than all the rest of his wonderful creation.

This lesson should lead to a deeper appreciation of that fact.

INTRODUCTION

A. NO HAWKS, NO HARVEST

In a certain area in the midwestern U.S., farmers grow clover for seed. One year the crop looked especially good. The plants grew luxuriantly, bloomed prolifically, and had few problems from disease or parasites. But when harvest time came, the farmers were disappointed. Their crops produced few seeds.

An expert was brought in to try to find out what caused the failure. This particular variety of clover could not be pollinated by honeybees, but required bumblebees. He soon discovered that there were almost no bumblebees in the entire area. He did find, however, that the fields were overrun with field mice. Many of the farmers also raised chickens in open lots. The baby chickens were easy prey for chicken hawks, and so two or three years earlier the farmers had declared open season on the hawks, practically exterminating them in the entire area.

The pieces of the puzzle were beginning to fall into place. When the hawks were eliminated, the mice population, with no natural enemies, exploded. Mice, it was found, destroyed bumblebee nests, and so there were no bumblebees to pollinate the clover, and thus no seed.

This incident indicates how delicately balanced the forces of nature are. When we change one small item in the system, we run a risk of upsetting that balance. Often we do this quite ignorantly, because we are just beginning to learn a few of the wonderful things God has provided in his creation. As Christians we should treat the world about us with awe and respect, learning all we can about it so that we can treat it more wisely.

DEVOTIONAL READING
ISAIAH 40:25-31
LESSON SCRIPTURE
PSALM 104
PRINTED TEXT
PSALM 104:24-34

Jul
7

LESSON AIMS

As a result of studying this lesson, each student should:

1. Describe responses that recognize God as Creator.

2. Develop/express worship responses to God who created and sustains the earth.

KEY VERSE

How many are your works, O LORD! In wisdom you made them all; the earth is full of your creatures. —Psalm 104:24

LESSON 6 NOTES

WHAT DO YOU THINK?

As for the origin of the universe, some say any explanation of what exists requires some faith. Whether one chooses to believe in the eternal existence of matter, in a big bang that began the universe, in evolution, or in some other theory that does not include a Creator or to look at what is and agree that a marvelous designer has been at work, each view comes down to faith

Do you agree or disagree? Why?

What do you make of Paul's assertion in Romans 1:19, 20?

Visual 6 of the visuals packet illustrates verse 24. Display it as you begin your Bible study today.

B. LESSON BACKGROUND

The author of this psalm is unknown, nor is there any agreement about when it was written. There is little in the psalm that even hints about its authorship or date. Some feel that it was designed to be sung by an individual in the worship in the temple. Certainly the psalm would lend itself to that purpose, because the pronouns *my* and *I* appear at the beginning and near the end.

The psalm opens with words of praise to God, who created the physical universe. In language that is both rich and colorful, the writer mentions many aspects of God's creation—the sky, the sea, the mountains, the vegetation, the animals. But, to the psalmist, God is more than a Creator; he also sustains the world he has created. God established the earth and then placed limits on the seas (vv. 5-9). He made the springs that feed the streams that quench the thirst of the wild animals, and he sends the rain that waters the mountains (vv. 10-13). Verses 14-18 tell that he makes grass grow for the cattle and provides food for man, while the mountains and forests give habitat for the animals and birds. The sun and moon mark daylight during which man works, and darkness in which beasts prowl (vv. 19-23).

The writer sees a God who is both powerful and loving. As a result he is filled with both awe and joy. This is his mood as he raises his voice in praise to God. As we study this psalm in detail, we should share his worshipful attitude.

I. GOD'S WISDOM IN CREATION (PSALM 104:24-26)

A. HIS BOUNDLESS WORKS (v. 24)

24. How many are your works, O LORD! In wisdom you made them all; the earth is full of your creatures.

All of nature is a revelation of God's power and majesty. On occasion God has revealed himself to man directly, but these occasions are relatively rare. On the other hand, at every tick of a watch God's works speak of his power. Only one who is spiritually blind would fail to see this. We gaze into the heavens and with the naked eye see thousands of stars, but with the telescope we can detect countless millions. The microscope unlocks miniature worlds that increase our awe of the Creator.

In wisdom you made them all. The ancient psalmist lacked the technology that we have to probe the secrets of the universe; but in the intricate workings of what he could see, he marveled at God's wisdom. How much greater our reverence should be! With our tools we see a universe far more complicated than the psalmist could even dream of.

B. THE WONDERS OF THE SEA (vv. 25, 26)

25, 26. There is the sea, vast and spacious, teeming with creatures beyond number—living things both large and small. There the ships go to and fro, and the leviathan, which you formed to frolic there.

Teeming with creatures beyond number. The psalmist's knowledge of the vast oceans and the life they contain was slight compared to what scientists know today. Yet even he knew that the number of sea animals was beyond counting. The more we understand about the oceans, the more we marvel at the bounty of God's creation. He made the whales, the most massive creatures on land or sea, and he made the tiny plankton upon which the whales feed.

On the surface of the seas sail the fleets of the nations, carrying men and their products great distances. Ships of today are more and bigger and swifter than those seen by the psalmist, but God made the oceans big enough for all of them.

Leviathan may be a name for any big creature that plays in the water. Some students think the one described in Job 41 is a crocodile, but it seems more probable that our text speaks of a dolphin or a whale.

THIS GREAT SEA

The psalmist is awed by God's greatness as seen his creation. The many evidences on land are called to mind, but he also contemplates the vast and mysterious sea. Here is an awesome testimony to the might and majesty of the Creator.

Lord Byron's long poem, "Childe Harold's Pilgrimage," contains some of the most beautiful and vivid thoughts ever expressed about "this great and wide sea."

> Roll on, thou deep and dark blue Ocean—roll!
> Ten thousand fleets sweep over thee in vain;
> Man marks the earth with ruin—his control
> > Stops with the shore;—upon the watery plain
> > The wrecks are all thy deed, nor doth remain
> A shadow of man's ravage, save his own,
> > > When, for a moment, like a drop of rain,
> > > He sinks into thy depths, with bubbling groan—
> > Without a grave—unknelled, uncoffined, and unknown.

This awareness of man's frailty and finiteness compared with the expanse and power of the sea is followed shortly by a magnificent passage explaining and extolling the ocean as an unequaled and unparalleled expression of the wondrous wisdom of God.

> Thou glorious mirror, where the Almighty's form
> Glasses itself in tempests; in all time,
> Calm or convulsed—in breeze, or gale, or storm—
> > Icing the Pole, or in the torrid clime
> > Dark-heaving—boundless, endless, and sublime—
> The image of Eternity.
> > > > > > > —J. G. V. B.

II. GOD PROVIDES (PSALM 104:27-30)

A. HE GIVES FOOD (vv. 27, 28)

27, 28. These all look to you to give them their food at the proper time. When you give it to them, they gather it up; when you open your hand, they are satisfied with good things.

Some believe in a Creator God, who, once he had made the physical universe, retired from it, leaving it to run on its own. These deists believe that God no longer intervenes in the world, either to care for his creation or to answer prayers. This is certainly not the view of the psalmist. He sees God on every hand sustaining his creation. All living creatures depend upon God for their sustenance. As we learn more about our environment, we have growing appreciation for the intricate balance necessary to sustain life. We have also learned some of the devastating results when man upsets this balance.

We also learn how God has built into nature recuperative power that allows life to be revived when disaster strikes. Few things are more disheartening than to see a once majestic forest that has been ravaged by fire. All life has been destroyed—it seems—and one would guess that years must elapse before life could be restored. But the very next spring, green shoots begin to appear. Some seeds are brought in by wind or birds or animals, a method of replanting planned by God. However, some seeds have been there all along, waiting for a fire. The seeds of certain conifers, such as the lodge pole pine, are locked inside such tight cones that only the heat of a blazing forest fire can release them. Then after the fire that has been so devastating, they spring into life. All across nature we see similar examples of God's provision. How can anyone doubt his existence and his love?

WHAT DO YOU THINK?

There are some who say God did indeed create the universe, but since then he has not been involved in it. How would you respond to such a claim?

B. He Gives and Takes Life (v. 29)

29. When you hide your face, they are terrified; when you take away their breath, they die and return to the dust.

When God turns away from his creation, trouble comes to all his creatures. Drought or flood or fire may destroy habitat and food supply. God does not reject his creation whimsically, but rather when his holy will has been violated. Human sinfulness contributes to the suffering of nature. "We know that the whole creation has been groaning as in the pains of childbirth right up to the present time ... as we wait eagerly for our ... redemption" (Romans 8:22, 23).

When God created Adam, he breathed into him the breath of life and he became a living being (Genesis 2:7). When that breath is withdrawn, man ceases to live and returns to the dust from which he came. "The dust returns to the ground it came from, and the spirit returns to God who gave it" (Ecclesiastes 12:7).

C. He Gives Renewal (v. 30)

30. When you send your Spirit, they are created, and you renew the face of the earth.

The creation of new life is an ongoing process. Even as some die and return to dust, others are being called into existence and given the breath of life. God's initial creative acts were completed in six days, but his renewal of life never ceases. *You renew the face of the earth.* We see this happening every springtime; we see it happening after a disastrous fire or flood; we see it happening continually as animals and people die and new generations are born.

THE CREATOR SPIRIT

In verse 30 of our text, "you send your Spirit" could be translated, "you send your breath." Either translation tells us God is personally active in the continuing creation of living things. The complex process by which the face of the earth is renewed is no mindless, mechanical process. It is due to the creating power of God flowing through the natural order. Wordsworth may have felt that when he wrote:

> And I have felt
> A presence that disturbs me with the joy
> Of elevated thoughts; a sense sublime,
> Of something far more deeply interfused,
>
> . . . .
>
> A motion and a spirit, that impels
> All thinking things, all objects of all thought,
> and rolls through all things.
>
> —J. G. V. B.

III. MAN'S RESPONSE (PSALM 104:31-34)

A. He Praises God's Glory (v. 31)

31. May the glory of the Lord endure forever; may the Lord rejoice in his works.

This is not only a prayer to God in Heaven; it is also a reminder to people on earth. May they use their voices to give glory and honor and praise to the Creator, and may they live their lives in a way that will make him happy.

B. He Sees God's Power (v. 32)

32. He who looks at the earth, and it trembles, who touches the mountains, and they smoke.

In recent years hurricanes, earthquakes, floods, and volcanic eruptions remind us of God's power latent in the earth he has created. These displays of power also remind us of how puny we are in contrast. We now have a better understanding of

---

WHAT DO YOU THINK?

That God chooses to love sinners adds to his glory, and out of his love he has provided a means of escape from condemnation (Romans 5:8-11). The sacrifice of Jesus on our behalf satisfies the claim of justice, and allows God to extend forgiveness and eternal life to believers. Clearly, God takes joy in this work of salvation, since he is the one who initiated it (John 3:16). We glorify God for creating us and for recreating us in Christ.

What kind of emotional response do you feel when you consider that God takes joy in your salvation? What kind of action responses are appropriate to express your feelings?

WHAT DO YOU THINK?

Is the psalmist saying God is the direct cause of natural disasters, with his "look" and his "touch" (v. 32)? If we believe that God is all-knowing, all-powerful, and full of love, how can we explain natural disasters?

(Consider the effect of the sin of man on the entire created order [Romans 8:22] and the possible involvement of Satan [Job 1:6-22].)

Are natural disasters punishment for sin (Deuteronomy 11: 16, 17)? Always? Sometimes? Never?

the laws that work to unleash the vast powers of nature, but we are still powerless to do anything about them.

C. HE SINGS PRAISES (v. 33)

33. I will sing to the LORD all my life; I will sing praise to my God as long as I live.

Of all of God's creatures, only man uses his voice to praise the Lord in songs like the one we are reading. God gave us voices to communicate with our fellowmen, but he intended that we also lift them up to him in songs of praise and thanksgiving. As the psalmist contemplates God's power in nature and his renewal of life, he uses his voice to break out in exultant praise of Jehovah.

"Let those refuse to sing who never knew our God," wrote Isaac Watts in "We're Marching to Zion." But how could any who have seen God's handiwork in nature "refuse to sing"? How could any who have known God's grace fail to lift up his or her voice and *sing praise*?

Christianity has produced a larger, more varied body of hymns and songs to praise God than has any other religion. Christian music varies from culture to culture, and even between generations within a culture. God is pleased with a variety of music forms that offer to him the sincere praise of his people. This very psalm was probably used in public worship in the temple.

D. HE REJOICES IN GOD (v. 34)

34. May my meditation be pleasing to him, as I rejoice in the LORD.

We worship God in our songs, but we also worship him in our meditations and prayers. In the busy world in which we live, most of us do not spend enough time in meditation. Our world is so intrusive that it is difficult to find even a few minutes when the noise and clatter about us do not break into our thoughts. We may wish for a slower, simpler life-style, but few of us have that option. We try to set aside a bit of time each day for devotions, but outside a monastery such a routine is difficult to maintain. Still, there are those occasional moments when we are able to enter into this special relationship with God. It may happen when we stand on a mountain overlook and see his majesty stretched out before us, or when a golden sun sends its rays across the radiant garb of autumn trees, or when winter casts a blanket of pristine snow and glistening ice across the landscape. Perhaps it is when in the middle of a sleepless night we find ourselves drawn closer to God. The important thing is to take advantage of the moment when it comes—and worship.

CONCLUSION

When man is confronted by the power and magnitude of God's handiwork in creation, how should he respond? Some are totally oblivious to everything about them. They not only fail to notice God's world of nature, they are equally unconcerned about the technological wonders that make their lives easy and comfortable. Caught up in their own concerns, they never give even a nod to the majesty of the world that surrounds them. They are, as Browning says, "finished and finite clods, untroubled by a spark."

Others live their lives openly or covertly in rebellion against God. They ignore the evidence of God about them, because to acknowledge this evidence would require them to acknowledge his power and his authority. To acknowledge this would require them to acknowledge that he has authority over their lives. This they are unwilling to do.

Others see God, not only in nature, but in science and technology. They see God in the vast expanse of space revealed by the instruments of science, a universe far greater than a person with the unaided eye could even dream of. They watch in

---

WHAT DO YOU THINK?

How important do you think our worship is to God? How important do you think it is to most Christians? What characterizes the life of a believer who takes worship seriously? What kind of "meditation" do you think is "pleasing" to God?

WHAT DO YOU THINK?

Corporate worship is important, and so is private worship. How helpful do you think each of the following devotional practices are? What other suggestions can you make for meaningful private worship?

• Having a quiet time in the morning or evening for Bible reading, meditation, and prayer

• Using a Bible study guide or devotional guide

• Listening to worship tapes or the Bible on tape while commuting to work or while working at home

• Meditating and praying while exercising

PRAYER

O mighty Creator and loving Father, we come before you recognizing your power and wisdom in creation. Give us a better understanding of the world you have created and placed us in, and teach us how to protect and use it for your glory. Open before us paths of service. In Jesus' name we pray. Amen.

THOUGHT TO REMEMBER

This is my Father's world,
I rest me in the thought
Of rocks and trees, of skies and
    seas—
His hand the wonders wrought.
    —Maltbie D. Babcock (1901)

DAILY BIBLE READINGS

    Monday, July 1—*The Lord as Creator* (Psalm 33:1-9)

    Tuesday, July 2—*Creation by God's Word* (Genesis 1:1-8)

    Wednesday, July 3—*Separation of Land and Water* (Genesis 1:9-13)

    Thursday, July 4—*Celestial Bodies Provide Light* (Genesis 1:14-19)

    Friday, July 5—*Animals Created by God* (Genesis 1:20-25)

    Saturday, July 6—*People to Dominate the Earth* (Genesis 1:26-31)

    Sunday, July 7—*Made to Need Each Other* (Genesis 2:18-24)

reverent amazement as men unlock the secrets of electronics, genetics, and the subatomic realm, secrets that God in his wisdom put there. Persons who are so endowed and so blessed respond in several ways.

A. AWE

As we come to understand the complexity of the world about us, we are driven to our knees in awe. The human body, for example, must maintain a delicate chemical balance if it is to function properly. Even the presence or absence of a few milligrams of this chemical or that can make the difference between health and sickness. Stop for a moment and consider human vision. The light rays emitted from some distant star can strike the eye and create an image that is transmuted into electrical energy that carries a message to the brain. One would have to be a clod indeed if he did not stand in awe of the Creator of such a marvelous process!

B. HUMILITY

We live in an age that prizes its independence. We create our own little worlds in which we are self-sufficient. Such a world is an illusion; it doesn't exist. In the very act of breathing, we recognize our dependence upon our Creator. After all, he created the air, and he gave us the ability to breathe it. Should not we with every breath humbly accept our dependence?

However, this humility is not that of a slave of a tyrannical despot. We are slaves indeed, but of no despot! And we are much more. We are children of a loving heavenly Father. The rich bounty he heaps upon us every day ought to instill within us a sense of dependent humility.

C. WORSHIP

A person who humbly acknowledges God as the source of every good and perfect gift (James 1:17) will naturally want to praise him. Those who refuse to trust God will still worship, but they will turn to false worship. "For although they knew God, they neither glorified him as God nor gave thanks to him, but their thinking became futile and their foolish hearts were darkened. Although they claimed to be wise, they became fools and exchanged the glory of the immortal God for images made to look like mortal man and birds and animals and reptiles" (Romans 1:21-23).

Few people in our culture would bow down before animals or idols of wood or stone. They turn to more sophisticated idols—money, power, pleasure, things. The principle is the same, however. Whether persons are primitive barbarians or sophisticated moderns, they worship those things they have put first in their lives.

D. SERVICE

Christians usually unite their hearts to worship together. We find strength and encouragement in that. Our worship is not complete, however, when the benediction is said and the building where we meet is vacated. Worship finds its fulfillment beyond the walls of the church building. A vital worship service not only will encourage its participants to seek areas *where* they may serve, it also will provide some help and direction in *how* they may serve. A worship service that lifts us to an emotional high and makes us feel good falls short if it does not send us forth with directions about how and where we may serve.

The same is true of a Sunday school class meeting. It would be quite appropriate at this point to ask students to discuss ways in which they are currently serving the Lord. Then have them go beyond this to mention other possible ways to serve. Encourage them to be as specific as possible in their suggestions.

Discovery Learning

This page contains an alternate lesson plan emphasizing learning activities. Classes desiring such student involvement will find these suggestions helpful. The next page is a reproducible activity page to further enhance discovery learning.

LEARNING GOALS

As a result of participating in this class session, a learner should:

1. Describe responses that recognize God as Creator.

2. Develop/express worship responses to God who created and sustains the earth.

INTO THE LESSON

Before class write the following instructions on the chalkboard: *Describe places you have visited that display God's creation.* Ask your learners to describe places they have visited that display the beauty of God's creation. Write the names of the places mentioned on the board under your instructions. Be prepared to mention a common place yourself, e.g., the Grand Canyon, to encourage more people to participate. Not everyone has gone to far-off places, but all have been to a forest or local park.

After you have allowed time for people to describe the visible beauty of our invisible Creator, write the word *revelation* on the board above the list of places. Explain that not all of God's revelation is in the Bible. We learn much about a skilled craftsman by scrutinizing his work, and we learn much about God through his creation (Romans 1:20). If time permits, you may want to read the story *No Hawks, No Harvest,* found on page 385.

OPTION

Display a variety of pictures that show beautiful landscapes and other displays of God's marvelous creation. Discuss how these sights reveal something of God to us; then proceed as described in the second paragraph above.

OPTION

Use the reproducible activity "Looking for God's Handiwork" on page 392 to begin your lesson.

INTO THE WORD

After your learners have taken time to reflect on God's wonderful works that are on display all around us, divide them into smaller study groups of five to seven members. Each group will need a reader, a recorder, and a reporter. The reader's task will be to read Psalm 104 aloud to the group. The recorder will take notes on what the group discovers. The reporter will summarize the group's findings to the whole class when the group is asked to report. (You could assign each group a portion of Psalm 104

instead of the entire chapter. This would allow time for fuller discussion.)

Your prompts for the group should include the following two questions:

1. *What did the psalmist learn about God from nature?* Responses should include: God is the Creator; he sustains the world he has created; he provides for his creatures; he gives renewal; he is powerful; he is loving; and he is wise. Use material from the Lesson Background and sections I and II to help you here.

2. *What have you learned about God from nature?* One response might be that he is a God of order and detail. The class should have no trouble adding to this list.

When you call for the group reports, make a list of their findings on the chalkboard. (If time is short, ask the groups to mention only responses that have not already been given by a group before them.)

INTO LIFE

One of the ways God reveals himself to us is through nature. Concentrate on specific ways the learners can respond to what they know about God from nature. Use material from the conclusion of the lesson to guide your class discussion. Don't limit your responses to the four given by the lesson writer—awe, humility, worship, and service. Encourage each learner to choose one specific attitude or act and then commit himself or herself to putting this into practice in the week ahead. On an index card have each one write a characteristic of God and a planned response. For example, "Because God created and cares for nature, I will pay more attention to recycling around my home, starting this week." The pattern for the learner to follow is first to state the characteristic of God (*Because God...*) and then to add his or her planned response (*I will...starting this week*). Be ready to share your response with the class. Invite others to read their cards aloud as time permits. Encourage each learner to put the card in a visible place as a reminder of his or her commitment. Suggest the dashboard of the car or a bathroom mirror.

Conclude your time together with a silent prayer time as each learner humbly enters God's presence and praises him for his wonderful works.

OPTION

Use the reproducible activity "Creation and Re-Creation" on page 392. Discuss; then close with prayer.

Looking for God's Handiwork

Some people are totally oblivious to God's handiwork in nature. Others see God everywhere. In the sentences below are parts of God's handiwork. Circle God's creations when you find them. The first is an example for you follow: the "sea" is one of God's creations. (There is one in each of the other four statements.)

1. We praise a Creator who loves us.

2. Whenever you are outside, listen and you will hear the sounds of his creation.

3. Ask yourself, "How can I praise God for his creation?"

4. Adam and Eve were the crown to God's creation.

5. Plan daily time with God to acknowledge him as your Creator.

Creation and Re-Creation

How is salvation in Christ related to God's glory and his desire to rejoice in his works? Look up the Scriptures and answer the questions on the chart below. By the time you finish, you will see how the Lord can "rejoice in his works"—especially his work of salvation!

QUESTION	SCRIPTURE	ANSWER
1. By what pattern did God create people?	Genesis 1:26, 27	
2. God created us capable of being tempted and capable of sin, so that the obedience we give is a true sign of faith and devotion. How well have we done on that?	Romans 3:23	
3. What does justice demand for sinners?	Genesis 1:17; Romans 6:23	
4. God takes no delight in seeing his created beings condemned. On what basis did God act to save people—who obviously could not save themselves?	Romans 5:8; John 3:16	
5. The sacrifice of Jesus on our behalf satisfies the claim of justice, and allows God to extend forgiveness. What is the result of forgiveness?	Romans 6:22, 23	
6. What has been God's plan for us all along?	Romans 8:29, 30	

Salvation restores to us God's original design so that we can be "conformed to the likeness of his Son," and "glorified" by the Father. We glorify him for creating us and for re-creating us in Christ.

Answers—Looking for God's Handiwork: 1 sea; 2 earth; 3 sky; 4 man; 5 land.
Creation and Re-Creation: 1 in the likeness and image of God; 2 all have sinned; 3 death; 4 love; 5 eternal life; 6 conformed to the likeness (image) of his Son (cf. "In the image of God," Genesis 1:27).

PRAISING GOD FOR MIGHTY ACTS

LESSON 7

WHY TEACH THIS LESSON?

This is an exciting unit of study. Its theme is so appropriate to worship that you may find your class sessions taking on more of a worship tone than one of study. That is all right. These lessons are designed to encourage worship, both corporate and private. The real goal is not just to encourage worship in your time spent together, but in your students' daily lives.

Use this look at God's mighty acts first as a reminder for yourself—a reminder not just of what you read about God's doing, but what he has done in your own life! Spend some time in quiet reflection and personal worship of our great God even as you prepare to teach. Then, as you lead this session, challenge your students to consider God's mighty acts often, and to pause for praise each time they do.

INTRODUCTION

A. 10,000 DISCOVERIES

Thomas Edison was a prodigious inventor. To him is credited the electric light bulb, the phonograph, the motion picture projector, and a variety of other original inventions or improvements on someone else's design. His long search and numerous failures in seeking the correct filament material for his light bulb are legendary. At one point, an associate is reported to have asked him if he weren't becoming discouraged with his failures. Edison is said to have responded, "I have not failed. I have discovered 10,000 things that won't work!"

What if Edison had not kept a record of his efforts? How could he ever have remembered all the different materials he had already tried without success? He may well have tried the same materials again and again and never found the right one.

This is the value of looking back. Edison's friend Henry Ford apparently did not appreciate such retrospection. "History is bunk," he is reported to have said on one occasion. Edison could not have agreed.

Nor could the ancient Israelites. Wise men among them never forgot their past or how they got where they were. They knew they were a special people. They knew God had intervened in history on their behalf. Their teachers talked about their past. Their prophets called them to repentance on the basis of their history. They even sang about their past when they came to the temple to worship. Psalm 105 is an example of such a song.

B. LESSON BACKGROUND

Many believe that this psalm was designed to be used in public worship. Verses 1-15 appear in 1 Chronicles 16:8-22 as part of the song David gave to the musicians when the ark of the covenant was brought to Jerusalem. This was undoubtedly a joyous occasion calling for praise and thanksgiving. It was also a

DEVOTIONAL READING
PSALM 106:1-12

LESSON SCRIPTURE
PSALM 105

PRINTED TEXT
PSALM 105:1-11, 43-45

Jul
14

LESSON AIMS

As a result of studying this lesson each student should:

1. List some of the marvelous works of God's providence.

2. Explain how recalling God's past provision builds faith in his continued providence.

3. Express thanksgiving and praise for God's provision.

KEY VERSE

Give thanks to the LORD, call on his name; make known among the nations what he has done.
—Psalm 105:1

Display visual 7 from the visuals packet as you begin the Bible study. (See page 395.)

WHAT DO YOU THINK?

While worship styles vary from place to place, certain elements of Christian worship are fairly constant. As you think about worship at your church, how do you celebrate "what [God] has done" in each of the following? Which of God's "wonderful acts" (v. 2) are most often celebrated in this way?

- *Singing*
- *Prayers*
- *The giving of offerings*
- *Communion*
- *Sermons*
- *Other?*

WHAT DO YOU THINK?

"Let the hearts of those who seek the LORD rejoice." Would you characterize your church as rejoicing in its worship services? Why or why not? Are most Christians you know joyful? Why or why not? What can you do to make your worship more joyful? Do you think that would produce more joy in the lives of the church's members? Why or why not?

time for renewing the covenant and for exhorting the people to live according to God's commandments.

The people had come through some difficult times during the reign of Saul and during the early years of David's reign. The nation had been repeatedly harassed by the Philistines, and internal strife fueled by Saul's jealousy of David had been equally damaging. Now things were looking up, and they could rejoice. But it was also a time for taking stock of what had happened to them and why it had happened. It was a time to renew their commitment to God. The psalmist helped them do this by singing about their history.

I. A CALL TO PRAISE (PSALM 105:1-6)

A. GIVE THANKS AND PRAISE (vv. 1-3)

1. Give thanks to the LORD, call on his name; make known among the nations what he has done.

The first six verses of this psalm serve as an introduction, setting the tone for the rest of the song. This opening verse is a call for thanksgiving, always an appropriate way to address our Lord, the giver of all our benefits. Worshipers are to *call on his name*—Jehovah or Yahweh, the special name that belongs only to the real God.

A major reason for thanksgiving was the way Jehovah had blessed his people, calling them out of Egypt, keeping them during their wandering in the desert, and then leading them into the promised land. The people were not to keep these blessings a secret among themselves. They were to *make known among the nations what he has done*. The Israelites were to tell the facts of their history to the tribes around them.

2. Sing to him, sing praise to him; tell of all his wonderful acts.

It was quite natural for their gratitude to break forth in song. God's people are singing people. Those who have alienated themselves from God have less to sing about. "Let those refuse to sing who never knew our God." At the triumphal entry, Jesus told the Pharisees praise is so natural that the stones would cry out if his disciples kept silent (Luke 19:39, 40).

While the *praise* is to be directed to God, other people were to be addressed in these songs, too. God's *wonderful acts* were to be told, not only in Israel, but to other peoples (v. 1). Paul urges the same balance in Christian worship, encouraging the Ephesians to "speak *to one another* in psalms, hymns and spiritual songs," and also "sing and make music in your heart *to the Lord*" (Ephesians 5:19).

3. Glory in his holy name; let the hearts of those who seek the LORD rejoice.

People of the world *glory* in their wealth or their power, but the people of God find glory in his *name*. The word LORD (spelled with small capitals) is used to translate the Hebrew word *Jehovah* or *Yahweh*. This is the unique name of God, who is the God of the covenant, the God of Abraham, Isaac, and Jacob. To avoid the danger of misusing this name (Exodus 20:7), the Jews eventually considered this name so *holy* that they would not pronounce it, even when they were reading Scripture. As a result, later generations forgot how to pronounce the word. It has come into English as *Jehovah*, but many scholars today prefer *Yahweh*.

It is widely believed that the followers of God are a rather solemn bunch, rarely finding joy in life. Nothing could be farther from the truth, as the writer here indicates. While it is true that God first of all requires his people to be holy (1 Peter 1:16), holiness and happiness are not mutually exclusive. The truth is that the happiest people in the world are those who have surrendered their lives to God. They may not experience the worldly pleasures that others crave, but they have a hope in eternity that assures them of everlasting joy.

B. SEEK THE LORD (v.4)

4. Look to the LORD and his strength; seek his face always.

God's search for man is a theme that runs through the entire Bible. Even as God searches for man, however, man must also seek God, actively and diligently. To *look to the Lord* is to desire his presence and his favor. As we seek his presence, we also seek *his strength*. We can be certain that Satan does all he can to discourage us in this search for God, but God gives us strength to continue our search.

THE SEARCH FOR STRENGTH

After a protracted illness, a special diet supplement may be taken to speed recovery. Some liquid preparations are full of minerals and vitamins that help "recharge" us physically.

At times there is also a weakening of our spiritual and ethical resources. A constant attrition is caused by our contacts with much that is bitter, cruel, cynical, and superficial. Our efforts to comfort and cheer others may subtract from our own store of inner vitality.

In the Twenty-third Psalm, David says of the Lord, "He restores my soul." Isaiah 40:31 says, "Those who hope in the Lord will renew their strength." Paul writes in Philippians 4:13, "I can do everything through him who gives me strength." Psalm 138:3 gives beautiful testimony to the resources we have in our heavenly Father: "When I called, you answered me; you made me bold and stouthearted."

Verse 4 of our text urges us, "Look to the LORD and his strength." He is indeed the Sun of our soul who gives us warmth, light, energy, and all we need for guidance, growth, goodness, and, finally, glory. Let us "seek his face always"!

—J. G. V. B.

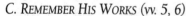

Visual 7

C. REMEMBER HIS WORKS (vv. 5, 6)

5, 6. Remember the wonders he has done, his miracles, and the judgments he pronounced, O descendants of Abraham his servant, O sons of Jacob, his chosen ones.

We are prone to forget the good things God has done for us and remember only the times he didn't give us exactly what we wanted. We need to have our memories jogged so that we won't forget, but also so that we may pass these memories on to our children and our grandchildren.

His *wonders* means the miracles *he has done*. The miraculous delivery from Egypt loomed large in Hebrew history. *The judgments* were punishments inflicted on Israel or others. God's people were to remember the happy occasions when God rescued them or blessed them, but they were also to remember the times his holy wrath had fallen on them.

The Israelites were reminded that they were children of *Abraham*, inheritors of the promise made to him. They would remember that in his life Abraham saw both God's wonders and his judgment. The most amazing of God's wonders in Abraham's life must surely have been the birth of his son Isaac. And as he watched the smoke arise from Sodom and Gomorrah, he knew this was God's judgment upon them for their wickedness (Genesis 19:27, 28).

II. GROUNDS FOR PRAISE (PSALM 105:7-11)

A. THE LORD IS GOD (v. 7)

7. He is the LORD our God; his judgments are in all the earth.

The writer hails the Lord, that is, Yahweh, as the God of the Israelites. He called them out, entered into a covenant with them, and richly blessed them. But Yahweh was not the God of the Israelites only. *His judgments are in all the earth*. The tribal gods of the pagan peoples around the Israelites were not real gods. Yahweh is real.

WHAT DO YOU THINK?

Often the focus of our worship is on the mighty deeds of God recorded in the Bible. God continues to answer prayers and to reclaim lives given to him, and he should receive glory and thanksgiving for those works as well as his mighty works in history.

In some worship meetings, Christians "testify," recounting how God has intervened to work a great blessing in their own lives. Does your church ever do this? If so, what benefit do you receive from it? Have you ever been embarrassed by a testimony? Why or why not? Why do you think some churches do not do this?

If your church does not, why not? What would you think if someone stood up in your service and gave a testimony?

How to Say It
Gomorrah. Guh-MOR-uh.
Sodom. SOD-um.

Option

Your students who enjoy cross-word puzzles will like the reproducible page 400. Answers to the puzzle follow:

Across	Down
4. window	1. Jonah
5. Joseph	2. words
8. flood	3. furnace
9. Joshua	6. Paul
10. Elijah	7. body
13. Peter	8. family
14. Jerusalem	11. Esther
17. pray	12. ten
18. snake	15. staff
21. Isaac	16. manna
23. water	19. Gabriel
24. Judas	20. Sinai
25. apostles	22. Abraham
26. love	24. Jacob
27. David	

What Do You Think?

God made a promise to Abraham because of Abraham's faith. The promise was that Abraham's descendants would be blessed as the people of God and live in the land of Canaan. Paul says we can be included in that promise through faith (Romans 4:16, 17). The most significant aspect of the covenant with Israel seems to have been the land. What is most significant to you about the covenant of faith? Why? What is different about your behavior because of this promise?

In his covenant with Abraham he promised to bless Abraham, but he also promised to bless "all peoples on earth" through him (Genesis 12:3). That blessing came down through Abraham's son Isaac, through Jacob and the nation of Israel, and ultimately through God's own Son, Jesus Christ. But as God's blessings extend to the whole earth, so also do his judgments.

B. God Remembers His Covenant (v. 8)

8. He remembers his covenant forever, the word he commanded, for a thousand generations.

God had kept his part of the covenant. That was the reason for the strong exhortation in verse 5, urging the people to remember their part. *For a thousand generations.* Century after century God kept his end of the bargain, but again and again the people failed to live up to their commitment. As a result, God promised to establish a new covenant with his people: "'The time is coming,' declares the Lord, 'when I will make a new covenant with the house of Israel and with the house of Judah'" (Jeremiah 31:31). This new covenant or new testament was established by Christ (Matthew 26:28).

C. A Covenant With All Israel (vv. 9, 10)

9, 10. The covenant he made with Abraham, the oath he swore to Isaac. He confirmed it to Jacob as a decree, to Israel as an everlasting covenant.

God's covenant with Abraham is first recorded in Genesis 12:1-3. God repeated the promise, along with a dramatic display of his presence, in Genesis 15:5-21. In Genesis 17:1-22 it is repeated yet again. The promise was later affirmed to Isaac (Genesis 26:2-5) and then Jacob (Genesis 28:10-15). After Jacob wrestled with an angel, he was given the new name of Israel (Genesis 32:24-28). Later this name was applied to the whole nation of his descendants. That seems to be the meaning of *Israel* in this verse.

One God, Different Men

In verses 9 and 10 we read of God's covenant made with Abraham, then with Isaac, and later with Jacob and Israel as a nation. It was a promise to give them the land of Canaan, a promise conditioned on their obedience to the Lord. There was and is but one God, but he deals in promises and pledges with generations of men as they come, live their lives, and go into eternity.

There is a beautiful chapter in the apocryphal book of *Ecclesiasticus* that begins,

> Let us now praise famous men,
> And our fathers in their generations.

The chapter is a recital of the dedication and deeds of many of the outstanding people of Israel's history, beginning with Enoch.

Now we have accepted God's new covenant sealed by the blood of Jesus. Our responsibility is to be faithful in our generation.

—J. G. V. B.

D. The Covenant Fulfilled (v. 11)

11. "To you I will give the land of Canaan as the portion you will inherit."

Centuries earlier the land had been promised to Abraham (Genesis 17:8). He had lived there as a wandering shepherd. After centuries in Egypt, God led Abraham's people back to that land. *The portion you will inherit* is literally "the cord of your inheritance," suggesting that Canaan had been measured out with a cord. A brief description of how the land was portioned out among the tribes of Israel is recorded in Numbers 34.

III. A CLOSING EXHORTATION (PSALM 105:43-45)

A. BASIS FOR THE EXHORTATION (vv. 43, 44)

43. He brought out his people with rejoicing, his chosen ones with shouts of joy.

God brought the Israelites out of Egypt with a tremendous display of his power. The ten plagues, along with the miraculous crossing of the Red Sea, convinced even the most skeptical that God was leading the people (Exodus 14:31). Once the people were safely out of the reach of Pharaoh, Moses led them in a great song of *rejoicing*. We are told that Miriam, Moses' sister, led the women with music, singing, and dancing (Exodus 15). Praising God with songs was certainly a normal response after such a great deliverance.

44. He gave them the lands of the nations, and they fell heir to what others had toiled for.

After reminding the people how the Israelites praised God following their escape from the Egyptians, the psalmist reminds them that they have much more for which to be thankful. The land that God led them into was already a developed land. The Canaanites, whom the Israelites replaced, had spent centuries building houses, walling cities, digging wells, clearing fields, and planting vineyards. The hard work had been done; all the Israelites had to do was to move in.

In some respects we are like these ancient Israelites. Our generation has inherited a land that has been richly developed by the hard work of those who have gone before us. We are the heirs of a government that grants us religious freedom, a blessing still denied in many places around the world. We live in an age of technological conveniences hardly dreamed of in earlier days. In spite of our blessings we never seem satisfied, always wanting more. It is perhaps not entirely coincidental that "Count Your Blessings," which we used to sing regularly, is now missing from many of our song books!

B. ISRAEL'S RESPONSIBILITY (v. 45)

45. ... that they might keep his precepts and observe his laws. Praise the LORD.

God fulfilled every promise he made to his people. With these blessings, however, came responsibilities. The tragedy of the Israelites was their short memory. When they accepted God's covenant, they undoubtedly intended to keep their end of the bargain. After a time, however, they became involved in enjoying their blessings and they forgot to observe God's statutes. They failed to pass along to all their children the faith that had brought them to the promised land. They turned to the idols of Canaan and brought disgrace upon themselves.

This script sounds all too familiar, and certainly it should, for we are seeing the same process unfold in our own land. We have forgotten the blessings we have received and have turned to the idols of possessions and pleasures.

CONCLUSION

A. WHEN THE SINGING STOPS

Worship in the early church was simple and probably rather spontaneous. Only after the passage of considerable time did more rigid patterns develop. As people settled into these rituals, worship lost some of its spontaneity. The people felt comfortable in these patterns and became uneasy when anyone tried to change them. If a person tried to institute much change, he might be accused of being a heretic.

Our culture has a frightening way of intruding into our Christian faith and bringing changes. Some of them are good, but some of them are bad. Those who oppose innovations are right in keeping out worldly elements that may

---

WHAT DO YOU THINK?

The lesson writer says "praising God with songs was certainly a normal response after such a great deliverance." Have you ever responded to God's blessing with spontaneous song? If so, to what were you responding? How important do you think singing is to most Christians? Why?

WHAT DO YOU THINK?

The lesson writer says, "We are seeing the same process [as in Israel] unfold in our own land. We have forgotten the blessings we have received and have turned to the idols of possessions and pleasures." What "idols" do you see people turning to today? What blessings are especially being ignored? How can people be challenged to give up their "idols" and turn to the Lord?

WHAT DO YOU THINK?

What kind of changes have taken place in your church's worship services over the past five years? If no major changes have occurred, do you think some should? Why or why not?

If there have been changes, how would you evaluate them? Are they helpful in promoting true worship, or do you think they are worldly in nature? What makes you think so?

PRAYER

Dear Father, let our hearts sing our praises to you. Let our voices exalt you. Kindle in our hearts the memories of all that you have done for us. Help us to understand your statutes. Give us the strength to keep your laws. Above all, teach us to trust in you as the hope of our salvation. In Jesus' name we pray. Amen.

THOUGHT TO REMEMBER

"It is only as men begin to worship that they begin to grow."
—Calvin Coolidge

DAILY BIBLE READINGS

Monday, July 8—Covenant Initiated by God (Genesis 17:1-8)

Tuesday, July 9—A Helper Provided (Exodus 4:10-17)

Wednesday, July 10— Dependent on God's Mercies (Deuteronomy 8:1-10)

Thursday, July 11—Praise, Prayer, and Confession (Psalm 106:1-12)

Friday, July 12—Confident of God's Help (Isaiah 26:7-15)

Saturday, July 13—God's Discipline (Jeremiah 32:17-25)

Sunday, July 14—God's Provisions for Humankind (Luke 1:67-79)

erode the faith, but in defending present patterns they may reject elements that are good.

The New Testament gives us very little specific information about how Christians worshiped in the first century. Early Christians put more emphasis on people's attitudes when they worshiped and on how they lived after the worship service ended.

Many Christians are disturbed by changes they see being instituted in worship. They don't know the newer songs and are uncomfortable with some of the more relaxed and spontaneous behavior. It is right to be concerned, for every generation must evaluate changes in worship patterns lest we become enthralled with practices and values that reflect the world rather than the Scriptures. However, change in Christian worship has been a continuing process over the past two thousand years, and change will continue for another two thousand years, if the Lord delays his coming. Change is not necessarily bad. We need to examine each change to see what it is and what it does.

More important than worship styles is what happens when the singing ends. God accepts any worship that is in keeping with his laws and that comes from grateful, joyous hearts. If a worship service is followed by changes in people's lives, making them more loving, more generous, more responsible, and more faithful in their commitment to the Lord, then we ought to rejoice. If our worship fails to remind us of God's nature and his will, then we, like the ancient Israelites, are worshiping in vain. What happens in your church after the singing stops?

B. WHERE HAVE YOU BEEN?

Most of us have had the experience of traveling down an interstate highway and not paying much attention to where we were. By remembering the exits that we had passed, however, we could orient ourselves on the map and determine where we were. In other words, we knew where we were by remembering where we had been.

That is what Psalm 105 is all about. The Israelites throughout their history were surrounded by enemies who wished nothing more than to do them in. This psalm recounts their history as a means of giving them assurance. It tells how God called Abraham and made a covenant with him. That covenant was renewed with the descendants of Abraham. God watched over and protected his people. An outstanding example of that protection was their deliverance from Egypt.

As the Israelites sang this psalm or listened to it, they knew where they were in history. Even more important, they knew Whose they were. In the trying times they faced, that knowledge gave them great assurance.

We share many things with the ancient Israelites. We worship the same God—Jehovah. The Israelites were his chosen people under the Old Covenant. Christians are his chosen people under the New Covenant. The Israelites were often led to pursue false gods, and in the process they lost their way. They needed to be reminded of where they had been in order to know where they were. We too have often been led astray, enticed by the world. We have lost our way; and to find our way back, we need to know where we have been. For that reason we need to study the Old Testament to learn what God has done for his people under the Old Covenant, and we need to study the New Testament to understand where he wants us to go today. We also need to study the history of the church in order to see some of the mistakes others have made and the results of those mistakes. We need to learn of the faith and courage of some of the saints who worked and suffered so that we may enjoy the blessings God has in store for his own. Let the Bible be our road map to let us see where the church has been, where we are now, and where we ought to be headed.

Discovery Learning

This page contains an alternate lesson plan emphasizing learning activities. Classes desiring such student involvement will find these suggestions helpful. The next page is a reproducible activity page to further enhance discovery learning.

LEARNING GOALS

As a result of participating in this class session, a learner should:

1. List some of the marvelous works of God's providence.

2. Explain how recalling God's past provision builds faith in his continued providence.

3. Express thanksgiving and praise for God's provision.

INTO THE LESSON

Before class draw two columns on the chalkboard or on a poster. Write the following headings above your columns: *Joyful Times* and *Difficult Times*.

Begin the lesson by pointing out that life is not all joyful nor all difficult, but rather a combination of the two. We all desire more joyful times, but both have their places in our family life. Ask each learner to take a few moments to think back over his or her family's history and write down a brief description of joyful and difficult times that come to mind. Encourage all to emphasize the joyful times, but not to ignore the difficult times. Each should prepare a sheet of paper that is divided as the board is. People will need time to think, so allow several minutes for this writing.

Ask for volunteers who are willing to tell about some of the joyful times from their family's past. Repeat the same type of reporting for difficult times. If your learners like to share in this way, you may have to limit each to one response from each category. Be ready to tell something from your family history as well.

OPTION

Distribute copies of the crossword puzzle on page 400. Give the students five minutes to complete the puzzle. Observe that just as it required them to recall some of God's mighty acts to complete the puzzle, today's lesson reminds us we need to recall his mighty acts to remain faithful to him in the present. (See page 396 for answers to the puzzle.)

INTO THE WORD

Divide your class into three study groups. Each group will need a reader, a recorder, and a reporter. One of the assignments below should be given to each study group to get the thinking started. To save time you can write out the Scripture reference and assignment for each group on a separate index card before class. Then distribute the cards to your groups when you divide the class.

Assignments

1. Psalm 105:1-6   List the ten imperatives
2. Psalm 105:7-11, 42-45   Describe the covenant
3. Psalm 105:12-41   Summarize God's helpful acts

Write the following phrase on the board before the groups start: "How God's intervention influences our future." Ask the groups to keep this thought uppermost in mind as they complete their assignments. Use the following information to clarify the assignments.

Group 1: As you list the ten imperatives, consider how these would be influenced by a past relationship between God and his people.

Group 2: While describing the covenant between God and the Israelites, consider how a past promise influenced the future relationship.

Group 3: In summarizing God's helpful acts, be thinking about how these past actions influenced God's people in the future.

To ensure that every group gets a chance to report, set a time limit of four minutes for each group to summarize its study. Suggest that a member of the reporting group watch the clock and say "time" when four minutes are up. Use the lesson material in sections I, II, and III to prepare you for any questions the class may ask concerning what they read in Psalm 105.

INTO LIFE

Have the learners look over the sheets where they listed joyous and difficult times in the history of their families. Ask them to consider how God may have intervened in these circumstances. Ask several class members to describe how they see God's hand in the events they have listed. How have they grown from these experiences? In what ways do they find themselves better able to minister to others because of them? From which did they learn more, the "good" times or the "bad"? Why?

After a brief discussion, close the class session with sentence prayers thanking God for his presence in our past, present, and future.

Remembering His Mighty Acts

Psalm 105 encourages us to remember God's marvelous works in history. Recalling God's past provisions builds faith in his continued providence. To complete the crossword puzzle successfully (and to build your faith), you will need to remember some of God's mighty acts.

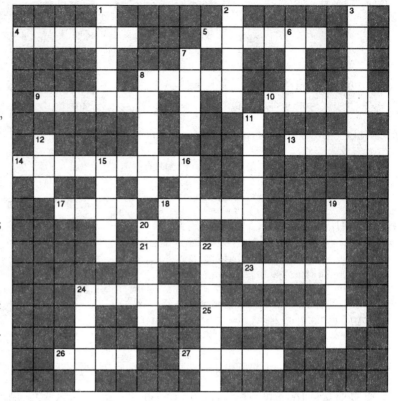

OLD TESTAMENT ACTS OF GOD

DOWN

1. He lived in cramped quarters for 3 days and 3 nights
2. God formed his creation with these
3. Three brave Israelites refused to worship the golden statue and were thrown in
11. She risked her life to save her people and God saved her
15. Moses carried it and God used it
16. Food God provided to those wandering in the wilderness
20. Mountain where God gave rules to his people
22. He lived in the city of Haran, but God had other plans for him
24. He became wealthy in spite of his uncle's deception

ACROSS

5. One day he was in a prison and the next he was ruler over Egypt
8. Noah built an ark to escape this
9. God listened to this man and made the sun stand still
10. This prophet stopped the rain
14. God used Nehemiah to rebuild the walls of this important city
21. A son born to aged parents according to God's promise
27. He knew a slingshot would suffice if God is on your side

NEW TESTAMENT ACTS OF GOD

DOWN

6. A man with a mission that was changed
7. A common metaphor for the church
8. Paul gave guidelines for this in Ephesians 5 and Colossians 3
12. One came back, but Jesus healed how many?
19. He announced the birth of Jesus

ACROSS

4. During a sermon Eutychus dozed off and then fell from here
13. Even when in prison he slept like a baby
17. What Jesus did regularly
18. One of these bit Paul when he was on the island of Malta
23. Jesus was the first to walk on this
24. A man with an evil plan
25. Jesus chose 12 of these

PRAISING GOD
FOR DELIVERANCE

LESSON 8

WHY TEACH THIS LESSON?

It used to be that discussions of "deliverance" in Sunday school classes were confined to spiritual issues like deliverance from sin or from the power of Satan. Examples of biblical characters like David, who were also delivered from very physical dangers, were relevant as illustrations of God's power to deliver.

More and more, however, the message of physical deliverance is becoming very relevant. David's case becomes an example, a model, not just an illustration. Because they take a stand for biblical standards of morality and decency, Christians are being attacked with slander and sometimes even physical violence today. More and more the promise of deliverance will be what brings comfort and peace of mind to these embattled saints.

Perhaps your students have been feeling the pressure of standing for the truth. If so, this lesson can help ease their fears and encourage them to continue the fight.

INTRODUCTION

A. IN PROTECTING HANDS

In the early months of the Protestant Reformation, the pope sent a representative to try to persuade Martin Luther to abandon his activities. The representative, a skilled theologian, did his best to show Luther the error of his ways; but Luther was also a theologian and a student of the Bible. He was able to answer every challenge thrust at him.

Finally the papal envoy realized that Luther would not be changed by argument, and so he turned to threats. "Dr. Luther," he said, "the pope has more power in his little finger than all these German princes put together. If he unleashes that power, where will you be then?"

Unmoved by the threats, Luther calmly replied, "I'll be right where I am now—in the protecting hands of the Almighty." In his faith Luther was reflecting the faith shown by the writer of the thirty-fourth Psalm: "The angel of the Lord encamps around those who fear him" (Psalm 34:7).

B. LESSON BACKGROUND

The structure of this psalm is unusual. Each verse starts with a different letter in the Hebrew alphabet. Verse 1 begins with the first letter, *aleph.* Verse 2 begins with the second letter, *beth,* and so on through the alphabet. (There are twenty-two letters in the Hebrew alphabet.) We don't know why the author used this acrostic literary form. Perhaps it was to make the psalm easier for singers to memorize. Perhaps it was a popular form at that particular period in history. Several other psalms are similar in style. For whatever reason, the writer used this form as a framework upon which to build his poem, much as English

DEVOTIONAL READING
PSALM 121:1-8

LESSON SCRIPTURE
PSALM 34

PRINTED TEXT
PSALM 34:2-10, 18-22

Jul
21

LESSON AIMS

As a result of studying this lesson, each student should:

1. Describe the Lord as a God of deliverance.

2. Cite examples of God's deliverance or rescue of the faithful.

3. Express appreciation for the deliverance God provides.

KEY VERSE

The LORD is close to the brokenhearted and saves those who are crushed in spirit.
—Psalm 34:18

LESSON 8 NOTES

WHAT DO YOU THINK?

Like the psalmist, we may "boast in the Lord," or "glorify the Lord" in our times of worship. What are some other ways we can do this? What purpose do you think it serves to "boast in the Lord" and "exalt his name"?

(See Matthew 5:16; Psalm 44:8; 1 Corinthians 1:29-31.)

WHAT DO YOU THINK?

David said the Lord "delivered me from all my fears." Yet Saul was still pursuing him, trying to kill David. God is able to relieve our fears even before circumstances change. Fear is an internal reaction, an attitude, based upon perceptions of what may (or may not) occur.

What, then, do you think should be one's reaction today to dangerous or hostile situations? How can a Christian find the same deliverance from fear even when the threatening situation may not be removed?

OPTION

Use the reproducible activity "Hymn Study" on page 408 to explore the concept of God's deliverance and to praise him for deliverance. This can be done individually or in small groups.

writers for many years have used limericks or various sonnet forms for their work.

The title of Psalm 34 ascribes it to David during the time when he was fleeing from King Saul. David found refuge in Gath, a Philistine city (1 Samuel 21:10-15). There he met Abimelech, the king (also known as Achish). When Achish was told that this was the general who had defeated the Philistines in battle, David became fearful for his life. To escape he pretended to be insane. Displeased with such a demented person, the king sent him away. David then took refuge in the cave of Adullam, located southwest of Jerusalem. There he was surrounded by friends, and for a while was relatively safe from Saul.

I. A SONG OF PRAISE (PSALM 34:2-7)
A. FREELY GIVEN (vv. 2, 3)
2, 3. My soul will boast in the LORD; let the afflicted hear and rejoice. Glorify the LORD with me; let us exalt his name together.

In verse 1 the psalmist affirmed that he would bless the Lord at all times. Certainly this included the good times, but it also included the bad times. David was in a life-and-death struggle. His effort to find a safe refuge with Abimelech had failed, and now he had to endure the life of a fugitive. His safety was uncertain even when he was hiding in a remote cave among friends. Still he declared he would praise the Lord.

This vow to praise the Lord regardless of circumstances finds fulfillment in verses 2 and 3. We read in 1 Samuel 22:2 that when David was at Adullam, "all those who were in distress or in debt or discontented gathered around him, and he became their leader. About four hundred men were with him." Such a sizable group of followers, a motley crew of down-and-outers, placed a heavy responsibility on David; and this psalm may have been written in part to reassure them and direct them to God as the source of power.

Boasting is not ordinarily considered a virtue, but David had no intention of boasting in his own strength. Rather, his boasting would be *in the Lord*. The *afflicted* (the *King James Version* has "humble") would respond gladly to the Lord when they understood that he was the source of their power. Certainly the group that was attracted to David would be considered humble and afflicted. In verse 3 David encourages them to join with him in glorifying the Lord. There are times when it is most appropriate for an individual to pour out his heart in praise to God. There are other occasions when corporate praise is proper, and this was one of those times. This group of outcasts lifting their voices would praise God, but their song would also lift their spirits and bring encouragement.

B. A CRY FOR HELP (vv. 4, 5)
4, 5. I sought the LORD, and he answered me; he delivered me from all my fears. Those who look to him are radiant; their faces are never covered with shame.

David's flight to the Philistines had proved to be unwise. He had looked for safety with them instead of trusting wholly in the Lord. He had come to recognize his folly and had come to God. When he humbly *sought the Lord*, the Lord *answered* his prayer for protection. God not only delivered him from physical danger, but also delivered him from fear. In many situations fear is a more dangerous enemy than physical danger. Physical danger often arises suddenly and just as suddenly passes, but fear can linger to gnaw at our insides. Medical science now recognizes that anxiety can cause heart and circulatory problems and lead to ulcers and many other ills. Fear weakens us physically and erodes our resolve. Freed of this fear, David had every reason to praise God.

Jesus on occasion also spoke to this problem. "Do not let your hearts be troubled," he said, and lifted the eyes of his disciples to the hope of Heaven for reassurance (John 14:1-3). John dealt with the same subject: "There is no fear in love. But perfect love drives out fear, because fear has to do with punishment. The one who fears is not made perfect in love" (1 John 4:18).

All who trust in God will have their fears lifted from their hearts. They will be *radiant*. Trusting in the Lord puts a glow in their countenances and joy in their lives.

THE GLOW OF GLORY

Our faces have a way of revealing the emotional state we are experiencing. We often see a friend with a gloomy or downcast look, so much so that we ask, "What's wrong?" Sometimes there is a happy aura about one's expression, and we say, "What are you so happy about?"

In verse 5 of today's text we are told that those trusting in God and looking to him are "radiant." The blessing of trusting in God shows in their faces.

When Moses came down from Mount Sinai after receiving the Ten Commandments, he "was not aware that his face was radiant" (Exodus 34:29). That radiance passed away, but as Christians we are changed "with ever-increasing glory" as we look to God in Christ (2 Corinthians 3:7-18). What a great promise and reassurance this is! As we look to the Lord Jesus our faces express the glow with which our trust in him fills our lives.

—J. G. V. B.

C. THE CRY ANSWERED (vv. 6, 7)

6, 7. This poor man called, and the LORD heard him; he saved him out of all his troubles. The angel of the LORD encamps around those who fear him, and he delivers them.

This repeats the sentiments found in verse 4. Now David writes in the third person, but he is still speaking about himself. *This poor man* is David. He was poor indeed. His life was in jeopardy, and he had no powerful friends to whom he could turn. In his extremity he turned to God, who *heard* his prayer. The eternal King does not play favorites. High or low, rich or poor, every person has access to the heavenly throne. David was still pursued by the troops of Saul, but his fear was swept away when the Lord heard his prayer.

The *angel of the Lord* appears in Scripture as God's special agent in dealing with man. Sometimes he is the agent of judgment and destruction (2 Samuel 24:16; 2 Kings 19:35). In other situations he protects and delivers (Exodus 14:19, 20). That is obviously his role in the passage we are studying. Like a mighty army, the angel of the Lord surrounds *those who fear him,* giving them protection and deliverance.

II. KNOWING GOD (PSALM 34:8-10)

A. THROUGH EXPERIENCE (v. 8)

8. Taste and see that the LORD is good; blessed is the man who takes refuge in him.

Persons who have walked with God most of their lives know from experience that he has protected them and delivered them. They have "tasted" his blessings. There are others whose faith may be completely intellectual. In their own lives they have never felt God's strong presence. David invites such people to open their hearts so they can experience him. Intellectual faith is important, of course, but it is never complete in itself. It needs the support of knowing firsthand God's blessings. Since David had just gone through a harrowing experience, he was in an excellent position to invite others to share in the same joy.

WHAT DO YOU THINK?

Have you ever known a Christian whose face seemed "radiant" with the joy of the Lord? If so, what kept that person so joyful? David seems to suggest that kind of radiance is normal. Why do you think it seems so rare today—or do you? Explain.

WHAT DO YOU THINK?

What do you know about the ministry of angels? Do you often think about their presence or count on their protection? Why or why not?

(See Genesis 16:7-11; Psalm 91:11; Luke 16:22; Hebrews 1:13, 14.)

WHAT DO YOU THINK?

Most believers have a personal story of how they came to love God. It is good for us to share those stories and be encouraged by God's blessing in different lives. What was your first "taste" that convinced you God is good? What has added to your confidence since then? What would you recommend for those who are not sure?

The Lord is close to the brokenhearted and saves those who are crushed in spirit.

Use visual 8 of the visuals packet to illustrate verse 18.

B. THROUGH HIS CARE (vv. 9, 10)

9. Fear the LORD, you his saints, for those who fear him lack nothing.

To *fear* God is to give him humble reverence that leads to a faithful observance of his laws. Anyone who claims to be a follower of God must demonstrate that fact by leading a life of obedience. The *saints* in the Old Testament period were people devoted to God. In the New Testament all Christians are called saints. This does not so much describe the level of their moral attainment as it describes their status before God. Every saint is one who has been "set apart" (the literal meaning of the word) or dedicated to God.

The saints enjoy the knowledge that they will *lack nothing*. They learn to distinguish their desires from their needs. Most of us are still trying to do this. Only a few have been in situations where we had nothing but the bare essentials needed to sustain life. Those who have had that experience have come to realize how little it takes to survive. Further, we should understand God's promise in an eternal sense. In the past, many saints have refused to give up their faith and have perished because they lacked food, shelter, and clothing. To them the Lord says, "Great is your reward in heaven" (Matthew 5:11, 12).

10. The lions may grow weak and hungry, but those who seek the LORD lack no good thing.

The lion, frequently referred to as king of the beasts, is feared by other animals. But at times even powerful *lions* do not find prey, and as a result go *hungry*. The point the psalmist is making is that strength and cunning are not always enough to keep one from experiencing want. By contrast, *those who seek the Lord* will find that their needs are met. The world does not readily comprehend this paradox. Jesus expressed a similar idea when he affirmed that the meek "will inherit the earth" (Matthew 5:5).

III. GOD AND HIS PEOPLE (PSALM 34:18-22)

A. GOD IS NEAR (v. 18)

18. The LORD is close to the brokenhearted and saves those who are crushed in spirit.

The Lord is everywhere, and so he is near everyone. And yet in a sense he is especially close to those who are *brokenhearted*. The brokenhearted here are not those so crushed that they give up their faith, neither are they those who meet trouble with stubborn rebellion. They are the humble and contrite, those who yield themselves to God's will. They are the ones who will be blessed. The world often honors those who are bold and aggressive, even arrogant. But in both the Old and New Testaments we find God honoring those who are humble and submissive before him. For example, in Micah 6:8 we read, "He has showed you, O man, what is good. And what does the Lord require of you? To act justly and to love mercy and to walk humbly with your God." In the Sermon on the Mount Jesus expressed the same idea in these words: "Blessed are the poor in spirit, for theirs is the kingdom of heaven" (Matthew 5:3).

God offers salvation to those of a contrite spirit. This is not to say they will escape all danger and all suffering. God does not assure us that life will be a bed of roses if we submit to him. But we do have the assurance that when suffering and sorrows come, he will provide the strength to triumph over them.

WHAT DO YOU THINK?

When the psalmist speaks of the "brokenhearted" and those "crushed in spirit," he seems to be referring not merely to those who are humble, but to those who have been through some kind of humbling or crushing experience. Have you or someone close to you ever been in that kind of situation and experienced the truth of this verse (18)? If so, how did you find the Lord close, and what did his presence do for you?

THE TOUCH OF TENDERNESS

Many of us know what it is to be "brokenhearted." Some have trusted in another's faithfulness and have been betrayed. Some have lost loving life partners through death. Some have met failure in some great endeavor. The psalmist is not singing of such tragedies so much as of the condition of the heart—a heart neither rebelling nor giving up hope, but humbly submitting to God.

What an assurance we have in the statement that our heavenly Father is near us! Jesus reminds us in Luke 12:6, "Are not five sparrows sold for two pennies? Yet not one of them is forgotten by God." As a stanza from Civilla D. Martin's hymn says so vividly:

"Let not your heart be troubled,"
   His tender word I hear,
And resting on his goodness,
   I lose my doubts and fears;
Tho' by the path he leadeth
   But one step I may see:
His eye is on the sparrow,
   And I know he watches me.

—J. G. V. B.

B. GOD DELIVERS HIS OWN (vv. 19, 20)

19, 20. A righteous man may have many troubles, but the LORD delivers him from them all; he protects all his bones, not one of them will be broken.

A righteous man may have many troubles. The saints have ample evidence of the truth of this statement. Some suffer because they are righteous. The pages of the history of the church are stained with the blood of martyrs who suffered because they refused to compromise their faith. Sometimes, however, the righteous suffer because they have sinned. The righteous, like everyone else, may succumb to temptation; and when this happens, they suffer the consequences just as any other sinner. In some situations people suffer, not because they are sinners, but because they are foolish or ignorant. A child who plays with matches and as a result is burned is not a sinner. He or she is simply ignorant.

From recent events in his own life, David recognized that the life of the faithful is not always healthy and wealthy. When a righteous man falls into sin and suffers as a result, God uses chastening to cleanse and purge him from that sin. This idea is expressed in Hebrews 12:6: "The Lord disciplines those he loves, and he punishes every one he accepts as a son."

All his bones is to be understood as the whole body. While this refers to protection from physical harm, its meaning can be extended to the spiritual realm, where God has promised protection for his own.

C. THE WICKED SHALL PERISH (v. 21)

21. Evil will slay the wicked; the foes of the righteous will be condemned.

Justice is not perfect in this life; the righteous often suffer and the wicked seem to prosper. And yet justice is often meted out. One who sets out upon a life of violence comes to a violent end: a person who is motivated by hatred becomes the object of hatred.

The psalmist may have had more in mind than justice in this life. He may have been looking to the ultimate judgment with God as the supreme judge. In that day all of us will stand guilty before him. Our only hope is that we have "one who speaks to the Father in our defense—Jesus Christ, the Righteous One" (1 John 2:1). We escape the penalty we deserve because Jesus bore it for us.

D. THE LORD REDEEMS (v. 22)

22. The LORD redeems his servants; no one will be condemned who takes refuge in him.

HOW TO SAY IT

Abimelech. Uh-BIM-eh-lek.
Achish. AY-kish.
Adullam. a-DULL-lum.
aleph (Hebrew). AH-lef.
beth (Hebrew). bayth or bait.
Philistine. Fih-LISS-teen
   or FIL-iss-teen.

WHAT DO YOU THINK?

Sometimes the righteous suffer because they are righteous, sometimes because they sin, and sometimes because they are ignorant or foolish. What other reasons may cause the righteous to suffer? How does one know which of these has brought suffering—and thus how to respond? If I suffer because of sin or foolishness, I need to change. But if I suffer for righteousness, I dare not change! How do I know which is which?

OPTION

Use the reproducible activity "Tracking God's Deliverance" on page 408 to help the students be more aware of God's deliverance in their own lives.

PRAYER

Dear Father, we realize that we are often burdened by problems because we don't call upon you. Teach us to "approach the throne of grace with confidence, so that we may receive mercy, and find grace to help us in our time of need." In Jesus' name we pray. Amen.

THOUGHT TO REMEMBER

Prayer is the golden key that opens Heaven.

DAILY BIBLE READINGS

Monday, July 15—Victory in Battle (Psalm 18:6-19)

Tuesday, July 16—Delivered From Enemies (2 Samuel 22:1-7)

Wednesday, July 17—Delivered From Burning (Daniel 3:24-30)

Thursday, July 18—Delivered From Prison (Acts 12:6-11)

Friday, July 19—Delivered From Shipwreck (Acts 27:39-44)

Saturday, July 20—Delivered From Temptation (1 Corinthians 10:6-13)

Sunday, July 21—Delivered to Heavenly Kingdom (2 Timothy 4:9-18)

God takes care of his own. No Bible truth is more certain than this. We doubt that David had more than a faint glimpse of the salvation God has in store for the faithful. Yet in this verse David seems to envision more than just physical redemption. We have a much fuller understanding of God's plans for the righteous because he sent his Son to reveal those plans to us. Should we not then lift our hearts in more joyous song because we have so much more for which to be thankful?

CONCLUSION

A. THE ONLY WAY YOU CAN LOOK IS UP

"When you're at the bottom of a well, the only way you can look is up," my grandmother used to say. This statement summarized her outlook on life. And it was a most appropriate philosophy, for she knew little but hard times and sickness. Yet in spite of all of this, she was a happy person, always singing or humming a hymn as she went about her daily work. As a young girl she had committed her life to the Lord, and through the years that commitment grew and deepened. She knew that no matter what blows life dealt her, no matter how bad things might seem, she could always look up to the Lord and pray. And she never doubted for a moment that God would answer her prayer, not always in the way she had asked, but always in his way and in his time.

My grandmother lived and died in obscurity. Few people remember her, even in the little town where she spent all her life. No monuments have been erected to her honor, and they haven't named any streets or buildings after her. And yet she left behind a more important memorial than these, a living memorial. More than a half dozen of her grandchildren and great-grandchildren are today ministers, ministers' wives, or missionaries, and most of the others are active in the Lord's work.

In her own quiet way Grandmother was able to pass along to her descendants that serene faith that sustained her through all kinds of difficulties. But she had no exclusive claim on that faith. Any one of us can lay hold of it. It was the kind of faith that sustained David during his many trials. We are not told how he acquired his faith, but we can be sure he learned it from his parents and his friends and from God's Word. Just as important was his growth in that faith. As life battered and bruised him, he did not spend much time feeling sorry for himself or becoming bitter. Instead he looked increasingly to God, not only for help, but to praise him.

B. DIALING THE DIVINE 911

When we moved into our present home, our county was considered a rural area. But the city soon began to encroach upon our rustic environment, bringing with it many of the amenities and the problems of a big city. The fire department was practically nonexistent, and so a volunteer fire department was organized. The sheriff's department was enlarged. Then came water lines with fire hydrants so the fire department could effectively fight fires. Our telephone system was enhanced so that we could dial 911 for help in an emergency.

In spite of all the money and efforts expended to make our county safer, most of the residents here don't feel as safe as we did twenty years ago. Even though we can dial 911 in an emergency and expect to get help much quicker than we used to, yet that doesn't seem enough.

As our concern for our safety grows, we who are Christians need to be reminded that we have a divine 911 that we can call and expect an immediate response. We can call out to God for help at any time. He never leaves his post, never becomes unconcerned, and never sleeps. "Indeed, he who watches over Israel will neither slumber nor sleep" (Psalm 121:4). If our call is to be effectual, however, we must keep the lines open by regular prayer, Bible study, and meditation.

Discovery Learning

This page contains an alternate lesson plan emphasizing learning activities. Classes desiring such student involvement will find these suggestions helpful. The next page is a reproducible activity page to further enhance discovery learning.

LEARNING GOALS

As a result of this lesson the students should be able to:

1. Describe the Lord as a God of deliverance.

2. Cite examples of God's deliverance or rescue of the faithful.

3. Express appreciation for God's deliverance.

INTO THE LESSON

Begin today's lesson by displaying a poster with the following question written in large letters: "When should Christians praise God?" Brainstorm and list situations when people should praise God. Acknowledge all answers listed. Then tell the class, "Today we hear the psalmist call us to praise God with him. It is easy to praise God for his blessings in good times. But the psalmist also models praising God as we ask his help in some of the difficulties of life."

Ask class members to tell of Bible characters who praised God while or after they experienced troubles or difficulties in their lives (for example, Miriam's singing and dancing, Exodus 15:20, 21; Paul and Silas in prison, Acts 16:19-25). Today's lesson is David's praise for God's deliverance from a very difficult situation and a reminder of God's presence when we face life's difficulties.

OPTION

Use the reproducible activity "Hymn Study" on page 408. Students can work individually or in small groups; then discuss their findings together. You may even want to sing one of the hymns.

INTO THE WORD

Early in the week ask a student to prepare a three- to five-minute lecture on the lesson background for Psalm 34, focusing on the story of David in 1 Samuel 21:10-15. Give the student a copy of the second paragraph of the "Lesson Background" section.

Probably you or your church library can lend the student a Bible dictionary in which he or she can find additional material about the Philistines and Achish, their king.

Begin this portion of the study with the student's presentation on the background of Psalm 34. Then display a poster with the heading "Word Pictures of God's Care and Deliverance." Ask students to watch for word pictures in the text that illustrate God's care for us.

Read today's Scripture, Psalm 34:2-10, 18-22, aloud. Allow students to share the word pictures or illustrations they find. These may include "delivered me from all my fears" (v. 4), "the angel of the Lord encamps around those who fear him" (v. 7), "those who seek the Lord lack no good thing" (v. 10), "The Lord is close" (v. 18), "he protects all his bones" (v. 20), and others.

As the students list their findings on the poster, discuss the significance of each, using thoughts from the comments on the text in this book.

INTO LIFE

This psalm is a grand assurance of God's care. Point to the poster on which were listed the assurances David gave. Be sure the following are included: God is near (v. 18); God delivers his servants (vv. 19, 20); the wicked will perish (v. 21); the Lord redeems his servants (v. 22).

Ask, "When God promises such care to his people, why do some Christians have trouble, poverty, sickness, and suffering of other kinds?" The Bible has more than one answer to the question of why good people suffer: suffering is discipline (Proverbs 3:11, 12; Hebrews 12:4-11); suffering is a test (Job 1:8-12; 2:3-10); suffering is a means to maturity (James 1:2-4; Romans 5:3, 4); faithfulness in spite of suffering brings glory to God (1 Peter 4:16); faithful endurance is rewarded in Heaven (Matthew 5:11, 12). God does not promise we will not suffer, but he does assure us of his presence and care.

David's experience of affliction and God's care is a testimony to us. One of the great things Christians learn as we experience suffering or difficulty is that God is near.

Ask class members, "What can we who are Christians do to foster David's attitude of confidence in our daily lives? Is there some special thought or exercise we can foster to help us remember God's presence?" Let the class discuss answers that are given.

Ask class members to think of a Christian who is suffering or brokenhearted. Ask each class member to make a commitment to pray daily for seven days for the person he or she has selected. Close with a prayer that all class members may see God helping them this week.

OPTION

Use the reproducible activity "Tracking God's Deliverance" on page 408 to help the students be more aware of God's deliverance in their own lives. Close with prayer.

Hymn Study

Look up the following hymns in a hymnal: A Mighty Fortress Is Our God; Day by Day (by Carolina Sandel Berg, not the Godspell version); God Will Take Care of You; Great Is Thy Faithfulness; Hiding in Thee; O God, Our Help in Ages Past; Praise to the Lord, the Almighty; We Praise Thee, O God, Our Redeemer. Read the words to each hymn; then write a few phrases or words from each that relate to God's deliverance of his people.

(If time allows, use the index to find additional hymns that describe or praise God for his protection and deliverance.)

Tracking God's Deliverance

In the space below is a time line. It begins with your birth and ends with the present. Put marks on the time line to denote several occasions when you experienced God's deliverance in your life. Below the mark, give the deliverance a title (example: "The Close Call;" of "Money from Nowhere"). Then gather with two or three others, and allow those who want to share an event from their "Deliverance Time line" to do so with the group.

Birth _____ Present

PRAISING GOD WHO KNOWS AND CARES

LESSON 9

WHY TEACH THIS LESSON?

"Honesty," Elton John sang a few years back, "is hardly ever heard." Things have not improved in the years since that song was written. Honesty is still a rare commodity. Ours is an age of deception, wearing a mask, putting on a good front. "Perception is reality." Sometimes we have to strip away the front, remove the mask, and stop the deception. Perception is just that, and it may not be real at all.

This lesson challenges the mask wearer in each of us. First it challenges us to be honest with God. He sees behind our masks anyway. Without our masks we can be honest with each other. Be sensitive as you lead this session. Some people have had their masks on for a long time. It may hurt when the mask starts to come off.

Above all else, be sure to leave your own mask at home when you come to teach this lesson.

INTRODUCTION

A. LOOKING IN ALL DIRECTIONS

A father involved his son in a scheme to steal some apples from a neighbor. As they approached the orchard, the father told the boy to look to the north and east to see if anyone was watching. The father looked to the south and west. "Do you see anyone, Son?" asked the father.

"No, nobody in my direction," he replied.

"I don't see anyone in my direction, so let's sneak in."

"But, Dad, you didn't look in every direction," protested the lad.

"Sure we did," came the father's response. "You looked to the north and east and I looked to the south and west."

"But, Dad, you forgot to look up."

The father stood silent for a moment, and finally replied, "You're right, Son. Let's go home." The son remembered what we all at times may forget. We may be clever enough to hide our deeds from our fellowmen, but we cannot hide from God.

B. LESSON BACKGROUND

The heading of Psalm 139 carries these words: "Of David," but it is generally agreed that this heading is not a part of the original writing. Some scholars think the language of the psalm indicates a later date and another author. But the content of the psalm seems worthy of David, and there is no proof that he is not the author.

I. GOD'S KNOWLEDGE OF US (PSALM 139:1-6)

A. HE OBSERVES ALL OUR WAYS (vv. 1-3)

1-3. O LORD, you have searched me and you know me. You know when I sit and when I rise; you perceive my thoughts from afar. You discern my going out and my lying down; you are familiar with all my ways.

DEVOTIONAL READING
1 PETER 5:6-11
LESSON SCRIPTURE
PSALM 139
PRINTED TEXT
PSALM 139:1-14, 23, 24

LESSON AIMS

As a result of studying this lesson, each student should:

1. Identify instances of God's omniscience and omnipresence.

2. Explain how God's omni-qualities provide comfort and encouragement.

3. Plan ways to share the benefits of God's omni-nature with others.

Jul
28

KEY VERSE

Search me, O God, and know my heart; test me and know my anxious thoughts.
—Psalm 139:23

The writer says his life is an open book before Jehovah; there are no secrets. In recent years we have read about public officials who have recorded their thoughts and deeds in diaries or on tape. When controversy arose and they were questioned about these records, they have often shown great reluctance to make them public. In some cases it has taken subpoenas or other legal action to open up these records. God doesn't need a search warrant or a subpoena. He knows us inside and out.

God knows our activities. He knows when we *sit* down for a meal or a rest, and when we *rise* up to engage in some other activity. He knows our *thoughts* even before we think them. After all, he created our brains and designed the way our minds function.

He watches over us when we travel, and no path is too obscure for him to find. If we follow the path of righteousness, he certainly knows that; but just as certainly he knows when we choose paths of wickedness. The psalmist sums it up by saying, *you are familiar with all my ways.*

B. HE KNOWS OUR WORDS (vv. 4-6)

4. Before a word is on my tongue you know it completely, O LORD.

God's omniscience, his power to know everything, is illustrated in another way. He knows every *word* the psalmist speaks. It is as if God has a vast cosmic recorder. No conversation, no matter how private, escapes his notice. He hears persons plotting crimes or other misdeeds. He hears the offhanded remarks that often more accurately reveal our real character than do our guarded statements. He even hears us when we talk to ourselves.

But there is a positive side to this. God also hears the kind things we say or the words of encouragement we give to others. He hears us when we share the gospel with those who so desperately need it. He knows when we lift our voices in praise to him.

5. You hem me in—behind and before; you have laid your hand upon me.

God is not some far-off king who only occasionally looks in on his subjects. Jehovah is involved in every aspect of human behavior. God does not play favorites: every human being receives his attention regardless of rank. He is actively involved in giving direction to our lives. In times past he has directly revealed himself to men, as when he called Moses to lead the Israelites out of Egypt (Exodus 3), or when he called Isaiah to become a prophet to his people (Isaiah 6). In most situations, however, God leads us providentially. Often we are not even aware of his leading until long after the event. But even a delayed knowledge of his presence is reassuring.

6. Such knowledge is too wonderful for me, too lofty for me to attain.

As the writer contemplates God's knowledge and power, he is brought to his knees in humility. How could it be otherwise? Pity the poor atheist who arrogantly asserts that there is no God. To be able to make such an assertion, he would have to be as omniscient as God. He would have to know everything, for the one thing unknown might be that there is a God.

The psalmist's words remind us of Job's experience. When Job had talked glibly about himself, God asked him a series of questions that exposed his ignorance. Humbled by this, Job cried out, "I know that you can do all things; no plan of yours can be thwarted. You asked, 'Who is this that obscures my counsel without knowledge?' Surely I spoke of things I did not understand, things too wonderful for me to know." Then he concluded, "I despise myself and repent in dust and ashes" (Job 42:2, 3, 6).

The apostle Paul expressed the same idea: "Where is the wise man? Where is the scholar? Where is the philosopher of this age? Has not God made foolish the wisdom of the world? . . . For the foolishness of God is wiser than man's wisdom, and the weakness of God is stronger than man's strength" (1 Corinthians 1:20, 25).

II. GOD'S VAST DOMAIN (PSALM 139:7-14)

A. NO PLACE TOO FAR (vv. 7, 8)

7. Where can I go from your Spirit? Where can I flee from your presence?

Verse 7 poses two rhetorical questions that are expanded in the verses that follow. We see here a transition from God's omniscience to his omnipresence: that is, the fact that God is everywhere. Suppose one sought to escape from God. Where could one flee to avoid him? From the psalmist's answers, it is clear that God is not limited to one spot at any given time. That fact is frightening to those who seek to avoid God, but it is a source of assurance to those who trust in him.

8. If I go up to the heavens, you are there; if I make my bed in the depths, you are there.

Up to the heavens. . . . in the depths. The translation of this verse is something of a problem. In Hebrew, even as in our own language, the word *heaven* can be used of the atmosphere in the physical world or of the eternal home of God. Likewise, sheol, here translated "the depths" has a variety of meanings, including the grave, Hell, or the abode of the dead. The *New International Version* has taken the terms to be the two extremes in the physical universe—up in the heavens (sky) or down in the depths. Earlier versions took them to be the extreme eternal regions—Heaven or Hell. Both views seem to make the point that at either extreme to which a person might go to flee from God, he or she cannot go far enough to escape.

Some would have a problem taking these terms to refer to the eternal dwellings. First, it seems illogical that one would go to Heaven to escape God. Second, the idea of God's presence in Hell is startling. Hell has traditionally been understood as a separation from God. This is all purely hypothetical, however. First, man under his own power could never enter Heaven in the first place. And God's separation from Hell is his own doing. Hell could not shut him out if he chose to go there.

So either view is plausible. The writer searches for every hiding place. From one extreme to the other, there is no place where one could hide from God.

THE INESCAPABLE GOD

In verse 7 of Psalm 139 the questions are asked, "Where can I go from your Spirit? Where can I flee from your presence?"

The British poet, Francis Thompson, dealt at length with this matter in "The Hound of Heaven." Picturing God pursuing one as a criminal is tracked down by authorities using bloodhounds, the poem is quite autobiographical. Thompson had made many mistakes in his life. He had dropped out of medical college and had left his home and gone to London. He became a drug addict, lost touch with all his family, and became destitute. He wrote of his long "running away" from his heavenly Father:

I fled him down the nights and down the days;
I fled him down the arches of the years;
I fled him down the labyrinthine ways
Of my own mind; and in the mist of tears
I hid from him and under running laughter.

But all this flight was in vain. At point after point in the poem, a section concludes with a statement by God about how inescapable he is: At last Thompson gives up and surrenders to God.

We can't escape from God. But why should we want to? He pursues us so he can save us, bless us, and pour out his love upon us. —J. G. V. B.

B. EXTENDS ACROSS THE SEA (vv. 9, 10)

9, 10. If I rise on the wings of the dawn, if I settle on the far side of the sea, even there your hand will guide me, your right hand will hold me fast.

Since neither the heavens nor the depths could offer a hiding place from God, the writer now turns to other possibilities. Morning light sweeps swiftly westward over land and sea. If he could go like that to the remotest part of the ocean, still God would be with him.

Your hand will guide me. There is no place so remote that God would not be there to guide him. *Your right hand will hold me fast.* This may mean that God's hand would be there to restrain him, or that God's hand would be there to sustain him. In either case, his point is clear: God would be there.

C. INCLUDES THE NIGHT (vv. 11, 12)

11, 12. If I say, "Surely the darkness will hide me and the light become night around me," even the darkness will not be dark to you; the night will shine like the day, for darkness is as light to you.

Since distance cannot separate the writer from God, can darkness surround him with a robe that even God's vision cannot penetrate? With electric lights both in our homes and in our streets, we can scarcely imagine how dark a moonless night can be without these conveniences. The psalmist echoes a statement we find in Job 34:22: "There is no dark place, no deep shadow, where evildoers can hide."

Even the most intense darkness we can imagine cannot shield us from God's scrutiny. As far as God is concerned, *the night* shines *like the day.* Since God is not a physical being, his vision is not limited to that which can be seen by physical eyes. The psalmist has explored just about all the possibilities of a person who would limit God's omniscience and omnipresence. A god who could not be everywhere is not the almighty God the psalmist worships. Nor could he be the almighty God if one's activities could be shielded from him by a blanket of night.

D. PRECEDES BIRTH (v. 13)

13. For you created my inmost being; you knit me together in my mother's womb.

Jehovah God, who created the heavens and the earth, who made the vast seas and the majestic mountains, is just as much concerned about the individual, even the unborn infant. We know much more about the process of conception, gestation, and birth than did the ancients. Still, when we contemplate the process that culminates in birth, we cannot help being filled with awe and wonder. The writer shared that wonder and awe, and readily recognized that God was involved in it. God was as much concerned about him when he was an unborn fetus as when he became a mature adult. Persons who are ready to terminate an unwanted pregnancy by abortion will do well to give some thought to this verse.

E. LEADS TO PRAISE (v. 14)

14. I praise you because I am fearfully and wonderfully made; your works are wonderful, I know that full well.

After contemplating the vast universe that God had made, the psalmist was compelled to raise his voice in praise of the Creator. We are indeed *fearfully and wonderfully made.* Even the psalmist's meager understanding of the body's functions led him to praise God. Modern science is probing ever deeper into the mysteries of the human body. Even though we know vastly more than we did a

WHAT DO YOU THINK?

Most of us are self-conscious about parts of our bodies that we feel are too long or too short, too round or too flat, too heavy or too thin. We may consider that we are far from the ideal, but we must agree with the psalmist that we are "fearfully and wonderfully made." Our advanced knowledge of the human body gives us all the more reason to come to that conclusion. What aspect of the human body do you find most fascinating? Why? How does that declare the power of God?

generation ago, we still have not unlocked all the secrets of its functions. What we do know should cause us to fall on our faces and praise our Maker. Yet all too often we casually ignore all of this and forget him who designed us and made us.

WHAT OUR BODIES TELL US

When we want to emphasize the reality of the work of God in the world, we don't have to look farther than our own bodies. Think of all the evidences of design and planning they reveal!

First is our *skin*. This is a marvelous covering over our entire bodies, from the soles of our feet to the tops of our heads. It tucks everything in and keeps us from oozing out all over. Further, it has thousands of pores through which perspiration can flow to cool us.

How interesting is our *digestive system!* We eat food, aided by saliva excreted in our mouths. It passes into our stomachs, where chemical agents process it into nutrients that blood carries to cells throughout our whole body. The waste is also processed for disposal through channels prepared for this purpose.

There are all the *special function organs* of our bodies—the heart, lungs, liver, kidneys, and others. There are the *eyes* with all their intricacy, the *ears,* and the *nostrils* with their delicate power of smelling.

There is the *brain* with its power of conceptualizing and problem solving. How marvelous are its abilities to control body movements, and also to dream dreams and envision possibilities and design futures!

Truly does the psalmist say, "I am fearfully and wonderfully made."

—J. G. V. B.

III. GOD'S SEARCHING (PSALM 139:23, 24)

A. GOD'S SEARCHING NEEDED (v. 23)

23. Search me, O God, and know my heart; test me and know my anxious thoughts.

In verses 19-22 the writer speaks out against the wicked, those who speak with evil intent and who misuse the name of the Lord. He expresses his hatred for those who hate God. He is certain that God will slay the wicked. Clearly, he is distancing himself from the wicked—"I count them my enemies"—and aligning himself with God.

The psalmist has no doubt about whose side he is on. He understands that God knows every thought and motive of his heart, and he is willing to let God search for any improper thoughts or feelings that might be harbored there. The writer may seem a bit too sure of himself, even to the point of arrogance, supposing that his life can stand the close scrutiny of God's penetrating eye. But see the next verse.

B. THE PURPOSE OF GOD'S SEARCH (v. 24)

24. See if there is any offensive way in me, and lead me in the way everlasting.

This call for God to search his heart was not really an exercise in spiritual arrogance. The psalmist had a purpose in this search. If God found anything undesirable there, he wanted him to cleanse his heart and set his feet upon the path that leads to everlasting life. In this he showed an openness to God's leading, a willingness to remove whatever was wrong.

We are like the psalmist in that we too must constantly search for anything in our hearts that may be foreign to God's holiness. But we enjoy one very important advantage over him. We have Christ as our example and the New Testament as a direct guide. We will not be held guiltless if we neglect either of these.

WHAT DO YOU THINK?

"Search me, O God, and know my heart...." What is the point? Haven't we just established that God already knows everything? The psalmist, however, has a practical motive in mind. He is eager for God to examine his thoughts and motives to disclose any wickedness found there. It is an act of submission. (See v. 24b.)

How important do you think it is to submit to God in this way? What kind of attitude is required to be able to say "Search me...test me...find my faults"? Do you think that is easy or hard for people in our culture today? Why? What can we do to make it easier?

Use visual 9 of the visuals packet to illustrate the psalmist's prayer in verses 23 and 24.

Prayer

All-knowing, all-seeing God, our heavenly Father, we come to you with thanks that you are concerned about us as individuals. Search our hearts, O Lord, and cleanse us from any offensive thought or deed, and lead us in the way everlasting. In Jesus' name we pray. Amen.

Thought to Remember

We cannot get away from God, though we can ignore him.

Daily Bible Readings

Monday, July 22—God Is Mindful of Us (Psalm 115:3-15)

Tuesday, July 23—God Is Aware (Luke 12:1-9)

Wednesday, July 24—God Cares (1 Peter 5:6-11)

Thursday, July 25—God Strengthens (Isaiah 41:8-13)

Friday, July 26—God Perseveres (Isaiah 46:3-11)

Saturday, July 27—God Sees All (Hebrews 4:1-13)

Sunday, July 28—God Is Our Confidence (Romans 8:26-35)

CONCLUSION

A. "You Cannot Hide From God"

Years ago we used to sing a song in church, "You Cannot Hide From God." As one reads the words of the song, one cannot avoid the conclusion that the writer was familiar with Psalm 139. Part of the chorus went like this:

> You cannot hide from God.
>> Wherever you go,
>> Whatever you do,
> You cannot hide from God;
>> His eye is fixed on you.

I was always a bit apprehensive when I sang this song. I had ways of avoiding the surveillance of my parents, but I wasn't sure I could escape God's constant scrutiny. Mentally I kept looking over my shoulder to see if God really was there with his eye fixed on me.

I haven't heard the song in years. Of course the music is a bit old-fashioned, and the lyrics are simplistic. But perhaps a more important reason we don't sing it is that the whole idea of a God constantly watching us goes against the contemporary emphasis on individual autonomy. We really don't want to have anything to do with a God who is something of a cosmic "Big Brother." After all, we have a right to privacy.

But in insisting upon our privacy even from God, we may be paying a rather high price. If we reject the idea of a God who watches us, we also lose the idea of a God who watches *over* us. The closing stanza of the song turns to this very theme:

> If you would save your sinful soul,
> If you would be made pure and whole,
> If you would reach the highest goal,
>> Your soul must hide in God.

Exactly! An all-seeing, all-knowing God may be a threat to us if we are determined to go our own way rather than his. But if we are willing to surrender ourselves *to* him, we will no longer have to hide *from* him. We will be able to rejoice in the comfort and protection we have when we hide *in* him.

B. Never Alone

In the 1950s *The Lonely Crowd* was a widely read sociological study. One of the points made by the book was that as our society becomes more urbanized, we are brought into contact with more and more people every day. Yet the paradox is that the more people we meet each day the lonelier we become. The reason is not hard to find. The more people we contact each day the less time we have to develop a trusting, intimate relationship with any one person. In the four decades since the book was published, the situation has not improved; indeed, it has become much worse.

Amidst the growing crowd, people are lonelier than ever. As a result, they enter into all kinds of relationships, many of which prove disappointing or disastrous, leaving them lonelier than ever. But we can have a fellowship with God that supports and sustains. And the church, through its members, can help bring people into that fellowship. More than at any other time in history, Christians need to be reaching out to the lonely crowd to show people that they never need to be alone.

Discovery Learning

This page contains an alternate lesson plan emphasizing learning activities. Classes desiring such student involvement will find these suggestions helpful. The next page is a reproducible activity page to further enhance discovery learning.

LEARNING GOALS

As a result of this lesson the students should be able to:

1. Identify and list instances of God's omniscience and omnipresence.

2. Explain how God's omni-qualities provide comfort and encouragement.

3. Plan ways to share the benefits of God's omni-nature with others.

INTO THE LESSON

Begin this lesson by dividing the class into pairs (not immediate family members). Ask each student to share with his partner any information he will about himself (biographical data, interests, little-known facts, etc.) for two minutes. The other partner is to make some brief notes. Then reverse roles and have the second partner tell information while the first takes notes for two minutes.

After the sharing exercise, ask for volunteers, each of whom will report to the class one interesting fact about his partner that he did not know before.

Say, "Probably the information you revealed to your partner was information you are willing for everyone to know. But what you *did not* say may also be significant. There are parts of our lives that we will not tell just anyone. There may be hurts that are too deep, activities of which we are not proud, or personal problems that we just don't care to discuss with everyone. We need a close friend with whom we can share the more intimate portions of our lives. And we treasure a friend who knows and understands us intimately. God can be that friend."

Today's psalm is written by one who treasured the intimate knowledge and presence of God. The psalmist invites God thus: "Search me, O God, and know my heart; test me and know my anxious thoughts" (139:23). This is a wonderful devotional psalm that not only teaches us something about the character of God, but also invites a closer and deeper relationship with him. Do we really want God to know all about us? Are we willing to tell him everything we do, everything we think, all our most secret feelings?

INTO THE WORD

Prior to the reading of today's Scripture lesson, give each student a piece of paper with two headings over two columns. Printed over the top of column one should be the words *Evidences or Illustrations of God's Omniscience.* Printed over column two should be the words *Evidences or Illustrations of God's Omnipresence.* Ask students to define "omniscience" and "omnipresence." (The prefix *omni* means "all.") *Omniscience* is knowledge of all things. *Omnipresence* is presence in all places at all times. Omniscience and omnipresence are two aspects of God's nature that transcend our own. Another is omnipotence, which means all power. After discussing those words, read the Scripture aloud clearly and slowly while students listen and write evidences in the appropriate columns.

An interesting alternative would be to play a dramatic recording of Psalm 139 while students listen and make notes.

After the reading, have students share their notes while one student makes a master list on two pieces of poster board.

Ask these discussion questions:

1. Contrast verses 1 and 23, 24. Verse 1 tells us God has already searched the heart of the psalmist. Verses 23 and 24 invite God to continue the searching of his heart. Why do you think the psalmist would offer that invitation to God? Why does he ask God to search his thoughts and know his heart?

2. What do verses 23 and 24 imply about the character and values of the psalmist?

INTO LIFE

Continue with the discussion questions to bring the Scripture into life.

1. Some adults may be frightened by the idea that a higher power than themselves sees and knows their every thought and action. Others would find that comforting. Why would some be frightened and why would some find this comforting?

2. Should Christians find God's knowledge and presence intimidating and frightening, or find his knowledge and presence comforting, or both? Why? How do you think God uses his knowledge of us?

3. Ask class members to share any new or reinforced perceptions of God they have gained from Psalm 139. Ask, "If you were to write or lead a prayer right now, what appreciation or understanding of God would you express to him?"

Distribute copies of "You Choose" on page 416. Allow about five minutes for the students to complete one of the activities; then ask volunteers to share the results of their work.

You Choose . . .

Below are several options of activities to help you apply the truths of Psalm 139. After reading verses 1-14, 23, 24, select one of the projects below.

PERSONAL PRAYER

Write a prayer to God thanking him for his intimate presence in your life. Express to him how his presence provides strength, support, and encouragement. Try to be specific in how his presence affects you.

PERSONALIZED PARAPHRASE

Reread Psalm 139:1-14. Write these verses in a way that conveys the thoughts, but applies them to your own situation. (For example: Lord, You have looked at me through and through and You know me inside and out. You know when I relax in my easy chair and watch television—and when I get up and get going . . .)

PERSONAL LETTER

Think of a friend who is encountering a difficult time. Write a letter of encouragement to him or her based upon the promise of God's presence. You may not decide to send the letter. But perhaps it will bring encouragement if you do. Be sure not to use a lot of clichés. Just try to be honest and encouraging. (Note: it is important to be sensitive to confidentiality. You might be wise not to share with others in class to whom you are writing—depending upon the situation.)

PERSONAL REMINDER

Write yourself a note that will remind you of God's presence when you are in difficult or stressful situations. In your reminder, identify specific situations you tend to encounter during which you need to remember this great promise (example, during heavy traffic on the way home from work; or during times when income doesn't match expenses). Suggest ways that meditating on God's caring and powerful presence can enable you to overcome in these situations.

God Is With Us (Psalms)
Unit 2. Responding to God
(Lessons 10-13)

TRUST IN GOD

LESSON 10

WHY TEACH THIS LESSON?

The deliverance theme is common in the Psalms. We have seen it once in our brief study already (lesson 8). One might wonder, then, what the value is in teaching another lesson so soon on the same theme.

Actually, the theme is somewhat different. The earlier lesson focused on the deliverer and praised God. This lesson focuses on the one to be delivered and challenges trust.

This lesson and the rest of the lessons for this month are aimed at challenging the learners to a specific response. Urge your students to trust God today, and this week, and the rest of their lives. He is worthy of trust; he is the deliverer.

INTRODUCTION

A. LATCHSTRING ON THE OUTSIDE

A Quaker family who lived on the frontier of the newly settled Pennsylvania colony was having family devotions. They chose for their Bible study that evening a passage from one of the psalms that spoke of God's deliverance of his people. As they prepared to retire, the father pulled the latchstring inside so the door could not be opened from the outside.

"Father, why did you place the latchstring inside?" asked one of the children. "If we trusted in God like the man who wrote the psalm, we wouldn't have to be afraid of anyone." Moved by the child's faith, the father placed the latchstring on the outside of the door.

In the middle of the night, they heard the door open and heard men whispering. Then the door was closed again and the men were heard no more. When the family arose in the morning, they discovered that every other house in the village had been burned and the people massacred. Amid their sorrowing over their neighbors, they paused to give thanks for their own deliverance. Only years later did they learn what had happened. An old Indian told how he had led a raiding party to the village, intending to destroy it and kill everyone in it. When he saw the latchstring on the outside of the door, however, he knew that the people in the house were Quakers and trusted in God. He also knew that the Quakers had treated the Indians fairly, and so their lives were spared.

B. LESSON BACKGROUND

The superscription, which is not a part of the original psalm, assigns Psalm 40 to David. Other authors have been suggested, but the situation that seems to provide background for the psalm fits the life of David. In fact, the psalm could very well describe either of two different crises in his life. One occurred during the reign of Saul, when David was forced to flee for his life and live for some time as a fugitive from the king who tried to kill him. (He was joined by other men who were out of favor with the king, about four hundred of them. They hid in the desert for years, as we read in 1 Samuel 22:1—30:31.) The other situation came later in David's career, when his son Absalom attempted to seize the throne and threatened his life. This danger did not last so long, but it

DEVOTIONAL READING
PSALM 36:5-12
LESSON SCRIPTURE
PSALM 40
PRINTED TEXT
PSALM 40:1-5, 9-11, 16, 17

LESSON AIMS

As a result of studying this lesson, each student should:

1. Conclude that God delivers and blesses those who suffer.

2. Contrast biblical strategies for responding to suffering with strategies typically proposed.

3. Plan a response to suffering that will exalt the Lord.

Aug
4

KEY VERSE

Blessed is the man who makes the Lord his trust.
—Psalm 40:4

brought death to David's son and terrible grief to David. The record of it is found in 2 Samuel, chapters 15–18.

I. THE PSALMIST'S DELIVERANCE (PSALM 40:1-5)

A. HE WAITED PATIENTLY (v. 1)

1. I waited patiently for the LORD; he turned to me and heard my cry.

The psalmist waited patiently under trying circumstances. This is not just a case of being inconvenienced. We today are likely to become irritated and upset about little things—like being caught in a traffic jam or delayed at the checkout counter. These situations, however, do not even compare with David's. David was in a life and death struggle.

He turned to me. God heard the psalmist's prayer, not as just one among many, but he gave it his full attention. The image here pictures God as turning to listen or leaning forward to give his attention. It is a comfort to any who suffer to know that God gives this kind of attention whenever we *cry* to him.

B. HIS DELIVERANCE CAME (v. 2)

2. He lifted me out of the slimy pit, out of the mud and mire; he set my feet on a rock and gave me a firm place to stand.

The *pit* was a terrible place to be. If this verse is taken literally, it indicates that the psalmist had been thrust into a muddy cistern or some similar pit. (See Jeremiah 38:1-13 for that prophet's experience in a miry dungeon.) The soft *mud* in the bottom, accumulated over years, might be a foot or more deep. This made it very difficult to move one's feet. Further, there might be considerable water in the cistern, adding to the difficulty and danger.

On the other hand, this verse may be figurative, referring to a political or military crisis that brought considerable agony. In this case the mud would represent some confining and/or dangerous situation.

Whatever the situation was, God rescued the psalmist from the crisis, set his feet firmly *on a rock,* perhaps even saved his life. Being free on solid ground, he could now move in the direction he believed the Lord was calling him.

C. HE HAS A NEW SONG (v. 3)

3. He put a new song in my mouth, a hymn of praise to our God. Many will see and fear and put their trust in the LORD.

Praising God through *song* is a natural response for people who have known his deliverance. We are not told what the new song was, but it was given by God and it involved *praise* of God. We are reminded of the song of rejoicing raised by the Israelites after their deliverance from the Egyptians at the Red Sea (Exodus 15:1-18). The deliverance that God had provided would be witnessed by many. It would produce reverent *fear* among them, and they would *trust in the Lord.* God's mighty works usually produce one of two responses. Some people become angry and rebellious, and their opposition to God is intensified. The pharaoh of Egypt and many religious leaders in Jesus' day provide good examples of this response. The other response is to come to trust in God or to become an even stronger believer in him. Many who witnessed Jesus' miracles belong in this category.

A NEW SONG

It is a human characteristic to sing. The ideas and emotions that are vital to us and vibrant in us tend to be expressed in those lyrical measures that we call "song." Of course there are many songs to be sung. We give voice in our love songs to our

WHAT DO YOU THINK?

The psalmist "waited patiently for the Lord." Many of us, on the other hand, are familiar with waiting impatiently. Instead of feeling the quiet confidence that comes from trusting God, we become worried and upset. Our anxiety may make us physically ill, or it may move us to some drastic action.

Why do you think some people are able to wait patiently, and others seem unable to? What is the key to being able to trust God and wait patiently? Can one develop this ability? If so, how?

WHAT DO YOU THINK?

This picture of mire and rock has been applied as a metaphor of salvation. Sin is the miry clay that has us trapped, and the rock is Jesus Christ. Many different types of addictions or compulsive behaviors can entrap people like mire and mud. Recovery groups can be very helpful, but the most effective deliverance is that which comes from God.

Practically speaking, how does that deliverance happen? If someone confessed to you a situation that had him or her trapped, as if in a pit of mire, how would you respond? Would you just say, "Trust God"? How does one do that?

need for human affection, for tenderness of touch, for the deepest levels of sharing one's life with another. Sentiments of familiarity and love of our natural surroundings lead to songs of patriotism and celebration of our heritage.

In some cultures, songs of melancholy and monotony tell of the pitiful round of similar days, the sorrow and unremitting toil of existence. Much Oriental temple music is such a combination of sad, minor-key tones.

The psalmist tells us he can sing a *new* song. He does not just call upon God for help, but *praises* him for what he already has done.

A similar note is found in the book of Revelation. The redeemed express their joy in God's saving love in Jesus, the Lamb of God. They sing a *new* song—no longer one of despair, or gloom, or hopeless longing. "Worthy art Thou . . . for Thou wast slain, and didst purchase for God with Thy blood men from every tribe and tongue and people and nation" (Revelation 5:9, *New American Standard Bible*).

During our lifetimes we sing many songs. Across the years we give voice to lyrics of love, patriotism, and college *alma maters*. But the most important song is the new one that tells of sin and death escaped, and righteousness and life achieved through him who loves us, Jesus our Lord.

—J. G. V. B.

D. BLESSED IS THE MAN WHO TRUSTS THE LORD (v. 4)

4. Blessed is the man who makes the LORD his trust,
who does not look to the proud, to those who turn aside to false gods.

Those who put their trust in the Lord will enjoy greater blessings than those who put their trust in men or money. *Does not look to the proud.* Some people attempt to gain the favor of men who are proud of their wealth or power, even if the wealth or power has been won by dishonesty. Some commentators take this to refer to those who followed Absalom in his rebellion against David, though the reference to *false gods* does not fit that occasion. Some versions have *lies*, however, instead of *false gods*. If this is correct, then the reference to the dishonesty and treason of the conspirators makes perfect sense (2 Samuel 15—18).

E. GOD'S WORKS ARE WONDERFUL (v. 5)

5. Many, O LORD my God, are the wonders you have done. The things you planned for us no one can recount to you; were I to speak and tell of them, they would be too many to declare.

Not only was the writer thankful for God's deliverance; he also expressed appreciation for God's other *wonders*. The ancient Israelites lived closer to nature than most of us do, so they were more aware of God's works in nature. Their pastoral lives allowed them to observe the starry heavens, the growing plants, the animals. This made them more respectful of nature and more reverent toward the God who had created it.

Most of us today live in cities or are caught up in the busy rush of urban life. The bright lights of the city cause the stars to pale into insignificance, and buildings and paved streets have eliminated most of the flora and fauna that were an important part of ancient pastoral life. As a result, we rarely stand in awe of the vast celestial canopy or watch with interest the plant and animal life about us. Thus we miss the sense of awe and reverent fear of God that the ancients knew.

The things you planned for us. Jehovah God is much more than just a mighty Creator of the physical world. He never ceases to show his concern for his creation. The human race, the crown of his creation, is especially the center of his attention. The psalmist readily recognizes that he can't begin to number the ways that God is involved in human affairs.

Happy is the person who trusts in the Lord.

Visual 10 of the visuals packet illustrates verse 4. Display it and discuss how the person pictured may be trusting the Lord.

WHAT DO YOU THINK?

The psalmist said God's wonderful works were "too many to declare." Still it's helpful to list some from time to time. Naming some of God's wonderful works glorifies and exalts him. Doing so can help us overcome discouragement, overcome envy, and overcome doubt. As we name God's works, we realize anew how great God is and how blessed we are.

What other benefits can you think of? Of all that have been named, which is most significant to you? Why?

II. THE PSALMIST'S RESPONSE TO GOD'S DELIVERANCE (PSALM 40:9-11)

In verse 6 the writer says, "Sacrifice and offering you did not desire." Of course he is not opposing the sacrifices required by God's law. He is saying God wants something more. Many were going through the motions of worship by offering the appropriate sacrifices, but this was just an empty exercise that left their hearts unchanged.

The psalmist's criticism of vain sacrifices was not unique. Samuel said to King Saul, "To obey is better than sacrifice, and to heed is better than the fat of rams" (1 Samuel 15:22). God expressed the same idea through Amos: "Even though you bring me burnt offerings and grain offerings, I will not accept them. Though you bring choice fellowship offerings, I will have no regard for them" (Amos 5:22). The offering of sacrifices should not be stopped, but reverence and obedience should be added.

A. HE PREACHED RIGHTEOUSNESS (vv. 9, 10)

9. I proclaim righteousness in the great assembly; I do not seal my lips, as you know, O LORD.

Sermons are not the only way of preaching. The writer was a musician; perhaps he often proclaimed righteousness in his singing. Large parts of the prophetic books of the Bible are poetic. The prophets may have sung them to throngs of listeners. Some modern songs also preach righteousness, if we listen to the words we are singing. "Yield Not to Temptation" is an example. Of course there is much prose preaching, too. See Moses' long address in Deuteronomy, or read Christian sermons in the book of Acts.

The great assembly. Three times a year all Israel gathered for a great religious festival. Acts 2 records Peter's sermon to such an *assembly.* There were other great assemblies too. Joshua assembled many of the people at Shechem to hear his farewell address (Joshua 24:1). Ezra and others read the law to a great assembly on the first day of the seventh month (Nehemiah 8:2, 3).

Standing before such an assembly is not quite the same as standing in a church service, however, even though the *King James Version* uses the word *congregation.* In our church services, everyone is pretty sympathetic with one's own position. Even when there is disagreement, most of the people remain encouraging. In a national assembly, much wider diversity would be present. The "enemies" the psalmist has written about and from whom he has prayed for deliverance would be present there. It was a bold act to "proclaim righteousness" before such an assembly.

I do not seal my lips. The message of righteousness was not welcomed by everyone, and it took courage for the psalmist to speak up as he did. But he was quite willing to risk disfavor with his opponents in order to remain faithful to the truth. That situation has not changed greatly. A person who contends for righteousness today may be ostracized or even attacked for the stand he or she takes.

10. I do not hide your righteousness in my heart; I speak of your faithfulness and salvation. I do not conceal your love and your truth from the great assembly.

The psalmist had not hid God's righteousness in his heart in some kind of secret piety. He had proclaimed it every chance he had, and with it he had proclaimed God's *faithfulness,* his *salvation,* his *love,* and his *truth.* No doubt he understood that it was not enough just to say the right things; he needed every day to demonstrate righteousness in his activities. Our faith, too, ought to produce lives that illustrate that faith. Many today have grown cynical about preaching and reject it out of hand, but a Christian life will silence these critics as words cannot.

WHAT DO YOU THINK?

Today we are told, "Faith is a personal matter. It has no place in public life." By that standard politicians can claim a "personal faith" but act in public as if biblical standards are irrelevant. As a result, standards of right and wrong have been so compromised and rewritten that what God considers sin is now protected, and appealing for righteousness is considered bigoted.

How can Christians take a stand, like the psalmist, and "proclaim righteousness"? What do you think will happen to Christians who do? To those who don't?

(See John 3:20; 15:18-21; Ezekiel 33:1-9.)

B. HE LOOKED TO THE LORD TO PRESERVE HIM (v. 11)

11. Do not withhold your mercy from me, O LORD; may your love and your truth always protect me.

In the previous verses the writer set forth his faithfulness to God. He has faithfully proclaimed God's righteousness. He has not withheld God's truth from the people. Now he asks God not to withhold his *mercy*.

Faithfulness to God does not guarantee freedom from trouble. Job, for example, though he was faithful to God, did not escape painful trials. Yet those who are faithful have one definite advantage. They know how to call upon God in prayer for his blessings. God intends for us to lay our problems before him, to pray with the anticipation that he will hear us and deal with us according to his purposes.

In spite of his rejoicing in the Lord, the psalmist still faced serious problems. He tells some of them in verses 12-15. His troubles had surrounded him. It is not surprising that he had become faint of heart. Further, he recognized that his own sins had "overtaken" him. It is quite possible that his sins had contributed to some of his troubles. Even when we have been faithful to the Lord, the problems that we face are sometimes the result of our own shortcomings.

The psalmist asks to be delivered from his trials. At the same time, he asks God to overcome those who have brought these trials upon him. He asks that they be "put to shame and confusion," "turned back in disgrace," and "appalled at their own shame." This may seem to fall short of Jesus' teaching to love our enemies and pray for them. We must note, however, that the psalmist prayed for the defeat of their evil purposes rather than for injury or death to the persons themselves.

III. THE PSALMIST'S PRAYER (PSALM 40:16, 17)

A. LET THE LORD BE MAGNIFIED (v. 16)

16. But may all who seek you rejoice and be glad in you; may those who love your salvation always say, "The LORD be exalted!"

In verses 12-15 the writer unburdened himself before the Lord. For a little while he thought of himself and all of his problems. Now his thoughts turn again to God. His self-pity turns to rejoicing, and he calls for others to join him in that rejoicing. Those who have known the Lord's salvation ought to exalt him. We can certainly agree with the psalmist at this point. At times our problems may seem overwhelming, but when we stop to count our blessings, the problems melt into insignificance.

GLADNESS IN GOD

One of the qualities of the religious faith of the Hebrew people was their joy in their Lord. The psalms are full of the praise of God, and a constant note in worship is the expression of gladness in God's service. The people of many other nations believed in deities who were easily offended and under whose wrath the worshipers cowered in abject fear. Some of these religions required their devotees even to sacrifice their own babies as offerings. It is difficult to see how such worship of Moloch or other gods could be anything but a source of grief and despair.

A characteristic note of New Testament worship is that of gladness and exultation, as expressed in the beginning of a fine hymn by Henry Van Dyke:

> Joyful, joyful, we adore Thee,
> God of glory, Lord of love.

Not long after this we come to these joyous lines:

HOW TO SAY IT

Absalom. AB-suh-lum.
Arimathea. Air-uh-muh-THEE-uh
  (th *as in* thin).
Moloch. MO-lock.
Shechem. SHEK-um.

WHAT DO YOU THINK?

The psalmist urges those who love God's salvation to say continually, "The Lord be exalted!" If one is not prone to praising God, frequently misses worship services, participates little in the singing and other praises, does this suggest that person does not love his salvation? Why or why not?

What does it mean to "love" God's salvation? If one truly understands from what and to what we have been saved, is any other response possible? Why or why not?

What Do You Think?

At the beginning of our text, the psalmist said he had waited patiently. In verse 17 he says, "O my God, do not delay." Has his patience run out? Tell why you think so or think not. What other reasons can you think might explain this phrase in verse 17?

(Compare 1 Corinthians 16:22b; Revelation 22:20.)

Prayer

Dear Father, we come before you, poor and needy as we are, seeking your wisdom to guide us and your strength to uphold us. Put a song of praise and thanksgiving in our hearts, and put it on our lips that all may know of the salvation you offer. In Jesus' name. Amen.

Thought to Remember

Gratitude is born in hearts that pause to count past blessings.

Daily Bible Readings

Monday, July 29—Wait Patiently (Psalm 37:1-7)

Tuesday, July 30—Take Refuge (Psalm 118:1-9)

Wednesday, July 31—Trust God Forever (Isaiah 26:1-6)

Thursday, Aug. 1—Taught by God (Isaiah 50:4-11)

Friday, Aug. 2—Hampered by Fear (Proverbs 29:22-27)

Saturday, Aug. 3—Protected by God (Psalm 31:11-24)

Sunday, Aug. 4—Surrounded by Love (Psalm 32:6-11)

Thou art giving and forgiving,
    Ever blessing, ever blest,
Well-spring of the joy of living,
    Ocean-depth of happy rest!

The essential message of the church is "the gospel," which of course means "the good news." The message is not what bad things God might do to us, but rather the marvelous good things he has done for us in the sending of Jesus and in his redemptive love.

—J. G. V. B.

B. God Is His Deliverer (v. 17)

17. Yet I am poor and needy; may the Lord think of me. You are my help and my deliverer; O my God, do not delay.

When the writer contemplates how blessed he is, he sinks to his knees in humility. With all his blessings he is still *poor and needy*. There is no way that he can defeat his enemies through his own strength. He is forced to rely upon God to deliver him. *Do not delay.* Even in his humility he shows a trace of impatience: "Hurry up, God; deliver me now!" Doesn't that sound like us?

CONCLUSION

A. Songs of Praise

The writers of the psalms lived thousands of years ago in a culture that seems almost primitive to us. Yet the songs of praise they lifted up to God rival or surpass anything we produce today. There are reasons for this. For one thing, most of the psalmists were farmers and shepherds who spent much of their time outdoors. Their extensive contact with nature made them appreciate its wonders. It was only natural for them to revere the God who had created the physical world.

Another reason they so readily praised God was that they knew they had to depend on him for their livelihood. He supplied the rain and sunshine needed for their crops; he protected their fields from plagues of locusts. Today we are less inclined to turn to God than we are to resort to science and technology for our help. We feel more comfortable with this arrangement because we have a better chance of controlling science than we have of controlling God.

So when we sing our songs, let us sing them with understanding. Let us note that many of our songs use themes familiar to the psalmists. Realizing this may help us recapture the simple but dynamic faith that characterized their lives.

B. Salvation

The writer of this psalm rejoiced as he looked to God for salvation. Probably he had in mind salvation from his enemies who surrounded him. The faith that God could provide him salvation under such distressing circumstances seemed reason enough for him to offer up praise and thanksgiving to his divine benefactor.

We too have the assurance that God watches over us, helps us through our day-to-day problems, and guides us through our major crises. Besides that, we have the promise of eternal salvation. Our praise ought to be far greater than that of the psalmist.

Courageously he stood before the people and proclaimed God's righteousness. At times he faced opposition from his enemies, but that did not keep him from being a bearer of good news. With such an example before us, shall we not be bearing witness to all the good things our Lord has done for us and has promised to everyone who will accept him?

Discovery Learning

This page contains an alternate lesson plan emphasizing learning activities. Classes desiring such student involvement will find these suggestions helpful. The next page is a reproducible activity page to further enhance discovery learning.

LEARNING GOALS

From this week's study, students of this lesson should be able to:

1. Conclude that God delivers and blesses those who suffer.

2. Contrast biblical strategies for responding to suffering with strategies typically proposed.

3. Plan a response to suffering that will exalt the Lord.

INTO THE LESSON

Write these questions on the chalkboard before the class arrives:

What is the greatest difficulty you have faced in your life?

How were you delivered from this difficulty?

How do you feel about the person who helped to rescue you?

When the class arrives, ask the students to form pairs and exchange answers to these questions. Circulate among your class members so you can tell when most of the students have had an opportunity to tell their stories. (Note: if your class is not accustomed to this kind of sharing, it will help everyone feel more comfortable if you tell your story first.)

Ask several students to give their answers to the last question with the whole group. (It is hoped that one of their responses will be that a student has come to *trust* the person who saved him or her from difficulty. If this is not one of the responses, you should add it to the list at this point.)

Explain to them that the psalmist had also faced great difficulty in his life and his reaction to being rescued can be found in Psalm 40.

INTO THE WORD

Ask your class to form five groups and assign each of the groups one of the following Psalms:

Psalm 28
Psalm 31
Psalm 37
Psalm 40
Psalm 56

Ask them to make a list of the circumstances in the life of the psalmist that caused him to trust in God. Then, ask them to summarize the main reasons the psalmist gives for trusting God.

When the groups are finished, lead them in a discussion how the psalmist's response to these various circumstances (trust in God and singing his praise) differs from the way the world might respond to the same circumstances. After a few minutes, discuss how the psalmist's response is like or different from the way most Christians today would respond. Is the Christian's response more like the psalmist's or more like the world's? Why? Is that as it should be? Why or why not?

OPTION

If your classroom does not allow you to break up into groups easily, you may do this as a large group activity by using the top section of the reproducible sheet on the next page. Have the students work with the reproducible page individually; then discuss their results as a group.

INTO LIFE

Read the first five verses of Psalm 69 followed by the first five verses of Psalm 40 (or have two students read these verses, one after the other). Ask your students what they think happened between the writing of these psalms. How did the psalmist go from standing in the slimy pit to standing on the solid rock? How did his perspective change?

Suggest to your students that the difference can be found in an abiding trust of God. It can also be found in verbal praise of what he has done.

Pass out slips of paper and ask your students to write a short hymn or prayer of praise for what God has done for them. Suggest that they choose one of the reasons the psalmist gives for trusting God that really challenges them. Ask them to write a short paragraph to express why this is important to them.

OPTION

Plan to close the class session by singing a familiar praise chorus. If you do not feel comfortable leading singing, ask someone in the class (in advance) to help you with this, or use a cassette player and ask everyone to sing along.

Close the class session with sentence prayers of thanksgiving for God's trustworthiness.

God Can Be Trusted!

List in the spaces provided the circumstances in the life of the psalmist that led to trust in God.

Psalm 28

Psalm 31

Psalm 37

Psalm 40

Psalm 56

Summarize the main reasons the psalmist gives in the passages above for trusting in God.

What was the psalmist's response to the trustworthiness of God?

OBEY GOD'S LAWS

WHY TEACH THIS LESSON?

The Bible has many uses. Some people use it for decoration. A large attractive Bible sits prominently on their coffee table or a shelf. It is dusted regularly, but seldom opened.

For others, it is a place to keep records. Inside the large family Bible is often a place to record births, deaths, and marriages. Such records have even been accepted as legal documents when birth records were not available!

Still others find the Bible is important in achieving a certain level of status among other believers. Carrying a Bible is considered a visible display that one is a Christian.

All these uses are inadequate however, without the one reason the Bible was given, "… so that the man of God may be thoroughly equipped for every good work" (2 Timothy 3:17).

It is interesting, if nothing else, that the longest psalm is devoted to the importance and value of God's Word. Perhaps some of your students have taken the Bible for granted. Perhaps some have never considered its nature. Use this lesson to show them, and to challenge them to put this great book to use. Not just on the coffee table, but in their lives!

INTRODUCTION

A. GOD'S ROAD MAP

Traveling in an unfamiliar part of the country, I missed a turn. After a few miles, I realized that I was lost. I pulled over to the side of the road and searched in my glove compartment for a map. I found a map of the area, but I still had a problem. The map was not detailed enough to help me find my way on the back road where I was. Then I found a more detailed map. Following it, I was soon back on a marked highway and feeling greatly relieved. Then suddenly I came to a dead end. The map I was following was an old one. A new highway had been built, and the old highway ended at a stream over which there was no bridge.

There was nothing to do but to find some help. Finally I came to a service station where I bought an up-to-date map. Following it, I was able to reach my destination.

Life itself can be like my experience. Often we try to negotiate the highway of life guided only by our own sense of direction. This is a sure way to get lost. Then we turn to other plans. Some are not detailed enough; others are out-of-date. This lesson offers a map for traveling life's highway from birth to our heavenly reward. God's law, God's Word, is that map. Following it will insure us a safe journey.

B. LESSON BACKGROUND

Psalm 119, containing 176 verses, is the longest psalm. Its structure is unusual. It is divided into twenty-two stanzas, one for each letter of the Hebrew alphabet. This makes it one of the most unusual of the alphabetic psalms. All eight verses of the first stanza begin with the letter *aleph,* the first letter in the Hebrew alphabet. All the verses in the second stanza begin with *beth,* the second letter, and so on through the entire psalm.

DEVOTIONAL READING
MATTHEW 7:21-28

LESSON SCRIPTURE
PSALM 119:1-16, 45, 105, 129, 130

PRINTED TEXT
PSALM 119:1-16, 45, 105, 129, 130

LESSON AIMS

As a result of studying this lesson, each student should:

1. List blessings that result from knowing and obeying God's Word.

2. Commit to improving personal Bible study habits.

Aug
11

KEY VERSE

Your word is a lamp to my feet and a light for my path.
—Psalm 119:105

LESSON 11 NOTES

Through all twenty-two stanzas, the writer emphasizes knowing and obeying God's law. To provide variety, he uses several synonyms for "law." Among these are "statutes," "decrees," "word" or "words," "precepts," "commands," and "promises."

I. BLESSEDNESS OF OBEDIENCE (PSALM 119:1-8)

A. INTEGRITY OF HEART (vv. 1-3)

1-3. Blessed are they whose ways are blameless, who walk according to the law of the LORD. Blessed are they who keep his statutes and seek him with all their heart. They do nothing wrong; they walk in his ways.

Blessed does not come from the Hebrew word meaning "to bless," but from a word that means "happy." *Blessed* is an appropriate translation, however; for if one is truly happy, it is because he is blessed of God. One *whose ways are blameless* describes one who follows God's leading completely, one who keeps himself "from being polluted by the world" (James 1:27). *The law of the Lord.* Sometimes this expression refers specifically to the law of Moses, but in this case it seems to include all of God's Word.

Statutes comes from a word that means "to witness" or "to testify." God's commandments testify to his divine nature and to man's duty. *Seek him with all their heart.* This was at the center of the Old Testament law: "Love the Lord your God with all your heart and with all your soul and with all your strength" (Deuteronomy 6:5). Jesus reaffirmed this (Matthew 22:37, 38).

They do nothing wrong.. This does not suggest that anyone can be morally perfect and never sin. John says, "If we claim to be without sin, we deceive ourselves and the truth is not in us" (1 John 1:8). We all stray from the path occasionally. God's Word, however, is never the cause of our wandering. As long as we follow its precepts, we do nothing wrong. Our problem is that we do not follow God's Word perfectly.

Wrong is derived from a word that means "to turn" or "to twist." The blessed man neither turns from God's way nor twists his commandments.

B. CONSISTENCY IN CONDUCT (vv. 4, 5)

4, 5. You have laid down precepts that are to be fully obeyed. Oh, that my ways were steadfast in obeying your decrees!

To be pleasing to God we must be consistent in walking in his way. He has laid out for us a definite course of conduct, and he expects us to follow it. To wander wherever our whims may take us cannot be pleasing to God, and it can be disastrous to us. To pursue a consistent course is not easy. Even the apostle Paul struggled with temptations that could have led his feet astray (Romans 7:21-23). Psalm 1 indicates how a person may stray. First, one walks "in the counsel of the wicked," then stands "in the way of sinners," and finally sits "in the seat of mockers."

C. AVOIDANCE OF SHAME (v. 6)

6. Then I would not be put to shame when I consider all your commands.

When one turns from the ways of God, he or she may suffer physically; but often a more intense suffering comes from the *shame* that wicked deeds bring. A good name that has become soiled by sin never can be restored to its original purity, nor can one ever completely regain the trust of others when sin has destroyed that trust.

D. RESULTING PRAISE (vv. 7, 8)

7, 8. I will praise you with an upright heart as I learn your righteous laws. I will obey your decrees; do not utterly forsake me.

WHAT DO YOU THINK?

The psalmist calls for being "steadfast in obeying" God's decrees. That, like most worthwhile objectives, takes initiative and discipline. Most believers agree that they should obey diligently, but many are not very diligent, choosing to obey when it's convenient. Why is that? What has been most helpful to you in encouraging diligent obedience? What would you recommend to someone who knows the right thing but has trouble doing it?

WHAT DO YOU THINK?

Parents, teachers, and other authority figures are cautioned against using shame as a motivation because it is damaging to one's self-esteem. Positive reinforcement of desired behavior is preferred. There is a shame, however, that is completely internal. It comes from an accusing conscience when we know we have done something wrong.

Which do you think is mentioned in verse 6 of the text, internal or external? Why? Is there a proper way for someone to appeal to another's internal sense of shame—his or her conscience—to encourage right behavior? If so, how?

Praise toward God came naturally to the psalmist, not just from his lips but from his *heart*. This praise was not just the gushing forth of strong emotions; it was based on knowledge of God and his Word.

We are not born with a knowledge of God. We acquire that knowledge through experience. Some of that experience is unplanned; it just happens. We view the vast expanse of the heavens or we see a majestic mountain raising its snowy head above its surroundings, and deep down we sense the existence of a power greater than ourselves. However, recognizing God's power in nature does not necessarily lead us to see his love and concern for us. For that we need special revelation through the Scriptures. We do not come to understand the Scriptures effortlessly through some magical process. Rather, we must devote long, arduous hours to study if we are to understand God's will for us. That is the reason Sunday school and every other educational activity within the church is so important.

Studying the Scriptures as simply an intellectual pursuit is not what the writer had in mind. His studies led him to keep God's statutes. Any study of God's Word that does not lead to a change in attitudes and actions is less than Christian education.

Do not utterly forsake me. These words suggest that there may have been some crisis in the psalmist's life, some suffering or some threat that turned him to God for help. Possibly he had turned from God's way and needed to be forgiven. His need was so pressing that he feared that God was forsaking him. Most of us can identify with the writer, for we have passed through times of fear and despair, times when we have pleaded for God to be with us. We can take comfort in his promise never to forsake us (Hebrews 13:5).

II. HOLY ADVICE (PSALM 119:9-16)

A. Heed the Word (vv. 9, 10)

9, 10. How can a young man keep his way pure? By living according to your word. I seek you with all my heart; do not let me stray from your commands.

Verse 9 introduces the second stanza in this psalm. It is labeled *beth*, the second letter in the Hebrew alphabet, and each verse in the stanza begins with this letter.

The stanza begins with a question that every young person ought to face. The writer may be an older man giving advice to a younger one. Every generation in one way or another passes along certain values to the next generation. The teaching of values may be done carefully and systematically, with constant reinforcement from the lives of the teachers. On the other hand, it may be done haphazardly by parents and church leaders, or what is worse, by outside forces that contradict what parents teach.

Young people today are bombarded by media crosswinds that blow in every direction. Is it any wonder that some young people are like rudderless ships, turning this way and that with each wind change? The tragedy is that some are blown upon reefs that destroy them morally and physically. Will God hold guiltless the older generation that stands by and allows this to happen?

Unlike some leaders, who seem to have lost their sense of direction, the psalmist knew how a young man can make his way clear: *By living according to your word.* The writer had followed God with all his heart, and now he was trying to teach others the truths he had learned. He knew the value of example, for he prayed that God would not let him wander from his commandments.

CLEANSING AND CORRECTION

Many problems arise in a young person's way. There is a temptation to think one is especially girded with strength. There is an awareness that one is better looking than are older people. There is an adroitness in doing physical acts that older people

---

How to Say It

aleph (Hebrew). AH-leff.
Amnon. AM-nun.
beth (Hebrew). bayth or bait.
Rehoboam. Re-ho-BO-um.
Tamar. TAY-mer.

What Do You Think?

Do you think it is harder for a young man to keep his way pure than for a young woman? Why or why not? For a young man than for an old man? Why or why not? Why do you think the psalmist asks about a "young man" instead of person generally?

may be less competent to perform. One is keenly aware of what one's peers are wearing, saying, and doing; one feels a pressure to conform. Sexual impulses may be extremely urgent in youth, and one may act rashly.

Rehoboam, Solomon's son, was strong, vain, arrogant, and impulsive. He acted as his young companions advised: proudly, thoughtlessly, and boastfully. As a result, he caused the Hebrew kingdom to split apart and brought about years of bloodshed. He did not take heed to his way according to God's Word (1 Kings 12:1-20).

One of David's sons, Amnon, became enamored of his half-sister, Tamar. His desire for her led to deception and rape. Tamar's brother then killed Amnon and fled out of the country (2 Samuel 13). So David's family was disrupted because young Amnon did not take heed to his way and cleanse it.

It can be said that *awareness* is the first thing a young person needs, awareness of God's Word by which his or her life can be cleansed. The Word of the Lord is what can purify, perfect, and protect a young person. —J. G. V. B.

WHAT DO YOU THINK?

How important do you think memorizing Scripture is? How does it protect against sin? Why do you think more people do not try to memorize Scripture regularly?

(See Matthew 4:1-10; Ephesians 6:10-18.)

B. INSURANCE AGAINST SIN (vv. 11, 12)
11, 12. I have hidden your word in my heart that I might not sin against you. Praise be to you, O LORD; teach me your decrees.

It is the *word* in our hearts, not a book in the house, that keeps us from doing wrong. That word cannot be implanted in our hearts by some surgical process, nor is there a pill that can put it there. It finds a home in our hearts by a process of diligent study. This is a strong argument for encouraging people, especially young people, to memorize Scripture.

C. PROCLAIM THE WORD (vv. 13, 14)
13, 14. With my lips I recount all the laws that come from your mouth. I rejoice in following your statutes as one rejoices in great riches.

We have an obligation to share our knowledge of God with others. As we do this, we share in the joy it brings to those who learn. We realize another blessing, too. As we teach others, our own knowledge and understanding grow.

Many things can cause people to rejoice: wealth, power, family, and service to God, to name a few. What brings joy to a person depends on that person's values. If one searches for joy only in wealth, power, or even family, he or she may be terribly disappointed. All of these may turn sour, and certainly they all will pass. Faithful service to God lasts into eternity. That is why the psalmist found joy in God's Word *as one rejoices in great riches.*

WHAT DO YOU THINK?

Are there meditation techniques that you have found helpful? Describe them.

D. MEDITATE ON THE WORD (vv. 15, 16)
15, 16. I meditate on your precepts and consider your ways. I delight in your decrees; I will not neglect your word.

Much can be said in favor of memorizing portions of God's Word. Thus we hide his precepts in our hearts and minds (v. 11). We need to go beyond knowing the words, however. We must ponder them, meditate over them.

Meditation is a mental lingering over an idea or a text. In meditating, one may restate a thought many times, each time emphasizing a different word, looking for additional understanding. One may restate a verse and inject his or her own name, thus making the verse very personal. Some have prayed a verse or passage back to God, letting it be the focus of the prayer. Others have found setting a text to music to be very helpful.

In our increasingly complicated world, we seem to find little time for this kind of meditation. But the complexity of our world is one of the reasons it is so important that we do. We need to spend time pondering God's principles so that we know how to apply them to specific situations for which are no easy answers. Where, for example, does one find texts to deal with the ethical issues being raised by the science of genetic engineering? What Scriptures does one quote to cope with all of the complex problems that arise when the government increasingly becomes involved in our lives? For this reason we must study the Scriptures and meditate over them to find the general principles that God has established to meet any problem that life may present.

Meditation is important for another reason. It causes one to examine the inner recesses of one's own heart and to measure its contents by God's standards. Christians have an obligation to relate their faith to the world; but in order to do this effectively, their own hearts must be right. In our busy schedules we struggle to find time for this kind of meditation; and worse, when we have a little extra time, we hardly know what to do with it.

Many of us deal with Bible study as if it were a business responsibility: a serious responsibility, to be sure, but still a responsibility. The psalm writer, on the other hand, found delight in God's statutes. He approached Bible study as we approach a hobby—something we look forward to with delight, something we enjoy while we are engaged in it.

III. A WALK IN THE WORD (PSALM 119:45, 105, 129, 130)

A. IT BRINGS FREEDOM (v. 45)

45. I will walk about in freedom, for I have sought out your precepts.

We hear much today about political freedom. People have suffered, even died for it. We understand people's willingness to sacrifice for political freedom, even though such freedom brings its own burdens and responsibilities. The psalmist's concern was for spiritual *freedom*, a far more important kind. Persons who know and follow God's law enjoy important blessings. However, those who follow God's commandments in a legalistic way are still under bondage. Such were the Pharisees in Jesus' day. One goal should be to grow in understanding until we follow God's law, not because we feel we have to, but because we love God so much that we want to. One who attains this level of discipleship enjoys real freedom that no one can take away.

B. IT BRINGS LIGHT (v. 105)

105. Your word is a lamp to my feet and a light for my path.

Stumbling around in a dark room is a disturbing experience. How much more threatening it is to try to find one's way in a darkened moral situation without any spiritual *light*! The consequences can be painful, even disastrous. Our society seems to be in that kind of a situation. We stagger from one crisis to another, only to be confronted with a still more serious problem—all because we have no light. To be more precise, we have an available light, the Bible; but many people prefer humanistic theories that only compound the darkness.

LIGHTED STEPS

The psalmist tells us God's Word is a lamp that lights his pathway. The picture here is not a long road brightly illuminated with electric lights. Rather, it is a scene of gloom with no gleam of light in the surrounding blackness. Only a few steps ahead are lit by a lamp.

This is an experience we have many times in our Christian walk. We may be going through a trying time. Someone close to us may be very ill, loved ones on whom we have depended in crises may seem indifferent to or unaware of our needs. Our duties may press upon us. We may be unable to see how we can comfort and cheer and challenge others who need our help. We need to let God's truth help us to see just

PRAYER

Amid the darkness that surrounds us, Father, we pray for light. Show us how to use the light you have given us through the Scriptures to guide our footsteps. Show us how to share this light with others. In the name of Jesus, the light of the world, we pray. Amen.

WHAT DO YOU THINK?

If the Bible is so valuable, why do so many Christians know so little about it? What could be done in your church to encourage Bible knowledge? How helpful do you think each of the following might be? Why?
- *Listen to the Bible on tape*
- *Report the number of Bibles carried to church*
- *Give opportunity for people to use their Bibles while at church.*
- *Sermon series on a Bible book*
- *Give people time to find a text and follow along during a sermon*
- *Memorization projects or contests*

DAILY BIBLE READINGS

Monday, Aug. 5—Keep God's Laws (Deuteronomy 26:15-19)

Tuesday, Aug. 6—Be Strong and of Good Courage (Joshua 1:1-9)

Wednesday, Aug. 7—To Obey Is Better Than Sacrifice (1 Samuel 15:22-29)

Thursday, Aug. 8—Ready for Rain (Genesis 6:11-22)

Friday, Aug. 9—Nothing Left Undone (Joshua 11:10-15)

Saturday, Aug. 10—Holding Fast to the Lord (2 Kings 18:1-8)

Sunday, Aug. 11—Learned Obedience (Hebrews 5:1-10)

one step at a time. We can't do it all at once—and can't do it *at all* unless we let the light lead us little by little.

—J. G. V. B.

C. IT BRINGS UNDERSTANDING (vv. 129, 130)

129, 130. Your statutes are wonderful; therefore I obey them. The unfolding of your words gives light; it gives understanding to the simple.

God's *statutes are wonderful* in that they reveal to us his power and majesty, his love and mercy. There is no way that we can understand all these things apart from his revelation. That revelation culminated in his Son, Jesus Christ. In him we are able to understand why we are here and where we are going. This understanding is not confined to just a handful of scholars hidden away in some ivory tower. The way of salvation has been made simple enough that all may find it.

THE GREAT PSALM

If ever a literary production deserved to be called "great," Psalm 119 certainly qualifies. It is great in *length*. Its 176 verses make it the longest of the psalms. It is great in *literary finesse* and intricacy. It goes through the Hebrew alphabet and gives each letter a section of eight verses, each one of which starts with that letter. The psalm is great in *its theme*, which is the Word of God, the commandments, precepts, testimonies, and statutes of the Lord. All of these many verses say something uplifting, challenging, or comforting about God's truth in relationship to human life.

However, while this psalm is a vivid example of literary artistry, its aim is not to amaze us with the virtuosity of the writer. Rather, its aim is to help us see the wonder of God's Word and to see how it relates to our guidance, challenge, comfort, and renewal.

—J. G. V. B.

CONCLUSION

It is a well-documented fact that the majority of Christians know little about the Bible. There was a time when editorials and political speeches abounded in Bible quotations and allusions. No more! And most people would not understand the biblical references if they were used.

How did this sorry state of affairs come about? We can point to the growing secularization of our society, for one thing. We have become so obsessed with things of this world that eternal matters are ignored. We may also point to the growing pluralism of our society. In our efforts to provide freedom of religion for every sect under the sun, we have accomplished freedom *from* religion for many. As a result, the study of the Bible and even its distribution are severely restricted in our public schools. The practical result is that the one book that has had the greatest impact on our civilization is hidden from our children.

What can we do about the situation? We have several options. One, we can stand around and complain, wringing our hands in impotency. Two, we can work through legal process to get court decisions changed. This, however, is a long, expensive process with no assurance of success. Three, we can use the opportunities we have right at hand to teach people the Bible. Parents can teach it to their children in their homes. We can encourage greater participation in the educational programs offered in our churches. And we can develop new and creative educational programs to meet the changing circumstances in our society.

Suppose we are stumbling down a rough pathway in the dark. Suppose we have a lantern, oil, and matches, and yet we refuse to use them to provide light for our path. Such reluctance to use what we have would be called foolish. We have the means to provide light, God's Word, to sweep away the moral darkness that surrounds us. Are we any less foolish if we don't find ways to use it?

Discovery Learning

This page contains an alternate lesson plan emphasizing learning activities. Classes desiring such student involvement will find these suggestions helpful. The next page is a reproducible activity page to further enhance discovery learning.

LEARNING GOALS

From this week's study, students of this lesson should be able to:

1. List blessings that result from knowing and obeying God's Word.

2. Commit to improving personal Bible study habits.

INTO THE LESSON

Before your students arrive in the classroom, write the letters W, O, R, and D vertically on the left side of the chalkboard, leaving plenty of space to write. If you do not have a chalkboard, hang four large pieces of paper or posterboard on a wall and put one letter on each one.

As your students enter the classroom, encourage each to think of a word that tells something about the Bible that begins with one of these letters and write it after the letter on the board (or posters).

After everyone has had opportunity to participate in this activity, encourage several class members to share the reasons for the words they chose.

INTO THE WORD

Move into the study of Psalm 119 by giving a brief background of this psalm taken from the Scripture study. Be sure to mention that this Psalm is a wonderful, intricate acrostic poem. The psalmist has taken the twenty-two letters of the Hebrew alphabet and divided the psalm into twenty-two sections with each section representing a different letter of the alphabet. Each verse in each section begins with the same letter. Several of the psalms are acrostics since this helped people to remember the verses. However, this is the greatest example of an acrostic psalm and shows not only the psalmist's devotion to the Word of God but his commitment to detail.

After giving some background, help the students to get into the psalm on their own, using the reproducible sheet on the next page. (Below are some definitions that will help you give structure to the discussion of the terms the psalmist uses to describe God's Word.)

Ask a student to read aloud Psalm 119:1-16; 45, 105, 129, 130. Then ask the students to look for examples of the following terms in the text, define them, and state what benefit the psalmist attributes to each.

• *Law*—basically means instruction by God about how to live in order to please him. Law is God's instruction about reality. There is nothing arbitrary about it.

• *Precept*—something revealed by God that is to be guarded and obeyed (i.e. his covenant).

• *Command*—an order to be obeyed, it carries the authority of the one who issued it.

• *Statute*—a decree issued by the sovereign Lord.

• *Word*—what proceeds from the mouth of God. Can also mean a promise. While men's words are often undependable, God's words are sure.

After the students have had time to complete their assignments, ask for reports. Write the five words on the chalkboard, or project them with an overhead projector, and then make notes under or next to each one, based on information supplied by the students.

OPTION

Divide the class into at least five small groups and assign one of the terms to each group. You may want to suggest they look at more of the psalm than just the lesson verses if they are only looking for the one term.

INTO LIFE

Ask, "What does this psalm say about our attitude toward obeying God's Word?" Your discussion should reveal some of the following: we should seek God *wholeheartedly* (vv. 2, 10), give *complete* obedience (v. 4), be *steadfast* in obedience (v. 5), consider disobedience *shameful* (v. 6), obedience should invoke *praise* and not complaint (vv. 7, 12), God's Word should cause *pleasure* (vv. 14, 16).

Sum up this discussion by saying something like, "Many times Christians approach Bible study as a chore, and it become laborious to them. The psalmist had a very different attitude, as we have seen. How do we develop such attitudes?" Discuss briefly; then suggest some of the practices mentioned in the text might help. Ask the students to list as many specific practices as they can find. Possible answers include pray for steadfastness (v. 5), consider (that is, give serious thought to) the Lord's commands (v. 6), combine Bible study with praise (v. 7), desire purity (v. 9), memorize Scripture (v. 11), tell others what you learn (v. 13), do not neglect the Word (v. 16).

Ask your students to write down one or two specific practices (from this list or otherwise) that would improve their own Bible study habits. They need not share these with anyone, but encourage them to write something.

Close the session with prayer, asking God to direct your students' individual Bible study for his glory.

A Magnificent Poem

Below are listed some of the terms the psalmist uses to describe the Word of God. Find each of these terms in Psalm 119. From the context, write a brief definition of each one in the space provided below. Also indicate how this understanding of the Bible affects the way you read and obey it.

Law

Statute

Precept

Word

Command

Picture This

Look up each of the following verses and tell which picture means the most to you and why.

Psalm 119:105 Lamp

Jeremiah 23:29 Fire/hammer

Ephesians 6:17 Sword

1 Peter 2:2   Milk

Psalm 19:10   Gold/honey

Luke 8:11   Seed

REPENT AND CONFESS

LESSON 12

WHY TEACH THIS LESSON?

The Bible tells us all have sinned (Romans 3:23). It tells us there is not a one of us who is righteous, "not even one" (Romans 3:10). It tells us to repent (Acts 2:38). And there, perhaps, we draw up short. Repent? That's one of those words you only hear in church. Just exactly what does it mean? How does one do it?

There are classic answers, but today's lesson gives something even better. It gives an example. It shows us a real person struggling with real guilt for real sin. If ever your students were tempted to think the Bible doesn't work in "the real world," today's lesson should forever put that doubt to rest. The world of the Bible *is* the real world. And the real God has the answer for our real problems—beginning with the very real problem of sin.

INTRODUCTION

A. DO YOU HAVE TO SAY, "I'M SORRY"?

One of the popular movies of a couple decades ago featured the line, "Love means you never have to say, 'I'm sorry.'" In fact, one of the songs from the movie, which became quite a hit in its own right, carried the same title. Some would question the wisdom of that philosophy.

Interestingly, the Bible never says we ought to say, "I'm sorry." Many people equate repentance with being sorry, but that is not accurate. Repentance is more than sorrow. Sorrow—godly sorrow—will *lead to* repentance (2 Corinthians 7:10), but sorrow by itself is not enough. Sorrow alone may produce nothing more than bitter remorse, by which Judas went out and hanged himself.

Should we say, "I'm sorry"? Not if we think that is the end of the matter. Sorrow by itself is an emotional response. If, when the emotion cools, there is no firm resolve to change in attitude and behavior, then we have not come to repentance.

The writer of the fifty-first Psalm does not actually say he was "sorry." He doesn't need to. His emotion is obvious in the writing. But so is his repentance, his firm resolve to serve the Lord, teaching other "sinners" like himself to "turn back" to the Lord (v. 13). Three thousand years later, he is still turning sinners back to the Lord through his writing.

B. LESSON BACKGROUND

The superscription credits this psalm to David, and indicates that it was written at one of the most painful crises of his life. The background for the psalm is the prophet Nathan's confrontation with David after he had committed adultery with Bathsheba and had conspired to have her husband, Uriah, murdered (2 Samuel 11, 12). David might have responded to Nathan with anger and threats, but instead he confessed his guilt and voiced his repentance.

I. A PLEA FOR FORGIVENESS (PSALM 51:1-4)

A. A CRY FOR MERCY (v. 1)

1. Have mercy on me, O God, according to your unfailing love; according to your great compassion blot out my transgressions.

DEVOTIONAL READING
EZEKIEL 18:25-32

LESSON SCRIPTURE
PSALM 51

PRINTED TEXT
PSALMS 51:1-13, 17

LESSON AIMS

As a result of studying this lesson, each student should:

1. Describe how God's unfailing love restores sinners.

2. Praise God for the purity that comes from forgiveness of sin.

KEY VERSE

Create in me a pure heart, O God, and renew a steadfast spirit within me.

—Psalm 51:10

Aug
18

LESSON 12 NOTES

WHAT DO YOU THINK?

David confessed his guilt and turned to God for cleansing. Contrast that with modern ways of dealing with guilt. Why are these other ways inadequate? How can people be persuaded to follow God's way instead of each of these?
* *Denial*
* *Rationalization*
* *Blame others (or blame circumstances)*
* *Counseling*
* *Others?*

WHAT DO YOU THINK?

Since God made us, sustains us, and gives us every good thing, certainly he has a right to draw the boundaries of acceptable behavior. We cannot sin without disregarding his claim on us. Thus David acknowledges, "Against you, you only, have I sinned." Does that suggest we have no need to apologize when we wrong another person? Why or why not? If someone who had been unfaithful to his or her spouse confided in you that he or she was going to confess the sin to God but not to the spouse, what would you advise? Why?

It is interesting that throughout this psalm David never addresses God as Jehovah. Perhaps he felt himself so unworthy that he dared not use the name that was so closely associated with the special covenant between Jehovah and Israel. David knew he had violated this covenant, and perhaps he felt that he could address God only as *Elohim,* the Creator God.

David asked first of all for mercy. He knew very well that he deserved punishment. Only by God's mercy could he hope to escape it. David stood where every one of us must stand—before a righteous God, a God of justice. If he were not also a God of mercy, our pleas for forgiveness would be futile. David asked that God in mercy would *blot out* his transgressions. He thought of his sins being inscribed in a divine record book. He wanted the bookkeeper to cross them out, eradicate them.

B. A PLEA FOR CLEANSING (v. 2)

2. Wash away all my iniquity and cleanse me from my sin.

David now changed his figure from bookkeeping to laundering. Not content with a clearing of the divine record, he wanted personal cleansing that would purge him of the sins that defiled him. His act of adultery was not the whole problem. That would not have happened if his heart had been clean. He sought to be thoroughly cleansed so that future temptations would not find him vulnerable.

Jesus later pointed out this great truth. Sin is not the outward act alone, but the condition of the heart that allows temptation to take root and grow until it results in overt action (Mark 7:21-23). If we are to live moral lives, we must ask God to purge our hearts of those things that defile us.

THE CALL FOR CLEANSING

Shakespeare's *Macbeth* provides a dramatic statement of how one feels when the soul is stained with sin. Macbeth has taken part in a bloody murder with a dagger. Now his hands are stained with blood. As he looks at them, the enormity of his guilt becomes increasingly clear to him.

> Will all great Neptune's ocean wash this blood
> Clean from my hand? No, this my hand will rather
> The multitudinous seas incarnadine,
> Making the green one red.

David likewise was aware of the terrible deeds he had done. He had committed adultery, and had added to that the sin of murder. He had used others in his sordid plot to bring about the death of brave, faithful, and earnest Uriah. It is startling to think that the same David who could compose the Twenty-third Psalm could fall into this complex of sins.

"Wash away all my iniquity and cleanse me from my sin," he cried. That shows how keenly he was aware of the slime and muck of sin that lay on his soul. As Christians we find there are times when in word or deed or in cowardly silence we soil ourselves with the clinging filth of sin. What a consolation it is to know "the blood of Jesus . . . purifies us from all sin"! "If we confess our sins, he is faithful and just to forgive us our sins, and to purify us from all unrighteousness" (1 John 1:7, 9).

—J. G. V. B.

C. AN ACKNOWLEDGMENT OF SIN (vv. 3, 4)

3, 4. For I know my transgressions, and my sin is always before me. Against you, you only, have I sinned and done what is evil in your sight, so that you are proved right when you speak and justified when you judge.

In our courts today, we see accused people denying their guilt, or blaming others for their problems, or trying to plea-bargain for a lesser sentence. Without making any reservations or blaming someone else for his problems, David admitted his guilt; nor did he attempt to plea-bargain to get a lighter sentence. *My sin is always before me.* David may have concealed his sins from most of the world, but he could not hide from his own conscience. It kept his sins ever before him. Nathan's accusation reminded him that he was not hidden from God either. He could find no peace until he had unburdened his soul before the Lord.

Against you, you only, have I sinned. In committing adultery and murder, David had, of course, sinned against others, but this paled in significance next to his sin against God. He recognized this when Nathan confronted him: "I have sinned against the Lord" (2 Samuel 12:13). We may sin against God without sinning against other persons, but we cannot sin against our fellowmen without sinning against God.

So that you are proved right. In confessing his sin, David acknowledged that God would be perfectly just in condemning him. This raises a profound theological issue. How can God, who is just and holy, overlook human sin? He cannot! That is the reason Christ died. And having paid the price, he can now extend his grace through his Son, Jesus Christ (Romans 3:23-26).

II. A CONFESSION OF SIN (PSALM 51:5-9)

A. AN ADMISSION OF GUILT (vv. 5, 6)

5. Surely I was sinful at birth, sinful from the time my mother conceived me.

Some theologians see this verse as proof of man's inherent depravity; others take it as a hyperbole confessing David's own complete sinfulness. We shall leave that argument to the theologians. David may be saying he was born into a sin-filled world, but he is not using that to excuse his own sins, as do some today when they blame all their problems on society. Quite the contrary, David is taking the responsibility for his own sinfulness, not trying to blame others for it.

6. Surely you desire truth in the inner parts; you teach me wisdom in the inmost place.

God is not satisfied with an external appearance of righteousness, which one might attain through careful attention to the ritualistic provisions of the law. Rather, God requires *truth in the inner parts.* He makes us to know such truth when we study and meditate on the Scriptures. (See Psalm 119:15.)

TRUTH WITHIN

A visit to the doctor will illustrate the truth of verse 6. Seldom, if ever, is the doctor content with an examination of the outside of the body. He will at least use his stethoscope to listen to the "inner parts." If necessary, he will look inside with an X-ray or ultrasound machine. The doctor knows a look within tells more about a patient's condition than does a look at the outside.

David was aware that God wanted "truth in the inner parts." He appeared as a king, in royal splendor and public acceptance; but within he had lacked integrity, honesty, purity, sympathy, constancy. Instead there had been selfishness, lust, callousness, faithlessness.

The *appearance* of righteousness, the mouthing of platitudes, and the assuming of a religious attitude are not enough for us. No, our heavenly Father desires "truth in the inner parts." May we not have to learn this as David did through moral collapse, rebuke, tragedy, sorrow, and remorse. "Blessed are the pure in heart, for they will see God" (Matthew 5:8).
—J. G. V. B.

B. A FURTHER PLEA FOR CLEANSING (v. 7)

7. Cleanse me with hyssop, and I will be clean; wash me, and I will be whiter than snow.

HOW TO SAY IT

Bathsheba. Bath-SHE-buh.
Elohim (Hebrew). El-o-HEEM.
Nicodemus. Nick-uh-DEE-mus.
Uriah. Yu-RYE-uh.

WHAT DO YOU THINK?

Verse 5 doesn't sound very "positive." What would the modern "self-esteem" proponents think of this verse? Is it really necessary for us to be so self-deprecating to be forgiven by God? Why or why not? (See James 4:6.) What should be our estimation of ourselves as we stand before our holy God? Is it possible to be (or sound) too humble? Why or why not?

WHAT DO YOU THINK?

David wanted a "pure heart" and a "steadfast spirit." How important in facing future temptations do you think that would be to him? Why?

If a fellow believer told you she struggled with a recurring temptation and said, "I'm already guilty; what difference will doing it again make?" how would you respond?

OPTION

Use the reproducible activity on page 440 to explore the path that leads to sin, and the path that leads back to a "pure heart." The diagram below will provide some of the answers

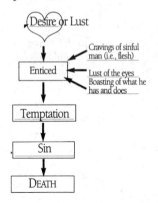

Visual 12 of the visuals packet is a poignant illustration of verse 10. Display it at this time.

Hyssop is a small shrub. Under the Old Testament law it was used in certain ceremonial activities for cleansing, such as the cleansing of a person with an infectious skin disease or one who had touched a dead body (Leviticus 14:1-7; Numbers 19:14-19). David here uses the term figuratively as another way of expressing his desire to be cleansed of sin.

Whiter than snow. Snow falls occasionally in Palestine, and it was the whitest thing the psalmist could think of. Nothing is whiter than a blanket of fresh-fallen snow.

C. A PLEA FOR JOY (vv. 8, 9)

8, 9. Let me hear joy and gladness; let the bones you have crushed rejoice. Hide your face from my sins and blot out all my iniquity.

Pardon brings peace of heart and mind, but the psalmist seems to be asking for more. He wants again to experience *joy and gladness.* Following his confrontation with Nathan, David had gone through a period of dark despair while his child lay dying (2 Samuel 12:13-18). Only comfort from the Lord could restore joy after those dark hours.

The bones you have crushed. We take this to be figurative. The emotional pain David suffered was like the pain one would suffer from broken bones. Even as he pleads for God to send him joy, he again asks that God will *blot out* all his sins.

III. A PLEA FOR RESTORATION (PSALM 51:10-13, 17)

A. A PRAYER FOR A CLEAN HEART (v. 10)

10. Create in me a pure heart, O God, and renew a steadfast spirit within me.

David prayed for cleansing from past sins, but he wanted more than that. He wanted a clean heart so he would not succumb to temptation and sin again. Interestingly, he asked for a new clean heart, not a cleansing of his old heart. The kind of spiritual change that David wanted was a radical change. This was the kind of change Jesus demanded when he told Nicodemus that he must be born again (John 3:3). Paul expressed a similar idea: "If anyone is in Christ, he is a new creation" (2 Corinthians 5:17).

As Christians we need to be concerned about efforts to solve some of the pressing problems of our society—poverty, poor health, crime, violence. We ought to work for and support laws that will improve these conditions. But we need to realize that the passing of laws can have little effect on these problems unless people's hearts are changed. Christians have the message that can change people's hearts. That's the reason we must give top priority to evangelism and Christian nurture.

B. A PLEA FOR ACCEPTANCE (v. 11)

11. Do not cast me from your presence or take your Holy Spirit from me.

When we come to realize the magnitude of our own sinfulness, we realize that a great chasm exists between ourselves and God. We also realize that it is humanly impossible to bridge that chasm. We know that we deserve to be cast out. No wonder there is a note of desperation in David's plea.

The *Holy Spirit* came on David when he was anointed king (1 Samuel 16:13). He knew that he could lose the Spirit, for he certainly was aware that the Spirit had departed from King Saul because of his disobedience (1 Samuel 16:14). Christians receive the Holy Spirit at their baptism (Acts 2:38). We need to understand that we also can grieve (Ephesians 4:30) or even quench the Spirit (1 Thessalonians 5:19).

C. A PLEA FOR SALVATION (v. 12)

12. Restore to me the joy of your salvation and grant me a willing spirit, to sustain me.

Earlier, David had faithfully followed God. God had saved him from many perils, and David had known *joy*. Sin had taken away that joy, and David wanted it back again. Many people who have fallen into sin know the soul-sickness that overwhelms them, and bringing agony to their hearts and driving sleep from the night. In Psalm 6:6 David mentions his own agonies: "I am worn out from groaning; all night long I flood my bed with weeping and drench my couch with tears."

Grant me a willing spirit, to sustain me. David wanted a spirit that would be willing to obey God. When a person is truly repentant, he or she wants to learn God's will and to obey that will.

SALVATION'S JOY

One reason David fell into sin was that he had lost the joy of God's salvation. It had become a happier thing to please himself than it was to please God.

To be saved from sin, Satan, and death is always a cause for rejoicing. We have reason to be "joyful in hope" (Romans 12:12). Paul admonished Christians to "rejoice in the Lord" (Philippians 3:1).

It is remarkable that the early pilgrims who settled New England held a thanksgiving observance when they did. Far from England's cozy, settled towns, on the edge of a vast unknown wilderness, with few material blessings, they still rejoiced in their survival. They were grateful for so little, while we sometimes are gloomy with so much.

We need to retain or to regain our joy in God's salvation. David's religious life must have become routine. His sense of God's presence and glory, which shines in many of his psalms, had become dull. He prayed for a restoration of joy.

—J. G. V. B.

D. A COMMITMENT TO SERVICE (v. 13)

13. Then I will teach transgressors your ways, and sinners will turn back to you.

When one has completely surrendered to God, that person looks for ways to serve him. One of the most obvious ways a believer can serve God is to share with others the faith that brought release from bondage to sin and restored joy to life. That's exactly what David promised to do: *Then I will teach transgressors your ways.* In many situations the best witness to God's grace is a person who was submerged in sin and then rescued. The alcoholic who has thrown off the chains of addiction is likely to be a better witness to a drinking alcoholic than one who has never tasted strong drink. Such a person can say, "I have walked where you have walked; I know where you hurt." As a grievous sinner, David could speak understandingly to another sinner.

When the great prophet Isaiah was confronted by a vision of the Lord, he felt himself undone because he knew the impurity of his life and of his people. The Lord first cleansed him and then challenged him to a special ministry. Isaiah's response was unhesitating: "Here am I. Send me!" (Isaiah 6:1-8). Even as he made the commitment, the prophet must have realized that the task would be difficult if not futile (Isaiah 6:9, 10). Those who have been cleansed by God do not volunteer with reservations, however; they volunteer and place their complete trust in God.

E. THE RIGHT SACRIFICE (v. 17)

17. The sacrifices of God are a broken spirit; a broken and contrite heart, O God, you will not despise.

In the Mosaic law, God instituted an elaborate system of *sacrifices* and offerings. The priests observed detailed rituals in making these offerings. These rituals were designed to make people conscious of their sins and to cause them to repent. In many cases they produced this result. On the other hand, many people carefully

WHAT DO YOU THINK?

The lesson writer says David's sin had taken away the joy of his salvation. The illustration writer suggests David sinned because he had already lost the joy of salvation. With whom do you agree? Why? What strengths do you find in each position? In light of this discussion, how would you advise a Christian who was struggling with a guilty conscience?

WHAT DO YOU THINK?

The bumper sticker says, "Christians are not perfect—just forgiven." Would you put such a sticker on your car? Why or why not? What do you think that suggests to non-Christians? Could it open the door to help you share Christ with someone? If so, how?

WHAT DO YOU THINK?

Suppose the Bible had glossed over the faults of all the heroes and told only of their faith and obedience. How would that affect your faith? Why is it helpful to read about severe moral lapses by the saints of old?

(See 1 Corinthians 10:6)

observed the rituals without ever experiencing a change in heart. The psalmist in this verse expresses what God really wants: *a broken and contrite heart.* God did not ask that the rituals be suspended; he asked that they lead to the desired end. We would be quite wrong to interpret this verse to mean that God wants us to abandon all rituals in our worship. Our concern should be that our rituals produce contrite hearts.

CONCLUSION

A. AWARENESS OF SIN

Satan has a way of blinding us to our sins until events force us to confront them. That was David's experience when Nathan finally faced him. We need to understand, however, that something more than this confrontation was involved. The prophet's message would have been so many words in the wind if David had not been taught God's standards for human conduct.

The Scriptures do not tell us how David came to a knowledge of God, but we can make a reasonable guess. The Old Testament placed upon the father the responsibility for the religious training of his children (Deuteronomy 6:4-9; Joshua 4:20-24). It is apparent that Jesse, David's father, lived up to this obligation. Then David's long, lonely hours as a shepherd opened his heart to the truths about God that nature reveals. After David became king, he had frequent contact with priests and prophets, whose teachings deepened his understanding of God and sensitized his conscience to God's will. Therefore Nathan's words quickly brought him to his knees in repentance. Had David been a barbarous savage, he might have had Nathan executed on the spot. Had he been a highly educated and sophisticated modern pagan, he likely would have sneered or laughed at Nathan and continued on his sinful way.

Our society is showing signs that it is plunging toward moral collapse. Many of our prominent leaders display an utter disregard for God's commandments against lying, stealing, and adultery. Thousands of young people roam the streets armed to the teeth, ready to snuff out a human life at the bat of an eye. How did we get in such a tragic situation? Many reasons may be cited, but the fundamental problem is that we have taken sin too lightly. As a result, we have not challenged sin when we have discovered it. By this same attitude, parents have failed to teach their children the important truths about God. Without understanding the seriousness of sin, we have felt no urgency to tell neighbors the good news of Christ. We've been so busy making money or building careers or seeking pleasure that we have neglected God's mandates.

What can we do about the situation? First of all, like David we need to repent of our sins, whether of omission or commission, and pray that God will extend forgiveness to us. Then, like David, we must teach transgressors God's ways. Some of us need to become involved in formal teaching in Sunday school, Vacation Bible School, or Christian camps. All of us can teach in family situations or in informal one-to-one situations. We need to take seriously both sin and its cure!

B. THE PERFECT SACRIFICE

In certain Old Testament rituals, the perfect sacrifice was a lamb without spot or blemish. Under the New Covenant, the perfect sacrifice is Jesus, "the Lamb of God, who takes away the sin of the world." But from us God still wants "a broken and contrite heart." In our worship we need to lay aside the distractions of the world and enter into our songs, our prayers, our meditations, and the Lord's Supper with such a heart. If we do, we have the assurance that God will not despise our worship.

Discovery Learning

This page contains an alternate lesson plan emphasizing learning activities. Classes desiring such student involvement will find these suggestions helpful. The next page is a reproducible activity page to further enhance discovery learning.

LEARNING GOALS

As a result of this lesson students should be able to:

1. Describe how God's unfailing love restores sinners.

2. Praise God for the purity that comes from forgiveness of sin.

INTO THE LESSON

Before class prepare a grid on the chalkboard or on a poster with seven squares aligned vertically and seven squares aligned horizontally, intersecting at the second letter of each. Put a hyphen between the fifth and sixth squares on the horizontal alignment. Prepare fourteen pieces of paper to fit the squares. On each, write one letter of the following words: *confess* and *cover-up*. (Prepare a few extra letters if you want some "stoppers.")

To begin the lesson, tell the class you're going to play a game like the TV version of *Scrabble*. Divide the class into two teams. Place a "C" in the first horizontal square and give team one this clue: "It can keep you warm or keep you guilty." Then show two letters. The team tries to figure out the word (*cover-up*) with the fewest number of letters shown as possible. The team chooses one of the letters you have shown, and you position it on the grid. They can try to guess the answer or take the next letter. If they cannot solve it, they ask for two new letters. Play continues until the team guess the solution or makes a wrong guess. Then it's the other team's turn. (If you use a "stopper," that is, a letter that does not fit in the word, play goes to the other team when a stopper is chosen.)

Team two begins with the "O" of confess already positioned. Give the clue: "David did it; Nixon didn't." Play proceeds as above.

When both words are revealed, observe that these words show two ways of dealing with sin: cover it up, and stay guilty, or confess it and find forgiveness. Today's lesson will explore how to do the latter.

INTO THE WORD

Ask the students to read 2 Samuel 11 and 12 silently, or divide the class into small groups and have one person in each group read the passage aloud. Then have them answer the following questions. (Make copies of the questions or to have them displayed at the front of the room on a poster, projected with an overhead projector, etc.) Allow ten minutes; then ask for reports. If you use groups, ask a different group to report on each section.

Part One: Sin (2 Samuel 11:1-5)

1. What situation became a temptation for David?

2. How did David handle the temptation?

Part Two: Cover-up (2 Samuel 11:6-27)

1. What did David try to do to cover-up his sin?

2. When that didn't work, what extreme measure did David take?

Part Three: Exposure (2 Samuel 12:1-25)

1. What was the point of Nathan's parable?

2. How did David respond when the prophet pronounced him guilty of wrongdoing?

Have someone read Leviticus 20:10 aloud. Ask, "Why do you think David and Bathsheba weren't put to death, as the law said?" Discuss that for a few minutes without pronouncing anyone "right" or "wrong." Then say, "Let's see what the Word of God has to say."

Ask a student to read Psalm 51 aloud. As the psalm is read, have the rest of the class listen for the *reasons* for David's forgiveness and the *results* of David's forgiveness.

Discuss these two issues after the psalm is read. Observe that David gives no reason from his own behavior. He could not earn forgiveness. The only reason is God's grace. Note how that is expressed in the following: "mercy" (v. 1), "unfailing love" (v. 1), "compassion" (v. 1), "wash" (v. 2, 7), "cleanse" (v. 2, 7), verse 9, verse 12, verse 14a. David does promise a response, however. But be sure to note these actions do not secure forgiveness; they are the results of David's forgiveness: verse 13, verse 14b, righteous sacrifices (v. 19).

Ask the class to look at 1 John 1:5-10 and note the parallels to Psalm 51. Are the steps to repentance similar in the two passages? What are the steps?

OPTION

Follow the discussion of reasons and results by using the activity on the reproducible page 440.

INTO LIFE

Read Psalm 51:17. Ask your students what they think David meant by this statement. As you discuss this, observe that no sacrifice could remove David's guilt. The only sacrifice he could offer was a humble heart seeking God's grace. That is still true for us.

Close your class session with sentence prayers of thanksgiving for God's cleansing and for the joy that dwells in a forgiven heart.

Temptation, Sin, and Forgiveness

Sin is not something that strikes suddenly without warning. If we are perceptive, we can generally see it coming. Use the chart below to visualize the process.

Read James 1:13-15. Fill in the blanks in the center of the chart with information from this passage.

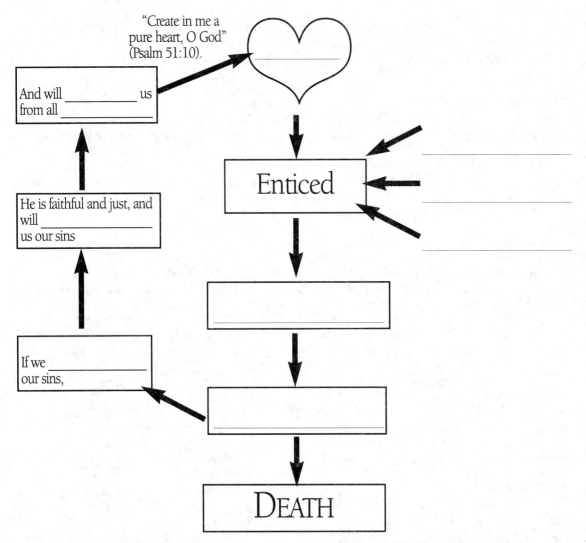

Read 1 John 2:16. What kinds of things become the enticements that lead to temptation? Write them in the three blanks near the "enticement" section of the chart.

Now read 1 John 1:9. Fill in the steps that lead back to a pure heart.

Review the chart. How does David's experience follow this path?

How have you seen the same process active in your own life?

WORSHIP AND WITNESS
| LESSON 13 |

WHY TEACH THIS LESSON?

The past few years have brought a renewed emphasis on worship. Worship styles, music, and instrumentation are all seeing great changes. Churches are even adding staff to facilitate better worship practices.

Today's lesson text, then, could not be more appropriate. It tells us, whatever the style, be sure you worship God and "ascribe to the Lord the glory due his name." Whether your church's worship is contemporary or traditional, liturgical or relaxed, this lesson will challenge your students to worship "in spirit and in truth."

INTRODUCTION

A. GIVING THE BEST

In Yucatan, Mexico, stand the remains of an ancient temple and altar. On this altar a young maiden would be placed; then a priest with a stone knife would rip her heart from her body and hold it aloft as a sacrifice to the Mayan god.

Archaeologists excavating the ancient city of Carthage in North Africa uncovered hundreds of small urns near a temple to one of the Carthaginian gods. When the excavators opened these urns, they found charred bones of tiny babies. It is quite evident that this was no ordinary cemetery, but was the final resting place for the remains of babies sacrificed in the temple.

We shudder as we realize how brutal many of the ancient religions were. Yet even as we abhor their brutality, we are forced to give grudging respect to the devotion of these ancient peoples who were willing to sacrifice their most precious possession, a child, to their gods. Are we equally devoted to Jehovah God? We are not for a moment suggesting that we engage in human sacrifice, but we are insisting that we ought to worship with the same wholehearted devotion that these ancient pagans did.

The truth is that many of us enter worship rather casually. We go through certain ceremonies in a perfunctory way, or we fail to concentrate on what we are doing, allowing our thoughts to roam wherever they will. Psalm 96 can be a healthy antidote to some of these weaknesses in our worship.

B. LESSON BACKGROUND

Psalm 96 is a joyous song of praise and worship of Jehovah. It has none of the soul-wrenching agony of Psalm 51 or the systematic tribute to the law found in Psalm 119. It is a happy song, the type of song one would sing in a worship service. It is longer and more detailed than a contemporary "praise chorus," but is similar in some respects. It has no superscription to tell of its author or its date.

I. A SONG (PSALM 96:1-3)

A. A NEW SONG (v. 1)

1. Sing to the LORD a new song; sing to the LORD, all the earth.

When we put our trust in Jehovah and devote our lives to doing God's will, we feel a new joy, a new confidence, a new strength. These break out in such singing as we have not done before. The psalmist calls *all the earth* to sing thus.

DEVOTIONAL READING
PSALM 98:1-9
LESSON SCRIPTURE
PSALM 96
PRINTED TEXT
PSALM 96

LESSON AIMS

As a result of studying this lesson each student should:

1. Summarize the Psalmist's reasons for praising and serving God.

2. Express praise and worship for the Lord, who is "most worthy of praise."

KEY VERSE

Sing to the LORD, praise his name; proclaim his salvation day after day. —Psalm 96:2

Aug
25

LESSON 13 NOTES

Visual 13 quotes verse 2 of the text. Have it displayed as your students arrive for class.

B. A SONG OF SALVATION (v. 2)

2. Sing to the LORD, praise his name; proclaim his salvation day after day.

Singing praises to Jehovah and blessing his name are vital to our worship, but they have a definite purpose beyond worship. This purpose is to *proclaim his salvation.* In the Old Testament, salvation often means protection or rescue from national or personal enemies, but sometimes it means deliverance from sin. See Psalm 51:14 in last week's lesson, for example. The New Testament concentrates on this latter meaning, for it tells us of God's Son who came to save us from our sins.

One can *proclaim* God's salvation not only by telling about it, but also by living a joyous, victorious life that exemplifies God's moral standards.

Not limited to special days or situations, this demonstration is to happen *day after day.* This verse should be heeded by Christians who attend church on Sunday and then live the rest of the week pretty much as the pagans about them do.

SING TO THE LORD

One peculiar human quality is the gift of song. While birds "sing" their songs, most of them are stereotyped melodies that are seemingly encoded into their makeup. So it is that each species of bird has his own special "song," which is usually a mating call. Of course, most also have alarm calls and calls to their chicks. And mockingbirds may really learn new songs.

Human beings have many songs to express the various pleasures, pains, yearnings, and forebodings of life. So we have songs of love, patriotism, battle, and nostalgia, plus rollicking songs of fun and exuberance. Of all our songs, however, the most wonderful and evocative are our songs of devotion, our lyrics of aspiration toward God, and our exalted praise to our Creator and the Guarantor of our well-being.

One of the characteristics of the psalms is their expression of praise for God's creative work. Even more deep are the phrasings of awareness of God's desire and ability to save humanity from sin and sorrow and death. This becomes even more prominent in our songs of relationship with Jesus, the Messiah, our Savior and Lord.

Compare the minor tonality and monotonous chants of Buddhist and Hindu devotion. There is seemingly no bright delight in a loving and saving God. How marvelous is the cry, "Sing to the LORD. . . . Sing to the LORD, praise his name; proclaim his salvation day after day"!

—J. G. V. B.

C. A MISSIONARY SONG (v. 3)

3. Declare his glory among the nations, his marvelous deeds among all peoples.

It is not enough just to sing among ourselves about God's dominion over all the peoples of the world. His glory must be declared *among all peoples.* When God called Abraham, he promised to bless him and then through him to bless all the nations of the world (Genesis 12:3). Scattered here and there through the Old Testament are clear indications that God never changed his concern for the whole world. Unfortunately, these points of light were largely obscured by the Israelites' concern for themselves. Christians have received a much firmer and clearer mandate to go into all the world, yet among most Christians this mandate does not take high priority. Dare we criticize the ancient Israelites for their narrow parochialism, when ours is even worse?

WHAT DO YOU THINK?

We are told to declare God's glory among the nations, or peoples (v. 3). What are the implications of that in regard to each of the following:

• *Supporting missionary efforts*

• *Reaching out to other ethnic groups locally*

• *Being sure our worship is meaningful to unbelievers and visitors*

How can our worship services be improved to deal with these implications?

II. REASONS FOR THE SONG (PSALM 96:4-6)

A. GOD'S GREATNESS (v. 4)

4. For great is the LORD and most worthy of praise; he is to be feared above all gods.

Greatness, whether it be in a person, a place, or a thing, normally elicits *praise.* How much more, then, should we praise Jehovah God, whose greatness is unique, one of a kind, far surpassing the greatness of everything else! We know God is greater than anything else, because he made everything else.

He is to be feared above all gods. The writer is not saying that other gods really exist, but he recognizes that many people think they exist. This was true among Israel's neighbors, who worshiped such imaginary gods as Baal, Chemosh, Dagon, Asherah, and others. In the long history of Israel many of her people were enticed by such false gods and began to worship them. The writer, rather than trying to prove that these gods really didn't exist, chose instead to urge the people to serve Jehovah because he is greater than all the so-called gods.

B. GOD THE CREATOR (vv. 5, 6)

5. For all the gods of the nations are idols, but the LORD made the heavens.

Idols. This Hebrew word primarily means *empty* or *nothing.* It is a fitting name for the gods invented by men. Many of the people worshiped images of wood, stone, or metal; but their worship was in vain because there was nothing behind those images. The apostle Paul echoed this sentiment when he wrote, "We know that an idol is nothing at all in the world" (1 Corinthians 8:4). The pagan idols *were* nothing and therefore could *do* nothing. Jehovah God, on the other hand, *made the heavens!* The writers of the psalms pointed frequently to the starry heavens as evidence of God's greatness and majesty. This was an impressive argument for people who spent much time out in the open where they could view the stars in all their splendor.

6. Splendor and majesty are before him; strength and glory are in his sanctuary.

Jehovah God is himself more glorious than anything else, but his surroundings are glorious too. This certainly is true in Heaven (Revelation 4). The word *sanctuary,* however, usually means the Holy of Holies in the tabernacle or temple. There Jehovah communed with his people from his place between the golden cherubim on the ark of the covenant (Exodus 25:22). The cherubim and the ark therefore were as majestic and beautiful as human hands could make them.

STRENGTH AND BEAUTY

It is a rare find that combines strength and beauty. Beautiful things are often fragile and evanescent, like spiderwebs or rainbows. Beauty frequently is related to the delicate, the intricate, and the dainty. Strength is associated with bigness, such things as bulging biceps and huge earth-moving machines.

One of the most striking combinations of strength, utility, and loveliness is found in the great suspension bridges of our land—such structures as the George Washington Bridge spanning the Hudson River, the Golden Gate Bridge across San Francisco Bay, and the Mackinac Bridge crossing the Straits of Mackinac between lakes Michigan and Huron.

Someone has called these beautiful suspension bridges "symphonies in steel." Viewed from a distance they are wonderful by day and fairylike when illuminated by thousands of sparkling lights by night. Yet they are fortresses of great strength, too.

Just as these mighty bridges combine the beauty of symmetry and proportion with the strength of steel and concrete, so God's power in our lives is a combination of strength and beauty. His love is strong and true, his Word a fortress of power and promise. Yet the quality of life he seeks to inspire in us involves kindness and gentleness, humility and helpfulness, compassion and tenderness. Truly, strength and beauty are in his sanctuary.

—J. G. V. B.

III. THE WORSHIP OF JEHOVAH (PSALM 96:7-9)

A. GIVE GLORY TO HIM (v. 7)

7. Ascribe to the LORD, O families of nations, ascribe to the LORD glory and strength.

WHAT DO YOU THINK?

We see no idols of wood and stone today. People today are caught up in worshiping material things, entertainment icons, sports heroes, pleasure, fame, personal achievement, and nature, among other things. Of course, they would not call it "worship." Do you think it is harder to win modern idolaters to the Lord than it was to win people who worshiped literal idols? Why or why not? How are modern "pagans" like the ancient pagans? How are they different?

WHAT DO YOU THINK?

The lesson writer notes that the furnishings in the sanctuary of the tabernacle/temple "were as majestic and beautiful as human hands could make them." Some today say that means modern church buildings should be ornate and majestic, as beautiful as we can make them. Others argue that church buildings should be modest, with more money spent on ministry and missions. What do you think?

Since Christians are God's sanctuary today (1 Corinthians 6:19), does this suggest we should be dressed in a special way for worship? Why or why not?

Families of nations. This call to worship was not directed exclusively to the Israelites but to all the nations of the world. This reinforces the idea introduced earlier in this psalm that Jehovah God is not a tribal deity who confines his activities to one small group of people.

For *ascribe* to God *glory and strength* earlier versions had "give" him these things. While *ascribe* might be an uncommon word in our vocabularies, it is an improvement. We cannot *give* God glory or strength; he has these things by his nature. We make a similar error when we say "*make* Christ Lord." He *is* Lord; we cannot add to or subtract from that any more than we can add to or subtract from God's glory. But we can recognize these qualities, we can ascribe to him these things, we can honor him as Lord because of his divine glory and unsurpassed strength.

B. BRING GIFTS TO HIM (v. 8)

8. Ascribe to the LORD the glory due his name; bring an offering and come into his courts.

Every human being has an obligation to glorify the Lord's *name.* That we have often failed to do this only increases our debt to him. The praise and glory offered God here foreshadow the praise and glory that are his in Heaven. For example, the four beasts "never stop saying: 'Holy, holy, holy is the Lord God Almighty.'" The twenty-four elders fall down before God, saying, "You are worthy, our Lord and God, to receive glory and honor and power" (Revelation 4:8, 10, 11).

Worshipers were instructed to *bring an offering* when they came to the place of worship. Similar instructions are given in 1 Chronicles 16:29. This is good advice for God's people today.

C. WORSHIP IN HOLINESS (v. 9)

9. Worship the LORD in the splendor of his holiness; tremble before him, all the earth.

God demands that all who come before him to worship must come *in the splendor of his holiness.* Holiness is at the very heart of the worship of Jehovah. As such, it stands in stark contrast to the worship of pagan gods, in which holiness played no part. Pagan gods were often depicted as powerful and awe-inspiring, but anything but holy. Thus, the behavior of their worshipers was also unholy, even immoral.

Worship acceptable to God has several requirements. First, its intent and activities must be in keeping with his will. Human sacrifice or sexual orgies, often practiced by devotees of pagan gods, are totally unacceptable to Jehovah. Worship of Jehovah must be pure. The Jewish priests donned clean linen when they brought offerings before God. The clean garments represented the moral cleanliness that God requires of his worshipers. This same emphasis is made in Psalm 24:3, 4: "Who may ascend the hill of the Lord? Who may stand in his holy place? He who has clean hands and a pure heart, who does not lift up his soul to an idol or swear by what is false."

Worship must be sincere if it is to be acceptable. It is only a meaningless routine if the heart is not in it. Many of us at times have been guilty of entering into worship while our thoughts were a thousand miles away.

Finally, our worship must be joyous. If there is one thing we should gather from our study of the psalms, it is that we should come before God with thankful, joyous hearts.

IV. THE UNIVERSAL WORSHIP (PSALM 96:10-13)

A. AMONG THE NATIONS (v. 10)

10. Say among the nations, "The LORD reigns." The world is firmly established, it cannot be moved; he will judge the peoples with equity.

WHAT DO YOU THINK?

What is the importance of bringing an offering when one comes to worship? Do you see offerings as an act of worship or merely a pragmatic act necessary to pay the bills? Why?

How might failure to present an offering convey one or more of the following messages?
* *pride*
* *ingratitude*
* *lack of trust in God*
* *envy*

WHAT DO YOU THINK?

When the psalmist said we should worship God "in the splendor of his holiness," he likely had in mind the vain, vulgar, and immoral excesses of pagan worship. These have no place in the worship of Jehovah. What other characteristics of worship are consistent with the splendor of his holiness? What would be out of place?

(See John 4:23; 1 Corinthians 14:40.)

WHAT DO YOU THINK?

Do you find impending judgment a reason to worship and rejoice today? Why or why not?

The psalmist has been encouraging his people to enter into a joyous worship of Jehovah. Now he turns his attention to the *nations*. They, too, have an obligation to worship God because he is their king also, even if they have not recognized him. In their ignorance the nations have not given Jehovah the recognition due him. As a result, their lives have been lived in darkness. They "exchanged the truth of God for a lie, and worshiped and served created things rather than the Creator" (Romans 1:25).

The psalmist now lays upon his own people the task of enlightening those living in darkness. The nations need to hear this message because the time is coming when God will *judge the people with equity*. The responsibility of declaring that message has been passed on to the church.

B. In Nature (vv. 11, 12)

11, 12. Let the heavens rejoice, let the earth be glad; let the sea resound, and all that is in it; let the fields be jubilant, and everything in them. Then all the trees of the forest will sing for joy.

The psalmist personifies the forces of nature and has them join in the praise of God. Hebrew poets frequently used this device. They had the *heavens* declaring God's glory, floods and *trees* clapping their hands, and mountains skipping like rams. There is a sense in which nature is involved in God's plan for the universe. Nature has suffered because of man's sinfulness. Paul tells us that "the whole creation has been groaning as in the pains of childbirth right up to the present time" as a result of this sin (Romans 8:22).

C. Because of Judgment (v. 13)

13. They will sing before the Lord, for he comes, he comes to judge the earth. He will judge the world in righteousness and the peoples in his truth.

This psalm deals with Jehovah as King. In ancient Israel the king often served as a *judge* over his subjects. Solomon, for example, established a great reputation as a judge (1 Kings 3:16-28). The general tenor of this psalm is joyous and optimistic, but if God judges the *world in righteousness*, then the outcome will not be happy for everyone. In fact, none of us wants justice when we stand before the great Judge; we want grace and mercy instead.

Some commentators see this as a messianic psalm. They see the coming judge as Christ returning to claim the church as his own and to mete out justice to the wicked. Such an interpretation certainly would not be foreign to the book of Psalms.

Judging Righteously With Truth

Man Child in the Promised Land tells of a boy who grew up in a very depressed area of an American city. He came from a home with dedicated parents; but he fell in with bad associates, became a criminal, and eventually went to prison. He said his parents counseled him to "be good," but among his friends being "good" meant stealing without getting caught!

There can be judgment that is entirely wrong because those judging are wicked, and there is no real understanding about what is true. Jesus was judged to be worthy of death, but there was no righteousness or truth in the decision that convicted him.

The psalmist tells us that God is evaluating men's conduct and that he will judge the people righteously. His righteousness is absolutely valid and unwavering. God's ethical standards are found in the Old Testament law where he is revealed as holy, with integrity that is absolute. Further, he shall judge the world

How to Say It

Chemosh. KEE-mosh.
Dagon. DAY-gon.
Asherah. Uh-SHE-ruh.

What Do You Think?

Name some examples of judgment that is not done "in righteousness" or "in truth." Who is likely to be the victim(s) of such judgment? What implications do you think the Lord's judgment has for such judges? for the victims? What ought to be the response of Christians who witness such judgment in light of the impending judgment of the Lord?

PRAYER

Dear Lord, teach us to sing a new song, not just with our lips but with our hearts as well. Help us to know the joy that comes to those who worship you in the "splendor of your holiness." Show us how and where we may serve when we leave the place of worship. In Jesus' name we pray. Amen.

THOUGHT TO REMEMBER

"Enter to worship; depart to serve."

DAILY BIBLE READINGS

Monday, Aug. 19—In Spirit, the Only Way (John 4:19-26)

Tuesday, Aug. 20—A Warm Invitation (Psalm 95:1-7)

Wednesday, Aug. 21—Preparation Required (Psalm 96:1-9)

Thursday, Aug. 22—Heaven's Command (Revelation 14:1-7)

Friday, Aug. 23—All People to Be Told (Isaiah 43:8-13)

Saturday, Aug. 24—Appointed to Witness (Acts 22:6-16)

Sunday, Aug. 25—Make Disciples of All Nations (Matthew 28:16-20)

with *his* truth. This will not be the truth as men may bend and distort it, but as the Holy God reveals and enforces it.

The question is unavoidable—where do we stand? We and our fellows make judgments now, but the day arrives when *he* comes. Then "he will judge the world in righteousness and the peoples in his truth."

—J. G. V. B.

CONCLUSION

A. RIGHT AFTER THE BENEDICTION

Many years ago a man was visiting in a small town in eastern Pennsylvania. When Sunday came, he wanted to attend church. The only church in town was that of the Quakers, so he went there.

In the old-fashioned Quaker meeting everyone sat quietly until someone was "moved by the Spirit" to speak. The visitor entered the building and sat quietly with the others. After fifteen or twenty minutes no one had spoken. The visitor turned to a man sitting beside him and asked, "When does the service begin?"

"Right after the benediction, friend," came the reply. "Right after the benediction."

Exactly! Service in the name of God ought to follow worship. If worship does not result in Christian service, then something is lacking in the worship. Psalm 96 envisions a joyous time of worship when the name of God is exalted, but the psalmist is also concerned about what happens when the worship ends. Worshipers are told to "declare his glory among the nations" (v. 3), "bring an offering" (v. 8), and "say among the nations, 'The LORD reigns'" (v. 10).

The mandate for Christian service is not limited to the professional clergy. Each one of us has an obligation to use his or her talents, time, and resources to glorify the Lord. Most of us will not be called to serve as missionaries on some distant shore, nor to proclaim the message from the pulpit. However, one may teach a Sunday school class, serve as a nursery attendant, or direct traffic in the church parking lot. We may visit the sick, counsel the discouraged, or share our faith with non-Christians. Most of us can witness in the school, marketplace, work place, or even at home.

B. SINGING A NEW SONG

Occasionally we hear people complain about the new music being used in our worship services. They are upset that the old familiar hymns and gospel songs are being replaced by "praise choruses" with new tunes and new lyrics. Are these the "new songs" mentioned by the psalmist?

Not necessarily. The new song of Psalm 96 is much like an older song we read in 1 Chronicles 16:23-33. It was new, however, to people who had not been singing it. It was new to people who had not been worshiping in the beauty of holiness. It was new to people who never had thought of telling the pagans about the Lord. To all such people it came with new enthusiasm, new optimism, new joy. Some modern songs may likewise tell the old, old story with new vigor and challenge.

Our concern for singing a new song ought to go beyond new tunes and new lyrics. It ought to lead us to worship with renewed enthusiasm. It should cause us to come before the Lord "in the splendor of his holiness" by purging our hearts of those things that stand between us and him. It ought to cause us to cast aside the idols of power, pride, and possessions. When we have done these things, we will indeed be singing a new song.

Discovery Learning

*This page contains an alternate lesson plan emphasizing learning activities. Classes
desiring such student involvement will find these suggestions helpful. The next page
is a reproducible activity page to further enhance discovery learning.*

LEARNING GOALS

As a result of participating in this lesson, your students
should be able to:

1. Summarize the psalmist's reasons for praising and
serving God.

2. Express praise and worship for the Lord, who is
"most worthy of praise."

INTO THE LESSON

As your class members arrive, hand them a small slip
of paper with the following questions: "What is your favorite hymn or song? What makes it so meaningful to
you?"

Ask them to be thinking about these questions while
the social and organizational activities are being cared for
before the lesson time.

When you are ready to begin the lesson, ask for several
volunteers to share their answers with the whole group.
Then point out that today they will be studying a praise
song that was used in temple worship in the Old Testament.

INTO THE WORD

Divide the class "down the middle." Designate the
group on your right as group 1, the group on your left as
group 2. Distribute copies of the reproducible page 448
and use the upper half to read Psalm 96 antiphonally.
Have everyone stand up for this reading.

(It would be entirely appropriate to pause for prayer
after this reading.)

Have the class sit down and point out that Psalm 96
was sung by temple singers as the Ark of the Covenant
was carried into Jerusalem (see 1 Chronicles 16:23-33). It
is a call for all of the created world to praise God as King.

Move into a study of the psalm by using the following
questions. You may decide to break your class up into
smaller groups to complete this study. Each group should
appoint a recorder (to write down the group's answers)
and a reporter (to report the group's findings to the
class).If you have a small enough class, it may be better to
work through the questions all together, discussing the
answers as you go.

• Look at verses 1-3 and 7-9. What are some ways of
worshiping the Lord? (Possible answers include
singing, proclaiming his salvation, declaring his glory
and deeds, giving offerings, "trembling" before him.)

• Look at verses 4-6 and 10. What are some reasons
for praising God? (Possible answers include he is
great; he is most worthy of praise; he is no idol, he
created the heavens, splendor, majesty, strength, and
glory accompany him, he reign, he is the righteous
judge.)

• How does the creation praise God? (The psalm personifies some of the aspects of nature to suggest
praise. One way the creation praises God is by testi-
fying to his greatness. Another way is by being submissive to him—it fulfills its purpose as it was
created to do.)

• How is the prospect of judgment a reason to praise and
worship God? (His right to judge is reason enough to
worship him: he is sovereign. That he judges in righteousness and truth is further reason. That he grants
mercy in his judgment—not mentioned in the
psalm—may be the Christians' greatest cause for
praising him.)

• What one thing most hinders you from "singing to the
Lord a new song"?

INTO LIFE

These verses in Psalm 96 have often been referred to as
a universal call to praise. Ask your students to list three
things for which they are extremely grateful to God. Then
ask them to think of ways they can express their gratitude
to him for these things.

Distribute copies of the reproducible page 448. Ask
the students to answer the three multiple choice questions on their own; then discuss the results. Follow that
with a discussion of the following open-ended sentences.
Write them on the chalkboard or display them with an
overhead projector.

• My understanding of praise and worship is…

• One thing that really helps me to worship is…

• One thing that hinders my worship is…

• One thing I will do this week to improve my preparation for worship is…

Ask the students to complete the second activity from
the reproducible page. Discuss the results if there is tim
Then sing a praise song together and then ask your clas
members to pray in small groups. Suggest that the focus
of these prayers be a thanksgiving to God for being their
source of joy and song.

Sing a New Song

Use the following to read Psalm 96 antiphonally.

GROUP 1

Sing to the LORD a new song;
Sing to the LORD, praise his name;
Declare his glory among the nations,

For great is the LORD and most worthy of praise;
For all the gods of the nations are idols,
Splendor and majesty are before him;

Ascribe to the LORD, O families of nations,
Ascribe to the LORD the glory due his name;
Worship the LORD in the splendor of his holiness;
Say among the nations, "The LORD reigns."
it cannot be moved;

Let the heavens rejoice,
let the sea resound,
let the fields be jubilant,
Then all the trees of the forest will sing for joy;
for he comes,

GROUP 2

sing to the LORD, all the earth.
proclaim his salvation day after day.
his marvelous deeds among all peoples.

he is to be feared above all gods.
but the LORD made the heavens.
strength and glory are in his sanctuary.

ascribe to the LORD glory and strength.
bring an offering and come into his courts.
tremble before him, all the earth.
The world is firmly established,
he will judge the peoples with equity.

let the earth be glad;
and all that is in it;
and everything in them.
they will sing before the LORD,
he comes to judge the earth.

ALL TOGETHER
He will judge the world in righteousness and the peoples in his truth.

It's Sunday Morning, and . . .

1. To prepare to worship on Sunday morning, I usually…
☐ Get to church on time.
☐ Get to church early so I can be well-prepared to worship.
☐ Arise early to spend a quiet time with God before I leave for the church building.
☐ Avoid any late activities on Saturday evening so I get a good night's sleep.
☐ Set the alarm as late as possible in the hope that I will arrive before the first song is finished.

2. During the worship service, I usually focus my attention on…
☐ The interesting people around me.
☐ Trying to stay awake.
☐ My responsibilities.
☐ The worship leaders.
☐ The presence of the Lord.

3. After worship on Sunday, I usually try to…
☐ Hurry home to catch the ball game on TV.
☐ Try to find my friends to catch up on the news.
☐ Discuss the sermon in the car on the way home.
☐ Recommit myself to spiritual growth during the week.
☐ Tell others about the joy of worship.